DICTIONARY OF AMERICAN LITERARY CHARACTERS

SECOND EDITION

DICTIONARY OF AMERICAN LITERARY CHARACTERS

SECOND EDITION

VOLUME I
1789–1960

Edited by Benjamin Franklin V

Revised by American BookWorks Corporation

☑®

Facts On File, Inc.

Dictionary of American Literary Characters, Second Edition

Copyright © 2002 by American BookWorks Corporation

An American BookWorks Corporation Project

Original Edition Copyright © 1990 by Bruccoli Clark Layman, Inc., and Facts On File, Inc.

Facts On File, Inc.
132 West 31st Street
New York NY 10001

Library of Congress Cataloging-in-Publication Data

Dictionary of American literary characters / edited by Benjamin Franklin, V; revised by American BookWorks Corporation.—2nd ed.
    p. cm.
  Includes indexes.
  Contents: v. 1. 1789–1960—v. 2. 1961–2000.
  ISBN 0-8160-4262-4 (set) (acid-free paper)
    1. American fiction—Dictionaries. 2. Characters and characteristics in literature—Dictionaries.
I. Franklin, Benjamin, 1939– II. American BookWorks Corporation.

PS374.C43 D5 2001
813.009'27'03—dc21   2001033270

Facts On File books are available at special discounts when purchased in bulk quantities for businesses, associations, institutions or sales promotions. Please call our Special Sales Department in New York at (212) 967-8800 or (800) 322-8755.

You can find Facts On File on the World Wide Web at http://www.factsonfile.com

Text design and layout by Rachel L. Berlin
Cover illustration by Smart Graphics
Cover design by Cathy Rincon

Printed in the United States of America

VB FOF 10 9 8 7 6 5 4 3 2 1

This book is printed on acid-free paper.

CONTENTS

ACKNOWLEDGMENTS

I would like to thank several people for their contributions beyond the call of duty. Rebecca Feind researched and provided the publication dates for the hundreds of novels in these volumes. Elaine Bender and Robert Geary helped to select and review the lists of books. My wife, Valerie Grayson, provided endless research assistance and editorial suggestions, as well as continued support during this project.

Fred N. Grayson, President
American BookWorks Corporation

PREFACE

This second edition of the *Dictionary of American Literary Characters* describes the major characters in significant American novels—in addition to those in some uncelebrated novels and in a sampling of best-sellers—from 1789 through 2000. By *novels* we mean long works of fiction, or what is presented as fiction. A few of the books are often referred to as novellas, and some others as nonfiction novels.

We have added hundreds of new works and thousands of new characters, primarily from novels published between 1979, where the first edition stopped, to 2000. We have tried to include a wider sampling of literary, popular, and genre fiction. The books that have been added to this edition were selected by various methods. We chose novels that won or were shortlisted for major book awards: the Pulitzer Prize, National Book Award, PEN/Faulkner, Edgar Allan Poe, and others. We also selected novels that were in the top five of major national and regional best-seller lists, and were on those lists for at least three months, since the mid-1970s. Finally, we received valuable suggestions from our contributors and relied on several literature professors to oversee the list, suggest new titles, eliminate others, and generally review the submissions. Because a novelist is included does not mean that characters from all of his or her novels are described.

Users of this book who cannot recall the name of a character in a novel, and therefore cannot turn directly to the desired character's entry, should consult the author index, which lists characters alphabetically by novel. The title index is a new feature for readers who know the title of the novel but not the author.

The two volumes of this edition are divided chronologically. Volume I covers novels published from 1789 through 1960; Volume II covers novels published from 1961 through 2000. Some novelists appear in both volumes, as noted in the author index. Each character has one entry, whether the character appears in one novel or in several; cross-references direct readers to the appropriate volume if the same character appears in novels published before and after 1960.

The entries are factual; they contain little interpretation. Although some characters, such as Babe Ruth and George Washington, are historical figures, they are treated in the same manner as obviously fictional characters.

DICTIONARY OF AMERICAN LITERARY CHARACTERS

SECOND EDITION

A Daughter of Nimni and Ohiro-Moldona-Fivona in Herman Melville's *Mardi.*

Aaron Hebrew son of Amram, brother of Miriam (and perhaps of Moses), and first high priest of the Israelites; killed and entombed by Moses on Mount Hor in Zora Neale Hurston's *Moses, Man of the Mountain.*

Horace Abbeville Bigamist and debtor; commits suicide after settling accounts with Lee Chong the grocer by exchanging a fish-meal storage building for his debt in John Steinbeck's *Cannery Row.*

Aunt Abby (Nab) Maiden sister and ward of John Bellmont; tries to protect Frado from Mrs. Bellmont in Harriet E. Wilson's *Our Nig.*

Abe Son of Lucy; slave who is sent to sea, where he dies trying to assist distressed sailors in John Pendleton Kennedy's *Swallow Barn.*

Uncle Abednego Elderly black man from the almshouse who is the Birdsongs' gardener in Ellen Glasgow's *The Sheltered Life.*

James Abel Poor Farm inmate and witch digger in Jessamyn West's *The Witch Diggers.*

Mary Abel Poor Farm inmate and witch digger; sets the fire that kills Christian Fraser in Jessamyn West's *The Witch Diggers.*

Abrazza Bachelor king of Bonovona in Herman Melville's *Mardi.*

Achille See Lafitte.

Noah Ackerman Lonely Jewish social worker whose marriage to Hope Plowman deeply enriches his life; drafted into the army during World War II, where he is subjected to anti-Semitic taunts and distinguishes himself as a hero, in Irwin Shaw's *The Young Lions.*

Robert Ackley Ill-groomed student who lives next to Holden Caulfield at Pencey Prep in J. D. Salinger's *The Catcher in the Rye.*

Elizabeth (Lizzie) Acton Guileless sister of Robert Acton; marries Clifford Wentworth in Henry James's *The Europeans.*

Mrs. Acton Invalid mother of Robert and Lizzie Acton in Henry James's *The Europeans.*

Robert Acton Sophisticated, well-traveled cousin of William Wentworth; courts Eugenia Münster in Henry James's *The Europeans.*

Walter (Wat, Watty) Adair North Carolina Tory sympathizer who betrays Arthur Butler; captured following the battle of King's Mountain; dies of a bite from a rabid wolf in John Pendleton Kennedy's *Horse-Shoe Robinson.*

Adam Texas soldier who has an affair with Miranda; dies from influenza in Katherine Anne Porter's *Pale Horse, Pale Rider.*

Alice (Lady Alicia, Alys Tuttle) Adams Daughter of Virgil Adams; has a summer-long romance with Arthur Russell, but gives up her dreams of a life in high society and enrolls in a business college in Booth Tarkington's *Alice Adams.*

Amos Adams Philosophic and idealistic editor of the *Harvey Tribune;* husband of Mary Adams, father of Grant Adams, and grandfather of Kenyon Adams in William Allen White's *In the Heart of a Fool.*

Grandfather Adams Grandfather of Stephen Grendon; takes Grendon's side in arguments and teaches him that all love is just a fight against time in August Derleth's *Evening in Spring;* also appears in *The Shield of the Valiant.*

Grant Adams Father of Kenyon Adams; carpenter, reformer, and labor organizer in love with Laura Nesbit Van Dorn and killed by an anti-union mob in William Allen White's *In the Heart of a Fool.*

Jake Adams Streetwise eighteen-year-old who makes his living in the drug underworld of St. Louis; main character in Herbert Simmons's *Corner Boy.*

John Adams See Alexander Smith.

John R. Adams Major, veteran of the Philippine campaign, and commander of the First Marine battalion in France during World War I in Thomas Boyd's *Through the Wheat.*

Kenyon Adams Illegitimate son of Grant Adams and Margaret Müller; reared as the son of Amos and Mary Adams; musician and artist who marries Lila Van Dorn in William Allen White's *In the Heart of a Fool.*

Mary Sands Adams Wife of Amos Adams and mother of Grant Adams; with the help of James Nesbit, claims her grandson Kenyon Adams as her own son in William Allen White's *In the Heart of a Fool.*

Mildred Adams See Mildred Adams Gale.

Mrs. Adams Wife of Virgil Adams and mother of Alice and Walter Adams; nags her husband to start his own factory so she and their daughter can join high society in Booth Tarkington's *Alice Adams.*

Old Man Adams Father of Jake Adams; factory worker close to retirement in Herbert Simmons's *Corner Boy.*

Phil Adams Boyhood friend of Tom Bailey; teaches Bailey self-defense; becomes the consul at Shanghai in Thomas Bailey Aldrich's *The Story of a Bad Boy.*

Virgil (Virg) Adams Father of Alice and Walter Adams; longtime loyal employee of J. A. Lamb who starts his own glue factory but is eventually bought out by Lamb, in Booth Tarkington's *Alice Adams.*

Walter (Wallie) Adams Son of Virgil Adams; despises the high society his mother and sister Alice aspire to; takes up with disreputable companions and becomes an embezzler in Booth Tarkington's *Alice Adams.*

Captain Willie Adams Boat owner who warns Harry Morgan that Morgan's bootlegging has been discovered in Ernest Hemingway's *To Have and Have Not.*

Frances (F. Jasmine, Frankie) Addams Twelve-year-old protagonist infatuated with her brother and his bride; disrupts their wedding in an attempt to accompany them on their honeymoon in Carson McCullers's *The Member of the Wedding.*

Jarvis Addams Older brother of Frankie Addams; bridegroom in Carson McCullers's *The Member of the Wedding.*

Royal Quincy Addams Jewelry store owner, father of Frankie and Jarvis Addams, and employer of Berenice Sadie Brown in Carson McCullers's *The Member of the Wedding.*

Judah Addison Investor in Frank Cowperwood's natural gas project in Theodore Dreiser's *The Titan.*

Adele Daughter of Lillian Beye in Anaïs Nin's *Ladders to Fire* and *Seduction of the Minotaur.*

Adeppi Young orphaned street singer in the Italian village of Castiglione; befriends Nino and lives with Arsella and Pipistrello in John Hawkes's *The Goose on the Grave.*

Adler Member of Ward Bennett's crew seeking and failing to reach the North Pole; loyally remains with Bennett afterwards, encouraging him to make another voyage to the Arctic, in Frank Norris's *A Man's Woman.*

Dr. Adler Vain physician and professor of internal medicine who lives in comfortable retirement in New York's Hotel Gloriana; uncaring father of Tommy Wilhelm in Saul Bellow's *The Victim.*

Liza Adler Marxist who corresponds with Paul Hobbes in John Clellon Holmes's *Go.*

Myron (Mike) Adler Successful and even-tempered businessman who, out of friendship and concern, reveals Joseph's decline into bad temper in Saul Bellow's *Dangling Man.*

Adraste Maid of Helen; becomes pregnant by Damastor in John Erskine's *The Private Life of Helen of Troy.*

Anthony (Toni) Adverse Illegitimate son of Maria Bonnyfeather and heir of John Bonnyfeather; has many adventures in his travels as he makes his fortune in Hervey Allen's *Anthony Adverse.*

Aegisthus Lover of Clytemnestra; conspires with her to murder Clytemnestra's husband, Agamemnon; killed by Orestes in John Erskine's *The Private Life of Helen of Troy.*

After Birth Tycoon See Salvador Hassan O'Leary.

Agamemnon Brother of Menelaos and husband of Clytemnestra; killed by Clytemnestra and her lover Aegisthus in John Erskine's *The Private Life of Helen of Troy.*

Agatha Beauty parlor assistant and girlfriend of Raymond; at Raymond's request, she visits the ailing Jake Brown in Claude McKay's *Home to Harlem.*

Bill Agatson Former Harvard University student who drinks heavily and craves excess; killed in the New York subway in John Clellon Holmes's *Go.*

Aglone Former slave who lives with the Pinseau family after the Civil War as their cook and housekeeper in Grace King's *The Pleasant Ways of St. Médard.*

Agocho (Agocho Koh Tli-chu, Fig Tree John, John, Red Fire Bird) Apache Indian who seeks revenge on all whites for his wife's murder in Edwin Corle's *Fig Tree John.*

Mme. Agoropoulos Woman kept from the social gatherings of the Cabala; honored when Alix d'Espoli accepts her invitation in Thornton Wilder's *The Cabala.*

Ahab Captain of the *Pequod* whose pursuit of Moby-Dick leads to the death of everyone aboard the ship except Ishmael in Herman Melville's *Moby-Dick.*

Gil Ahab Night-shift worker whose truck is used to transport workers to the Past Bay Manufacturing Company factory during the strike; religious fanatic in Robert Cantwell's *The Land of Plenty.*

Mickey Ahearn Unmarried mother of a child she calls Willy and sends via railroad freight to Will Brady in Wright Morris's *The Works of Love.*

Ah Fong Chinese baker on Manukura who dies in the hurricane before he can return to China in Charles Nordhoff and James Norman Hall's *The Hurricane.*

K. Y. Ahmed See Salvador Hassan O'Leary.

Aimata See Pomaree Vahinee I.

Mollie Ainslie Massachusetts teacher who becomes a major landowner in Kansas; marries Hesden Le Moyne in Albion W. Tourgee's *Bricks Without Straw.*

Oscar Ainslie Brother of Mollie Ainslie; makes Mollie promise, as he is dying of consumption, that she will remain in a healthful Southern climate in Albion W. Tourgee's *Bricks Without Straw.*

Noel (Saul Ehrmann) Airman Songwriter with a crooked arm who is the social director and head of the entertainment staff at South Wind, an adult camp; love of Marjorie Morningstar in Herman Wouk's *Marjorie Morningstar.*

Robert Aitken Philadelphia printer who hires Thomas Paine to start the *Pennsylvania Magazine,* only to fire him when Paine starts writing too plainly about American independence, in Howard Fast's *Citizen Tom Paine.*

A. J. (Merchant of Sex) Financier of Islam Inc.; international playboy and practical joker in William S. Burroughs's *Naked Lunch;* sponsor of Homer Mandrill for president in *Exterminator!;* also appears in *The Soft Machine* and *The Wild Boys.*

Alamo Lead steer of the Del Sol trail herd that travels from Texas to Abilene in Emerson Hough's *North of 36.*

Alan Husband of Sabina in Anaïs Nin's *A Spy in the House of Love.*

Alanno Chief of Hio-Hio who criticizes King Bello in Herman Melville's *Mardi.*

Bert Albany Former miner who works in Zar's saloon; courts and marries a prostitute, with whom he leaves Hard Times when Clay Turner returns to raze the town, in E. L. Doctorow's *Welcome to Hard Times.*

Alberta Maid with mixed blood who is the object of Gamaliel Bland Honeywell's early desires in Ellen Glasgow's *The Romantic Comedians.*

Salathiel (Little Turtle) Albine Child captured and reared by Indians; eventually works his way from life in the forest to one in civilization in Philadelphia, in Hervey Allen's *The Forest and the Fort, Bedford Village,* and *Toward the Morning.*

Helen Albury Sister of Robert Albury determined to prove her brother's innocence in Dashiell Hammett's *Red Harvest.*

Robert Albury Assistant cashier of the First National Bank in Personville who is desperately in love with Dinah Brand, embezzles money to court her, and is charged with the murder of Donald Willsson in Dashiell Hammett's *Red Harvest.*

Harriet Bumstead Alden Mother of Oliver Alden in George Santayana's *The Last Puritan.*

Nathaniel Alden Boston landlord and half brother of Peter Alden in George Santayana's *The Last Puritan.*

Oliver Alden Idealistic student of philosophy; the last Puritan in George Santayana's *The Last Puritan.*

Peter Alden Father of Oliver Alden in George Santayana's *The Last Puritan.*

Roberta (Mrs. Clifford Golden, Mrs. Carl Graham, Ruth Howard) Alden Lover of Clyde Griffiths and pregnant by him; falls from a boat and drowns as Griffiths fails to rescue her in Theodore Dreiser's *An American Tragedy.*

Thomas (Tom, Tommy) Alden Davenport author who sponsors Felix Fay at literary activities, even though Fay is a socialist, in Floyd Dell's *Moon-Calf.*

Aline Aldridge See Aline Aldridge Grey.

Rodney Aldwick　Friend of Neil Kingsblood; turns against his friend when Kingsblood's black ancestry is discovered in Sinclair Lewis's *Kingsblood Royal*.

Aleema　Priest from Amma who is killed by Taji in Herman Melville's *Mardi*.

Alex (Uncle Alex)　Alabama farmer, husband of Caroline, and employer and benefactor of Ollie in George Wylie Henderson's *Ollie Miss and Jule*.

Dr. Alexander　Assistant lecturer in biodynamics and government agent; brings Adam Krug to a university meeting the night Krug's wife, Olga, dies; later exterminated for bungling in Vladimir Nabokov's *Bend Sinister*.

Aunt Alexandra　Sister of Atticus Finch and aunt of Scout and Jem Finch; moves into the Finch home to help turn Scout into a southern lady in Harper Lee's *To Kill a Mockingbird*.

Alex Alexson　Second husband of Sophia Grieve Ryder in Djuna Barnes's *Ryder*.

Alfrado (Frado, Nig)　Spirited mulatto girl indentured to the Bellmont family; tells the story of her mistreatment and growth to adulthood in Harriet E. Wilson's *Our Nig*.

Alfred (Alfy)　Bouncer, protector, and watchman of the Bear Flag restaurant, a bar and brothel, in John Steinbeck's *Cannery Row*.

Kirby Allbee　Anti-Semite and weak-willed drunk who blames Asa Leventhal for his own moral degeneration, persecuting and finally attempting to murder him in retaliation, in Saul Bellow's *The Victim*.

Betsy Allbright　Romantic, much-married, and retired actress in Ludwig Bemelmans's *Dirty Eddie*.

Bobbie Allen　Waitress and prostitute who is Joe Christmas's first love in William Faulkner's *Light in August*.

Ethan (Ticonderoga) Allen　Enormous prisoner of war in Pendermis Castle, Falmouth, England, whom Israel Potter observes, in Herman Melville's *Israel Potter*.

Liddy Allen　Maid of Rachel Innes; believes murder and break-ins are the work of ghosts in Mary Roberts Rinehart's *The Circular Staircase*.

Madge Allen (Kramer)　Puma trainer who goes on a short trip to Mexico with Frank Chambers in James M. Cain's *The Postman Always Rings Twice*.

Miss Allen　Nurse at St. Vincent's Hospital; befriends and loves Jason Wheeler in Albert Halper's *Union Square*.

Reverend Allen　Hypocritical minister in Winston Churchill's *Richard Carvel*.

Abigail Allerton　Friend of Hamm Rufe; forced to resign her university history assistantship because of her frankness in writing the political history of the town of Franklin in Mari Sandoz's *Capital City*.

Anna Allston　Cousin and friend of Cornelia Wilton; becomes ill and dies following the disappearance of her husband, Lewis Barnwell, shortly after their wedding in Caroline Gilman's *Recollections of a Southern Matron*.

Almanni　Warrior who rules Odo during Media's absence in Herman Melville's *Mardi*.

Elizabeth Almond　Aunt of Catherine Sloper; hosts a party at which Catherine meets Morris Townsend in Henry James's *Washington Square*.

Marian Almond　Pretty cousin of Catherine Sloper; marries Arthur Townsend and introduces Catherine to Arthur's cousin, Morris Townsend, in Henry James's *Washington Square*.

Almsbury　See John Randolph, Earl of Almsbury.

Lady Emily Almsbury　Meek and faithful wife of John Randolph, Earl of Almsbury, in Kathleen Winsor's *Forever Amber*.

Frank Alpine　Gentile drifter who becomes assistant storekeeper in Bernard Malamud's *The Assistant*.

Gerald (Jerry) Alsop　Self-styled moral adviser with deep respect for conventions and clean living whose close friendship with George Webber breaks down at Harvard when Webber begins to question Alsop's values in Thomas Wolfe's *The Web and the Rock*.

Alva　Son of an American mulatto mother and Filipino father; employed as a presser in a costume house; has an affair with Emma Lou Morgan and fathers an illegitimate child by Geraldine in Wallace Thurman's *The Blacker the Berry*.

Captain Alvarado　Friend of Madre Maria del Pilar; urges Esteban to go to sea with him as an escape from the loss of Thornton Wilder's *The Bridge of San Luis Rey*.

Madame (Manueleta [Manuelata] Hernandez) Alvarez　Ambitious, aristocratic, Spanish-born wife of President Alvarez of Olancho in Richard Harding Davis's *Soldiers of Fortune*.

Pepe Alvarez　Prizefighter once managed by Ed Sansom; former lover of Randolph Lee Skully and the focus of his life in Truman Capote's *Other Voices, Other Rooms*.

President Alvarez　President of Olancho who aspires to establish a dictatorship but is overthrown and executed in Richard Harding Davis's *Soldiers of Fortune*.

Barone Alvarito　Duck-hunting companion of Col. Richard Cantwell in Ernest Hemingway's *Across the River and into the Trees*.

Elizabeth Thornwell (Betty) Alvin   Granddaughter of Cornelia Thornwell; leaves her parents' comfortable home to live modestly with her grandmother; becomes an antiestablishment activist; marries a socialist journalist and fights to save Sacco and Vanzetti from execution in Upton Sinclair's *Boston*.

Blessed (Bles) Alwyn   Favorite pupil of Mary Taylor; lover and later husband of Zora; fails as a Washington politician and returns to Alabama to help blacks free themselves from the sharecropping system in W. E. B. Du Bois's *The Quest of the Silver Fleece*.

Amber   See Amber St. Clare.

George Amberson   Brother of Isabel Amberson Minafer and uncle of George Amberson Minafer; former congressman and a business failure in Booth Tarkington's *The Magnificent Ambersons*.

Isabel Amberson   See Isabel Amberson Minafer.

Major Amberson   Head of a prominent family whose fortunes dwindle so much that he leaves no estate in Booth Tarkington's *The Magnificent Ambersons*.

Ambrosius   Young Franciscan monk who, in 1680, murders Benedicta, the hangman's daughter, to save her from a romance with Rochus in Ambrose Bierce's adaptation of *The Monk and the Hangman's Daughter*.

Amelia   Black maid and youthful friend of the narrator of Aline Bernstein's *The Journey Down*.

Prince Amerigo   Italian nobleman who marries Maggie Verver and who had a previous attachment to Charlotte Stant in Henry James's *The Golden Bowl*.

Bob Ames   Cousin of Mrs. Vance; encourages Carrie Meeber to become an actress in Theodore Dreiser's *Sister Carrie*.

Cathy Ames   See Cathy Ames Trask.

Dalton Ames   Lover of Caddy Compson and the father of Quentin Compson II in William Faulkner's *The Sound and the Fury*.

Mat Ames   Youth who leads a group of boys in the snowball fight against the boys led by Jack Harris in Thomas Bailey Aldrich's *The Story of a Bad Boy*.

Catherine Amesbury   See Cathy Ames Trask.

David Ben Ami   Israeli member of the Palmach; uses biblical passages as military strategies in Leon Uris's *Exodus*.

Amigo   Mexican cowhand for Major Willard Tetley; convinces the lynch mob to seek the rustlers on a trail different from that pursued by Sheriff Risley in Walter Van Tilburg Clark's *The Ox-Bow Incident*.

Jasper Ammen   Egoist who, as a study, plots the murder of a stranger in Conrad Aiken's *King Coffin*.

Amos   Prosperous member of the Chicago Stock Exchange who disapproves of his impractical and nonmaterialistic brother, Joseph, in Saul Bellow's *Dangling Man*.

Mr. Amos   Valet of Congressman Doolittle; keeps Sara Andrews informed of his employer's failing health in W. E. B. Du Bois's *Dark Princess*.

Amram   Hebrew father of Aaron and Miriam, and perhaps of Moses as well; slave in Goshen in Zora Neale Hurston's *Moses, Man of the Mountain*.

Mrs. Amsden   American expatriate and friend of Evalina Bowen; concerned with the affairs of others in William Dean Howells's *Indian Summer*.

Jules Amthor   Psychic consultant in Raymond Chandler's *Farewell, My Lovely*.

Amula   Young woman jealous of the attention Rochus gives Benedicta; comforts Ambrosius before his execution in Ambrose Bierce's adaptation of *The Monk and the Hangman's Daughter*.

Amy   Aunt of Miranda; romanticized by her family as a model of Southern beauty; marries Gabriel Breaux, her longtime suitor, and dies shortly thereafter of tuberculosis in Katherine Anne Porter's *Old Mortality*.

Amyas le Poulet   See Clarence.

Anacleto   Eccentric Filipino manservant excessively devoted to Alison Langdon; disappears shortly after her death in Carson McCullers's *Reflections in a Golden Eye*.

Dame Anaitis (Lady of the Lake)   Ruler of the enchanted island Cocaigne; becomes Jurgen's first wife when he begins a yearlong dalliance in the dream realm in pursuit of his wife Dame Lisa in James Branch Cabell's *Jurgen*.

Jack Analysis   Journalist of Greek parentage and former lover of Molly Calico in Peter De Vries's *The Mackerel Plaza*.

Albert Ancke   Times Square night person and drug addict in John Clellon Holmes's *Go*.

Alfred (Al) Anderson   Proprietor of Al's Lunch Wagon; sympathetic to the Communist labor organizers; helps feed the strikers in John Steinbeck's *In Dubious Battle*.

Andy Anderson   Chief bugler of G Company; feels his position threatened by Robert E. Lee Prewitt; coauthors "The Re-Enlistment Blues" with Prewitt and Sal Clark in James Jones's *From Here to Eternity*.

Bess (Bessie) Anderson   Daughter of Tillie and Ern Anderson and sister of Nonnie and Ed Anderson; college-educated maid in Lillian Smith's *Strange Fruit*.

Betty Anderson   Daughter of mill workers; becomes pregnant by Rodney Harrington and is bought off by his father, Leslie Harrington, in Grace Metalious's *Peyton Place*.

Brigham M. (Brig) Anderson   Senior senator from Utah and chairman of the Senate Foreign Relations Subcommittee on the nomination of Robert Leffingwell in Allen Drury's *Advise and Consent*.

Charley Anderson   World War I ace who has a mercurial career as an airplane parts manufacturer after the war; his obsession with the stock market and his lack of moral principles lead to his ruin in John Dos Passos's *U.S.A.* trilogy.

Ed (Eddie) Anderson   Son of Tillie and Ern Anderson, brother of Nonnie and Bessie Anderson, and killer of Tracy Deen in Lillian Smith's *Strange Fruit*.

Ern Anderson   Husband of Tillie Anderson and father of Nonnie, Bessie, and Ed Anderson in Lillian Smith's *Strange Fruit*.

Homer Anderson   Sociologist and factory personnel administrator and neighbor of Gertie and Clovis Nevels in Harriette Arnow's *The Dollmaker*.

Jaw Buster Anderson   Neighbor of Nunn Ballew, fox hunter, and owner of a logging truck often used to transport neighbors to town from their isolated community in Harriette Arnow's *Hunter's Horn*.

Mrs. Anderson   Neighbor of Gertie and Clovis Nevels and wife of Homer Anderson; brings Gertie the message that the wife of a factory executive wants dolls to be carved for a Christmas bazaar in Harriette Arnow's *The Dollmaker*.

Nonnie (Non) Anderson   Daughter of Tillie and Ern Anderson and sister of Bessie and Ed Anderson; black lover of Tracy Deen and mother of their unborn child in Lillian Smith's *Strange Fruit*.

Dr. Robert Anderson   Principal of a southern black school; moves to New York, where he meets and marries Anne Grey, in Nella Larsen's *Quicksand*.

Tillie Anderson   Mother of Nonnie, Bessie, and Ed Anderson and wife of Ern Anderson; works in white households as a cook in Lillian Smith's *Strange Fruit*.

Andreas   Franciscan Superior of the Monastery of Berchtesgaden in Ambrose Bierce's adaptation of *The Monk and the Hangman's Daughter*.

Andrés   Member of Pablo's partisan group in Ernest Hemingway's *For Whom the Bell Tolls*.

Andrew   Suitor and spiritual adviser of Mary Pinesett, husband of Doll, elder at Heaven's Gate Church, blacksmith, and carpenter at Blue Brook Plantation in Julia Peterkin's *Scarlet Sister Mary*.

Captain Donald Andrews   Math expert and friend of Captain Nathaniel Hicks; Acting Chief of the Statistical Section in James Gould Cozzens's *Guard of Honor*.

Gerald Andrews   Neighbor of Adah Logan and friend of the Mitchells; soldier killed during World War II in Susan Glaspell's *Judd Rankin's Daughter*.

Sara Andrews   See Sara Andrews Towns.

Walter Andrews   Man who, seventy years earlier, owned the property and mansion which is the poorhouse in John Updike's *The Poorhouse Fair*.

Andrei Androfski   Brother of Deborah Bronski, friend of Alexander Brandel and Christopher de Monti, and lover of Gabriela Rak; leads the Warsaw Ghetto Revolt in Leon Uris's *Mila 18*.

Andy   Freedman who tells Comfort Servosse about the local chapter of the Union League; caretaker at Warrington Place who tends to the dying Servosse in Albion W. Tourgee's *A Fool's Errand*.

Sister Angelica   Nun who is Father Trask's apprentice; helps lead the wake for Chalmers Egstrom in William Goyen's *In a Farther Country*.

Angélique   Discarded mistress of Count Armand de Sacy; courtesan living in forced exile at Bréda in Arna Wendell Bontemps's *Drums at Dusk*.

Dr. Angelo   Handsome middle-aged Italian physician at the Diamond County Home for the Aged; treats George Lucas's chronic ear infection in John Updike's *The Poorhouse Fair*.

Earl Angstrom   Husband of Mary Angstrom and father of Rabbit and Miriam Angstrom; works as a printer in John Updike's *Rabbit, Run* and *Rabbit Redux*.

Harry (Rabbit) Angstrom   Husband of Janice Springer Angstrom and father of Nelson Angstrom; talented former basketball player entangled in adult responsibilities in John Updike's *Rabbit, Run*. See also Volume II.

Janice Springer (Jan) Angstrom   Wife of Rabbit Angstrom and mother of Nelson Angstrom; accidentally drowns her infant daughter in John Updike's *Rabbit, Run*. See also Volume II.

Mary Angstrom   Wife of Earl Angstrom and mother of Rabbit and Miriam Angstrom in John Updike's *Rabbit, Run*; suffers from Parkinson's disease in *Rabbit Redux*.

Miriam (Mim) Angstrom   Younger sister of Rabbit Angstrom in John Updike's *Rabbit, Run* and *Rabbit Redux*.

Nelson Frederick Angstrom   Son of Janice and Rabbit Angstrom in John Updike's *Rabbit, Run*. See also Volume II.

Rebecca June Angstrom   Infant daughter of Janice and Rabbit Angstrom; drowns in a bathtub in John Updike's *Rabbit, Run*.

Arch Anker   See The County Clerk.

Ann   Traveling companion and supporter of Francis Starwick in Thomas Wolfe's *Of Time and the River*.

Annatoo   Wife of Samoa; lost at sea in Herman Melville's *Mardi*.

Anna Annesley   Genteel sister-in-law of John Osborne; cares for Mildred and Helen Osborne following their mother's death in Paul Laurence Dunbar's *The Love of Landry*.

Annette   Discarded mistress of Count Armand de Sacy; courtesan living in forced exile at Bréda in Arna Wendell Bontemps's *Drums at Dusk*.

Annixter   Wheat rancher in the San Joaquin Valley who attempts to influence the state's railroad commission and fails; shot by a railroad agent in Frank Norris's *The Octopus*.

Anselm (Arthur, Saint Anselm)   Religious poet and bitter friend of Stanley in William Gaddis's *The Recognitions*.

Anselmo   Old man who is Robert Jordan's guide in Ernest Hemingway's *For Whom the Bell Tolls*.

Mr. Antolini   Former English teacher of Holden Caulfield at Elkton Hills and a refuge for Holden in New York City; gives Holden a pat on the head, a drunkenly intimate gesture that frightens Holden away, in J. D. Salinger's *The Catcher in the Rye*.

Spiros Antonapoulos   Moronic deaf-mute idealized by John Singer; dies of nephritis in an insane asylum in Carson McCullers's *The Heart Is a Lonely Hunter*.

Antone   Middle-aged Portuguese sailor flogged for fighting aboard the *Neversink* in Herman Melville's *White-Jacket*.

Brother (Father) Antonio   Capuchin monk with a mysterious past; model for Miriam's artwork; killed by Donatello in Nathaniel Hawthorne's *The Marble Faun*.

Marc Antony   Nephew of Julius Caesar; caught attempting to seduce Cleopatra and leaving Rome soon after, in Thornton Wilder's *The Ides of March*.

Aonetti (Deer Eyes)   Indian maiden enamored of Koningsmarke in James Kirke Paulding's *Koningsmarke*.

Apeyahola (Indian Jory)   American sailor imprisoned by Tripoli pirates; Creek Indian, trader, pioneer, and cofounder of a town in Oklahoma in H. L. Davis's *Harp of a Thousand Strings*.

Catharine Bosworth Apley   Boston aristocrat chosen by George Apley's family to be his wife in John P. Marquand's *The Late George Apley*.

Eleanor (El) Apley   Daughter of George and Catharine Apley; rebels against her social class and marries an outsider in John P. Marquand's *The Late George Apley*.

George William Apley   Boston aristocrat and lawyer; son of Thomas Apley, husband of Catharine Apley, and father of John and Eleanor Apley; upholds the family tradition and social convention in John P. Marquand's *The Late George Apley*.

John Apley   Son of George and Catharine Apley; rebels against family tradition but returns to assume his role as head of the family and as a proper Bostonian in John P. Marquand's *The Late George Apley*.

Thomas Apley   Boston aristocrat and textile merchant; molds his son George Apley into a proper Bostonian while maintaining an illegitimate family in New York in John P. Marquand's *The Late George Apley*.

William Apley   Manager of the Apley family textile mills; considers his nephew George incompetent to enter the business in John P. Marquand's *The Late George Apley*.

Alf Applegate   Elderly bachelor neighbor of the Birdwells in Jessamyn West's *The Friendly Persuasion*.

Mr. Applegate   Vicar of Christ Church in St. Botolph's; alcoholic whose weakness is responsible for his colorful sermons in John Cheever's *The Wapshot Scandal*.

Stella Appleton   First girlfriend of Eugene Witla in Theodore Dreiser's *The "Genius."*

Apraxine   One of the many ill or handicapped people cared for by Chrysis in Thornton Wilder's *The Woman of Andros*.

Rachel (Little Mother) Apt   Leader of a group of Jewish resistance fighters battling the Nazis from well-concealed bunkers and in the sewers of occupied Warsaw in John Hersey's *The Wall*.

Arai   Younger daughter of Eakahau and Mata, sister of Marama, and servant to Madame de Laage; survives the hurricane in Charles Nordhoff and James Norman Hall's *The Hurricane*.

Julius Arcenaux   Owner of a grocery store, the central gathering place on the Isle aux Chiens, in Shirley Ann Grau's *The Hard Blue Sky*.

Cora (Mamma) Archbald   Widowed daughter-in-law of General Archbald; reared on *Little Women*, she tries to rear her daughter, Jenny Blair Archbald, in the same manner in Ellen Glasgow's *The Sheltered Life*.

General David (Grandfather) Archbald Patriarch who idealizes Eva Birdsong in Ellen Glasgow's *The Sheltered Life.*

Etta (Aunt Etta) Archbald Daughter of General Archbald; invalid, hysterical, and unmarried aunt of Jenny Blair Archbald in Ellen Glasgow's *The Sheltered Life.*

Isabella (Aunt Isabella) Archbald Bold and beautiful aunt of Jenny Blair Archbald; marries Joseph Crocker in Ellen Glasgow's *The Sheltered Life.*

Jenny Blair Archbald Woman who, at age nine, begins keeping a secret with George Birdsong and, at age eighteen, thinks she is in love with him in Ellen Glasgow's *The Sheltered Life.*

Alan Archdale White counsel for Peter in DuBose Heyward's *Porgy.*

Adeline Archer Widowed mother of Newland Archer in Edith Wharton's *The Age of Innocence.*

Alice Archer Sensitive friend of Sally Manchester and Cecilia Vaughan; dies of a broken heart when Cecilia, her best friend, marries Arthur Kavanagh, Alice's secret love, in Henry Wadsworth Longfellow's *Kavanagh.*

Dallas Archer Son of Newland and May Archer in Edith Wharton's *The Age of Innocence.*

Isabel Archer Charming, intellectual, strong-willed heroine who seeks to expand her life experiences in Europe; marries Gilbert Osmond in Henry James's *The Portrait of a Lady.*

Iva Archer Miles Archer's wife, with whom Sam Spade is attempting to end an affair, in Dashiell Hammett's *The Maltese Falcon.*

John Archer Doctor who assists Perry Dart in solving a murder case in Rudolph Fisher's *The Conjure Man Dies.*

Lew Archer California private detective; the hero in eighteen of Ross Macdonald's novels starting with *The Moving Target.*

May Archer See May Welland.

Miles Archer Sam Spade's partner, who is murdered while shadowing Brigid O'Shaughnessy and Floyd Thursby at the beginning of Dashiell Hammett's *The Maltese Falcon.*

Newland Archer Fiancé of May Welland; falls in love with his cousin, Ellen Olenska, in Edith Wharton's *The Age of Innocence.*

Doctor Howard Archie Small-town doctor who recognizes the musical intelligence of Thea Kronborg; helps her move to Chicago to study music and underwrites her studies in Germany in Willa Cather's *The Song of the Lark.*

Arfretee Wife of Deacon Ereemear Po-Po in Herman Melville's *Omoo.*

Argo Sister of Pamphilus in Thornton Wilder's *The Woman of Andros.*

Arheetoo Tahitian casuist who asks Typee to forge documents in Herman Melville's *Omoo.*

Madge Arlen Friend of India Bridge and member of the Women's Auxiliary in Evan Connell's *Mrs. Bridge* and *Mr. Bridge.*

Henry Armstid Poor farmer in William Faulkner's *As I Lay Dying, Light in August, The Hamlet, The Town,* and *The Mansion.*

Martha (Lula) Armstid Wife of Henry Armstid in William Faulkner's *As I Lay Dying, Light in August,* and *The Hamlet.*

Arnold (Aubrey Wallace) Armstrong Son of Paul Armstrong; as Aubrey Wallace he marries and abandons Lucy Haswell; murdered in Mary Roberts Rinehart's *The Circular Staircase.*

Fanny B. (F. B. A.) Armstrong Wife of Paul Armstrong; insists that Rachel Innes give up her lease to Sunnyside in Mary Roberts Rinehart's *The Circular Staircase.*

Louise Armstrong Daughter of Paul Armstrong; secretly returns to Sunnyside when she discovers her father's plot in Mary Roberts Rinehart's *The Circular Staircase.*

Paul Armstrong President of the Traders' Bank who embezzles money and frames John Bailey for the crime in Mary Roberts Rinehart's *The Circular Staircase.*

Clifford Armytage See Merton Gill.

Armenta Arnez Middle-class high school girl to whom Jake Adams is attracted in Herbert Simmons's *Corner Boy.*

Edna Arnez Wife of Henry Arnez and mother of Armenta Arnez in Herbert Simmons's *Corner Boy.*

Henry Arnez Husband of Edna Arnez and father of Armenta Arnez in Herbert Simmons's *Corner Boy.*

Arnold Heavyset young man who lives with his parents; eventually goes to live in the house of Christina Goering with his father and Lucie Gamelon in Jane Bowles's *Two Serious Ladies.*

Benedict Arnold American Revolutionary War colonel who leads an overland attack on Quebec in Kenneth Roberts's *Arundel.*

Julie Hempel Arnold Schoolgirl friend of Selina Peake Dejong; the friendship is renewed later in life in Edna Ferber's *So Big.*

Alcée Arobin Seducer who has an affair with Edna Pontellier in Kate Chopin's *The Awakening.*

Quintus Arrius   Roman tribune who, while in command of a ship, recognizes the slave Judah Ben-Hur's strength and eminence; is fair-minded, kind, and compassionate; is saved by Ben-Hur when pirates attack their ship and names Ben-Hur his legal heir, providing for him thusly; eventually returns to Rome and becomes a duumvir, bequeathing at his death all his riches to Ben-Hur in Lew Wallace's *Ben-Hur: A Tale of the Christ.*

Arrowhead   Untrustworthy Tuscarora Indian who informs the French of the relief party's position in James Fenimore Cooper's *The Pathfinder.*

Joyce Lanyon Arrowsmith   See Joyce Lanyon.

Leora Tozer Arrowsmith   See Leora Tozer.

Martin Arrowsmith   Medical doctor and researcher frustrated by the commercial and confining aspects of his work in Sinclair Lewis's *Arrowsmith.*

Arsella   Servant of a contessa; wife of Pipistrello; Adeppi stays with her family in John Hawkes's *The Goose on the Grave.*

Arthur   Headmaster of a boys' boarding school and companion of Mrs. Montague; patrols Hill House by night with a revolver in Shirley Jackson's *The Haunting of Hill House.*

Arthur (Jones)   King of England who, while posing as a peasant with Hank Morgan, is captured and sold into slavery; rescued by Clarence in Samuel Langhorne Clemens's *A Connecticut Yankee in King Arthur's Court.*

Stephan Asche   See Wyatt Gwyon.

Susan Ash   Maid of Beale Farange in Henry James's *What Maisie Knew.*

Colonel Argall Ashendyne   Father of Medway Ashendyne; leads the family's attempt to force traditional womanhood on his granddaughter, Hagar Ashendyne, in Mary Johnston's *Hagar.*

Hagar Ashendyne   Independent girl who grows to overcome her family and culture; becomes a famous author and an advocate for women's rights in Mary Johnston's *Hagar.*

Medway Ashendyne   Father of Hagar Ashendyne; travels to Europe during her childhood; when he is injured, Hagar assumes responsibility for him in Mary Johnston's *Hagar.*

Benish (Rabbi Benish) Ashkenazi   Revered leader in the Jewish community of Goray, Poland, and father of Levi Ashkenazi; temporarily exiled from Goray after the Chmielnicki massacre of 1648; later returns and remains studiously faithful to the Torah and Jewish tradition, rejecting the Sabbatai Zevi sect as blasphemous, in Isaac Bashevis Singer's *Satan in Goray.*

Levi Ashkenazi   Youngest son of Rabbi Benish Ashkenazi; disdains his father's orthodoxy and leads the followers of Sabbatai Zevi in Isaac Bashevis Singer's *Satan in Goray.*

Lady Brett Ashley   English fiancée of Michael Campbell and former lover of Robert Cohn; has an affair with Pedro Romero in Ernest Hemingway's *The Sun Also Rises.*

Senator Godfrey Ashley   A leading citizen of and chronicler of important social activities in Far Edgerley; junior warden of St. John's Episcopal Church in Constance Fenimore Woolson's *For the Major.*

Jefferson Ashton   Inexperienced and opportunistic attorney retained to defend six black men accused of raping a white woman in T. S. Stribling's *Unfinished Cathedral.*

Julia Ashton   American poet in London during World War I and wife of Rafe Ashton in H. D.'s *Bid Me to Live.*

Rafe Ashton   Poet and soldier married to Julia Ashton but having an affair with Bella Carter in H. D.'s *Bid Me to Live.*

Joe Askew   Army officer who sets up an airplane parts business in partnership with Charley Anderson after the war; when the business is successful, Anderson, who had been living with the Askew family, sells his partner out in a stock exchange deal in John Dos Passos's *U.S.A.* trilogy.

Askwani   White youth reared by the Cherokee of Crow Town; devoted protégé of Ewen Warne; husband of Ruhama Warne in H. L. Davis's *Beulah Land.*

Col. Robert (Bob) Assingham   Retired British army officer and husband of Fanny Assingham; listens to his wife's schemes with detachment in Henry James's *The Golden Bowl.*

Fanny Assingham   American-born wife of the retired British army officer Robert Assingham; becomes a confidante of Maggie Verver and breaks the golden bowl in Henry James's *The Golden Bowl.*

Theodore (Teddy) Ast   Women's garment salesman and manufacturer; gets out of his partnership with Harry Bogen in Apex Modes before it goes bankrupt in Jerome Weidman's *I Can Get It for You Wholesale;* starts his own garment firm and steals Martha Mills from Bogen in *What's in It for Me?*

Asta   Schnauzer of Nick and Nora Charles in Dashiell Hammett's *The Thin Man.*

China Aster   Candlemaker from Marietta, Ohio, whose attempts to repay loans drive him into poverty in Herman Melville's *The Confidence-Man.*

Mack Aston   Dance-marathon contestant in Horace McCoy's *They Shoot Horses, Don't They?*

Atherton   Boston attorney and friend of Bartley Hubbard in William Dean Howells's *A Modern Instance.*

Miss Atkins   Orphanage dietician whom Joe Christmas sees having sex with an intern in William Faulkner's *Light in August.*

George P. Atkinson   Manufacturer of cotton seed products and employer of Mamba in DuBose Heyward's *Mamba's Daughters.*

Lissa Atkinson   Mulatto daughter of Hagar and granddaughter of Mamba; talented singer who appears in a black folk opera at the Metropolitan Opera House in DuBose Heyward's *Mamba's Daughters.*

Miss Maudie Atkinson   Neighbor who defends Atticus Finch to his children; her house is burned down in Harper Lee's *To Kill a Mockingbird.*

Gordon Atterbury   Rejected suitor of Alison Parr in Winston Churchill's *The Inside of the Cup.*

Atti   Lioness kept by King Dahfu in the lower reaches of his castle; aids the transformation of Eugene Henderson from pig man to leonine kingly spirit in Saul Bellow's *Henderson the Rain King.*

Atwater   Architect of expensive homes in Henry Blake Fuller's *The Cliff-Dwellers.*

Mr. Aubineau   Henpecked host in James Kirke Paulding's *The Dutchman's Fireside.*

Mrs. Aubineau   Shrewish hostess in James Kirke Paulding's *The Dutchman's Fireside.*

Audrey   Name assumed at majority by the narrator's wife, Aurora, in Peter De Vries's *The Tunnel of Love.*

Augie (Little Augie, Little Poison)   Tiny black jockey born with a caul; succeeds despite a series of setbacks; protagonist of Arna Wendell Bontemps's *God Sends Sunday.*

Julia Cornelia Augusta   Wealthy young Roman who befriends the destitute Hipparchia in H. D.'s *Palimpsest.*

Augustin   Member of Pablo's partisan group in Ernest Hemingway's *For Whom the Bell Tolls.*

Augustine   Sober French maid of Eugenia Münster in Henry James's *The Europeans.*

Aurora   See Audrey.

Henry (Hank) Austin   Father of four children who is fired from his job as truckman by Old Running Water in Albert Halper's *Union Square.*

Avery   Original owner of the Silver Sun Saloon; tries to persuade Molly Riordan to kill Clay Turner; dies when Turner burns the Silver Sun in E. L. Doctorow's *Welcome to Hard Times.*

Avey   Independent northern black woman; the narrator mistakes her indifference toward him as indolence in Jean Toomer's *Cane.*

Buchanan Malt (Malty) Avis   West Indian friend of Banjo in Claude McKay's *Banjo.*

Dr. Marcus J. Axelrod   Boyhood friend of Herman Gold and prosperous Lower East Side physician in Michael Gold's *Jews without Money.*

Bartolomeo Aymo   Ambulance driver in the command of Frederic Henry; shot and killed by fellow Italian soldiers in the confusion of a retreat in Ernest Hemingway's *A Farewell to Arms.*

Ayres   British army major who attends the yacht party in William Faulkner's *Mosquitoes.*

Azarina   Black servant of Eugenia Münster in Henry James's *The Europeans.*

Fernande (Nande) Azeredo   Exotic Frenchwoman who has an affair with Sam Dodsworth in Sinclair Lewis's *Dodsworth.*

President Azureus   Head of the university who calls a meeting to require the faculty to sign papers of allegiance to the new regime; Adam Krug, whose wife dies only hours before the meeting, alone refuses to sign the declaration in Vladimir Nabokov's *Bend Sinister.*

Eleazar (Reb Eleazar) Babad Wealthiest man in Goray before the 1648 invasion and massacre; afterward, a widower, wanderer, and father who abandons Rechele Babad to relatives in Isaac Bashevis Singer's *Satan in Goray*.

Rechele Babad Epileptic daughter of Reb Eleazar Babad, wife of Reb Itche Mates in an unconsummated marriage, and mistress and later wife of Reb Gedaliya; called a prophetess by the people of Goray, she is tormented and impregnated by Satan in Isaac Bashevis Singer's *Satan in Goray*.

Babbalanja Philosopher from Odo and Taji's companion in Herman Melville's *Mardi*.

Eunice Littlefield Babbitt See Eunice Littlefield.

George F. (Georgie) Babbitt Realtor and faithful Zenith civic booster who fails to find happiness upholding community values in Sinclair Lewis's *Babbitt;* also appears in *Elmer Gantry*.

Katherine (Tinka) Babbitt Daughter of George and Myra Babbitt; adored by her father in Sinclair Lewis's *Babbitt*.

Myra Thompson Babbitt Patient wife of George Babbitt; mother of Katherine, Theodore, and Verona Babbitt in Sinclair Lewis's *Babbitt*.

Theodore Roosevelt (Ted) Babbitt Son of George and Myra Babbitt; would-be automobile mechanic who elopes with Eunice Littlefield in Sinclair Lewis's *Babbitt*.

Verona (Rone) Babbitt Daughter of George and Myra Babbitt; Bryn Mawr graduate who marries Kenneth Escott in Sinclair Lewis's *Babbitt*.

Dwight Babcock Stodgy member of the Knickerbocker Trust Company who is Patrick Dennis's trustee and Mame Dennis's nemesis in Patrick Dennis's *Auntie Mame* and *Around the World with Auntie Mame*.

Meyer Babushkin Partner of Harry Bogen in Apex Modes, a women's garments manufacturing company; goes to jail because of Bogen's stealing from the firm in Jerome Weidman's *I Can Get It for You Wholesale*.

Jesus de Baca Old, poor priest of Isleta whose sole worldly possession is a wooden parrot in Willa Cather's *Death Comes for the Archbishop*.

Bach Crippled ex-Nazi married to a woman who is half-Jewish in Thomas Berger's *Crazy in Berlin*.

Richard Bache Son-in-law of Benjamin Franklin; gets Thomas Paine a job as a tutor when Paine first arrives in America in Howard Fast's *Citizen Tom Paine*.

Linda (Lin) Bachofen Beautiful blonde government enforcer and sister of Mariette Bachofen; comes with her fiancé to arrest Mr. Ember and later appears with another fiancé, Doctor Alexander, to arrest Adam and David Krug; executed for her mistakes in Vladimir Nabokov's *Bend Sinister*.

Mariette (Mariechen) Bachofen Young sister of Linda Bachofen who becomes David Krug's nurse; probably informs on Adam Krug; dies after being raped by forty soldiers in Vladimir Nabokov's *Bend Sinister*.

Abra Bacon Young woman engaged to marry Aron Trask but who feels unworthy of his extreme virtue and trapped by his narrow view of life and love; realizes that Caleb Trask is the one she truly loves in John Steinbeck's *East of Eden*.

Lillian Bacon Dance-marathon partner of Pedro Ortega; violently attacked by Ortega when he learns that Rocky Gravo attempted to seduce her in Horace McCoy's *They Shoot Horses, Don't They?*

Ray Badger Ne'er-do-well first husband of Melissa Scaddon Wapshot; jewel thief and rival to Moses Wapshot in John Cheever's *The Wapshot Chronicle.*

Proctor (Proc) Baggart Bigoted and disreputable magistrate charged with keeping blacks subservient and with maintaining law and order in the district outside Charleston where Charles Raymond's Phosphate Mining Company is located in DuBose Heyward's *Mamba's Daughters.*

John (Alex, Alexander Graham, Jack) Bailey Bank cashier accused of murdering Arnold Armstrong and of causing the Traders' Bank to fail; disguises himself as a gardener in order to clear his name in Mary Roberts Rinehart's *The Circular Staircase.*

Thomas (Tom) Bailey Youth who has numerous adventures in Rivermouth; narrator of Thomas Bailey Aldrich's *The Story of a Bad Boy.*

Bump Baily Outfielder for the Knights, practical joker, and lover of Memo Paris; dies going after a fly ball in Bernard Malamud's *The Natural.*

Joe Baily Rival of Augie; a bad nigger who contends with Tom Wright for the affection of Florence Dessau in Arna Wendell Bontemps's *God Sends Sunday.*

Lulu Bains Daughter of a church deacon; Elmer Gantry narrowly escapes having to marry her, although he later has an affair with her, in Sinclair Lewis's *Elmer Gantry.*

Jeff Baird Director of comedy films who gives Merton Gill his first starring role, in Harry Leon Wilson's *Merton of the Movies.*

Helen Baker Friend of Larry Donovan; works at a hot dog stand in Jack Conroy's *The Disinherited.*

Jordan Baker Dishonest friend of Daisy Buchanan; romantically involved with Nick Carraway in F. Scott Fitzgerald's *The Great Gatsby.*

Lou Garbo (Left Bank, Montana Lou) Baker Bohemian and writer; mistress of Jesse Proctor in Wright Morris's *The Huge Season.*

Miss Baker Elderly woman who falls in love with Old Grannis in Frank Norris's *McTeague.*

Mrs. Samuel Baker Widow of a Washington lobbyist and client of John Carrington, to whom she reveals the improper dealings of Senator Ratcliffe, in Henry Adams's *Democracy.*

Steve Baker Actor on the Cotton Blossom who leaves the showboat with his wife Julie Dozier in Edna Ferber's *Show Boat.*

Annabel Balch Fiancée of Lucius Harney and rival of Charity Royall in Edith Wharton's *Summer.*

George Baldwin Unscrupulous attorney who rises to the top of his profession and becomes the third husband of Ellen Thatcher in John Dos Passos's *Manhattan Transfer.*

Baldy Scotch sailor aboard the *Neversink* whose life is saved by Cadwallader Cuticle in Herman Melville's *White-Jacket.*

Balfour Merchant who rescues Constantia Dudley from a group of ruffians; Constantia rejects him after a subsequent courtship in Charles Brockden Brown's *Ormond.*

Lord Balham Englishman and commissioner for refugees of the Society of Nations; Mary Douglas solicits his aid in blocking the expulsion order for German and Austrian refugees in Martha Gellhorn's *A Stricken Field.*

Professor Ball Headmaster of an academy for boys and a leader of the Free Farmers' Brotherhood of Protection and Control, a vigilante organization designed to control tobacco prices by any means necessary, in Robert Penn Warren's *Night Rider.*

John (Old John, Uncle John) Ballew Second cousin of Nunn Ballew; prosperous, highly respected farmer in Harriette Arnow's *Hunter's Horn;* sells land to Gertie Nevels in *The Dollmaker.*

Lee Roy Ballew Eldest son of Nunn and Milly Ballew; assumes responsibilities as man of the house while his father fox hunts in Harriette Arnow's *Hunter's Horn.*

Lucy Ballew Youngest daughter of Nunn and Milly Ballew in Harriette Arnow's *Hunter's Horn.*

Milly Ballew Long-suffering, hardworking wife of Nunn Ballew and mother of five living children and two others who died young in Harriette Arnow's *Hunter's Horn.*

Nunnely Danforth (Nunn) Ballew Kentucky fox hunter obsessed with chasing the fox called King Devil; husband of Milly Ballew in Harriette Arnow's *Hunter's Horn.*

Suse Ballew Intelligent, sensitive adolescent daughter of Nunn and Milly Ballew; longs to escape her family's poverty in Little Smokey Creek, Kentucky, in Harriette Arnow's *Hunter's Horn.*

William Danforth (Bill Dan) Ballew Baby son of Nunn and Milly Ballew in Harriette Arnow's *Hunter's Horn.*

Balthasar Egyptian companion of Sheik Ilderim and friend of Judah Ben-Hur; father of the lovely but cunning Iras; helps Ben-Hur defeat his enemy, the Roman Messala, and helps Ben-Hur find his imprisoned mother and sister; after the miracle of curing the female Hurs' leprosy, becomes a follower of Jesus Christ in Lew Wallace's *Ben-Hur: A Tale of the Christ.*

Baltimore   Black cook aboard the *Julia* who delivers the round robin to the English consul on Tahiti in Herman Melville's *Omoo*.

Lord Baltimore   See Charles Calvert, Lord Baltimore.

Hugo Bamman   World War I ambulance driver, freelance journalist and documentary novelist, communist, and former schoolmate of the narrator in Edmund Wilson's *I Thought of Daisy*.

Catherine Banahan   Fiancée of Studs Lonigan; conceives their child, although he dies before they can wed, in James T. Farrell's *Judgment Day*.

Cesare (Rico) Bandello   Ambitious and ruthless gang leader who takes over Sam Vettori's gang; enjoys seven years of success and fame before he is forced to flee Chicago and is killed in Toledo, Ohio, in William Riley Burnett's *Little Caesar*.

Isabel (Bell) Banford   Apparently the illegitimate daughter of Pierre Glendinning II; she and Pierre Glendinning III pretend to be married in Herman Melville's *Pierre*.

Thomas Buckminster (Tommy) Bangs   Sociable, mischievous boy in Louisa May Alcott's *Little Men*.

William Hays (Will) Banion   Kentuckian who leads the Liberty covered wagon train in Emerson Hough's *The Covered Wagon*.

Banjo   See Lincoln Agrippa Daily.

Freddie Banks   Twelve-year-old boyfriend of Jane Baxter in Booth Tarkington's *Seventeen*.

Joseph Banks   President of the Royal Society who secures Roger Byam a midshipman's berth on HMS *Bounty* so Byam can compile a dictionary of the Tahitian language; provides for Byam's defense after he is returned to England as a mutineer in Charles Nordhoff and James Norman Hall's *Mutiny on the Bounty*.

Si Banks   Leftist writer and friend of the narrator in Edmund Wilson's *Memoirs of Hecate County*.

Wallace Banks   Obsequious friend of William Baxter; usually gets the unenviable jobs of master of ceremonies and money taker for the jaunts of the young townspeople in Booth Tarkington's *Seventeen*.

Judge Goodwill Banner   Owner of the New York Knights baseball team in Bernard Malamud's *The Natural*.

Roger Bannon   Ambitious building contractor who attracts Grace Caldwell Tate in John O'Hara's *A Rage to Live*.

Henry (Hank) Banta   Mean boy, a compound of deceit and resentment, who causes Ralph Hartsook trouble in Edward Eggleston's *The Hoosier School-Master*.

Jean (The Homesteader, St. John the Baptist) Baptiste   Black homesteader; would-be lover of Agnes Stewart and husband of Orlean McCarthy in Oscar Micheaux's *The Homesteader*.

Antonina Barabo   Elder daughter of Signor Barabo; fascinated by the power of Il Gufo, she declares her love and offers herself to him in John Hawkes's *The Owl*.

Ginevra Barabo   Younger sister of Antonina Barabo; attacked by Il Gufo's pet owl in John Hawkes's *The Owl*.

Signor Barabo   Father of Antonina and Ginevra Barabo; tries to obtain the release of a prisoner to marry Antonina in John Hawkes's *The Owl*.

Tommy Barban   Soldier of fortune who becomes Nicole Warren Diver's second husband in F. Scott Fitzgerald's *Tender Is the Night*.

Arthur Barber   Student council president who tries to convince Dr. Charles Osman to change his mind about failing Raymond Blent in Howard Nemerov's *The Homecoming Game*.

Márgara Bárcenas   Beautiful daughter of a fugitive of the Revolution and lover of Domingo Vizquez de Anda in Josefina Niggli's *Step Down, Elder Brother*.

Edith Barclay   Secretary to Frank Hirsh; later becomes his second mistress but leaves for Chicago after Agnes Hirsh discovers their affair in James Jones's *Some Came Running*.

Jane Mason Barclay   Wife of John Barclay and mother of Jeanette Barclay; her death from typhoid fever is indirectly caused by her husband's greed in William Allen White's *A Certain Rich Man*.

Jeanette Barclay   Daughter of John and Jane Barclay; marries Neal Dow Ward after her father is rid of his fortune in William Allen White's *A Certain Rich Man*.

John (Johnnie) Barclay   Capitalist who founds the Golden Belt Wheat Company monopoly; husband of Jane Barclay and father of Jeanette Barclay; after his wife's death, he dismantles his fortune and returns to Sycamore Ridge in William Allen White's *A Certain Rich Man*.

Amanda (Miss Manda) Barcroft   Jilted lover of Harley Drew in Shelby Foote's *Love in a Dry Season*.

Florence (Miss Flaunts) Barcroft   Invalid sister of Amanda Barcroft in Shelby Foote's *Love in a Dry Season*.

Major Malcolm Barcroft   Cotton factor in Bristol, Mississippi, and father of Amanda and Florence Barcroft in Shelby Foote's *Love in a Dry Season*.

Bardianni   Sage who influences Babbalanja in Herman Melville's *Mardi*.

Carbon Bareau   Mountaineer who identifies Arnaud du Tilh as his nephew in Janet Lewis's *The Wife of Martin Guerre.*

Mr. Barham   English visitor to Kentucky in James Kirke Paulding's *Westward Ho!*

Damon Barker   Lost father of Agnes Deming and loyal father-surrogate to Jo Erring and Ned Westlock in E. W. Howe's *The Story of a Country Town.*

Ned Barker   Bullying, blundering boy in Louisa May Alcott's *Little Men.*

Catherine Barkley   English volunteer hospital worker in Italy at the beginning of World War I; falls in love with Frederic Henry and dies of hemorrhaging after the Caesarean delivery of their stillborn son in Ernest Hemingway's *A Farewell to Arms.*

King Barlo   Charismatic black preacher and field laborer famous for his cane-cutting and his attractiveness to women in Jean Toomer's *Cane.*

Joel Barlow   American expatriate in France who helps arrange for the publication of Thomas Paine's *The Age of Reason* in Howard Fast's *Citizen Tom Paine.*

Augustus Barnard   Spirited friend of Arthur Gordon Pym; arranges Pym's stowaway on the *Grampus*; wounded in the re-taking of the ship from mutineers; dies from exposure and malnutrition in Edgar Allan Poe's *The Narrative of Arthur Gordon Pym.*

Mr. Barnard   Father of Augustus Barnard and captain of the *Grampus*; set adrift when the ship's crew mutinies in Edgar Allan Poe's *The Narrative of Arthur Gordon Pym.*

Benecia Wallin Barnes   Wife of Solon Barnes and mother of five children, including Etta and Stewart Barnes, in Theodore Dreiser's *The Bulwark.*

Etta Barnes   Daughter of Solon and Benecia Barnes; disregards her parents' wishes and attends the University of Wisconsin; mistress of Willard Kane; returns home following the suicide of her brother Stewart Barnes in Theodore Dreiser's *The Bulwark.*

Hannah and Rufus Barnes   Quaker parents of Solon Barnes in Theodore Dreiser's *The Bulwark.*

Jacob (Jake) Barnes   American newspaperman in Paris rendered impotent by a war wound; narrator of Ernest Hemingway's *The Sun Also Rises.*

Lett Barnes   Poet and friend of Julia Ashton in H. D.'s *Bid Me to Live.*

Mattie Barnes   Original dance-marathon partner of Kid Kamm; collapses and is eliminated from the competition in Horace McCoy's *They Shoot Horses, Don't They?*

Solon Barnes   Quaker farmer and businessman who attempts to be both successful and a good Quaker in Theodore Dreiser's *The Bulwark.*

Stewart (Stew) Barnes   Son of Solon and Benecia Barnes; commits suicide following his involvement in the death of Psyche Tanzer in Theodore Dreiser's *The Bulwark.*

Anna Allston Barnwell   See Anna Allston.

Bill Barnwell   Slave beaten by his master Lewis Barnwell in Caroline Gilman's *Recollections of a Southern Matron.*

Lewis Barnwell   Girlhood boyfriend of Cornelia Wilton; disappears shortly after his marriage to Anna Allston in Caroline Gilman's *Recollections of a Southern Matron.*

Amadeus Baroque   Mill worker who finds and reads the only extant manuscript of Doctor Sax, written under the pen name Adolphus Asher Ghoulens, in Jack Kerouac's *Doctor Sax.*

Augustus M. Barr   Unscrupulous ex-minister; steals Peter Kaden's beloved in Oscar Micheaux's *The Homesteader.*

Lilli Barr   See Ellen Tolliver.

Celestine Barre   Wife of Raoul Barre in Allen Drury's *Advise and Consent.*

Raoul Barre   French ambassador to the United States; with his wife, Celestine Barre, and the British ambassador, expresses the NATO countries' viewpoint in Allen Drury's *Advise and Consent.*

Delia Barron   Unrelenting flirt whose interest in George Birdsong causes one of Eva Birdsong's early attacks of neuralgia in Ellen Glasgow's *The Sheltered Life.*

Grace Barron   Wife of Virgil Barron and friend of the Bridges; commits suicide in Evan Connell's *Mrs. Bridge* and *Mr. Bridge.*

Virgil Barron   Bank executive, husband of Grace Barron, and friend of the Bridges in Evan Connell's *Mrs. Bridge* and *Mr. Bridge.*

Wilkie Barron   Acquaintance of Jeremiah Beaumont in law school and successful politician; preserves Beaumont's manuscript and shoots himself tidily through the heart in Robert Penn Warren's *World Enough and Time.*

Barrow   Friend of Berkeley (Howard Tracy) in Samuel Langhorne Clemens's *The American Claimant.*

G. H. Barrow   Randy labor lobbyist whom J. Ward Morehouse uses to forge a cooperative spirit between management and labor; lover of Mary French in John Dos Passos's *U.S.A.* trilogy.

Bart   Hangman who executes Ben Harper in Davis Grubb's *The Night of the Hunter.*

Lily Bart   Well-bred but poor New York socialite whose futile attempts to arrange a suitable marriage for herself initiate the central plot of Edith Wharton's *The House of Mirth.*

Bartlett   Rancher who sways the mob to the idea of lynching the rustlers in Walter Van Tilburg Clark's *The Ox-Bow Incident.*

Edith Bartlett   Nineteenth-century fiancée of Julian West in Edward Bellamy's *Looking Backward.*

Barton   Twenty-first-century minister who preaches to thousands via telephone in Edward Bellamy's *Looking Backward.*

Mistress Bartram   Teacher who bears a child by Portius Wheeler; the child is named Rosa Tench after Bartram marries Jake Tench in Conrad Richter's *The Fields;* becomes a recluse in *The Town.*

Brush Bascom   Political manipulator and dispenser of bribes in Winston Churchill's *Mr. Crewe's Career.*

Chaplain Bascom   Baptist chaplain and friend of Father Donovan; rushes to save Donovan but is crushed by the same lorry that kills his friend in John Horne Burns's *The Gallery.*

Bashti   Island chief who leads the destruction of the Arangi and is Jerry's keeper in Jack London's *Jerry of the Islands.*

Jethro Bass   Devious political boss who is personally a kind and genuinely concerned leader; loves Cynthia Ware; guardian of Cynthia Wetherell in Winston Churchill's *Coniston.*

Claude Bassett   Educated orphan and drifter; seasonal husband of Maggie Moore who returns every winter and leaves every spring until his death in Betty Smith's *Maggie-Now.*

Ethel Bassett   First wife of Will Brady; spends their wedding night rolled in a sheet and later abandons him in Wright Morris's *The Works of Love.*

Georgie (The Little Gentleman) Bassett   Boy whose excellent behavior and refined ways irritate Penrod Schofield in Booth Tarkington's *Penrod, Penrod and Sam,* and *Penrod Jashber.*

Bastock   Driver for Huguenine's circus who trains Caroline Trid to be Carolina, lady high rider, in Walter D. Edmonds's *Chad Hanna.*

Bat   Motion picture mechanic who lives at Queenie's Boarding House; part of the group that sings with George Brush in Thornton Wilder's *Heaven's My Destination.*

Obed (Dr. Battius) Bat   Naturalist full of book knowledge but deficient in common sense; accompanies Ishmael Bush and clan onto the prairie; serves as a comic foil to Natty Bumppo in James Fenimore Cooper's *The Prairie.*

Henry Bates   Mulatto lover of Teresa Cary; forced away on the day of their elopement by Teresa's mother, Olivia Cary, in Jessie Redmon Fauset's *Comedy, American Style.*

James Bates   Dance-marathon contestant who, with his wife, Ruby, is Robert Syverten's and Gloria Beatty's best friend in the marathon in Horace McCoy's *They Shoot Horses, Don't They?*

Josep Bates   New England tutor of Cornelia Wilton and her brothers in Caroline Gilman's *Recollections of a Southern Matron.*

Ruby Bates   Dance partner and wife of James Bates; her participation in a marathon while pregnant is protested by the Mothers' League for Good Morals in Horace McCoy's *They Shoot Horses, Don't They?*

Sue Lathrop Bates   Head of Chicago society in Henry Blake Fuller's *With the Procession;* also appears in *The Cliff-Dwellers.*

Hymie Bateshaw   Mad pseudoscientist who studies boredom and thus claims to have discovered how to generate life; survives the shipwreck of the Sam MacManus with Augie March, whom he attacks viciously, in Saul Bellow's *The Adventures of Augie March.*

Miss Priscilla Batte   Majestic teacher at Dinwiddie Academy for Young Ladies, guardian of the old order, and matchmaker in Ellen Glasgow's *Virginia.*

Camille Turner Batterson   Retired teacher of writing and symbol of civilized behavior in Randall Jarrell's *Pictures from an Institution.*

Cynthia Battiloro   Former love of William Demarest, whom she meets unexpectedly aboard ship in Conrad Aiken's *Blue Voyage.*

Max Battisfore   Sheriff of Iron Cliffs County in Robert Traver's *Anatomy of a Murder.*

Baucis   Male slave on the Sawyer plantation; accompanies the Laceys to Beulah and returns with them to the Tidewater in Mary Lee Settle's *Beulah Land.*

Eva (Greek) Baum   Femme fatale of Earl Horter in Wright Morris's *Love among the Cannibals.*

Baxter   See Hagar.

Ezra Ezekial (Pa, Penny) Baxter   Honest and hardworking man who affectionately oversees the boyhood of his son, Jody Baxter, in Marjorie Kinnan Rawlings's *The Yearling.*

Jane (Little Jane) Baxter   Ten-year-old sister of William Baxter; pesters her brother while he is suffering the pangs of adolescent love in Booth Tarkington's *Seventeen.*

Jody Baxter   Adolescent who adopts an orphaned fawn; matures when his mother shoots the fawn to save the family food supply in Marjorie Kinnan Rawlings's *The Yearling.*

Mrs. Baxter   Patient, sympathetic, and long-suffering mother of William Baxter; tries to cope with her son's infatuation with

Miss Lola Pratt during his seventeenth summer in Booth Tarkington's *Seventeen*.

Ory (Ma) Baxter Hardworking mother of Jody Baxter in Marjorie Kinnan Rawlings's *The Yearling*.

Sarah Baxter Devoted friend of Constantia Dudley; reveals to Constantia a connection between Ursula Monrose and Ormond; loses her husband and their two daughters to yellow fever in Charles Brockden Brown's *Ormond*.

William Sylvanus (Silly Bill) Baxter Seventeen-year-old who makes a fool of himself when he falls in love with Miss Lola Pratt in Booth Tarkington's *Seventeen*.

Alice (Alie) Beach Younger sister of Lucy Beach; at forty-three, senses that her life lacks meaning but ignores her sister's encouragement to leave their mother in William Maxwell's *Time Will Darken It*.

Lucy Beach Older sister of Alice Beach; given musical training but denied a career by her mother; expresses her frustration near the end of William Maxwell's *Time Will Darken It*.

Major General Ira N. (Bus) Beal Commander at Ocanara Army Air Base whose leadership is tested when black officers attempt to use the officers' club in James Gould Cozzens's *Guard of Honor*.

Miss Beale Temperance and religious activist who teaches Patience Sparhawk about people's obsessive roles in Gertrude Atherton's *Patience Sparhawk and Her Times*.

Mrs. Beale See Mrs. Beale Farange.

John Bear Deaf-mute Pawnee Indian who helps Molly Riordan when she is burned; flees town when Clay Turner appears for a second time in E. L. Doctorow's *Welcome to Hard Times*.

Dr. Shakespeare Agamemnon Beard Black founder of the National Social Equality League in George S. Schuyler's *Black No More*.

Angus Beaton Arrogant art director of the magazine *Every Other Week* in William Dean Howells's *A Hazard of New Fortunes*.

Beatty Captain of the firemen who burn books in Ray Bradbury's *Fahrenheit 451*.

Gloria Beatty Cynical aspiring actress who convinces Robert Syverten to enter the dance marathon with her; killed by Syverten at her request in Horace McCoy's *They Shoot Horses, Don't They?*

Emily Crayton Beauchamp Daughter of Colonel Crayton and only true friend of Charlotte Temple among the gentility in the United States; writes to Charlotte's parents in England to explain the plight of their daughter in Susanna Rowson's *Charlotte*.

Henry Beauchamp Son of Lucas and Mollie Beauchamp in William Faulkner's *Go Down, Moses*.

Hubert Beauchamp Plantation owner and uncle of Ike McCaslin in William Faulkner's *Go Down, Moses*.

James Thucydides (Tennie's Jim, Thucydus) Beauchamp Son of Tomey's Turl and Tennie Beauchamp in William Faulkner's *Go Down, Moses*; grandfather of Bobo Beauchamp in *The Reivers*.

Lucas Quintus Carothers McCaslin Beauchamp Son of Tomey's Turl and Tennie Beauchamp; accused of murdering Vinson Gowrie; appears in William Faulkner's *Go Down, Moses*; *Intruder in the Dust*; and *The Reivers*.

Molly (Mollie) Beauchamp Wife of Lucas Beauchamp in William Faulkner's *Go Down, Moses* and *Intruder in the Dust*.

Philip Manigault Beauchamp Soldier who helps execute General Gragnon in William Faulkner's *A Fable*.

Samuel Worsham Beauchamp Grandson of Lucas and Molly Beauchamp; executed for killing a Chicago policeman in William Faulkner's *Go Down, Moses*.

Sophonsiba Beauchamp See Sophonsiba Beauchamp McCaslin.

Tennie Beauchamp Wife of Tomey's Turl and mother of James Thucydides (Tennie's Jim, Thucydus), Lucas, and Sophonsiba Beauchamp in William Faulkner's *Go Down, Moses*; great-grandmother of Bobo Beauchamp in *The Reivers*.

Tomey's Turl Beauchamp Husband of Tennie Beauchamp and father of James Thucydides (Tennie's Jim, Thucydus), Lucas, and Sophonsiba Beauchamp in William Faulkner's *Go Down, Moses*; a character of the same name appears in *The Town*.

Julius Beaufort Husband of Regina Beaufort; wealthy banker of mysterious origins and dissipated habits in Edith Wharton's *The Age of Innocence*.

Regina Dallas Beaufort Wife of Julius Beaufort and ostentatious hostess of old New York society in Edith Wharton's *The Age of Innocence*.

Jeremiah (Jerry, William K. Grierson) Beaumont Altruist and author of the manuscript that provides the plot of the novel; kills Colonel Cassius Fort, escapes from jail, but is caught and decapitated in Robert Penn Warren's *World Enough and Time*.

Ned Beaumont Gambler who investigates murder charges against his friend, political boss Paul Madvig, in Dashiell Hammett's *The Glass Key*.

Rachel Jordan Beaumont Wife of Jeremiah Beaumont and former lover of Colonel Cassius Fort, father of her first child, in Robert Penn Warren's *World Enough and Time*.

Beauty (Chips)   Ugly carpenter aboard the *Julia* in Herman Melville's *Omoo*.

Martinette de Beauvais (Ursula Monrose)   Purchaser of the lute Constantia Dudley sells to alleviate her family's financial distress; revealed to be the sister of Ormond, from whom she was separated during adolescence, in Charles Brockden Brown's *Ormond*.

Tug Beavers   Poor-white teamster on a railroad construction gang who is murdered by Peck Bradley in T. S. Stribling's *Teeftallow*.

Becky   White southerner who bears two black sons; dies alone, rejected by both black and white religious communities, in Jean Toomer's *Cane*.

Duncan Bedford   Son of Malcolm and Sarah Bedford; after serving in the Confederate army, he returns to Portobello plantation and marries Julia Valette Somerville in Stark Young's *So Red the Rose*.

Lieutenant Bedford   Platoon leader in France during World War I who is killed at the battle of Soissons in Thomas Boyd's *Through the Wheat*.

Malcolm (Mac) Bedford   Husband of Sarah Tate Bedford, father of Duncan Bedford, and owner of Portobello plantation in Natchez; joins the Confederate army and dies of typhus in Stark Young's *So Red the Rose*.

Sarah Tate (Sallie, Tait) Bedford   Wife of Malcolm Bedford and mother of Duncan Bedford; widowed during the Civil War, she manages Portobello plantation until Duncan returns from the army in Stark Young's *So Red the Rose*.

Record Head (Bednarski) Bednar   Veteran Chicago police captain who bears the guilt of the criminals with whom he has dealt in Nelson Algren's *The Man with the Golden Arm*.

Mrs. Beech   President of the Women's City Club interested in political reform in Chicago; in an attempt to join forces with others who share her reform interests, she is one of the white guests at Sara Andrews Towns's dinner party in W. E. B. Du Bois's *Dark Princess*.

Cyrus U. (Beeky) Beekman   Cunning and devious opportunist and Union army officer who exploits southern whites and blacks; carpetbag candidate for governor of Alabama who advocates a New South commercial ethic in T. S. Stribling's *The Forge and The Store*.

Sir Francis (Piggie) Beekman   Wealthy man attracted to Lorelei Lee; she is affectionate to him long enough to gain a diamond tiara that his wife desires for herself in Anita Loos's *Gentlemen Prefer Blondes*.

Gracie Beekman   See Gracie Vaiden.

Hiram Beers   Horse trainer and menial-for-hire for Norwood; serves as an ambulance driver during the Civil War and becomes Reuben Wentworth's stable hand in Henry Ward Beecher's *Norwood*.

Shep Beery   Accomplice of Gerry Kells in Paul Cain's *Fast One*.

S. Behrman   Railroad agent in the San Joaquin Valley who manipulates the law to the disadvantage of the wheat growers in Frank Norris's *The Octopus*.

Thami Beidaoui   Family outcast; Moroccan friend and victim of Nelson Dyar in Paul Bowles's *Let It Come Down*.

Carl Belcher   Incompetent night foreman at the Past Bay Manufacturing Company factory who precipitates the strike in Robert Cantwell's *The Land of Plenty*.

Belcour   Unscrupulous friend of Jack Montraville; convinces Montraville to desert Charlotte Temple on the claim that she is faithless; dies at the hands of Montraville when Montraville learns of the deception in Susanna Rowson's *Charlotte*.

Amy Belden   Widow who helps Mary Leavenworth and Henry Clavering elope, and who hides the maid Hannah Chester after the murder of Horatio Leavenworth, in Anna Katharine Green's *The Leavenworth Case*.

Gilbert Belden   Partner with David Marshall in a wholesale grocery in Henry Blake Fuller's *With the Procession*.

Belinda (Marie O'Neill)   Movie star at Olympia Studios; married to Maurice Cassard in Ludwig Bemelmans's *Dirty Eddie*.

Bell   Proprietor of a sugar plantation in Taloo; married to a beautiful woman from Sydney in Herman Melville's *Omoo*.

Joe Bell   Lexington Avenue bartender who takes messages for Holly Golightly in Truman Capote's *Breakfast at Tiffany's*.

Belladonna   Female piglet in Ludwig Bemelmans's *Dirty Eddie*.

Blondy Belle   Former moll and girlfriend of Little Arnie Worch; takes up with Rico Bandello and alerts him to Arnie's cheating on Rico in William Riley Burnett's *Little Caesar*.

Claire de Bellegarde   See Claire de Bellegarde de Cintré.

Emmeline de Bellegarde   Murderer of her husband and mother of Claire de Cintré; opposes the marriage of Claire and Christopher Newman in Henry James's *The American*.

Henri-Urbain de Bellegarde   Husband of Emmeline de Bellegarde and father of Claire, Urbain, and Valentin de Bellegarde; murdered by his wife and Urbain because he opposed Claire's first marriage in Henry James's *The American*.

Madame Urbain de Bellegarde   Unhappily married wife of Urbain de Bellegarde; encourages Christopher Newman's suit of Claire de Cintré in Henry James's *The American*.

Urbain de Bellegarde   Eldest son of Emmeline de Bellegarde, with whom he plots to kill his father; despises Christopher Newman in Henry James's *The American*.

Valentin de Bellegarde   Younger brother of Urbain de Bellegarde and friend of Christopher Newman; killed by Stanislas Kapp in a duel over Noémie Nioche in Henry James's *The American*.

Clare Bellew   See Clare Kendry.

John Bellew   White husband of Clare Kendry; businessman and former South American adventurer; after discovering Clare is black, he confronts her in a Harlem apartment, where she falls to her death, in Nella Larsen's *Passing*.

Margery Bellew   Daughter of John Bellew and Clare Kendry; attends boarding school in Switzerland in Nella Larsen's *Passing*.

Bellingham   Governor of Massachusetts Bay who wants to take Pearl from her mother, Hester Prynne, in Nathaniel Hawthorne's *The Scarlet Letter*.

Louis (Schemer) Bellini   Family man who leads a double life; dies from a gunshot wound suffered in a robbery in William Riley Burnett's *The Asphalt Jungle*.

John R. (Boss) Bellmann   Politician elected on a reform platform and later murdered in Paul Cain's *Fast One*.

James Bellmont   Abolitionist sympathizer who befriends Frado; business associate of his brother, Lewis Bellmont, and husband of Susan Bellmont; dies after a lingering illness in Harriet E. Wilson's *Our Nig*.

Jane Bellmont   Invalid daughter of John and Mrs. Bellmont; marries George Means against her mother's will in Harriet E. Wilson's *Our Nig*.

Jenny Bellmont   Young woman from a poor family in the West; marries Jack Bellmont and suffers the hatred and lies of her mother-in-law, Mrs. Bellmont, in Harriet E. Wilson's *Our Nig*.

John Bellmont   Kind patriarch of the Bellmont family who tries to protect Frado from the cruelty of Mrs. Bellmont in Harriet E. Wilson's *Our Nig*.

John (Jack) Bellmont   Youngest son of John and Mrs. Bellmont; befriends Frado (Alfrado), a girl of mixed race indentured to his family, and defies his mother and sister on her behalf, claiming her as his protégé; husband of Jenny Bellmont in Harriet E. Wilson's *Our Nig*.

Lewis Bellmont   Son of John and Mrs. Bellmont; lives in Baltimore, where he is associated in business first with his brother James and later with his brother Jack in Harriet E. Wilson's *Our Nig*.

Mary Bellmont   Younger daughter of John and Mrs. Bellmont; follows her mother's example in tormenting Frado, whom Mary attempts to kill by hurling a knife at her, in Harriet E. Wilson's *Our Nig*.

Mrs. Bellmont   Tyrannical and sadistic persecutor of Frado; professed Christian and wife of John Bellmont in Harriet E. Wilson's *Our Nig*.

Susan Bellmont   Descendant of a wealthy Baltimore family; wife of James Bellmont in Harriet E. Wilson's *Our Nig*.

Bello   Humpbacked ruler of Dominora in Herman Melville's *Mardi*.

A. M. Belshue   Atheistic and freethinking jeweler and husband of Nessie Sutton; commits suicide in T. S. Stribling's *Teeftallow*.

Bembo (Mowree)   New Zealand harpooner who, as temporary captain of the *Julia,* tries to wreck the ship near Tahiti in Herman Melville's *Omoo*.

Elijah Westlake (Lige) Bemis   County attorney, federal judge, and protector of John Barclay's monopoly in William Allen White's *A Certain Rich Man*.

Ben (Old Ben)   Slave and house servant of Moseley Sheppard in Arna Wendell Bontemps's *Black Thunder*.

Ben   Drug supplier and friend of Arthur Ketcham in John Clellon Holmes's *Go*.

Ben   Name used for two slaves, designated big Ben and little Ben, who are opossum hunters in John Pendleton Kennedy's *Swallow Barn*.

Ben   Large and menacing gangster whom Christina Goering meets in a bar; he deserts her in Jane Bowles's *Two Serious Ladies*.

Budda Ben   Crippled son of Maum Hannah and adviser to Mary Pinesett; banished from Heaven's Gate Church for cursing, but later reinstated, in Julia Peterkin's *Scarlet Sister Mary*.

Belle Mitchell Benbow   Mother of Titania Mitchell, divorced from Harry Mitchell, and married to Horace Benbow; appears in William Faulkner's *Sartoris* (*Flags in the Dust*) and *Sanctuary*.

Horace Benbow   Attorney in William Faulkner's *Sartoris* (*Flags in the Dust*) and *Sanctuary*.

Narcissa Benbow   See Narcissa Benbow Sartoris.

Albert F. Bendix   Brother of H. W. and R. N. Bendix; famous for giving large tips in Henry Miller's *Black Spring*.

H. W. Bendix   Brother of Albert F. and R. N. Bendix; wealthy merchant who complains about the quality of merchandise and services in Henry Miller's *Black Spring*.

R. N. Bendix   Brother of Albert F. and H. W. Bendix; unable to visit the tailor shop because he has had his legs amputated in Henry Miller's *Black Spring*.

Baldwin (Bawley) Benedict   Unmarried uncle of Bick Benedict; runs a small cattle operation in Edna Ferber's *Giant*.

Luz Benedict (I)   Sister of Bick Benedict; manages the Reata household and helps oversee the ranch in Edna Ferber's *Giant*.

Luz Benedict (II)   Daughter of Bick and Leslie Benedict in Edna Ferber's *Giant*.

Jordan (Jordy) Benedict the Fourth   Son of Jordan and Leslie Benedict and husband of Juana Benedict; becomes a physician in Edna Ferber's *Giant*.

Jordan (Bick) Benedict the Third   Husband of Leslie Lynnton Benedict and father of Jordy Benedict and Luz Benedict II; manages Reata, the huge family cattle estate, in Edna Ferber's *Giant*.

Juana Benedict   Wife of Jordy Benedict in Edna Ferber's *Giant*.

Leslie Lynnton (Les) Benedict   Wife of Bick Benedict and mother of Jordy Benedict and Luz Benedict II; forsakes her pleasant Virginia homestead for the rigors of rural Texas and the husband she loves in Edna Ferber's *Giant*.

Benedicta   Apparently the illegitimate daughter of a hangman but actually the daughter of the Saltmaster and the hangman's wife; secretly loves Ambrosius, a monk, who murders her in Ambrose Bierce's adaptation of *The Monk and the Hangman's Daughter*.

Cleo Benham   Wife of Elmer Gantry and mother of their two children in Sinclair Lewis's *Elmer Gantry*.

Judah Ben-Hur   Young Jewish son of the deceased Prince Ben-Hur of Jerusalem; handsome, strong, devoted to his family; wrongly enslaved for a supposed assassination attempt by Messala, a friend-turned-enemy, who is a Roman subject; is delivered from slavery years later by a Roman tribune who was friends with his father, eventually becoming the man's legal heir; exacts revenge on Messala by defeating him in a chariot race; through much effort finds his long-lost mother and sister and has them cured of their lately-acquired leprosy by the young Jesus Christ, who he tries to save from death in Lew Wallace's *Ben-Hur: A Tale of the Christ*.

Tirzah Ben-Hur   Beautiful Jewish sister of Judah Ben-Hur; kind and guileless in her youth; is imprisoned with her mother by the Roman Messala after an unfortunate accident involving her brother; is stricken with leprosy while imprisoned for eight years; is eventually saved by agents of her brother and is cured of leprosy by a young Jesus Christ in Lew Wallace's *Ben-Hur: A Tale of the Christ*.

Casimir (Casey) Benkowski   Washed-up Polish boxer, minor hood, and Bruno (Lefty) Bicek's boxing manager in Nelson Algren's *Never Come Morning*.

Issachar Bennet   Shaker missionary who helps Jerry Fowler rescue Norah Sharon in Walter D. Edmonds's *Erie Water*.

Ward Bennett   Arctic explorer who courts Lloyd Searight, contributing to the death of Richard Ferriss as he does so, in Frank Norris's *A Man's Woman*.

Lov Bensey   Railroad coal chute worker whose child wife, Pearl Lester Bensey, abandons him in Erskine Caldwell's *Tobacco Road*.

Pearl Lester Bensey   Daughter of Ada Lester; abandons her husband, Lov Bensey, in Erskine Caldwell's *Tobacco Road*.

Bob Benson   Friend of Jule Jackson in New York; helps Jule become a printer's apprentice in George Wylie Henderson's *Jule*.

Elspeth (Aunt Jetty) Bent   Granddaughter of Jess and Eliza Birdwell and daughter of Mattie Birdwell and Gardiner Bent in Jessamyn West's *The Friendly Persuasion* and *Except for Me and Thee*.

Gardiner (Gard) Bent   Fiancé and then husband of Mattie Birdwell in Jessamyn West's *The Friendly Persuasion* and *Except for Me and Thee*.

Mattie Bent   See Martha Truth Birdwell.

Horace Bentley   Generous friend of the poor after being ruined by Eldon Parr in Winston Churchill's *The Inside of the Cup*.

Jesse Bentley   Son of Tom Bentley; assumes responsibility for the Bentley farm after his father's retirement; injured by his grandson David Hardy in Sherwood Anderson's *Winesburg, Ohio*.

Katherine Bentley   Wife of Jesse Bentley; dies giving birth to Louise Bentley in Sherwood Anderson's *Winesburg, Ohio*.

Louise Bentley   See Louise Bentley Hardy.

Nat Benton   Stockbroker who advises Charley Anderson, allowing him to garner enough of stock in Askew-Merritt to sell out his senior partner, Joe Askew; Benton supplies Anderson with tips throughout the market boom in John Dos Passos's *U.S.A.* trilogy.

Dr. (Doc) Benway   Mad scientist and surgeon; manipulator and coordinator of symbol systems and expert in all phases of interrogation, brainwashing, and control; director of the Reconditioning Center in William S. Burroughs's *Naked Lunch;* also appears in *Nova Express, The Soft Machine,* and *Exterminator!*

Natalie Benziger   See Natalie Benziger Eaton.

Zeydel (Reb Zeydel) Ber   Ritual slaughterer, widower, uncle of Rechele Babad, and son-in-law of Granny; provides food, clothing, and shelter for Rechele until his death in Isaac Bashevis Singer's *Satan in Goray.*

Montgomery (Monty) Beragon (Bergoni)   Polo-playing lover and later husband of Mildred Pierce; wastes Mildred's money and betrays her by sleeping with her daughter, Veda Pierce, in James M. Cain's *Mildred Pierce.*

Marquis René-Victor de Bercy   French nobleman engaged to Thérèse de Fontenay in H. L. Davis's *Harp of a Thousand Strings.*

Marija Berczynskas   Cousin of Ona Rudkus; lends money to Jurgis Rudkus to buy a house; becomes a prostitute to support the family in Upton Sinclair's *The Jungle.*

Minna Bergen   Spoiled neighbor of Ada Fincastle and Ralph McBride; pursues Ralph in Ellen Glasgow's *Vein of Iron.*

Helga Bergenstrohm   Wife of Swede Bergenstrohm; washerwoman and cook for the miners; fights with Molly Riordan over feeding Jimmy Fee in E. L. Doctorow's *Welcome to Hard Times.*

Swede Bergenstrohm   Hardworking husband of Helga Bergenstrohm; killed by Clay Turner in E. L. Doctorow's *Welcome to Hard Times.*

Vinny Bergerac   Madcap boyhood friend of Jack Duluoz; known for cursing in Jack Kerouac's *Doctor Sax, Maggie Cassidy,* and *Book of Dreams.*

Alexandra Bergson   Smart, ambitious, but lonely farmer who becomes successful because she plans for the future in Willa Cather's *O Pioneers!*

Emil Bergson   Restless, college-educated brother of Alexandra Bergson; loves Marie Shabata and is killed by her husband, Frank Shabata, in Willa Cather's *O Pioneers!*

John Bergson   Swedish immigrant; hardworking but unsuccessful farmer who leaves his farm to his daughter, Alexandra Bergson, in Willa Cather's *O Pioneers!*

Lou Bergson   Greedy and bigoted brother of Alexandra Bergson; becomes a populist agitator in Willa Cather's *O Pioneers!*

Mrs. Bergson   Wife of John Bergson; longs for Sweden in Willa Cather's *O Pioneers!*

Oscar Bergson   Greedy and bigoted son of Mr. and Mrs. John Bergson; resents his brother Emil Bergson's intellectual tenden-

cies and his sister Alexandra Bergson's farming success in Willa Cather's *O Pioneers!*

Kirkcudbright Llanover Marjoribanks Sellers (Howard Tracy), Viscount Berkeley   Son of the Earl of Rossmore; wishes to renounce his title and live in America; falls in love and marries Sally Sellers in Samuel Langhorne Clemens's *The American Claimant.*

O. J. Berman   Hollywood agent who helps change Holly Golightly from a hillbilly to a potential starlet in Truman Capote's *Breakfast at Tiffany's.*

Jefferson (Jeff) Bernard   Aged recluse whose explanation of Mildred Latham's past to Sidney Wyeth causes Wyeth to return to her in Oscar Micheaux's *The Forged Note.*

Bernice   See Bernice Stockton.

Madame Anna Bernstein   Member of the Cabala and the power behind the German banking house in Thornton Wilder's *The Cabala.*

Lieutenant Paco Berrendo   Member of Captain Mora's fascist group in Ernest Hemingway's *For Whom the Bell Tolls.*

Blues Berry   Prisoner in the stockade; beaten to death by guards led by Fatso Judson in James Jones's *From Here to Eternity.*

Dolek Berson   Member of the Nazi-dominated Judenrat forced to coordinate the so-called resettlement of Polish Jews; becomes the strategic leader of the final battle against total Nazi destruction of the Warsaw ghetto in John Hersey's *The Wall.*

Bertha   See Chatelaine of La Trinité.

Bertha Mae   Teenaged lover of Jule Jackson; eventually moves with him from Alabama to New York in George Wylie Henderson's *Jule.*

Louis Berthold   French journalist with ever-changing politics; colleague of Mary Douglas in Martha Gellhorn's *A Stricken Field.*

Bertie   Victim of Harry Cresswell's sexual abuse and mother by him of a mulatto child, Emma, in W. E. B. Du Bois's *The Quest of the Silver Fleece.*

Alexander (Alex) BeShears   Store owner and neighbor of the Vaidens; father of Ponny BeShears and victim of the Leatherwood gang's violence in T. S. Stribling's *The Forge and The Store.*

Ponny BeShears   Daughter of Alex BeShears, lover of Polycarp Vaiden, and first wife of Miltiades Vaiden; dies during childbirth; appears in T. S. Stribling's *The Forge and The Store.*

Bess   Mistress of Crown, who deserts her; taken in by Porgy, from whom she runs away, in DuBose Heyward's *Porgy.*

Travis (Blix) Bessemer   Friend of Condé Rivers; helps Rivers become a writer and falls in love with him in the process in Frank Norris's *Blix.*

Bessie   Girlfriend of Van Norden; obsessed with technique in Henry Miller's *Tropic of Cancer.*

Lulu Bett   Spinster sister of Ina Bett Deacon; released from domestic drudgery when she marries, inadvertently, Ninian Deacon, a man already married; marries Neil Cornish in Zona Gale's *Miss Lulu Bett.*

Mrs. Bett   Mother of Ina and Lulu Bett and mother-in-law of Dwight Deacon, in whose house she lives, in Zona Gale's *Miss Lulu Bett.*

Thomas (Tommy) Bettersworth   Small-town businessman who is killed in a fight over his wife's reputation in Mary Austin's *A Woman of Genius.*

Betty   Fiancée of Miss Lonelyhearts in Nathanael West's *Miss Lonelyhearts.*

Lillian Beye   Woman always fighting inner turmoil and seeking self-fulfillment; pianist in Anaïs Nin's *Ladders to Fire, Children of the Albatross,* and *Seduction of the Minotaur.*

Friedrich (Fritz) Bhaer   Kindly, eccentric German tutor who marries Jo March in Louisa May Alcott's *Little Women;* also appears in *Little Men.*

Jo March Bhaer   See Jo March.

Robin (Rob, Robby) Bhaer   Enthusiastic chatterbox at Plumfield; son of Jo and Friedrich Bhaer in Louisa May Alcott's *Little Men.*

Bianca   Former lover of Bill Agatson and former fiancée of Arthur Ketcham in John Clellon Holmes's *Go.*

Billy Biasse   Friend of Jake Brown and host to the longshoremen's gaming rendezvous in Claude McKay's *Home to Harlem.*

Bruno (Lefty) Bicek   Polish hood and boxer who betrays his girlfriend Steffi Rostenkowski into prostitution and who commits a senseless murder in Nelson Algren's *Never Come Morning.*

Alexander Biddenhurst   English visitor to Virginia by way of Philadelphia; proponent of liberty and agitator of the revolt against planter-aristocrats in Henrico County, Virginia, in Arna Wendell Bontemps's *Black Thunder.*

Wing (Adolph Myers) Biddlebaum   Former teacher who works on farms in Winesburg, Ohio; morbidly obsessed with his hands because of a scandal that nearly resulted in his lynching in Sherwood Anderson's *Winesburg, Ohio.*

Bidet   French commander in William Faulkner's *A Fable.*

Paul (Polly) Biegler   Lawyer from Michigan's Upper Peninsula who defends Frederic Manion; narrator of Robert Traver's *Anatomy of a Murder.*

Big Bertha of Heaven   See Blackman.

Ruby Big Elk   Daughter of the former chief of the Osage nation, wife of Cimarron Cravat, and mother of two children in Edna Ferber's *Cimarron.*

Big Ellis   Kentucky farmer and drinking partner of Burley Coulter in Wendell Berry's *Nathan Coulter* and *A Place on Earth.*

Big Turtle   Shawnee Indian who captures Salathiel Albine and gives him the name of Little Turtle in Hervey Allen's *The Forest and the Fort.*

Reverend Doctor James Bigelow   Traveling evangelist who shocks George Brush in Thornton Wilder's *Heaven's My Destination.*

Roxie Biggers   Sister of Perry Northcutt; pietistic busybody and gossip who is opposed to Sunday baseball in T. S. Stribling's *Teeftallow.*

Lyde (Little) Biggs   Cynical, swaggering swindler in E. W. Howe's *The Story of a Country Town.*

Luther Biglin   Jailer in William Faulkner's *The Mansion.*

Big-Tooth   Mid-Pleistocene ancestor of the narrator, member of a race about to make evolutionary gains in Jack London's *Before Adam.*

Bildad   An owner of the *Pequod* in Herman Melville's *Moby-Dick.*

John Little Bilham   Aspiring artist who is a friend of Chad Newsome and a confidant of Lambert Strether; becomes engaged to Mamie Pocock in Henry James's *The Ambassadors.*

Bill   Editor of Miranda in Katherine Anne Porter's *Pale Horse, Pale Rider.*

Lucius Binford   Common-law husband of Reba Rivers in William Faulkner's *Sanctuary, The Mansion,* and *The Reivers.*

Doc Bingham   Disreputable book peddler who hires Mac in Chicago and, after being caught in bed with a farmer's wife, flees, leaving Mac stranded in rural Michigan in John Dos Passos's *U.S.A.* trilogy.

Jo-Lea Bingham   Pregnant daughter of Timothy Bingham in Robert Penn Warren's *The Cave.*

Thomas (Tom) Bingham   Architect who encourages his friend David Marshall to endow a college building in Henry Blake Fuller's *With the Procession.*

Timothy Bingham   Father of Jo-Lea Bingham and chief stockholder, president, and cashier of the People's Security Bank of

Johntown, Tennessee; arranges for Jo-Lea to have an abortion in Robert Penn Warren's *The Cave.*

Harvey Birch   Mysterious peddler thought to be a spy for the British army but who is, in fact, George Washington's most trusted agent; his actions are marked by a selfless devotion to his country in James Fenimore Cooper's *The Spy.*

Master Lazarus Birchem   Schoolmaster in James Kirke Paulding's *Koningsmarke.*

Harriet Bird   Beautiful woman who shoots athletes with silver bullets in Bernard Malamud's *The Natural.*

Henry Bird   Employee of the Free Press who fights with Bartley Hubbard over Hannah Morrison in William Dean Howells's *A Modern Instance.*

Miss Iris (Aunt Iris) Bird   Crippled biology teacher; a spinster who chaperones a beach house party for Cress Delahanty and friends in Jessamyn West's *Cress Delahanty.*

Pete Bird   Unemployed, debt-plagued amateur poet and friend of Daisy Meissner in Edmund Wilson's *I Thought of Daisy.*

Senator and Mrs. Bird   Ohio couple who aid Eliza and Harry Harris as they flee the Shelby estate in Harriet Beecher Stowe's *Uncle Tom's Cabin.*

Miss Birdseye   Elderly philanthropist and leader of New England reform movements who dies at Marmion, the summer cottage of Olive Chancellor, in Henry James's *The Bostonians.*

Dabney Birdsong   Brilliant engineer and architect who becomes the lover of Annabel Upchurch, his childhood friend, after she marries Judge Honeywell in Ellen Glasgow's *The Romantic Comedians.*

Eva Howard Birdsong   Famous Queensborough beauty of the 1890s who gives up a career in opera for the great passion of loving the unfaithful George Birdsong in Ellen Glasgow's *The Sheltered Life.*

George Birdsong   Charming but struggling attorney who marries Eva Howard; lover of Memoria and other women, including Jenny Blair, in Ellen Glasgow's *The Sheltered Life.*

Eliza Cope Birdwell   Recorded Quaker minister and wife of Jess Birdwell in Jessamyn West's *The Friendly Persuasion* and *Except for Me and Thee.*

Jane Birdwell   Younger daughter of Jess and Eliza Birdwell in Jessamyn West's *The Friendly Persuasion.*

Jesse Griffith (Jess) Birdwell   Quaker nurseryman and husband of Eliza Birdwell in Jessamyn West's *The Friendly Persuasion* and *Except for Me and Thee.*

Joshua (Josh) Birdwell   Son of Jess and Eliza Birdwell in Jessamyn West's *The Friendly Persuasion* and *Except for Me and Thee.*

Laban (Labe) Birdwell   Son of Jess and Eliza Birdwell in Jessamyn West's *The Friendly Persuasion* and *Except for Me and Thee.*

Little Jess Birdwell   Youngest child of Jess and Eliza Birdwell in Jessamyn West's *The Friendly Persuasion* and *Except for Me and Thee.*

Martha Truth (Mattie) Birdwell   Daughter of Jess and Eliza Birdwell; marries Gardiner Bent; appears in Jessamyn West's *The Friendly Persuasion* and *Except for Me and Thee.*

Sarah Birdwell   Daughter of Jess and Eliza Birdwell who dies young; appears in Jessamyn West's *The Friendly Persuasion* and *Except for Me and Thee.*

Stephen (Steve) Birdwell   Youngest son of Jess and Eliza Birdwell; marries Lidy Cinnamond in Jessamyn West's *The Friendly Persuasion.*

Kareen Birkman   Young girlfriend and lover left behind by Joe Bonham in Dalton Trumbo's *Johnny Got His Gun.*

Mike Birkman   Father of Kareen Birkman in Dalton Trumbo's *Johnny Got His Gun.*

B. D. Bisbee   Friend of Chad Hanna, advance man for Huguenine's circus, and eventually part-owner of the circus in Walter D. Edmonds's *Chad Hanna.*

Bernice Bishop   Welfare worker who with Mr. Rayber attempts to get Francis Marion Tarwater away from his greatuncle; failing, she marries Rayber but deserts him after bearing their idiot son, Bishop Rayber, in Flannery O'Connor's *The Violent Bear It Away.*

Clare Bishop   Former mistress and secretary of Sebastian Knight during the six years in which he wrote his first two novels; eventually marries someone else and dies without ever speaking to V. in Vladimir Nabokov's *The Real Life of Sebastian Knight.*

Ephraim (Eef) Bishop   Sheriff in William Faulkner's *The Mansion.*

Jesse Bishop   Congressional Medal of Honor winner and member of the 918th Bomb Group; dies in battle in Beirne Lay, Jr., and Sy Bartlett's *Twelve O'Clock High!*

Meg Bishop   Judgmental journalist who accuses Mrs. Karen Stone of escapism as a way to forget her husband in Tennessee Williams's *The Roman Spring of Mrs. Stone.*

Agate Bissell   Strong-willed servant-for-hire who does her Christian duty for all the citizens of Norwood; serves as a hospital administrator and member of the Sanitary Commission during the Civil War and marries Parson Buell after his first wife dies in Henry Ward Beecher's *Norwood.*

Joe (Iddiboy, Iddyboy) Bissonnette   Muscular boyhood friend of Jack Duluoz in Jack Kerouac's *Doctor Sax* and *Maggie Cassidy.*

Roderick Magsworth (Roddy) Bitts, Junior Scion of a snobbish, well-to-do family; his infrequent encounters with Penrod Schofield usually come to disastrous conclusions in Booth Tarkington's *Penrod, Penrod and Sam,* and *Penrod Jashber.*

Luella Bixby Aunt of Serena Lindley; member of numerous church societies and organizations for social improvement in Mary Austin's *Santa Lucia.*

Bea Sorenson Bjornstam See Bea Sorenson.

Capitola Black See Capitola Le Noir.

Josina Kugler Black Owner of the Black Motor Company in Mari Sandoz's *Capital City.*

Mr. Black Ironside minister; usually humane man and a saint of misery until World War I unleashes his sermons on God's righteous wrath in Ellen Glasgow's *Vein of Iron.*

Black Donald Wily chief of a bandit gang and supposed henchman of the villain Gabriel Le Noir; befriended by Capitola Le Noir in E.D.E.N. Southworth's *The Hidden Hand.*

Mrs. Blackett Aged but cheerful and self-reliant widowed mother of Mrs. Almira Blackett Todd and William Blackett in Sarah Orne Jewett's *The Country of the Pointed Firs.*

William Blackett Neat, handsome, and shy farmer/fisherman who is the brother of Mrs. Almira Todd; marries Esther Hight, whom he has secretly courted for forty years, in Sarah Orne Jewett's *The Country of the Pointed Firs.*

Jerry Blackford Tenant farmer, husband of Judith Pippinger, and father of three children in Edith Summers Kelley's *Weeds.*

Judith Pippinger (Judy) Blackford Daughter of Bill and Annie Pippinger, wife of Jerry Blackford, and mother of three children in Edith Summers Kelley's *Weeds.*

Wyeth Blackford Feckless best friend of Anson Page and curator of a hunt club in Hamilton Basso's *The View from Pompey's Head.*

Black Guinea (Ebony, Guinea) Crippled blackman who catches coins in his mouth in Herman Melville's *The Confidence-Man.*

Blackman (Big Bertha of Heaven) Itinerant fundamentalist preacher who conducts a revival in Irontown, Tennessee, in T. S. Stribling's *Teeftallow.*

Black Warrior Primitive Indian philosopher in James Kirke Paulding's *Westward Ho!*

Black Wolf College-educated Sioux Indian who is a friend of Aaron Gadd; murdered and scalped by the Ojibway Indians in Sinclair Lewis's *The GodSeeker.*

Amory Blaine Romantic egotist in and hero of F. Scott Fitzgerald's *This Side of Paradise.*

Beatrice O'Hara Blaine Extravagant and alcoholic mother of Amory Blaine in F. Scott Fitzgerald's *This Side of Paradise.*

Edith Lawrence Blair Childhood friend of Ruth Holland; stops seeing her after Ruth runs away with Stuart Williams, a married man, in Susan Glaspell's *Fidelity.*

Hugh Blair Editor in chief of *The Townsman* in Peter De Vries's *The Tunnel of Love.*

James Blair Friend of Samuele; graduate of Harvard University in classical studies who travels to Europe as an archaeological adviser to a film company in Thornton Wilder's *The Cabala.*

Jenny Blair See Jenny Blair Archbald.

Ben Blake Aspiring law student and first serious boyfriend of Francie Nolan in Betty Smith's *A Tree Grows in Brooklyn.*

Betty Blake Daughter of Rachel Colbert Blake; dies in an outbreak of diphtheria in Willa Cather's *Sapphira and the Slave Girl.*

Harry Blake Boyhood friend of Tom Bailey; inveterate carver of his initials in Thomas Bailey Aldrich's *The Story of a Bad Boy.*

Mabel Blake Widowed mother of Tony Blake; stabbed to death by Erskine Fowler in Richard Wright's *Savage Holiday.*

Macijah Blake Citizen of New Economy; informs Preacher of Pearl and John Harper's presence in the town in Davis Grubb's *The Night of the Hunter.*

Mary (Molly) Blake Daughter of Rachel Colbert Blake; survives a diphtheria epidemic in Willa Cather's *Sapphira and the Slave Girl.*

Michael Blake United States congressman from Virginia; husband of Rachel Colbert Blake; dies of yellow fever during an epidemic in Willa Cather's *Sapphira and the Slave Girl.*

Mrs. Blake Employment agency worker; advises Emma Lou Morgan to return to school and helps her find temporary work in Wallace Thurman's *The Blacker The Berry.*

Nathaniel (Nat) Blake Orphaned street musician who is sent to Plumfield in Louisa May Alcott's *Little Men.*

Rachel Colbert Blake Daughter of Sapphira and Henry Colbert; widow of Michael Blake; helps her mother's slave Nancy escape to Canada in Willa Cather's *Sapphira and the Slave Girl.*

Tony Blake Young son of Mabel Blake; accidentally falls from the balcony of his apartment after being frightened by the sudden appearance of Erskine Fowler in Richard Wright's *Savage Holiday.*

William Blake   English poet and illustrator who helps Thomas Paine flee from England after Paine's *The Rights of Man* creates a furor in Howard Fast's *Citizen Tom Paine.*

Captain Blakely   Presiding officer at the courtmartial of Lieutenant Steve Maryk for mutiny in Herman Wouk's *The Caine Mutiny.*

Roger Blakesley   Rival of Charles Gray; loses the bank vice-presidency to Gray in John P. Marquand's *Point of No Return.*

Clinton W. Blalock   Friend who tries to get Lee Youngdahl a teaching position at Harvard in Mark Harris's *Wake Up, Stupid.*

Estel Blanc   Abyssinian mortician and an eccentric; first person Malcolm visits on his journey through life in James Purdy's *Malcolm.*

Augusta Blanchard   Young American painter who belongs to the artistic fraternity of Rome; fiancée of Mr. Leavenworth in Henry James's *Roderick Hudson.*

Bland   Master-at-arms who runs an alcohol-smuggling ring aboard the *Neversink* in Herman Melville's *White-Jacket.*

Gerald Bland   Harvard classmate of Quentin Compson I in William Faulkner's *The Sound and the Fury.*

Madame Sisseretta (Mrs. Sari Blandine) Blandish   Owner of a Harlem hair-straightening parlor; when the Black-No-More process makes all blacks white, she develops a process to stain white skin light brown in George S. Schuyler's *Black No More.*

Ethel Blaney   Teacher and sister of Elizabeth Blaney Morison in William Maxwell's *They Came Like Swallows.*

Jim Blankenship   Chief minister of the Pine Street Methodist Church; initiator of extravagant fund-raising schemes for building a large nonsectarian cathedral in T. S. Stribling's *Unfinished Cathedral.*

A. Hebert Bledsoe   President of a southern black college who expels the narrator and sends him to New York in Ralph Ellison's *Invisible Man.*

Chris Bledsoe   Nephew of Lee Buck Cal; attracted to Louisa Sheridan, who feels herself falling in love with him; killed in a feud in Harriette Simpson Arnow's *Mountain Path.*

Bleecker   Host of the party at which George Kelcey gets drunk in Stephen Crane's *George's Mother.*

Raymond (Ray) Blent   Star football player who purposely fails two courses to cover up accepting a bribe to lose a game; boyfriend of Lily Sayre in Howard Nemerov's *The Homecoming Game.*

Colonel Bletheram   Rakish octogenarian in Ellen Glasgow's *The Romantic Comedians;* also appears in *They Stooped to Folly.*

William Bligh   Captain of the HMS *Bounty* whose harsh treatment of his men leads them to rebel in Charles Nordhoff and James Norman Hall's *Mutiny on the Bounty;* set adrift with eighteen men in a small boat and brings all but one of them to safety in *Men Against the Sea.*

Mr. Blimin   Member of the Communist Party's Central Committee in New York; questions Lionel Lane about his true identity and political beliefs and about the murders of Langley Herndon, Gilbert Blount, and Jack Hilton in Richard Wright's *The Outsider.*

Blind Pig (Piggy-O)   Blind, filthy drug deliverer and later drug dealer in Nelson Algren's *The Man with the Golden Arm.*

Mr. Blint   Member of the Ververs' social circle who is the object of Lady Castledean's romantic interest in Henry James's *The Golden Bowl.*

Betty Bliss   Plump, earnest graduate student of Russian; writes a paper on Dostoyevski for Professor Pnin in Vladimir Nabokov's *Pnin.*

Mattie Bliss   See Nina Carrington.

Mabel Blitch   See Mabel Blitch Lipscomb.

Blix   See Travis Bessemer.

Doremus (Reme) Blodgett   Hosiery salesman who is the first of many people to be shocked by George Brush's unusual theories in Thornton Wilder's *Heaven's My Destination.*

Joseph Bloeckman (Black)   Movie producer in F. Scott Fitzgerald's *The Beautiful and Damned.*

Hafen Blok   Hessian deserter and Indian fighter; heavy drinking, storytelling vagrant in John Pendleton Kennedy's *Swallow Barn.*

Moll (Mother Blonay) Blonay   Poor, elderly, potion-selling woman living in a hovel near Dorchester, South Carolina; assists her son Ned Blonay in betraying Major Singleton's partisan band to the British in William Gilmore Simms's *The Partisan.*

Ned (Goggle) Blonay   Son of Moll Blonay; betrays Major Singleton's partisan band to the British in William Gilmore Simms's *The Partisan.*

Lydia (Lily, Lurella, Lyddy) Blood   Niece of Maria Latham and the Erwins and granddaughter of Deacon Latham; becomes, on her trip to Venice, the Lady of the Aroostook; marries James Staniford in William Dean Howells's *The Lady of the Aroostook.*

Isaac Nathan Bloom   Army private who boxes for the regimental team; commits suicide after being implicated in a military investigation of homosexual activity in James Jones's *From Here to Eternity.*

Pear Blossom   Young slave who becomes Wang Lung's mistress in Pearl Buck's *The Good Earth;* after Wang Lung's death, she cares for his and O-lan's retarded daughter; following the daughter's death, she enters a nunnery in *Sons.*

Angus Blount   Young scamp who jilts Annabel Upchurch in Ellen Glasgow's *The Romantic Comedians.*

Eva Blount   Artist married to Gilbert Blount; becomes involved in an affair with Lionel Lane after Blount's death; commits suicide by jumping from a window of an apartment building in Richard Wright's *The Outsider.*

Gilbert (Gil) Blount   Communist Party official married to Eva Blount; attempts to recruit Lionel Lane; murdered by Lane in Langley Herndon's apartment in Richard Wright's *The Outsider.*

Jake Blount   Itinerant labor organizer who confides his dreams to the deaf-mute John Singer in Carson McCullers's *The Heart Is a Lonely Hunter.*

Blue   Self-appointed mayor and chronicler of Hard Times; marries Molly Riordan and cares for Jimmy Fee; ambushes and mortally wounds Clay Turner; narrator of E. L. Doctorow's *Welcome to Hard Times.*

Walden Blue   Tenor saxophonist in John Clellon Holmes's *The Horn.*

Blue Back   Old Oneida Indian and friend of Gil Martin in Walter D. Edmonds's *Drums along the Mohawk.*

Blue Billie   Childhood foe and later ally of Jimmie Johnson in Stephen Crane's *Maggie: A Girl of the Streets;* hoodlum whose impending fight with George Kelcey is interrupted by news of Kelcey's mother's illness in *George's Mother.*

Julian Blumberg   Weak, struggling novelist and screenwriter who unwittingly becomes a ghostwriter for Sammy Glick in Budd Schulberg's *What Makes Sammy Run?*

Jack Blunt   "Irish cockney" sailor aboard the Highlander who uses hair darkener and tries to interpret his dreams in Herman Melville's *Redburn.*

Gilly (Prince) Bluton   Sensuous, hedonistic, aggressive mulatto who attempts to seduce Lissa Atkinson; employee of and informer for Proctor Baggart; murdered by Hagar in DuBose Heyward's *Mamba's Daughters.*

Cornelia Bly   Abstract artist and mistress of Augie Poole; bears a child by Poole that Poole unwittingly adopts in Peter De Vries's *The Tunnel of Love.*

Major Boam   Frequent visitor to the Wandrous home; his pedophiliac behavior traumatizes Gloria Wandrous in John O'Hara's *Butterfield 8.*

Milly Boardman   Teenaged daughter of Quincy Boardman and student at a Massachusetts boarding school in Albert Halper's *Union Square.*

Quincy (Boardie) Boardman   Widower father of Milly Boardman; executive who lives, with his mistress Margie, in the Glen Cove Apartments in Albert Halper's *Union Square.*

Boaz   Martian army sergeant in Kurt Vonnegut's *The Sirens of Titan.*

Bobbie   Homosexual friend of Alva in Wallace Thurman's *The Blacker the Berry.*

Helen Bober   Twenty-three-year-old daughter of Morris and Ida Bober; pursued by Frank Alpine in Bernard Malamud's *The Assistant.*

Ida Bober   Wife of Morris Bober in Bernard Malamud's *The Assistant.*

Morris Bober   Jewish storekeeper in Bernard Malamud's *The Assistant.*

Gabriella Bodeen   Glamorous actress with whom Lee Youngdahl believes himself in love in Mark Harris's *Wake Up, Stupid.*

William Yancey Bodine   Organizer of a secret association to advance Americanism and to persecute Jews, blacks, and Catholics in T. S. Stribling's *Unfinished Cathedral.*

Léry Bogard   Scholar who accompanies Samuele to the Villa Horace for a week visit as the guest of Marie-Astrée-Luce de Morfontaine in Thornton Wilder's *The Cabala.*

Mrs. Bogart   Strict Baptist and neighbor of the Kennicotts in Sinclair Lewis's *Main Street.*

Harry (Heshalle, Heshie) Bogen   Women's garment manufacturer who steals from his own firm, Apex Modes, and makes his partner, Meyer Babushkin, take the blame and go to jail; narrator of Jerome Weidman's *I Can Get It for You Wholesale;* enters into partnership with and steals from Hrant Yazdabian; has his own money stolen by Martha Mills, his girlfriend; narrator of *What's in It for Me?*

Mrs. Bogen   Mother of Harry Bogen in Jerome Weidman's *I Can Get It for You Wholesale;* becomes ill and dies while Harry is trying to escape to Europe in *What's in It for Me?*

Elizaveta Innokentievna Bogolepov   See Dr. Elizaveta Innokentievna Bogolepov Pnin Wind.

Harry Bohn   Friend of Luke Lampson; born of his dead mother's body; helps to bury Hattie Lampson in John Hawkes's *The Beetle Leg.*

Miss Boke   Fat and friendly newcomer whose monopolization of William Baxter at Miss Lola Pratt's going-away party almost induces him to commit mayhem in Booth Tarkington's *Seventeen.*

Paul (Kid Faro, Scot, Scotch, Scotcho, Scotty) Boldieu   Baseball pitcher and boyhood friend of Jack Duluoz in Jack Kerouac's *Doctor Sax, Maggie Cassidy,* and *Book of Dreams.*

Joe Boleo   Skilled woodsman and courier for the American forces in the Mohawk Valley; instrumental in saving Gil Martin's family from destruction in Walter D. Edmonds's *Drums Along the Mohawk.*

Brother Bolo   Priest who smuggles religious artifacts out of Castiglione; friend of Dolce, with whom he made a hair shirt out of rat skins for Arsella's mother, in John Hawkes's *The Goose on the Grave.*

Rachel Bolt   Confidante and New York guide of Hagar Ashendyne; recovers from her husband's abuse in Mary Johnston's *Hagar.*

Harry (Bury) Bolton   Mysterious friend of Redburn; crushed to death between a whale and a ship in Herman Melville's *Redburn.*

Oliver Bolton   Farmer and caretaker of the Kilburn estate in William Dean Howells's *Annie Kilburn.*

Pauliny Bolton   Wife of Oliver Bolton and proud housekeeper of the Kilburns in William Dean Howells's *Annie Kilburn.*

Ruth Bolton   Philadelphia Quaker; medical student and girlfriend of Philip Sterling in Samuel Langhorne Clemens and Charles Dudley Warner's *The Gilded Age.*

Bombie of the Frizzled Head (Snow Ball)   Witchlike black servant of Heer Peter Piper in James Kirke Paulding's *Koningsmarke.*

Charles Bon   Probably the son of Thomas Sutpen and his first wife, Eulalia Bon; engaged to his probable half sister Judith Sutpen in William Faulkner's *Absalom, Absalom!*

Charles Etienne Saint-Valery Bon   Son of Charles Bon and his octoroon mistress; father of Jim Bond in William Faulkner's *Absalom, Absalom!*

Eulalia Bon   See Eulalia Bon Sutpen.

Napoleon Bonaparte   French ruler and lover of Angela Guessippi in Hervey Allen's *Anthony Adverse.*

Napoleon Bonaparte   French dictator who seeks Thomas Paine's support to add legitimacy to his regime in Howard Fast's *Citizen Tom Paine.*

Remi Boncoeur   Prep school friend of Sal Paradise; works as a barracks guard in Jack Kerouac's *On the Road.*

Hamish (Old Man Bond, 'Sieur' Amsh, Alec Hinks, Captain Strike-down-then-make-the-Palaver) Bond   Slave runner turned New Orleans plantation owner who buys the mulatto Amantha Starr and takes her as a mistress; hangs himself while a captive of Rau-Ru and black rioters in 1866 in Robert Penn Warren's *Band of Angels.*

Jim Bond   Idiot son of Charles Etienne Saint-Valery Bon and a black woman in William Faulkner's *Absalom, Absalom!*

Aldo Bonello   Italian ambulance driver in the command of Frederic Henry during the retreat from Caporetto; wanders off with the hope of being taken prisoner by the Germans in Ernest Hemingway's *A Farewell to Arms.*

Blanche Lebanon Timberlane Boneyard   First wife of Cass Timberlane in Sinclair Lewis's *Cass Timberlane.*

Ann Chapin Bongiorno   See Ann Chapin.

Charley Bongiorno   Jazz saxophonist and Ann Chapin's first husband in John O'Hara's *Ten North Frederick.*

Joe Bonham   American soldier who suffers nearly complete physical incapacitation as the result of wounds received in World War I; his dreams and reminiscences comprise Dalton Trumbo's *Johnny Got His Gun.*

Dolly Bonner   Mistress of Milton Loftis in William Styron's *Lie Down in Darkness.*

Nicholas de Bonneville   French newspaper editor who helps shelter Thomas Paine in Paris and who later sends his family to Paine in America during the Napoleonic regime in Howard Fast's *Citizen Tom Paine.*

John Bonnyfeather   Prominent Leghorn merchant; maternal grandfather of Anthony Adverse, whom he gives a surname and educates, in Hervey Allen's *Anthony Adverse.*

Maria (Marquise da Vincitata) Bonnyfeather   Mother, by Denis Moore, of Anthony Adverse in Hervey Allen's *Anthony Adverse.*

Booker   Middle-aged pool hall owner who allows his customers—mostly corner boys—to play dice in the back room in Herbert Simmons's *Corner Boy.*

Calvin (Uncle Cal) Bookwright   Bootlegger in William Faulkner's *The Town, The Mansion,* and *The Reivers.*

Odum Bookwright   Wealthy farmer and one of the buyers of Old Frenchman's Place; appears in William Faulkner's *The Hamlet* and *The Mansion.*

Daniel Boone   Frontiersman who marries Diony Hall Jarvis and Evan Muir in Elizabeth Madox Roberts's *The Great Meadow.*

Borabolla   Fat king of Mondoldo in Herman Melville's *Mardi.*

Isabelle Borgé   First love of Amory Blaine while he is at Princeton in F. Scott Fitzgerald's *This Side of Paradise.*

Boris   Weather prophet living with Henry Miller at the Villa Borghese in Henry Miller's *Tropic of Cancer.*

Borowski   Accordion-playing friend of Henry Miller; gives Miller lunch on Wednesdays in Henry Miller's *Tropic of Cancer*.

Sergeant Leonard Borth   Fearless M.P. in charge of security during the Allied occupation of Adano in John Hersey's *A Bell for Adano*.

Catharine Bosworth   See Catharine Bosworth Apley.

Jacob (Jake) Botcher   Behind-the-scenes political manipulator and dispenser of bribes in Winston Churchill's *Mr. Crewe's Career*.

Doctor Botot   Wealthy widower and physician who cares for the residents of St. Médard parish in Grace King's *The Pleasant Ways of St. Médard*.

Pierre Bouc   See Piotr.

Boukman   Ugly, menacing black leader of a group of rebel slaves in Arna Wendell Bontemps's *Drums at Dusk*.

Raoul de Bourggraff   Masterful art department head at Olympia Studios in Ludwig Bemelmans's *Dirty Eddie*.

Garan Bourke   New York lawyer who rescues his lover Patience Sparhawk from execution for murder in Gertrude Atherton's *Patience Sparhawk and Her Times*.

Dolly Boutts   Flirt interested in John Gwynne; rival of Isabel Otis in Gertrude Atherton's *Ancestors*.

Matt Bowden   Opportunist who pursues Major Grumby in William Faulkner's *The Unvanquished*.

Charles Bowen   Elderly friend of Laura Fairford; philosophizes about the male passion for moneymaking that relegates women to the periphery of men's lives in Edith Wharton's *The Custom of the Country*.

Effie Bowen   Daughter of Evalina Bowen and admirer of Theodore Colville in William Dean Howells's *Indian Summer*.

Evalina Ridgely (Lina) Bowen   Widow who marries her friend Theodore Colville; mother of Effie Bowen and temporary guardian of Imogene Graham in William Dean Howells's *Indian Summer*.

Frederika Bowers   Chief mistress of Prince Cabano; helps her rival Estella Washington escape from Cabano in Ignatius Donnelly's *Caesar's Column*.

James (Jim) Bowers   Employee at a funeral home owned by Tyree Tucker; proposes marriage to Emma Tucker after Tyree Tucker's death in Richard Wright's *The Long Dream*.

Madison Bowers   Fashionable but excellent Chicago voice teacher with whom Thea Kronborg studies in Willa Cather's *The Song of the Lark*.

Deighton Boyce   Free-spirited father of Selina Boyce; commits suicide within sight of the coast of Barbados after trying to find himself in New York in Paule Marshall's *Brown Girl, Brownstones*.

Ina Boyce   Sister of Selina Boyce; quiet, soft-spoken young woman who is devoted to her church; settles into an uneventful life and a dull marriage in Paule Marshall's *Brown Girl, Brownstones*.

Selina (Deighton Selina) Boyce   Daughter of Silla and Deighton Boyce and sister of Ina Boyce; unsettled heroine who returns to the Caribbean after becoming disillusioned with America in Paule Marshall's *Brown Girl, Brownstones*.

Silla (Silla-gal) Boyce   Wife of Deighton Boyce and mother of Selina and Ina Boyce; driven woman determined to control the lives of those in her family in Paule Marshall's *Brown Girl, Brownstones*.

Beverly (Bev) Boyd   Homosexual college instructor rejected by Peter Gale in Louis Adamic's *Grandsons*.

Gordon Boyd   Wild boyhood friend of Walter McKee; writer and self-proclaimed failure in Wright Morris's *The Field of Vision* and *Ceremony in Lone Tree*.

Mrs. Boyd   See Daughter.

J. Boyer   Accomplished clergyman attracted to Eliza Wharton in Hannah Webster Foster's *The Coquette*.

Orren Boyle   Failing industrialist who seeks government protection against free market competition in Ayn Rand's *Atlas Shrugged*.

Eloisa Brace   Resident at the fourth address to which Mr. Cox sends Malcolm; painter who often invites musicians to her house in James Purdy's *Malcolm*.

Jerome Brace   Ex-convict and husband of Eloisa Brace; because he sees Malcolm as the spirit of life, begs Malcolm for his friendship in James Purdy's *Malcolm*.

Henry Bradford   Saloon owner who nearly beats Adolph Myers (Wing Biddlebaum) to death because Myers supposedly molested Bradford's son in Sherwood Anderson's *Winesburg, Ohio*.

Bradish   New York artist friend and studio mate of Richard Dale in Sarah Orne Jewett's *A Marsh Island*.

Jessie Bradley   First wife of George Ogden; her spending ruins Ogden financially in Henry Blake Fuller's *The Cliff-Dwellers*.

Peck Bradley   Poor-white hill man who is lynched for murdering Tug Beavers in T. S. Stribling's *Teeftallow*.

Brady   Irish schoolmaster who cares for Morton Goodwin and Kike Lumsden; marries Lumsden's mother in Edward Eggleston's *The Circuit Rider*.

Cecilia Brady   Daughter of Pat Brady; her love for Monroe Stahr is unrequited; narrator of F. Scott Fitzgerald's *The Last Tycoon*.

Pat Brady   Father of Cecilia Brady and treacherous partner of Monroe Stahr in F. Scott Fitzgerald's *The Last Tycoon.*

Will Jennings Brady   Unsuccessful entrepreneur, hotel lobby dweller; dies while dressed for the role of Santa Claus in Wright Morris's *The Works of Love.*

Willy Brady, Jr.   Son of Mickey Ahearn adopted by Will Brady in Wright Morris's *The Works of Love.*

Clinton Bragg   Early suitor and second husband of Mateel Shepherd, whose first husband, Jo Erring, kills him in E. W. Howe's *The Story of a Country Town.*

Braid-Beard   See Mohi.

Abbie Brainard   Daughter of Abigail and Erastus Brainard; second wife of George Ogden in Henry Blake Fuller's *The Cliff-Dwellers.*

Abigail Brainard   Wife of Erastus Brainard and mother of Abbie, Burton, and Marcus Brainard in Henry Blake Fuller's *The Cliff-Dwellers.*

Burton Tillinghast (Burt) Brainard   Son of Abigail and Erastus Brainard and vice president of his father's bank; his financial schemes drive the family into poverty in Henry Blake Fuller's *The Cliff-Dwellers.*

Cornelia McNabb Tillinghast (Nealie) Brainard   Waitress and then stenographer in the Clifton; wife of Burt Brainard in Henry Blake Fuller's *The Cliff-Dwellers.*

Erastus M. Brainard   Husband of Abigail Brainard and father of Abbie, Burton, and Marcus Brainard; president of the Underground National Bank; killed by his son Marcus in Henry Blake Fuller's *The Cliff-Dwellers.*

Marcus Brainard   Son of Abigail and Erastus Brainard; frustrated artist who kills his father, strangles his brother, Burt, and commits suicide in Henry Blake Fuller's *The Cliff-Dwellers.*

Marigold Shoemaker Brainerd   Philadelphian living in Paris; rival of Aileen Cowperwood for the affections of Bruce Tollifer in Theodore Dreiser's *The Stoic.*

Kate Helen Branch   Mother of Burley Coulter's bastard son in Wendell Berry's *Nathan Coulter.*

Battle John Brand   Hellfire and brimstone revival preacher in Harriette Arnow's *Hunter's Horn* and *The Dollmaker.*

Charlotte Wentworth Brand   See Charlotte Wentworth.

Dinah Brand   Golddigger who provides information and companionship to the Op in Dashiell Hammett's *Red Harvest.*

Mr. Brand   Unitarian minister who courts Gertrude Wentworth but who ultimately marries Charlotte Wentworth in Henry James's *The Europeans.*

Alexander (Alex) Brandel   Father of Wolf Brandel and friend of Andrei Androfski; historian of the Warsaw ghetto and leader of the Bathyran Zionist Executive Council; scholar and pacifist turned activist; diarist/journalist in Leon Uris's *Mila 18.*

Wolf Brandel   Son of Alexander Brandel and lover of Rachel Bronski; leads survivors from the Warsaw ghetto in Leon Uris's *Mila 18.*

George Sylvester Brander   Ohio senator who dies before he can marry his lover Jennie Gerhardt in Theodore Dreiser's *Jennie Gerhardt.*

Backwater Brandon   Tidewater gentleman living in Fluvanna County; never adapts to frontier ways and so is always at odds with his neighbors in Mary Lee Settle's *O Beulah Land.*

Constancia Brown (Constance, Lady Macbeth, Mrs. Shakespeare) Brandon   Garrulous, pretentious hostess of a salon in Harlem's Striver's Row; satirized, along with an outrageous assortment of her guests, in Countee Cullen's *One Way to Heaven.*

Cousin Annie Brandon   See Annie Brandon O'Neill.

Dr. George Brandon   Husband of Constancia Brandon in Countee Cullen's *One Way to Heaven.*

Stuart Brandon   Wastrel brother of Mamie Brandon Catlett and father of Annie Brandon O'Neill in Mary Lee Settle's *Know Nothing.*

Percy Brandreth   Petitioner for Mrs. Munger; male lead in *Romeo and Juliet* in William Dean Howells's *Annie Kilburn.*

Mrs. Homer Branney   See Mabel Blitch Lipscomb.

Bob Brannom   Corrupt district attorney who is killed by Dix Handley in William Riley Burnett's *The Asphalt Jungle.*

Alice Brannon   Little-mourned wife of Biff Brannon; dies following surgery in Carson McCullers's *The Heart Is a Lonely Hunter.*

Bartholomew (Biff) Brannon   Methodical and observant café owner who is fond of freaks; husband of Alice Brannon in Carson McCullers's *The Heart Is a Lonely Hunter.*

Bras-Coupé   Former African prince; tortured and dies following an attempted escape from slavery in George Washington Cable's *The Grandissimes.*

Etta Brashear   Cincinnati working woman who befriends Susan Lenox; marries a rich brewer in order to avoid a life of poverty and prostitution in David Graham Phillips's *Susan Lenox.*

Richard Braxley   Lawyer for Major Roland Forrester; tries to cheat Edith Forrester of her inheritance in Robert Montgomery Bird's *Nick of the Woods.*

Braxton   Unemployed gambler and hustler; shares an apartment with Alva in Wallace Thurman's *The Blacker The Berry.*

Catherine Bread   Servant of the de Bellegardes; reveals to Christopher Newman that Emmeline and Urbain de Bellegarde killed Urbain's father in Henry James's *The American*.

Gabriel (Gabe) Breaux   Drinker and gambler who courts and marries Amy in Katherine Anne Porter's *Old Mortality*.

Gavin Breckbridge   Fiancé of Drusilla Hawk; killed at Shiloh in William Faulkner's *The Unvanquished*.

Edmonia Honeywell Bredalbane   Liberated, promiscuous, oft-married twin sister of Judge Gamaliel Bland Honeywell in Ellen Glasgow's *The Romantic Comedians*.

Ralph Bredalbane   Young and poor fourth husband of Edmonia Bredalbane, on whose money he lives, in Ellen Glasgow's *The Romantic Comedians*.

Nathan Brederhagan   Profligate rake who stabs Christina Jansen during an attempted rape in Ignatius Donnelly's *Caesar's Column*.

Hallie Breedlove   Mulatto prostitute with a fierce sense of independence in Nelson Algren's *A Walk on the Wild Side*.

Monica Breedlove   Neighbor and friend of Christine Penmark; senses fear and worry in Christine, but is oblivious to the evil in Rhoda Penmark, in William March's *The Bad Seed*.

Charlie Breene   Wealthy suitor of Dorothy Shaw; their marriage is cruelly opposed by his parents; when he is penniless and her husband is dead, they marry in Anita Loos's *But Gentlemen Marry Brunettes*.

Captain Elijah (Lige) Brent   Riverboat captain and devoted friend of Colonel Carvel, and therefore of the South, in Winston Churchill's *The Crisis*.

Ellen Brent   Pregnant wife of Henry Brent; scared into her grave by her husband's mad delusions in Andrew Lytle's *A Name for Evil*.

Frederick (Fred, Freddie) Brent   Ward of Hester Prime; Baptist pastor in Dexter, Ohio, who leaves his post in disgrace and migrates to Cincinnati, where he meets his father, a born-again Christian, in Paul Laurence Dunbar's *The Uncalled*.

Henry Brent   Haunted man who undertakes the restoration of his ancestor's farm; narrator of Andrew Lytle's *A Name for Evil*.

Major Brent   Former owner of The Grove and felt to be its ghostly inhabiter by his descendant Henry Brent in Andrew Lytle's *A Name for Evil*.

Margaret (Mag, Margar't) Brent   Wife of Tom Brent and mother of Frederick Brent; dies from alcoholism in Paul Laurence Dunbar's *The Uncalled*.

Robert Brent   New York playwright who helps Susan Lenox become an actress and dies through the plotting of her jealous lover, Freddie Palmer, in David Graham Phillips's *Susan Lenox*.

Tom Brent   Drunkard who abuses and later abandons his wife, Margaret Brent, and son, Frederick Brent; becomes a born-again Christian and is reunited with his son in Paul Laurence Dunbar's *The Uncalled*.

Rev. Evan Brewster   Minister of the Ebenezer Baptist Church in Sinclair Lewis's *Kingsblood Royal* and *Cass Timberlane*.

Maud Brewster   Shipwrecked woman rescued by the *Ghost*; assists Hump Van Weyden in navigating the ship to the United States in Jack London's *The Sea Wolf*.

Brock (Brock Chamberlain) Brewton   Son of Lutie Brewton and Brice Chamberlain, although Colonel James B. Brewton refuses to accept this fact; becomes a gambler and then an outlaw; killed by a posse in Conrad Richter's *The Sea of Grass*.

Harry (Hal) Brewton   Nephew of Colonel James Brewton; becomes a medical doctor; narrator of Conrad Richter's *The Sea of Grass*.

Colonel James B. (Jim) Brewton   Powerful cattle baron and rancher who battles against nester settlements until government laws restrain his actions; welcomes the return of his errant wife Lutie in Conrad Richter's *The Sea of Grass*.

Lutie Cameron Brewton   Wife of Colonel James B. Brewton; has an affair with Brice Chamberlain and has a son by him; deserts her family because of boredom with pioneer life, but returns home fifteen years later in Conrad Richter's *The Sea of Grass*.

Margaret Brice   Mother of Stephen Brice in Winston Churchill's *The Crisis*.

Stephen Atterbury (Steve) Brice   Antislavery lawyer who marries Virginia Carvel in Winston Churchill's *The Crisis*.

Virginia Carvel Brice   See Virginia Carvel.

Bridesman   Flight commander in William Faulkner's *A Fable*.

Bridewell   First lieutenant aboard the *Neversink* in Herman Melville's *White-Jacket*.

Hannah Bridewell   See Hannah Bridewell Catlett.

Carolyn (Corky) Bridge   Daughter of Walter and India Bridge; marries and moves to Parallel, Kansas, in Evan Connell's *Mrs. Bridge* and *Mr. Bridge*.

Douglas Bridge   Son of Walter and India Bridge; frequently in trouble as a child; later joins the army in Evan Connell's *Mrs. Bridge* and *Mr. Bridge*.

India Bridge Wife of Walter Bridge and mother of Ruth, Carolyn, and Douglas Bridge in Evan Connell's *Mrs. Bridge* and *Mr. Bridge*.

Ma'am Bridge Washerwoman for Clarissa Packard's mother in Caroline Gilman's *Recollections of a Housekeeper*.

Ruth Bridge Daughter of Walter and India Bridge; moves to New York City and takes a job with a women's magazine in Evan Connell's *Mrs. Bridge* and *Mr. Bridge*.

Walter Bridge Husband of India Bridge and father of Ruth, Carolyn, and Douglas Bridge; dies in his Kansas City law office in Evan Connell's *Mrs. Bridge* and *Mr. Bridge*.

Jim Bridger Mountaineer who aids the wagon train and Molly Wingate in Emerson Hough's *The Covered Wagon*.

Cicily Carver Bridges See Cicily Carver Bridges Lancaster.

James (John) Bridges One of three Englishmen, sympathetic to the American cause, who send Israel Potter as courier to Benjamin Franklin in Herman Melville's *Israel Potter*.

Charley Bridwell Reclusive father of Jed Bridwell in Vardis Fisher's *In Tragic Life*.

Jed Bridwell Untamed boy who lives across Snake River from Vridar Hunter in Vardis Fisher's *In Tragic Life;* also appears in *Orphans in Gethsemane*.

Lela Bridwell Mother of Jed Bridwell and friend of Prudence Hunter; leaves her husband, Charley Bridwell, after years of suffering with him in Vardis Fisher's *In Tragic Life*.

Henry (Harry) Brierly College friend of Philip Sterling, with whom Brierly goes west to make money in railroads; business partner of Beriah Sellers; loves but is rejected by Laura Hawkins in Samuel Langhorne Clemens and Charles Dudley Warner's *The Gilded Age*.

Hortense Briggs Shop employee admired by Clyde Griffiths in Theodore Dreiser's *An American Tragedy*.

Mona Brigstock Owen Gereth's vulgar and domineering fiancée and, finally, wife in Henry James's *The Spoils of Poynton*.

Mrs. Brigstock Mother of Mona Brigstock and mistress of the Waterbath estate in Henry James's *The Spoils of Poynton*.

Bella (Belle) Brill Daughter of Clothilde Wright and cousin of Jim Calder; makes opportunistic marriages with Joe Stowe and Allen Southby in John P. Marquand's *Wickford Point*.

Clothilde Brill See Clothilde Brill Wright.

Harry Brill Parasitical son of Clothilde Wright and cousin of Jim Calder; preoccupied with maintaining his social position in John P. Marquand's *Wickford Point*.

Brimmer Communist labor organizer in F. Scott Fitzgerald's *The Last Tycoon*.

Judge Brisdine Comical judge who loses his coat and shoes during the Confederate raid on Chambersburg in Hervey Allen's *Action at Aquila*.

Grace Brissenden Gossip married to Guy Brissenden, a man nearly half her age, in Henry James's *The Sacred Fount*.

Guy (Briss) Brissenden Young man married to Grace Brissenden, a woman nearly twice his age; acts as a front for the affair between Gilbert Long and Lady John in Henry James's *The Sacred Fount*.

Russ Brissenden Socialist poet who encourages and inspires Martin Eden; commits suicide in Jack London's *Martin Eden*.

Mr. Britten Employee of Henry Dalton; questions Bigger Thomas about the disappearance of Mary Dalton in Richard Wright's *Native Son*.

Nan Britton Faithful maid and confidante of Amber St. Clare in Kathleen Winsor's *Forever Amber*.

Donald R. Broadbent Inept counsel for the State Senate Standing Committee on Education, Welfare, and Public Morality investigating the propriety of an attempt to purchase a brilliant child in John Hersey's *The Child Buyer*.

Thomas Broaden Prosperous, college-educated mulatto banker who promotes high culture in the upper echelon of the black community in DuBose Heyward's *Mamba's Daughters*.

Dorothy (Dotty) Brock American Red Cross worker in Luxembourg and lover of Lieutenant Colonel John Dawson Smithers in Martha Gellhorn's *Wine of Astonishment*.

Lucius Brockway Supervisor at Liberty Paints in Ralph Ellison's *Invisible Man*.

Sally Broke Snobbish young society woman in Winston Churchill's *Coniston*.

Austin (Irwin Swenson) Bromberg Erudite essayist and owner of an impressive private library; host of Leo Percepied in Jack Kerouac's *The Subterraneans;* mentioned in *Book of Dreams*.

Deborah Androfski Bronski Sister of Andrei Androfski, wife of Paul Bronski, and lover of Christopher de Monti; becomes active in the Warsaw ghetto resistance in Leon Uris's *Mila 18*.

Paul Bronski Husband of Deborah Bronski; heads the Jewish Civil Authority for Warsaw after the Nazi occupation; commits suicide in Leon Uris's *Mila 18*.

Rachael Bronski Daughter of Paul and Deborah Bronski and lover of Wolf Brandel; resistance fighter in the Warsaw ghetto in Leon Uris's *Mila 18*.

George H. Bronson   Newly elected prosecuting attorney who sees the trial of Ralph Hartsook as an opportunity to distinguish himself in Edward Eggleston's *The Hoosier School-Master.*

Daisy (Posy, Mrs. Shakespeare Smith) Brooke   Twin sister of Demijohn Brooke in Louisa May Alcott's *Little Women;* also appears in *Little Men.*

John Brooke   Sensible tutor of Theodore Laurence; marries Meg March in Louisa May Alcott's *Little Women;* also appears in *Little Men.*

John (Demi, Demijohn) Brooke   Twin brother of Daisy Brooke and son of Meg and John Brooke in Louisa May Alcott's *Little Women;* also appears in *Little Men.*

Margaret March Brooke   See Margaret March.

Mrs. Edward (Mrs. Brook) Brookenham   Daughter of Lady Julia and leader of a social group; ambitious mother of Nanda Brookenham in Henry James's *The Awkward Age.*

Fernanda (Nanda) Brookenham   Daughter of Mrs. Brookenham; loves Van Vanderbank; lives in London with her godfather, Mr. Longdon, in Henry James's *The Awkward Age.*

J. Jerome (Jerry) Brophy   District attorney who offers to dismiss a rape charge against Ralph Detweiler if Arthur Winner will support his quest for a judgeship in James Gould Cozzens's *By Love Possessed.*

Brower   Insurance adjuster and roommate of George Ogden in Henry Blake Fuller's *The Cliff-Dwellers.*

Theodore Brower   Settlement house resident who courts Jane Marshall in Henry Blake Fuller's *With the Procession.*

Benson Brown   Light-skinned black man attracted to Emma Lou Morgan; eventually marries Gwendolyn Johnson in Wallace Thurman's *The Blacker the Berry.*

Berenice Sadie Brown   Black cook and confidante of Frankie Addams in Carson McCullers's *The Member of the Wedding.*

Biglow (Papa Biglow) Brown   Magnificent ginger-colored giant and rival of Augie for the affection of Della Green in Arna Wendell Bontemps's *God Sends Sunday.*

Bo-Jo Brown   Harvard football hero and classmate of Harry Pulham; organizes their twenty-fifth class reunion in John P. Marquand's *H. M. Pulham, Esquire.*

Bubber Brown   Comical friend of Jinx Jenkins in Rudolph Fisher's *The Walls of Jericho* and *The Conjure-Man Dies.*

Bunny Brown   Harlem friend of Max Disher; becomes white through the Black-No-More process and helps Disher run the Knights of Nordia in George S. Schuyler's *Black No More.*

Charles Brown   Beloved of Mary Conant banished from New England because he is an Episcopalian; returns to wed Conant and adopt her half-Indian son in Lydia Maria Child's *Hobomok.*

Cyril Brown   Marine killed on Saipan in Leon Uris's *Battle Cry.*

Dick Brown   Humpbacked, cheerful boy in Louisa May Alcott's *Little Men.*

Fats Brown   Bartender at the Grove in Richard Wright's *The Long Dream.*

Frederick (Steely) Brown   Ten-year-old son of Paul and Mae Brown; reader sees ghetto life from his viewpoint in Julian Mayfield's *The Long Night.*

Honey Camden Brown   Foster brother of Berenice Sadie Brown; imprisoned for breaking into a drugstore in Carson McCullers's *The Member of the Wedding.*

Jake Brown   Longshoreman who returns to Harlem longing to embrace friends and familiar places; meets the girl of his dreams, Felice, his first night home, loses her the next day, therefore spending the rest of the novel trying to find his "little brown" in Claude McKay's *Home to Harlem;* expatriate returning to the United States from Marseilles in *Banjo.*

Jayhu (Jehu) Brown   Union man whose cough keeps him from being drafted into the Confederate army; assists Union prisoners of war who escape from Salisbury prison in Albion W. Tourgee's *A Fool's Errand.*

Joe Brown   See Lucas Burch.

Mae Brown   Long-suffering wife of Paul Brown, by whom she is temporarily deserted, and mother of Steely Brown in Julian Mayfield's *The Long Night.*

Mike Brown   Revolutionary War veteran; drunken farmer and blacksmith whose family deserts him in John Pendleton Kennedy's *Swallow Barn.*

Paul Brown   Father of Steely Brown and husband of Mae Brown; defeated by ghetto life in Julian Mayfield's *The Long Night.*

Recktall Brown   Corrupt businessman who talks Wyatt Gwyon into forging paintings in William Gaddis's *The Recognitions.*

Sergeant William (Willie) Brown   Misogynistic soldier in Norman Mailer's *The Naked and the Dead.*

Elizabeth Browne   See Elizabeth Browne Rogers.

Adrian Pericles Brownwell   Owner and editor of the Sycamore Ridge *Banner* whose modest wealth saves John Barclay's bank early in Barclay's career and who, with Barclay's help, marries Molly Culpepper in William Allen White's *A Certain Rich Man*.

Molly Culpepper Brownwell   Daughter of Martin Culpepper and wife of Adrian Brownwell; loves Bob Hendricks in William Allen White's *A Certain Rich Man*.

Rev. Calvin Bruce   Chicago minister in Charles M. Sheldon's *In His Steps*.

Colonel Bruce   Commander of the station outpost in Robert Montgomery Bird's *Nick of the Woods*.

Dr. Bruce (Doc)   Black physician and business partner of Tyree Tucker in Richard Wright's *The Long Dream*.

Victor Bruge   Friend of Stewart Barnes; gives Psyche Tanzer a fatal dose of a drug he believes is an aphrodisiac in Theodore Dreiser's *The Bulwark*.

Eddie Brunner   Platonic friend of Gloria Wandrous; struggles to find work as a commercial artist while working as a night man in a brothel in John O'Hara's *Butterfield 8*.

Elizabeth Martin Brush   See Elizabeth Martin.

George Marvin (George Busch, James Bush, Jim) Brush   Innocent, religiously and socially conservative representative of a textbook company in Thornton Wilder's *Heaven's My Destination*.

Marcus Junius Brutus   Former enemy of Caesar; recalled from Gaul by Caesar to become Praetor; one of Caesar's assassins in Thornton Wilder's *The Ides of March*.

Malcolm (Malc) Bryant   Anthropologist-sociologist who analyzes the class structure of the town of Clyde in John P. Marquand's *Point of No Return*.

Lacy Gore Buchan   Fifteen-year-old son of Major Lewis Buchan; friend of George Posey and in love with Jane Posey; tries to understand both the Buchan and Posey families; joins the Confederate army after the death of his father; narrator of Allen Tate's *The Fathers*.

Major Lewis Buchan   Father of Semmes, Susan, and Lacy Buchan; member of an old Virginia family; remains loyal to the Union but is killed by the Union army in Allen Tate's *The Fathers*.

Semmes (Brother Semmes) Buchan   Son disowned by Major Lewis Buchan; Virginia native who joins the Confederate army against his father's wishes; loves and plans to marry Jane Posey; killed by George Posey in Allen Tate's *The Fathers*.

Susan Buchan   See Susan Buchan Posey.

Daisy Fay Buchanan   Wife of Tom Buchanan and treacherous lost love of Jay Gatsby in F. Scott Fitzgerald's *The Great Gatsby*.

Doctor Buchanan   Golf partner and doctor of Judge Honeywell in Ellen Glasgow's *The Romantic Comedians*.

Rosemarie (Rosie) Buchanan   Friend of Ray Smith and mistress of Cody Pomeray; leaps off an apartment building to her death during an attack of paranoia in Jack Kerouac's *The Dharma Bums*; also appears in *Book of Dreams* and *Big Sur*.

Tom Buchanan   Unfaithful millionaire husband of Daisy Buchanan in F. Scott Fitzgerald's *The Great Gatsby*.

Buchwald   Army private who helps execute General Gragnon in William Faulkner's *A Fable*.

Buck   Dog who leads a dog team and twice saves the life of John Thornton, whose death Buck mourns, in Jack London's *The Call of the Wild*.

Buckingham   See George Villiers.

David A. Buckley   State's attorney who prosecutes Bigger Thomas for the murder of Mary Dalton in Richard Wright's *Native Son*.

Eleanor Apley Budd   See Eleanor Apley.

Irma Barnes Budd   Wealthy American heiress and wife of Lanny Budd in Upton Sinclair's *Dragon's Teeth*.

Lanning Prescott (Lanny) Budd   Wealthy American son of an arms manufacturer; helps secure the release of Johannes and Freddi Robin from the Nazis in Upton Sinclair's *Dragon's Teeth*.

William (Baby, Beauty, Billy) Budd   Handsome sailor aboard the *Rights-of-Man* impressed into service on the *Indomitable*; when falsely accused of planning a mutiny, he accidentally kills his accuser John Claggart in Herman Melville's *Billy Budd*.

Buell   Intelligent, unemotional minister of Norwood whose sermons are filled with carefully crafted scholarship and who marries Agate Bissell after the death of his first wife in Henry Ward Beecher's *Norwood*.

Dr. Samuel Buggerie   White statistician who discovers that over half the Anglo-Saxon population of the United States has black ancestors; eventually lynched in George S. Schuyler's *Black No More*.

Herr Ottokar Bukuwky   Employee of the von Studenitz family and husband of Frau Natalie Schuschnigg; instrumental in arranging restoration of Rudolf Stanka to family position in Louis Adamic's *Cradle of Life*.

Bulkington   Popular crewman from the *Grampus* who signs aboard the *Pequod* in Herman Melville's *Moby-Dick*.

Joe Bullitt   Friend of William Baxter; one of Baxter's rivals for the affections of Miss Lola Pratt in Booth Tarkington's *Seventeen*.

Absalom Bulrush Poor white man whose farm is mortgaged to Frank Meriwether in John Pendleton Kennedy's *Swallow Barn*.

Nathaniel (Deerslayer, Hawkeye, Leather-stocking, la Longue Carabine, Natty, Pathfinder) Bumppo White woodsman and guide with knowledge of Indian ways; helps Chingachgook rescue Wah-ta!-Wah and protects the Hutter family in James Fenimore Cooper's *The Deerslayer*; guide and escort to Major Heyward and the Munro sisters in *The Last of the Mohicans*; experiences love for Mabel Dunham in *The Pathfinder*; comes into conflict with the settlers of Templeton in *The Pioneers*; dies on the prairie in *The Prairie*.

Dr. Bumstead Father of Harriet Bumstead Alden; briefly cares for Peter Alden in George Santayana's *The Last Puritan*.

Harriet Bumstead See Harriet Bumstead Alden.

Byron Bunch Mill worker who befriends Lena Grove in William Faulkner's *Light in August*.

Addie Bundren First wife of Anse Bundren and mother of five children, one of whom, Jewel, is fathered by the minister Whitfield; following Addie's death, the family carries her body to Jefferson in William Faulkner's *As I Lay Dying*.

Anse Bundren Husband of Addie Bundren and father of four children; honors his wife's request to be buried in Jefferson, Mississippi; remarries soon after Addie's funeral in William Faulkner's *As I Lay Dying*.

Cash Bundren Son of Anse and Addie Bundren; carpenter who builds his mother's coffin in William Faulkner's *As I Lay Dying*.

Darl Bundren Son of Anse and Addie Bundren; committed to an asylum in William Faulkner's *As I Lay Dying*.

Dewey Dell Bundren Daughter of Anse and Addie Bundren; impregnated by Lafe in William Faulkner's *As I Lay Dying*.

Jewel Bundren Son of Addie Bundren and her lover Whitfield in William Faulkner's *As I Lay Dying*.

Vardaman Bundren Son of Anse and Addie Bundren in William Faulkner's *As I Lay Dying*.

Bundy (Old Bundy) Aging, bald, and extremely thin slave with a predilection for alcohol; dies as a result of a whipping administered by Thomas Prosser in Arna Wendell Bontemps's *Black Thunder*.

Bungs Cooper aboard the *Julia* in Herman Melville's *Omoo*.

Doctor Burch Young New York doctor who loves Dorinda Oakley and guides her emotional recovery and intellectual development in Ellen Glasgow's *Barren Ground*.

Lucas Burch (Joe Brown) Braggart mill worker and bootlegger who fathers Lena Grove's child in William Faulkner's *Light in August*.

Calvin Burden (I) Father of Nathaniel Burden; John Sartoris kills Burden and Calvin Burden II in William Faulkner's *Light in August*.

Calvin Burden (II) Son of Nathaniel and Juana Burden; John Sartoris kills Burden and Calvin Burden I in William Faulkner's *Light in August*.

Ellis (Scholarly Attorney) Burden Lawyer who marries Jack Burden's mother and moves her from Arkansas to Burden's Landing; leaves her when Jack is about six years old in Robert Penn Warren's *All the King's Men*.

Jack (Jackie, Jackie-Bird, Jackie-Boy) Burden Student of history, friend of Anne and Adam Stanton, son of Judge Irwin, and cynical right-hand man for Willie Stark; narrator of Robert Penn Warren's *All the King's Men*.

Jim Burden Lawyer for a railroad company who recalls his friendship with Ántonia Shimerda; narrator of Willa Cather's *My Ántonia*.

Joanna Burden Daughter of Nathaniel Burden and his second wife; lover of Joe Christmas, who murders her, in William Faulkner's *Light in August*; also appears in *The Mansion*.

Juana Burden First wife of Nathaniel Burden and mother of Calvin Burden II in William Faulkner's *Light in August*.

Martha Burden White New York artist friend of Angela Murray in Jessie Redmon Fauset's *Plum Bun*.

Milly Burden Defiant and unsettling secretary of Virginius Littlepage; seduced, impregnated, and abandoned by Martin Welding in Ellen Glasgow's *They Stooped to Folly*.

Nathaniel Burden Father of Calvin Burden II (by Juana Burden) and Joanna Burden (by his second wife) in William Faulkner's *Light in August*.

Alberta Ross Burdick See Alberta Ross.

Clark Burdon Gunman and homesteader who befriends Clay Clavert in H. L. Davis's *Honey in the Horn*.

Wally Burgan Shady lawyer and former business partner of Herbert Pierce; lover of Mildred Pierce in James M. Cain's *Mildred Pierce*.

Nancy Burke Assistant costume designer and friend of Delia Poole in Janet Flanner's *The Cubical City*.

Sadie Burke Private secretary to and mistress of Willie Stark; her jealousy leads to Stark's assassination in Robert Penn Warren's *All the King's Men*.

Studsy Burke Ex-convict, owner of the speakeasy The Pigiron Club in Dashiell Hammett's *The Thin Man*.

George Burkin Fellow inmate of George Brush in an Ozarksville, Missouri, jail in Thornton Wilder's *Heaven's My Destination*.

Burleigh Lawyer who gains acquittal for Royal Earle Thompson in Katherine Anne Porter's *Noon Wine*.

John Burleson Friend of Melville Gurney and chief of the county Ku Klux Klan; speaks out against murdering Comfort Servosse and tends to the dying Servosse; ultimately denounces the Klan in Albion W. Tourgee's *A Fool's Errand*.

Henry Burlingame III Gifted tutor who gives Ebenezer Cooke an unusually comprehensive education in John Barth's *The Sot-Weed Factor*.

Robert Burlingham Showboat owner and Susan Lenox's protector in David Graham Phillips's *Susan Lenox*.

Johnny Burnecker Well-meaning Iowa farm youth who joins the army and is inspired by the example of Noah Ackerman in Irwin Shaw's *The Young Lions*.

Frank Burnham Stunt pilot killed in an airplane crash in William Faulkner's *Pylon*.

Mr. Burns Employment manager at the Cosmodemonic Telegraph Company of North America in Henry Miller's *Tropic of Capricorn*.

Beauregard Jackson Pickett (Beau) Burnside Southern millionaire who marries Mame Dennis after she sells him twenty pairs of roller skates; dies thirteen months after their wedding in Patrick Dennis's *Auntie Mame*.

Elmore Jefferson Davis Burnside Obnoxious southerner, ladies' underwear salesman, and cousin of Mame Dennis's dead husband; tries to court Mame until her nephew arranges to have him arrested by Fascists in Patrick Dennis's *Around the World with Auntie Mame*.

Mame Dennis Burnside See Mame Dennis.

Aaron Burr Conspirator to conquer and rule in Mexico; opponent of Thomas Jefferson; acquitted at a trial for treason in Mary Johnston's *Lewis Rand*.

Henry Burrage Son of Mrs. Burrage; Harvard student who proposes marriage to Verena Tarrant in Henry James's *The Bostonians*.

Mrs. Burrage Society hostess who entertains Verena Tarrant in New York in Henry James's *The Bostonians*.

Nathaniel Burrington Father of Calvin Burden I in William Faulkner's *Light in August*.

Anthony (Tony) Burton President of the Stuyvesant Bank who awards the vice-presidency of the bank to Charles Gray in John P. Marquand's *Point of No Return*.

Bertrand Burton Manservant of Ebenezer Cooke; temporarily becomes a king in John Barth's *The Sot-Weed Factor*.

Doc Burton Physician who treats the migrant workers and supports their strike in John Steinbeck's *In Dubious Battle*.

Ralph Burton English officer friendly to Johnny Lacey; brings Lacey news of Braddock's death after the defeat outside Fort Duquesne in Mary Lee Settle's *O Beulah Land*.

Thomas Burton One of the soldiers who tries to make a deal with Richard Mast for the pistol Mast possesses in James Jones's *The Pistol*.

Tom (Big Boy) Burwell Southern black laborer who resents white Bob Stone's advances toward his girlfriend Louisa; in self-defense he cuts Stone's throat and is lynched by a white mob in Jean Toomer's *Cane*.

Asa Bush Firstborn son of Ishmael and Esther Bush; shot in the back by his uncle, Abiram White, who tries to blame Natty Bumppo for Asa's murder, in James Fenimore Cooper's *The Prairie*.

Esther (Eester) Bush Powerful and fearless wife of Ishmael Bush; concurs with Ishmael in imposing a death sentence on her brother, Abiram White, in James Fenimore Cooper's *The Prairie*.

Ike (Al Kennedy) Bush Fighter dissuaded from taking a dive by the Op in Dashiell Hammett's *Red Harvest*.

Ishmael (the Great Buffalo) Bush Squatter, patriarch, and law unto himself; husband of Esther Bush and brother-in-law of Abiram White; with White, kidnapper of Inez de Certavallos in James Fenimore Cooper's *The Prairie*.

Ambrose Bushfield Frontiersman in James Kirke Paulding's *Westward Ho!*

Otto Bussen Mathematics student at the University of Berlin; roomer in Rosa Reichl's boardinghouse in Katherine Anne Porter's *The Leaning Tower*.

Buster (Bus) Friend and playmate of Sandy Rodgers; passes for white in Langston Hughes's *Not Without Laughter*.

Seth Buswell Owner and editor of the *Peyton Place Times* who gives Allison MacKenzie her first job in Grace Metalious's *Peyton Place*.

Butler Mysterious stranger who abducts Ellen Langton; falls from a cliff and dies while fighting Fanshaw in Nathaniel Hawthorne's *Fanshawe*.

Aileen (Ai) Butler See Aileen Butler Cowperwood.

Arthur Butler Patriot hero captured by the Tories; rescued by Horse Shoe Robinson in time to fight at King's Mountain; husband of Mildred Lindsay in John Pendleton Kennedy's *Horse Shoe Robinson.*

Edward Malia (Eddie) Butler   Father of Aileen Butler; uses his political influence to ruin Frank Cowperwood in Theodore Dreiser's *The Financier.*

Eugenie Victoria (Bonnie Blue) Butler   Daughter of Scarlett O'Hara and Rhett Butler; killed in a horse-riding accident in Margaret Mitchell's *Gone with the Wind.*

Rhett K. Butler   Successsful blockade runner during the Civil War; third husband of Scarlett O'Hara, whom he leaves, in Margaret Mitchell's *Gone with the Wind.*

Widow Butler   Invalid mother of Butler; lives with her sister in Nathaniel Hawthorne's *Fanshawe.*

Clara Butterworth   Daughter of Tom Butterworth and student at Ohio State University; thoughtful young woman who marries Hugh McVey in Sherwood Anderson's *Poor White.*

Tom Butterworth   Ohio farmer and father of Clara Butterworth; invests in the factory that produces Hugh McVey's inventions in Sherwood Anderson's *Poor White.*

Roger Byam   Midshipman on the HMS *Bounty* who narrates the events of the voyage to Tahiti, his efforts to compile a dictionary of the Tahitian language, the mutiny, his return to England in chains, and his narrow escape from being hanged as a mutineer in Charles Nordhoff and James Norman Hall's *Mutiny on the Bounty.*

Peter Bye   Doctor of mixed racial heritage; husband of Joanna Marshall in Jessie Redmon Fauset's *There Is Confusion.*

Mr. Byfield   Track coach of Homer Macauley at Ithaca High School; prejudiced against students from immigrant families in William Saroyan's *The Human Comedy.*

Mrs. Bywaters   Frederick County postmistress who helps Nancy escape to Canada in Willa Cather's *Sapphira and the Slave Girl.*

C

Prince Cabano (Jacob Isaacs)   Jewish banker and a leader in the Oligarchy who attempts to deflower Estella Washington; killed during an apocalyptic revolution in Ignatius Donnelly's *Caesar's Column.*

Lionel Cabot   Best friend of Ulysses Macauley in William Saroyan's *The Human Comedy.*

Rheinhold Cacoethes   San Francisco literary critic in Jack Kerouac's *The Dharma Bums.*

Matteo Cacopardo   Sulfur processor who advises Major Joppolo to secure a bell for the town in John Hersey's *A Bell for Adano.*

Mr. Cadwalader   Leader of the Progressive group and official head of the Farmer-Labor Party in Chicago with whom Mrs. Beech seeks an alliance in W. E. B. Du Bois's *Dark Princess.*

Alex Cady   Bigoted and violent poor-white tenant farmer who persecutes blacks; destroys a wagon belonging to Miltiades Vaiden and leads a mob that lynches Toussaint Vaiden in T. S. Stribling's *The Store.*

Eph Cady   Son of Alex Cady; assassinates Miltiades Vaiden in T. S. Stribling's *Unfinished Cathedral.*

Augustus (Gus) Caesar   Former slave of Richard Cameron; rapes Marion Lenoir and is lynched by the Ku Klux Klan in Thomas Dixon's *The Clansman.*

Gaius Julius Caesar   Dictator of Rome whose death occurs on the ides of March in Thornton Wilder's *The Ides of March.*

Rollo Cage   Loyal white friend of Jule Jackson and son of a store owner in George Wylie Henderson's *Jule.*

Eddie Cahow   Ubiquitous barber with genealogical genius in Wright Morris's *The Man Who Was There* and *The Home Place.*

Amanda (Mandy) Cain   Adulteress whose infidelity, discovered by Ellen Chesser, causes the suicide of Cassie Beal MacMurtrie in Elizabeth Madox Roberts's *The Time of Man.*

Joel Cairo   Homosexual pursuer of the jewel-encrusted statuette who forms a temporary alliance with Brigid O'Shaughnessy in Dashiell Hammett's *The Maltese Falcon.*

Corie Cal   See Corie Calhoun.

Haze Cal   See Haze Calhoun.

Rie Cal   See Rie Calhoun.

Calamity Jane (Martha Jane Canary)   Childhood friend of Morissa Kirk; drunkenly taunts Morissa about being illegitimate in Mari Sandoz's *Miss Morissa.*

Joseph P. (Gentleman Joe) Calash   Highwayman who helps Daniel Harrow escape a beating and who is later helped to escape by Harrow and Molly Larkins, only to be shot by a posse, in Walter D. Edmonds's *Rome Haul.*

Jim Calder   Successful writer of magazine fiction and cousin of the Brills; alternately drawn to and repelled by Wickford Point; narrator of John P. Marquand's *Wickford Point.*

Brock Caldwell   Idle, sarcastic older brother of Grace Caldwell Tate; gradually matures and becomes head of the Caldwell family in John O'Hara's *A Rage to Live.*

Duck Caldwell   Hired worker for the Crooms; represents a high manifestation of ordinary life in Lionel Trilling's *The Middle of the Journey.*

Dr. Edward (Ned) Caldwell Father of William Caldwell; beloved country doctor injured in a buggy accident in Mary Austin's *Santa Lucia*.

Emily Caldwell Wife of Duck Caldwell and lover of John Laskell; her unreality distances the Crooms in Lionel Trilling's *The Middle of the Journey*.

Grace Brock Caldwell See Grace Brock Caldwell Tate.

Professor Caldwell Professor of English who helps Martin Eden expand his interests in Jack London's *Martin Eden*.

Susan Caldwell Daughter of Duck and Emily Caldwell; John Laskell becomes friendly with her in Lionel Trilling's *The Middle of the Journey*.

William (Billy) Caldwell Ebullient daughter of Doctor Caldwell; loved by Edward Jasper and successfully courted by George Rhewold in Mary Austin's *Santa Lucia*.

Bud Calhoun Lazy genius inventor who joins revolutionaries in Kurt Vonnegut's *Player Piano*.

Corie (Corie Cal) Calhoun Wife of Lee Buck Calhoun and mother of Rie Calhoun and five other children in Harriette Simpson Arnow's *Mountain Path*.

Gerald (Bull's-eye, Jerry) Calhoun Former college quarterback ashamed of his father; in love with Sue Murdock, daughter of his employer, Bogan Murdock, in Robert Penn Warren's *At Heaven's Gate*.

Haze (Haze Cal) Calhoun Brother, neighbor, and moonshining partner of Lee Buck Calhoun in Harriette Simpson Arnow's *Mountain Path*.

Lee Buck Calhoun Calhoun family patriarch, farmer, school trustee, moonshiner, fiddler, and landlord of Louisa Sheridan in Harriette Simpson Arnow's *Mountain Path*.

Mabel Calhoun Daughter of Haze Calhoun; cousin and schoolmate of Rie Calhoun in Harriette Simpson Arnow's *Mountain Path*.

Rie (Rie Cal) Calhoun Oldest daughter of Lee Buck and Corie Calhoun; student of Louisa Sheridan in Harriette Simpson Arnow's *Mountain Path*.

Professor Seth Calhoun Bigot and author of *The Menace of the Negro to Our American Civilization*; invited by Constancia Brandon to speak at a soiree in her salon in Countee Cullen's *One Way to Heaven*.

Molly Calico Clerk of the zoning board and later parish secretary; clandestinely courted and affianced by Andrew Mackerel during the period of mourning for his late wife; finally marries Mike Todarescu in Peter De Vries's *The Mackerel Plaza*.

Pippa Calico Mother of Molly Calico and temporary housekeeper for Andrew Mackerel in Peter De Vries's *The Mackerel Plaza*.

Zeb Calloway See Boone Caudill.

Calpurnia Last wife of Caesar; they are married weeks before his death in Thornton Wilder's *The Ides of March*.

Calpurnia Housekeeper for the Finch family and mother substitute for Scout and Jem Finch in Harper Lee's *To Kill a Mockingbird*.

Charles Calvert, Lord Baltimore Lord Proprietary of the Province of Maryland in John Barth's *The Sot-Weed Factor*.

Clay Calvert Orphan adopted by Uncle Preston Shiveley in H. L. Davis's *Honey in the Horn*.

Thomas Cambridge Maternal uncle of Clara and Theodore Wieland; reveals to Clara that Theodore killed his own wife and children at Carwin's instigation in Charles Brockden Brown's *Wieland*.

Ben Cameron Confederate colonel who organizes the Ku Klux Klan to overthrow the black-dominated government of Reconstruction in Thomas Dixon's *The Clansman*.

Henry Cameron Pioneer in modern architecture; defies mediocrity but finally is crushed by it in Ayn Rand's *The Fountainhead*.

Kenneth Cameron New York producer who marries Kim Ravenal in Edna Ferber's *Show Boat*.

Kim Ravenal Cameron Daughter of Magnolia and Gaylord Ravenal; New York actress who marries Kenneth Cameron in Edna Ferber's *Show Boat*.

Dr. Lemuel (Bracciani) Cameron Site director of Talifer Missile Base known for his ruthlessness and brilliance; discredited in a congressional hearing in John Cheever's *The Wapshot Scandal*.

Margaret Cameron Sister of Ben Cameron; loves Phil Stoneman in Thomas Dixon's *The Clansman*.

Richard Cameron Father of Ben and Margaret Cameron; physician who identifies Augustus Caesar as Marion Lenoir's assailant in Thomas Dixon's *The Clansman*.

Camille Second wife of Dean Moriarty; following a third marriage, he returns to her in Jack Kerouac's *On the Road*.

Flora Camp Youngest daughter of Tom Camp; abducted and killed, apparently by Dick, in Thomas Dixon's *The Leopard's Spots*.

Reuben (Reub) Camp Unsuccessful farmer who agrees with many of Homos's criticisms of America in William Dean Howells's *A Traveler from Altruria*.

Tom Camp   Poor, crippled Confederate veteran who becomes insane after his daughters are killed by blacks in Thomas Dixon's *The Leopard's Spots.*

Michael (Mike) Campbell   Heavy-drinking British fiancé of Lady Brett Ashley in Ernest Hemingway's *The Sun Also Rises.*

Nicholas Campbell   First love of Phebe Grant and the husband of one of her friends in Jessie Redmon Fauset's *Comedy, American Style.*

Camper   Traveler who helped to build the dam originally and who witnessed the mud slide that killed Mulge Lampson; helps to bury Hattie Lampson in John Hawkes's *The Beetle Leg.*

Luis Campion   Homosexual expatriate in F. Scott Fitzgerald's *Tender Is the Night.*

Akiva Ben Canaan   Brother of Barak Ben Canaan and uncle of Ari and Jordana Ben Canaan; heads illegal terrorist activities against the British forces in Palestine in Leon Uris's *Exodus.*

Ari Ben Canaan   Lover of Kitty Fremont; soldier in the Israeli War of Independence and smuggler of Jews into Palestine, his home, in Leon Uris's *Exodus.*

Barak Ben Canaan   Father of Ari and Jordana Ben Canaan and brother of Akiva Ben Canaan; political head of Palestine in Leon Uris's *Exodus.*

Jordana Ben Canaan   Sister of Ari Ben Canaan and lover of David Ben Ami; Israeli sabra and fighter in Leon Uris's *Exodus.*

Martha Jane Canary   See Calamity Jane.

Canby   Eponymous owner of the only saloon in the town of Bridger's Wells in Walter Van Tilburg Clark's *The Ox-Bow Incident.*

Candy   See Candy Christian.

Candy   Aging ranch hand who dreams of making a new start with George Milton and Lennie Small in John Steinbeck's *Of Mice and Men.*

Mrs. Candy   Housekeeper and cook for Doremus Jessup; quiet supporter of the New Underground in Sinclair Lewis's *It Can't Happen Here.*

Lash Canino   Killer in Raymond Chandler's *The Big Sleep.*

Gerald (Chief) Cantley   White chief of police who receives kickbacks from Tyree Tucker's illegal businesses; murders Tyree Tucker and arrests Fish Tucker for attempted rape in Richard Wright's *The Long Dream.*

Richard (Dick, Ricardo) Cantwell   American army officer who, fatally ill, returns to Venice to visit a lover and hunt for ducks in Ernest Hemingway's *Across the River and into the Trees.*

John Canty   Cruel father of Tom Canty; introduces Edward Tudor, disguised as Tom Canty, to thieves and beggars in Samuel Langhorne Clemens's *The Prince and the Pauper.*

Tom Canty   Boy from the London slums who looks exactly like Edward Tudor; exchanges identity with Edward and learns the burdensome duties of royal life in Samuel Langhorne Clemens's *The Prince and the Pauper.*

Charles Cap   Sea captain who is uneasy on land and inland waters in James Fenimore Cooper's *The Pathfinder.*

Luigi and Angelo Capello   Italian twins blamed for the murder of York Driscoll in Samuel Langhorne Clemens's *Pudd'nhead Wilson.*

Mrs. Capon   Woman with whom Frado leaves her son until she can regain strength and find a livelihood in Harriet E. Wilson's *Our Nig.*

Captain   Lover of Ida Farange while she is married to Sir Claude in Henry James's *What Maisie Knew.*

Captain Bob   Tahitian jailer and linguist in Herman Melville's *Omoo.*

Caraher   Anarchist saloon keeper in the San Joaquin Valley who influences Presley to bomb S. Behrman's home in Frank Norris's *The Octopus.*

Richard (Dick) Caramel   Successful novelist and friend of Anthony Patch in F. Scott Fitzgerald's *The Beautiful and Damned.*

Judge Darwin Carberry   Judge who ultimately frees George Brush from an Ozarksville, Missouri, jail in Thornton Wilder's *Heaven's My Destination.*

Carey   Slave of Frank Meriwether; coachman and butler in John Pendleton Kennedy's *Swallow Barn.*

Carl   Former lover from whom the narrator receives a bottle of brandy she later gives to her new suitor, a talented and passionate young writer, in Aline Bernstein's *The Journey Down.*

Carl   Farm boy who is the first love of Rose Dutcher in Hamlin Garland's *Rose of Dutcher's Coolly.*

Carl (Joe)   Writer who has written no book; hates Paris in Henry Miller's *Tropic of Cancer.*

Crazy Carl   Retarded adult in the town of Maxwell, Georgia, on whose word Henry McIntosh is mistakenly identified as the murderer of Tracy Deen in Lillian Smith's *Strange Fruit.*

Carlo   Handsome, teenaged hand-organ player aboard the *Highlander* in Herman Melville's *Redburn.*

Christina Carlson   See Christina Jansen.

Claudia Carlstadt Woman hired by Frank Cowperwood to seduce the mayor of Chicago so Cowperwood can blackmail him in Theodore Dreiser's *The Titan*.

Lady (Corinna) Carlton Beautiful wife of Bruce Carlton; her faithfulness eventually persuades him to give up his relationship with Amber St. Clare in Kathleen Winsor's *Forever Amber*.

Lord (Bruce) Carlton Dashing cavalier, privateer, only real love of Amber St. Clare, and father of two of her children; begins a King's grant plantation in Virginia with his wife, Corinna, in Kathleen Winsor's *Forever Amber*.

Carma Muscular black southerner whose denial of adultery results in her husband's being sentenced to a chain gang in Jean Toomer's *Cane*.

Carmelo Hired hand of Sparicio; works the tiller and sings a Mediterranean ballad in Lafcadio Hearn's *Chita*.

Frank Carmichael Chief of police in Peter De Vries's *Comfort Me with Apples*.

John Carmichael Hard-drinking executive of a meat-packing firm in Robert Herrick's *The Memoirs of an American Citizen*.

Frank Carmody Writer and drug addict; companion of Adam Moorad and Leo Percepied in Jack Kerouac's *The Subterraneans*.

Lucette Carmody Crippled child evangelist whose preaching fascinates both Mr. Rayber and young Francis Marion Tarwater in Flannery O'Connor's *The Violent Bear It Away*.

Carnashan Alcoholic messenger hired by Henry Miller in Henry Miller's *Tropic of Capricorn*.

Cassius P. (Cash) Carney Boyhood friend of John Wickliff Shawnessy; financier in Ross Lockridge, Jr.'s *Raintree County*.

Caroline Wife of Uncle Alex; nurses Ollie from wounds received in a knife fight in George Wylie Henderson's *Ollie Miss*; appears also in *Jule*.

Aunt Caroline Relative with whom Henry Miller spends a summer; notable for her kindness to him and her pockmarked face in Henry Miller's *Tropic of Capricorn*.

Belle Carpenter Employee in a millinery shop who allows herself to be courted by George Willard because of her distrust of Ed Handby in Sherwood Anderson's *Winesburg, Ohio*.

Carey Carr Minister who presides at the funeral of Peyton Loftis; confidant of Helen Loftis in William Styron's *Lie Down in Darkness*.

Nick Carraway Neighbor and befriender of Jay Gatsby; narrator of F. Scott Fitzgerald's *The Great Gatsby*.

Sir Robert Carre Military leader for Governor Lovelace in James Kirke Paulding's *Koningsmarke*.

Lieutenant Colonel Benny Carricker Young fighter pilot and war hero whose punching of a black pilot is partly responsible for triggering unrest among black officers in James Gould Cozzens's *Guard of Honor*.

Sister Carrie See Caroline Meeber.

John Carrington Washington lawyer whom Senator Ratcliffe sends to Mexico in order to get him away from Madeleine Lee in Henry Adams's *Democracy*.

Nina (Mattie Bliss) Carrington Chambermaid at the hotel where Paul Armstrong fakes his death; tries to blackmail Frank Walker in Mary Roberts Rinehart's *The Circular Staircase*.

Madam Marion More Morris Carroll Second wife of Major Carroll, stepmother of Sara Carroll, and mistress of the Carroll Farms; forced by her husband's mental decline to protect him and the community from each other in Constance Fenimore Woolson's *For the Major*.

Sara Carroll Daughter of Major Carroll and beloved of Frederick Owen; responds diplomatically to the needs of both her father and stepmother, Marion More Carroll, in Constance Fenimore Woolson's *For the Major*.

Scar Carroll Son of Major Carroll and Marion More Carroll and stepbrother of Sara Carroll in Constance Fenimore Woolson's *For the Major*.

Major Scarborough Carroll Owner of the Carroll Farms, first citizen of Far Edgerley, and senior warden of St. John's Episcopal Church; subject of protective attention from his wife Marion More Carroll and daughter, Sara Carroll, as senility and blindness threaten his position in the community in Constance Fenimore Woolson's *For the Major*.

Amy Carruthers Wealthy North Carolina socialite who becomes Harley Drew's lover in Shelby Foote's *Love in a Dry Season*.

Jeff Carruthers Husband and cousin of Amy Carruthers in Shelby Foote's *Love in a Dry Season*.

Christopher (Kit) Carson Mountaineer and scout who brings news of the discovery of gold in California in Emerson Hough's *The Covered Wagon*.

Edward (Ed, Kit, Pimples) Carson Acne-ridden seventeen-year-old apprentice mechanic to Juan Chicoy; interested in the electrifying Camille Oaks in John Steinbeck's *The Wayward Bus*.

Frederic Augustus Carson Suitor of Nina Gordon, whom he loses to Edward Clayton, in Harriet Beecher Stowe's *Dred*.

Kit (Christóbal) Carson Explorer, trapper, and Indian hunter; friend of Bishop Latour in Willa Cather's *Death Comes for the Archbishop*.

Alisande de la Carteloise See Sandy.

Bella Carter   Mistress of Rafe Ashton in H. D.'s *Bid Me to Live.*

Cyrus Carter   President of a railroad, employer of Oliver Tappan, and uncle of Madeline Carter in Hjalmar Hjorth Boyesen's *The Golden Calf.*

Madam Fannie Rosalie de Carter   Neighbor of Aunt Hager Williams; fights for women's suffrage and prohibition in Langston Hughes's *Not Without Laughter.*

Gil Carter   Rowdy best friend of Art Croft in Walter Van Tilburg Clark's *The Ox-Bow Incident.*

Hattie (Hattie Starr) Carter   Proprietor of a Louisville brothel; mother of Berenice Fleming in Theodore Dreiser's *The Stoic* and the *Titan.*

John T. Carter   Southern gentleman serving in the Union army during the Civil War who marries Lillie Ravenel despite the objections of her father; dies in battle shortly after the discovery of his affair with Lillie's aunt, Mrs. Larue, in John William DeForest's *Miss Ravenel's Conversion from Secession to Loyalty.*

Lillie Ravenel Carter   Louisiana belle who, through a series of adventures and marriages, becomes firmly attached to the Union cause in the Civil War in John William DeForest's *Miss Ravenel's Conversion from Secession to Loyalty.*

Madeline Carter   Aristocratic New Yorker and niece of Cyrus Carter; marries Oliver Tappan and inspires his corruption in Hjalmar Hjorth Boyesen's *The Golden Calf.*

Ravenel (Ravvie) Carter   Son of John and Lillie Ravenel Carter; his presence and need for attention occupies Lillie after her husband's infidelity is discovered in John William DeForest's *Miss Ravenel's Conversion from Secession to Loyalty.*

Ted Carter   Young man who, to the chagrin of his social-climbing family, loves the socially unacceptable Selena Cross in Grace Metalious's *Peyton Place.*

Charles Carteret   Friend of Nick Dormer; urges Dormer to enter politics in Henry James's *The Tragic Muse.*

Major Philip Carteret   Aristocratic white newspaper owner and adversary of Dr. William Miller in Charles W. Chesnutt's *The Marrow of Tradition.*

Colonel Comyn Carvel   Grandson of Dorothy Manners and Richard Carvel; father of Virginia Carvel; proslavery aristocrat in Civil War St. Louis in Winston Churchill's *The Crisis.*

Dorothy Manners Carvel   See Dorothy Manners.

Grafton Carvel   Deceitful, unprincipled uncle of Richard Carvel in Winston Churchill's *Richard Carvel.*

Lionel Carvel   Kindly man who rears the orphaned Richard Carvel in Winston Churchill's *Richard Carvel.*

Philip Carvel   Ne'er-do-well son of Grafton Carvel in Winston Churchill's *Richard Carvel.*

Richard (Dick) Carvel   Manly Marylander who suffers greatly as an American supporter during the Revolutionary War; husband of Dorothy Manners; narrator of Winston Churchill's *Richard Carvel.*

Virginia (Jinny) Carvel   Descendant of Richard Carvel; spirited and high-minded supporter of her Maryland ancestors and of slavery; marries Stephen Brice in Winston Churchill's *The Crisis.*

Alden Carver, Junior   Bachelor brother of Stephen Carver; succeeds his father as a bank president; appears in Margaret Ayer Barnes's *Years of Grace* and *Wisdom's Gate.*

Cicily Carver   See Cicily Carver Bridges Lancaster.

Cicily (Silly) Carver   Unmarried sister of Stephen Carver in Margaret Ayer Barnes's *Years of Grace.*

Jane Ward (Mumsy) Carver   Daughter of John and Lizzie Ward, wife of Stephen Carver, and mother of three children, including Cicily Carver; despite her education and opportunities, she accepts a conventional life in Margaret Ayer Barnes's *Years of Grace* and *Wisdom's Gate.*

Captain Jonathan Carver   Officer in Rogers' Rangers who later betrays Major Robert Rogers in Kenneth Roberts's *Northwest Passage.*

Lawyer Carver   Attorney who reads Peregrine Lacey Catlett's will to the Catlett family in Mary Lee Settle's *Know Nothing.*

Maury Carver   Loudmouth member of Johnny Catlett's militia unit in Mary Lee Settle's *Know Nothing.*

Mother Carver   Wise old frontier woman who settles with her family at Beulah; tries to help Sally Lacey adapt to frontier life but is scorned in Mary Lee Settle's *O Beulah Land.*

Preston Carver   Eighteen-year-old dandy and subordinate officer in Johnny Catlett's Confederate army unit in Mary Lee Settle's *Know Nothing.*

Stephen Carver   Boston banker married to Jane Ward Carver; father of three children, including Cicily Carver, in Margaret Ayer Barnes's *Years of Grace* and *Wisdom's Gate.*

Francis Carwin   Biloquist who wreaks havoc on the lives of Clara Wieland, her family, and her friends in Charles Brockden Brown's *Wieland.*

Christopher Blanchard (Chris) Cary, Jr.   Son of Olivia Cary; saved from her influence by his father and his wife's claiming of their black heritage in Jessie Redmon Fauset's *Comedy, American Style.*

Christopher Fidele Cary Husband of Olivia Cary; a doctor who refuses to pass for white in Jessie Redmon Fauset's *Comedy, American Style.*

Edward Cary Son of Warwick Cary, brother of Judith Cary, nephew of Fauquier Cary, and husband of Désirée Gaillard; fights with the Confederate navy in Virginia and Mississippi in Mary Johnston's *The Long Roll* and *Cease Firing.*

Fairfax Cary Brother of Ludwell Cary; postpones engagement to Unity Dandridge to pursue his brother's murderer in Mary Johnston's *Lewis Rand.*

Fauquier Cary Uncle of Judith and Edward Cary and cousin of Richard Cleave; Whig veteran of the Mexican War who wants to preserve the Union, until the battle at Fort Sumter; promoted to the rank of general and loses an arm at Sharpsburg; appears in Mary Johnston's *The Long Roll* and *Cease Firing.*

Judith Jacqueline Cary Daughter of Warwick Cary, sister of Edward Cary, and niece of Fauquier Cary; attends wounded Confederate troops in Richmond, and marries Richard Cleave; appears in Mary Johnston's *The Long Roll* and *Cease Firing.*

Lucy Cary Aunt of Judith and Edward Cary and sister of Fauquier Cary; makes shirts, from family curtains, for Confederate troops in Mary Johnston's *The Long Roll.*

Ludwell Cary Brother of Fairfax Cary; rival in politics and romance of Lewis Rand, by whom he is murdered, in Mary Johnston's *Lewis Rand.*

Oliver Cary Dark-skinned son of Olivia Cary; driven to suicide by his mother's treatment of him in Jessie Redmon Fauset's *Comedy, American Style.*

Olivia Blanchard Cary Upper-class, light-skinned woman who eventually destroys two of her children by her obsession with skin color in Jessie Redmon Fauset's *Comedy, American Style.*

Teresa (Tess, Treesa) Cary Light-skinned mulatto daughter of Olivia Cary; forced by her mother to give up her dark-skinned lover to marry the white Aristide Pailleron in Jessie Redmon Fauset's *Comedy, American Style.*

Prince Casamassima Young and exceedingly wealthy Italian prince married to Christina Light in Henry James's *Roderick Hudson;* pursues his runaway wife in an attempt to convince her to return home in *The Princess Casamassima.*

Princess Casamassima See Christina Light.

Maurice (Joe) Cassard French screenwriter who marries Belinda in Ludwig Bemelmans's *Dirty Eddie.*

Casse-tête Thief executed with Stefan in William Faulkner's *A Fable.*

Maggie (M. C.) Cassidy First love of Jack Duluoz; ultimately rejects him in Jack Kerouac's *Maggie Cassidy;* mentioned in *Book of Dreams* and *Desolation Angels.*

Cassy (Miss Cassy) Mysterious, unwilling slave mistress to Simon Legree; manages the escape of herself and Emmeline, her daughter, with the help of Uncle Tom and is reunited by chance with Eliza Harris in Harriet Beecher Stowe's *Uncle Tom's Cabin.*

Alejandro Castillo Younger son of the valley's richest man and lover of the beautiful Maria de las Garzas; friend of Bob Webster; married to a woman he does not love; dies tragically in Josefina Niggli's *Mexican Village.*

Joaquín Castillo Older son of the valley's richest man; leaves Hidalgo to fight in the Revolution of 1910; returns incognito as an actor with a wandering troupe and reclaims his position in the village, eventually becoming a close friend of Bob Webster, in Josefina Niggli's *Mexican Village.*

James Castle Elkton Hills student who commits suicide rather than retract his statement accusing another student of conceit in J. D. Salinger's *The Catcher in the Rye.*

Lady Castledean Member of the Ververs' social circle who is romantically interested in Mr. Blint in Henry James's *The Golden Bowl.*

Castlemaine See Barbara Palmer, Lady Castlemaine.

Jim Casy Former preacher who baptized the infant Tom Joad (II); inspires Tom to correct some social wrongs in John Steinbeck's *The Grapes of Wrath.*

Abiah Cathcart Stolid New Englander who rises from poverty to become a leading citizen of Norwood, owning the best set of matched horses in town and fathering an enormous family, in Henry Ward Beecher's *Norwood.*

Alice Cathcart Friend of Rose Wentworth; joins Wentworth and Agate Bissell in Northern hospital duty during the Civil War, only to see her true love, Thomas Heywood, die fighting for the South at Gettysburg, in Henry Ward Beecher's *Norwood.*

Barton Cathcart Son of Abiah and Rachel Cathcart; practical yet mystical graduate of Amherst who becomes the Norwood schoolmaster; rises to a Union generalship in the Civil War despite being wounded and captured several times; marries Rose Wentworth in Henry Ward Beecher's *Norwood.*

Rachel Liscomb Cathcart Sensitive wife of Abiah Cathcart; passes on some of her mystical spirit to her son Barton Cathcart in Henry Ward Beecher's *Norwood.*

Andrew (Andy) Cather Husband of Bertha Cather; at age twelve he found the body of his drowned mother; narrates part of Conrad Aiken's *Great Circle.*

Bertha (Berty) Cather　Wife of Andrew Cather; has an affair with Tom Crapo in Conrad Aiken's *Great Circle.*

David Cather　Uncle of Andrew Cather and brother of John Cather; drowns with his lover Doris Cather in Conrad Aiken's *Great Circle.*

Doris Cather　Mother of Andrew Cather; drowns with her lover David Cather in Conrad Aiken's *Great Circle.*

John Cather　Father of Andrew Cather in Conrad Aiken's *Great Circle.*

Queen Catherine (Infanta Catherine of Portugal)　Barren queen of Restoration England's Charles II; tolerates his many mistresses out of love for him and the hope that she will eventually give him a legitimate heir to the English throne in Kathleen Winsor's *Forever Amber.*

George Catherwood　Brother of Tom Catherwood; Confederate soldier in a divided family in Winston Churchill's *The Crisis.*

Tom Catherwood　Brother of George Catherwood; Union soldier in a divided family in Winston Churchill's *The Crisis.*

Ezekiel (Zeke) Catlett　Eldest son of Jeremiah and Hannah Catlett; marries Sara Lacey and becomes Johnny Lacey's heir; kills Witcikti, using the English tomahawk once stolen from Witcikti himself, in Mary Lee Settle's *O Beulah Land.*

Hannah Bridewell Catlett　London pickpocket transported to Virginia; as a captive of Shawnee Indians, she is the first white settler to see Beulah land; killed by Witcikti in the last Indian raid at Beulah; wife of Jeremiah and mother of Ezekiel and Rebecca Catlett in Mary Lee Settle's *O Beulah Land.*

Jeremiah Catlett　Illiterate farmer and New Light preacher led to escape his indentures, travel west, rescue Hannah Bridewell Catlett, his future wife, in the wilderness, and move to Beulah, where he is killed in the last Indian raid; father of Ezekiel and Rebecca Catlett in Mary Lee Settle's *O Beulah Land.*

Johnny Catlett　Younger son of Leah and Peregrine Lacey Catlett; leaves Beulah to avoid commitment to Melinda Lacey; goes to Missouri and Kansas, but returns to take over Beulah from his father; eventually enlists in the Confederate army but without believing in the southern position or the possibility of success in Mary Lee Settle's *Know Nothing.*

Leah Cutwright Catlett　Descendant of Doggo Cutwright; Ohio-born wife of Peregrine Lacey Catlett and mother of Lewis, Johnny, and Lydia Catlett; an outsider who is initially an abolitionist, she becomes willing to sell slaves and more approving of slavery than is her husband in Mary Lee Settle's *Know Nothing.*

Lewis Catlett　Elder son of Leah and Peregrine Lacey Catlett; inherits his mother's antislavery attitudes, religious piety, and sense of being an outsider; becomes a preacher and an abolitionist; leaves Beulah and eventually enlists in the Union army in Mary Lee Settle's *Know Nothing.*

Lydia Catlett　See Lydia Catlett Neill.

Mamie Brandon Catlett　Descendant of Backwater Brandon and the Kreggs; daughter-in-law of Ezekiel Catlett and mother of Peregrine Lacey Catlett in Mary Lee Settle's *Know Nothing.*

Peregrine Lacey Catlett　Grandson of Ezekiel Catlett, proprietor of Beulah, husband of Leah Cutwright Catlett, and father of Lewis, Johnny, and Lydia Catlett and of the slave Toey; deplores the responsibilities of being a slave owner and supports the Union in Mary Lee Settle's *Know Nothing.*

Rebecca (Becky) Catlett　Daughter of Jeremiah and Hannah Catlett and sister of Ezekiel Catlett in Mary Lee Settle's *O Beulah Land.*

Sara Lacey (Mrs. Ezekiel Catlett) Catlett　Daughter of Johnny and Sally Lacey, sister of Peregrine and Montague Lacey, and wife of Ezekiel Catlett; only child of Johnny Lacey to share his love for Beulah land and his egalitarian ideas, she eventually inherits Beulah in Mary Lee Settle's *O Beulah Land.*

Sara Lacey (Mrs. Lewis Catlett) Catlett　Daughter of Brandon and Sally Lacey; beautiful child who, as an adult, becomes gawky, religious, and conscious of being a poor relation; marries Lewis Catlett and adopts his attitudes in Mary Lee Settle's *Know Nothing.*

Jeremiah Catlin　Union soldier from Lane County, Tennessee, who is imprisoned by the Confederates; husband of Marcia Vaiden in T.S. Stribling's *The Store.*

Jerry Catlin the Second　Son of Jerry and Marcia Catlin; seduces Pammy Lee Sparkman; Methodist minister infatuated with Sydna Crowninshield Vaiden but who marries Aurelia Swartout; appears in T. S. Stribling's *The Store* and *Unfinished Cathedral.*

Marcia Vaiden Catlin　See Marcia Vaiden.

Gaius Valerius Catullus　Young poet with great potential; first an enemy of Caesar and then a friend; loves Clodia Pulcher, who rejects him, in Thornton Wilder's *The Ides of March.*

Boone (Zeb Calloway) Caudill　Fledgling mountain man who leaves his Kentucky home to trap furs in the Rocky Mountains in A. B. Guthrie's *The Big Sky.*

Allie Caulfield　Sensitive younger brother of Holden Caulfield; dies of leukemia in J. D. Salinger's *The Catcher in the Rye.*

D. B. Caulfield　Older brother of Holden Caulfield; writer of sensitive short stories who now writes movie scripts in Hollywood in J. D. Salinger's *The Catcher in the Rye.*

Holden Caulfield　Seventeen-year-old prep school dropout who recounts the events leading to his confinement in a sanitorium; narrator of J. D. Salinger's *The Catcher in the Rye.*

Phoebe Josephine Caulfield Ten-year-old sister of Holden Caulfield; writes short stories about Hazle Weatherfield in J. D. Salinger's *The Catcher in the Rye.*

Rita Cavanagh Actress turned lyric poet and Greenwich Village celebrity in Edmund Wilson's *I Thought of Daisy.*

Dorinda (D'rindy) Cayce Attractive daughter of John Cayce; scorns the suit of Rick Tyler and believes that Hiram Kelsey is similar to an Old Testament prophet in Mary Noailles Murfree's *The Prophet of the Great Smoky Mountains.*

John Cayce Moonshiner and father of Dorinda Cayce in Mary Noailles Murfree's *The Prophet of the Great Smoky Mountains.*

Mr. Cedarquist Wealthy manufacturer and shipbuilder who sees a great future in grain exports to the Far East in Frank Norris's *The Octopus.*

Mrs. Cedarquist Wife of Mr. Cedarquist and supporter of the arts, including artists of dubious merit, in Frank Norris's *The Octopus.*

Cinquo (Sinker) Centavos Young Mexican horse wrangler with the Del Sol trail herd in Emerson Hough's *North of 36.*

Inez de Certavallos Sixteen-year-old daughter of a wealthy Spanish nobleman in Louisiana and bride of Duncan Uncas Middleton; kidnapped on her wedding night by Abiram White and Ishmael Bush; later rescued by Middleton, with the help of Natty Bumppo, in James Fenimore Cooper's *The Prairie.*

Jud Chain Professional gambler and business associate of Bo Mason in Wallace Stegner's *The Big Rock Candy Mountain.*

Lieutenant Commander Jack Challee Navy judge advocate who prosecutes Lieutenant Steve Maryk for mutiny in Herman Wouk's *The Caine Mutiny.*

Beryl Challenor Childhood friend and playmate of Selina Boyce; values prestige and material gain in Paule Marshall's *Brown Girl, Brownstones.*

Percy Challenor Father of Beryl Challenor and a leader of the Association of Barbadian Homeowners and Businessmen in Paule Marshall's *Brown Girl, Brownstones.*

Brice Chamberlain Prominent lawyer who supports the nesters; paramour of Lucie Brewton and father of Brock Brewton; becomes judge of the district court in Conrad Richter's *The Sea of Grass.*

Frank Chambers Drifter who works for Nick Papadakis and is the lover of Cora Papadakis; with Cora, he murders Nick, but is acquitted; later convicted of murdering Cora, who dies accidentally, in James M. Cain's *The Postman Always Rings Twice.*

George (Fat) Chance Portly inspector and chief of detectives in Peter De Vries's *The Mackerel Plaza.*

Vic Chance Airplane builder in William Faulkner's *Pylon.*

Kate Chanceller Feminist, socialist, and student at Ohio State University; becomes a good friend of Clara Butterworth in Sherwood Anderson's *Poor White.*

Olive Chancellor Radical Boston spinster who opposes the marriage of her protégée Verena Tarrant in Henry James's *The Bostonians.*

Luke Channell Disgusting rogue and secret first husband of Amber St. Clare in Kathleen Winsor's *Forever Amber.*

Mrs. Luke Channell See Amber St. Clare.

Christina Channing Singer with a symphony orchestra and mistress of Eugene Witla in Theodore Dreiser's *The "Genius."*

Madame de Chantelle Mother-in-law of Anna Leath; represents aristocratic French propriety in spite of her American origins in Edith Wharton's *The Reef.*

Mateo Chapa Mestizo chauffeur whose entrepreneurial ambitions and intelligence accelerate his rise in the Monterrey business world; marries Sofia Vázquez de Anda in Josefina Niggli's *Step Down, Elder Brother.*

Joseph Benjamin (Joby, Joe) Chapin, Jr. Son of Edith and Joe Chapin I; jazz pianist unappreciated by his parents; works for the OSS in John O'Hara's *Ten North Frederick.*

Ann Chapin Daughter of Edith and Joe Chapin I in John O'Hara's *Ten North Frederick.*

Benjamin Chapin Father of Joe Chapin I in John O'Hara's *Ten North Frederick.*

Charlotte Hofman Chapin Wife of Benjamin Chapin and mother of Joe Chapin I in John O'Hara's *Ten North Frederick.*

Edith Stokes Chapin Wife and widow of Joe Chapin I in John O'Hara's *Ten North Frederick.*

Joseph (Joe) Benjamin Chapin Gibbsville, Pennsylvania, lawyer who aspires to be president of the United States in John O'Hara's *Ten North Frederick.*

Celia Chapman Eighteen-year-old cleaning woman who loves Leon Fisher in Albert Halper's *Union Square.*

Charitas Conventional neighbor of Helen; shocked by Helen's views of love and morality; forces her son Damastor to leave home after he impregnates Helen's maid Adraste in John Erskine's *The Private Life of Helen of Troy.*

Charlemont St. Louis merchant who bankrupts himself to help a needy friend in Herman Melville's *The Confidence-Man.*

Charles II See Charles Stuart.

Anatole Charles   Art dealer who sponsors a show of Eugene Witla's work in Theodore Dreiser's *The "Genius."*

Nick Charles   Out-of-retirement private detective in Dashiell Hammett's *The Thin Man.*

Nora Charles   Wealthy wife of Nick Charles in Dashiell Hammett's *The Thin Man.*

Vera Charles   Famed actress and best friend of Mame Dennis in Patrick Dennis's *Auntie Mame* and *Around the World with Auntie Mame.*

Inez Dresden Charlesbois   Piano and accordion teacher idealized by Cress Delahanty until Cress learns of her affair with Don Rivers in Jessamyn West's *Cress Delahanty.*

Luther Charlesbois   Husband of Inez Charlesbois in Jessamyn West's *Cress Delahanty.*

Lester Charley   Bookstore owner and later a canaller who rents a room to Jerry and Mary Fowler in Walter D. Edmonds's *Erie Water.*

Ed Charney   Gibbsville bootlegger and keeper of Helene Holman in John O'Hara's *Appointment in Samarra.*

Duke of Chartersea   Degenerate, immoral suitor of Dorothy Marmaduke and rival of Richard Carvel in Winston Churchill's *Richard Carvel.*

Jack Chase   Respected British captain of the main-top aboard the *Neversink;* deserts ship to fight for Peru; secures liberty for the crew in Rio in Herman Melville's *White-Jacket.*

Jasper Chase   Local society novelist in love with but rejected by Rachel Winslow in Charles M. Sheldon's *In His Steps.*

Chatelaine of La Trinité (Bertha)   Chatelaine of a community in the High Alps; travels through Europe with Aurelia West, dilettantes, and minor nobles in Henry Blake Fuller's *The Chatelaine of La Trinité.*

Ellen Chauncey   Pleasant young woman Ellen Montgomery meets at the Marshmans' Christmas dinner; they become bosom friends in Susan Warner's *The Wide, Wide World.*

Comte Raymond de Chelles   Third husband of Undine Spragg; enraged when Undine attempts to sell his family's Louis Quinze tapestries hanging in his chateau de Saint Désert in Edith Wharton's *The Custom of the Country.*

Countess Raymond de Chelles   See Undine Spragg.

Coralie Chépé   Governess for the Talbot family before the Civil War; strips their abandoned house of its remaining valuables and refuses to help them when they return to New Orleans destitute after the war in Grace King's *The Pleasant Ways of St. Médard.*

Mary Cherry   Opinionated spinster who moves from family to family in the Natchez plantation society; during the Civil War, sneaks messages and medicines through the picket lines in Stark Young's *So Red the Rose.*

Pete (The Smoothie) Cheshire   Ex-convict and attempted blackmailer in Peter De Vries's *Comfort Me with Apples.*

Stella Chesney   Beautiful actress, fugitive from a jealous lover in Mexico, and finally wife of Augie March and starlet in the French movie *Les Orphelines* in Saul Bellow's *The Adventures of Augie March.*

Ellen (Ellie) Chesser   Daughter of an itinerant farmer; engaged to Jonas Prather but marries Jasper Kent and has many children in Elizabeth Madox Roberts's *The Time of Man.*

Henry Chesser   Itinerant farmer who is the husband of Nellie Chesser and the father of Ellen Chesser in Elizabeth Madox Roberts's *The Time of Man.*

Nellie Chesser   Wife of Henry Chesser and mother of Ellen Chesser in Elizabeth Madox Roberts's *The Time of Man.*

Hannah Chester   Maid to Eleanore and Mary Leavenworth; discovered to be missing following the murder of Horatio Leavenworth in Anna Katharine Green's *The Leavenworth Case.*

Crystal Chickering   Fiancée, then wife of Chick Swallow in Peter De Vries's *Comfort Me with Apples.*

Alice Chicoy   Querulous, bored, and alcoholic wife of Juan Chicoy; helps at her husband's diner and fears that Juan will leave her in John Steinbeck's *The Wayward Bus.*

Juan Chicoy   Irish-Mexican mechanic, bus driver, and owner of a gas station/diner; considers abandoning his mud-stuck bus and his troublesome passengers to start a carefree life away from his gas station and his alcoholic wife in John Steinbeck's *The Wayward Bus.*

Roger Chillingworth   Name assumed by the husband of Hester Prynne; conceals his identity, with Hester's help, in order to seek revenge on Arthur Dimmesdale, his wife's lover, in Nathaniel Hawthorne's *The Scarlet Letter.*

Chinatown   See Chinatown Moss.

Ching   Honest and industrious farmer and overseer of Wang Lung's land in Pearl Buck's *The Good Earth.*

Chingachgook (Great Serpent, Indian John, John Mohegan)   Noble Indian who is the last of his tribe, the father of Uncas, and the companion of Natty Bumppo; enlists Bumppo's help in rescuing Wah-ta!-Wah in James Fenimore Cooper's *The Deerslayer;* helps Bumppo fight Magua in *The Last of the Mohicans;* helps Bumppo guide Mabel Dunham to her father in *The Pathfinder;* converted to Christianity, he lives in a cabin near Templeton, where he dies in a fire, in *The Pioneers.*

Elly Chipley (Lenore La Verne)   Actress on the *Cotton Blossom* in Edna Ferber's *Show Boat*.

Chips   See Beauty.

Aunt Chloe   Wife of Uncle Tom and mother of three children; suffers greatly when Tom is sold and attempts to earn the money to buy Tom back by cooking on other plantations in Harriet Beecher Stowe's *Uncle Tom's Cabin*.

Aunt Chloe   Black nurse of Tom Bailey in New Orleans in Thomas Bailey Aldrich's *The Story of a Bad Boy*.

Chloris   Denizen of the enchanted forest Leuke; becomes Jurgen's second wife after his apotheosis as a solar legend and subsequent exile from Cocaigne following the vernal equinox in James Branch Cabell's *Jurgen*.

Chief Choate   Full-blooded Indian corporal who boxes on the regimental team in James Jones's *From Here to Eternity*.

Lee Chong   Chinese grocer who owns and operates the largest and most eclectically stocked general store in the Cannery Row section of Monterey, California, in John Steinbeck's *Cannery Row*.

Choucoune   Tiny mulatto modiste who sometimes sews at Bréda in Arna Wendell Bontemps's *Drums at Dusk*.

Emilia Chrabotzky   Catholic widow of a professor and mother of Halina Chrabotzky; beloved friend of Yasha Mazur in Isaac Bashevis Singer's *The Magician of Lublin*.

Halina Chrabotzky   Sickly daughter of Emilia Chrabotzky; her youth, beauty, and precocity sexually attract Yasha Mazur, unbeknown to Emilia, and to Yasha's admitted shame, in Isaac Bashevis Singer's *The Magician of Lublin*.

Chremes   Father of Philumena; does not understand why Simo does not insist that Pamphilus marry Philumena in Thornton Wilder's *The Woman of Andros*.

Bill Christian   Member of the board of directors of the Association of Growers of Dark Fired Tobacco, an organization designed to influence tobacco prices; supporter of the night riders in Robert Penn Warren's *Night Rider*.

Candy Christian   Innocent who, in her search for love, has a number of bizarre sexual encounters in Terry Southern and Mason Hoffenberg's *Candy*.

Fletcher Christian   Master's mate on HMS *Bounty* who marries Maimiti and who leads the rebellion against Captain Bligh in Charles Nordhoff and James Norman Hall's *Mutiny on the Bounty;* leads a group of mutineers and Tahitians to an isolated island where he attempts to establish a democracy, only to see it fail when the tension between the Tahitians and the whites erupts into violence, to which he falls victim, in *Pitcairn's Island*.

Jack Christian   Identical twin of Sidney Christian, husband of Livia Christian, and uncle of Candy Christian, whom he seduces on the floor of her father's hospital room, in Terry Southern and Mason Hoffenberg's *Candy*.

Livia Christian   Vulgar, sex-starved wife of Jack Christian and aunt of Candy Christian in Terry Southern and Mason Hoffenberg's *Candy*.

Lucille (Sukie) Christian   Daughter of Bill Christian and lover of Percy Munn in Robert Penn Warren's *Night Rider*.

Sidney Christian   Father of Candy Christian; suffers a partial lobotomy at the hands of his gardener but reappears as a dung-covered holy man in Terry Southern and Mason Hoffenberg's *Candy*.

Uncle Willy Christian   Drugstore operator in William Faulkner's *The Town, The Mansion,* and *The Reivers*.

Christine   Blonde wife of Max; impregnated by Gene Pasternak in John Clellon Holmes's *Go*.

Joe Christmas   Possibly a mulatto who is the lover and murderer of Joanna Burden; castrated by Percy Grimm in William Faulkner's *Light in August*.

Chrono   Son of Malachi Constant and Beatrice Rumfoord in Kurt Vonnegut's *The Sirens of Titan*.

Chrysis   The woman of Andros who comes to Brynos, to the dismay of the Greek citizens there whose sons frequent her dinners and discussions, in Thornton Wilder's *The Woman of Andros*.

Chub   Irish immigrant and Presbyterian minister; friend of Frank Meriwether, collector of the classical library, and tutor in John Pendleton Kennedy's *Swallow Barn*.

Alfred Churchill   Rambunctious son of the Churchills who grows to manhood in Henry Wadsworth Longfellow's *Kavanagh*.

Edward Churchill   Uncle of Jacqueline Churchill, whose marriage to Lewis Rand he opposes; Federalist and veteran of Yorktown in Mary Johnston's *Lewis Rand*.

Jacqueline Churchill   Niece of Edward Churchill; refuses Ludwell Cary's marriage proposal and offends her family by marrying Lewis Rand in Mary Johnston's *Lewis Rand*.

Mary Churchill   Wife of Churchill; encourages her husband to write and scolds him when he does not do so in Henry Wadsworth Longfellow's *Kavanagh*.

Mr. Churchill   Schoolmaster who tries unsuccessfully to write a romance in Henry Wadsworth Longfellow's *Kavanagh*.

Horace (Woody) Church-Woodbine   Irresponsible banjo player from a family of wealthy horse fanciers; employer of Badfoot Dixon and Augie in Arna Wendell Bontemps's *God Sends Sunday*.

Cicero   Roman senator who becomes one of the conspirators against Caesar in Thornton Wilder's *The Ides of March*.

Cinder   Rival of Mary Pinesett; lover of July, whom she wins by means of a love charm, in Julia Peterkin's *Scarlet Sister Mary*.

Lidy Cinnamond   Wife of Stephen Birdwell and lover of Mel Venters in Jessamyn West's *The Friendly Persuasion*.

Claire de Bellegarde de Cintré   Young widow whose family hopes she will marry a rich man; becomes a nun because her family will not let her marry Christopher Newman in Henry James's *The American*.

John (Jemmy Legs) Claggart   Master-at-arms aboard the *Indomitable* who, upon falsely accusing Billy Budd of planning a mutiny, is killed by Budd in Herman Melville's *Billy Budd*.

Claire   Discarded mistress of Count Armand de Sacy; courtesan living in forced exile at Bréda in Arna Wendell Bontemps's *Drums at Dusk*.

Harry Clammidge   Publisher of the *Picayune Blade* and employer of Chick Swallow in Peter De Vries's *Comfort Me With Apples*.

DeYancey Clanahan   Grandson of Tip Clanahan; defense attorney for Daniel Ponder in Eudora Welty's *The Ponder Heart*.

Tip Clanahan   Friend of Sam Ponder; judge who helps commit Daniel Ponder to an asylum in Jackson, Mississippi, in Eudora Welty's *The Ponder Heart*.

Mr. Clancy   General manager of the Cosmodemonic Telegraph Company; hires Henry Miller to spy on and fire employees in Henry Miller's *Tropic of Capricorn*.

Captain Daniel Clapsaddle   Bluff American patriot in Winston Churchill's *Richard Carvel*.

Hugh Clapton   Royalist clergyman and teacher of Johnny Fraser in James Boyd's *Drums*.

Clara   Middle child of the three orphans in the care of Rachel Cooper in Davis Grubb's *The Night of the Hunter*.

Clarence (Amyas le Poulet)   Sixth-century associate of Hank Morgan; with Morgan's help, publishes a newspaper in Samuel Langhorne Clemens's *A Connecticut Yankee in King Arthur's Court*.

Clarendon   See Edward Hyde, Earl of Clarendon.

Edward Hyde, Earl of Clarendon   Highly influential, envied, and disliked Chancellor of Restoration England who aids Charles II but finally falls out of favor and is ousted from power in Kathleen Winsor's *Forever Amber*.

Claret   Captain of the *Neversink* in Herman Melville's *White-Jacket*.

Clarice   Illegitimate daughter of Arthur Wiatte, niece of Euphemia Lorimer, and fiancée of Clithero Edny in Charles Brockden Brown's *Edgar Huntly*.

Sister Clarisse   Widow to whom Hubert Cooley is attracted in Julian Mayfield's *The Hit*.

Paul Clark   Suave rival of Homer Zigler for the affections of Frances Harbach in Clyde Brion Davis's *The Great American Novel*.

Robert (Bob, David Hawke) Clark   Writer and teacher whom Vridar Hunter meets in New York in Vardis Fisher's *No Villain Need Be*; also appears as David Hawke in *Orphans in Gethsemane*.

Salvatore (Friday, Sal) Clark   Bugler for G Company; shares Andy Anderson's and Robert E. Lee Prewitt's love of the blues in James Jones's *From Here to Eternity*.

Sam Clark   Owner of a hardware store and friend of Will Kennicott in Sinclair Lewis's *Main Street*.

Seward Trewlove Clark   Unitarian minister from California who predicts a murder aboard ship in Conrad Aiken's *Blue Voyage*.

Clarke   Overseer in Kirby and John's mill in Rebecca Harding Davis's *Life in the Iron Mills*.

Henry Clarke   Capable certified public accountant with Glymmer, Read who is relatively unaffected by the firm's bankruptcy in Nathan Asch's *The Office*.

Mlle. Claude   Prostitute with whom Henry Miller briefly thinks he is in love in Henry Miller's *Tropic of Cancer*.

Sir Claude   Dashing young man with an eye for the ladies who marries Ida Farange and becomes involved with Mrs. Beale Farange; loving stepfather of Maisie Farange in Henry James's *What Maisie Knew*.

Clausen   Sexually frustrated murderer and suicide in Henry Miller's *Tropic of Capricorn*.

Henry Ritchie (Le Roy Robbins) Clavering   Englishman who secretly marries Mary Leavenworth in Anna Katharine Green's *The Leavenworth Case*.

Lee (Clavey) Clavering   New York journalist and playwright who offers his lover Countess Marie Zattiany a return to youthful passion in Gertrude Atherton's *Black Oxen*.

Clif Clawson   Medical school roommate of Martin Arrowsmith; drops out of school and becomes an automobile salesman in Sinclair Lewis's *Arrowsmith*.

Collis Clay   Unsuccessful suitor of Rosemary Hoyt in F. Scott Fitzgerald's *Tender Is the Night*.

Robert Clay   Adventurer and self-taught engineer in charge of an iron-mining operation in Olancho; enamored of socialite Alice Langham in Richard Harding Davis's *Soldiers of Fortune*.

Anne Clayton   Owner, with her brother Edward Clayton, of Magnolia Grove plantation; institutes educational and disciplinary reforms on the plantation, which arouse the ire of her neighbors, in Harriet Beecher Stowe's *Dred*.

Edward Clayton   Son of Judge Clayton and fiancé of Nina Gordon; sides increasingly with the abolitionists until he is forced to give up the plantation system and move to Canada with his emancipated slaves in Harriet Beecher Stowe's *Dred*.

Judge Clayton   Father of Edward and Anne Clayton; as a North Carolina superior court judge, he is forced to overturn a ruling that Edward won ensuring humane treatment of slaves in Harriet Beecher Stowe's *Dred*.

Sean Cleary   Unprincipled, self-serving director of guidance for the public schools of Pequot; aids Wissey Jones's attempt to purchase a child genius for experimental research in John Hersey's *The Child Buyer*.

Richard (Dick, Philip Deaderick) Cleave   Captain of the 65th Virginia Infantry under General Jackson; temporarily disgraced and forced to fight under an assumed name, but restored to command; marries Judith Cary after heroic action and revelation of a rival's plotting; appears in Mary Johnston's *The Long Roll* and *Cease Firing*.

Hattie Clegg   Old-maid neighbor of the Ganchions who moves to Houston in William Goyen's *The House of Breath*.

Clematis (Clem)   Mongrel dog of Genesis; his antics embarrass William Baxter in Booth Tarkington's *Seventeen*.

Clemence   Black street woman who assists Palmyre la Philosophe in seeking revenge on Agricola Fusilier in George Washington Cable's *The Grandissimes*.

Karen Hansen Clement   Surrogate daughter of Kitty Fremont, lover of Dov Landau, and Jewish refugee in Cyprus; killed during the Israeli War of Independence in Leon Uris's *Exodus*.

Mrs. Clement   Prostitute whom Bert Albany trades for another prostitute in E. L. Doctorow's *Welcome to Hard Times*.

Laurence G. Clements   Scholar at Waindell College; his wife rents a room to Timofey Pnin until their daughter returns and forces Pnin to move out in Vladimir Nabokov's *Pnin*.

Cleo   Piano player with Walden Blue in John Clellon Holmes's *The Horn*.

Cleopatra   Queen of Egypt and lover of Caesar, by whom she has borne a son; visits Rome on a state visit in Thornton Wilder's *The Ides of March*.

Gaston Cleric   Classical scholar and teacher who inspires Jim Burden in Willa Cather's *My Ántonia*.

Helena (Hellen) Cleves   Friend and employer of Constantia Dudley; her reputation is ruined by Ormond's refusal to marry her; dies of yellow fever in Charles Brockden Brown's *Ormond*.

Brother Tod Clifton   Member of the Brotherhood who is killed by the police and becomes a Brotherhood martyr in Ralph Ellison's *Invisible Man*.

Schuyler Clinton   New York senator and chairman of the Foreign Relations Committee; admirer of Madeleine Lee in Henry Adams's *Democracy*.

Frances Clyne   Lover of Robert Cohn in Ernest Hemingway's *The Sun Also Rises*.

Clytemnestra   Sister of Helen and wife of Agamemnon; conspires with her lover Aegisthus to murder Agamemnon; killed in turn by her son Orestes in John Erskine's *The Private Life of Helen of Troy*.

Charles (Cobby) Cobb   Greedy and crafty bookie who helps finance a jewelry robbery in William Riley Burnett's *The Asphalt Jungle*.

Georgiana Cobb   Fiancée of her neighbor Adam Moss in James Lane Allen's *A Kentucky Cardinal*; dies after giving birth to their son, Adam Cobb Moss, in *Aftermath*.

Joe R. Cobb   Air exec with the 918th Bomb Group in Beirne Lay, Jr., and Sy Bartlett's *Twelve O'Clock High!*

Joseph Cobb   Brother of Georgiana Cobb; West Point cadet in James Lane Allen's *A Kentucky Cardinal*; also appears in *Aftermath*.

Margaret Cobb   Mother of Georgiana Cobb in James Lane Allen's *A Kentucky Cardinal* and *Aftermath*.

Sylvia Cobb   Sister of Georgiana and Joseph Cobb; flirts with Adam Moss in James Lane Allen's *A Kentucky Cardinal*; also appears in *Aftermath*.

Ensign Peregrine Cockburn   English cousin of Johnny Lacey; sent to Virginia as part of Braddock's force against Fort Duquesne; killed by Indians and stripped of his possessions by Squire Raglan in Mary Lee Settle's *O Beulah Land*.

Jack Cockerell   Head of the English department at Waindell College; does near-perfect but mean impersonations of Timofey Pnin in Vladimir Nabokov's *Pnin*.

Cockney   See Shorty.

Dan Cody   Millionaire miner who employs the young James Gatz for five years; leaves money to Gatz, which he does not receive, in F. Scott Fitzgerald's *The Great Gatsby*.

Anna Cohen　Worker burned to death in a fire at Mine. Soubrine's, a fashionable millinery shop in John Dos Passos's *Manhattan Transfer*.

Joey Cohen　Russian-born childhood friend of Michael Gold in Michael Gold's *Jews without Money*.

Robert Cohn　Jewish-American novelist in Paris; in love with and violently jealous of Lady Brett Ashley in Ernest Hemingway's *The Sun Also Rises*.

Henry Colbert　Miller and husband of Sapphira Dodderidge Colbert; gives their daughter, Rachel Colbert, money to smuggle Nancy to Canada in Willa Cather's *Sapphira and the Slave Girl*.

Martin Colbert　Rakish nephew of Henry Colbert; his repeated advances toward Nancy cause her to escape to Canada in Willa Cather's *Sapphira and the Slave Girl*.

Rachel Colbert　See Rachel Colbert Blake.

Sapphira Dodderidge (Sapphy, The Mistress) Colbert　Wealthy Virginia slave owner, wife of Henry Colbert, and mother of Rachel Colbert in Willa Cather's *Sapphira and the Slave Girl*.

Colbrook　Marine corporal aboard the *Neversink* who saves White-Jacket from a flogging in Herman Melville's *White-Jacket*.

Edward (Cap) Colburne　New England lawyer who relinquishes Lillie Ravenel to John Carter and serves as a captain under Carter in the Civil War; marries Lillie after Carter's death in John William DeForest's *Miss Ravenel's Conversion from Secession to Loyalty*.

Lillie Ravenel Carter Colburne　See Lillie Ravenel Carter.

Cold Cuts　Alcoholic nightclub singer who works in a morgue and speaks sixteen languages; friend of Jay in Anaïs Nin's *A Spy in the House of Love*.

Ellen Coldfield　See Ellen Coldfield Sutpen.

Goodhue Coldfield　Father of Ellen and Rosa Coldfield in William Faulkner's *Absalom, Absalom!*

Rosa Coldfield　Daughter of Goodhue Coldfield in and one of the narrators of William Faulkner's *Absalom, Absalom!*

George (Stuffy) Cole　Big boy with an overindulgent mother in Louisa May Alcott's *Little Men*.

King Cole　Marine whose guitar playing entertains his platoon mates; wounded in France during World War I in Thomas Boyd's *Through the Wheat*.

Pauline (M. C. Number Two, Moe) Cole　High school cheerleader and girlfriend abandoned by Jack Duluoz in favor of Maggie Cassidy in Jack Kerouac's *Maggie Cassidy*; mentioned in *Book of Dreams* and *Desolation Angels*.

Raymond Cole　Fighter and heavy drinker; combat veteran who freezes to death in a cornfield in James Jones's *Some Came Running*.

William Cole　Boatswain on HMS *Bounty* whose loyalty to Captain Bligh and his regard for Admiralty law cause him to be set adrift with Bligh after the mutiny in Charles Nordhoff and James Norman Hall's *Mutiny on the Bounty*; his faith in God and Bligh, as well as his great strength, help him survive being cast adrift at sea in *Men Against the Sea*.

Alice E. Coleman　Wife of a northerner who, after being ambushed, dies in her arms in Albion W. Tourgee's *A Fool's Errand*.

Claris Coleman　Daughter of Colonel Coleman and first lover of Clay-Boy Spencer in Earl Hamner, Jr.'s *Spencer's Mountain*.

Daisy Meissner Coleman　Broadway chorus girl and wife of Ray Coleman in Edmund Wilson's *I Thought of Daisy*.

Ray Coleman　Husband of Daisy Meissner Coleman; reporter for the *Telegram-Dispatch* and then for the tabloid *Daily Sketch* in Edmund Wilson's *I Thought of Daisy*.

Vance R. (Professor, Slim) Coleman　Book salesman and would-be entrepreneur; friend of Sidney Wyeth in Oscar Micheaux's *The Forged Note*.

Clarence Colfax　Hotheaded but noble Confederate soldier; suitor of Virginia Carvel in Winston Churchill's *The Crisis*.

John Collier　Bearer of a marriage proposal from James Hopkins to Sally Oldham; she encourages Collier to advance his own suit and becomes his wife in Lydia Maria Child's *Hobomok*.

Sally Oldham Collier　Friend of Mary Conant; rejects the written marriage proposal of James Hopkins in favor of its bearer, John Collier, in Lydia Maria Child's *Hobomok*.

Collins　American sailor who often pays for drinks and entertainment for Henry Miller, Kruger, and Fillmore in Henry Miller's *Tropic of Cancer*.

Henry Collins　Rich, cranky Englishman who marries Marian Forrester and makes her final years secure in Willa Cather's *A Lost Lady*.

Jasper Collins　Companion of Larry Donovan and Nat Moore in the search for jobs and a meaningful life in Jack Conroy's *The Disinherited*.

Kitty (Mrs. Benjamin Watson, Mrs. Catherine) Collins　Maid at the Hutter house; married to Benjamin Watson, who returns to her after an absence of ten years, in Thomas Bailey Aldrich's *The Story of a Bad Boy*.

Rupe (Rupie) Collins　Bully who encourages Penrod Schofield's antics to take a more aggressive form in Booth Tarkington's *Penrod*.

Collyer British adjutant in William Faulkner's *A Fable*.

Ann Colt Wife of Timothy Colt; shy, awkward former English major who remains devoted to her husband despite his affair with Eileen Shallcross; returns to him after his trial in Louis Auchincloss's *The Great World and Timothy Colt*.

Timothy (Timmy) Colt Idealistic but angry young lawyer who becomes a partner in a large Manhattan law firm and almost destroys his career and marriage through unethical conduct; husband of Ann Colt in Louis Auchincloss's *The Great World and Timothy Colt*.

Colton Unknown outsider who becomes the first elected sheriff of Tooms County, Alabama, and vows to destroy blacks any way possible to prevent them from advancing in W. E. B. Du Bois's *The Quest of the Silver Fleece*.

Anabel Colton Friend of Isabel Otis, wife of Tom Colton, and a mother submerged in domesticity in Gertrude Atherton's *Ancestors*.

Thomas (Tom) Colton Practical California businessman, husband of Anabel Colton, politician eager to become a United States senator, and rival of John Gwynne in Gertrude Atherton's *Ancestors*.

Ralph Coltsworth Suitor preferred by Hagar Ashendyne's family; opposes Hagar's beliefs, but is determined to marry her until she resists his physical advances in Mary Johnston's *Hagar*.

Bess Columbine Mistress and partner in crime of Blackjack Mallard; jealous of Mallard's friendship with Amber St. Clare in Kathleen Winsor's *Forever Amber*.

Theodore Colville Newspaper editor living in Florence; briefly engaged to Imogene Graham, but marries the more suitable Evalina Bowen in William Dean Howells's *Indian Summer*.

Benjamin (Benjy, Maury) Compson Idiot son of Caroline Bascomb and Jason Lycurgus Compson III; brother of Caddy Compson, Quentin Compson I, and Jason Compson IV; castrated and committed to an asylum; appears in William Faulkner's *The Sound and the Fury* and *The Mansion*.

Candace (Caddy) Compson Daughter of Caroline Bascomb and Jason Lycurgus Compson III; sister of Benjy Compson, Quentin Compson I, and Jason Compson IV; mother of Quentin Compson II; appears in William Faulkner's *The Sound and the Fury* and *The Mansion*.

Caroline Bascomb Compson Wife of Jason Lycurgus Compson III; mother of Benjy and Caddy Compson, Quentin Compson I, and Jason Compson IV in William Faulkner's *The Sound and the Fury*.

Jason Lycurgus Compson (I) Indian agent who trades a racing mare to Ikkemotubbe for a square mile of land that becomes the center of Jefferson, Mississippi; appears in William Faulkner's *The Sound and the Fury* and *Requiem for a Nun*.

Jason Lycurgus Compson (II) Hunter and Civil War general; only real friend of Thomas Sutpen; appears in William Faulkner's *The Sound and the Fury; Absalom, Absalom!; The Unvanquished; Go Down, Moses; Intruder in the Dust; Requiem for a Nun; The Town;* and *The Reivers*.

Jason Lycurgus Compson (III) Husband of Caroline Bascomb; father of Benjy and Caddy Compson, Quentin Compson I, and Jason Compson IV; appears in William Faulkner's *The Sound and the Fury* and *Absalom, Absalom!*

Jason Lycurgus Compson (IV) Son of Caroline Bascomb and Jason Lycurgus Compson III; brother of Benjy and Caddy Compson and Quentin Compson I; appears in William Faulkner's *The Sound and the Fury, The Town,* and *The Mansion*.

Quentin Compson (I) Son of Caroline Bascomb and Jason Lycurgus Compson III; brother of Benjy and Caddy Compson and Jason Compson IV; following a year at Harvard, he commits suicide; appears in William Faulkner's *The Sound and the Fury; Absalom, Absalom!*

Quentin Compson (II) Illegitimate daughter of Caddy Compson and Dalton Ames; appears in William Faulkner's *The Sound and the Fury* and *The Mansion*.

Ben Compton Radical intellectual devoted to proletarian issues who is jailed for subversive activities in John Dos Passos's *U.S.A.* trilogy.

Gladys Compton Secretary whom J. Ward Morehouse asks to watch over Janey Williams and whose family, as a result, boards her temporarily; sister of Ben Compton in John Dos Passos's *U.S.A.* trilogy.

Charlie Comstock Reformed alcoholic, pious parishioner of Andrew Mackerel, and copublisher of the Globe in Peter De Vries's *The Mackerel Plaza*.

Lord (Jack) Comyn Generous nobleman secretly sympathetic to the American cause; friend of Richard Carvel in Winston Churchill's *Richard Carvel*.

Charles Hobomok Conant Son of Mary Conant and Hobomok in Lydia Maria Child's *Hobomok*.

Mary Conant Bride of Hobomok and later of Charles Brown; mother of Charles Hobomok Conant and heroine of Lydia Maria Child's *Hobomok*.

Mrs. Mary Conant Daughter of an English earl, wife of Roger Conant, and mother of Mary Conant; dies in the Puritan settlement at Salem in Lydia Maria Child's *Hobomok*.

Roger Conant   Stern Puritan father of Mary Conant and husband of Mrs. Mary Conant; forbids his daughter to marry the Episcopalian Charles Brown in Lydia Maria Child's *Hobomok.*

Catherine M. (Cate) Conboy   Daughter of Lincoln and Elizabeth Conboy; loves Christian Fraser but marries Ferris Thompson in Jessamyn West's *The Witch Diggers.*

Elizabeth (Lib) Conboy   Wife of Lincoln Conboy and mother of Catherine, James, and Emma Conboy in Jessamyn West's *The Witch Diggers.*

Emma Jane (Em) Conboy   Younger daughter of Lincoln and Elizabeth Conboy in Jessamyn West's *The Witch Diggers.*

James (Dandie, Jim) Conboy   Son of Lincoln and Elizabeth Conboy; marries Poor Farm inmate Norah Tate in Jessamyn West's *The Witch Diggers.*

Lincoln (Link) Conboy   Superintendent of Poor Farm, husband of Elizabeth Conboy, and father of Catherine, James, and Emma Conboy in Jessamyn West's *The Witch Diggers.*

Sophie Concord   Negro nurse and friend of Neil Kingsblood in Sinclair Lewis's *Kingsblood Royal.*

Count Condu   Hungarian vampire imagined by Jack Duluoz in Jack Kerouac's *Doctor Sax.*

Mame and Max Confrey   Restaurateurs in William Faulkner's *Light in August.*

Congo   Sailor without attachments or responsibilities; he is an intellectual anarchist against whom free-spirited but otherwise encumbered characters are measured in John Dos Passos's *Manhattan Transfer.*

Jim Conklin   Tall soldier fatally wounded in battle; Henry Fleming witnesses his grotesque death throes in Stephen Crane's *The Red Badge of Courage.*

Alec Connage   Princeton classmate of Amory Blaine and brother of Rosalind Connage in F. Scott Fitzgerald's *This Side of Paradise.*

Rosalind Connage   Great love of Amory Blaine; marries a rich man in F. Scott Fitzgerald's *This Side of Paradise.*

Stephen Conner   Current superintendent of the Diamond County Home for the Aged; holds certain ideals about serving humanity and the need for impartiality in dealing with the residents; stoned by some of the old people in John Updike's *The Poorhouse Fair.*

Betsy Jekyll Connolly   See Betsy Jekyll.

Hector Connolly   Irish-Catholic newspaperman and author; marries Betsy Jekyll in Nancy Hale's *The Prodigal Women.*

Lizzie Connolly   Occasional girlfriend of Martin Eden in Jack London's *Martin Eden.*

Professor Connolly   Fawning head of the drama department at Webster, an Ivy League school, whom Victor Milgrim courts in hopes of obtaining an honorary degree in Budd Schulberg's *The Disenchanted.*

Phil Connor   Boss of Ona Rudkus; coerces her into having sex with him in Upton Sinclair's *The Jungle.*

Walt Connor   Night-shift worker at the Past Bay Manufacturing Company factory who is promoted by Carl Belcher and sides with management during the strike; briefly kidnaps Marie Turner and has a relationship with Rose MacMahon in Robert Cantwell's *The Land of Plenty.*

Mary Connynge   Deceitful mistress of John Law and, later, of Philippe of Orleans in Emerson Hough's *The Mississippi Bubble.*

Gabriel (John Doe, Johnny Dumbledee, Gabe) Conroy   Gentle giant of a man; good but somewhat clumsy protagonist of Bret Harte's *Gabriel Conroy.*

Grace Conroy   See Doña Dolores Salvatierra.

Olympia (Olly) Conroy   Dutiful wife of Gabriel Conroy in Bret Harte's *Gabriel Conroy.*

Malachi (Space Wanderer, Unk) Constant   Millionaire, messiah, and space traveler in Kurt Vonnegut's *The Sirens of Titan.*

Contessa   Elderly woman who arranges meetings between handsome Italian gigolos she calls *marchettas* and rich men and women; introduces Mrs. Karen Stone to Paolo in Tennesee Williams's *The Roman Spring of Mrs. Stone.*

The Continental Op   Nameless detective for the Continental Detective Agency who heads the investigation into corruption in Personville in Dashiell Hammett's *Red Harvest.*

Bill Conway   Boyhood foe of Tom Bailey, until Tom beats him in a fight; tells Ezra Wingate that Tom and others stole Ezra's stagecoach; becomes a grocer with Seth Rodgers in Thomas Bailey Aldrich's *The Story of a Bad Boy.*

Durfee (Duff) Conway   Jazz cornet player executed for murder in Shelby Foote's *Jordan County.*

Nora Conway   Mother of Duff Conway in Shelby Foote's *Jordan County.*

Widow Conway   Dressmaker and mother of Bill Conway in Thomas Bailey Aldrich's *The Story of a Bad Boy.*

John Coode   Antithesis of Lord Baltimore; possible hero, possible villain, or possible figment of the imagination in John Barth's *The Sot-Weed Factor.*

Signora Coogan   Rich woman who pays for the companionship of Paolo and takes him to Capri; ridiculed by Paolo and the Contessa in Tennessee Williams's *The Roman Spring of Mrs. Stone*.

Al Cook   See Alexandr Petrovich Kukolnikov.

Lois Cook   Unkempt author of *The Gallant Gallstone* who exalts decadence in order to spite beauty in Ayn Rand's *The Fountainhead*.

Thomas (Tommy) Cook   Law clerk who takes over Mr. Talbot's practice during the Civil War but relinquishes it to Talbot when he returns to New Orleans after the war in Grace King's *The Pleasant Ways of St. Médard*.

Wilmer Cook   Boyish thug who works for Casper Gutman and whom Sam Spade calls a gunsel in Dashiell Hammett's *The Maltese Falcon*.

Anna Cooke   Twin sister of Ebenezer Cooke who, Henry Burlingame suggests, might be in reality the woman Cooke really loves in John Barth's *The Sot-Weed Factor*.

Ebenezer (Eben) Cooke   American-born Londoner forced to cross the Atlantic to claim his father's Maryland estates in John Barth's *The Sot-Weed Factor*.

Judge Charlie Cool   Defender and protector of Dolly Talbo; proposes to her shortly before her death in Truman Capote's *The Grass Harp*.

Joe Cool   Prison inmate who entrusts Erwin Riemenschneider with Cool's big robbery plan, provided that Riemenschneider will try to get Cool paroled, in William Riley Burnett's *The Asphalt Jungle*.

Gertrude Cooley   Long-suffering wife of Hubert Cooley and mother of James Lee Cooley in Julian Mayfield's *The Hit*.

Hubert Cooley   Fifty-year-old husband of Gertrude Cooley and father of James Lee Cooley in Julian Mayfield's *The Hit*.

James Lee Cooley   Twenty-six-year-old son of Hubert and Gertrude Cooley, lover of Essie Turner in Julian Mayfield's *The Hit*.

Seabright B. (Seab) Cooley   Senior senator from South Carolina and president pro tempore of the Senate who helps defeat two of his enemies, the president and the president's nominee for secretary of state, in Allen Drury's *Advise and Consent*.

Coonskins   See Pitch.

Rachel Cooper   Elderly woman who takes in Pearl and John Harper after their flight down the river; protects the children from Preacher in Davis Grubb's *The Night of the Hunter*.

Coot   See Asa Bruce Harcoot.

Carmen Sylva (Sylvy) Cope   Cousin and fiancée of Christian Fraser; loses him first to Catherine Conboy and then to death in Jessamyn West's *The Witch Diggers*.

Benedict Mady Copeland   Ascetic black physician committed to racial progress; his children ignore his teachings in Carson McCullers's *The Heart Is a Lonely Hunter*.

Grandpapa Copeland   Elderly preacher; father and final refuge of Benedict Mady Copeland in Carson McCullers's *The Heart Is a Lonely Hunter*.

Ted (Teddy) Copeland   First fiancé of Aline Grey, dies of the flu during World War I in Sherwood Anderson's *Dark Laughter*.

William (Willie) Copeland   Son of Benedict Mady Copeland and brother of Portia; negligent prison guards cause the amputation of his feet from frostbite in Carson McCullers's *The Heart Is a Lonely Hunter*.

Beverly Copfee   Prostitute employed by Maurice Cassard in Ludwig Bemelmans's *Dirty Eddie*.

Frieda Copperfield   Wife of J. C. Copperfield, friend of Christina Goering, and intimate companion of Pacifica in Jane Bowles's *Two Serious Ladies*.

J. C. Copperfield   Husband of Frieda Copperfield; enthusiastic man who loves to travel; Frieda finally leaves him in Jane Bowles's *Two Serious Ladies*.

Corbitant   Enemy of Hobomok and the Puritan settlers in Lydia Maria Child's *Hobomok*.

Fidsey Corcoran   Young hoodlum whom George Kelcey helps win a fistfight in Stephen Crane's *George's Mother*.

Jesus Maria Corcoran   Alcoholic, dissipated acquaintance of Pilon, who invites Corcoran to live with him because Corcoran has three dollars, in John Steinbeck's *Tortilla Flat*.

Anna Bellingham Corey   Wife of Bromfield Corey; opposes the attachment of her son, Tom Corey, to Penelope Lapham in William Dean Howells's *The Rise of Silas Lapham*.

Bromfield Corey   Boston aristocrat who tries to accept the relationship of his son, Tom Corey, with the Laphams in William Dean Howells's *The Rise of Silas Lapham*.

Judge Leonidas Corey   Member of the educational committee in Morganville, Oklahoma; tries to interest George Brush in Corey's daughter in Thornton Wilder's *Heaven's My Destination*.

Mississippi Corey   Daughter of Judge Leonidas Corey; dines with George Brush and shocks him with her references to drinking and smoking in Thornton Wilder's *Heaven's My Destination*.

Mister Corey   Minister imported by Sally Lacey for Sara Lacey's marriage to Ezekiel Catlett in Mary Lee Settle's *O Beulah Land*.

Tom Corey   Son of Bromfield and Anna Corey; employee in Silas Lapham's paint factory who marries Penelope Lapham in William Dean Howells's *The Rise of Silas Lapham.*

Frank (Frankie, Mark) Cornelius   Dying tubercular who is the object of Cress Delahanty's infatuation in Jessamyn West's *Cress Delahanty.*

Joyce Cornelius   School bus driver and wife of Frank Cornelius in Jessamyn West's *Cress Delahanty.*

Neil Cornish   Piano teacher and would-be law student who marries Lulu Bett in Zona Gale's *Miss Lulu Bett.*

Cornwallis   Head of the British forces in the South; graciously receives Mildred and Henry Lindsay in John Pendleton Kennedy's *Horse-Shoe Robinson.*

Corporal   See Stefan.

Alfredo Corregio   Portuguese fisherman who lives for a time with his family in the Meserve's servant house before returning to the shrimping business to handle Jim Meserve's boats in Zora Neale Hurston's *Seraph on the Suwanee.*

Corruthers   Political crony of Sammy Scott; known for his underground dirty work in W. E. B. Du Bois's *Dark Princess.*

Sheldon Corthell   Esthete who courts Laura Dearborn and then attempts to win her once more after her marriage to Curtis Jadwin in Frank Norris's *The Pit.*

Edith Cortright   American-born widow of a British diplomat; lover and traveling companion of Sam Dodsworth in Sinclair Lewis's *Dodsworth.*

Mrs. Costello   Aunt of Frederick Winterbourne; thinks that the Millers are common, dreadful, and vulgar in Henry James's *Daisy Miller.*

Euphrasia (Phrasie) Cotton   Spinster housekeeper of Hilary Vane; friend of Austen Vane in Winston Churchill's *Mr. Crewe's Career.*

Burley (Uncle Burley) Coulter   Wayward bachelor brother of Jarrat Coulter; his wild antics provide down-home Kentucky humor in Wendell Berry's *Nathan Coulter, A Place on Earth,* and *The Memory of Old Jack.*

David (Dave) Coulter   Father of Jarrat and Burley Coulter and Grandpa to Nathan Coulter in Wendell Berry's *Nathan Coulter;* also appears in *The Memory of Old Jack.*

Jarrat Coulter   Widowed subsistence tobacco farmer in Port William, Kentucky; father of Tom Coulter and Daddy to Nathan Coulter in Wendell Berry's *Nathan Coulter, A Place on Earth,* and *The Memory of Old Jack.*

Nathan Coulter   Kentucky tobacco farmer and second husband of widowed Hannah Feltner; narrator of Wendell Berry's *Nathan Coulter;* also appears in *A Place on Earth* and *The Memory of Old Jack.*

Tom Coulter   Oldest son of Jarrat Coulter; leaves home after a fight with his father; killed during World War II in Wendell Berry's *A Place on Earth;* also appears in *Nathan Coulter.*

Count of Monte Beni   See Donatello.

Countess   Physically ugly but wealthy American lover of Beale Farange while he is married in Henry James's *What Maisie Knew.*

The County Clerk (Arch Anker)   Obscene civil servant working out of the Old Court House in Pigeon Hole; person to whom civil cases are referred so they will not be resolved in William S. Burroughs's *Naked Lunch* and *The Soft Machine.*

Olive de Courcy   Red Cross volunteer in France who passes out stocks of American supplies to the villagers in Willa Cather's *One of Ours.*

Landry Court   Boyish suitor of Laura Dearborn and worshipful colleague of Curtis Jadwin at the Chicago Board of Trade; marries Laura's sister Page Dearborn and remains determined to become like Jadwin, despite Jadwin's failure as a speculator, in Frank Norris's *The Pit.*

Jim Courtney   Police captain killed by Rico Bandello in the New Year's Eve holdup of the Casa Alvarado nightclub in William Riley Burnett's *Little Caesar.*

Miles Coverdale   Narrator who observes the people and events at Blithedale and who claims to have loved Priscilla in Nathaniel Hawthorne's *The Blithedale Romance.*

Daisy Patricia Cowan   Sister of Jim Cowan and fiancée of Phillip Laurie in Nathan Asch's *Pay Day.*

Eugene Cowan   Brother of Jim and Daisy Cowan; killed at Verdun in Nathan Asch's *Pay Day.*

James (Jim) Cowan   Dissatisfied bookkeeper who wants to be a traveling salesman and who wanders around New York on the night of the Sacco-Vanzetti executions in Nathan Asch's *Pay Day.*

Martha Cowan   Mother of Jim and Daisy Cowan; tries to keep the family together in Nathan Asch's *Pay Day.*

Ebenezer Cowley   Owner of Cowley & Son's store whose reputation as queer torments his son Elmer Cowley in Sherwood Anderson's *Winesburg, Ohio.*

Elmer Cowley   Junior partner of Cowley & Son's store; beats George Willard and leaves Winesburg in a frustrated attempt to deal with his family's reputation as queer in Sherwood Anderson's *Winesburg, Ohio.*

Aileen Butler (Ai, Mrs. Montague) Cowperwood Mistress of Frank Cowperwood in Theodore Dreiser's *The Financier;* unhappily married wife of Cowperwood in *The Stoic* and *The Titan.*

Frank Algernon (Dickson, Montague) Cowperwood Stockbroker and friend of Philadelphia politicians; husband of Lillian Semple Cowperwood and lover of Aileen Butler; convicted and jailed for unscrupulous business deals in Theodore Dreiser's *The Financier;* released from jail, he is active in the natural gas business; marries Aileen Butler in *The Titan;* attempts to monopolize the London streetcar and subway system; dies in *The Stoic.*

Henry Worthington Cowperwood Father of Frank Cowperwood; resigns his bank presidency following Frank's involvement in a scandal in Theodore Dreiser's *The Financier.*

Lillian Semple (Anna Wheeler) Cowperwood Widow of Alfred Semple and first wife of Frank Cowperwood in Theodore Dreiser's *The Financier;* also appears in *The Stoic,* where she is called Anna Wheeler, and *The Titan.*

Hillary Cox Innocent disfigured by an anarchist's bomb in Robert Herrick's *The Memoirs of an American Citizen.*

Mr. Cox Astrologer who meets Malcolm on a hotel bench and helps introduce him to life by sending him to the homes of acquaintances in James Purdy's *Malcolm.*

Coyotito Infant son of Kino and Juana; refused medical treatment after being stung by a scorpion because his parents are poor; shot to death by a thief in John Steinbeck's *The Pearl.*

Crab Teacher at Swallow Barn; preceptor of Ned Hazard in John Pendleton Kennedy's *Swallow Barn.*

Thomas Craig Employee of Stephen Dudley; his embezzlement causes Dudley's financial ruin; kills Dudley, at Ormond's bidding, and is himself killed by Ormond in Charles Brockden Brown's *Ormond.*

Keg Head Cramer Neighbor of Nunn Ballew; crass, self-righteous father-in-law of Lureenie Cramer in Harriette Arnow's *Hunter's Horn.*

Lureenie Cramer Mother of three at age twenty; dreamer deserted by her husband, Rans Cramer; nearly starves to death with her family; dies in childbirth in Harriette Arnow's *Hunter's Horn.*

Mark Cramer Son of Keg Head Cramer; works in Detroit and fathers a child by Suse Ballew out of wedlock in Harriette Arnow's *Hunter's Horn.*

Rans Cramer Husband who deserts Lureenie Cramer; flees the community to avoid arrest and returns after he gets religion in Harriette Arnow's *Hunter's Horn.*

Emile Cramner Grocery delivery boy with whom Melissa Wapshot has an affair in John Cheever's *The Wapshot Scandal.*

Agatha Cramp Wealthy white woman dedicated to social service to blacks but opposed to an integrated neighborhood in Rudolph Fisher's *The Walls of Jericho.*

Esther Crane Daughter of a prosperous black grocer; fascinated by King Barlo in Jean Toomer's *Cane.*

Helga Crane Daughter of a Danish immigrant mother and black American father; resigns as a teacher and travels to Harlem and Denmark; becomes the sickly and overburdened wife of the Reverend Mr. Pleasant Green in Nella Larsen's *Quicksand.*

Jasper Crane Black Virginian who claims to live with his brother in Harlem; meets Emma Lou Morgan in a movie theater, borrows five dollars from her, and vanishes in Wallace Thurman's *The Blacker the Berry.*

Kelcey Crane Young trumpeter in John Clellon Holmes's *The Horn.*

Nebraska (Bras) Crane Part-Cherokee Indian boyhood friend of George Webber in Thomas Wolfe's *You Can't Go Home Again* and *The Web and the Rock.*

Thomas (Tom) Lowell Crapo Friend of Andrew Cather and lover of Cather's wife Bertha Cather in Conrad Aiken's *Great Circle.*

Crash Naval officer convicted of having an illicit affair with a fourteen-year-old Polynesian female in Herman Melville's *Omoo.*

Cimarron (Cim) Cravat Son of Sabra and Yancey Cravat and husband of Ruby Big Elk; field geologist in Edna Ferber's *Cimarron.*

Donna Cravat Daughter of Sabra and Yancey Cravat and wife of the multimillionaire Tracy Wyatt in Edna Ferber's *Cimarron.*

Sabra Venable Cravat Daughter of Felice and Lewis Venable, wife of Yancey Cravat, and mother of Cimarron and Donna Cravat; strong pioneer who becomes an important newspaper editor and an Oklahoma congresswoman in Edna Ferber's *Cimarron.*

Yancey (Cimarron) Cravat Husband of Sabra Venable Cravat and father of Cimarron and Donna Cravat; lawyer and newspaperman who becomes governor of the Oklahoma Territory and then joins Teddy Roosevelt's Rough Riders in Edna Ferber's *Cimarron.*

Marcella L. (Queenie) Craven Owner of Queenie's Boarding House in Kansas City, where George Brush stays; devout Catholic in Thornton Wilder's *Heaven's My Destination.*

Brandon Crawford Brother-in-law of Sally Lacey, helps Johnny Lacey with his land claims and is elected with him to the House of Burgesses in Mary Lee Settle's *O Beulah Land.*

Janie Mae Crawford Heroine who becomes the wife of Logan Killicks, Jody Starks, and Vergible Woods before becoming completely herself in Zora Neale Hurston's *Their Eyes Were Watching God.*

Melancthon Crawford   American sailor imprisoned by Tripoli pirates; Indian trader and pioneer who is a cofounder of a town in Oklahoma in H. L. Davis's *Harp of a Thousand Strings.*

Miss Stephanie Crawford   Gossipy neighbor of Atticus Finch and one of the family who constantly spread rumors about Boo Radley in Harper Lee's *To Kill a Mockingbird.*

Colonel Crayton   Father of Mrs. Beauchamp and husband of Mademoiselle La Rue in Susanna Rowson's *Charlotte.*

Mrs. Crayton   See Mademoiselle La Rue.

William Cream   Barber who offers no trust to his customers in Herman Melville's *The Confidence-Man.*

Captain Joe Cree   First husband of Julia Cropleigh Cree and pillar of the community; his suicide sets in motion the events of Andrew Lytle's *The Velvet Horn.*

Julia Cropleigh Cree   Youngest of the orphaned Cropleigh children and mother of Lucius Cree; object of the long-suffering love of Pete Legrand, the crazed passion of her brother, Duncan Cropleigh, and the formal devotion of her husband, Joe Cree, in Andrew Lytle's *The Velvet Horn.*

Lucius Cree   Son of Joe and Julia Cropleigh Cree; forced to face the mystery of his family's past when his father commits suicide in Andrew Lytle's *The Velvet Horn.*

Catherine Creek   Black woman who insists she is an Indian; from childhood on, lives with the Talbo sisters, adoring Dolly and despising Verena, in Truman Capote's *The Grass Harp.*

Carrie Cressler   Confidante of Laura Dearborn; encourages Laura to marry Curtis Jadwin in Frank Norris's *The Pit.*

Charles (Charlie) Cressler   Dealer in grain at the Chicago Board of Trade who is ruined by speculation and commits suicide in Frank Norris's *The Pit.*

Harry Cresswell   Congressman who opposes the education of his black tenants; son of Colonel St. John Cresswell, husband of Mary Taylor, and father of Bertie's mulatto child Emma in W. E. B. Du Bois's *The Quest of the Silver Fleece.*

Helen Cresswell   Self-centered daughter of Colonel St. John Cresswell and wife of John Taylor in W. E. B. Du Bois's *The Quest of the Silver Fleece.*

Mary Taylor Cresswell   See Mary Taylor.

Colonel St. John Cresswell   Southern aristocrat who owns almost everything in Tooms County, Alabama; father of Helen and Harry Cresswell in W. E. B. Du Bois's *The Quest of the Silver Fleece.*

Creuzot   Tall, fair-skinned Frenchman who operates his own print shop; afflicted with a lung disease in Arna Wendell Bontemps's *Black Thunder.*

Alice Pomfret Crewe   See Alice Pomfret.

Humphrey Crewe   Unskilled amateur politician who becomes increasingly shrewd and reforming; unsuccessful suitor of Victoria Flint and husband of Alice Pomfret in Winston Churchill's *Mr. Crewe's Career.*

Tony Crews   Black poet; Emma Lou Morgan meets him at a rent party in Wallace Thurman's *The Blacker the Berry.*

Cribbens (Crib)   Prospector with whom McTeague discovers gold in the Panamint Range in Frank Norris's *McTeague.*

Cribiche   Young orphan reared by Père Philéas in Grace King's *The Pleasant Ways of St. Médard.*

Avis Criley   See Avis Criley Elderman.

Bradd Criley   Grand Republic attorney, friend of Cass Timberlane, and lover of Jinny Timberlane in Sinclair Lewis's *Cass Timberlane.*

Crimson Rambler   See Clarence Rambo.

John Cripps   Illiterate and cruel husband of Sue Seymour Cripps; following her death, turns their children's home into a low tavern in Harriet Beecher Stowe's *Dred.*

Sue Seymour (Suse) Cripps   Daughter of formerly aristocratic Virginian parents and wife of the illiterate John Cripps; owner of Tiff Peyton; dies in poverty after the birth of her third child in Harriet Beecher Stowe's *Dred.*

Amy Crittenden   Mother of John Buddy Pearson and wife of Ned Crittenden in Zora Neale Hurston's *Jonah's Gourd Vine.*

Ned Crittenden   Stepfather of John Buddy Pearson and husband of Amy Crittenden in Zora Neale Hurston's *Jonah's Gourd Vine.*

Elizabeth Crittendon   Southern lady who has an affair with Nathaniel Franklin after he burns her house in Hervey Allen's *Action at Aquila.*

Margaret Crittendon   Daughter of Elizabeth Crittendon; has an affair with a doomed Confederate soldier in Hervey Allen's *Action at Aquila.*

Joseph Crocker   Handsome carpenter whom Isabella Archbald elects to marry in Ellen Glasgow's *The Sheltered Life.*

Art Croft   Narrator of Walter Van Tilburg Clark's *The Ox-Bow Incident.*

Staff Sergeant Samuel (Sam) Croft Fascistic commander of a reconnaissance unit who arranges the death of Robert Hearn in Norman Mailer's *The Naked and the Dead.*

Professor Crofts Condescending Emersonian scholar and Shep Stearns's former teacher in Budd Schulberg's *The Disenchanted.*

Mrs. Crofut Woman who George Brush believes has many daughters, when in fact she operates a house of prostitution, in Thornton Wilder's *Heaven's My Destination.*

Miss Croly Grade-school teacher of Felix Fay; encourages Fay to use his imagination in Floyd Dell's *Moon-Calf.*

Hugh and Sarah Hutchins (Widow Hutchins) Crombie Operators of the Hand and Bottle Inn in Nathaniel Hawthorne's *Fanshawe.*

Jabberwhorl (Jab) Cronstadt Friend of Henry Miller; provides one free meal per week for Miller in Henry Miller's *Tropic of Cancer;* poet, musician, weatherman, herbologist, and linguist in *Black Spring.*

Katya Cronstadt Daughter of Jabberwhorl Cronstadt in Henry Miller's *Black Spring.*

Eugene (Gene) Crook Crooked banker who swindles Jean Baptiste in Oscar Micheaux's *The Homesteader.*

Dr. Junius (Doc) Crookman Black biologist and physician who develops the Black-No-More process to make blacks white in George S. Schuyler's *Black No More.*

Crooks Black ranch hand who hesitatingly befriends Lennie Small in John Steinbeck's *Of Mice and Men.*

Arthur Croom Friend of John Laskell; arranges for Laskell's care during his illness in Lionel Trilling's *The Middle of the Journey.*

Nancy (Nan) Croom Wife of Arthur Croom; refuses to accept the reality of death in Lionel Trilling's *The Middle of the Journey.*

George Crooper Cousin of Johnnie Watson; his prodigious appetite causes him trouble, to the delight of William Baxter, Johnnie Watson, and Joe Bullitt, in Booth Tarkington's *Seventeen.*

Beverly Cropleigh Woodsman and eldest of the Cropleigh siblings; retreats to Parcher's Cove after his parents are killed in a steamboat disaster in Andrew Lytle's *The Velvet Horn.*

Dickie Cropleigh Physician and brother of Julia Cropleigh Cree in Andrew Lytle's *The Velvet Horn.*

Duncan Cropleigh Jealous brother of Julia Cropleigh Cree and probable biological father of her son, Lucius Cree; blown up with his brother Beverly in a dynamite explosion during the Civil War in Andrew Lytle's *The Velvet Horn.*

Jack (Uncle Jack) Cropleigh Brother of Julia Cropleigh Cree and garrulous uncle of Lucius Cree; tries to instruct and protect his nephew, in the lunging in front of the bullet intended for Lucius; principal narrator of Andrew Lytle's *The Velvet Horn.*

Julia Cropleigh See Julia Cropleigh Cree.

Anthony (Anthony Cruz) Cross Poor, light-skinned love and eventual mate of Angela Murray in Jessie Redmon Fauset's *Plum Bun.*

Lucas Cross Drunken shack-dweller whose abuse of his stepdaughter, Selena Cross, drives her to murder him and causes the suicide of his wife, Nellie Cross, in Grace Metalious's *Peyton Place.*

Nellie Cross Wife of Lucas Cross and mother of Selena Cross; hangs herself in the MacKenzie home as a result of her husband's raping and impregnating her daughter in Grace Metalious's *Peyton Place.*

Selena Cross Daughter of Nellie Cross, stepdaughter of Lucas Cross, and best friend of Allison MacKenzie; kills her abusive stepfather during an attempted rape and is acquitted of the murder but henceforth shunned by the respectable townspeople in Grace Metalious's *Peyton Place.*

Crotti Cocaine merchant involved in a struggle for control of Los Angeles in Paul Cain's *Fast One.*

Martha Crouch Wife of Samuel Crouch; landlady and secret lover of N'Gana Frimbo in Rudolph Fisher's *The Conjure-Man Dies.*

Samuel (Easley Jones) Crouch Harlem mortician, husband of Martha Crouch, and landlord of N'Gana Frimbo, whom Crouch kills in Rudolph Fisher's *The Conjure-Man Dies.*

Crown Catfish Row cotton stevedore and lover of Bess; murders Robbins and is fatally stabbed by Porgy in DuBose Heyward's *Porgy.*

Alberta Sydna Crowninshield See Alberta Sydna Crowninshield Vaiden.

Drusilla Lacefield (Dru) Crowninshield Daughter of Caruthers Lacefield; elopes with Emory Crowninshield the day before she is to marry Miltiades Vaiden; mother of Sydna Crowninshield; appears in T. S. Stribling's *The Forge, The Store,* and *Unfinished Cathedral.*

Emory Crowninshield Southern genteel aristocrat and husband of Drusilla Lacefield; Confederate major and ardent defender of chattel slavery; appears in T. S. Stribling's *The Forge.*

Kate Croy Secret fiancée of Merton Densher and friend of the dying Mildred Theale; plots to have Densher marry Theale and inherit her money in Henry James's *The Wings of the Dove.*

Sarah Croyden   Actress, confidante of Olivia Lattimore, and abandoned lover and later the wife of Leon Lawrence in Mary Austin's *A Woman of Genius*.

Cruz   Indian woman, addict, and companion of Tristessa in Jack Kerouac's *Tristessa*.

Anthony Cruz   See Anthony Cross.

Cuckoo   Mistress of Old Lord in the House of Hwang; procuress who moves to Wang Lung's home as Lotus's meddling servant in Pearl Buck's *The Good Earth*.

Cudjoe   Deformed slave fiercely faithful to Lafitte in Joseph Holt Ingraham's *Lafitte*.

Daddy Cudjoe   Conjure doctor at Blue Brook Plantation; dispenser of a successful love charm to Cinder and of an unsuccessful antidote to Mary Pinesett in Julia Peterkin's *Scarlet Sister Mary*.

Moll Cudlip   Cutpurse sentenced for life to Australia; escapes and lives with her aborigine lover in Charles Nordhoff and James Norman Hall's *Botany Bay*.

Cuffee   Slave and miller at Beulah; sold as punishment for trying to run away in Mary Lee Settle's *Know Nothing*.

Lieutenant Culpepper   Third-generation army officer; serves as defense counsel for Robert E. Lee Prewitt's trial in James Jones's *From Here to Eternity*.

Martin (Mart) Culpepper   Town developer and partner of John Barclay; saved from disgrace and financial ruin when his daughter, Molly Culpepper, marries Adrian Brownell in William Allen White's *A Certain Rich Man*.

Molly Culpepper   See Molly Culpepper Brownwell.

Lieutenant Jack Culver   Lawyer on Marine reserve duty and closest friend of Captain Mannix; one of the men ordered on a useless thirty-six-mile hike in William Styron's *The Long March*.

Thwaite Cumberly   Philadelphian hired by MacDougal to work with Marietta McGee-Chavéz to populate her Spain in William Goyen's *In a Farther Country*.

Major General Edward Cummings   Commander of troops on the island of Anopopei; predicts a totalitarian future for America in Norman Mailer's *The Naked and the Dead*.

John Cunningham   Father of Avis Cunningham Everhard; physics professor who is fired for publishing a prolabor book; disappears during the rise of the Iron Heel in Jack London's *The Iron Heel*.

Miz Cunningham   Woman who looks after John and Pearl Harper while Willa Harper is at work; attempts to coerce John into revealing the whereabouts of hidden money in Davis Grubb's *The Night of the Hunter*.

Cupid   Arrogant, perverted policeman in Wright Morris's *My Uncle Dudley*.

Dan Cupid   Mischievous grandson of Bombie of the Frizzled Head in James Kirke Paulding's *Koningsmarke*.

Miss Lavinia Curdy   Friend of Gin-head Susy; searches successfully for a lover in Claude McKay's *Home to Harlem*.

Curley   Part-owner of a ranch who vows to kill Lennie Small for having raped Curley's wife in John Steinbeck's *Of Mice and Men*.

Curley   Friend admired by Henry Miller because he has no morals or sense of shame; has affairs with three women at the same time in Henry Miller's *Tropic of Capricorn*.

Ned Currie   Reporter for the *Winesburg Eagle* who leaves his lover Alice Hindman for greater opportunities in Chicago in Sherwood Anderson's *Winesburg, Ohio*.

James (Peppercorn) Curry   British dragoon who bribes Wat Adair to betray Arthur Butler; killed at King's Mountain in John Pendleton Kennedy's *Horse-Shoe Robinson*.

Curtin (Curtis, Curty)   American drifter who meets Dobbs in a Mexican oil camp and joins him on a search for gold in B. Traven's *The Treasure of the Sierra Madre*.

Cadwallader Cuticle   Surgeon aboard the *Neversink* who is interested in morbid anatomy; saves the life of Baldy and kills another sailor by operating on him unnecessarily in Herman Melville's *White Jacket*.

Wycliffe (Wick) Cutter   Merciless moneylender who tries to seduce Ántonia Shimerda; murders his wife and commits suicide in Willa Cather's *My Ántonia*.

Doggo Cutwright   Braggart, provincial soldier, and lazy settler at Beulah; moves west beyond Beulah because he hates all symbols of refinement, but leaves his children behind so they can be educated; eventually sides with Johnny Lacey's political opponents in Mary Lee Settle's *O Beulah Land*.

Jacob Cutwright   Drunkard and brother of Doggo Cutwright; tears up and fouls Jarcey Pentecost's books before leaving Beulah with a band of white outlaws who raid the settlement during Johnny Lacey's absence in Mary Lee Settle's *O Beulah Land*.

Leah Cutwright   See Leah Cutwright Catlett.

Maggie Cutwright   Half-Indian wife of Doggo Cutwright; insulted by the women of Beulah, she steals Sally Lacey's china cup before leaving the settlement in Mary Lee Settle's *O Beulah Land*.

Anton Cuzak   Husband of Ántonia Shimerda at the conclusion of Willa Cather's *My Ántonia*.

Lily Shane de Cyon   See Lily Shane.

René de Cyon   French diplomat who marries Lily Shane in Louis Bromfield's *The Green Bay Tree.*

Cytheris   Famous actress who instructs Pompeia for a part in the Mysteries; visits Turrinus in his self-imposed exile in Thornton Wilder's *The Ides of March.*

Casimir (Polack) Czienwicz   Polish-American soldier who believes he can beat the system in Norman Mailer's *The Naked and the Dead.*

Daisy Dacey Traveling companion of Pauline Faubion in Conrad Aiken's *Blue Voyage*.

Daddy Talented and exuberant actor; father of the narrator of Aline Bernstein's *The Journey Down*.

Daddy Faith Preacher who conducts a riverside baptismal service in William Styron's *Lie Down in Darkness*.

Herbert Hamilton Dade Young entrepreneur whose courtship of Margaret Schofield is undermined by her brother, Penrod Schofield, in Booth Tarkington's *Penrod Jashber*.

Private Luther Dade Confederate rifleman from Mississippi; narrates part of Shelby Foote's *Shiloh*.

Anne Dadier Pregnant wife of Richard Dadier in Evan Hunter's *The Blackboard Jungle*.

Richard (Richie, Rick) Dadier First-year teacher at a New York vocational school who wins the respect of the problem student Gregory Miller in Evan Hunter's *The Blackboard Jungle*.

Steven (Steve) Dagg Drunken, malingering, and scavenging backwoodsman who serves as a foot soldier under General Jackson; delivers a false message, which leads to the destruction of Richard Cleave's Stonewall Brigade; deserts the military to live with a widow in the mountains; appears in Mary Johnson's *The Long Roll* and *Cease Firing*.

Daggoo Black harpooner for Flask in Herman Melville's *Moby-Dick*.

Urban Dagonet Grandfather of Ralph Marvell and head of the prestigious old New York family whose locus is a house on Washington Square in Edith Wharton's *The Custom of the Country*.

Dahfu King of the Wariri tribe of African lion worshippers; former medical student and later philosophical mentor and friend of Eugene Henderson in Saul Bellow's *Henderson the Rain King*.

Gjermund Dahl Norwegian political leader in O. E. Rölvaag's *Peder Victorious* and *Their Father's God*.

Katrina Nilssen Dahl Maternal aunt of Helga Crane and wife of Poul Dahl; encourages Helga to marry an artist in Copenhagen and remain in Denmark in Nella Larsen's *Quicksand*.

Mona Dahl Best friend of Dolores Haze at Beardsley School; knows about Haze's involvement with Clare Quilty and helps her keep secrets from Humbert Humbert in Vladimir Nabokov's *Lolita*.

Poul Dahl Uncle by marriage of Helga Crane and husband of Katrina Dahl; encourages Helga to become an expatriate and remain in Denmark in Nella Larsen's *Quicksand*.

Claude Daigle Schoolmate of Rhoda Penmark; murdered by Rhoda because he received a penmanship medal that Rhoda thought she should have won in William March's *The Bad Seed*.

Lincoln Agrippa (Banjo) Daily Black American expatriate ilving in Marseilles; hangs out with a group of black expatriates from Africa and the Caribbean in Claude McKay's *Banjo*.

Hube Dakens River flatboatman in H. L. Davis's *Beulah Land*.

Richard (Dick) Dale Wealthy young New York painter who becomes more serious about both his life and his art after spending a month on a New England farm in Sarah Orne Jewett's *A Marsh Island*.

Sheridan Dale Shady lawyer who heads the trusts and estates department and becomes managing partner of Sheffield, Knox after the death of Henry Knox; under his influence Timothy Colt commits a breach of trust in Louis Auchincloss's *The Great World and Timothy Colt.*

Suzanne Dale Daughter of Eugene Witla's landlady; attracts Witla, whom she distracts from his work, in Theodore Dreiser's *The "Genius."*

Annie D'Alfonso See Annie Landry.

Ignatius (Inky) D'Alfonso Marooned skipper of the *Pixie* who becomes the lover and then husband of Annie Landry in Shirley Ann Grau's *The Hard Blue Sky.*

Cal Dalhart Cowboy who falls in love with Taisie Lockhart and murders his rival, Del Williams, in Emerson Hough's *North of 36.*

Major Dalleson Officer who accidentally wins the Battle of Anopopei in Norman Mailer's *The Naked and the Dead.*

Julia Sherringham Dallow Widow engaged to Nick Dormer until he chooses art over politics in Henry James's *The Tragic Muse.*

Amy Paget Dalrymple Attractive, opulent neighbor of Virginius Littlepage; seeks Littlepage's legal advice in Ellen Glasgow's *They Stooped to Folly.*

Henry G. Dalton Father of Mary Dalton; wealthy philanthropist who hires Bigger Thomas as a chauffeur in Richard Wright's *Native Son.*

Mary Dalton Daughter of the wealthy Dalton family and girlfriend of Jan Erlone sympathetic to Communist ideology; suffocated with a pillow by Bigger Thomas in Richard Wright's *Native Son.*

Mrs. Dalton Blind wife of Henry G. Dalton and mother of Mary Dalton in Richard Wright's *Native Son.*

Damastor Cowardly son of Charitas; forced to leave home after impregnating Adraste in John Erskine's *The Private Life of Helen of Troy.*

Stuart Dameron Chief of the Campbell County Ku Klux Klan in Thomas Dixon's *The Leopard's Spots.*

Cross (Lionel Lane) Damon Postal worker believed by his family and friends in Chicago to have been killed in a train accident; escapes to New York, where he assumes another identity, commits three murders, and is himself murdered by members of the Communist Party, in Richard Wright's *The Outsider.*

Damuddy Grandmother of Benjy and Caddy Compson, Jason Compson IV, and Quentin Compson I in William Faulkner's *The Sound and the Fury.*

Dan Rough, rebellious orphan in Louisa May Alcott's *Little Men.*

Danby Dissolute American husband of Handsome Mary in Herman Melville's *Redburn.*

Molly Dance Whore and mother of ten; lover of Wendell Ryder and Dr. Matthew O'Connor in Djuna Barnes's *Ryder.*

Claude Dancer Lawyer who takes over Mitch Lodwick's prosecution of Frederic Manion in Robert Traver's *Anatomy of a Murder.*

Francisco Domingo Carlos Andres Sebastian (Frisco) d'Anconia Successful industrialist who destroys his international copper empire when he joins the strike in Ayn Rand's *Atlas Shrugged.*

Unity Dandridge Niece of Edward Churchill and cousin of Jacqueline Churchill; engaged to Fairfax Cary in Mary Johnston's *Lewis Rand.*

Danforth See Gerald Stanhope.

Cornelia Dangerfield Wife of Cuthbert Dangerfield in James Kirke Paulding's *Westward Ho!*

Colonel Cuthbert Dangerfield Displaced Virginian and founder of a Kentucky frontier village in James Kirke Paulding's *Westward Ho!*

Leonard Dangerfield Son of Cornelia and Cuthbert Dangerfield; politician in James Kirke Paulding's *Westward Ho!*

Mrs. Samuel Dangerfield See Amber St. Clare.

Samuel Dangerfield Extremely wealthy elderly commoner and second husband of Amber St. Clare; gives her second child by Bruce Carlton his name and then dies, leaving her a rich widow, in Kathleen Winsor's *Forever Amber.*

Virginia Dangerfield Daughter of Cornelia and Cuthbert Dangerfield; high-spirited heroine of James Kirke Paulding's *Westward Ho!*

The Dankster (Board-Her-in-the-Smoke) Mainmastman aboard the *Indomitable* who tells Billy Budd that John Claggart dislikes Budd in Herman Melville's *Billy Budd.*

Dan'l Black servant of Mulberry Sellers in Samuel Langhorne Clemens's *The American Claimant.*

Ragnar Danneskjold Aristotelian philosopher who turns pirate in order to exact justice in Ayn Rand's *Atlas Shrugged.*

Danny Happily vagrant and alcoholic young man who inherits two small houses and quickly finds himself beset by friends who come to live in his houses; becomes so depressed from the restrictive lifestyle of owning property that he dies from a fall, his houses burn, and all his friends disperse after his burial in John Steinbeck's *Tortilla Flat*.

Danton   Leader of the French Jacobites who, opposed to Thomas Paine and the Girondists, unleashes the Terror on France, only to be a victim of it himself, in Howard Fast's *Citizen Tom Paine*.

Julia (Donna Julia) d'Aquilanera   Daughter of Leda Matilda Colonna d'Aquilanera and half sister of Marcantonio d'Aquilanera in Thornton Wilder's *The Cabala*.

Leda Matilda Colonna, La Duchessa d'Aquilanera   Mother of Marcantonio and Julia d'Aquilanera; enlists Samuele's help in curbing Marcantonio's sensual lifestyle in Thornton Wilder's *The Cabala*.

Marcantonio d'Aquilanera   Son of Leda Matilda Colonna d'Aquilanera; adopts a life of dissipation and commits suicide in Thornton Wilder's *The Cabala*.

Monsignor Thayer Darcy   Worldly Roman Catholic priest who becomes a father-substitute for Amory Blaine in F. Scott Fitzgerald's *This Side of Paradise*.

Victoria Dare   Frequenter of Washington parties; keeps Madeleine Lee and Sybil Ross informed of the latest gossip; engaged to Lord Dunberg in Henry Adams's *Democracy*.

Austin Darnley   Father of James and Rose Darnley; English vicar and philosophical adviser to Oliver Alden in George Santayana's *The Last Puritan*.

James (Jim, Lord Jim) Darnley   Captain of the yacht owned by Peter Alden and friend of Oliver Alden in George Santayana's *The Last Puritan*.

Rose Darnley   Sister of James Darnley; rejects the marriage proposal of Oliver Alden in George Santayana's *The Last Puritan*.

George Darrow   Middle-aged diplomat and former suitor of Anna Leath; when they renew their relationship, he lies about his connection with Sophy Viner, with whom he has had an affair, in Edith Wharton's *The Reef*.

Perry Dart   Police detective in Rudolph Fisher's *The Conjure-Man Dies*.

Beagle Hamlet Darwin   Character in a novel Balso Snell reads; impregnates Janey Davenport but will not marry her in Nathanael West's *The Dream Life of Balso Snell*.

Basil Dashwood   Actor who marries Miriam Rooth in Henry James's *The Tragic Muse*.

Miriam Rooth Dashwood   See Miriam Rooth.

Lou Da Silva   Chairman of the student honor committee and forceful advocate of Raymond Blent's eligibility to play football in Howard Nemerov's *The Homecoming Game*.

Dates   Servitor to the Glendinnings in Herman Melville's *Pierre*.

Daughter (Mrs. Boyd)   Companion of Gordon Boyd; poses as his wife in Wright Morris's *Ceremony in Lone Tree*.

Kitty Daumler   Earthy and uncomplicated mistress of Joseph for a brief time in Saul Bellow's *Dangling Man*.

Dauphin (Edmund Kean, Elexander Blodgett, Looy the Seventeen, Harvey Wilks)   Confidence man and accomplice of the Duke of Bridgewater in Samuel Langhorne Clemens's *Adventures of Huckleberry Finn*.

Janey Davenport   Character in a novel Balso Snell reads; wants Snell to kill Beagle Darwin in Nathanael West's *The Dream Life of Balso Snell*.

Keith Davenport   Commanding officer of the 918th Bomb Group who overidentifies with his men; replaced by Frank Savage in Beirne Lay, Jr., and Sy Bartlett's *Twelve O'Clock High!*

David   American youth living in Paris and trying to come to terms with his sexual identity; breaks his engagement to Hella when he falls in love with Giovanni; narrator of James Baldwin's *Giovanni's Room*.

Arthur Davies   General-store owner who opposes the lynch mob but rides with it in hopes of averting the hanging in Walter Van Tilburg Clark's *The Ox-Bow Incident*.

Avis Davis   House-party participant, identical twin of Mavis Davis, and schoolmate of Cress Delahanty in Jessamyn West's *Cress Delahanty*.

Exum Davis   Confederate veteran who, because he sells land and stock to his black hands, is threatened by the Regulators in Albion W. Tourgee's *A Fool's Errand*.

John (Jack) Davis   Young Goose Creek native recruited for Major Singleton's partisan band; his love for Bella Humphries embroils him in a dispute with Sergeant Hastings in William Gilmore Simms's *The Partisan*.

Lancy Davis   White-hating black youth killed in a race riot in Carson McCullers's *The Heart Is a Lonely Hunter*.

Louise (Lou) Davis   College-educated girlfriend of Jule Jackson in New York; has an affair with Jeff Gordon in George Wylie Henderson's *Jule*.

Mavis Davis   House party participant, identical twin of Avis Davis, and schoolmate of Cress Delahanty in Jessamyn West's *Cress Delahanty*.

Mississippi Davis   Driver of rigs for hire in New Orleans in Arna Wendell Bontemps's *God Sends Sunday*.

Peggy Davis   Attractive widow returning to Wales; the Welsh Rarebit in Conrad Aiken's *Blue Voyage*.

Seneca Davis   Uncle of Frank Cowperwood and owner of a Cuban sugar plantation in Theodore Dreiser's *The Financier*.

Hope Davison   Friend of Sally Forbes; secretly in love with Lymie Peters in William Maxwell's *The Folded Leaf*.

Phoebe Davison   Granddaughter of Garrett Pendergass and true love of Salathiel Albine in Hervey Allen's *Bedford Village*.

Charles Proctor Dawn   Attorney engaged by Helen Albury to defend her brother and whom the Op is accused of murdering in Dashiell Hammett's *Red Harvest*.

Dave Dawson   Albino conjure man; kidnapped to locate a lode of gold on Ty Ty Walden's farm in Erskine Caldwell's *God's Little Acre*.

Francis (Frank) Dawson   Schoolmaster in colonial North Carolina who avoids punishment for his rebellion by fleeing to Tennessee in Caroline Gordon's *Green Centuries*.

Jocasta Dawson   See Jocasta Dawson Outlaw.

Joe Dawson   Laundry room supervisor of Martin Eden in Jack London's *Martin Eden*.

Mr. and Mrs. Luke Dawson   Wealthiest couple in Gopher Prairie in Sinclair Lewis's *Main Street*.

Clara Day   Daughter of Traverse Rocke's benefactor and later fiancée of Rocke in E.D.E.N. Southworth's *The Hidden Hand*.

Norma Day   Girlfriend of Eddie Brunner; lends clothes to Gloria Wandrous in John O'Hara's *Butterfield 8*.

Diana (Di) Deacon   Daughter of Dwight Deacon; talked out of eloping with Bobby Larkin by Lulu Bett in Zona Gale's *Miss Lulu Bett*.

Dwight Herbert (Bertie) Deacon   Husband of Ina Deacon and brother-in-law of Lulu Bett; dentist and justice of the peace who inadvertently marries his brother Ninian Deacon to Lulu Bett in Zona Gale's *Miss Lulu Bett*.

Ina Bett (Inie) Deacon   Sister of Lulu Bett, wife of Dwight Deacon, and stepmother of Diana Deacon in Zona Gale's *Miss Lulu Bett*.

Ninian Deacon   Globe-trotting brother of Dwight Deacon; husband of Lulu Bett until his long-lost wife is discovered to be alive in Zona Gale's *Miss Lulu Bett*.

Jim Deakins   Young sidekick of Boone Caudill; killed by Caudill, who suspects Deakins of making love to Teal Eye, in A. B. Guthrie's *The Big Sky*.

Fred Dealey   Realistic judge who believes that whatever happens, happens because a lot of other things have happened already in James Gould Cozzens's *By Love Possessed*.

Laura Dearborn   See Laura Dearborn Jadwin.

Page Dearborn   Younger sister of Laura Dearborn; ingénue who loves her sister's former suitor Landry Court in Frank Norris's *The Pit*.

Deborah (Deb)   Cousin of Hugh Wolfe; her theft of a pocketbook results in his imprisonment in Rebecca Harding Davis's *Life in the Iron Mills*.

Miss Debry   Day-nurse of John Laskell in Lionel Trilling's *The Middle of the Journey*.

Alma Mathews Deen   Mother of Tracy and Laura Deen and wife of Dr. Tutwiler Deen; driving force to get Tracy married and in the church in Lillian Smith's *Strange Fruit*.

Laura Deen   Sister of Tracy Deen and daughter of Alma and Dr. Tutwiler Deen; northern-educated young southern woman in Lillian Smith's *Strange Fruit*.

Tracy Deen   Son of Alma and Dr. Tutwiler Deen and brother of Laura Deen; white lover of a black woman, Nonnie Anderson; murdered by Ed Anderson in Lillian Smith's *Strange Fruit*.

Dr. Tutwiler (Tut) Deen   Husband of Alma Deen and father of Tracy and Laura Deen; physician to White Town of Maxwell, Georgia, in Lillian Smith's *Strange Fruit*.

Lord Deepmore   English aristocrat who becomes friendly with Noémie Nioche in Henry James's *The American*.

Deerslayer   See Nathaniel Bumppo.

Bernadine (Nedra) Deevers   Friend and schoolmate of Cress Delahanty in Jessamyn West's *Cress Delahanty*.

Dirk (So Big, Sobig) Dejong   Son of Selina and Pervus Dejong; studies architecture and becomes a bond salesman in Edna Ferber's *So Big*.

Pervus Dejong   Truck farmer and widower who marries Selina Peake in Edna Ferber's *So Big*.

Selina Peake Dejong   Daughter of Simeon Peake; teacher in a country school near Chicago who marries Pervus Dejong and becomes a successful truck farmer following his death; mother of Dirk Dejong in Edna Ferber's *So Big*.

General Johann De Kalb   German commander of the Continental Regulars under Horatio Gates at the Battle of Camden in William Gilmore Simms's *The Partisan.*

Crescent (Cress, Cressy) Delahanty   Daughter of John and Gertrude Delahanty who grows from twelve to sixteen in Jessamyn West's *Cress Delahanty.*

Gertrude Delahanty   Wife of John Delahanty and mother of Cress Delahanty in Jessamyn West's *Cress Delahanty.*

John Delahanty   Rancher, school board clerk, husband of Gertrude Delahanty, and father of Cress Delahanty in Jessamyn West's *Cress Delahanty.*

Delaney   Foreman of the Quien Sabe ranch discharged because of Annixter's jealousy; joins the railroad agents who oppose the wheat ranchers in the San Joaquin Valley; dies during a gunfight with the ranchers in Frank Norris's *The Octopus.*

Della   Schofield family cook who manages to keep Penrod Schofield out of trouble in her domain in Booth Tarkington's *Penrod, Penrod and Sam,* and *Penrod Jashber.*

Alfred Delmer   Antique dealer who rents out upstairs rooms to male university students; landlord of Spud Latham and Lymie Peters in William Maxwell's *The Folded Leaf.*

Pauline Delos   Bisexual mistress of Earl Janoth and sometime lover of George Stroud; killed by Janoth in Kenneth Fearing's *The Big Clock.*

William Demarest   Author traveling by ship from New York to London in Conrad Aiken's *Blue Voyage.*

Demetrius   Poet who invites Hedylus to a school in Alexandria in H. D.'s *Hedylus.*

Agnes Deming   Daughter of Damon Barker; schoolteacher and later the wife of Ned Westlock in E. W. Howe's *The Story of a Country Town.*

Demion   Former lover of Hedyle who befriends her son Hedylus in H. D.'s *Hedylus.*

Marthe (Magda) Demont   Sister of Marya and Stefan in William Faulkner's *A Fable.*

Salvatore (Sal) De Muccio   Son of Italian immigrants, owner of Superior Shoeshine Parlor, and husband of Reenie O'Farron in Betty Smith's *Tomorrow Will Be Better.*

Jim Denby   Boyfriend of Gertrude Donovan in Nathan Asch's *The Office.*

Homer Denham   Orphan befriended by Jess Birdwell in Jessamyn West's *The Friendly Persuasion.*

Stephen Denleigh   Doctor who successfully courts Laurentine Strange in Jessie Redmon Fauset's *The Chinaberry Tree.*

Mame (Auntie Mame) Dennis   Flamboyant heiress whose unorthodox ideas and lifestyle are the basis of Patrick Dennis's *Auntie Mame* and *Around the World with Auntie Mame.*

Michael Dennis   Son of Patrick Dennis and Pegeen Ryan in Patrick Dennis's *Around the World with Auntie Mame.*

Patrick Dennis   Young boy who comes of age under the influence of his flamboyant aunt; narrator of Patrick Dennis's *Auntie Mame* and *Around the World with Auntie Mame.*

Pegeen Dennis   See Pegeen Ryan.

Wallace French (Wally) Dennis   Writer and winner of the Parkman College Creative Writing Fellowship; lover of Dawn Hirsh; killed in the Korean War in James Jones's *Some Came Running.*

Will Dennison   Friend of David Stofsky in John Clellon Holmes's *Go.*

Merton Densher   Journalist secretly engaged to Kate Croy; plots with Croy to marry the dying Mildred Theale and inherit her money; cannot go through with the plot, and refuses Theale's fortune when he inherits it in Henry James's *The Wings of the Dove.*

Bobby Denton   Revivalist preacher in Kurt Vonnegut's *The Sirens of Titan.*

George (Crazy George) Denton   Insane friend of Henry Miller in Henry Miller's *Black Spring.*

Thomas Denton   Union man who is the intended victim of a Ku Klux Klan ambush in Albion W. Tourgee's *A Fool's Errand.*

Virginia Depre   See Virginia Du Pre.

Annie Derrick   Wife of Magnus Derrick, with whom she lives on a wheat ranch; refined woman fearful of nature in Frank Norris's *The Octopus.*

Harran Derrick   Loyal son of Magnus and Annie Derrick and one of the ranchers slain by the railroad agents at the irrigation-ditch gunfight in Frank Norris's *The Octopus.*

Lyman Derrick   San Francisco attorney with gubernatorial ambitions; betrays his father, Magnus Derrick, and other San Joaquin Valley wheat ranchers in order to obtain the railroad's support in Frank Norris's *The Octopus.*

Magnus Derrick   Proprietor of the Los Muertos wheat ranch in the San Joaquin Valley; resorts to bribery to effect a change of grain-hauling rates and loses his reputation and sanity in the process as the railroad finally defeats him in Frank Norris's *The Octopus.*

Count Armand De Sacy   Parisian visiting the Haitian estate of his cousin, the absent owner of Bréda, in Arna Wendell Bontemps's *Drums at Dusk*.

Diron Desautels   Handsome young nephew of Philippe Desautels and member of Les Amis des Noirs, an antislavery faction; with Toussaint, coprotagonist of Arna Wendell Bontemps's *Drums at Dusk*.

Philippe Desautels   Elderly aristocrat recently fired as naval commissioner of Colonial Haiti in Arna Wendell Bontemps's *Drums at Dusk*.

Dorothy la Désirée (Heart's Desire, Madame Dorothy)   First true love of Jurgen; appears to him as the perfect woman and epitome of lost love throughout his yearlong journey in James Branch Cabell's *Jurgen*.

Colonel Potem (Potestatem Dedimus Smith) Desmit   Son of Peter Smith; owner of numerous North Carolina plantations, where he breeds slaves scientifically; owner of Nimbus, whom Desmit cheats in the sale of the Red Wing plantation, in Albion W. Tourgee's *Bricks without Straw*.

Lorency Desmit   See Lorency.

Nimbus Desmit   See Nimbus.

Bernie Despain   Bookie who holds IOUs from Taylor Henry and who owes Ned Beaumont money in Dashiell Hammett's *The Glass Key*.

Princess Alix d'Espoli   Member of the Cabala; brilliant conversationalist who, although married, falls in love with many younger men, including James Blair, in Thornton Wilder's *The Cabala*.

Raoul-Ernest-Louis Desrivières   Husband of Aimée Peyronnette and father of Mayotte; shot to death in Lafcadio Hearn's *Youma*.

Florence Dessau   Churchgoing New Orleans woman who captures Augie's attention and at whose heels Joe Baily and Tom Wright follow; involved in a secret affair with Horace Church-Woodbine in Arna Wendell Bontemps's *God Sends Sunday*.

Dessie   Girlfriend of Henry McIntosh and maid in Tom Harris's household in Lillian Smith's *Strange Fruit*.

Anne Dettrey   Clever magazine editor who is a friend and supporter of Phil Green, unaware he is not really Jewish, in Laura Z. Hobson's *Gentleman's Agreement*.

Helen Detweiler   Secretary of Arthur Winner and sister of Ralph Detweiler; commits suicide because of troubles brought by her brother in James Gould Cozzens's *By Love Possessed*.

Ralph Detweiler   Brother of Helen Detweiler; charged with rape; his subsequent flight contributes to his sister's suicide in James Gould Cozzens's *By Love Possessed*.

Jack Devlin   Childhood friend and later fiancé of Derrick Thornton; although a socialist and a pacifist, he fights in World War I and is killed in action in Helen Hooven Santmyer's *Herbs and Apples*.

DeVoss   Manager of the Bronze Peacock nightclub in William Riley Burnett's *Little Caesar*.

Josiah Devotion   See Squire Raglan.

Colonel Devries   War hero and congressman in William Faulkner's *The Mansion*.

Paul Dexter   Regular customer at the tailor shop; moves to New York from Indiana in Henry Miller's *Black Spring*.

Mammy Diana   Slave who prophesies marriage between the Hazard and Tracy families as the only way of settling the lawsuit over worthless land in John Pendleton Kennedy's *Swallow Barn*.

Dick   Communist organizer and ladies' man known as a bedroom radical in John Steinbeck's *In Dubious Battle*.

Dick   Dishonest black who is lynched for apparently having murdered Flora Camp in Thomas Dixon's *The Leopard's Spots*.

Dick   Cartoon editor for *The Townsman*; friend and neighbor of Augie Poole; narrator of Peter De Vries's *The Tunnel of Love*.

Nathaniel G. Dick   Union colonel in William Faulkner's *The Unvanquished*.

Danny Dickerson   Pathetic, has-been performer who approaches Miranda about an unfavorable review she gave him in Katherine Anne Porter's *Pale Horse, Pale Rider*.

Geordie Dickson   Jazz singer discovered by Edgar Pool in John Clellon Holmes's *The Horn*.

Bud Diefendorf   Former physicist turned philosopher, Buddhist, and janitor; friend of Ray Smith in Jack Kerouac's *The Dharma Bums*.

Christian Diestl   Ex-communist German officer who joins the Nazi party and gradually becomes a fanatical fascist, losing moral principles in a series of brutal acts; killed by Michael Whitacre at the end of World War II in Irwin Shaw's *The Young Lions*.

Bob (Bobby) Dietz   Son of the Reata ranch boss; becomes a self-employed agronomist after refusing to operate the ranch in Edna Ferber's *Giant*.

Digby   Owner of the Past Bay Manufacturing Company in Robert Cantwell's *The Land of Plenty*.

Gracie Dill   See Gracie Vaiden.

William Howard Taft ('Bama) Dillert Flamboyant gambler and drinker; protector of Dave Hirsh in James Jones's *Some Came Running.*

John (Johnny) Dillinger Head of a gang of robbers in William Riley Burnett's *High Sierra.*

Dilsey See Dilsey Gibson.

Abner Dilworthy United States senator investigated for bribery in Samuel Langhorne Clemens and Charles Dudley Warner's *The Gilded Age.*

Mr. Dimick Insurance man from Albany, New York, and a courier of messages for the New Underground in Sinclair Lewis's *It Can't Happen Here.*

Arthur Dimmesdale Minister, lover of Hester Prynne, and father of Pearl; dies after acknowledging his paternity of Pearl in Nathaniel Hawthorne's *The Scarlet Letter.*

Nancy Dimock Mistress of the Blue Ball Inn and friend of the Lindsays, Arthur Butler, and Horse Shoe Robinson in John Pendleton Kennedy's *Horse-Shoe Robinson.*

Dinadan Camelot humorist who tells old jokes in Samuel Langhorne Clemens's *A Connecticut Yankee in King Arthur's Court.*

Dinah First wife of Hart Kennedy in John Clellon Holmes's *Go.*

Myrtle Dinardo Parasol-wielding accomplice of Mother Ormsby in upstaging the navy during ceremonies dedicating the USS *Ormsby* in Wright Morris's *Man and Boy.*

Mabel Budd Detaze (Beauty) Dingle Oft-married mother of Lanny Budd in Upton Sinclair's *Dragon's Teeth.*

Parsifal Dingle Latest husband of Mabel Dingle; spiritualist and devotee of New Thought literature in Upton Sinclair's *Dragon's Teeth.*

Willie Dinsmore Playwright from whom Michael Lovett gets a boardinghouse room in Norman Mailer's *Barbary Shore.*

Thomas Parke D'Invilliers Literary Princeton classmate of Amory Blaine in F. Scott Fitzgerald's *This Side of Paradise.*

Dirty Eddie Black piglet from a San Fernando Valley farm who achieves stardom in a musical film in Ludwig Bemelmans's *Dirty Eddie.*

Max (Matthew [Matt] Fisher, William Small) Disher Harlem man about town and first recipient of the Black-No-More treatment; after becoming white, marries the daughter of the Imperial Grand Wizard of the Knights of Nordica in George S. Schuyler's *Black No More.*

Ditcher Barrel-chested black overseer on the Bowler plantation; champion fistfighter until conquered by Gabriel Prosser; the two become friends and cogenerals in the slave uprising in Arna Wendell Bontemps's *Black Thunder.*

Ditmas Cynical and freethinking engineer on a railroad construction gang who is the chief proponent of Sunday baseball in T. S. Stribling's *Teeftallow.*

Nicole Warren Diver Wealthy young woman who suffers a mental collapse as a result of an incestuous relationship with her father; wife of Dick Diver in F. Scott Fitzgerald's *Tender Is the Night.*

Richard (Dick) Diver Brilliant young psychiatrist who undergoes a process of decline after marrying mental patient Nicole Warren in F. Scott Fitzgerald's *Tender Is the Night.*

Bad-foot (Mistah Bad-foot Man) Dixon Clubfooted stableman who gives Augie a home and a chance to become a jockey in Arna Wendell Bontemps's *God Sends Sunday.*

Djuna Dancer, friend and possibly lover of Lillian, and lover of Rango; appears in Anaïs Nin's *Ladders to Fire, Children of the Albatross, The Four-Chambered Heart, A Spy in the House of Love,* and *Seduction of the Minotaur.*

Dill Doak Black burlesque entertainer who tries to convert Cass McKay to communism in Nelson Algren's *Somebody in Boots.*

Ben Doaks Cattle herder and farmer who loves Lethe Sayles in Mary Noailles Murfree's *In the Clouds.*

Dobbs (Dobby) American drifter in Mexico; works in an oil camp and lives as a panhandler before searching for gold in B. Traven's *The Treasure of the Sierra Madre.*

Doc Owner of the Western Biological Laboratory, a marine-specimen supply company, in John Steinbeck's *Cannery Row.*

Doc Easygoing physician aboard the *Reluctant;* friend and confidant of Mr. Roberts in Thomas Heggen's *Mister Roberts.*

Uncle Doc Friend of Jake Brown; owns a saloon that the longshoremen frequent in Claude McKay's *Home to Harlem.*

Pardon Dodge Frontier settler who kills Richard Braxley while Braxley is abducting Edith Forrester in Robert Montgomery Bird's *Nick of the Woods.*

Brent Dodsworth Son of Fran and Sam Dodsworth and a student at Yale University in Sinclair Lewis's *Dodsworth.*

Emily Dodsworth See Emily Dodsworth McKee.

Frances Voelker (Fran) Dodsworth Europhile wife of Sam Dodsworth; runs off with her lover, Count Kurt von Obersdorf, in Sinclair Lewis's *Dodsworth.*

Samuel (Sam, Sammy) Dodsworth President of Revelation Motor Company in Zenith; travels with his wife, Fran, to

Europe, where their marriage breaks up, in Sinclair Lewis's *Dodsworth.*

Abel Doe   Renegade white man who has become a Piankeshaw Indian warrior in Robert Montgomery Bird's *Nick of the Woods.*

Telie Doe   Daughter of Abel Doe and guide to Captain Roland and Edith Forrester in Robert Montgomery Bird's *Nick of the Woods.*

Charles (Charley) Doheny   Irish farmer who is the brother of Susie Doheny and the friend of Peder Holm in O. E. Rölvaag's *Peder Victorious* and *Their Father's God.*

Susie Doheny   Devout Irish Catholic neighbor of the Norwegian Holms in O. E. Rölvaag's *Peder Victorious;* marries the Lutheran Peder Holm, and religion becomes the basis for conflict between them in *Their Father's God.*

Professor (Dr.) Dohmler   Swiss psychiatrist and mentor of Dick Diver in F. Scott Fitzgerald's *Tender Is the Night.*

Dolce   Priest who stays at the Caffé Gatto; as a novice, he and Brother Bolo made a hair shirt of rat skins for Arsella's mother in John Hawkes's *The Goose on the Grave.*

Della Dole   Former lover of Jule and rival of Ollie; dies before the conclusion of George Wylie Henderson's *Ollie Miss.*

Doll   Unpleasant wife of Andrew and rival of Mary Pinesett in Julia Peterkin's *Scarlet Sister Mary.*

Doña Clara   See Doña Clara de Montemayor.

Donald   Flamboyant, effeminate man who becomes one of Sabina's lovers but treats her as a mother figure in Anaïs Nin's *A Spy in the House of Love.*

Donald   Lover of Michael in Anaïs Nin's *Children of the Albatross.*

Vincent (Socks) Donald   Promoter of the dance marathon; loses his struggle against the Mothers' League for Good Morals after a shooting in the bar adjoining the dance hall in Horace McCoy's *They Shoot Horses, Don't They?*

Donatello (Count of Monte Beni)   Faunlike Italian who loves Miriam Schaefer and kills Brother Antonio in Nathaniel Hawthorne's *The Marble Faun.*

Eddie Donato   Sicilian grocery store owner who hides Dix Handley and Erwin Riemenschneider in William Riley Burnett's *The Asphalt Jungle.*

Donjalolo (Fonoo)   Effeminate ruler of Juam in Herman Melville's *Mardi.*

Lady Agnes Donner   Mother of Biddy, Grace, Nick, and Percy Dormer in Henry James's *The Tragic Muse.*

Sean Xavier (Mike) Donnigan   Master construction worker and friend of Howard Roark in Ayn Rand's *The Fountainhead.*

Father Donovan   Catholic chaplain and friend of Chaplain Bascom; run over by an English lorry while trying to save a young girl in John Horne Burns's *The Gallery.*

Gertrude (Gert, Gerty) Donovan   Stenographer-typist for Glymmer, Read; consents to marry Jim Denby when she discovers that she is unable to marry one of the firm's junior partners in Nathan Asch's *The Office.*

Larry Donovan   Young workingman who travels through the American Midwest in the years leading up to the Great Depression in search of jobs and a meaningful life; narrator of Jack Conroy's *The Disinherited.*

Larry Donovan   Rakish railroad conductor who plans to marry Ántonia Shimerda, but abandons her after impregnating her in Willa Cather's *My Ántonia.*

Tom Donovan   Former Catholic priest, coal miner, labor organizer, and father of Larry Donovan in Jack Conroy's *The Disinherited.*

Neloa (Nell) Doole   Wife of Vridar Hunter; in order to punish him for her frustrating life with him, she commits suicide; appears in Vardis Fisher's *In Tragic Life, Passions Spin the Plot, We Are Betrayed,* and *Orphans in Gethsemane.*

Gene Doolie   Heroin customer of William Lee; possibly a police informer in William S. Burroughs's *Junkie.*

Congressman Doolittle   White legislator whose vacant seat Sammy Scott and Matthew Towns attempt to win in W. E. B. Du Bois's *Dark Princess.*

Hiram Doolittle   Templeton architect who has Natty Bumppo imprisoned for hunting out of season in James Fenimore Cooper's *The Pioneers.*

Doom   See Ikkemotubbe.

Earl of Dorincourt   See John Arthur Molyneux Errol.

Bridget (Biddy) Dormer   Younger sister of Nick Dormer; loves Peter Sherringham in Henry James's *The Tragic Muse.*

Grace Dormer   Older sister of Nick Dormer in Henry James's *The Tragic Muse.*

Nicholas (Nick) Dormer   Man who chooses art over politics, which leads Julia Sherringham Dallow to break their engagement in Henry James's *The Tragic Muse.*

Percival (Percy) Dormer   Older brother of Nick Dormer in Henry James's *The Tragic Muse.*

Dorris Artistic dancer barred by class differences from a romance with the brother of her employer in Jean Toomer's *Cane*.

Bertha Dorset Wealthy New York socialite who tries to conceal her own infidelity by insinuating that her husband, George Dorset, is involved with Lily Bart in Edith Wharton's *The House of Mirth*.

George Dorset Unhappily married, wealthy businessman who falls in love with Lily Bart but is rejected by her in Edith Wharton's *The House of Mirth*.

Fidelia (Delia) Dosson Sister of Francie Dosson in Henry James's *The Reverberator*.

Francina (Francie) Dosson Daughter of Whitney Dosson; gives an interview to her friend George Flack which, when published, scandalizes her family in Henry James's *The Reverberator*.

Whitney Dosson Wealthy American who takes his daughters, Delia and Francie Dosson, to Europe in Henry James's *The Reverberator*.

Dot See Dorothy Powers.

Lob (Jumping Sturgeon) Dotterel Busybody constable adopted by the Indians in James Kirke Paulding's *Koningsmarke*.

Douceline Mother of Youma; dies when her son is young in Lafcadio Hearn's *Youma*.

Thomas Dougherty Butler in the Leavenworth house who discovers the body of Horatio Leavenworth in Anna Katharine Green's *The Leavenworth Case*.

Douglas Man who reads the governess's manuscript about Miles, Flora, and the ghosts in Henry James's *The Turn of the Screw*.

Mary Douglas American Journalist and anti-Fascist in Czechoslovakia between the time of the Munich Pact and the Anschluss in Martha Gellhorn's *A Stricken Field*.

Old Douglas Racist who initially denies Jule Jackson a membership card in Typographical Union No. 6 in George Wylie Henderson's *Jule*.

Widow Douglas Sister of Miss Watson and guardian of Huck Finn in Samuel Langhorne Clemens's *The Adventures of Tom Sawyer* and *Adventures of Huckleberry Finn*.

Chet Douglass Student at Devon School and rival of Gene Forrester for class academic honors in John Knowles's *A Separate Peace*.

Monsieur Douperie French dancing master driven to distraction by his student Teague Oregan in Hugh Henry Brackenridge's *Modern Chivalry*.

Douris Ruler of Samos in Hellenistic times, lover of Hedyle, and patron of Hedyle's son, Hedylus, in H. D.'s *Hedylus*.

Hettie Dowler Zenith church secretary who attempts to blackmail her lover, the Methodist minister Elmer Gantry, in Sinclair Lewis's *Elmer Gantry*.

Oscar Dowler Husband of Hettie Dowler; helps his wife attempt to blackmail Elmer Gantry in Sinclair Lewis's *Elmer Gantry*.

Margo Dowling Chorus girl who marries unhappily and is unable to rid herself permanently of her leeching Cuban husband; mistress of Charley Anderson in John Dos Passos's *U.S.A.* trilogy.

Frances Lonigan Dowson See Frances Lonigan.

Fay Doyle Wife of Peter Doyle; writes to Miss Lonelyhearts and seduces him in Nathanael West's *Miss Lonelyhearts*.

Peter Doyle Crippled husband of Fay Doyle; shoots Miss Lonelyhearts in Nathanael West's *Miss Lonelyhearts*.

Count Alphonse (Henri) D'Oyley Twin brother and nemesis of Lafitte in Joseph Holt Ingraham's *Lafitte*.

Beckwith Dozer Proud black man who becomes the central figure in racially tense Winfield County, Mississippi, in Elizabeth Spencer's *The Voice at the Back Door*.

Julie Dozier Actress who is forced to leave the *Cotton Blossom* when people learn that her mother is black in Edna Ferber's *Show Boat*.

Hubert Drake Brother of Temple Drake in William Faulkner's *Sanctuary*.

Judge Drake Father of Hubert and Temple Drake in William Faulkner's *Sanctuary*.

Susanna Drake Lovely, scarred, and mad Southern belle who marries John Wickliff Shawnessy; dies during the Civil War in Ross Lockridge, Jr.'s *Raintree County*.

Temple Drake See Temple Drake Stevens.

Dred See Dred Vesey.

Inez Dresden See Inez Dresden Charlesbois.

Harley Drew Owner of the largest ranch in Bridger's Wells; sells Donald Martin the cattle Martin is accused of rustling in Walter Van Tilburg Clark's *The Ox-Bow Incident*.

Harley Drew Ambitious cotton merchant and banker engaged to Amanda Barcroft; lover of Amy Carruthers in Shelby Foote's *Love in a Dry Season*.

Rev. John Jennison Drew Pastor of the Chatham Road Presbyterian Church, of which George Babbitt is a member, in Sinclair Lewis's *Babbitt*.

Percy Northumberland Driscoll Father of Thomas A. Becket Driscoll and brother of York Driscoll; rears Valet de Chambre in Samuel Langhorne Clemens's *Puddnhead Wilson.*

Thomas à Becket (Chambers, Valet de Chambre) Driscoll Son of Percy Driscoll; switched at birth with Valet de Chambre and reared as a slave named Chambers in Samuel Langhorne Clemens's *Pudd'nhead Wilson.*

York Leicester Driscoll Judge and leading citizen of Dawson's Landing; murdered by Valet de Chambre in Samuel Langhorne Clemens's *Pudd'nhead Wilson.*

George Drobes Bronx suitor of Marjorie Morningstar in Herman Wouk's *Margorie Morningstar.*

Natasha and Otto (Vanya) Drollinger Married couple who are non-Communist Russophiles and residents of the Glen Cove Apartments in Albert Halper's *Union Square.*

Charles H. (Charlie) Drouet Traveling salesman and first lover of Carrie Meeber in Theodore Dreiser's *Sister Carrie.*

Henry Iverson Dround Old-fashioned and philanthropic meat packer in Robert Herrick's *The Memoirs of an American Citizen.*

Jane Dround Forceful and brilliant wife of Henry Dround and adviser of Edward Van Harrington in Robert Herrick's *The Memoirs of an American Citizen.*

Dr. Roy Drover President of the Federal Club, from which Neil and Robert Kingsblood resign, in Sinclair Lewis's *Kingsblood Royal;* friend of Cass Timberlane in *Cass Timberlane.*

Drucilla Black cook for Moseley Sheppard in Arna Wendell Bontemps's *Black Thunder.*

Kate Drummond New York roommate of Ann Chapin; lover of Joe Chapin I in John O'Hara's *Ten North Frederick.*

Christine (Chris) and Mela (Mely) Dryfoos Daughters of Jacob Dryfoos who are eager to find their place in New York society in William Dean Howells's *A Hazard of New Fortunes.*

Conrad Dryfoos Son of Jacob Dryfoos and publisher of *Every Other Week;* killed while helping the people involved in a streetcar strike in William Dean Howells's *A Hazard of New Fortunes.*

Jacob Dryfoos Millionaire from oil found on his farm; backer of the magazine *Every Other Week* who has difficulty fitting into high society in William Dean Howells's *A Hazard of New Fortunes.*

Jack Duane Jail inmate with Jurgis Rudkus; introduces Jurgis to a life of crime and Chicago politics in Upton Sinclair's *The Jungle.*

Larry Duane Young lawyer married to a daughter of Henry Knox; defends Timothy Colt in his trial for breach of trust in Louis Auchincloss's *The Great World and Timothy Colt.*

Captain Clarence Duchemin Enthusiastic voluptuary of the Reports Section at Ocanara Army Air Base whose influence secures an apartment for himself, Captain Nathaniel Hicks, and Captain Donald Andrews in James Gould Cozzens's *Guard of Honor.*

Dr. Pete Duchesne Physician and hero of Bret Harte's *Gabriel Conroy.*

Pompey Ducklegs Slave of Cuthbert Dangerfield in James Kirke Paulding's *Westward Ho!*

Bernard Ducrot Aide to the retired Archbishop Latour in Willa Cather's *Death Comes for the Archbishop.*

Dudley Caretaker at Hill House and husband of Mrs. Dudley in Shirley Jackson's *The Haunting of Hill House.*

Bruce (John Stockton) Dudley Dissatisfied newspaper reporter who flees from his job and his wife in Chicago and returns to his boyhood home of Old Harbor, Indiana, under an assumed name; runs away with the wife of the richest man in town in Sherwood Anderson's *Dark Laughter.*

Constantia (Constance) Dudley Young woman whose efforts to support her father and herself lead her into a battle of wills with the sinister Ormond in Charles Brockden Brown's *Ormond.*

Mrs. Dudley Officious housekeeper and cook who refuses to stay at Hill House after dark in Shirley Jackson's *The Haunting of Hill House.*

Stephen Dudley Father of Constantia Dudley; supported by Constantia after he loses his business to Thomas Craig's embezzlement; murdered by Craig in Charles Brockden Brown's *Ormond.*

Angus Duer Medical school classmate of Martin Arrowsmith; Arrowsmith's rival for the affections of Leora Tozer in Sinclair Lewis's *Arrowsmith.*

Margaret (Margy) Duff First lover of Eugene Witla in Theodore Dreiser's *The "Genius."*

J. D. Duffey Well-known moonshiner in Harriette Arnow's *Hunter's Horn.*

Tiny Duffy Lieutenant governor under Willie Stark and Stark's reminder to himself of political corruption; sets in motion the events leading to Stark's assassination in Robert Penn Warren's *All the King's Men.*

Maribeth Dufour Schoolmate of Cress Delahanty, house party participant, and niece of Miss Iris Bird in Jessamyn West's *Cress Delahanty.*

Yuro Dug Husband of Dora Dugova and father of Zorka Dugova; imprisoned for robbery; murderer of several foster children in Louis Adamic's *Cradle of Life.*

Sheik Dugan Bullying thug who terrorizes Sammy Glick in elementary school and later becomes his factotum in Budd Schulberg's *What Makes Sammy Run?*

Dora (Doramamo) Dugova Croatian peasant who is the wife of Yuro Dug, mother of Zorka Dugova, and foster mother of Rudolf Stanka; murderer of several foster children in Louis Adamic's *Cradle of Life.*

Zorka Dugova Peasant daughter of Dora Dugova and Yuro Dug; marries Rudolf Stanka in Louis Adamic's *Cradle of Life.*

Leo Dugovka Gentile friend of David Schearl in Henry Roth's *Call It Sleep.*

Duke Patient, long-suffering dog of Penrod Schofield; his loyalty to his master results in his being subjected to numerous experiments in Booth Tarkington's *Penrod, Penrod and Sam,* and *Penrod Jashber.*

The Duke (Herr Duke) German cannibal who carves up and devours a child in John Hawkes's *The Cannibal.*

Duke of Bridgewater (Bilgewater, David Garrick, William Wilks) Confidence man and accomplice of the Dauphin in Samuel Langhorne Clemens's *Adventures of Huckleberry Finn.*

Nathaniel (Nat, Sir Nat) Dukinfield Dissipated, sports-loving baronet who attracts Johnny Fraser at Edenton in James Boyd's *Drums.*

Ange (Angie, Angy, Ma, Memère) Duluoz See Volume II.

Catherine (Nin, Ti Nin) Duluoz See Volume II.

Emil Alcide (Emilio, Emil Kerouac, Emil Pop, Leo, Pa) Duluoz See Volume II.

Gerard (Gerardo, Ti Gerard) Duluoz See Volume II.

Jean Louis (Jack, Jackie, Jacky, J.D., John, Ti Jean, Ti Loup, Ti Pousse [Little Thumb], Zagg, Zaggo) Duluoz See Volume II.

Du Mesne French-Canadian guide and boatman for John Law in Emerson Hough's *The Mississippi Bubble.*

Peter Dumphy Conniving villain; specialist in California land fraud schemes in Bret Harte's *Gabriel Conroy.*

Royal Dumphry Homosexual expatriate in F. Scott Fitzgerald's *Tender Is the Night.*

René Dumur Suitor of Annette Slogum; castrated by Butch Haber in Mari Sandoz's *Slogum Home.*

Lord Dunbeg Irishman visiting Washington to study Americans; fascinated by Victoria Dareto, to whom he becomes engaged, in Henry Adams's *Democracy.*

Charles Duncan New England tutor of Cornelia Wilton and her brothers in Caroline Gilman's *Recollections of a Southern Matron.*

Duncan of Lundie Commander of Tort Oswego in James Fenimore Cooper's *The Pathfinder.*

Lieutenant Dundy Police detective antagonistic toward Sam Spade who is investigating the murders of Miles Archer and Floyd Thursby in Dashiell Hammett's *The Maltese Falcon.*

Charley Dunham Friend of James Staniford; marries Miss Hibbard in William Dean Howells's *The Lady of the Aroostook.*

Mabel (Magnet) Dunham Daughter of Serjeant Dunham and the only woman Natty Bumppo ever loves; loves and marries Jasper Western in James Fenimore Cooper's *The Pathfinder.*

Mrs. Dunham See Miss Hibbard.

Serjeant Dunham Father of Mabel Dunham, whom he wishes to marry Natty Bumppo; killed in an ambush in James Fenimore Cooper's *The Pathfinder.*

Ed Dunkel Complacent friend of Dean Moriarty in Jack Kerouac's *On the Road.*

Brace Dunlap Suitor of Benny Phelps; conspires with Jubiter Dunlap to kill their brother, Jake Dunlap, and frame Silas Phelps in Samuel Langhorne Clemens's *Tom Sawyer, Detective.*

Doctor J. Dunlap Hospital director who fondles the unconscious Candy Christian in Terry Southern and Mason Hoffenberg's *Candy.*

Jake Dunlap Jewel thief murdered by his brothers Brace and Jubiter Dunlap in Samuel Langhorne Clemens's *Tom Sawyer, Detective.*

Jubiter Dunlap Twin brother of Jake Dunlap; conspires with his brother Brace Dunlap to kill Jake and frame Silas Phelps in Samuel Langhorne Clemens's *Tom Sawyer, Detective.*

Brother Dunwoodie Leader of the August evangelist tent revival; at Alma Deen's request, he counsels Tracy Deen into church and marriage in Lillian Smith's *Strange Fruit.*

Peyton Dunwoodie Major of the Virginia dragoons who is torn between his friendship with Henry Wharton and the patriot cause; marries Frances Wharton and later becomes a general in James Fenimore Cooper's *The Spy.*

Louis Eugene (Julian Morris) Dupont Visitor to Carroll Farms who is revealed to be Marion More Carroll's lost son in Constance Fenimore Woolson's *For the Major.*

Virginia (Miss Jenny) Du Pre (Depre) Sister of John Sartoris in William Faulkner's *Sartoris* (*Flags in the Dust*), *Sanctuary, The Unvanquished, Requiem for a Nun, The Town,* and *The Mansion.*

Julian Durgo   Detective sergeant who investigates the rape of Laura Manion and the shooting of Barney Quill in Robert Traver's *Anatomy of a Murder.*

Mrs. John Durham   Aristocratic former slave owner who rears Allan McLeod in Thomas Dixon's *The Leopard's Spots.*

Rev. John Durham   North Carolina preacher who turns down a lucrative Job offer from a Boston church in Thomas Dixon's *The Leopard's Spots.*

André Duroy   Sculptor and first boyfriend of Jane Ward in Margaret Ayer Barnes's *Years of Grace.*

John Dutcher   Farmer and father of Rose Dutcher; reluctantly supports Rose's university education and life in the city in Hamlin Garland's *Rose of Dutcher's Coolly.*

Rose (Rosie) Dutcher   Farm girl reared by her father, John Dutcher; college graduate whose independence and natural grace gain her access to Chicago society; marries Warren Mason in Hamlin Garland's *Rose of Dutcher's Coolly.*

Gora Dwight   Novelist aware of the recklessness of Lee Clavering and Mary Ogden's passion in Gertrude Atherton's *Black Oxen.*

Nelson Dyar   New York bank teller who travels to Tangier; protagonist of Paul Bowles's *Let It Come Down.*

Billie Dyer   Son of Malcolm Dyer and friend of Paul Hardin; recipient of a dog cart made by J. Hardin; drowned in a swimming accident in Brand Whitlock's *J. Hardin & Son.*

Dave Dyer   Gopher Prairie druggist in Sinclair Lewis's *Main Street.*

Malcolm Dyer   Father of Billie and Winona Dyer; wealthy landowner and idol of Paul Hardin; dies of pneumonia after rescuing Evelyn Walling from an icy creek in Brand Whitlock's *J. Hardin & Son.*

Winona (Winifred, Winnie) Dyer   Daughter of Malcolm Dyer and wife of Paul Hardin; temporarily separated from her husband when his affair with Evelyn Walling is exposed in Brand Whitlock's *J. Hardin & Son.*

Dyke   Wrongfully discharged railroad employee who turns to hop-growing, only to be ruined by the railroad's shipping rates; becomes a train robber in Frank Norris's *The Octopus.*

Roy (Mad Dog) Earle Pardoned convict who is sent to California to rob a resort hotel; hunted down and killed after he becomes America's New Public Enemy No. 1 in William Riley Burnett's *High Sierra*.

Edward Easterly Partner of the late Mr. Job Grey and executor of the Grey fortune; chairman of the Republican State Committee of New Jersey in W. E. B. Du Bois's *The Quest of the Silver Fleece*.

William Washington Eathorne President of the First State Bank of Zenith; works with George Babbitt to increase Sunday school enrollment in Sinclair Lewis's *Babbitt*.

Brother Eaton Second Avenue evangelist in Henry Miller's *Black Spring*.

Martha Johnson Eaton Wife of Samuel Eaton and mother of Alfred Eaton; falls in love with two other men and becomes an invalid alcoholic in John O'Hara's *From the Terrace*.

Mary St. John Eaton Woman who breaks off her engagement to another man to marry Alfred Eaton in John O'Hara's *From the Terrace*.

Natalie Benziger Eaton Young Mountain City woman with whom Alfred Eaton falls in love at first sight; becomes Eaton's mistress and later his wife in John O'Hara's *From the Terrace*.

Raymond Alfred Eaton Second son of Samuel and Martha Eaton; after World War I he becomes a private banker in New York; an assistant secretary to the navy in World War II in John O'Hara's *From the Terrace*.

Rowland Eaton First son of Alfred and Mary Eaton; World War II navy pilot who dies on a training mission in John O'Hara's *From the Terrace*.

Samuel Eaton Father of Alfred Eaton and autocratic owner of Eaton Iron & Steel in John O'Hara's *From the Terrace*.

Janet Eberly Crippled woman loved by Sam McPherson in Sherwood Anderson's *Windy McPherson's Son*.

Ebony See Black Guinea.

Jack Eccles Episcopalian minister who counsels Rabbit Angstrom in John Updike's *Rabbit, Run*.

Lucy Eccles Wife of Jack Eccles; physically attracted to Rabbit Angstrom in John Updike's *Rabbit, Run*.

Simeon Ecuyer Swiss soldier-of-fortune in charge of Fort Pitt; appears in Hervey Allen's *The Forest* and *The Fort* and *Bedford Village*.

Eddie Part-time bartender who supplies the Palace Flophouse and Grill with stolen liquor in John Steinbeck's *Cannery Row*.

Eddie Store clerk who brings the resurrected road runner to Marietta McGee-Chavéz in William Goyen's *In a Farther Country*.

Martin (Bill) Eden Sailor who becomes a successful author; commits suicide when he is unable to find happiness in Jack London's *Martin Eden*.

Michael (Mike) Eden Former psychology professor who works to rescue Jews from Nazi Germany; meets Marjorie Morningstar on a ship sailing to France in Herman Wouk's *Marjorie Morningstar*.

Carothers (Roth) Edmonds Son of Zack Edmonds and father of McCaslin Edmonds in William Faulkner's *Go Down, Moses; Intruder in the Dust; The Town;* and *The Reivers*.

Carothers McCaslin (Old Cass) Edmonds   Woodsman and father of Zack Edmonds in William Faulkner's *Go Down, Moses; The Town;* and *The Reivers.*

Zachary Taylor (Zack) Edmonds   Son of McCaslin Edmonds; almost murdered by Lucas Beauchamp; appears in William Faulkner's *Go Down, Moses* and *The Reivers.*

Clithero Edny   Deranged Irishman who murders Arthur Wiatte; attempts further murder because of insane delusions; ultimately commits suicide in Charles Brockden Brown's *Edgar Huntly.*

Edouard   Friend of Nino; attacked by his former partner, Jacopo, in John Hawkes's *The Goose on the Grave.*

First Lieutenant James A. Edsell   Champion of justice and equality whose pleasure in making trouble renders his liberal principles suspect in James Gould Cozzens's *Guard of Honor.*

Agnes and Esther Edwards   Elderly aunts of Guy Grand in Terry Southern's *The Magic Christian.*

Edward Edwards   Captain of HMS *Pandora* who, sent to capture mutineers, captures and returns to England both the guilty and innocent, and treats them all inhumanely, in Charles Nordhoff and James Norman Hall's *Mutiny on the Bounty.*

Foxhall (Fox) Edwards   Editor, mentor, and best friend of George Webber in Thomas Wolfe's *You Can't Go Home Again.*

Henry Edwards   Elderly friend of Julien La Brierre; dies at Viosca's Point before La Brierre can reach him in Lafcadio Hearn's *Chita.*

Josh Edwards   Teacher whose students destroy his prized record collection in Evan Hunter's *The Blackboard Jungle.*

Oliver Edwards   See Oliver Effingham.

Ralph Edwards   Pharmacy student who seduces Barbara Mintner at a drive-in theater in Terry Southern's *Flash and Filigree.*

Oliver (Oliver Edwards) Effingham   Young hunter who returns to Templeton to claim land once owned by his father but now owned by judge Marmaduke Temple; marries Elizabeth Temple in James Fenimore Cooper's *The Pioneers.*

Mrs. Efrim   Operator of a small store where George Brush assists a thief in taking her money in order to prove his theory of ahimsa in Thornton Wilder's *Heaven's My Destination.*

Norah Egan   Chicago prostitute and Cass McKay's only love in Nelson Algren's *Somebody in Boots.*

Egbert   Disciple of Mark Winsome; tells the story of China Aster in Herman Melville's *The Confidence-Man.*

Chalmers Egstrom   Fat, laughing man who brings a mandolin with strings made of a woman's hair into Marietta McGee-

Chavéz's Spain; dies and is resurrected in William Goyen's *In a Farther Country.*

Harriet Ehrlich   Fiancée, then wife of Ron Patimkin in Philip Roth's *Goodbye, Columbus.*

Billy Ehrmann   Son of a Supreme Court justice, brother of Saul Ehrmann (Noel Airman), student at Columbia University, and suitor of Marjorie Morningstar in Herman Wouk's *Marjorie Morningstar.*

Saul Ehrmann   See Noel Airman.

Frederick Eichner   Renowned dermatologist who causes a fatal automobile accident and inexplicably attacks and later kills his patient Felix Treevly in Terry Southern's *Flash and Filigree.*

William Einhorn   Full-time employer and part-time mentor of Augie March during March's high school years; paralytic schemer, bluffer, survivor, womanizer, and philosopher of high aspirations in Saul Bellow's *The Adventures of Augie March.*

Gus Eisman   "Button King" who is interested in educating his mistress, Lorelei Lee; she remains attentive to him throughout her adventures and does not drop him until she marries Henry Spoffard in Anita Loos's *Gentlemen Prefer Blondes.*

Charles Francis (Charley) Eitel   Movie director who eventually testifies before an antisubversive congressional committee in Norman Mailer's *The Deer Park.*

Pepe El Culito   See Salvador Hassan O'Leary.

Eladio   Member of Pablo's partisan group in Ernest Hemingway's *For Whom the Bell Tolls.*

Elder   See Nung En.

Avis Criley Elderman   Sister of Bradd Criley; cares for Jimmy Timberlane in Sinclair Lewis's *Cass Timberlane.*

Mr. Eldridge   Maternal grandfather of Charlotte Temple; despite his grief at the loss of Charlotte, he manages to enjoy her child for several years in Susanna Rowson's *Charlotte.*

El Hombre Invisible   See William Lee.

Elijah   Mysterious figure who warns Ishmael and Queequeg about Ahab in Herman Melville's *Moby-Dick.*

Elinor   Married woman who leaves her family to join Francis Starwick in France; supports Starwick financially and is erroneously thought to be his mistress in Thomas Wolfe's *Of Time and the River.*

Maggie (Mag) Ellersley   Friend of the Marshall family; wife of Henderson Neal and then of Peter Marshall; successful businesswoman after Peter's death in Jessie Redmon Fauset's *There Is Confusion.*

Bob Ellgood　Robust brother of Geneva Ellgood; farms scientifically and takes an interest in Dorinda Oakley in Ellen Glasgow's *Barren Ground*.

Geneva Ellgood　Wealthy, ugly blonde whose family pressures Jason Greylock to marry her after she claims they were engaged in New York; drowns on Dorinda Oakley's wedding day in Ellen Glasgow's *Barren Ground*.

James (Jim) Ellgood　Father of Geneva and Bob Ellgood; experimental and successful stock farmer who forces Jason Greylock to marry Geneva in Ellen Glasgow's *Barren Ground*.

Francis Bosworth (Frank) Ellinger　Handsome bachelor of ambiguous morals, lover of Marian Forrester during her husband's illness, and husband of Constance Ogden in Willa Cather's *A Lost Lady*.

Ed Elliott　Boyhood friend of Niel Herbert, whom Elliott tells, much later, about the final years and death of Marian Forrester, in Willa Cather's *A Lost Lady*.

Edward Elton (Ed, Eddie) Ellis　Worker at Red Cloud Agency and friend of gamblers and horse thieves; husband of Morissa Kirk in Mari Sandoz's *Miss Morissa*.

Morissa Kirk Ellis　See Morissa Kirk.

Kitty Ellison　Cousin of Richard Ellison; befriends Isabel March in William Dean Howells's *Their Wedding Journey*.

Lucy Ellison　Classmate of Mollie Ainslie; teacher at Red Wing school, until her marriage to an army officer, in Albion W. Tourgee's *Bricks Without Straw*.

Richard and Fanny Ellison　Married couple traveling across New York and Canada in William Dean Howells's *Their Wedding Journey*.

William Elphinstone　Master-at-arms's mate on HMS *Bounty* who is set adrift with Captain Bligh in Charles Nordhoff and James Norman Hall's *Mutiny on the Bounty*; the ordeal at sea causes his mind to snap in *Men Against the Sea*.

Elsa　Young German woman living with Henry Miller and Boris in Henry Miller's *Tropic of Cancer*.

Elspeth　Haglike mother of Zora; allows Harry Cresswell and his cronies to carouse with the young girls in her cabin in W. E. B. Du Bois's *The Quest of the Silver Fleece*.

Elzbieta (Teta Elzbieta)　Stepmother of Ona Rudkus in Upton Sinclair's *The Jungle*.

Mr. Ember　Obscure scholar, translator of Shakespeare, and friend of Adam Krug, with whom he carries on a lengthy conversation about Hamlet; later arrested for his association with Krug in Vladimir Nabokov's *Bend Sinister*.

Fortune Emerson　Half sister of Captain Morgan Montgomery and strict guardian of Ellen Montgomery when Ellen's parents go abroad in Susan Warner's *The Wide, Wide World*.

Enoch Emery　Young man with "wise blood" who steals a mummy from the zoo museum to be the new Jesus for Hazel Motes's Church Without Christ; later disappears wearing a gorilla suit in Flannery O'Connor's *Wise Blood*.

Stan Emery　Would-be architect who feels imprisoned within the artlessness of the buildings and the intellectual stagnation of New York; burns the building in which he lives in a suicidal gesture in John Dos Passos's *Manhattan Transfer*.

Emil　Quick-tempered, restless boy in Louisa May Alcott's *Little Men*.

George Emlen　Obnoxious businessman whom Timothy Colt represents in several corporate transactions; as trustee of Emlen family holdings, Colt helps George by concealing the true value of stock in a textile firm, thus breaking his trust to other family members, in Louis Auchincloss's *The Great World and Timothy Colt*.

Emma　Mulatto daughter of Harry Cresswell and Bertie; grows into a fine young woman with Zora's guidance in W. E. B. Du Bois's *The Quest of the Silver Fleece*.

Emmanuel　Mexican gardener who, upon being caught having sex with Candy Christian, attacks her father with a trowel in Terry Southern and Mason Hoffenberg's *Candy*.

Emmeline　Beautiful young slave bought by Simon Legree to be his mistress; escapes with Cassy to Canada and then to Europe in Harriet Beecher Stowe's *Uncle Tom's Cabin*.

Alonzo D. (Lon) Emmerich　Corrupt criminal lawyer who commits suicide rather than face exposure and prison in William Riley Burnett's *The Asphalt Jungle*.

Emmy　Housekeeper for the Mahons; loves Donald Mahon before and after his injuries in William Faulkner's *Soldiers' Pay*.

Governor Endicott　Chief magistrate of the Puritan settlement at Salem; banishes Charles Brown in Lydia Maria Child's *Hobomok*.

Endymion　Slave of Mildred Lindsay in John Pendleton Kennedy's *Horse-Shoe Robinson*.

Caroline Walker English　Wife of Julian English in John O'Hara's *Appointment in Samarra*.

Julian McHenry English　Unhappy Gibbsville Cadillac dealer; protagonist in John O'Hara's *Appointment in Samarra*; also appears in *A Rage to Live*.

William Dilworth English　Prominent Gibbsville doctor and father of Julian English in John O'Hara's *Appointment in Samarra*; appears in *Ten North Frederick*.

Bartholomew Enright Broadway producer to whom Lee Youngdahl takes his play in Mark Harris's *Wake Up, Stupid*.

Envelove Head of the legal department at Olympia Studios in Ludwig Bemelmans's *Dirty Eddie*.

Ephum Loyal slave in Winston Churchill's *The Crisis*.

Horst von Epp Head of the Department of Propaganda and Press in Warsaw after Nazi occupation; friend of Christopher de Monti in Leon Uris's *Mila 18*.

Clem Ergot Brother of Jody Ergot; old-time vaudeville hoofer who works as a Russian agent to represent the United States in an unfavorable light in William S. Burroughs's *Naked Lunch*.

Jody Ergot Brother of Clem Ergot; with him, works as a Russian agent to discredit the United States in William S. Burroughs's *Naked Lunch*.

Lord Eric Lover of Ida Farange during her marriage to Sir Claude in Henry James's *What Maisie Knew*.

Augusta Erlich Mother of a college friend of Claude Wheeler; befriends Wheeler with adoration and introduces him to a social and cultural arena in Willa Cather's *One of Ours*.

Jan Erlone Communist party member and boyfriend of Mary Dalton; secures an attorney to defend Bigger Thomas after Thomas is charged with Mary's murder in Richard Wright's *Native Son*.

Jo Erring Uncle and closest friend of Ned Westlock; divorces Mateel Shepherd and kills her second husband, Clinton Bragg; commits suicide in E. W. Howe's *The Story of a Country Town*.

Captain Cedric Errol Third son of the Earl of Dorincourt; marries an American, fathers Cedric Errol, and dies young in Frances Hodgson Burnett's *Little Lord Fauntleroy*.

Cedric (Ceddie, Lord Faunderoy) Errol American-born grandson of the Earl of Dorincourt; returns to England as his grandfather's heir in Frances Hodgson Burnett's *Little Lord Fauntleroy*.

John Arthur Molyneux (Earl of Dorincourt) Errol British nobleman who disinherits his son yet brings his grandson, Cedric Errol, to England as his heir in Frances Hodgson Burnett's *Little Lord Fauntleroy*.

Mrs. Cedric (Dearest) Errol American widow of Captain Cedric Errol and mother of Cedric Errol in Frances Hodgson Burnett's *Little Lord Fauntleroy*.

Henshaw Erwin Second husband of Josephine Erwin; eccentric Englishman fascinated by the United States in William Dean Howells's *The Lady of the Aroostook*.

Josephine Erwin Aunt of Lydia Blood; invites Lydia to visit her in Italy in William Dean Howells's *The Lady of the Aroostook*.

Joaquín Escalona Mayor of a Mexican village; captures Miguel and Miguel's bandits in B. Traven's *The Treasure of the Sierra Madre*.

Baron Carola von Eschenbach Practical joker who once worked in Hollywood; claims to have been wealthy, but is now broke and has a venereal disease in Henry Miller's *Black Spring*.

Kenneth Escott Newspaper reporter with liberal political views; marries Verona Babbitt in Sinclair Lewis's *Babbitt*.

Verona Babbitt Escott See Verona Babbitt.

Frank Esel Painter summering in Norwood who, rejected by Rose Wentworth, becomes a superior artist before becoming a Union colonel in Barton Cathcart's regiment during the Civil War in Henry Ward Beecher's *Norwood*.

Esme Schizophrenic model for Wyatt Gwyon in William Gaddis's *The Recognitions*.

Jean Espagnol Soldier of fortune who identifies Arnaud du Tilh in Janet Lewis's *The Wife of Martin Guerre*.

Elena Esposito Mistress of Charles Eitel and later of Marion Faye in Norman Mailer's *The Deer Park*.

Constance (Connie) Estabrook Aunt of Margery Estabrook; stops interfering with Stephen Grendon's love for Margery when he points out some of Connie's son's clandestine activities in August Derleth's *Evening in Spring*.

Margery Estabrook Protestant girlfriend of Stephen Grendon in August Derleth's *Evening in Spring*.

Esteban Identical twin of Mañuel; goes to sea with Captain Alvarado to cope with his grief over Mañuel's death; dies in the fall of the bridge in Thornton Wilder's *The Bridge of San Luis Rey*.

Estelle Secretary at a New York export firm with whom Paul Hobbes is unable to consummate an affair in John Clellon Holmes's *Go*.

Esther Lover of Gabriel Grimes and mother of Royal; dies in childbirth in James Baldwin's *Go Tell It on the Mountain*.

Esther Beautiful Jewish daughter of Simonides; generally timid and modest; is willing to become the mistress of Judah Ben-Hur to ensure her father's comfort; becomes, instead, Ben-Hur's wife and mother of his two children in Lew Wallace's *Ben-Hur: A Tale of the Christ*.

Princess Lili Estradina Eminent figure in Paris's Faubourg Saint Germain society; lively companion of Undine Spragg and cousin of Raymond de Chelles in Edith Wharton's *The Custom of the Country*.

Eteoneus Gatekeeper who believes that men should be brute-like and that women should submit to men in John Erskine's *The Private Life of Helen of Troy*.

Etta   Spoiled but attractive fifteen-year-old niece of Joseph; her taunts lead Joseph to family violence in Saul Bellow's *Dangling Man.*

Eugenio   Courier traveling with the Millers in Henry James's *Daisy Miller.*

Eunice   Mother of Tomasina and wife of Thucyclides in William Faulkner's *Go Down, Moses.*

Eusabio   Navajo friend of Bishop Latour; appeals to Latour to help the Navajos, who are being driven from their land, in Willa Cather's *Death Comes for the Archbishop.*

Kate Eustis   Wife of Luther Eustis; narrates part of Shelby Foote's *Follow Me Down.*

Luther Dade (Luke Gowan) Eustis   Religious fundamentalist, murderer of Beulah Ross, and central narrator of Shelby Foote's *Follow Me Down.*

Brownie Evans   Son of Lije and Rebecca Evans, husband of Mercy McBee, and capable sidekick of Dick Summers in A. B. Guthrie's *The Way West.*

Janice Evans   Bride of Jarvis Addams; Frankie Addams disrupts their wedding in Carson McCullers's *The Member of the Wedding.*

Lije Evans   Missouri farmer who travels to Oregon with a wagon train; husband of Rebecca Evans and father of Brownie Evans in A. B. Guthrie's *The Way West.*

Rebecca (Becky) Evans   Wife of Lije Evans and mother of Brownie Evans in A. B. Guthrie's *The Way West.*

Mrs. Eveleigh   Wealthy plantation widow whom Captain Porgy contemplates marrying in William Gilmore Simms's *Woodcraft.*

Avis Cunningham (Felice Van Verdighan) Everhard   Daughter of John Cunningham and wife of Ernest Everhard; author and narrator of a book, published in the distant future, that chronicles the rise of the Iron Heel in Jack London's *The Iron Heel.*

Ernest Everhard   Martyr of the anti-Oligarchy revolution who foresees the rise of the Iron Heel; husband of Avis Cunningham Everhard in Jack London's *The Iron Heel.*

Mark Eversley   Great tragic actor and mentor of Olivia Lattimore in Mary Austin's *A Woman of Genius.*

Mayella Violet Ewell   Abused daughter of Bob Ewell; accuses Tom Robinson of rape in Harper Lee's *To Kill a Mockingbird.*

Robert E. Lee (Bob) Ewell   Father of Mayella Ewell, accuser of Tom Robinson, and attempted murderer of Scout and Jem Finch in Harper Lee's *To Kill a Mockingbird.*

Walter Ewell   Hunter in William Faulkner's *Go Down, Moses; The Mansion;* and *The Reivers.*

Miss Ewing   Longtime legal secretary who becomes mentally unstable in William Maxwell's *Time Will Darken It.*

Mr. Eyebright   Prominent Union man to whom Ralph Kirkwood confesses the details of Jerry Hunt's murder; opposes the Ku Klux Klan; helps tend to the dying Comfort Servosse in Albion W. Tourgee's *A Fool's Errand.*

Gregario Fabbisogno   One of two carabinieri who attack and then release Jacopo; later beats Adeppi in John Hawkes's *The Goose on the Grave*.

Faber   Former professor of English who teaches Guy Montag about books and helps him escape arrest in Ray Bradbury's *Fahrenheit 451*.

Fabio   Troubled friend of Paolo; swindled by a corrupt Vatican-connected priest; Paolo wants Mrs. Karen Stone to help Fabio financially in Tennessee Williams's *The Roman Spring of Mrs. Stone*.

Moses Fable   President of Olympia Studios who suffers with Dirty Eddie's owners until the piglet becomes a box-office sensation in Ludwig Bemelmans's *Dirty Eddie*.

Battle (Fire-eater) Fairchild   Father of the bride, Dabney Fairchild, husband of Ellen Fairchild, and owner of the Delta plantation Shellmound in Eudora Welty's *Delta Wedding*.

Dabney (Miss Dab) Fairchild   Daughter of Battle and Ellen Fairchild; seventeen-year-old bride in Eudora Welty's *Delta Wedding*.

David Fairchild   Fashionable interior decorator known for his acerbic wit; confidant of Eileen Shallcross in Louis Auchincloss's *The Great World and Timothy Colt*.

Dawson Fairchild   Novelist who attends the yacht party in William Faulkner's *Mosquitoes*.

Denis Fairchild   Brother of Battle Fairchild and father of Maureen Fairchild; killed in France during World War I in Eudora Welty's *Delta Wedding*.

Ellen Dabney Fairchild   Pregnant wife of Battle Fairchild and Virginia-born mother of eight, including the bride, in Eudora Welty's *Delta Wedding*.

George Fairchild   Memphis lawyer, youngest brother of Battle Fairchild, and best man in the wedding of his niece Dabney Fairchild; risks his life to free his niece Maureen Fairchild's foot from the path of an oncoming train, in Eudora Welty's *Delta Wedding*.

India Primrose Fairchild   Nine-year-old daughter of Battle and Ellen Fairchild and first cousin of Laura McRaven in Eudora Welty's *Delta Wedding*.

Jim Allen Fairchild   Unmarried deaf sister of Battle Fairchild; lives at the Grove plantation in Eudora Welty's *Delta Wedding*.

Maureen Fairchild   Nine-year-old daughter of Denis Fairchild living with the Battle Fairchild family; suffers from brain damage and impaired speech after her mother drops her on her head in infancy in Eudora Welty's *Delta Wedding*.

Primrose Fairchild   Unmarried sister of Battle Fairchild; lives at the Grove plantation in Eudora Welty's *Delta Wedding*.

Roberta Reid (Robbie) Fairchild   Wife of George Fairchild; leaves her husband but returns to him at Shellmound before the wedding in Eudora Welty's *Delta Wedding*.

Roy Fairchild   Eight-year-old son of Battle and Ellen Fairchild; pushes his cousin Laura McRaven into the Yazoo River in Eudora Welty's *Delta Wedding*.

Shelley Fairchild   Eighteen-year-old oldest child of Battle and Ellen Fairchild; plans to go to Europe with an aunt after her sister Dabney's wedding in Eudora Welty's *Delta Wedding*.

Laura Fairford   Sister of Ralph Marvell and member of one of the old families of New York's Washington Square in Edith Wharton's *The Custom of the Country.*

Helen Fairwood   American tourist in Egypt; main character in H. D.'s *Palimpsest.*

Fakahau   Father of Marama, husband of Mata, and chief of the island of Manukura; shelters his fugitive son-in-law Terangi; dies during the hurricane in Charles Nordhoff and James Norman Hall's *The Hurricane.*

Julian Falck   Amherst College student and boyfriend of Sissy Jessup; sent to a concentration camp for having infiltrated the Minute Men as a member of the New Underground in Sinclair Lewis's *It Can't Happen Here.*

Reverend Falck   Episcopal minister and grandfather of Julian Falck; beaten to death in a concentration camp in Sinclair Lewis's *It Can't Happen Here.*

Sharon Falconer   Evangelist and faith healer whose assistant is Elmer Gantry; killed in a fire during a revival in Sinclair Lewis's *Elmer Gantry.*

Harley Falk   Itinerant cobbler with a blind horse; informs Mary Fowler of Jerry Fowler's affair with Norah Sharon in Walter D. Edmonds's *Erie Water.*

Falsgrave   Clergyman and frustrated suitor of Mary Glendinning in Herman Melville's *Pierre.*

Grace Fanhall   Socialite pursued and won by Billie Hawker; gives him three violets in Stephen Crane's *The Third Violet.*

Lieutenant Tod Fanning   Shipmate of Claude Wheeler aboard the *Anchises;* contracts pneumonia, but survives because of Wheeler's care, in Willa Cather's *One of Ours.*

Fanshawe   Serious Harley College student; loves Ellen Langton and rescues her from Butler, but does not marry her, in Nathaniel Hawthorne's *Fanshawe.*

Doctor Faraday   Large and genial New York surgeon who rescues Dorinda Oakley after she steps in front of a horse-drawn vehicle; gives Dorinda work and teaches her to think biologically in Ellen Glasgow's *Barren Ground.*

Beale Farange   Father of Maisie Farange; materialistic, showy man with lecherous tendencies; husband of both Ida Farange and Mrs. Beale Farange in Henry James's *What Maisie Knew.*

Ida Farange   Mother of Maisie Farange; similar to her husband Beale Farange in being materialistic and lascivious, but she is also moody and charming; wife of both Farange and Sir Claude in Henry James's *What Maisie Knew.*

Maisie Farange   Child who saw too much while in her innocence, acting as a cover for many adulterous affairs in Henry James's *What Maisie Knew.*

Mrs. Beale (Miss Overmore) Farange   Governess of Maisie Farange; involved with Sir Claude in Henry James's *What Maisie Knew.*

Farani   Husband of Hitia and son-in-law of Tavi and Marunga; survives the hurricane in Charles Nordhoff and James Norman Hall's *The Hurricane.*

Lou Farbstein   Cynical and fast-talking police beat reporter for the *World* newspaper in William Riley Burnett's *The Asphalt Jungle.*

Gertrude (Gerty) Farish   Destitute cousin of Lawrence Selden; remains a loyal friend to Lily Bart throughout Edith Wharton's *The House of Mirth.*

Jean Farlow   First cousin and wife of John Farlow and closest friend in Ramsdale of Charlotte Haze; with her husband, attends the Haze-Humbert wedding in Vladimir Nabokov's *Lolita.*

John Farlow   Husband of Jean Farlow; manages the Haze property after Charlotte Haze dies until the death of his own wife in Vladimir Nabokov's *Lolita.*

Gladys Farmer   Poor but extravagant high school teacher who is pursued by Bayliss Wheeler in Willa Cather's *One of Ours.*

Jeff Farnley   Best friend of alleged murder victim Larry Kinkaid, employee of Harley Drew, and focal point of the lynch mob in Walter Van Tilburg Clark's *The Ox-Bow Incident.*

Virgie Farnum   Friend of Silla Boyce; unlike most Barbadian women, has pale skin and gray eyes in Paule Marshall's *Brown Girl, Brownstones.*

Cecily Saunders Farr   Wife of George Farr, after having been engaged to Donald Mahon, in William Faulkner's *Soldiers' Pay.*

George Farr   Georgian who marries Cecily Saunders in William Faulkner's *Soldiers' Pay.*

M. J. Farr   District Attorney under whom Ned Beaumont ostensibly operates as a special investigator in Dashiell Hammett's *The Glass Key.*

Captain John Farrago   Bachelor, often disappointed in love, who travels between Pittsburgh and Philadelphia with his servant Teague Oregan, to whom Farrago administers lessons in servile behavior, in Hugh Henry Brackenridge's *Modern Chivalry.*

Mrs. Farrinder   Campaigner for the emancipation of women who is skeptical of inspirational views in Henry James's *The Bostonians.*

Ensign Farrington   Replacement officer aboard the USS *Caine* who assists Willie Keith in saving the ship after a kamikaze attack in Herman Wouk's *The Caine Mutiny.*

Father   Father of Henry Miller; becomes ill when he stops drinking, remains a semi-invalid for a year, and spends his free time sitting on a bench in the cemetery in Henry Miller's *Tropic of Capricorn*.

Sam Fathers   Son of Ikkemotubbe; teaches Ike McCaslin about the woods and hunting in William Faulkner's *Go Down, Moses;* also appears in *Intruder in the Dust* and *The Reivers*.

Pauline Faubion   Flirtatious American fleshpot in Conrad Aiken's *Blue Voyage*.

Faunderoy   See Moodie.

Lord Faunderoy   See Cedric Errol.

Faustin the Zombie   Witness to and commentator on, but not participant in, life in Anaïs Nin's *Children of the Albatross*.

Harriot (Rosebud) Fawcet   Companion to Mrs. Francis; dies after learning that her beloved, Tommy Harrington, is her half-brother in William Hill Brown's *The Power of Sympathy*.

Maria Fawcet   Mother, by J. Harrington, of Harriot Fawcet in William Hill Brown's *The Power of Sympathy*.

Felix Fay   Socialist reformer in Davenport, Iowa, in Floyd Dell's *Moon-Calf*.

John Fay   Bridge-building engineer who receives Hagar Ashendyne's declaration of love and promise of marriage as they drift off the coast of Brittany after a shipwreck in Mary Johnston's *Hagar*.

Fayaway   Female friend of Tommo in Herman Melville's *Typee*.

Marion (Marion O'Faye) Faye   Bisexual, pimp, drug dealer, and beat-nihilist; son of Dorothea O'Faye in Norman Mailer's *The Deer Park*.

Walter Feather   Saxophone player and rival of Willie Keith for the affections of May Wynn in Herman Wouk's *The Caine Mutiny*.

Fedallah   Mysterious Parsee whom Ahab smuggles aboard the *Pequod* in Herman Melville's *Moby-Dick*.

Samson-Aaron (The Uncle) Feder   Brother of Rose Morgenstern in Herman Wouk's *Marjorie Morningstar*.

Fee   Town carpenter and father of Jimmy Fee; killed by Clay Turner in E. L. Doctorow's *Welcome to Hard Times*.

Jimmy Fee   Orphan cared for by Blue and Molly Riordan, whom he accidentally kills, in E. L. Doctorow's *Welcome to Hard Times*.

Felice   "Little brown" whom Jake Brown believes is the love of his life and for whom he searches Harlem; they leave Harlem together for Chicago in Claude McKay's *Home to Harlem*.

Thea Fenchel   Heiress to a million-dollar mineral water business; brash and spoiled seeker after goddess-like perfection; her affair with Augie March lasts only as long as her abortive attempt in Mexico to hunt iguanas with eagles in Saul Bellow's *The Adventures of Augie March*.

Henry Fenn   Drunken lawyer and first husband of Margaret Miller; reformed railroad shopkeeper in William Allen White's *In the Heart of a Fool*.

Lee Fenner   Silent partner of the *Coast Guardian,* which publishes information damaging to John Bellmann, in Paul Cain's *Fast One*.

Captain Jack Fenwick   Half-mad mountaineer whose parents were killed by Indians; becomes a killer of Indians in Hervey Allen's *Bedford Village*.

Collin Talbo Fenwick   Southern boy who lives with his cousins, the Talbo sisters, during his adolescent years; narrator of Truman Capote's *The Grass Harp*.

Ferguson   Tory partisan leader killed at King's Mountain in John Pendleton Kennedy's *Horse-Shoe Robinson*.

Duncan Ferguson   Educated, moral, and philosophical servant who becomes Captain John Farrago's bog-trotter, after Teague Oregan is appointed as exciseman, in Hugh Henry Brackenridge's *Modern Chivalry*.

Helen (Fergy) Ferguson   Scottish nurse in Italy at the beginning of World War I; friend and confidante of Catherine Barkley in Ernest Hemingway's *A Farewell to Arms*.

Jeb Ferguson   Boorish farmer whom Susan Lenox is forced to marry and from whom she flees in David Graham Phillips's *Susan Lenox*.

Burgess, Claudia, and Octavia Fern   Sisters who own the Fern Grammar School, where Rhoda Penmark is enrolled, in William March's *The Bad Seed*.

Fernando (Fernandito)   Member of Pablo's partisan group in Ernest Hemingway's *For Whom the Bell Tolls*.

Luther Ferrari   High school boyfriend of Brenda Patimkin; teammate of Ron Patimkin and best man at his wedding in Philip Roth's *Goodbye, Columbus*.

Floyd Ferris   Major coordinator of the State Science Institute who is responsible for Project X and Project F in Ayn Rand's *Atlas Shrugged*.

Richard (Dick) Ferriss   Best friend of Ward Bennett; dies of typhoid fever when his nurse, Lloyd Searight, is prevented by Bennett from doing her duty in Frank Norris's *A Man's Woman*.

William Fetters   White cotton mill owner who exploits his employees and traffics in convict labor in Charles W. Chesnutt's *The Colonel's Dream*.

Jesus Fever   Ancient little black man who drives a mule and wagon; his death changes the life of his granddaughter, Missouri Fever, in Truman Capote's *Other Voices, Other Rooms.*

Missouri (Zoo) Fever   Granddaughter of Jesus Fever; her husband cut her throat when she was a teenaged bride; becomes a religious fanatic after being gang-raped in Truman Capote's *Other Voices, Other Rooms.*

Fibby   See Phoebe.

Fidelia   Young woman whose abduction before her marriage leads to Henry's suicide in William Hill Brown's *The Power of Sympathy.*

Achsa Fielding   Supposedly widowed English Jewess who promises to marry Arthur Mervyn in Charles Brockden Brown's *Arthur Mervyn.*

Roger Fielding   Rich white lover of Angela Murray in Jessie Redmon Fauset's *Plum Bun.*

Fig Tree John   See Agocho.

Mr. Filer   Agent of Olive Chancellor; tries to convince Verena Tarrant to go on stage in Henry James's *The Bostonians.*

Fillmore   Friend of Henry Miller; employed in the diplomatic service; assaulted by a prostitute, hospitalized, and forced to leave Paris in order to escape from Ginette in Henry Miller's *Tropic of Cancer.*

Ada Fincastle   Heroine who challenges Janet Rowan for the love of Ralph McBride, loses him, bears their child, marries him, but has difficulty keeping him in Ellen Glasgow's *Vein of Iron.*

Grandmother Fincastle   Mother of John Fincastle and grandmother of Ada Fincastle; of unquestioning religion, thinks her son a heretic in Ellen Glasgow's *Vein of Iron.*

John (Father) Fincastle   Presbyterian minister and philosopher of idealism who loses his church because of a book he publishes; spends his life as a poor schoolmaster; father of Ada Fincastle in Ellen Glasgow's *Vein of Iron.*

Maggie (Aunt Maggie) Fincastle   Sister of John Fincastle and aunt of Ada Fincastle; does not accept her brother's religious doubts in Ellen Glasgow's *Vein of Iron.*

Mary Evelyn (Mrs. John, Mother) Fincastle   Poor, orphaned Tidewater belle who marries John Fincastle, but who becomes uneasy in their life of poverty in Ellen Glasgow's *Vein of Iron.*

Atticus Finch   Father of Scout and Jem Finch and lawyer who defends Tom Robinson; right-minded citizen and parent who says it is a sin to kill a mockingbird in Harper Lee's *To Kill a Mockingbird.*

Jean Louise (Scout) Finch   Curious and defiant youngster who begins to accept her role as a female; daughter of Atticus Finch and narrator of Harper Lee's *To Kill a Mockingbird.*

Jeremy Atticus (Jem) Finch   Proud older brother of Scout Finch; comes to appreciate and understand his father, Atticus Finch, in Harper Lee's *To Kill a Mockingbird.*

Katharine Finch   Secretary to Paul Proteus in Kurt Vonnegut's *Player Piano.*

Miriam Finch   Sculptress and lover of Eugene Witla in Theodore Dreiser's *The "Genius."*

Sondra Finchley   Wealthy girlfriend of Clyde Griffiths, who sees in her a chance to improve his social standing, in Theodore Dreiser's *An American Tragedy.*

Fin-de-Siècle   Parisian count, writer, and traveling companion of Aurelia West and the Chatelaine in Henry Blake Fuller's *The Chatelaine of La Trinité.*

Sidney Fineman   Influential and pioneering Hollywood producer whose position as production chief is usurped by Sammy Glick in Budd Schulberg's *What Makes Sammy Run?*

Mike Fink   Mississippi River flatboatman and mail rider in Eudora Welty's *The Robber Bridegroom.*

Angela Finlay   Beautiful woman who provides an alibi for Alonzo D. Emmerich in William Riley Burnett's *The Asphalt Jungle.*

Huckleberry (George Jackson, George Peters, Huck, Sarah Mary Williams, Tom Sawyer) Finn   Son of Pap Finn; witnesses Injun Joe's murder of Dr. Robinson and rescues Widow Douglas in Samuel Langhorne Clemens's *The Adventures of Tom Sawyer;* runs away with Jim and narrates *Adventures of Huckleberry Finn;* accompanies Tom Sawyer on a balloon trip across North Africa and narrates *Tom Sawyer Abroad;* helps Tom Sawyer solve a murder and narrates Clemens's *Tom Sawyer, Detective.*

Pap Finn   Town drunk and father of Huckleberry Finn in Samuel Langhorne Clemens's *The Adventures of Tom Sawyer* and *Adventures of Huckleberry Finn.*

Edward Francis (Ed) Finnerty   Best friend of Paul Proteus; joins the Ghost Shirt revolution in Kurt Vonnegut's *Player Piano.*

Oliver Finnerty   Panderer, pimp, and peepshow proprietor in Nelson Algren's *A Walk on the Wild Side.*

Thomas (Colonel, Curn, Curny) Finnley   Iconoclastic and successful trumpeter in John Clellon Holmes's *The Horn.*

Finny   See Phineas.

Firebird   Wild horse of Leonora Penderton; throws Captain Penderton and brings about his chance meeting with the naked Private Ellgee Williams in Carson McCullers's *Reflections in a Golden Eye*.

Sweeney Fishberg   Grand Republic attorney and friend of Jinny Timberlane in Sinclair Lewis's *Cass Timberlane*.

Carry Fisher   Twice-divorced New York socialite who tries to help Lily Bart find a husband and, later, a job in Edith Wharton's *The House of Mirth*.

Helen Givens Fisher   Daughter of the Imperial Grand Wizard of the Knights of Nordica; marries whitened black man Matthew Fisher and gives birth to a mulatto son in George S. Schuyler's *Black No More*.

Leon Fisher   Idealistic communist artist and friend of Jason Wheeler; unhappily in love with Helen Jackson, but loved by Celia Chapman, in Albert Halper's *Union Square*.

Matthew (Matt) Fisher   See Max Disher.

Pop Fisher   Manager of the Knights and uncle of Memo Paris in Bernard Malamud's *The Natural*.

Eddy Fiske   Police officer who investigates Frederick Eichner's automobile accident in Terry Southern's *Flash and Filigree*.

Eddie Fislinger   College classmate of Elmer Gantry, president of the local YMCA, and Baptist minister in Sinclair Lewis's *Elmer Gantry*.

Captain Basil Fitz-Hugh   Handsome, genteel British nobleman who romances Mame Dennis and marries Vera Charles in Patrick Dennis's *Around the World with Auntie Mame*.

George P. (or M.) Flack   American reporter for *The Reverberator* who publishes a story about his friend Francie Dosson and her family in Henry James's *The Reverberator*.

Flag   Orphaned fawn Jody Baxter takes as a pet and companion in Marjorie Kinnan Rawlings's *The Yearling*.

Celia Flagg   Ex-wife of Mason Flagg; also loved by Peter Leverett in William Styron's *Set This House on Fire*.

Mason Flagg   American playboy living in Rome whose sadistic behavior and decadent lifestyle destroy many lives and culminate in the rape and murder of Francesca Ricci and his own subsequent death in William Styron's *Set This House on Fire*.

Jim Flaherty   Veteran Irish police detective who is Rico Bandello's antagonist and close observer in William Riley Burnett's *Little Caesar*.

Guy Flamm   Shady theatrical producer in Herman Wouk's *Marjorie Morningstar*.

Elizabeth (Betty) Flanagan   Washerwoman, cook, and petticoat doctor to the American troops in James Fenimore Cooper's *The Spy*.

Jack Flanders   Young man with a scarred face who wants to be an actor; enters Marietta McGee-Chavéz's Spain in William Goyen's *In a Farther Country*.

Flask (King-Post)   Third mate aboard the *Pequod* in Herman Melville's *Moby-Dick*.

Troy Flavin   Thirty-four-year-old Fairchild overseer from the Tishomingo Hills of Mississippi; marries Dabney Fairchild in Eudora Welty's *Delta Wedding*.

Berenice (Bevy, Kathryn Trent) Fleming   Daughter of Hattie Carter and lover of Frank Cowperwood in Theodore Dreiser's *The Titan;* moves to London with Cowperwood and plans to build a hospital after his death in *The Stoic*.

Henry (Flem) Fleming   Youthful Union soldier who deserts his regiment; a spurious wound emboldens him to return and fight fearlessly in Stephen Crane's *The Red Badge of Courage*.

Joe Fleming   Boxer who will not give up his sport despite the pleas of his girlfriend, Genevieve; killed in a prizefight in Jack London's *The Game*.

Robert Fleming   Solicitor who encourages Hugh Tallant to seek redress in England after the American Revolution and who later gets Tallant pardoned when Tallant returns to England after escaping from the Australian penal colony in Charles Nordhoff and James Norman Hall's *Botany Bay*.

Everell Fletcher   Son of William Fletcher and betrothed of Hope Leslie; captured by Indians and saved from execution by Magawisca in Catharine Maria Sedgwick's *Hope Leslie*.

Gid Fletcher   Avaricious blacksmith who captures Rick Tyler in Mary Noailles Murfree's *The Prophet of the Great Smoky Mountains*.

William Fletcher   Puritan settler, father of Everell Fletcher, and guardian of Faith and Hope Leslie in Catharine Maria Sedgwick's *Hope Leslie*.

Mr. Flick   Musician and shipboard gigolo with whom the narrator dances en route from Europe to America in Aline Bernstein's *The Journey Down*.

Wilbur Flick   Alcoholic scion of a wealthy family who, following the stock market crash, becomes a communist and a professional magician in Edmund Wilson's *Memoirs of Hecate County*.

Private Otto Flickner   Union cannoneer from Minnesota; narrates part of Shelby Foote's *Shiloh*.

Lucius Fliegend   Jewish owner of Fliegend Fancy Box and Pasteboard Toy Manufacturing Company, which employs Jinny Timberlane, in Sinclair Lewis's *Cass Timberlane*.

Luther Leroy (Lute) Fliegler   Employee of Julian English, to whom Fliegler gives good advice, in John O'Hara's *Appointment in Samarra*.

Augustus P. (Gus) Flint   Tyrannical railroad executive who controls state politics; father of Victoria Flint in Winston Churchill's *Mr. Crewe's Career*.

Jere Flint   Dance-marathon contestant who is unfairly eliminated from a derby race through the machinations of the marathon officials in Horace McCoy's *They Shoot Horses, Don't They?*

Victoria Flint   Privileged daughter of Augustus P. Flint; matures and becomes the wife of Austen Vane in Winston Churchill's *Mr. Crewe's Career*.

Evy Rommely Flittman   Older sister of Katie Nolan and refined aunt of Francie Nolan in Betty Smith's *A Tree Grows in Brooklyn*.

Captain Flood   Operator of a riverboat and friend of Johnny Fraser in James Boyd's *Drums*.

Dora Flood   Madam and proprietor of the Bear Flag Restaurant, a popular brothel, in John Steinbeck's *Cannery Row*.

Mrs. Flood   Landlady of Hazel Motes who, though at first attracted only by his money, becomes fascinated by his eyes after he blinds himself and takes him in before his death in Flannery O'Connor's *Wise Blood*.

Nora Flood   American socialite and lover of Robin Vote; after losing Robin to Jenny Petherbridge, she observes Robin's confrontation with the dog and Robin's bestial nature in Djuna Barnes's *Nightwood*.

Flopit   Spoiled lapdog of Miss Lola Pratt in Booth Tarkington's *Seventeen*.

Flora   Angelic girl under the care of the governess; sister of Miles; becomes frightened of and hateful toward the governess when the governess confronts her about the ghosts in Henry James's *The Turn of the Screw*.

Florimel   Vampire who becomes Jurgen's third wife during his sojourn in the Hell of his father following Jurgen's departure from Leuke in James Branch Cabell's *Jurgen*.

Flossie   Good-natured prostitute who appears to radiate health but afflicts both Dolly Haight and Vandover with a venereal disease in Frank Norris's *Vandover and the Brute*.

Effie (Mrs. Effie, Mrs. Senator James Knox Floud) Floud   Cousin of Egbert G. Floud and leader of the Red Gap social set; wants Marmaduke Ruggles to teach Egbert how to dress and behave as a gentleman in Harry Leon Wilson's *Ruggles of Red Gap*.

Egbert G. Floud   Cousin of Effie Floud; wins the valet Marmaduke Ruggles from George Augustus Vane-Basingwell in a poker game and takes Ruggles to the United States in Harry Leon Wilson's *Ruggles of Red Gap*.

Dick Foley   Continental Detective Agency operative who answers the Continental Op's call for assistance and quits the job because of his scrupulous attitude in Dashiell Hammett's *Red Harvest*.

Edward (Eddie) Foley   Junior partner with Glymmer, Read who, when the firm becomes bankrupt, turns to alcohol in Nathan Asch's *The Office*.

Peter Nielson Foley   Ineffectual pacifist and author of an unfinished manuscript, "The Strange Captivity," about the charismatic influence of Charles Lawrence, in Wright Morris's *The Huge Season*.

Alwin Folger   Aristocratic neighbor of the Crooms; host of John Laskell as Laskell recuperates from scarlet fever in Lionel Trilling's *The Middle of the Journey*.

Eunice (Eunie) Folger   Nursemaid for the son of Nancy and Arthur Croom in Lionel Trilling's *The Middle of the Journey*.

Mrs. Folger   Wife of Alwin Folger; her interest in John Laskell's intellectual life facilitates his recovery from scarlet fever in Lionel Trilling's *The Middle of the Journey*.

Willard Follansbee   Deputy who hopes to become sheriff of Winfield County, Mississippi; pawn of corrupt forces in Elizabeth Spencer's *The Voice at the Back Door*.

Catherine Follet   Daughter of Jay and Mary Follet and younger sister of Rufus Follet in James Agee's *A Death in the Family*.

Jay Follet   Father of Rufus Follet and husband of Mary Follet; dies in an automobile accident while driving home to Knoxville, Tennessee, after an emergency visit to his father, who was wrongly believed to be dying in James Agee's *A Death in the Family*.

Mary Follet   Pious, prudish wife of Jay Follet and mother of Rufus Follet; widowed when her husband dies in an automobile accident in James Agee's *A Death in the Family*.

Ralph Follet   Younger brother of Jay Follet and uncle of Rufus Follet; undertaker and an alcoholic; phones Jay with the mistaken news that their father is dying and sets Jay upon the Journey that ends with his death in an automobile accident in James Agee's *A Death in the Family*.

Rufus Follet   Six-year-old son of Jay and Mary Follet; protagonist of James Agee's *A Death in the Family*.

Louie (Nifty) Fomorowski   Drug dealer in Chicago's Polish neighborhoods in Nelson Algren's *The Man with the Golden Arm*.

Fondriere   Corporal who refuses to use his authority to order Grace to return the pistol stolen from Richard Mast in James Jones's *The Pistol*.

Fonoo   See Donjalolo.

Jeanne-Marie Ignace Thérèse Cabarrus de Fontenay   French noblewoman and former wife of Jean-Lambert Tallien in H. L. Davis's *Harp of a Thousand Strings.*

Sally Forbes   Daughter of a university professor and friend of Lymie Peters and Hope Davison; loves Spud Latham in William Maxwell's *The Folded Leaf.*

Father Vincent Forbes   Freethinking Catholic priest who introduces Theron Ware to higher criticism; Ware later wrongly suspects Forbes of an affair with Celia Madden in Harold Frederic's *The Damnation of Theron Ware.*

Jack Ford   Sly, tight-fisted boy in Louisa May Alcott's *Little Men.*

Buck Forrester   Neighbor who helps the Baxters when Penny Baxter becomes ill in Marjorie Kinnan Rawlings's *The Yearling.*

Daniel (Danny) Forrester   Marine radio operator wounded at Saipan in Leon Uris's *Battle Cry.*

Captain Daniel Forrester   Pioneer and railroad builder who loses his fortune rather than sacrifice his honor; marries Marian Ormsby after saving her life in Willa Cather's *A Lost Lady.*

Edith Forrester   Niece of Major Roland Forrester, cousin of Captain Roland Forrester, and heir to her uncle's wealth in Robert Montgomery Bird's *Nick of the Woods.*

Fodder-wing Forrester   Crippled boy who raises wild animals and who is Jody Baxter's best friend in Marjorie Kinnan Rawlings's *The Yearling.*

Gene Forrester   Best friend of Finny and probably the cause of the accident that cripples him; narrator of John Knowles's *A Separate Peace.*

Lem Forrester   Drunken, mean neighbor of the Baxters; becomes Oliver Hutto's enemy in Marjorie Kinnan Rawlings's *The Yearling.*

Marian Ormsby (Maidy) Forrester   Wife of Daniel Forrester, who is twenty-five years her senior, and first lady of Sweet Water; turns to alcohol and other men because of her husband's illness; as a widow marries Henry Collins, a rich Englishman, in Willa Cather's *A Lost Lady.*

Captain Roland Forrester   Cousin of Edith Forrester and nephew of Major Roland Forrester; written out of his uncle's will when he fights on the American side in the Revolutionary War in Robert Montgomery Bird's *Nick of the Woods.*

Major Roland (Roly) Forrester   Former Tory and wealthy uncle of Captain Roland Forrester and Edith Forrester; wishes to keep his wealth from his nephew in Robert Montgomery Bird's *Nick of the Woods.*

Fort   See Luther.

Colonel Cassius (Old Cass) Fort   Lawyer and prominent politician who becomes Jeremiah Beaumont's mentor; Beaumont kills him for seducing Rachel Jordan in Robert Penn Warren's *World Enough and Time.*

Malory Forten   Conventional young man discovered to be the half brother of Melissa Paul just before his marriage to her in Jessie Redmon Fauset's *The Chinaberry Tree.*

Hugh Fortescue   British seaman and New World colonist whose settlement disappears without a trace, giving rise to the legend of the Lost Colony, in Thomas Wolfe's *The Hills Beyond.*

Brother Fortinbride   Methodist preacher who once fought with John Sartoris's regiment in William Faulkner's *The Unvanquished.*

Susan Fosdick   Elderly widow famous for her skill at visiting; although called a strange sail for her tendency to arrive without warning, her entertaining stories make her a welcome guest in Sarah Orne Jewett's *The County of the Pointed Firs.*

Dr. Foster   Minister of India and Walter Bridge in Evan Connell's *Mrs. Bridge.*

Silas Foster   Farmer and overseer of Blithedale in Nathaniel Hawthorne's *The Blithedale Romance.*

Stephen (Steve) Foster   Patriot frontiersman who teaches woodcraft and the art of war to the young Henry Lindsay in John Pendleton Kennedy's *Horse-Shoe Robinson.*

Tom Foster   Young man who comes to Winesburg from Cincinnati; in a drunken state he fabricates a sexual encounter between himself and Helen White in Sherwood Anderson's *Winesburg, Ohio.*

Fouché   French minister of police in H. L. Davis's *Harp of a Thousand Strings.*

Captain Walter Fountain   Ohio native who dies in the first Confederate advance; narrates part of Shelby Foote's *Shiloh.*

Erskine Fowler   Retired insurance company employee partly responsible for the accidental death of Tony Blake; murderer of Mabel Blake in Richard Wright's *Savage Holiday.*

Jeremiah (Jerry) Fowler   Young man bound for the Holland Patent to buy farmland; instead buys the papers of Mary Goodhill, whom he later marries; carpenter who builds locks on the Erie Canal in Walter D. Edmonds's *Erie Water.*

Mary Goodhill Fowler   Indentured servant redeemed by Jerry Fowler; Fowler's long-suffering wife in Walter D. Edmonds's *Erie Water.*

Madeline Fox   Graduate student in English who is engaged to Martin Arrowsmith until he meets Leora Tozer in Sinclair Lewis's *Arrowsmith.*

Mardou (Irene May) Fox Independent black woman, former mental patient, and lover of Leo Percepied in Jack Kerouac's *The Subterraneans;* also appears in *Book of Dreams.*

Frado See Alfrado.

Eunice Fraley Elderly, timid New England spinster tyrannized by her mother in Sarah Orne Jewett's *A Country Doctor.*

Frampton Goose Creek native who, demented, avenges his wife's death in William Gilmore Simms's *The Partisan.*

Lancelot (Lance) Frampton Youth who, following his mother's murder, joins Major Singleton's group of partisans and becomes Singleton's protégé in William Gilmore Simms's *The Partisan;* partisan lieutenant of Captain Porgy in *Woodcraft.*

Dolph Franc Chief of a corrupt police force in William Riley Burnett's *The Asphalt Jungle.*

Francie Friend who visits the narrator and her young writer-lover at Ambleside and takes the pair on a tour of the English countryside in Aline Bernstein's *The Journey Down.*

Francie Girlfriend of Henry Miller; enjoys describing her sexual experiences with other men; attempts to seduce her brother in Henry Miller's *Tropic of Capricorn.*

Mrs. Francis Companion to Harriot Fawcet in William Hill Brown's *The Power of Sympathy.*

Dominique Francon Independent misanthrope and Howard Roark's mistress in Ayn Rand's *The Fountainhead.*

Andre Franconi Syphilitic barber, reputed Lothario, and resident of the Glen Cove Apartments in Albert Halper's *Union Square.*

Rose Frank Hostess of a party in Paris which the Walkers and Aline Aldridge attend and where Aline meets Fred Grey, her future husband, in Sherwood Anderson's *Dark Laughter.*

Frankie Mildly retarded boy befriended by Doc; institutionalized following his theft of an expensive clock to give as a birthday gift to Doc in John Steinbeck's *Cannery Row.*

Frankie Friend of Harry Morgan; introduces Morgan to Mr. Sing in Ernest Hemingway's *To Have and Have Not.*

Amy Forrester Franklin Recent bride of Dr. Deane Franklin; leaves him because of his friendship with Ruth Holland in Susan Glaspell's *Fidelity.*

Benjamin Franklin American statesman and philosopher who provides the means for Thomas Paine to immigrate to America in Howard Fast's *Citizen Tom Paine.*

Benjamin Franklin American ambassador to France to whom Israel Potter delivers a message in Herman Melville's *Israel Potter.*

Dr. Deane Franklin Unconventional small-town physician who helps and defends Ruth Holland in Susan Glaspell's *Fidelity.*

Julia Franklin Replacement for Charlotte Temple in the affections of Jack Montraville and eventually his wife in Susanna Rowson's *Charlotte.*

Nathaniel T. (Nat) Franklin Union army colonel who dies on his front porch while watching young soldiers march off to war with Spain in Hervey Allen's *Action at Aquila.*

Tommy Franklin Resident of the Diamond County Home for the Aged; files peachstones into the shapes of small animals and baskets to sell at the annual fair; befriends Elizabeth Heinemann and escorts her to meals in John Updike's *The Poorhouse Fair.*

Don Franyo Priest-tutor of Rudolf Stanka; uncovers Stanka's gift of communion with birds in Louis Adamic's *Cradle of Life.*

Franz Tall Germanic domestic boy in Louisa May Alcott's *Little Men.*

John (Johnny) Fraser, Jr. Loyalist turned patriot who is wounded aboard the Bonhomme Richard in James Boyd's *Drums.*

Christian J. (Christie) Fraser Insurance salesman who loves both Catherine Conboy and Sylva Cope in Jessamyn West's *The Witch Diggers.*

John (Dadder) Fraser Scotch Presbyterian loyalist, well-to-do farmer, and father of Johnny Fraser in James Boyd's *Drums.*

Simon Frasier Black attorney who represents blacks in the police and magistrate courts of Charleston in DuBose Heyward's *Porgy.*

Stephen Frazer Friend of Felix Fay, whom Frazer introduces to atheist thought, in Floyd Dell's *Moon-Calf.*

Fred Name Holly Golightly gives to the otherwise unnamed young writer and narrator of Truman Capote's *Breakfast at Tiffany's.*

Freddy Dance-marathon contestant who is eliminated when his partner is revealed to be a minor who ran away from home in Horace McCoy's *They Shoot Horses, Don't They?*

Doris Frederic English teacher and lover of 'Bama Dillert in James Jones's *Some Came Running.*

Frederick (Frederico, Rico) Controversial poet and novelist; friend of Julia Ashton in H. D.'s *Bid Me to Live.*

Elsa Frederick Wife of Frederick in H. D.'s *Bid Me to Live.*

Mr. Freed Manager at the St. Mark's Hotel who gives Sam Spade information from the hotel registry about Brigid O'Shaughnessy in Dashiell Hammett's *The Maltese Falcon.*

Dave Freeland Husband of Felise Freeland and Harlem socialite in whose apartment the confrontation between John Bellew and Clare Kendry, which ends in Clare's death, occurs in Nella Larsen's *Passing.*

Felise Freeland Member of Harlem's black bourgeoisie, wife of Dave Freeland, and friend of Irene Redfield; hosts a party at which Clare Kendry falls to her death from a sixth-floor window in Nella Larsen's *Passing.*

Lucy Freeman See Lucy Freeman Sumner.

Ludie Freeman First and favorite husband of Berenice Sadie Brown in Carson McCullers's *The Member of the Wedding.*

Katherine (Kitty) Fremont Friend of Mark Parker, lover of Ari Ben Canaan, and surrogate mother of Karen Clement; American Christian nurse in post–World War II refugee centers and in Israel in Leon Uris's *Exodus.*

Ezra French Bidwell, Ohio, farmer who influences Hugh McVey's ideas for a mechanical cabbage patch in Sherwood Anderson's *Poor White.*

Guinevere (Gwen) French English teacher at Parkman College and thwarted lover of Dave Hirsh; edits his comic combat novel after his death in James Jones's *Some Came Running.*

Col. Henry French Civil War veteran who offends his southern neighbors by his color-blind attitudes in business in Charles W. Chesnutt's *The Colonel's Dream.*

Mary French Devoted radical who works as secretary to G. H. Barrow and provides a home for Ben Compton when he gets out of jail in John Dos Passos's *U.S.A.* trilogy.

Robert Ball French Poet and retired English teacher; father of Gwen French; amateur philosopher and drinker in James Jones's *Some Came Running.*

Fortune Friendly Gambler and preacher who drives for Daniel Harrow; buys the *Ella-Romeyn* when Harrow returns to farming in Walter D. Edmonds's *Rome Haul.*

N'Gana Frimbo Harvard-educated Harlem conjure man and secret lover of his landlady Martha Crouch; killed by Samuel Crouch in Rudolph Fisher's *The Conjure-Man Dies.*

Colonel Nathan (One-Eye) Frisbie Abolitionist, house burner, and commander of the Union gunboat *Starlight* in Shelby Foote's *Jordan County.*

Frisco See Francisco d'Anconia.

Ethan (Ethe) Frome New England farmer whose life is ruined by poverty and his sickly, malicious wife, Zenobia Frome, in Edith Wharton's *Ethan Frome.*

Zenobia Pierce (Zeena) Frome Shrewish, hypochondriacal wife and cousin of Ethan Frome in Edith Wharton's *Ethan Frome.*

Frony See Frony Gibson.

Mark Frost Poet who attends the yacht party in William Faulkner's *Mosquitoes.*

Martin Frost Private detective hired by Frederick Eichner to investigate Felix Treevly in Terry Southern's *Flash and Filigree.*

Captain Frounier Cursing, toothless, ninety-one-year-old owner of a fleet of sailing vessels in Haiti in Arna Wendell Bontemps's *Drums at Dusk.*

Joseph Frowenfeld Young American pharmacist who marries Clotilde Nancanou and whose liberal views are opposed by the old Louisiana society in George Washington Cable's *The Grandissimes.*

Indiana Frusk See Indiana Frusk Rolliver.

Thomas (Happy Tom) Fry Cripple aboard the *Fidde* in Herman Melville's *The Confidence-Man.*

John Fryer Master of HMS *Bounty* who treats the crew decently, but who is forced to join Captain Bligh in being set adrift after the rebellion in Charles Nordhoff and James Norman Hall's *Mutiny on the Bounty;* because of his strength and navigational skills, he is of great assistance while adrift at sea in *Men Against the Sea.*

Lois Fuchs Large, earthy woman from Louisiana who tells of her passionate affair with a boy in William Goyen's *In a Farther Country.*

Otto Fuchs Hired man of the Burdens; admired by Jim Burden in Willa Cather's *My Ántonia.*

Dolores de la Fuente (y Someruelos) Second wife of Anthony Adverse in Hervey Allen's *Anthony Adverse.*

Elizabeth (E. F.) Fuess Deceased girlfriend of John Laskell in Lionel Trilling's *The Middle of the Journey.*

Fulkerson Magazine sponsor who convinces Basil March to edit *Every Other Week* in William Dean Howells's *A Hazard of New Fortunes.*

Governor Alvin Tufts (Allie) Fuller Former trick bicycle rider and racer who rises to great wealth and prominence; in his dislike of Reds, he refuses to grant Sacco and Vanzetti a new trial, despite evidence that Webster Thayer, who presided at the earlier trial, had engaged in numerous improprieties in Upton Sinclair's *Boston.*

Furman Southern jail inmate and model of audacity to Dudley Osborn in Wright Morris's *My Uncle Dudley.*

Flora Furness Daughter of Lily Furness, cousin of Stephen Carver, and schoolmate of Jane Ward in Margaret Ayer Barnes's *Years of Grace* and *Wisdom's Gate.*

Lily Furness   Mother of Flora Furness; commits suicide when Albert Lancaster, the man she loves, marries Muriel Lester in Margaret Ayer Barnes's *Years of Grace*.

Agricola (Agricole) Fusilier   Creole uncle of Honoré Grandissime in George Washington Cable's *The Grandissimes*.

Nick Fuso   Young mechanic and upstairs tenant of Morris Bober in Bernard Malamud's *The Assistant*.

Gabriel (Gabou) Servant of Louis Desriviéres and lover of Youma, whom he fails to rescue from a burning house, in Lafcadio Hearn's *Youma.*

Gabriel See Gabriel Breaux.

Reverend Gabrielsen Preacher who advocates English services in the Norwegian Lutheran Church; presses Peder Holm to join the ministry in O. E. Rölvaag's *Peder Victorious.*

Aaron Gadd New England carpenter, missionary to the Sioux Indians in the Minnesota territory, and later a builder in St. Paul; husband of Selene Lanark in Sinclair Lewis's *The God-Seeker.*

Elijah Gadd Brother of Aaron Gadd and labor organizer in the Minnesota territory in Sinclair Lewis's *The God-Seeker.*

Selene Lanark Gadd See Selene Lanark.

Uriel Gadd New England farmer, Calvinist deacon, and father of Aaron and Elijah Gadd; helps slaves escape to Canada in Sinclair Lewis's *The God-Seeker.*

Errante Gaetano Sleeping cart driver whose failure to leave the road leads to General Marvin's order forbidding carts to enter Adano in John Hersey's *A Bell for Adano.*

Gaffett Old seafarer who tells Captain Littlepage about a city of ghosts near the North Pole in Sarah Orne Jewett's *The Country of the Pointed Firs.*

Désirée Gaillard Wife of Edward Cary; attacked and killed by Sherman's drunken marauders in Mary Johnston's *Cease Firing.*

Bull (Old Bull, Seflor Gahr-va) Gaines Cincinnati-born, sixty-year-old morphine addict living in Mexico City in Jack Kerouac's *Tristessa* and *Desolation Angels.*

Bill Gains Friend and heroin connection of William Lee in New York; later comes to Mexico City in William S. Burroughs's *Junkie;* also appears in *Naked Lunch* and *The Soft Machine.*

Neil Gaither Woman John Wickliff Shawnessy should marry but does not in Ross Lockridge, Jr.'s *Raintree County.*

Andrew (Andy, George Andrews, Miles-Away-Andrews) Gale, Jr. Grandson of Slovenian immigrant Anton Galé and contributor to liberal causes; killed gang-land style in Louis Adamic's *Grandsons.*

Andrew (Andy) Gale, Sr. Son of Anton Galé and father of Andy, Margaret, and Peter Gale; worker who becomes a middle-class salesman in Louis Adamic's *Grandsons.*

Anthony Adams (Tony) Gale Son of Mildred Adams Gale and Jack Gale in Louis Adamic's *Grandsons.*

Jack Gale Grandson of Anton Galé and son of Tony Gale; murdered because of his I. W. W. organizing activities in Louis Adamic's *Grandsons.*

Margaret Gale See Margaret Gale Stedman.

Mildred Adams Gale Wife of Jack Gale and mother of Anthony Adams Gale; supporter of liberal causes in Louis Adamic's *Grandsons.*

Peter (Jack McLeish) Gale Rootless grandson of Anton Galé; assumes the identity of Jack McLeish, a character in his proposed novel "Grandsons," in Louis Adamic's *Grandsons.*

Tony Gale Steelworker son of Anton Galé and father of Jack Gale in Louis Adamic's *Grandsons.*

Anton Galé   Slovenian immigrant who is killed in the Haymarket Riot; father of Andrew Gale, Sr., and Tony Gale; grandfather of Andy, Margaret, Peter, and Jack Gale in Louis Adamic's *Grandsons*.

Honor Gallagher   Best friend in childhood of Cress Delahanty in Jessamyn West's *Cress Delahanty*.

Jane Gallagher   Former neighbor and friend of Holden Caulfield; always kept her kings in the back row when playing checkers; Holden worries about her date with Ward Stradlater in J. D. Salinger's *The Catcher in the Rye*.

Roy Gallagher   Boston-Irish soldier who suffers a nervous breakdown when he hears of his wife's death in Norman Mailer's *The Naked and the Dead*.

Gallegos   Corrupt priest who is suspended by Bishop Latour in Willa Cather's *Death Comes for the Archbishop*.

Sedaya (Sede) Gallet   Cherokee Indian who betrays a rebellious tribesman in return for Crow Town's exemption from removal; later the wife of Ewen Warne in H. L. Davis's *Beulah Land*.

Ike Galovitch   Hardheaded Yugoslavian-American platoon guide who dislikes Robert E. Lee Prewitt in James Jones's *From Here to Eternity*.

John Galt   Brilliant research engineer for Twentieth Century Motor Company; organizes a strike against self-immolation in Ayn Rand's *Atlas Shrugged*.

Lucie Gamelon   Cousin of Christina Goering's governess and later companion of Christina; eventually lives with Arnold in Jane Bowles's *Two Serious Ladies*.

David Gamut   Psalm singer accompanying Duncan Heyward and the Munroe sisters in James Fenimore Cooper's *The Last of the Mohicans*.

Berryben Ganchion   See Berryben Starnes.

Boy Ganchion   A main voice/narrator of William Goyen's *The House of Breath*.

Christy Ganchion   Son of Granny Ganchion; fails to save his wife from drowning in William Goyen's *The House of Breath*.

Folner (Follie) Ganchion   Son of Granny Ganchion; runs away with a circus and later commits suicide in William Goyen's *The House of Breath*.

Hannah (Granny) Ganchion   Mother of Christy and Folner Ganchion; grandmother of Boy Ganchion and Berryben Starnes in William Goyen's *The House of Breath*.

Benjamin (Ben) Harrison Gant   Beloved older brother of Eugene Gant in Thomas Wolfe's *Look Homeward, Angel*; dies of pneumonia caused by years of neglect by his parsimonious parents in *Of Time and the River*.

Eliza E. Pentland Gant   Wife of Oliver Gant and mother of Eugene Gant; her fear of poverty and fervent belief in the work ethic ultimately destroy her family in Thomas Wolfe's *Look Homeward Angel* and *Of Time and the River*.

Eugene Gant   Shy, studious boy from a large, parsimonious North Carolina family; his youth and young manhood are chronicled in Thomas Wolfe's *Look Homeward, Angel* and *Of Time and the River*.

Oliver Gant   Unfaithful husband of Eliza Gant and father of Eugene Gant; drunken womanizer who dies of cancer in Thomas Wolfe's *Look Homeward, Angel*.

Elmer Gantry   Midwesterner who, after working as a revivalist, becomes a powerful, less-than-ethical Methodist minister in Sinclair Lewis's *Elmer Gantry;* radio minister with ties to various charitable organizations that employ Gideon Planish in *Gideon Planish*.

Mrs. Elmer Gantry   See Cleo Benham.

Mrs. Logan Gantry   Dress shop owner with great hopes for her son, Elmer Gantry, in Sinclair Lewis's *Elmer Gantry*.

Louis Garafolo   Old boxing manager of Lee Youngdahl in Mark Harris's *Wake Up, Stupid*.

Sir Philip Gardiner   Villain who is unsuccessful in his attempt to abduct Hope Leslie in Catharine Maria Sedgwick's *Hope Leslie*.

Jeff Gardner   Bowlegged thug employed by Shad O'Rory; enjoys beating Ned Beaumont in Dashiell Hammett's *The Glass Key*.

Adela Gareth   Mother of Owen Gareth and mistress of Poynton; attempts to enlist Fleda Vetch's assistance in maintaining control of the Poynton furnishings in Henry James's *The Spoils of Poynton*.

Owen Gareth   Weak-willed son of Adela Gareth; attracted to Fleda Vetch but marries Mona Brigstock in Henry James's *The Spoils of Poynton*.

Tony Garido   Cuban husband of Margo Dowling who drives her away with his abuse and yet periodically seeks her help in John Dos Passos's *U.S.A.* trilogy.

Vin Garl   Day-shift worker at the Past Bay Manufacturing Company factory; Finnish immigrant and former Wobbly who proposes the strike in Robert Cantwell's *The Land of Plenty*.

Mary Garland   Cousin of Sarah Hudson and fiancée of Roderick Hudson; loved by Rowland Mallet, Hudson's patron, in Henry James's *Roderick Hudson*.

George D. Garnett (Garnet) Southern planter opposed to slavery; buys slaves and lets them work for their freedom; expelled from the Mayfield Baptist Church for supporting Comfort Servosse's sabbath school for freedom at Warrington; attacked unsuccessfully by the Ku Klux Klan in Albion W. Tourgee's *A Fool's Errand.*

Louisa Garnett (Garnet) Daughter of George Garnett; her hair turns from brown to white as a result of the Ku Klux Klan attack on her home in Albion W. Tourgee's *A Fool's Errand.*

Pete Garolian Serbian proprietor of the Crystal Lunchroom in Albert Halper's *Union Square.*

Helmeth Garrett Engineer and self-made man; Olivia Lattimore's first romance and later her lover; alienated from Lattimore when she refuses to halt her stage career should they marry in Mary Austin's *A Woman of Genius.*

Joe Garrity High school track coach of Jack Duluoz in Jack Kerouac's *Maggie Cassidy.*

Marie Garson Dime-a-dance woman on whom Roy Earle becomes emotionally dependent in William Riley Burnett's *High Sierra.*

Nat Garth Feebleminded adopted son of Nellie Garth Goodwin; becomes a thief so he can join Nellie in Australia, only to die en route, in Charles Nordhoff and James Norman Hall's *Botany Bay.*

Nellie Garth See Nellie Garth Goodwin.

Georgia Garveli Daughter of Pop Garveli and friend of Jake Adams, whose car crashes with Georgia in it, in Herbert Simmons's *Corner Boy.*

Pop Garveli Father of Georgia Garveli and friend of Jake Adams; white grocery store owner who operates a store in St. Louis's black belt in Herbert Simmons's *Corner Boy.*

Richard Garvin Investor in Consolidated Tractions; driven to financial ruin and suicide by Eldon Parr in Winston Churchill's *The Inside of the Cup.*

Maria de las Garzas Loveliest woman in Hidalgo, but an outcast; loves Alejandro Castillo and is murdered by his wife in Josefina Niggli's *Mexican Village.*

Amos G. Gashwiler Storekeeper in Simsbury, Illinois, who promises to hold Merton Gill's job in case Merton does not succeed in Hollywood in Harry Leon Wilson's *Merton of the Movies.*

Captain Amos Gaskens Former plantation owner who leads a band of Tories in William Gilmore Simms's *The Partisan.*

Charles (Charlie) Gaston Son of a Confederate hero and husband of Sallie Worth; organizes the Red Shirts in opposition to the Reconstruction government and is elected governor of North Carolina in Thomas Dixon's *The Leopard's Spots.*

Nelson (Nelse) Gaston Faithful slave of the Gastons; refuses to Join the Union League in Thomas Dixon's *The Leopard's Spots.*

Ben Gately Graduate of the United States Military Academy and commander of the Leper Colony in the 918th Bomb Group in Beirne Lay, Jr., and Sy Bartlett's *Twelve O'Clock High!*

Dr. Gates Former Confederate doctor who also practiced among the Northerners and thought secession was folly; cares for Comfort Servosse during Servosse's final illness in Albion W. Tourgee's *A Fool's Errand.*

General Horatio Gates Commander of the American forces at the Battle of Camden in William Gilmore Simms's *The Partisan.*

Jo Gates Formerly married girlfriend of the narrator in Edmund Wilson's *Memoirs of Hecate County.*

Jay (James Gatz) Gatsby Man of mysterious background who hosts lavish parties on Long Island in the 1920s; seeks to recover Daisy Buchanan's love in F. Scott Fitzgerald's *The Great Gatsby.*

Henry C. Gatz Father of James Gatz in F. Scott Fitzgerald's *The Great Gatsby.*

James Gatz See Jay Gatsby.

Adam Gaudylock Backwoodsman, friend of Lewis Rand, and innocent participant in a plan to settle the West in Mary Johnston's *Lewis Rand.*

Denny Gayde Escaped convict aided by the child Hagar Ashendyne; becomes a Socialist speaker in Mary Johnston's *Hagar.*

Squire Gaylord Publisher of the Free Press and father of Marcia Gaylord Hubbard in William Dean Howells's *A Modern Instance.*

Thomas (Tom) Gaylord Friend of Hilary and Austen Vane; lumber executive and political worker in Winston Churchill's *Mr. Crewe's Career.*

William (Bill) Gaylord American infantry lieutenant killed in action in World War II in Martha Gellhorn's *Wine of Astonishment.*

Major Gazaway Politician and soldier in John Carter's regiment; his connections keep him ahead of Edward Colburne despite Gazaway's obvious cowardice and ineptness at command in John William DeForest's *Miss Ravenel's Conversion from Secession to Loyalty.*

Charlie Geary Self-serving, manipulative Darwinian who strips Vandover of his inheritance in Frank Norris's *Vandover and the Brute.*

Orlando Geary   Early settler and deputy sheriff in Shoestring Valley, Oregon, in H. L. Davis's *Honey in the Horn*.

Reb Gedaliya   Ritual slaughterer, cabalist, and follower of Sabbatai Zevi; Satan figure who leads the townspeople of Goray into evil; seduces and then marries Rechele Babad; finally leaves Goray and turns apostate in Isaac Bashevis Singer's *Satan in Goray*.

Abigail (Aunt Abigail) Geddy   Member of the only colored family in Ironside; independent woman proud of her Indian blood and pragmatic about killing chickens in Ellen Glasgow's *Vein of Iron*.

Hans von Gehring   Facially scarred roomer at Rosa Reichl's boardinghouse; student on leave from Heidelberg University in Katherine Anne Porter's *The Leaning Tower*.

Arthur Gwynn Geiger   Pornography dealer and blackmailer who is murdered in Raymond Chandler's *The Big Sleep*.

Genesis   Black handyman of the Baxters; unintentionally but effectively deflates William Baxter's ego in Booth Tarkington's *Seventeen*.

Mr. Genesis   Father of Genesis; whittles toys for Jane Baxter in Booth Tarkington's *Seventeen*.

Genevieve   Girlfriend of Joe Fleming, with whom she pleads to give up boxing, in Jack London's *The Game*.

Genslinger   Newspaper editor loyal to railroad interests who reveals Magnus Derrick's resort to bribery as a means of reducing the rates for shipping wheat in Frank Norris's *The Octopus*.

Sarah Gentles   Wife of Van Harrington in Robert Herrick's *The Memoirs of an American Citizen*.

George III   King of England who hires Israel Potter as a gardener in Herman Melville's *Israel Potter*.

Tobey George   Army friend of Marcus Macauley; visits the Macauley family following Marcus's death in William Saroyan's *The Human Comedy*.

Georgia   Cousin of Daniel Verger, with whom she has an affair, in John Clellon Holmes's *Go*.

Georgiana   Girlfriend of Henry Miller known for having changed her name and for creating her own identity in Henry Miller's *Tropic of Capricorn*.

Letty Pace Gerald   Childhood sweetheart and later wife of Lester Kane, who cannot love her as he loved Jennie Gerhardt, in Theodore Dreiser's *Jennie Gerhardt*.

Geraldine   Girlfriend of Alva; becomes pregnant and gives birth to their illegitimate, deformed child in Wallace Thurman's *The Blacker the Berry*.

Gerard   Early lover of Lillian; frightened by her power in Anaïs Nin's *Ladders to Fire*.

Sophie Geratis   Greek chambermaid in a luxury hotel with whom Augie March has a brief affair during his period as a labor organizer for the CIO in Saul Bellow's *The Adventures of Augie March*.

Lieutenant David Gerhardt   Handsome officer from New York and friend of Claude Wheeler; respected by fellow soldiers because he could have been in the military band but chose to serve in the infantry in Willa Cather's *One of Ours*.

Genevieve (Jennie, Mrs. J. G. Stover) Gerhardt   Lover of George Brander, by whom she has a child; nurse and lover of Lester Kane; unwed mother who tries to improve her life but suffers many setbacks in Theodore Dreiser's *Jennie Gerhardt*.

Joe (Joey) Gerhardt   Childhood friend of Henry Miller; considered a gentleman for having beaten up another youth in Henry Miller's *Tropic of Capricorn*.

William Gerhardt   Father of Jennie Gerhardt, with whom he lives after his wife dies, in Theodore Dreiser's *Jennie Gerhardt*.

Germaine   Prostitute with gold teeth who becomes a friend of Henry Miller in Henry Miller's *Tropic of Cancer*.

Emmeline Gerrish   Childhood friend of Annie Kilburn and proud wife of William Gerrish in William Dean Howells's *Annie Kilburn*.

William B. (Bill) Gerrish   Successful businessman who leads the revolt against Julius W. Peck in William Dean Howells's *Annie Kilburn*.

George Gerry   Handsome New England lawyer; after being angered by Miss Nan Prince's rejection of his marriage proposal, he admires the dedication that leads her to choose a career in medicine; becomes more serious as a result of his relationship with Nan in Sarah Orne Jewett's *A Country Doctor*.

Gerta   Girlfriend of Jasper Ammen in Conrad Aiken's *King Coffin*.

Lucy Gessler   Neighbor of Mildred Pierce and bartender in Mildred's restaurant in James M. Cain's *Mildred Pierce*.

Sister Geter   Pentecostal Fire Baptized Believer who tries to evangelize Ray, Banjo, and the other expatriates in Claude McKay's *Banjo*.

Adolphus Asher Ghoulens   See Doctor Sax.

Cavaliere Giuseppino Giacosa   Former secret lover of Mrs. Light and father, by her, of Christina Light; escorts Christina and Mrs. Light to the watering-places of Europe in Henry James's *Roderick Hudson*.

Mr. Giardineri   Owner of the Aaron Burr, a local college restaurant; pretends to have contacts with organized crime concerning the bribe money Raymond Blent took to lose a football game in Howard Nemerov's *The Homecoming Game.*

Miss Dorothy Gibbs   Operator of the Female Institute in Thomas Bailey Aldrich's *The Story of a Bad Boy.*

Dilsey Gibson   Cook for the Compsons; married to Roskus Gibson and the mother of Frony, T. P., and Versh Gibson in William Faulkner's *The Sound and the Fury.*

Fannie Gibson   See Fannie Hamilton.

Frony Gibson   Daughter of Dilsey and Roskus Gibson; sister of T. P. and Versh Gibson in William Faulkner's *The Sound and the Fury.*

Jim Gibson   Journeyman harnessmaker who helps his employer Joseph Wainsworth improve his business; murdered by Wainsworth when he publicly humiliates Wainsworth for his old-fashioned business ways in Sherwood Anderson's *Poor White.*

Roskus Gibson   Husband of Dilsey; father of Frony, T. P., and Versh Gibson in William Faulkner's *The Sound and the Fury.*

T. P. Gibson   Son of Dilsey and Roskus Gibson; brother of Frony and Versh Gibson in William Faulkner's *The Sound and the Fury.*

Versh Gibson   Son of Dilsey and Roskus Gibson, brother of Frony and T. P. Gibson in William Faulkner's *The Sound and the Fury.*

Gignoux   Spy and traitor in Winston Churchill's *The Crossing.*

Gil   Proprietor of and bartender at Gil's Tavern who is able to place George Stroud with Pauline Delos on the day of her murder in Kenneth Fearing's *The Big Clock.*

Gloria Gilbert   See Gloria Gilbert Patch.

Ted Gilbert   Americanized Norwegian teacher who shocks Beret Holm by producing a play in O. E. Rölvaag's *Peder Victorious.*

Grace Giles   Black student at the University of Southern California; friendly toward Emma Lou Morgan but not popular with the other students in Wallace Thurman's *The Blacker the Berry.*

Jimmie Giles   Cheerful young porter who befriends Matthew Towns and is lynched after being accused of attacking a white woman in W. E. B. Du Bois's *Dark Princess.*

Colonel Barry Fitzgerald Macartney Gilfillan   British officer in James Kirke Paulding's *The Dutchman's Fireside.*

Father (Gilly) Gilhooley   Priest of the Lonigans in James T. Farrell's *Young Lonigan;* builds a new church as blacks move into the South Chicago neighborhood in *The Young Manhood of Studs Lonigan* and *Judgment Day.*

Merton (Clifford Armytage) Gill   Small-town store clerk who becomes a Hollywood film actor under the name of Clifford Armytage in Harry Leon Wilson's *Merton of the Movies.*

Miss Gillespie   Cold, defiant school principal who snubs Matthew Towns because he is a Pullman porter in W. E. B. Du Bois's *Dark Princess.*

Joe (Yaphank) Gilligan   Army private who helps care for Donald Mahon in William Faulkner's *Soldiers' Pay.*

Hayden Gillis   Representative of the governor of the Dakota Territory; consults with Blue about Hard Times in E. L. Doctorow's *Welcome to Hard Times.*

John Gilson   Schoolboy who, in order to impress his teacher, pretends to be Fyodor Dostoyevski's character Raskolnikov in Nathanael West's *The Dream Life of Balso Snell.*

Ginette   Prostitute involved with Fillmore; becomes pregnant and has a venereal disease in Henry Miller's *Tropic of Cancer.*

Gin-head Susy (Susy)   Woman with a "yellow complex" who searches for a lover; dispenses free gin at socials she gives in Brooklyn; Zeddy Plummer later becomes her live-in lover in Claude McKay's *Home to Harlem.*

Ginny   Roommate of Louella and volunteer Red Cross worker in John Horne Burns's *The Gallery.*

Joe Ginotta   Brother of Pete Ginotta; bootlegger and restaurant manager in William Faulkner's *Mosquitoes* and *Pylon.*

Pete Ginotta   Brother of Joe Ginotta; boyfriend of Jenny Steinbauer, with whom he attends the yacht party, in William Faulkner's *Mosquitoes;* also appears in *Pylon.*

Giovanelli   Handsome Italian who declares the innocence of his companion Daisy Miller following her death in Henry James's *Daisy Miller.*

Giovanni   Italian lover of David and rival of Hella in James Baldwin's *Giovanni's Room.*

Zito Giovanni   Former fascist informer who retains his position as town usher and becomes an assistant to Major Joppolo in John Hersey's *A Bell for Adano.*

Girard Girard   Billionaire notorious for being unfaithful to his wife; becomes enamored of Malcolm and wants to become his substitute father in James Purdy's *Malcolm.*

Madame (Doddy) Girard   Wife of Girard Girard; somewhat mad, she becomes obsessively infatuated with Malcolm and nurses him on his deathbed in James Purdy's *Malcolm.*

Christopher Gist   Indian agent who fails to understand why the Catawba warriors leave Braddock's camp in Mary Lee Settle's *O Beulah Land*.

Giulia   Young Italian woman who falls in love with an American captain and agrees to sleep with him on the night he must leave for the front in John Horne Burns's *The Gallery*.

Uncle Dan Givens   Notorious teller of tall tales about his past in Cudge Windsor's pool hall in Langston Hughes's *Not Without Laughter*.

Helen Givens   See Helen Givens Fisher.

Reverend Henry Givens   Former Ku Klux Klansman, now Imperial Grand Wizard of the Knights of Nordica; discovered to have black ancestors in George S. Schuyler's *Black No More*.

James Callowhill Gladwin   Spokesman for Masonry on the frontier in Hervey Allen's *Bedford Village*.

Gladys   Estranged wife of Cross Damon; refuses to grant him a divorce; demands that he borrow $800 and give her the title to the house and car in Richard Wright's *The Outsider*.

Gladys   Girlfriend of Fish Tucker; dies in a fire at the Grove in Richard Wright's *The Long Dream*.

Aunt Gladys   Newark relative with whom Neil Klugman lives in Philip Roth's *Goodbye, Columbus*.

E. M. Glavis   Husband of Ethel McCarthy Glavis in Oscar Micheaux's *The Homesteader*.

Ethel McCarthy Glavis   Sister of Orlean McCarthy; sides with their father, Newton Justine McCarthy, against Jean Baptiste in Oscar Micheaux's *The Homesteader*.

Dorothea Glendinning   Sister of Pierre Glendinning II; gives a portrait of him as a young man to Pierre Glendinning III in Herman Melville's *Pierre*.

Mary Glendinning   Wife of Pierre Glendinning II and mother of Pierre Glendinning III; disowns her son and makes Glendinning Stanly the beneficiary of her estate in Herman Melville's *Pierre*.

Pierre Glendinning (I)   Father of Pierre Glendinning II and horse-loving general in Herman Melville's *Pierre*.

Pierre Glendinning (II)   Father of Pierre Glendinning III and apparently the father of Isabel Banford in Herman Melville's *Pierre*.

Pierre Glendinning (III)   Son of Mary and Pierre Glendinning II; by pretending to be the husband of Isabel Banford, apparently his half sister, he causes the death of himself and others in Herman Melville's *Pierre*.

Nelly Glentworth   Nineteen-year-old engaged woman loved by the adolescent Tom Bailey in Thomas Bailey Aldrich's *The Story of a Bad Boy*.

Israel Glickstein   Brother of Sammy Glick; unlike his sibling, Israel observes the traditions of the Jewish faith in Budd Schulberg's *What Makes Sammy Run?*

Sammy (Sammele Glickstein) Glick   Ruthlessly ambitious copyboy who rises to the position of production chief of a major Hollywood studio in Budd Schulberg's *What Makes Sammy Run?*

Yuri Gligoric   Brash young poet and sexual rival of Leo Percepied in Jack Kerouac's *The Subterraneans*.

Gloriani   American sculptor of European extraction; member of the artistic fraternity in Rome and commentator on Roderick Hudson's sculptures in Henry James's *Roderick Hudson*.

Glover   Harley College student and friend of Edward Walcott in Nathaniel Hawthorne's *Fanshawe*.

Glycerium   Fifteen-year-old sister of Chrysis; falls in love with Pamphilus; before the question of their marriage is resolved, she dies in childbirth in Thornton Wilder's *The Woman of Andros*.

John T. Glymmer   Forceful senior partner of Glymmer, Read and former Secretary of the Treasury of the United States in Nathan Asch's *The Office*.

Goat   Young man with whom Salome Musgrove conspires to kill her stepdaughter Rosamond in Eudora Welty's *The Robber Bridegroom*.

God   The burning bush, Voice, Lord, pillar of cloud, and pillar of fire that guides Moses in Zora Neale Hurston's *Moses, Man of the Mountain*.

Louisa Goddard   Wealthy and frugal intellectual loved by Marmaduke Littlepage, whose brother, Virginius Littlepage, she has loved for more than thirty years, in Ellen Glasgow's *They Stooped to Folly*.

Michael Godfrey   Student debtor who tutors Amber St. Clare in upper-class speech and helps her escape from the criminal environment of Black Jack Mallard and Mother Red Cap in Kathleen Winsor's *Forever Amber*.

Gaston Godin   Bachelor professor of French at Beardsley College, friend of Humbert Humbert, and fancier of young boys; finds a home for Humbert and Dolores Haze near Beardsley School in Vladimir Nabokov's *Lolita*.

Reverend Marcus Augustus Godley   Bethel Church minister whose horse loses an unofficial race with Jess Birdwell's horse in Jessamyn West's *The Friendly Persuasion*.

Christina Goering   Friend of Frieda Copperfield and, for a while, lover of Andrew McClane in Jane Bowles's *Two Serious Ladies*.

Allan Gold Schoolmaster and scout for General Jackson; wounded in the battle at Gaines's Mill; transformed into a fierce warrior by action at Sharpsburg; appears in Mary Johnston's *The Long Roll* and *Cease Firing*.

Esther Gold Sister of Michael Gold; killed by a truck in New York's Lower East Side in Michael Gold's *Jews without Money*.

Herman Gold Rumanian-born father of Michael Gold; owns a suspender shop, but is reduced to painting houses and finally to peddling bananas in New York's Lower East Side in Michael Gold's *Jews without Money*.

Katie Gold Hungarian-born mother of Michael Gold in Michael Gold's *Jews Without Money*.

Michael (Mikey) Gold Jewish narrator who tells of his family's life in New York's Lower East Side in Michael Gold's *Jews without Money*.

Rosalie Goldbaum Naive young woman to whom Sammy Glick proposes in New York and then abandons when he moves to Hollywood in Budd Schulberg's *What Makes Sammy Run?*

Alvah Goldbook Poet and friend of Ray Smith; author of the poem "Wail" in Jack Kerouac's *The Dharma Bums*.

Laura (Daphne Fountain, Vivi Lamar, Diana Lord) Golden Successful actress who threatens John Wickliff Shawnessy's idealism in Ross Lockridge, Jr.'s *Raintree County*.

Dave Goldman Jewish childhood friend of Phil Green, recently discharged from the army; becomes the sounding board for Green's experiences and frustrations in Laura Z. Hobson's *Gentleman's Agreement*.

Sidney Jerome (Sid) Goldman Hard-hitting Jewish first baseman for the New York Mammoths in Mark Harris's *The Southpaw, Bang the Drum Slowly, A Ticket for a Seamstitch*, and *It Looked Like For Ever*.

Goldstein Broadway producer of lavish spectacles; loves Delia Poole in Janet Flanner's *The Cubical City*.

Joey Goldstein Jewish-American soldier in Norman Mailer's *The Naked and the Dead*.

Maxine Goldstein Former girlfriend of Jake Adams; seeks fame as a dancer in Herbert Simmons's *Corner Boy*.

Sandy Goldstone Son of the owner of Lamm's department store and suitor of Marjorie Morningstar in Herman Wouk's *Marjorie Morningstar*.

Doc Golightly Horse doctor from Tulip, Texas; took in Lulamae Barnes and her brother, Fred, as children and married the fourteen-year-old girl in Truman Capote's *Breakfast at Tiffany's*.

Holiday (Holly, Lulamae Barnes) Golightly Nineteen-year-old girl about town living in New York in the 1940s; married to Doc Golightly in Tulip, Texas, when she was fourteen in Truman Capote's *Breakfast at Tiffany's*.

Comrade General Golz (Hotze) Officer who orders Robert Jordan to blow up a bridge in Ernest Hemingway's *For Whom the Bell Tolls*.

John Golz Clean-cut young writer; downstairs neighbor and friend of Mardou Fox in Jack Kerouac's *The Subterraneans*.

Joseph (Joe, Spanish) Gomez Marine troublemaker who dies heroically at Saipan in Leon Uris's *Battle Cry*.

Captain Rogelio Gomez Republican army officer who escorts Andrés through the Republican lines in Ernest Hemingway's *For Whom the Bell Tolls*.

Goneril Vain and apparently deranged woman whose husband, John Ringman, leaves her in Herman Melville's *The Confidence-Man*.

Pepe Gonzales Clever jokester and friend of Bob Webster; one of his pranks settles a longstanding feud with a neighboring village in Josefina Niggli's *Mexican Village*.

Agnes Gooch Prim secretary who, under the influence of Mame Dennis, becomes pregnant; marries one of Patrick Dennis's schoolmasters moments before her baby is born in Patrick Dennis's *Auntie Mame*.

Eunice Goode Alcoholic expatriate and Nelson Dyar's sexual rival in Paul Bowles's *Let It Come Down*.

Mary Goodhill See Mary Goodhill Fowler.

Jim Goodhue Dispossessed Ohio farmer who befriends Roy Earle in William Riley Burnett's *High Sierra*.

Velma Goodhue Clubfooted woman in William Riley Burnett's *High Sierra*.

Goodman Son-in-law of Zuckor and minor employee of Glymmer, Read in Nathan Asch's *The Office*.

Francis (Frank) Goodman Cosmopolitan who encounters Mark Winsome, Egbert, and William Cream, among others, in Herman Melville's *The Confidence-Man*.

Lyra Goodman See Lyra Goodman Wilmington.

Mr. Goodman Unscrupulous secretary of Sebastian Knight; writes a biography of his former employer after Knight's death in Vladimir Nabokov's *The Real Life of Sebastian Knight*.

Washington Goodspeed Northern congressman with whom Hesden Le Moyne discusses the need for federal aid to local schools and other educational projects in Albion W. Tourgee's *Bricks Without Straw*.

Goodwell   Friend of Wellingborough Redburn; tries to care for Harry Bolton in New York in Herman Melville's *Redburn*.

Bella Goodwin   First wife of Dan Goodwin; though a free person, accompanies her convict husband to Australia; dies as they escape the penal colony in Charles Nordhoff and James Norman Hall's *Botany Bay*.

Dan Goodwin   English smuggler imprisoned in Australia; after his first wife dies and after he returns to England, he marries Nellie Garth, whereupon they immigrate to America, in Charles Nordhoff and James Norman Hall's *Botany Bay*.

Lee Goodwin   Bootlegger who is lynched in William Faulkner's *Sanctuary*.

Lewis (Marcus Burchard, Lew, Pinkey) Goodwin   Older brother of Morton Goodwin; outlaw believed to be dead but actually living as Burchard, a local sheriff, and Pinkey, a notorious desperado, in Edward Eggleston's *The Circuit Rider*.

Morton (Mort) Goodwin   Rough southern Ohio youth who, following his conversion to Methodism and subsequent rejection as a suitor by Patty Lumsden, becomes a circuit rider in Edward Eggleston's *The Circuit Rider*.

Nellie Garth Goodwin   Widowed owner of a small English farm who is sent to Australia for having harbored highwayman Tom Oakley; after escaping from the penal colony, she marries Dan Goodwin, with whom she immigrates to America, in Charles Nordhoff and James Norman Hall's *Botany Bay*.

Caspar Goodwood   Resolute American suitor of Isabel Archer in Henry James's *The Portrait of a Lady*.

Brother Joe C. Goodyhay   Minister in William Faulkner's *The Mansion*.

Goosey   Flute player who plays jazz with Banjo in Claude McKay's *Banjo*.

Gordon   Sculptor who attends the yacht party in William Faulkner's *Mosquitoes*.

Aunt Katy Gordon   See Aunt Katy.

Cora Gordon   See Cora Gordon Stewart.

Harry Gordon   Half brother of Nina and Tom Gordon and husband of Lisette Gordon; quadroon manager of Canema plantation who, inspired by Dred Vesey, flees the plantation for the Dismal Swamp and joins Edward Clayton as a free man in Canada in Harriet Beecher Stowe's *Dred*.

Helen Gordon   Unhappy wife of Richard Gordon in Ernest Hemingway's *To Have and Have Not*.

Jeff Gordon   Wealthy businessman and friend and lover of Louise Davis in George Wylie Henderson's *Jule*.

John Gordon   Uncle of Nina Gordon and owner of the plantation neighboring Canema; aids an indigent white family who are squatters on his land in Harriet Beecher Stowe's *Dred*.

Lisette Gordon   Wife of Harry Gordon; bought by Nina Gordon to protect Lisette from Tom Gordon's lecherous pursuit in Harriet Beecher Stowe's *Dred*.

Nina Gordon   Vivacious owner of Canema plantation and fiancée of Edward Clayton; undergoes conversion to Christianity and abolitionism in Harriet Beecher Stowe's *Dred*.

Richard (Dick) Gordon   Writer in Ernest Hemingway's *To Have and Have Not*.

Thomas (Tom) Gordon   Dissolute brother of Nina Gordon; inherits Canema plantation and begins leading lynch mobs that attack Edward Clayton and kill Dred Vesey in Harriet Beeher Stowe's *Dred*.

Hermann Wilhelm Göring   Nazi Reichminister who forces Johannes Robin to give his wealth to the Nazis; makes a deal with Lanny Budd for the release of Freddi Robin from Dachau in Upton Sinclair's *Dragon's Teeth*.

Dennis P. (Dinny) Gorman   Supporter of the Democratic Party in James T. Farrell's *Young Lonigan*; influential judge and member of the Order of Christopher in *The Young Manhood of Studs Lonigan* and *Judgment Day*.

Levi Gorringe   Lawyer and Methodist church trustee who befriends Alice Ware in Harold Frederic's *The Damnation of Theron Ware*.

Bill Gorton   Friend of Jake Barnes; accompanies Barnes on a trip to Spain in Ernest Hemingway's *The Sun Also Rises*.

Restore Gosling   Witness against Koningsmarke in James Kirke Paulding's *Koningsmarke*.

Maria Gostrey   Friend and confidante of Lambert Strether, with whom she ultimately falls in love; friend of Madame de Vionnet in Henry James's *The Ambassadors*.

August (Auggie) Gottlieb   Newspaperboy and leader of the neighborhood gang in William Saroyan's *The Human Comedy*.

Professor Max Gottlieb   Medical school bacteriology professor who is dismissed for his eccentric ideas but who later becomes director of the McGurk Institute of Biology in Sinclair Lewis's *Arrowsmith*.

Governor   Amateur naturalist and antiquarian; French and German cosmopolite who is the godfather and traveling companion of the Chatelaine in Henry Blake Fuller's *The Chatelaine of La Trinité*.

Governor   Governor of an unnamed state who impregnates Lily Shane but will not marry her in Louis Bromfield's *The Green Bay Tree.*

Harmon Gow   Former stage driver who tells the narrator part of Ethan Frome's story in Edith Wharton's *Ethan Frome.*

Judge James Bartholomew Gowan   Judge who serves as an authority figure for the young Ellen Chesser in Elizabeth Madox Roberts's *The Time of Man.*

Luke Gowan   See Luther Dade Eustis.

Bilbo Gowrie   Son of Nub Gowrie and twin of Vardaman Gowrie in William Faulkner's *Intruder in the Dust.*

Bryan Gowrie   Son of Nub Gowrie in William Faulkner's *Intruder in the Dust.*

Crawford Gowrie   Son of Nub Gowrie; military deserter who murders his brother Vinson Gowrie and Jake Montgomery in William Faulkner's *Intruder in the Dust.*

N. B. Forrest Gowrie   Son of Nub Gowrie in William Faulkner's *Intruder in the Dust.*

Nub Gowrie   Father of six sons and bootlegger in William Faulkner's *Intruder in the Dust, The Town,* and *The Mansion.*

Vardaman Gowrie   Son of Nub Gowrie and twin of Bilbo Gowrie in William Faulkner's *Intruder in the Dust.*

Vinson Gowrie   Youngest son of Nub Gowrie; murdered by his brother Crawford Gowrie in William Faulkner's *Intruder in the Dust.*

Dr. Frederika Gozar   Principal of Lincoln Elementary School and mentor of child-genius Barry Rudd; resists the bribes and seductive reasoning of Wissey Jones in an attempt to make Barry one of his specimens in John Hersey's *The Child Buyer.*

Grace   Soldier who fights for the pistol that Richard Mast possesses in James Jones's *The Pistol.*

Grace   Beautiful young nurse for Dr. Angelo; comes to the fair to meet her boyfriend and another couple; all four sneak up to the sick ward to deliver candies to the patients in John Updike's *The Poorhouse Fair.*

Mr. Gracie   Harvard undergraduate and friend of Henry Burrage in Henry James's *The Bostonians.*

Grady   Newspaper reporter in William Faulkner's *Pylon.*

Dr. Graf   Attending physician of John Laskell in Lionel Trilling's *The Middle of the Journey.*

Stanley Graff   Realtor with George Babbitt's agency; fired for dishonesty in Sinclair Lewis's *Babbitt.*

Grafton   Former lover of Delia Poole in Janet Flanner's *The Cubical City.*

Charles Gragnon   General against whom Stefan and others mutiny in William Faulkner's *A Fable.*

Alexander Graham   See John Bailey.

Eustace Graham   District attorney in William Faulkner's *Sartoris (Flags in the Dust)* and *Sanctuary.*

Imogene Graham   Protégée of Evalina Bowen and fiancée of Theodore Colville in William Dean Howells's *Indian Summer.*

Mr. Graham   Chairman of the Republican County Central Committee and one of the white guests at Sara Andrews Towns's dinner party in W. E. B. Du Bois's *Dark Princess.*

Mrs. Graham   Elderly New England widow whose wisdom and kindness make her a favorite confidante of both Dr. John Leslie and Nan Prince in Sarah Orne Jewett's *A Country Doctor.*

Mrs. Graham   Mother of Imogene Graham; requests that Imogene be released from her engagement to Theodore Colville in William Dean Howell's *Indian Summer.*

Gran Boz (La Grand' Bosse, Louis Caddo, Louis Cadeau, Ole Big Hump)   Humpbacked river pirate and trader who shelters Jeremiah and Rachel Beaumont after they escape from jail in Robert Penn Warren's *World Enough and Time.*

Gran Maestro (Grand Master)   Italian friend of Richard Cantwell; maitre d'hotel at the Gritti Palace in Ernest Hemingway's *Across the River and into the Trees.*

Julia Granby   Society friend of Eliza Wharton in Hannah Webster Foster's *The Coquette.*

Guy Grand   Eccentric billionaire who amuses himself by paying large sums of money for people to degrade themselves in Terry Southern's *The Magic Christian.*

Achille Grandissime   Cousin of Honoré Grandissime in George Washington Cable's *The Grandissimes.*

Honoré Grandissime   Member of the Creole aristocracy and head of the Grandissimes; marries Aurora Nancanou in George Washington Cable's *The Grandissimes.*

Honoré Grandissime f.m.c   Quadroon half brother of Honoré Grandissime; landlord who commits suicide because Palmyre la Philosophe refuses to marry him in George Washington Cable's *The Grandissimes.*

Sylvestre Grandissime   Nephew of Agricola Fusilier, from whom Grandissime is saved from dueling, in George Washington Cable's *The Grandissimes.*

Madame Grandoni   Friend and neighbor of Augusta Blanchard, friend of Mrs. Light and Christina Light, and confidante of Rowland Mallet in Henry James's *Roderick Hudson*.

Granger   Leader of a group of underground intellectuals who have memorized great works of literature in order to preserve them in a bookless society in Ray Bradbury's *Fahrenheit 451*.

Emmeline Grangerford   Deceased daughter of Colonel Grangerford; author of "Ode to Stephen Dowling Bots, Dec'd" in Samuel Langhorne Clemens's *Adventures of Huckleberry Finn*.

Colonel Saul Grangerford   Head of the Grangerford family that is feuding with the Shepherdsons; is killed in a battle with them in Samuel Langhorne Clemens's *Adventures of Huckleberry Finn*.

Sophia Grangerford   Daughter of Colonel Grangerford; elopes with Harney Shepherdson, thus precipitating a deadly battle between the Grangerfords and Shepherdsons, in Samuel Langhorne Clemens's *Adventures of Huckleberry Finn*.

Old Grannis   Elderly man who falls in love with Miss Baker in Frank Norris's *McTeague*.

Granny   Mother-in-law of Reb Zeydel Ber and grandmother figure to Rechele Babad; superstitious old woman whose stories of witches, goblins, and demons and whose death on the eve of Yom Kippur negatively influence the impressionable and epileptic Rechele in Isaac Bashevis Singer's *Satan in Goray*.

Granny   Deceased grandmother who had a profound influence on Lutie Johnson in Ann Petry's *The Street*.

S. Granquist   Accomplice of Gerry Kells; accused of murdering John Bellmann, whom she had tried to blackmail, in Paul Cain's *Fast One*.

Louisa Grant   Friend of Elizabeth Temple in James Fenimore Cooper's *The Pioneers*.

Phebe Grant   Light-skinned mulatto who refuses to pass for white; becomes the loyal wife of Christopher Cary, Jr., in Jessie Fauset's *Comedy, American Style*.

Bud Grantham   Father of Bella Grantham Tallant and friend and partner of Jimmy Tallant; like Jimmy, he undergoes a favorable character transformation in Elizabeth Spencer's *The Voice at the Back Door*.

Christabel Grau   Young landlady in love with Cass Timberlane in Sinclair Lewis's *Cass Timberlane*.

Hermione Gravell-Pitt   Con artist with prominent teeth; promises to have Mame Dennis presented at court but instead bilks her out of a great deal of money in Patrick Dennis's *Around the World with Auntie Mame*.

George Graves   Friend of Eugene Gant in Thomas Wolfe's *Look Homeward, Angel*.

Muley Graves   Oklahoma farmer and neighbor of the Joad family; tells Tom Joad II how their families were forced to abandon their farms and journey to California to find work in John Steinbeck's *The Grapes of Wrath*.

Rocky Gravo   Master of ceremonies for the dance marathon; known for his indiscretions with female contestants in Horace McCoy's *They Shoot Horses, Don't They?*

Gray Beaver   Cruel Indian master of White Fang; sells White Fang to Beauty Smith for a bottle of whiskey in Jack London's *White Fang*.

Belfreda Gray   Black maid of the Kingsbloods in Sinclair Lewis's *Kingsblood Royal*.

Charles (Charley) Gray   Lower-upper-class native of Clyde who becomes vice president of Stuyvesant Bank in John P. Marquand's *Point of No Return*.

John Gray   Father of Charles Gray; makes and loses several fortunes in John P. Marquand's *Point of No Return*.

Mortimer (Mort, Speedy, Tex) Gray   Marine who survives campaigns at Tarawa and Saipan in Leon Uris's *Battle Cry*.

Nancy (Nance) Gray   Wife of Charles Gray; helps her husband achieve business success in John P. Marquand's *Point of No Return*.

Lewin Lockridge Grayle   Devoted millionaire husband of the former Velma Valento in Raymond Chandler's *Farewell, My Lovely*.

Rev. Thomas Grayson   Educated mulatto minister from New York City who tries unsuccessfully to establish a new church for the black workers of the Phosphate Mining Company; assumes pastorate of a Harlem Episcopal church and helps Lissa Atkinson become a successful singer in DuBose Heyward's *Mamba's Daughters*.

Great World Snake (Palalakonuh, Serpent of Eternity, Snake of Evil, World Sun Snake)   Monstrous embodiment of evil defeated by the forces of good in an apocalyptic Judgment Day at the end of Jack Kerouac's *Doctor Sax*.

Montague Greaves   English engineer who interests Frank Cowperwood in the London subway system in Theodore Dreiser's *The Stoic*.

Al (Ed Charney, Anthony Joseph Murascho) Grecco   Driver and helper for Ed Charney in John O'Hara's *Appointment in Samarra*.

Maxwell Greech   Satanic-looking manager of South Wind camp for adults where Marjorie Morningstar meets Noel Airman in Herman Wouk's *Marjorie Morningstar*.

Della Green   Mulatto former prostitute who becomes Augie's mistress after his success as a jockey in Arna Wendell Bontemps's *God Sends Sunday.*

Harvey Green   Professional gambler who corrupts the youth of Cedarville and murders Willy Hammond in T. S. Arthur's *Ten Nights in a Bar-Room.*

Aunt Mehitable Green   Former slave and present conjure woman who informs Dorinda Oakley that Dorinda is pregnant in Ellen Glasgow's *Barren Ground.*

Micajah ('Cajah) Green   Sheriff of Shaftsville who identifies the location of the Cayce still and who loses his job because of his inability to capture Rick Tyler in Mary Noailles Murfree's *The Prophet of the Great Smoky Mountains.*

Mr. Green   Grand Dragon of the Ku Klux Klan convinced by Sara Andrews to support Matthew Towns's release from prison as a good political move in W. E. B. Du Bois's *Dark Princess.*

Pauly Green   World War II veteran and owner of a café in Bristol, Mississippi; fires his pistol at customers in Shelby Foote's *Jordan County.*

Philip (Phil, Schuyler) Green   Widowed thirty-five-year-old writer on his first magazine assignment; pretending he is Jewish, devises a new slant for articles on anti-Semitism in Laura Z. Hobson's *Gentleman's Agreement.*

Reverend Mr. Pleasant Green   Southern black preacher who meets Helga Crane in a Harlem storefront church, marries her, and returns with her to rural Alabama in Nella Larsen's *Quicksand.*

Schuyler Green   See Philip Green.

Tom (Tommy) Green   Bright and loving eight-year-old son of Phil Green; experiences ridicule from his peers because he pretends to be Jewish in Laura Z. Hobson's *Gentleman's Agreement.*

Greene   Young man who reports the alleged murder by rustlers of Larry Kinkaid in Walter Van Tilburg Clark's *The Ox-Bow Incident.*

General Nathanael Greene   American Revolutionary War general who tries to persuade Thomas Paine to join his command and who relies upon Paine to explain to the soldiers what they are fighting for, thereby keeping their allegiance, in Howard Fast's *Citizen Tom Paine.*

Pete Greene   Free black man; friend and coworker of Jim in Harriet E. Wilson's *Our Nig.*

Phillip (Phil) Greene   Famous editor and friend of Garvin Wales in Hamilton Basso's *The View from Pompey's Head.*

Faye Greener   Aspiring actress who cares only about advancing her career; romantically involved with Tod Hackett and Earle Shoop in Nathanael West's *The Day of the Locust.*

Harry Greener   Former vaudevillian clown who is the father of Faye Greener and a friend of Tod Hackett in Nathanael West's *The Day of the Locust.*

Dr. Fowler Greenhill   Medical doctor and husband of Mary Jessup Greenhill; executed by firing squad for refusing to become a medical officer in the Minute Men in Sinclair Lewis's *It Can't Happen Here.*

Mary Jessup Greenhill   Older daughter of Doremus Jessup and wife of Dr. Fowler Greenhill; joins the Corpo Women's Flying Corps and deliberately crashes her plane into Effingham Swan's in order to kill Swan in Sinclair Lewis's *It Can't Happen Here.*

Drexel Greenshaw   Black headwaiter in the Fiesole Room at the Pineland Hotel in Sinclair Lewis's *Kingsblood Royal.*

Lieutenant Barney Greenwald   Attorney for accused mutineer Lieutenant Steve Maryk in Herman Wouk's *The Caine Mutiny.*

Colonel Walter Greer   Holder of a life-grant for Red Wing plantation, which Potem Desmit buys and sells fraudulently to Nimbus, in Albion W. Tourgee's *Bricks Without Straw.*

Mrs. Greer   Disseminator of village gossip, especially about the Carroll Farms, in Constance Fenimore Woolson's *For the Major.*

Count Greffi   Ninety-four-year-old former diplomat who drinks champagne and plays billiards with Frederic Henry in Ernest Hemingway's *A Farewell to Arms.*

Billy Gregg   Seventy-year-old resident of the Diamond County Home for the Aged; former Newark electrician; small, angry man who, emboldened by George Lucas's bottle of rye, throws the first stones at Stephen Conner in John Updike's *The Poorhouse Fair.*

Franz Gregorovious   Swiss psychiatrist and disloyal partner of Dick Diver in a mental clinic in F. Scott Fitzgerald's *Tender Is the Night.*

Kaethe Gregorovious   Wife of Franz Gregorovious; resents Dick and Nicole Diver in F. Scott Fitzgerald's *Tender Is the Night.*

Mrs. Harry (Tishy) Grendon   Hostess of Nanda Brookenham in Henry James's *The Awkward Age.*

Stephen (Steve) Grendon   Successful author, member of the school board, and Sac Prairie celebrity in August Derleth's *The Shield of the Valiant;* Roman Catholic whose love for the Protestant Margery Estabrook is opposed by his family, except for Grandfather Adams; narrator of Derleth's *Evening in Spring.*

Will and Rose Grendon   Parents of Stephen Grendon in August Derleth's *Evening in Spring.*

Louis Grenier   A founder of Jefferson and original owner of Old Frenchman's Place in William Faulkner's *Intruder in the Dust, Requiem for a Nun, The Town,* and *The Reivers.*

Catherine (Katty) Grenville   Young woman who becomes romantically involved with Roger Bannon in John O'Hara's *A Rage to Live.*

Samuel (Sam) Gretry   Broker at the Chicago Board of Trade who handles Curtis Jadwin's attempt to corner the American wheat market in Frank Norris's *The Pit.*

Nancy Grewell   Black midwife who saves the infant Capitola Le Noir from being murdered at birth by her villainous uncle in E.D.E.N. Southworth's *The Hidden Hand.*

Aline Aldridge Grey   Wife of Fred Grey; fantasizes about one of her husband's workers, Bruce Dudley; pregnant by Dudley, she runs away with him in Sherwood Anderson's *Dark Laughter.*

Anne Grey   Widowed niece of Jeanette Hayes-Rore and member of Harlem's young black socialites; takes Helga Crane into her home as a guest; meets Robert Anderson through Helga and later marries him in Nella Larsen's *Quicksand.*

Fred Grey   Owner of a wheel factory in Old Harbor, Indiana, and husband of Aline Aldridge Grey; leads an unhapy life and eventually loses his wife to Bruce Dudley, one of his former workers, in Sherwood Anderson's *Dark Laughter.*

Mr. Job Grey   Deceased husband of Mrs. Grey in W. E. B. Du Bois's *The Quest of the Silver Fleece.*

Mrs. Grey   Wealthy New York widow of Job Grey; shows concern for blacks and promises financial support for Miss Sarah Smith's school in W. E. B. Du Bois's *The Quest of the Silver Fleece.*

Doctor Greylock   Cruel, drink-crazed father of Jason Greylock; lives amid his mixed-race offspring and backs Jason's marriage to Geneva Ellgood in Ellen Glasgow's *Barren Ground.*

Jason Greylock   Personable but weak-willed doctor who sacrifices himself for his father; seduces Dorinda Oakley, marries Geneva Ellgood, and succumbs to alcohol in Ellen Glasgow's *Barren Ground.*

Herbert Greyson   Young protector of Capitola Le Noir and later her husband in E.D.E.N. Southworth's *The Hidden Hand.*

Amelia de Grier   Wife of Wendell Ryder and mother of five in Djuna Barnes's *Ryder.*

Elizabeth Grier   Member of the Cabala who lives at the Palazzo Barberini; hosts numerous dinners in Thornton Wilder's *The Cabala.*

Jenny (Ma) Grier   Only female member of the lynch mob; uses her femininity to shame doubtful members of the mob into

certainty concerning the need for a hanging in Walter Van Tilburg Clark's *The Ox-Bow Incident.*

William K. Grierson   See Jeremiah Beaumont.

Gustus Thomas (Gus, Tom) Griff   Uncle of Tad; owner of a mill that is, presumably, destroyed by Mink Lorey in Mary Noailles Murfree's *In the Clouds.*

Leon Griffin   See Leon Lawrence.

Mrs. Griffin   Widow to whom Captain Porgy is attracted in William Gilmore Simms's *Woodcraft.*

Walter (Wat) Griffin   Whig farmer captured by the Tory Amos Gaskens; saved from hanging by Major Singleton in William Gilmore Simms's *The Partisan.*

Asa Griffiths   Traveling evangelist, husband of Elvira Griffiths, and father of Clyde Griffiths in Theodore Dreiser's *An American Tragedy.*

Clyde (Baker, Clifford Golden, Carl Graham, Harry Tenet) Griffiths   Son of Asa and Elvira Griffiths; lover of Roberta Alden, whom he plots to kill when he has the opportunity to raise his social standing by marrying Sondra Finchley; executed for having murdered Alden in Theodore Dreiser's *An American Tragedy.*

Elvira Griffiths   Traveling evangelist, wife of Asa Griffiths, and mother of Clyde Griffiths in Theodore Dreiser's *An American Tragedy.*

Samuel Griffiths   Uncle of Clyde Griffiths; gives his nephew an important job and introduces him to upper-class life in Theodore Dreiser's *An American Tragedy.*

Deborah Grimes   First wife of Gabriel Grimes; made sterile when raped by white men at the age of sixteen in James Baldwin's *Go Tell It on the Mountain.*

Elizabeth Grimes   Common-law wife of Richard and mother by him of John Grimes; marries Gabriel Grimes after Richard's suicide in James Baldwin's *Go Tell It on the Mountain.*

Florence Grimes   Oppressed black woman who desperately surrenders to Christianity; sister of Gabriel Grimes in James Baldwin's *Go Tell It on the Mountain.*

Gabriel Grimes   Deacon at the Temple of the Fire Baptized, a black evangelical church in Harlem; frustrated by years of white oppression, he is driven to violence and hypocrisy; stepfather of John Grimes and husband of Deborah Grimes and later Elizabeth Grimes in James Baldwin's *Go Tell It on the Mountain.*

John Grimes   Harlem adolescent who eventually commits himself to Christianity after a torturous search for his black identity in a white world; brother of Roy Grimes, stepson of Gabriel Grimes, and son of Elizabeth Grimes in James Baldwin's *Go Tell It on the Mountain.*

Roy Grimes   Rebellious black youth and brother of John Grimes in James Baldwin's *Go Tell It on the Mountain*.

Percy Grimm   National guardsman who castrates Joe Christmas in William Faulkner's *Light in August*.

Mr. Grimshaw   Teacher at the Temple Grammar School in Thomas Bailey Aldrich's *The Story of a Bad Boy*.

Grindle   Mystic leader of a utopian community who seduces Candy Christian in Terry Southern and Mason Hoffenberg's *Candy*.

Grippenwald   Veterinarian to Hollywood animals, including Dirty Eddie, in Ludwig Bemelmans's *Dirty Eddie*.

Griswold   Messenger hired by Henry Miller; former army sergeant who goes crazy and destroys the office; eventually promoted to a clerkship in Henry Miller's *Tropic of Capricorn*.

Colonel Sandy Griswold   Cavalry officer who aids the Del Sol cowboys during their troubles with Indians and rustlers in Emerson Hough's *North of 36*.

Griza   Computer operator at Talifer Missile Base who helps Coverly Wapshot do a computer analysis of Keats's poetry in John Cheever's *The Wapshot Scandal*.

William (Willie) Grogan   Night wire-chief and confidant of Homer Macauley; dies of a heart attack while receiving a telegraph message about Marcus Macauley's death in William Saroyan's *The Human Comedy*.

H. M. Grosbeake   Professor of philosophy and the narrator's spiritual mentor in Edmund Wilson's *I Thought of Daisy*.

Mrs. Grose   Housekeeper and motherly friend to the governess; gradually reveals the history of Bly in Henry James's *The Turn of the Screw*.

Mrs. Hugo Gross   See Felix Treevly.

Rhino (O–Daddy) Gross   Disqualified gynecologist, one-time abortionist, and maker of O-Daddy, The Condom of Tomorrow in Nelson Algren's *A Walk on the Wild Side*.

Velma Gross   Ex-convict and maker, with her husband, Rhino, of O-Daddy condoms in Nelson Algren's *A Walk on the Wild Side*.

Lena Grove   Poverty-stricken woman who travels to Jefferson in search of Lucas Burch, the father of her unborn child, in William Faulkner's *Light in August*.

Sally Grover   Associate of Horace Bentley and friend of the poor in Winston Churchill's *The Inside of the Cup*.

Major Grumby   Leader of Grumby's Independents who murders Rosa Millard and who in turn is murdered by her grandson,

Bayard Sartoris II; appears in William Faulkner's *The Unvanquished* and *The Hamlet*.

Ebenezer Gryce   New York police detective who investigates the murder of Horatio Leavenworth in Anna Katharine Green's *The Leavenworth Case*.

Percy Gryce   Dull but wealthy collector of Americana; one of several men Lily Bart attempts to marry in Edith Wharton's *The House of Mirth*.

Guenever   Queen; wife of Arthur in Samuel Langhorne Clemens's *A Connecticut Yankee in King Arthur's Court*.

Princess Guenevere (Phyllida)   Woman whom Jurgen rescues; through her, he becomes acquainted with Dame Analtis in James Branch Cabell's *Jurgen*.

Guerlac   See Henri Guerlac de Sabrevois.

Madame Martin Guerre   See Bertrande de Rols.

Martin Guerre   Husband of Bertrande de Rols; many years after deserting his wife, he returns to find her living with Arnaud du Tilh, who resembles Guerre and who has pretended to be him, in Janet Lewis's *The Wife of Martin Guerre*.

Monsieur Guerre   Demanding father of Martin Guerre; thrown from a horse and killed in Janet Lewis's *The Wife of Martin Guerre*.

Pierre Guerre   Brother of Monsieur Guerre; becomes head of the Guerre family following his brother's death in Janet Lewis's *The Wife of Martin Guerre*.

Sanxi Guerre   Son of Bertrande de Rols and Martin Guerre in Janet Lewis's *The Wife of Martin Guerre*.

Angela (Angela Maea) Guessippi   Lover of Anthony Adverse and later of Napoleon Bonaparte in Hervey Allen's *Anthony Adverse*.

Il Gufo (Padrone)   Hangman and only marriageable man in the village of Sasso Fetore (Tomb Stench); known as the owl; narrator of John Hawkes's *The Owl*.

Caporale Guiglielmo   One of two carabinieri who attack and then release Jacopo in John Hawkes's *The Goose on the Grave*.

John Guild   Police lieutenant investigating the murder of Julia Wolf and the disappearance of Clyde Wynant in Dashiell Hammett's *The Thin Man*.

Guillaume   Homosexual who humiliates Giovanni and is murdered by him in James Baldwin's *Giovanni's Room*.

Guinea   See Black Guinea.

Beverly Guinevere   See Beverly Guinevere McLeod.

Monina Guinevere   See Monina.

Luther Gulliday   Victim of Stuart McKay's murderous anger and resentment when Gulliday takes McKay's Job in Nelson Algren's *Somebody in Boots*.

Vergil Gunch   President of the Boosters' Club of which George Babbitt is a member; pressures Babbitt to join the Good Citizens' League in Sinclair Lewis's *Babbitt*.

Gun-Deck   Man-of-war's man aboard the *Highlander* in Herman Melville's *Redburn*.

Ma Gundel   Motherly waitress to and confidante of Moses Fable in Ludwig Bemelmans's *Dirty Eddie*.

Lucy Gurget   Cook for Solomon Tinkle and motherly friend of Daniel Harrow and Molly Larkins in Walter D. Edmonds's *Rome Haul*.

Forbes Gurney   Poet and lover of Stephanie Platow in Theodore Dreiser's *The Titan*.

General Marion Gurney   Confederate veteran and prominent politician who opposes Reconstruction; sends an anonymous warning that enables Lily Servosse to save her father and Thomas Denton from the Ku Klux Klan ambush; opposes his son's marriage to Lily in Albion W. Tourgee's *A Fool's Errand*.

Melville Gurney   Son of General Marion Gurney; sentinel during the Ku Klux Klan's abortive ambush of Thomas Denton; vows to marry Lily Servosse in Albion W. Tourgee's *A Fool's Errand*.

Mr. Gurney   Minister in Lionel Trilling's *The Middle of the Journey*.

Gus   Black youth assaulted by Bigger Thomas in Richard Wright's *Native Son*.

Gus (Brownie)   Friend of Melba; picks up Malcolm at the horticultural gardens and prepares him for marriage to Melba in James Purdy's *Malcolm*.

Ephraim (Eph) Guthrie   Low-key brother of Fee Guthrie in Mary Noailles Murfree's *In the "Stranger People's" Country*.

Felix (Fee) Guthrie   Owner of the stranger people's burial ground; loves Litt Pettingill intensely, and beats Leonard Rhodes savagely; dies because of a sheriff's mistake in Mary Noailles Murfree's *In the "Stranger People's" Country*.

Casper Gutman   Criminal mastermind whose research has identified the jewel-encrusted statuette given as a tribute to Charles V by the Hospitalers of St. John in the sixteenth century and whose ruthless persistence has led him to San Francisco in search of it in Dashiell Hammett's *The Maltese Falcon*.

Rhea Gutman   Daughter of Casper Gutman; drugged in Dashiell Hammett's *The Maltese Falcon*.

Guy (Cabin Boy, Paper Jack)   Captain of the *Julia* in Herman Melville's *Omoo*.

Captain Guy   Part owner and captain of the schooner *Jane Guy* who rescues Arthur Gordon Pym and Dirk Peters after the wreck of the *Grampus*; murdered with his crew on the island of Tsalal in Edgar Allan Poe's *The Narrative of Arthur Gordon Pym*.

James (Jeemes, Jim) Gwinnan   Judge at Mink Lorey's trial who is, Lorey thinks, in love with Lethe Sayles; disliked by Lorey's attorney Bob Harshaw in Mary Noailles Murfree's *In the Clouds*.

John Elton Cecil (Jack) Gwynne   American-born English aristocrat and lover of Isabel Otis; willing to give up his inherited seat in the British government for a political career in the United States in Gertrude Atherton's *Ancestors*.

Nell (Nelly) Gwynne   Famous actress and one of the many mistresses of Charles II in Kathleen Winsor's *Forever Amber*.

Lady Victoria Gwynne   Beautiful widowed mother of John Gwynne; forced to choose between the ennui of expected social-class behavior and the expression of her intellectual, sensuous nature in Gertrude Atherton's *Ancestors*.

Camilla Gwyon   Wife of Reverend Gwyon; dies when their son, Wyatt Gwyon, is three and haunts him throughout William Gaddis's *The Recognitions*.

Esther Gwyon   Aspiring writer and wife of Wyatt Gwyon in William Gaddis's *The Recognitions*.

Reverend Gwyon   Protestant minister who turns to pagan religion after the death of his wife in William Gaddis's *The Recognitions*.

Wyatt (Stephan Asche, Stephen) Gwyon   Painter who turns to forgery; later an expatriate in Spain; protagonist of William Gaddis's *The Recognitions*.

Gypsy (Zuleika)   Pony of Tom Bailey; becomes a trick pony in a circus in Thomas Bailey Aldrich's *The Story of a Bad Boy*.

H

Butch (Butch Braley) Haber Convict brother of Gulla Slogum; castrates René Dumur, Annette Slogum's suitor, on her mother's orders in Mari Sandoz's *Slogum House*.

Regula (Gulla) Haber See Regula Haber Slogum.

Eunice Habersham Spinster granddaughter of Doctor Habersham in William Faulkner's *Intruder in the Dust* and *The Town*.

Doctor Samuel Habersham Early settler of Jefferson in William Faulkner's *Intruder in the Dust, Requiem for a Nun,* and *The Town*.

Hugh Habershaw North Carolina Tory partisan who captures Arthur Butler; killed by Horse-Shoe Robinson in John Pendleton Kennedy's *Horse-Shoe Robinson*.

Dr. Habicht Father of Ferdinand and Minna; scholarly, idealistic German who educates the young Oliver Tappan in Hjalmar Hjorth Boyesen's *The Golden Calf*.

Ferdinand Habicht Ne'er-do-well brother of Minna Habicht; studies in a German university; upon returning to the United States, he borrows money from Oliver Tappan in Hjorth Boyesen's *The Golden Calf*.

Minna Habicht Simple, pretty, and uncorrupt daughter of Dr. Habicht; once engaged to Oliver Tappan in Hjorth Boyesen's *The Golden Calf*.

Jerome (Jerry) Hack Mediocre but reliable screenwriter at Olympia Studios in Ludwig Bemelmans's *Dirty Eddie*.

Philip (Phil) Hackett Respectable yet ultimately disloyal friend of Laurentine Strange in Jessie Redmon Fauset's *The Chinaberry Tree*.

Tod Hackett Lover of Faye Greener and painter for a movie studio who observes Hollywood decadence, which inspires his painting, *The Burning of Los Angeles,* in Nathanael West's *The Day of the Locust*.

Elmo C. Hacketts, Jr. Army private in Kurt Vonnegut's *Player Piano*.

Harriet N. Q. (Hattie) Haddock Wife of William P. Haddock and mother of Mildred Haddock in Donald Ogden Stewart's *Mr and Mrs Haddock Abroad*.

Mildred Haddock Ten-year-old daughter of Harriet and William Haddock in Donald Ogden Stewart's *Mr and Mrs Haddock Abroad*.

William P. (Will) Haddock Husband of Harriet Haddock and father of Mildred Haddock; takes his wife and daughter on a voyage to Europe, on which they have strange experiences, in Donald Ogden Stewart's *Mr and Mrs Haddock Abroad*.

Hadi Ja Child prostitute pursued by Nelson Dyar and Eunice Goode in Paul Bowles's *Let It Come Down*.

Brinker Hadley Class leader and politican who later joins the Coast Guard to avoid combat during World War II in John Knowles's *A Separate Peace*.

Mr. Hadley Father of Brinker Hadley and exponent of traditional values concerning patriotism and duty in John Knowles's *A Separate Peace*.

Mr. Hadwin Quaker benefactor of Arthur Mervyn; dies in the yellow-fever epidemic of 1793 in Charles Brockden Brown's *Arthur Mervyn*.

Hagar (Baxter)   Daughter of Mamba and mother of Lissa Atkinson; banned from Charleston because of her drunkenness and violent and disorderly conduct; murdered by Gilly Bluton in DuBose Heyward's *Mamba's Daughters*.

Hagen   Father of Johnny Hagen; longtime night-crew electrician at the Past Bay Manufacturing Company factory who is feared and distrusted by Carl Belcher; shot by police during the strike in Robert Cantwell's *The Land of Plenty*.

Herman Hagen   Head of the German department at Waindell College and Timofey Pnin's protector in Vladimir Nabokov's *Pnin*.

John (Johnny) Hagen   Son of Hagen; recently hired night-crew worker at the Past Bay Manufacturing Company factory who falls in love with Ellen Turner in Robert Cantwell's *The Land of Plenty*.

Steve Hagen   Second in command to Earl Janoth at Janoth Enterprises; conceives a plan to locate the unidentified witness who can link Janoth to the murder of Pauline Delos; a narrator of Kenneth Fearing's *The Big Clock*.

Paul (Paulie) Haggerty   Friend of Studs Lonigan in James T. Farrell's *Young Lonigan;* pressured into marrying; dies of a venereal disease in *The Young Manhood of Studs Lonigan*.

Mister Haggin   Plantation owner and Jerry's original master in Jack London's *Jerry of the Islands*.

Hagood   Newspaper editor in William Faulkner's *Pylon*.

Edgar Rice Burroughs Hagstrohm   Average man and inhabitant of the dystopian Homestead in Kurt Vonnegut's *Player Piano*.

Augustus M. Haguenin   Editor of a Chicago newspaper who endorses Frank Cowperwood's streetcar plans in exchange for a streetcar line past his office in Theodore Dreiser's *The Titan*.

Cecily Haguenin   Daughter of Augustus Haguenin and lover of Frank Cowperwood in Theodore Dreiser's *The Titan*.

Dolliver (Dolly) Haight   Virtuous man who contracts a venereal disease from the prostitute Flossie via a kiss upon his cut lip in Frank Norris's *Vandover and the Brute*.

Lonzo Hait   Husband of Mannie Hait in William Faulkner's *The Town;* mule and horse trader in *The Mansion*.

Mannie Hait   Wife of Lonzo Hait in William Faulkner's *The Town*.

Vashti (Vash) Hake   See Vashti Hake Snyth.

Hal   Soldier who wants to help the sorrowing world, but lands in a hospital with paranoia and delusions of persecution in John Horne Burns's *The Gallery*.

Arnold Haldmarne   Husband of Willa Haldmarne and father of Kerrin, Marget, and Merle Haldmarne; farmer who battles drought and depression in Josephine Johnson's *Now in November*.

Kerrin Haldmarne   Eldest daughter of Arnold and Willa Haldmarne; emotionally unstable; commits suicide in Josephine Johnson's *Now in November*.

Marget Haldmarne   Middle daughter of Arnold and Willa Haldmarne; narrator of Josephine Johnson's *Now in November*.

Merle Haldmarne   Youngest daughter of Arnold and Willa Haldmarne in Josephine Johnson's *Now in November*.

Willa Haldmarne   Wife of Arnold Haldmarne and mother of Kerrin, Marget, and Merle Haldmarne; dies of burns while trying to save the family farm from fire in Josephine Johnson's *Now in November*.

Bona Hale   White southerner attracted to Paul Johnson, a fellow student she suspects might be black, in Jean Toomer's *Cane*.

Mrs. Hale   Invalid wife of a clergyman; employs Frado after she leaves Mrs. Moore in Harriet E. Wilson's *Our Nig*.

Ruth Varnum (Mrs. Ned Hale) Hale   Widow and old acquaintance of Ethan Frome; declines to enlighten the narrator about Frome's story in Edith Wharton's *Ethan Frome*.

Dan Haley   Slave dealer who buys Harry Harris and Uncle Tom from the Shelbys in Harriet Beecher Stowe's *Uncle Tom's Cabin*.

James J. (Jim) Halford   Lover of Julia Maybury Stairs; leaves the United States believing that Julia will not accompany him in Mary Austin's *Santa Lucia*.

Colonel (Sir Peter) Halkett   Scottish regimental commander of the British army; possesses second sight and so knows the day he will die in Mary Lee Settle's *O Beulah Land*.

Betty Hall   Feminine sister of Diony Hall in Elizabeth Madox Roberts's *The Great Meadow*.

Diony Hall   See Diony Hall Jarvis.

George (Ike) Hall   Itinerant socialist who befriends Mac in John Dos Passos's *U.S.A.* trilogy.

James Hall   Cigar-smoking judge and source of Charlie Noble's story about John Moredock in Herman Melville's *The Confidence-Man*.

Polly Brook Hall   Mother of Diony Hall in Elizabeth Madox Roberts's *The Great Meadow*.

Thomas Hall   Father of Diony Hall and philosopher of the spread of civilization in Elizabeth Madox Roberts's *The Great Meadow*.

Betsey (Ma) Halleck   Matriarch of the family that transports Jerry and Mary Fowler to Utica; owner of a large farm at which Mary takes refuge when separating from Jerry in Walter D. Edmonds's *Erie Water.*

Ezra Ben Halleck   Wealthy Bostonian who remains loyal to Marcia Gaylord Hubbard during her divorce proceedings in William Dean Howells's *A Modern Instance.*

Douglas Halliday   Spoiled, angry son of Manley and Jere Halliday in Budd Schulberg's *The Disenchanted.*

Jere Halliday   See Jere Wilder-Halliday.

Manley Halliday   Brilliant, accomplished American novelist in decline, famous for his chronicling of the 1920s; an alcoholic in debt and poor health, he agrees to collaborate with a young junior writer on a screenplay for a low-budget college musical; a drinking spree culminates in his death in Budd Schulberg's *The Disenchanted.*

Rachel Halliday   Center of the Quaker household where Eliza Harris and her husband are reunited before being aided by the Quaker community on their flight north in Harriet Beecher Stowe's *Uncle Tom's Cabin.*

Hallie   See Hallie Breedlove.

Colonel Halloway   White lover of Sal Strange and father of Laurentine Strange in Jessie Redmon Fauset's *The Chinaberry Tree.*

Catherine (Katie) Halsey   Orphaned niece of Ellsworth Toohey vitiated by her uncle's counsel and Peter Keating's betrayal in Ayn Rand's *The Fountainhead.*

Fred Halsey   Black owner of a wagon shop who befriends Ralph Kabnis in Jean Toomer's *Cane.*

Lanning Halsey   Cousin of Delia Ralston; courts Clementina Lovell and plans to marry her after she is adopted by her wealthy aunt Delia in Edith Wharton's *The Old Maid.*

Doctor Ewing J. Halyard   State Department guide for the Shah of Bratpuhr in Kurt Vonnegut's *Player Piano.*

Carl Halzer   Farmer, labor organizer, and legislator in Mari Sandoz's *Capital City.*

Brother Hambro   Chief theoretician of the Brotherhood who teaches the narrator the Brotherhood's doctrine in Ralph Ellison's *Invisible Man.*

Hamilton   Surgeon aboard the HMS *Pandora* who tries to alleviate the inhumane treatment of the *Bounty* prisoners and who assists Roger Byam at Byam's trial in Charles Nordhoff and James Norman Hall's *Mutiny on the Bounty.*

Anise Hamilton   Girlfriend who provides Braxton with spending money until she discovers he is spending it on other women in Wallace Thurman's *The Blacker the Berry.*

Berry (Be'y) Hamilton   Hardworking, loyal butler falsely accused of stealing money from Francis Oakley and sentenced to ten years at hard labor; husband of Fannie Hamilton and father of Joe and Kitty Hamilton in Paul Laurence Dunbar's *The Sport of the Gods.*

Charles (Charlie) Hamilton   First husband of Scarlett O'Hara; dies from pneumonia and measles during the early stages of the Civil War in Margaret Mitchell's *Gone with the Wind.*

Fannie (Fannie Gibson) Hamilton   Housekeeper on the estate of Maurice Oakley, wife of Berry Hamilton, and mother of Joe and Kitty Hamilton; migrates to New York City, where she is tricked into marriage by a man who beats her and reduces her to poverty, in Paul Laurence Dunbar's *The Sport of the Gods.*

Joe Hamilton   Son of Berry and Fannie Hamilton; migrates to New York City, where he becomes a dandy, an alcoholic, and the murderer of his sweetheart, in Paul Laurence Dunbar's *The Sport of the Gods.*

Kitty (Kit) Hamilton   Daughter of Berry and Fannie Hamilton; becomes a vaudeville dancer and singer in Paul Laurence Dunbar's *The Sport of the Gods.*

Melanie Hamilton   See Melanie Hamilton Wilkes.

Roy Hamilton   Californian who has come east to discover the identity of his father; admired by Henry Miller in Henry Miller's *Tropic of Capricorn.*

Samuel (Sam) Hamilton   Salinas Valley farmer who befriends the settler Adam Trask and, just before he dies, convinces Trask to name Trask's sons and reveals that Trask's wife, Cathy Ames Trask, is operating a successful brothel in Salinas in John Steinbeck's *East of Eden.*

Sarah Jane (Pittypat) Hamilton   Spinster aunt of Charles and Melanie Hamilton; receives the mourning Scarlett O'Hara in Atlanta following the death of Charles Hamilton, Scarlett's first husband, in Margaret Mitchell's *Gone with the Wind.*

Will Hamilton   Son of Samuel Hamilton and business partner of Caleb Trask in the bean venture which makes them both wealthy during the wartime food shortages in John Steinbeck's *East of Eden.*

Jack Hamlin   Gambler with a heart of gold in Bret Harte's *Gabriel Conroy.*

Bert Hammer   American soldier; pal and bunkmate of Jacob Levy in Martha Gellhorn's *Wine of Astonishment.*

Caleb Hammil   Utica contractor who hires Jerry Fowler to build first canal locks in Walter D. Edmonds's *Erie Water.*

Hallie Rufer Hammond   Daughter of George Rufer, widow of Michael Hammond, and mother of Rufer Hammond; political radical in her youth and early in her marriage; owner of Hammonds, Franklin's largest department store, in Mari Sandoz's *Capital City*.

Lois Hammond Teacher whom Richard Dadier saves from rape and who tries to seduce Dadier in Evan Hunter's *The Blackboard Jungle*.

Miss Hammond Nurse who cares for Elsa Mason as she is dying from cancer in Wallace Stegner's *The Big Rock Candy Mountain*.

Reverend Hammond Pastor of the church attended by Bigger Thomas's mother; visits Thomas in jail and attempts to convert him to Christianity in Richard Wright's *Native Son*.

Rufer Hammond See Hamm Rufe.

Willy Hammond Young man from Cedarville who becomes a gambler and is murdered by Harvey Green in T. S. Arthur's *Ten Nights in a Bar-Room*.

Richard (Dicky) Hampshire Boyhood friend who draws cartoons with Jack Duluoz in Jack Kerouac's *Doctor Sax*.

Hope (Hub) Hampton (I) Sheriff of Yoknapatawpha County in William Faulkner's *The Hamlet, Intruder in the Dust, The Town, The Mansion,* and *The Reivers*.

Hope (Little Hub) Hampton (II) Son of Hub Hampton and sheriff of Yoknapatawpha County in William Faulkner's *The Mansion* and *The Reivers*.

Judge Horace Hanby Former carpetbag governor of a southern state; keeps the citizens of Bidwell, Ohio, informed about his prophetic and philosophical ideas of the future of industry in the Midwest in Sherwood Anderson's *Poor White*.

Samuel Hanby Puritanical principal of a black training school who demands the resignation of Ralph Kabnis in Jean Toomer's *Cane*.

Caroline Hand Wife of Hosmer Hand; lover of Frank Cowperwood in Theodore Dreiser's *The Titan*.

Hosmer Hand Investor who seeks revenge on Frank Cowperwood, who has been sleeping with Hand's wife, in Theodore Dreiser's *The Titan*.

John Handback Owner of a plantation store who cheats black as well as white sharecroppers; financially ruined because of Miltiades Vaiden's vengeance; appears in T. S. Stribling's *The Forge* and *The Store*.

Lucius Handback Son of John Handback; marries Sydna Crowninshield Vaiden; appears in T. S. Stribling's *The Store* and *Unfinished Cathedral*.

Ed Handby Bartender who courts Belle Carpenter and takes her from George Willard in Sherwood Anderson's *Winesburg, Ohio*.

Dix (Dixie, William Tuttle Jamieson) Handley Once-famous criminal who dies in his native South, ironically fulfilling his dream of returning, in William Riley Burnett's *The Asphalt Jungle*.

Hank Airport announcer in William Faulkner's *Pylon*.

Hank Friend of Joe Gilligan in William Faulkner's *Soldiers' Pay*.

Caroline Trid Hanna See Caroline Trid.

Chad Hanna Orphan hotel hostler who joins Huguenine's Great and Only International Circus, marries Caroline Trid, and becomes ringmaster in Walter D. Edmonds's *Chad Hanna*.

Maum Hannah Mother of Budda Ben and guardian of and midwife for Mary Pinesett; matriarch of Blue Brook Plantation and important member of Heaven's Gate Church in Julia Peterkin's *Scarlet Sister Mary*.

Hans German socialist, veteran of World War I, labor agitator, and Larry Donovan's political mentor in Jack Conroy's *The Disinherited*.

Beret Holm Hansa Wife of Per Hansa and mother of Peder Victorious Holm in O. E. Rölvaag's *Giants in the Earth*; widowed, she often succumbs to madness, but still establishes a successful farm as her children become Americanized, in *Peder Victorious* and *Their Father's God*.

Per (Peder) Hansa (Holm) Innovative pioneer farmer married to Beret Holm; leader of the Norwegian settlement in the Dakota territory; successfully battles nature, but dies in a winter storm, in O. E. Rölvaag's *Giants in the Earth*.

Minnie Meeber Hanson Sister of Carrie Meeber; Carrie lives with her in Theodore Dreiser's *Sister Carrie*.

Countess Berthe von Happel Viennese divorcée who marries into Boston society; only hostess who invites Sonia Marburg to her salon in Jean Stafford's *Boston Adventure*.

Count Rudolf von Hapsburg Lover of Zdenka von Studenitz, father of Rudolf Stanka, and murderer of a mistress; commits suicide in Louis Adamic's *Cradle of Life*.

Frances Harbach True love of Homer Zigler in Clyde Brion Davis's *The Great American Novel*.

Asa Bruce (Coot) Harcoot Former bank president who lives as a philosophical bum in Herb's Addition; built the first brick kilns in Franklin in Mari Sandoz's *Capital City*.

Gregory W. Harcourt Psychiatrist whose testimony for the prosecution is discredited by Paul Biegler in Robert Traver's *Anatomy of a Murder*.

Billie Harcum Stereotyped Memphis belle of Irwin K. Macgregor and later his wife in Wright Morris's *Love among the Cannibals*.

Tandy Hard   Winesburg citizen whose childhood encounter with a drunken stranger changes her life in Sherwood Anderson's *Winesburg, Ohio*.

Tom Hard   Religious fanatic who, with his daughter Tandy, befriends a drunken stranger in Sherwood Anderson's *Winesburg, Ohio*.

Hardee-Hardee   See Lem Hardy.

Gretchen Hardenburg   Unfaithful wife of Lieutenant Hardenburg; undermines the character of Christian Diestl by initiating an affair with him in Irwin Shaw's *The Young Lions*.

Lieutenant Hardenburg   Callous Nazi officer whose heinous crimes against humanity serve as an example for Christian Diestl in Irwin Shaw's *The Young Lions*.

Hard Heart   Noble Pawnee chieftain and ally of Natty Bumppo; kills enemy chief Mahtoree in fierce combat and claims his scalp in James Fenimore Cooper's *The Prairie*.

J. (Joshua) Hardin   Father of Paul Hardin; carriage maker and crusading prohibitionist who protests alone against the mob that lynched Smoke in Brand Whitlock's *J. Hardin & Son*.

Paul Hardin   Rebellious son of J. Hardin and husband of Winona Dyer; bank vice president who is a successful oil speculator and landowner in Brand Whitlock's *J. Hardin & Son*.

Winona Dyer Hardin   See Winona Dyer.

Annie Harding   High-spirited girl who comes to live at Plumfield in Louisa May Alcott's *Little Men*.

Reverend Hardman   Episcopal minister and Christian Socialist in Robert Herrick's *The Memoirs of an American Citizen*.

Alva Hardwick   Demented man employed by Donald Martin; accuses Juan Martinez of murdering Larry Kinkaid; lynched by the mob in Walter Van Tilburg Clark's *The Ox-Bow Incident*.

Albert Hardy   Father of John and Mary Hardy; allows Louise Bentley to board at his family's home while she attends school in Sherwood Anderson's *Winesburg, Ohio*.

Coach Hardy   Football coach for the College and plea bargainer for Raymond Blent's football career in Howard Nemerov's *The Homecoming Game*.

David Hardy   Son of Louise and John Hardy; leaves home after an incident in which he fears he has accidentally killed his grandfather, Jesse Bentley, in Sherwood Anderson's *Winesburg, Ohio*.

Harriet Hardy   Daughter of Albert Hardy; shuns Louise Bentley when the elder Hardy prefers Louise to her and her sister Mary Hardy in Sherwood Anderson's *Winesburg, Ohio*.

John Hardy   Winesburg banker and husband of Louise Hardy; works with Jesse Bentley to have David Hardy moved to Bentley's farm in Sherwood Anderson's *Winesburg, Ohio*.

Lem (Hardee-Hardee) Hardy   English military leader of Hannamanoo whom the natives tattoo in Herman Melville's *Omoo*.

Louise Bentley Hardy   Daughter of Jesse Bentley and mother of David Hardy; her cynicism isolates her from the rest of the townspeople in Sherwood Anderson's *Winesburg, Ohio*.

Mary Hardy   Daughter of Albert Hardy; her tryst with a young man strengthens Louise Bentley's resolve to have a suitor in Sherwood Anderson's *Winesburg, Ohio*.

Theo J. Hardy   New, honest, and hardworking police chief who is determined to reform the department in William Riley Burnett's *The Asphalt Jungle*.

Rev. Balthazar Harge   Superintendent of the Bois des Morts Mission in the Minnesota territory; convinces Aaron Gadd to become a missionary to the Indians in Sinclair Lewis's *The God-Seeker*.

Mercie Harge   Wife of Balthazar Harge; dies of consumption in Sinclair Lewis's *The God-Seeker*.

Daniel Harkavy   *Trade Journal* editor and friend of Asa Leventhal; warns Leventhal, as a fellow Jew, not to be hypersensitive or defensive about his Jewishness, in Saul Bellow's *The Victim*.

Joe Harland   Bum who has fallen from a position of prominence in the business world in John Dos Passos's *Manhattan Transfer*.

Whizzer Harlow   Old beatnik friend of Lee Youngdahl in Mark Harris's *Wake Up, Stupid*.

Rocco (Little Rock, Little Rock Harmony, Rock) Harmonia   Boyfriend of Winnie in John Clellon Holmes's *Go*.

Lucius Harney   Young architect who, on a visit to his cousin in North Dormer, becomes Charity Royall's lover and impregnates her in Edith Wharton's *Summer*.

Al Harper   Quick, conniving Hollywood agent in Budd Schulberg's *The Disenchanted*.

Ben Harper   Father of Pearl and John Harper; executed for robbery and murder in Davis Grubb's *The Night of the Hunter*.

Duncan (Happy) Harper   Racial moderate and candidate for sheriff in Winfield County, Mississippi; dies in a car wreck with a black man in his protection in Elizabeth Spencer's *The Voice at the Back Door*.

John Harper   Son of Ben and Willa Harper; flees with his sister Pearl rather than reveal to Preacher the whereabouts of stolen money he has sworn to his father to protect in Davis Grubb's *The Night of the Hunter.*

Joseph (Joe) Harper   Pal of Tom Sawyer in Samuel Langhorne Clemens's *The Adventures of Tom Sawyer.*

Louise Taylor (Tinker) Harper   Wife and eventual widow of Duncan Harper and object of Jimmy Tallant's romantic affection in Elizabeth Spencer's *The Voice at the Back Door.*

Pearl Harper   Younger sister of John Harper and daughter of Ben and Willa Harper; flees with her brother to avoid giving Preacher the stolen money hidden in her rag doll in Davis Grubb's *The Night of the Hunter.*

Willa Harper   Mother of Pearl and John Harper and widow of Ben Harper; marries and is murdered by Preacher in Davis Grubb's *The Night of the Hunter.*

Celia Hornby (Baby, Ceeley, Doll-Baby, HoneyBaby) Harrick   Wife of Jack Harrick and teacher in Robert Penn Warren's *The Cave.*

Jasper (Big Bubba) Harrick   Older son of John T. and Celia Hornby Harrick and a hero in the Korean War; dies trapped in a cave near Johntown, Tennessee, in Robert Penn Warren's *The Cave.*

John T. (Jack, Jumping Jack, Ole Jack) Harrick   Dying husband of Celia Hornby Harrick; soldier in World War II and blacksmith by trade; known as a hell-raiser in his younger days in Robert Penn Warren's *The Cave.*

Harriett   Maid and cook for India and Walter Bridge in Evan Connell's *Mrs. Bridge* and *Mr. Bridge.*

Kerfoot (Carl) Harriman   Marine sergeant in France during World War I who, upon learning of his girlfriend's interest in another man, shoots himself in the foot in Thomas Boyd's *Through the Wheat.*

Harrington   Father of Laurette Harrington; chairman of the board of World-Wide Studios responsible for the ousting of Sidney Fineman as production chief and the promotion of Sammy Glick to take his place in Budd Schulberg's *What Makes Sammy Run?*

Amelia Harrington   Wife of J. Harrington and mother of Tommy Harrington in William Hill Brown's *The Power of Sympathy.*

Edward Harrington   See Edward Van Harrington.

J. Harrington   Father, by his wife Amelia Harrington, of Tommy Harrington and, by Maria Fawcet, of Harriot Fawcet in William Hill Brown's *The Power of Sympathy.*

Laurette Harrington   Beautiful, arrogant daughter of the chairman of the board of World-Wide Studios; marries Sammy Glick in Budd Schulberg's *What Makes Sammy Run?*

Leslie Harrington   Wealthy mill owner who uses his money and power to control people in Grace Metalious's *Peyton Place.*

May Rudge Harrington   Wife of Will Harrington in Robert Herrick's *The Memoirs of an American Citizen.*

Myra Harrington   Sister of Tommy Harrington; loves Jack Worthy in William Hill Brown's *The Power of Sympathy.*

Rodney Harrington   Spoiled son of Leslie Harrington; selfish womanizer who impregnates Betty Anderson and is later killed in an automobile accident in Grace Metalious's *Peyton Place.*

Sarah Gentles Harrington   See Sarah Gentles.

Tommy Harrington   Moralist and amoroso and brother of Myra Harrington; commits suicide after discovering that his beloved, Harriot Fawcet, is his half sister in William Hill Brown's *The Power of Sympathy.*

Will Harrington   Principled and poor brother of Edward Van Harrington and husband of May Rudge Harrington in Robert Herrick's *The Memoirs of an American Citizen.*

Harris   New Orleans steamboat captain and market contractor; searches island and coastal areas for survivors following the storm that destroys Last Island in Lafcadio Hearn's *Chita.*

Charles Baker (Dill) Harris   Nephew of Miss Rachel Haverford and excitable summer neighbor of Scout and Jem Finch in Harper Lee's *To Kill a Mockingbird.*

Eliza Harris   Slave to the Shelbys, who have treated her almost as a daughter; wife of George Harris and mother of Harry Harris; flees with Harry across the partially frozen Ohio River to the North and then to Canada when she learns that Harry has been sold in Harriet Beecher Stowe's *Uncle Tom's Cabin.*

George Harris   Harvard-educated black who, unable to find work, turns to crime in Thomas Dixon's *The Leopard's Spots.*

George Harris   Husband of Eliza Harris and father of Harry Harris; skilled machinist who flees to Canada when his owner becomes threatened by Harris's superior talents in Harriet Beecher Stowe's *Uncle Tom's Cabin.*

Harry Harris   Son of the slaves Eliza and George Harris; taken north by his mother after she learns that he has been sold in Harriet Beecher Stowe's *Uncle Tom's Cabin.*

Jack Harris   Boyhood friend of Tom Bailey; leads boys in the snowball fight; dies in the battle of the Seven Pines in Thomas Bailey Aldrich's *The Story of a Bad Boy.*

Tom Harris   Leading Citizen of Maxwell, Georgia; owner of its sawmills and turpentine stills in Lillian Smith's *Strange Fruit.*

Frederick Harrison   Man who charters the *South Florida* and turns in Harry Morgan to the authorities in Ernest Hemingway's *To Have and Have Not.*

Mrs. Phelps (Dolly) Harrison   Wealthy Washington society leader and widow involved with Bob Mun in Allen Drury's *Advise and Consent.*

William (Willie) Harrison   Mill owner whose proposal of marriage Lily Shane rejects in Louis Bromfield's *The Green Bay Tree.*

Daniel (Dan, Dan'l) Harrow   Farmer who works as a driver, inherits a canal boat, becomes lover of Molly Larkins, and returns to farming in Walter D. Edmonds's *Rome Haul;* appears as a dairyman in *The Big Barn.*

Harry   English groom in William Faulkner's *A Fable.*

Harry   Brother of Amy and father of Miranda and Maria; shoots a man suspected of having kissed Amy in Katherine Anne Porter's *Old Mortality.*

Andor Harsanyi   Chicago pianist and teacher who encourages Thea Kronborg to study voice in Willa Cather's *The Song of the Lark.*

Bob Harshaw   Attorney who defends Mink Lorey and who becomes the enemy of James Gwinnan in Mary Noailles Murfree's *In the Clouds.*

Miss Hartley   Nurse from Mobile, Alabama, called to care for Helga Crane after the birth of Helga's fourth child in Nella Larsen's *Quicksand.*

Reverend Curtis Hartman   Presbyterian minister who is driven to distraction by his voyeuristic obsession with Kate Swift in Sherwood Anderson's *Winesburg, Ohio.*

George Hartshorn   Jealous white man who loves Slim Girl in Oliver La Farge's *Laughing Boy.*

Ralph Hartsook   Young schoolmaster whose first assignment is in the 1850s in Flat Creek, Indiana, where he matches wits with recalcitrant pupils and corrupt locals, but where he also finds love, in Edward Eggleston's *The Hoosier School-Master.*

Caroline Harvey   Society matron and wife of Willis Harvey; accepts and coaches Rose Dutcher in Chicago society in Hamlin Garland's *Rose of Dutcher's Coolly.*

Elbert Harvey   Son of Caroline and Willis Harvey; offers wealth and good character in his courtship of Rose Dutcher in Hamlin Garland's *Rose of Dutcher's Coolly.*

Willis Harvey   Wealthy, enlightened Chicago businessman and husband of Caroline Harvey in Hamlin Garland's *Rose of Dutcher's Coolly.*

James Trueman Harwell   Murderer of Horatio Leavenworth, whom he had served as secretary, in Anna Katharine Green's *The Leavenworth Case.*

Nat Haskell   Freedman who tells Comfort Servosse about overhearing Marcus Thompson relate how John Walters was murdered by a group of ten men, including Thompson himself, in Albion W. Tourgée's *A Fool's Errand.*

Bonny Fern Haskin   Childhood and adult companion of Larry Donovan and female counterpart of the itinerant male worker during hard times in the American Midwest in Jack Conroy's *The Disinherited.*

Hassan   See Salvador Hassan O'Leary.

Martha Hastings   See Martha Hastings King.

Sergeant Hastings   British sergeant serving in Dorchester, South Carolina; bully whose lust for Bella Humphries leads to his death in William Gilmore Simms's *The Partisan.*

Lucy Haswell   Wife of Arnold Armstrong, whom she knows as Aubrey Wallace; dies giving birth to their son, Lucien Wallace, in Mary Roberts Rinehart's *The Circular Staircase.*

Homer T. Hatch   Bounty hunter killed by Royal Earle Thompson in Katherine Anne Porter's *Noon Wine.*

Miss Hatchard   Cousin of Lucius Harney and supervisor of the North Dormer library in which Charity Royall works for a short time in Edith Wharton's *Summer.*

James Graves Hatcher   Professor of dramatics at Harvard who teaches Eugene Gant in Thomas Wolfe's *Of Time and the River.*

Tilda Hatter   Former landlady of Jinny Timberlane; plaintiff in a court case before Cass Timberlane in Sinclair Lewis's *Cass Timberlane.*

Angeline Hatton   See Angeline Meserve.

Hausenfield   Undertaker in the first Hard Times; placed alive in his own hearse by Clay Turner and sent to the flats, where he dies, in E. L. Doctorow's *Welcome to Hard Times.*

Herman Hauser   Owner of the Little Rialto burlesque house in Chicago in Nelson Algren's *Somebody in Boots.*

Hautia   Queen of Flozella a Nina who apparently captures Yillah in Herman Melville's *Mardi.*

Ernest Havel   Bohemian immigrant and Claude Wheeler's best boyhood friend in Willa Cather's *One of Ours.*

Miss Rachel Haverford   Neighbor of Atticus Finch and aunt of Dill Harris in Harper Lee's *To Kill a Mockingbird.*

T. Havisham   Attorney for the Earl of Dorincourt; brings Cedric Errol to England in Frances Hodgson Burnett's *Little Lord Fauntleroy.*

Ally Hawes   Poorest girl in North Dormer and friend of Charity Royall; sews for Annabel Balch in Edith Wharton's *Summer*.

Julia Hawes   North Dormer bad girl and sister of Ally Hawes; seen by Charity Royall carousing with Lawyer Royall in a nearby town in Edith Wharton's *Summer*.

Hawk   Talented military subordinate of Wang the Tiger; eventually establishes himself as leader of a rival bandit group and is then captured and killed by his former leader in Pearl Buck's *Sons*.

Dr. Archibald Hawk   Byronically romantic man who presents himself so as to be attractive to women; engaged to Gertrude Larkin, until she discovers that he desires her money, in Hjalmar Hjorth Boyesen's *The Mammon of Unrighteousness*.

Drusilla Hawk   See Drusilla Hawk Sartoris.

Louisa (Louise) Hawk   Mother of Drusilla Hawk in William Faulkner's *The Unvanquished*.

David Hawke   See Robert Clark.

Harrison (Woolf) Hawke   Fraudulent psychiatrist in Vardis Fisher's *No Villain Need Be*; also appears as Harrison Woolf in *Orphans in Gethsemane*.

William (Billie, Will) Hawker   Struggling artist in love with a woman of superior wealth and social status in Stephen Crane's *The Third Violet*.

Hawkeye   See Nathaniel Bumppo.

George Washington Hawkins   Brother of Laura and Henry Clay Hawkins; with Laura, plans to sell their land in Tennessee and build Knobs Industrial University for blacks in Samuel Langhorne Clemens and Charles Dudley Warner's *The Gilded Age*.

Henry Clay Hawkins   Brother of Laura and George Washington Hawkins; inept Confederate soldier who later, from his Australian business ventures, supports the Hawkins family in Samuel Langhorne Clemens and Charles Dudley Warner's *The Gilded Age*.

Hiram Adolphus Hawkins   Poet who dies of a broken heart when Cecilia Vaughan rejects him and marries Arthur Kavanagh in Henry Wadsworth Longfellow's *Kavanagh*.

Laura Van Brunt Hawkins   Daughter of the Van Brunts, who is adopted by the Hawkinses after the Van Brunts are thought to be killed in a steamboat crash; becomes an influential Washington lobbyist; murders George Selby, but is acquitted; dies believing she is a failure in Samuel Langhorne Clemens and Charles Dudley Warner's *The Gilded Age*.

Martha Hawkins   Kindly niece of Squire Hawkins; wins the affection of Bud Means in Edward Eggleston's *The Hoosier School-Master*.

Martha Amelia Hawkins   Sister of Adolphus Hawkins; helps him in his unsuccessful pursuit of Cecilia Vaughan in Henry Wadsworth Longfellow's *Kavanagh*.

Squire Hawkins   Former poor Yankee schoolmaster who becomes one of the influential men of Flat Creek, Indiana, in Edward Eggleston's *The Hoosier School-Master*.

Wibird Hawkins   Rivermouth minister in Thomas Bailey Aldrich's *The Story of a Bad Boy*.

Captain Andy Hawks   Owner of the *Creole Belle* and later of the showboat *Cotton Blossom* in Edna Ferber's *Show Boat*.

Asa Hawks   Bogus street preacher who pretends to be blind but actually lost his nerve in the attempt to blind himself; father of Sabbath Lily Hawks in Flannery O'Connor's *Wise Blood*.

Magnolia Hawks   See Magnolia Hawks Ravenal.

Parthenia Ann (Parthy) Hawks   Former teacher from Massachusetts, wife of Andy Hawks, and mother of Magnolia Hawks Ravenal in Edna Ferber's *Show Boat*.

Sabbath Lily Hawks   Illegitimate daughter of Asa Hawks; pursues Hazel Motes and tries to live with him when her father leaves town in Flannery O'Connor's *Wise Blood*.

Mary Hawley   Dance-marathon contestant who agrees to marry her partner Vee Lovell in a publicity-oriented wedding arranged by the managers of the contest in Horace McCoy's *They Shoot Horses, Don't They?*

August Hay   Former ice-cream vendor, now derelict resident of the Diamond County Home for the Aged; laughs at everything and shares George Lucas's bottle of rye at the fair in John Updike's *The Poorhouse Fair*.

Harry and Juanita Haydock   Owners of the Bon Ton Store in Sinclair Lewis's *Main Street*.

Sally Hayes   Friend Holden Caulfield takes to the theater; he invites her to run away with him in J. D. Salinger's *The Catcher in the Rye*.

Jeanette Hayes-Rore   Widow of a black Chicago politician; a race woman, active in Negro Women's Clubs; becomes the employer, benefactor, and friend of Helga Crane in Nella Larsen's *Quicksand*.

Clarence Hay-Lawrence   Pretentious, monocled chess opponent of William Demarest in Conrad Aiken's *Blue Voyage*.

Andrew Haynes   Schoolmaster in Harriette Arnow's *Hunter's Horn*.

Flagler Haynes   Book publisher, then editor of the *Booklover*, and finally publisher's reader and reviewer in Edmund Wilson's *Memoirs of Hecate County*.

Thomas Hayward   Cowardly midshipman who reveals his cruelty by testifying against both the mutineers and those who are forced to stay aboard the HMS *Bounty* after the mutiny in Charles Nordhoff and James Norman Hall's *Mutiny on the Bounty;* set adrift with Captain Bligh in *Men Against the Sea.*

Bill Haywood   IWW leader portrayed in John Dos Passos's *U.S.A.* trilogy.

Arthur (Art) Hazard   Black musician who teaches Rick Martin how to play the trumpet; member of Jeff Williams's band in Dorothy Baker's *Young Man with a Horn.*

Edward Hazard   Father of Walter Hazard and grandfather of Ned Hazard; ambitious politician whose misdirected schemes at agricultural improvement help encumber his estate and instigate the eventual lawsuit between Frank Meriwether and Isaac Tracy over worthless land separating their plantations in John Pendleton Kennedy's *Swallow Barn.*

Lucretia Hazard   See Lucretia Hazard Meriwether.

Ned Hazard   Son and heir of Walter Hazard and brother of Lucretia Hazard Meriwether; irresponsible but good-natured gentleman and sportsman who is expelled from Princeton; assists in operating Frank Meriwether's plantation in John Pendleton Kennedy's *Swallow Barn.*

Walter Hazard   Father of Ned Hazard and Lucretia Hazard Meriwether in John Pendleton Kennedy's *Swallow Barn.*

Charlotte Haze   See Charlotte Becker Haze Humbert.

Dolores (Dolly, Lo, Lolita) Haze   Precocious nymphet, daughter of Charlotte Haze, stepdaughter and mistress of Humbert Humbert, and wife of Richard Schiller in Vladimir Nabokov's *Lolita.*

Sidney Herbert Head   Banker married to and quickly divorced from Caddy Compson in William Faulkner's *The Sound and the Fury.*

Vince Healy   Famous newspaper reporter in William Riley Burnett's *High Sierra.*

Lieutenant Robert (Bobby) Hearn   Harvard-educated assistant to General Cummings; resists Cummings's authority and is made head of a reconnaissance patrol; dies by Japanese sniper fire after Sergeant Croft withholds information in Norman Mailer's *The Naked and the Dead.*

Arthur Heathcote   Englishman who unsuccessfully woos Mildred Osborne in Paul Laurence Dunbar's *The Love of Landry.*

Hector   Faithful hound of Natty Bumppo in James Fenimore Cooper's *The Prairie* and *The Pioneers.*

Mrs. Hedges   Mysterious woman who operates a whorehouse in the apartment building where Lutie Johnson lives; close friend and informal partner of Mr. Junto in Ann Petry's *The Street.*

Professor Hedron   Mathematician and childhood friend of Adam Krug; arrested and later commits suicide in prison in Vladimir Nabokov's *Bend Sinister.*

Hedyle   Athenian courtesan, consort of Douris of Samos, and mother of Hedylus in H. D.'s *Hedylus.*

Hedylus   Adolescent poet of the Hellenistic Age who rebels against his mother, Hedyle; invited by Demion to leave Samos for India in H. D.'s *Hedylus.*

Mrs. Heeny   Society manicurist and masseuse who provides Undine Spragg with social gossip in Edith Wharton's *The Custom of the Country.*

Mrs. Heimowitz   Mother of Murray Heimowitz and upstairs neighbor of Mrs. Bogen in Jerome Weidman's *I Can Get It for You Wholesale;* cares for the dying Mrs. Bogen in *What's in It for Me?*

Murray Heimowitz   Lawyer engaged to Ruthie Rivkin in Jerome Weidman's *What's in It for Me?*

Elizabeth Heinemann   Blind resident of the Diamond County Home for the Aged; speaks of her hopes for an afterlife in John Updike's *The Poorhouse Fair.*

Heinrich   Twelve-year prisoner of Dachau and Jacob Levy's guide to the concentration camp in Martha Gellhorn's *Wine of Astonishment.*

Helen   Girlfriend of Jim Cowan; she is with Eddie Mitchell the night of the Sacco-Vanzetti executions in Nathan Asch's *Pay Day.*

Helen   Wife of Menelaos and sister of Clytemnestra; her liberal views of love, morality, and life upset others in John Erskine's *The Private Life of Helen of Troy.*

Hella   Young American woman courted and later jilted by David in James Baldwin's *Giovanni's Room.*

Heimie Hellman   Bootlegging associate of Harry (Bo) Mason in Wallace Stegner's *The Big Rock Candy Mountain.*

Hello   Joint king, with Piko, of Diranda; they control the population size by holding deadly games in Herman Melville's *Mardi.*

Adam Helmer   Giant, womanizing woodsman who outruns a party of Mohawks to warn of an impending attack on German Flats in Walter D. Edmonds's *Drums Along the Mohawk.*

Olaf Eric Helton   Escapee from an insane asylum; makes Royal Earle Thompson's farm profitable in Katherine Anne Porter's *Noon Wine.*

August (Aug) Hempel   Father of Julie Hempel Arnold; butcher who later owns the Hempel Packing Company in Edna Ferber's *So Big.*

Ed Henderson   Brigadier general and bomber commander in Beirne Lay, Jr., and Sy Bartlett's *Twelve O'Clock High!*

Eugene H. (Captain Henderson, Gene, Henderson-Sungo, Leo E., Rain King, Sungo) Henderson   Twice-married American millionaire with a master's degree, a face like an "unfinished church," and a voice within crying "I want, I want" that drives him in an earnest search for higher reality in Africa; discovers his answer in service to others as a joyful affirmer and an aspiring physician in Saul Bellow's *Henderson the Rain King.*

Riley Henderson   Independent and admired friend of Collin Fenwick; helps fight the battlers of the tree house in Truman Capote's *The Grass Harp.*

Rose Henderson   First love of Felix Fay and lover, with him, of French literature in Floyd Dell's *Moon-Calf.*

Sam Henderson   Fat horse trader who is actually an undercover police agent pursuing Gentleman Joe Calash in Walter D. Edmonds's *Rome Haul.*

Will Henderson   Editor of the *Winesburg Eagle* in Sherwood Anderson's *Winesburg, Ohio.*

Miles Hendon   Former soldier who is the guardian and protector of Edward Tudor (disguised as Tom Canty); made an earl when Edward becomes king in Samuel Langhorne Clemens's *The Prince and the Pauper.*

Robert (Bob) Hendricks   Fund-raiser for John Barclay; loses Molly Culpepper to Adrian Brownwell, who murders Hendricks, although the death is ruled a suicide, in William Allen White's *A Certain Rich Man.*

Millicent (Milly) Henning   Childhood friend of Hyacinth Robinson; becomes acquainted with a group of revolutionaries in Henry James's *The Princess Casamassima.*

Henri   See Count Alphonse D'Oyley.

Henry   Lover of Fidelia, whose abduction leads to his suicide, in William Hill Brown's *The Power of Sympathy.*

Billy James Henry   Juilliard-trained bassist in John Clellon Holmes's *The Horn.*

Frederic Henry   American serving as a lieutenant in the Italian army at the beginning of World War I; deserts with his lover Catherine Barkley to neutral Switzerland, where she dies in childbirth; narrator of Ernest Hemingway's *A Farewell to Arms.*

Janet Henry   Daughter of Senator Henry; romantically pursued by Paul Madvig, whom she despises; falls in love with Ned Beaumont in Dashiell Hammett's *The Glass Key.*

Judge Henry   Employer of the Virginian in Owen Wister's *The Virginian.*

Senator Ralph Bancroft Henry   U.S. senator whose son is murdered in Dashiell Hammett's *The Glass Key.*

Taylor Henry   Son of Senator Henry; the last person to see his murdered father in Dashiell Hammett's *The Glass Key.*

Philip Henshaw   English engineer who interests Frank Cowperwood in the London subway system in Theodore Dreiser's *The Stoic.*

Arvay (Arvie) Henson   Poor backwoods heroine who marries Jim Meserve; sister of Larraine Henson Middleton and mother of Earl, Angeline, and Kenny Meserve in Zora Neale Hurston's *Seraph on the Suwanee.*

Larraine Henson   See Larraine Henson Middleton.

Matthew (Matt) Henson   Neighbor of Angela and Virginia Murray; eventual love of Virginia in Jessie Redmon Fauset's *Plum Bun.*

Niel Herbert   Friend of Daniel and Marian Forrester; goes east to study architecture in Willa Cather's *A Lost Lady.*

Jimmy Herf   Newspaperman who aspires to authorship; married, for a time, to Ellen Thatcher; the central observer of the action in John Dos Passos's *Manhattan Transfer.*

Grandmother Herkimer   Elderly woman influenced by Agee Ward; her funeral is detailed in Wright Morris's *The Man Who Was There.*

Nicholas Herkimer   Stolid, courageous commander of the American militia at the battle of Oriskany; dies after amputation of a leg fails to halt gangrene in Walter D. Edmonds's *Drums along the Mohawk.*

Herman   Drug addict who moves in with William Lee and sells marijuana with him in William S. Burroughs's *Junkie.*

Herman   Card shark who poses as a diamond trader to cover up his illicit trading in women; eventually runs away with Zeftel and operates a brothel with her in Buenos Aires in Isaac Bashevis Singer's *The Magician of Lublin.*

Herman   Black neighbor of Penrod Schofield; with his brother, Verman, Herman provides the manpower for Penrod's grand schemes in Booth Tarkington's *Penrod, Penrod and Sam,* and *Penrod Jashber.*

Annie Morris Herman   Spirited, supportive high school classmate of Ruth Holland in Susan Glaspell's *Fidelity.*

Hermione   Daughter of Helen and Menelaos; rejects her mother's views of love and morality and runs off with Orestes in John Erskine's *The Private Life of Helen of Troy.*

Langley Herndon Owner of the apartment building where Gilbert and Eva Blount live; argues with Gilbert about Gilbert's allowing Lionel Lane to live there despite rules excluding blacks; Lane murders both men in Richard Wright's *The Outsider*.

Isabel Herrick Physician who supports women's equality with men in career and marriage; marries Dr. Sanborn in Hamlin Garland's *Rose of Dutcher's Coolly*.

Josie (Jo) Herrick High-society woman whom Ross Wilbur rejects in favor of Moran Sternersen in Frank Norris's *Moran of the Lady Letty*.

David Herschmidt See David L. Hirsh.

Vic (Old Man) Herschmidt Father of Frank and David Hirsh; leaves his wife to elope with the doctor's wife; town drunk in James Jones's *Some Came Running*.

Earl of Hertford Uncle of Edward Tudor; advisor to Tom Canty (disguised as Edward) in Samuel Langhorne Clemens's *The Prince and the Pauper*.

Lorena (Rena) Hessenwinkle Secretary at the Friendly Hearth Wood Yard; former lover of Fen Redcliff, by whom she has a son, and later wife of Fen's brother, Tat Redcliff, in Josephine Pinckney's *Three O'Clock Dinner*.

Black Hetty Devoted servant to Colonel James B. Brewton's family; assigned to care for the children in Conrad Richter's *The Sea of Grass*.

Hevaneva Idol maker and canoe builder on Maramma in Herman Melville's *Mardi*.

Duncan Heyward British major charged with taking Cora and Alice Munro to Fort William Henry; led astray by Magua, Heyward enlists the help of Natty Bumppo, Chingachgook, and Uncas to protect the Munro sisters in James Fenimore Cooper's *The Last of the Mohicans*.

Thomas J. Heywood Virginia gentleman summering in Norwood who, feeling caught between two cultures and rejected by Rose Wentworth, becomes swept up in the war fever; fights for the South at Gettysburg in Henry Ward Beecher's *Norwood*.

Angeline (Angie) Hibbard Mother-in-law and ideological opposite of Caddy Hibbard; triumphs by outliving Caddy in Wright Morris's *The World in the Attic*.

Bud Hibbard Conventional rural boyhood friend whom Clyde Muncy revisits in Wright Morris's *The World in the Attic*.

Caddy Hibbard Childless daughter-in-law of Angie Hibbard: her death and funeral are the key events in Wright Morris's *The World in the Attic*.

Clark Hibbard Editor and publisher of the *Parkman Oregonian;* helps Frank Hirsh develop Parkman Village at the bypass in James Jones's *Some Came Running*.

Clinton Hibbard Deceased husband of Caddy Hibbard and son of Angie Hibbard; the basis of conflict between the two women in Wright Morris's *The World in the Attic*.

Miss Hibbard Wealthy, unattractive fiancée of Charley Dunham; marries Dunham in William Dean Howells's *The Lady of the Aroostook*.

Nellie Hibbard Wife considered by Bud Hibbard the finest creature on God's earth in Wright Morris's *The World in the Attic*.

Mistress Hibbins Sister of Governor Bellingham; hanged as a witch in Nathaniel Hawthorne's *The Scarlet Letter*.

Wild Bill Hickok Marshal of Hays City, Kansas, in Emerson Hough's *North of 36*.

Captain Nathaniel Hicks Former magazine editor who represents the viewpoint of the intelligent, reasonable civilian drafted to be a soldier in James Gould Cozzens's *Guard of Honor*.

Miss Hicks High school history teacher of Homer Macauley; tries to promote goodwill among students of different ethnic backgrounds in William Saroyan's *The Human Comedy*.

Mr. Hicks Prodigal son whose trip aboard the *Aroostook* fails to cure him of his alcoholism in William Dean Howells's *The Lady of the Aroostook*.

William Hicks Marine automatic rifleman in France during World War I who is transformed into a hardened veteran in Thomas Boyd's *Through the Wheat*.

Mrs. Higbee Housekeeper for Cass Timberlane in Sinclair Lewis's *Cass Timberlane*.

Mrs. J. Franklin Higby President of the Mothers' League for Good Morals in Horace McCoy's *They Shoot Horses, Don't They?*

Bernard Higginbotham Brother-in-law of Martin Eden; believes that Eden is a worthless drunk in Jack London's *Martin Eden*.

Dinah Blackford Higgins Sister of Wyeth Blackford and childhood sweetheart of Anson Page; marries Mico Higgins in order to restore her family's faded fortunes in Hamilton Basso's *The View from Pompey's Head*.

Hop Higgins Night watchman of Winesburg in Sherwood Anderson's *Winesburg, Ohio*.

Mico (Mickey) Higgins Outsider who becomes a successful entrepreneur and a social climber in Hamilton Basso's *The View from Pompey's Head*.

Ned Higgins Boy who visits Hepzibah Pyncheon's cent-shop in Nathaniel Hawthorne's *The House of the Seven Gables*.

Frances Higginson   College roommate of and later resident of the same New York apartment with Derrick Thornton in Helen Hooven Santmyer's *Herbs and Apples*.

Highboy   Husband of Portia and companion of her brother Willie Copeland in Carson McCullers's *The Heart Is a Lonely Hunter*.

Esther (Dunnet Shepherdess) Hight   Spinster shepherdess whose hard outdoor life supporting herself and her aged, difficult mother is rewarded when, at her mother's death, she marries William Blackett, who has courted her for forty years, in Sarah Orne Jewett's *The Country of the Pointed Firs*.

Gail Hightower   Presbyterian minister forced to resign from his church following his wife's suicide in William Faulkner's *Light in August*.

Mrs. Gail Hightower   Disturbed wife of Gail Hightower; commits suicide by jumping from a hotel window in Memphis in William Faulkner's *Light in August*.

Hilda (The Dove)   Copier of famous paintings in Rome who lives in a tower surrounded by doves and who witnesses the murder of Brother Antonio; marries Kenyon in Nathaniel Hawthorne's *The Marble Faun*.

Hildesheim   Physician who restores Miranda's health in Katherine Anne Porter's *Pale Horse, Pale Rider*.

Eliab Hill   Crippled black shoemaker, preacher, and teacher who is freed by Casaubon Le Moyne and who is taught to read and write by Hester Le Moyne; rescued from the Ku Klux Klan by Nimbus; receives a college education in the North in Albion W. Tourgee's *Bricks with Straw*.

Hillentafel   Father of Kuno; furniture maker in Texas in Katherine Anne Porter's *The Leaning Tower*.

Kuno Hillentafel   Dead friend of Charles Upton; inspires Upton's visit to Berlin in Katherine Anne Porter's *The Leaning Tower*.

Boyd (B. H.) Hiller   Estranged husband of Irene Blaney Hiller in William Maxwell's *They Came Like Swallows*.

Irene Blaney Hiller   Sister of Elizabeth Morison; estranged from Boyd Hiller, she considers his request for a reconciliation but chooses instead to help rear Elizabeth's children in William Maxwell's *They Came Like Swallows*.

John (Jack) Hilton   Communist Party member and member of the editorial board for the *Daily Worker;* murdered by Lionel Lane in Richard Wright's *The Outsider*.

Alice Hindman   Clerk in Winney's Dry Goods Store; spinster because of her devotion to her departed lover, Ned Currie, in Sherwood Anderson's *Winesburg, Ohio*.

Eupheus (Doc) and Mrs. Hines   Parents of Milly Hines and grandparents of Joe Christmas in William Faulkner's *Light in August*.

Milly Hines   Daughter of Eupheus and Mrs. Hines; dies giving birth to Joe Christmas in William Faulkner's *Light in August*.

Alec Hinks   See Hamish Bond.

Hipparchia   Greek poet-courtesan; lives with Marius and later Verrus in H. D.'s *Palimpsest*.

Buck Hipps   Texan who auctions the spotted horses in William Faulkner's *The Hamlet*.

Agnes Marie Towns Hirsh   Wife of Frank Hirsh and mother of Dawn and Walter Hirsh; hypochondriac who resents her husband's mistresses in James Jones's *Some Came Running*.

David L. (Dave, David Herschmidt) Hirsh   Talented writer and World War II veteran; loves Gwen French but marries Ginnie Moorehead, whose exhusband kills him, in James Jones's *Some Came Running*.

Dawn (Dawnie) Hirsh   Daughter of Frank and Agnes Hirsh and aspiring actress; lover of Wally Dennis but marries another man in order to forget him in James Jones's *Some Came Running*.

Mrs. Elvira Hirsh   Wife of Vic Hershmidt and member of the Church of Christ Saved in James Jones's *Some Came Running*.

Frank Hirsh   Leading citizen of Parkman, Illinois, and brother of Dave Hirsh; becomes a wealthy peeping tom in James Jones's *Some Came Running*.

Walter Hirsh   Seven-year-old adopted son of Frank and Agnes Hirsh; loves engineering and heavy equipment in James Jones's *Some Came Running*.

Hist-oh!-Hist   See Wah-ta!-Wah.

Mrs. Wally Bee Hitchcock   Woman encountered by Hazel Motes on his train ride to Taulkinham in Flannery O'Connor's *Wise Blood*.

Hitia   Daughter of Marunga and Tavi and wife of Farani; survives the hurricane, during which she gives birth to a son, in Charles Nordhoff and James Norman Hall's *The Hurricane*.

Hitihiti   Tahitian subchieftain with whom Roger Byam resides and who helps Byam compile a dictionary of the Tahitian language in Charles Nordhoff and James Norman Hall's *Mutiny on the Bounty*.

Adolf (the Führer, Adi Schicklgruber) Hitler   Leader of the National Socialist revolution in Germany; discusses politics and art with Lanny Budd in Upton Sinclair's *Dragon's Teeth*.

Hivohitee   Pontiff of Maramma in Herman Melville's *Mardi*.

Miss Hobbe   Landlady of Miranda; threatens to evict the ill Miranda in Katherine Anne Porter's *Pale Horse, Pale Rider*.

Kathryn (Cousin Angie) Hobbes   Cynical and aggressive wife of Paul Hobbes; has an affair with Gene Pasternak in John Clellon Holmes's *Go*.

Paul (H.) Hobbes   Twenty-five-year-old novelist and poet married for six years to Kathryn Hobbes; unable to consummate a relationship with Estelle in John Clellon Holmes's *Go*.

Corporal Hobbs   Joker from Oklahoma and radioman in William Styron's *The Long March*.

Roy Hobbs   Star outfielder for the New York Knights; a rookie in his late thirties who succumbs to a gambling scheme involving his team's owner in Bernard Malamud's *The Natural*.

Silas Hobbs   New York grocer and friend of Cedric Errol in Frances Hodgson Burnett's *Little Lord Fauntleroy*.

Hobomok   Noble Indian chieftain who weds Mary Conant but relinquishes her and their son on the return of Mary's first love, Charles Brown, in Lydia Maria Child's *Hobomok*.

Alison Parr Hodder   See Alison Parr.

John Hodder   Clergyman who reevaluates his religious beliefs in light of modern social problems; marries Alison Parr in Winston Churchill's *The Inside of the Cup*.

Baron (Putzi) von Hodenlohern   Nazi who nearly tricks Mame Dennis in Patrick Dennis's *Around the World with Auntie Mame*.

Eliphalet (Brother Hodges, 'Liph, 'Liphalet) Hodges   Husband of Hester Prime; adoptive father of Frederick Brent in Paul Laurence Dunbar's *The Uncalled*.

Captain Hodgson   Captain of the lifeboat station in San Francisco Bay who discovers Moran Sternersen's corpse and reports her murder to Ross Wilbur in Frank Norris's *Moran of the Lady Letty*.

James Vaiden Hodige   Mulatto great-grandson of Miltiades Vaiden; one of six blacks standing trial for raping a white woman; escapes to safety in T. S. Stribling's *Unfinished Cathedral*.

Fred Hoff   IWW instigator who recruits Mac to work for a Wobbly newspaper in John Dos Passos's *U.S.A.* trilogy.

Violet Mauling Hogan   Secretary to Thomas Van Dorn; becomes a prostitute after being widowed, but reforms with the help of Henry Fenn in William Allen White's *In the Heart of a Fool*.

Boon Hogganbeck   Hunter or stable hand in William Faulkner's *Go Down, Moses* (where he kills Old Ben), *Intruder in the Dust, The Town,* and *The Reivers*.

Lucius Priest Hogganbeck   Son of Boon and Corrie Hogganbeck in William Faulkner's *The Town, The Mansion,* and *The Reivers*.

Mrs. Hoggs   Woman who boards sick people who are wards of the state; betrays Frado, claiming she is not an invalid and is capable of work, in Harriet E. Wilson's *Our Nig*.

Prince Moritz Franz Ernst Felix von Hohenauer   Austrian diplomat who convinces Marie Zattiany to gain political power by marrying him rather than to marry Lee Clavering for love in Gertrude Atherton's *Black Oxen*.

Prince Arbogast (Arbo) von Hohengraetz   Liberal nobleman who directs Rudolf Stanka's maturation and reveals Stanka's true identity in Louis Adamic's *Cradle of Life*.

Dr. Rippleton Holabird   Head of the physiology department and later director of the McGurk Institute of Biology in Sinclair Lewis's *Arrowsmith*.

Holgrave   Daguerreotypist, descendant of Matthew Maule, and resident of the Pyncheon house; marries Phoebe Pyncheon in Nathaniel Hawthorne's *The House of the Seven Gables*.

Burne Holiday   Princeton friend of Amory Blaine; social reformer in F. Scott Fitzgerald's *This Side of Paradise*.

Cyrus (Cy) Holland   Unforgiving brother of Ruth Holland in Susan Glaspell's *Fidelity*.

Ruth Holland   Independent-minded, small-town young woman who scandalizes local society by running away with Stuart Williams, a married man, in Susan Glaspell's *Fidelity*.

Ted Holland   Supportive younger brother of Ruth Holland in Susan Glaspell's *Fidelity*.

Hollingsworth   Selfish reformer who uses Zenobia and who loves Priscilla in Nathaniel Hawthorne's *The Blithedale Romance*.

Ed Leroy Hollingsworth   Government agent who pursues and interrogates William McLeod; lover of Beverly Guinevere McLeod in Norman Mailer's *Barbary Shore*.

John (Jack) Hollister   Columnist and managing editor of the Fort Penn Sentinel whose casual friendship with Grace Caldwell Tate, his employer, leads to an affair with her in John O'Hara's *A Rage to Live*.

Jebb Holloway   Rival of Jasper Harrick and former basketball star; goes into the cave with Isaac Sumpter but lies about reaching the trapped Harrick in Robert Penn Warren's *The Cave*.

Holly   See Holly Webster Wiggen.

Anna Marie (And-Ongen) Holm (Hansa)   Daughter of Beret Holm and Per Hansa and sister of Peder Holm (Hansa) in O. E.

Rölvaag's *Giants in the Earth, Peder Victorious,* and *Their Father's God.*

Beret Holm   See Beret Holm Hansa.

Henry Percival Holm   Son of Store-Hans Holm in O. E. Rölvaag's *Peder Victorious.*

Ole Haldor (Olamand) Holm (Hansa)   Son of Per Hansa and Beret Holm in O. E. Rölvaag's *Giants in the Earth;* marries and moves farther west in *Peder Victorious.*

Peder Emmanuel (Lisj-Per, Patrick St. Olaf, Petie) Holm   Son of Peder Holm and Susie Doheny Holm; his parents' religious conflict leads to his being christened secretly by both his grandmother and his mother in O. E. Rölvaag's *Their Father's God.*

Peder Victorious (Permand) Holm   Son of Per Hansa and Beret Holm; focus of his mother's sanity and madness in O. E. Rölvaag's *Giants in the Earth;* marries Susie Doheny, an Irish Catholic, in *Peder Victorious;* abandons the ministry for politics in *Their Father's God.*

Per Holm   See Per Hansa.

Store-Hans (Hans Kristian) Holm (Hansa)   Son of Per Hansa and Beret Holm in O. E. Rölvaag's *Giants in the Earth;* marries and buys a farm in *Peder Victorious;* opposes his brother Peder Hansa's marriage and politics in *Their Father's God.*

Susie Doheny Holm   See Susie Doheny.

Helene Holman   Torch singer and Ed Charney's girlfriend in John O'Hara's *Appointment in Samarra.*

Bradley Holmes   Editor of Allison MacKenzie; becomes her lover without telling her he is married in Grace Metalious's *Peyton Place.*

Captain Dana E. (Dynamite) Holmes   Company commander and coach of the regimental boxing team; orders the Treatment for Robert E. Lee Prewitt after Prewitt refuses to box in James Jones's *From Here to Eternity.*

Mrs. Eliza Holmes   Bookish, meditative, and sentimental resident of Belleview; reveals that Tommy Harrington and Harriot Fawcet have the same father in William Hill Brown's *The Power of Sympathy.*

Jack Holmes   Parachute jumper and possibly the father of Jack Schumann in William Faulkner's *Pylon.*

Karen Holmes   Wife of Dana Holmes; has an affair with Milton Warden; leaves Oahu for the mainland after Holmes and Warden receive their orders to go overseas in James Jones's *From Here to Eternity.*

Alexander Holston   A founder of Jefferson in William Faulkner's *Absalom, Absalom!, Intruder in the Dust, Requiem for a Nun, The Town,* and *The Mansion.*

Andrew Holte   Minister who advocates abandoning the Norwegian for the evangelical in the Lutheran church in O. E. Rölvaag's *Peder Victorious;* also appears in *Their Father's God.*

Onnie Jay Holy   See Hoover Shoats.

Homos (Altrurian)   Visitor to America from the European utopia of Altruria; critic of American life in William Dean Howells's *A Traveler from Altruria.*

Little Homer Honey   Son of Sister Ida Honey and star of the Honey family; preaches, rope twirls, and helps with collections in Truman Capote's *The Grass Harp.*

Sister Ida Honey   Impoverished traveling revivalist; mother of fifteen children, most of them illegitimate, in Truman Capote's *The Grass Harp.*

Miss Honey   Second wife of Gabriel Breaux in Katherine Anne Porter's *Old Mortality.*

Annabel Upchurch Honeywell   See Annabel Upchurch.

Judge Gamaliel Bland Honeywell   Wealthy, decorous, and recently widowed man who marries Annabel Upchurch, a woman more than forty years his junior, in Ellen Glasgow's *The Romantic Comedians.*

Ezekiel Hook   See John Treeworgy.

John F. (Hookie) Hook   Ninety-four-year-old resident of the Diamond County Home for the Aged; respected former schoolteacher who sees his friend Billy Gregg as his final pupil in John Updike's *The Poorhouse Fair.*

Andrew (Andy) Hookans   Marine radio operator who loses a leg at Saipan in Leon Uris's *Battle Cry.*

Minna Hooven   Daughter of Mrs. Hooven; driven by want—because the railroad forced her out of her home—to prostitution in Frank Norris's *The Octopus.*

Mrs. Hooven   Mother of Minna Hooven; victim of the railroad's chicanery who, having lost her home, starves to death in Frank Norris's *The Octopus.*

James Hopkins   Rejected suitor of Sally Oldham in Lydia Maria Child's *Hobomok.*

Eliphalet Hopper   Sycophantic and unscrupulous war profiteer; suitor of Virginia Carvel in Winston Churchill's *The Crisis.*

Earl Horter   Writer of popular song lyrics who is attracted to Eva Baum; narrator of Wright Morris's *Love among the Cannibals.*

Ernest Horton Traveling novelty salesman from the Little Wonder Company who impresses the passengers on Juan Chicoy's bus with his ingenious merchandise, including the Little Wonder Artificial Sore Foot, in John Steinbeck's *The Wayward Bus.*

Ginger Horton Writer and friend of Guy Grand in Terry Southern's *The Magic Christian.*

Ely Houston New York district attorney who investigates the murders of Gilbert Blount, Langley Herndon, and Jack Hilton in Richard Wright's *The Outsider.*

Jack (Zack) Houston Farmer murdered by Mink Snopes; appears in William Faulkner's *The Hamlet, The Town,* and *The Mansion.*

Paul (Mr. Bug Gatherer) Hover Kentucky-born bee hunter who follows his beloved Ellen Wade onto the prairie; joins Natty Bumppo and Duncan Uncas Middleton in rescuing Inez de Certavallos in James Fenimore Cooper's *The Prairie.*

Howard (Howy) Experienced prospector who helps Dobbs and Curtin search for gold in B. Traven's *The Treasure of the Sierra Madre.*

Pembroke Howard Courtroom opponent of Pudd'nhead Wilson; prosecutes Luigi and Angelo Capello for the murder of York Driscoll in Samuel Langhorne Clemens's *Pudd'nhead Wilson.*

Pappy Howell Horse-race gambler found shot to death and robbed of his winnings, for which Wade Shiveley is unjustly blamed, in H. L. Davis's *Honey in the Horn.*

Hatton Howland Yankee husband of Angeline Meserve and entrepreneur land-developer in Zora Neale Hurston's *Seraph on the Suwanee.*

Rosemary Hoyt Beautiful young movie actress who falls in love with Dick Diver in F. Scott Fitzgerald's *Tender Is the Night.*

Bartley Hubbard Newspaperman married to Marcia Gaylord Hubbard; given to affairs and plagiarism; murdered by an outraged citizen in William Dean Howells's *A Modern Instance;* interviews Silas Lapham in *The Rise of Silas Lapham.*

Marcia Gaylord (Marsh) Hubbard Wife of Bartley Hubbard; after he deserts her, she divorces him in William Dean Howells's *A Modern Instance;* also appears in *The Rise of Silas Lapham.*

Hubert Maternal grandfather of Cress Delahanty in Jessamyn West's *Cress Delahanty.*

Zachary (Zack) Huddlestone New Yorker and friend of Mark Littleton in John Pendleton Kennedy's *Swallow Barn.*

Harley M. Hudson Vice president of the United States; appears weak until thrust into the presidency by the president's death in Allen Drury's *Advise and Consent.*

Roderick Hudson Young American sculptor studying art in Europe and patronized by Rowland Mallet; fiancé of Mary Garland, but in love with Christina Light; dies tragically in Henry James's *Roderick Hudson.*

Sarah Hudson Widowed mother of Roderick Hudson and cousin of Mary Garland; visits her son in Europe in Henry James's *Roderick Hudson.*

Mrs. Hudspeth Widow who trades horses with Jess Birdwell in Jessamyn West's *The Friendly Persuasion.*

Saved from Captivity (Cap) Huff Friend of Steven Nason; marches to Quebec with Benedict Arnold in Kenneth Roberts's *Arundel.*

Samuel (Sam) Hugg River barge captain and teller of tall tales in James Kirke Paulding's *Westward Ho!*

Alonzo Dent (A. D.) Huguenine Farmer who becomes a circus owner and struggles to recoup his investment in Huguenine's Great and Only International Circus in Walter D. Edmonds's *Chad Hanna.*

Bettina (Bettina Billings) Huguenine Wife of A. D. Huguenine; as Bettina Billings, she is the fat lady in Huguenine's circus; matronly protector of the circus workers in Walter D. Edmonds's *Chad Hanna.*

Andy Hull Son of a preacher; eighth-grade classmate of Suse Ballew in Harriette Arnow's *Hunter's Horn;* serves in Europe in World War II in *The Dollmaker.*

Charlotte Becker Haze Humbert Mother of Dolores Haze and second wife of Humbert Humbert; struck and killed by a car as she runs out of her house in a fit of anger against Humbert in Vladimir Nabokov's *Lolita.*

Humbert (Edgar H. Humbert, Hummy) Humbert European author who tells of his obsession with the nymphet Dolores Haze; narrator of Vladimir Nabokov's *Lolita.*

George Humbolt See Uncle Peepee Marshmallow.

Alice Humphreys Young woman who befriends and teaches Ellen Montgomery while Ellen lives with her aunt near Thirlwall; dies at age twenty-four in Susan Warner's *The Wide, Wide World.*

John Humphreys Ministerial student and brother of Alice Humphreys; becomes Ellen Montgomery's beloved teacher and finally her husband in Susan Warner's *The Wide, Wide World.*

Mr. Humphreys Country minister and father of Alice and John Humphreys; Ellen Montgomery moves to his home and cares for him after Alice's untimely death in Susan Warner's *The Wide, Wide World.*

Bella (Bell) Humphries   Daughter of Richard Humphries; her suitors include the British sergeant Hastings and the partisan John Davis in William Gilmore Simms's *The Partisan.*

Richard (Old Dick) Humphries   Taverner and father of Bella and William Humphries in William Gilmore Simms's *The Partisan.*

William (Bill) Humphries   Son of Richard Humphries and brother of Bella Humphries; trusted lieutenant of Major Singleton in William Gilmore Simms's *The Partisan.*

Adam B. Hunt   Ambitious party man but unsuccessful candidate for the gubernatorial nomination in Winston Churchill's *Mr. Crewe's Career.*

Jason Hunt   Husband of Nan Hunt and father of Cissy Hunt and Marcia Mae Hunt O'Donnell; wealthy, socially prominent, and politically influential figure in Elizabeth Spencer's *The Voice at the Back Door.*

Jerry (Uncle Jerry) Hunt   Crippled freedman and charismatic preacher whose warning saves Comfort Servosse from an ambush; hanged by the Ku Klux Klan following a vision in which he reveals the details of John Walter's murder in Albion W. Tourgee's *A Fool's Errand.*

Marjorie Angeline (Cissy) Hunt   Younger daughter of Nan and Jason Hunt and fiancée of Kerney Woolbright in Elizabeth Spencer's *The Voice at the Back Door.*

Nan Hunt   Patrician wife of Jason Hunt and mother of Marcia Mae Hunt O'Donnell and Cissy Hunt in Elizabeth Spencer's *The Voice at the Back Door.*

Angele Lorelei Lee Hunter   First lover, then mistress, and third wife of Vridar Hunter in Vardis Fisher's *Orphans in Gethsemane.*

Diana Hunter   Sister of Vridar Hunter and the only Hunter child who does not forsake the parents' Mormon strictures in Vardis Fisher's *In Tragic Life, Passions Spin the Plot, We Are Betrayed,* and *Orphans in Gethsemane.*

Dock Hunter   Good-humored brother of Joe Hunter in Vardis Fisher's *In Tragic Life* and *Orphans in Gethsemane.*

Joseph Charles (Joe) Hunter   Cold father of Vridar Hunter in Vardis Fisher's *In Tragic Life, Passions Spin the Plot, We Are Betrayed, No Villain Need Be,* and *Orphans in Gethsemane.*

Mertyl (Mert) Hunter   Cross-eyed and persecuted brother of Vridar Hunter in Vardis Fisher's *In Tragic Life, Passions Spin the Plot, We Are Betrayed, No Villain Need Be,* and *Orphans in Gethsemane.*

Neloa Doole Hunter   See Neloa Doole.

Prudence Branton Hunter   Stern mother of Vridar Hunter in Vardis Fisher's *In Tragic Life, Passions Spin the Plot, We Are Betrayed, No Villain Need Be,* and *Orphans in Gethsemane.*

Robert (Bob) Hunter   Black railway worker fired from his job; briefly involved with the Communist Party, whose members turn him in to the immigration authorities for deportation to Jamaica, in Richard Wright's *The Outsider.*

Sarah Hunter   Wife of Bob Hunter in Richard Wright's *The Outsider.*

Steve Hunter   Business school graduate who builds a factory to produce Hugh McVey's mechanical inventions and persuades local citizens to invest in it; shot and wounded by Joseph Wainsworth for contributing to the industrialization of the community, therefore changing it, in Sherwood Anderson's *Poor White.*

Vridar Baroledt (Vreed) Hunter   Child of a religious Utah family; grows up to be an intellectual and writes an autobiographical novel; appears in Vardis Fisher's *In Tragic Life, Passions Spin the Plot, We Are Betrayed, No Villain Need Be,* and *Orphans in Gethsemane.*

Edgar Huntly   Narrator who relates the tale of how his insane compulsions, although with good motives, misled him, bringing about disastrous consequences, in Charles Brockden Brown's *Edgar Huntly.*

Iris Hurley   God-fearing friend of Silla Boyce in Paule Marshall's *Brown Girl, Brownstones.*

Will Hurley   Drugstore clerk who unsuccessfully courts Alice Hindman in Sherwood Anderson's *Winesburg, Ohio.*

George W. (George Wheeler) Hurstwood   Married saloon manager who steals money from the saloon and flees to New York with his lover, Carrie Meeber; dies in a flophouse fire in Theodore Dreiser's *Sister Carrie.*

Julia Hurstwood   Estranged wife of George Hurstwood in Theodore Dreiser's *Sister Carrie.*

Eveline Hutchins   Friend and partner of Eleanor Stoddard who develops her interest in art and high culture into a social skill; her flirtatious manner attracts an array of well-heeled suitors despite her marriage in John Dos Passos's *U.S.A.* trilogy.

Sarah (Widow Hutchins) Hutchins   See Hugh and Sarah Hutchins Crombie.

Hetty Hutter   Simpleminded sister of Judith Hutter; loves Henry March; accidentally killed in an Indian attack in James Fenimore Cooper's *The Deerslayer.*

Judith Hutter   Beautiful stepdaughter of Thomas Hutter; tries unsuccessfully to inspire love in Natty Bumppo in James Fenimore Cooper's *The Deerslayer.*

Thomas (Thomas Hovey) Hutter   Stepfather of Judith and Hetty Hutter; lives on the ark that he built on Lake Glimmerglass; scalped by the Indians and laid to rest at the bottom of Glimmerglass in James Fenimore Cooper's *The Deerslayer.*

Grandma Hutto   Friend of Penny Baxter; once shared her home with the Baxter family in Marjorie Kinnan Rawlings's *The Yearling.*

Oliver Hutto   Seafaring son of Grandma Hutto; his love for Twink Weatherby causes his mother to move away in Marjorie Kinnan Rawlings's *The Yearling.*

Samuel (Sam) Huxley   Marine captain killed at Saipan in Leon Uris's *Battle Cry.*

Lord (Old Lord) Hwang   Patriarch of the House of Hwang in Pearl Buck's *The Good Earth.*

Liff Hyatt   Mountain child who occasionally works for farmers in Edith Wharton's *Summer.*

Mary Hyatt   Destitute mother of Charity Royall whom Charity does not know until she attends Mary's primitive burial on the Mountain in Edith Wharton's *Summer.*

Anne Hyde   Rather homely daughter of the Earl of Clarendon and wife of the Duke of York in Kathleen Winsor's *Forever Amber.*

Jesse Hyman   Son of Squire Nathaniel Hyman; because he favors Reconstruction, he is beaten by the Ku Klux Klan; sent to Kansas, where he is befriended by a preacher who was beaten at Flat Rock twelve years earlier, in Albion W. Tourgee's *A Fool's Errand.*

Squire Nathaniel Hyman   Neighbor of Comfort Servosse and a community spokesman in warning the Servosses against associating with Northern teachers from the freedmen's school at Verdenton; presides at the trial of three Negro men accused of murdering Tom Savage in Albion W. Tourgee's *A Fool's Errand.*

Mr. Hyslop   Secretary of A. J. in William S. Burroughs's *Naked Lunch.*

I Daughter of Nimni and Ohiro-Moldona-Fivona in Herman Melville's *Mardi*.

Idomeneus Unconventional suitor of Helen and the first soldier to return from the Trojan War in John Erskine's *The Private Life of Helen of Troy*.

Finger Idzikowski Friend and boxing trainer of Bruno (Lefty) Bicek; hexes Bicek's opponents in Nelson Algren's *Never Come Morning*.

Ike (Old Ike) Friend and heroin connection of William Lee in Mexico City in William S. Burroughs's *Junkie* and *Naked Lunch*.

Ikkemotubbe (Doom) Chickasaw chief in William Faulkner's *Absalom, Absalom!; Go Down, Moses; Requiem for a Nun; The Town;* and *The Reivers*.

(The Generous) Sheik Ilderim Egyptian horse trader who befriends Judah Ben-Hur during his quest for his lost mother and sister; is gracious and shrewd, possessing some of the finest horses in the Middle East; provides Ben-Hur with a chariot and stallions enough to defeat the Roman Messala in Lew Wallace's *Ben-Hur: A Tale of the Christ*.

Ned Inching London pickpocket imprisoned in Australia; escapes from the penal colony and returns to London in Charles Nordhoff and James Norman Hall's *Botany Bay*.

El Indio Morphine addict and friend of Tristessa in Jack Kerouac's *Tristessa*.

Inez Third wife of Dean Moriarty in Jack Kerouac's *On the Road*.

Arthur J. Ingles Husband of Cecilia Ingles; owner of the Clifton, a Chicago skyscraper, in Henry Blake Fuller's *The Cliff-Dwellers*.

Cecilia Ingles Wife of Arthur J. Ingles; rules Chicago society in Henry Blake Fuller's *The Cliff-Dwellers*.

Zell Ingram Commercial artist; friend of Jule Jackson and fellow resident at the YMCA in New York City in George Wylie Henderson's *Jule*.

Injun Joe Half-breed who murders Dr. Robinson and frames Muff Potter; dies when he is accidentally sealed in a cave in Samuel Langhorne Clemens's *The Adventures of Tom Sawyer*.

Raoul Innerarity Creole who helps Joseph Frowenfeld in Frowenfeld's drug store in George Washington Cable's *The Grandissimes*.

Gertrude Innes Niece of Rachel Innes and fiancée of John Bailey in Mary Roberts Rinehart's *The Circular Staircase*.

Halsey B. Innes Nephew of Rachel Innes; kidnapped when he discovers that Paul Armstrong is alive in Mary Roberts Rinehart's *The Circular Staircase*.

Rachel (Aunt Ray) Innes Middle-aged spinster who rents Sunnyside and who helps solve the murder of Arnold Armstrong; narrator of Mary Roberts Rinehart's *The Circular Staircase*.

Innis Tory partisan leader in Charleston, South Carolina, who imprisons Arthur Butler in John Pendleton Kennedy's *Horse-Shoe Robinson*.

Iras Beautiful Egyptian daughter of Balthasar and brief lover of Judah Ben-Hur; is greedy and conniving, wanting desperately the riches Roman life; becomes a spy for the Roman Messala and eventually leaves Ben-Hur for Messala; angry over the lack of riches and general abuse she encounters while Messala's mistress, she kills him and regrets her rejection of Ben-Hur in Lew Wallace's *Ben-Hur: A Tale of the Christ*.

Latham Ireland   Lawyer who rivals Martin Arrowsmith for the affections of Joyce Lanyon in Sinclair Lewis's *Arrowsmith*.

Irene   Adolescent friend of Hedylus who considers leaving Samos with him in H. D.'s *Hedylus*.

Daniel Webster (Dan) Irving   College professor blacklisted for his outspoken opposition to United States involvement with Russia during World War I; journalist who exposes the oil scandal in the Harding administration in Upton Sinclair's *Oil!*

Alexander Irwin   Young heavyweight boxer in whom Lee Youngdahl has an investment in Mark Harris's *Wake Up, Stupid*.

Judge Montague M. (Monty) Irwin   Respected citizen of Burden's Landing and father of the illegitimate Jack Burden; backs the political opposition to Willie Stark in Robert Penn Warren's *All the King's Men*.

Isaac   Elderly slave at Dove Cote; accompanies the Lindsays and Horse-Shoe Robinson on their visit to Cornwallis to assure Arthur Butler's fair treatment in John Pendleton Kennedy's *Horse-Shoe Robinson*.

Jacob Isaacs   See Prince Cabano.

Isaiah   Ex-slave and servant of Felice and Lewis Venable; runs away to Oklahoma with Sabra Venable and her new husband, Yancey Cravat, in Edna Ferber's *Cimarron*.

Ishmael   Narrator; sole survivor of the *Pequod*'s pursuit of Moby-Dick in Herman Melville's *Moby-Dick*.

Issetibbeha   Chickasaw chief in William Faulkner's *Go Down, Moses; Requiem for a Nun; The Town;* and *The Reivers*.

Itelo   Prince of the Arnewi tribe of African cow worshippers; welcomes Eugene Henderson to the drought-stricken village with a ritual wrestling match that Henderson wins, making Itelo a bosom friend, in Saul Bellow's *Henderson the Rain King*.

Ito   Giggling Japanese houseboy noted for his terrible driving in Patrick Dennis's *Auntie Mame* and *Around the World with Auntie Mame*.

Iva (née Almstadt)   Librarian and long-suffering wife of Joseph in Saul Bellow's *Dangling Man*.

Walter Ivans   Disgruntled associate of Paul Madvig's who feels that Madvig should arrange the release of his brother, Tim Ivans, in Dashiell Hammett's *The Glass Key*.

Crazy Ivar   Eccentric Norwegian hermit who works with animals on Alexandra Bergson's farm in Willa Cather's *O Pioneers!*

Jacataqua Abenaki Indian blood sister of Steven Nason; accompanies Benedict Arnold's army to Quebec in Kenneth Roberts's *Arundel*.

Jacinto Indian guide who shows Bishop Latour a sacred Indian cave in Willa Cather's *Death Comes for the Archbishop*.

Jack Writer and would-be painter adventuring in the drug underworld of Mexico City; narrator of Jack Kerouac's *Tristessa*.

Brother Jack Leader of the Brotherhood who recruits the narrator into his organization in Ralph Ellison's *Invisible Man*.

Captain Jack Keeper of a lifesaving station in San Francisco Bay who provides plots and details to the would-be author Condé Rivers in Frank Norris's *Blix*.

Esther Jack Stage-set designer, wife of Frederick Jack, and lover of George Webber in Thomas Wolfe's *You Can't Go Home Again* and *The Web and the Rock*.

Frederick (Fritz) Jack Wealthy New York businessman and husband of Esther Jack in Thomas Wolfe's *You Can't Go Home Again;* also appears in *The Web and the Rock*.

Jackson Worker who loses his arm in an industrial accident and is denied compensation by his employer in Jack London's *The Iron Heel*.

Jackson Illiterate atheist who bullies the *Highlander*'s sailors in Herman Melville's *Redburn*.

Art Jackson Parachute jumper in William Faulkner's *Pylon*.

Beth Jackson Senior nurse at the Hauptman Clinic in Terry Southern's *Flash and Filigree*.

Bill Jackson Mountaineer who helps Will Banion protect the wagon train; kills Sam Woodhull in Emerson Hough's *The Covered Wagon*.

Father Jackson Priest who comforts Mary Follet after the death of her husband in James Agee's *A Death in the Family*.

Harry Jackson Butler and chauffeur for Edith and Joe Chapin I; confidant of Ann Chapin in John O'Hara's *Ten North Frederick*.

Helen Jackson New Orleans Communist and resident of Twenty-Door City; mistress of Josie Morales and loved by Leon Fisher in Albert Halper's *Union Square*.

Jordan Jackson Poor white man who rises to the rank of lieutenant in the Confederate army; saves the life of Hesden Le Moyne in battle, and makes money in trade following the war; whipped by the Ku Klux Klan for running on the same political ticket as a black man and for advocating a political alliance of blacks and poor whites in Albion W. Tourgee's *Bricks Without Straw*.

Jule (Mr. Man, Schoolboy) Jackson Illegitimate son of Ollie and Big Jule, lover of Bertha Mae, and protagonist of George Wylie Henderson's *Jule*.

Sillerton Jackson Bachelor and social gossip in Edith Wharton's *The Age of Innocence;* mentioned in *The Old Maid*.

Stuart Jackson Wealthy midwestern suitor who is rejected by Adah Logan in Susan Glaspell's *Judd Rankin's Daughter*.

T5 Ronald Jackson Driver for Richard Cantwell in Ernest Hemingway's *Across the River and into the Trees*.

General Thomas Jonathan (Stonewall) Jackson   Professor of natural philosophy and military tactics at Virginia Military Institute; earns a reputation as an eccentric but brilliant tactician; apotheosized when accidentally killed by Confederate troops in Mary Johnston's *The Long Roll*.

Baron Jacobi   Bulgarian minister who lectures on the corruptness of Americans and who whacks Senator Ratcliffe with a cane; friend of Madeleine Lee in Henry Adams's *Democracy*.

Capt. Jacobi   Ship's captain of *La Paloma* who delivers a falcon statuette to Sam Spade in Dashiell Hammett's *Maltese Falcon*.

Constance Jacobs   Sister of Wilson Jacobs; befriends Mildred Latham in Oscar Micheaux's *The Forged Note*.

Samuel (Sammy) Jacobs   Elderly Jewish store owner who is disappointed when his son loses his job with Glymmer, Read in Nathan Asch's *The Office*.

Wilson Jacobs   Minister, fund-raiser for the YMCA, and brother of Constance Jacobs; falls in love with Mildred Latham in Oscar Micheaux's *The Forged Note*.

Jacopo   Accordion player in the Caffé Gatto; attacks his former partner, Edouard, in John Hawkes's *The Goose on the Grave*.

Ernestine (Winnie) Jacques   Long-lost sister whom Mildred Latham meets by coincidence; wife of the physician who treats Sidney Wyeth for typhoid in Oscar Micheaux's *The Forged Note*.

Father Jacques   Frontier priest in James Kirke Paulding's *Westward Ho!*

Curtis (J.) Jadwin   Real estate baron, romantic lover, and then the Great Bull of the Chicago Board of Trade; attempts to corner the American wheat market, losing his fortune and almost losing his wife, in Frank Norris's *The Pit*.

Laura Dearborn Jadwin   Wife of Curtis Jadwin; nearly driven insane by Jadwin's neglect in Frank Norris's *The Pit*.

Don Jaime   See Don Jaime de Ribera.

Jake   Faithful former slave of Richard Cameron; helps get Cameron released from jail in Thomas Dixon's *The Clansman*.

Jake   Black fisherman and resident of Catfish Row; killed in a Charleston hurricane in DuBose Heyward's *Porgy*.

Earl James   White playmate and friend of Sandy Rodgers; does not understand why Sandy is not admitted to Children's Day at the amusement park in Langston Hughes's *Not Without Laughter*.

Jefferson James   Physician and friend of Frank Cowperwood in Theodore Dreiser's *The Stoic*.

Laura James   First love of Eugene Gant; leaves Gant to marry her hometown boyfriend in Thomas Wolfe's *Look Homeward, Angel*.

Miss James   Telephone operator with Glymmer, Read who is relatively unconcerned when the firm declares bankruptcy in Nathan Asch's *The Office*.

Clive Jameson   Famous Civil War general and son of Isaac Jameson in Shelby Foote's *Jordan County*.

Dorothy Jameson   Painter who attends the yacht party in William Faulkner's *Mosquitoes*.

Isaac Jameson   First white settler and plantation developer on Lake Jordan in Shelby Foote's *Jordan County*.

Jamieson   Detective who investigates Arnold Armstrong's murder in Mary Roberts Rinehart's *The Circular Staircase*.

Mary (Bessie) Jamiesson   Resident of the Diamond County Home for the Aged; homely, heavy woman with a gift for flirting, affection, and patience; bears the emotional scars of having had a beautiful, unloving mother in John Updike's *The Poorhouse Fair*.

Tom Jamison   Hometown friend for whom a delirious soldier mistakes Henry Fleming in Stephen Crane's *The Red Badge of Courage*.

Duchess Jane   Friend of Mrs. Brookenham in Henry James's *The Awkward Age*.

Janey   Child protected by Hugh Wolfe and his relatives in Rebecca Harding Davis's *Life in the Iron Mills*.

Mrs. Janney   Mother of Rena Janney; killed in an automobile crash in August Derleth's *The Shield of the Valiant*.

Rena (Miss Lolly C., Mouse, Renchen) Janney   Girlfriend of Kivden Sewall and a victim of Sac Prairie gossip; moves to Madison to live with her mother and becomes a jazz singer in August Derleth's *The Shield of the Valiant*.

Earl Janoth   Publisher and head of Janoth Enterprises; lover and murderer of Pauline Delos; a narrator of Kenneth Fearing's *The Big Clock*.

Pauline Janowski   Adolescent who asks Henry Miller for a job as a messenger; he seduces her and leaves her on the highway in the middle of the night to hitch a ride to Cleveland in Henry Miller's *Tropic of Capricorn*.

Christina Jansen (Christina Carlson)   Wife of Maximilian Petion; poor music hall singer whom Nathan Brederhagan stabs during an attempted rape in Ignatius Donnelly's *Caesar's Column*.

Samuel Japson   Quaker trader who befriends Salathiel Albine; appears in Hervey Allen's *The Forest and the Fort* and *Bedford Village*.

Willard Jarkins   Broker for Frank Cowperwood; handles Cowperwood's interest in the London subway system in Theodore Dreiser's *The Stoic*.

Jarl (Skyeman, Viking)   Companion of Taji; killed by Aleema's sons in Herman Melville's *Mardi*.

Father Jarnatt   Village priest who befriends Jean Lambert Tallien in H. L. Davis's *Harp of a Thousand Strings*.

Berk Jarvis   Pioneer who marries Diony Hall; captured by Indians, but escapes and reclaims Diony, who has married Evan Muir, in Elizabeth Madox Roberts's *The Great Meadow*.

Diony Hall (Diny) Jarvis   Imaginative daughter of a planter family; marries Berk Jarvis, who is later captured by the Indians and presumed dead; marries Evan Muir, but chooses Jarvis over Muir when Jarvis returns, in Elizabeth Madox Roberts's *The Great Meadow*.

Elvira Jarvis   Mother of Berk Jarvis in Elizabeth Madox Roberts's *The Great Meadow*.

Major Gordon Jarvis   Defense counsel for Jacob Levy in Martha Gellhorn's *Wine of Astonishment*.

Paul Jarvis   Fiancé of Delia Poole; taken into his uncle's business and subsequently ordered to the Philippines in Janet Flanner's *The Cubical City*.

Edward K. (Jap) Jasper   Former medical student disabled by mental collapse; finally able to complete his studies after having served as Doctor Caldwell's faithful assistant; silently in love with William Caldwell in Mary Austin's *Santa Lucia*.

Madame de Jaume   Witty friend of Adela Gareth in Henry James's *The Spoils of Poynton*.

Jay   Pianist in a movie house, drunkard, and artist whose paintings decorate Mambo's nightclub; friend of Sabina and Djuna and husband of Lillian in Anaïs Nin's *Ladders to Fire, Children of the Albatross, The Four-Chambered Heart, A Spy in the House of Love,* and *Seduction of a Minotaur*.

Charlie Jay   Devil-may-care boyhood friend of Brock Caldwell; has sex with Grace Brock Caldwell when they both are teenagers; becomes mayor of Fort Penn in John O'Hara's *A Rage to Live*.

Jean   Soldier in William Faulkner's *A Fable*.

Jean-baby   Friend of Martin Frost; puts hashish in Frederick Eichner's drink in Terry Southern's *Flash and Filigree*.

Roscoe Jeffcoat   Jailer in Shelby Foote's *Follow Me Down*.

Jefferson (Jeff)   Impotent husband of Till and slave of Sapphira Dodderidge Colbert in Willa Cather's *Sapphira and the Slave Girl*.

Thomas Jefferson   President of the United States who helps Lewis Rand become an attorney; withholds a letter which would reveal Rand's part in the Burr conspiracy in Mary Johnston's *Lewis Rand*.

Thomas (Tom) Jefferson   Virginia gentleman who helps Thomas Paine formulate revolutionary ideas and who incorporates many of them in the Declaration of Independence in Howard Fast's *Citizen Tom Paine*.

Betsy Jekyll   Younger sister of Maizie Jekyll; fashion model and a free-spirited woman until she marries Hector Connolly in Nancy Hale's *The Prodigal Women*.

Minnie May Jekyll   Wife of Thomas Jekyll and mother of Maizie and Betsy Jekyll; urges her husband to move the family from Virginia to Massachusetts in Nancy Hale's *The Prodigal Women*.

Minnie May (Maizie) Jekyll   Virginia beauty who marries Lambert Rudd and has a nervous breakdown shortly after their daughter is born in Nancy Hale's *The Prodigal Women*.

Thomas (Tom) Jekyll   Lawyer from Virginia who never adjusts to life in the North after moving to Massachusetts with his family in Nancy Hale's *The Prodigal Women*.

Jinx Jenkins   Furniture mover and comical friend of Bubber Brown in Rudolph Fisher's *The Walls of Jericho; The Conjure-Man Dies*.

Leo (Dead-Eye) Jenks   Stupid sharpshooter who becomes sheriff of the second Hard Times; killed by Clay Turner in E. L. Doctorow's *Welcome to Hard Times*.

Captain Jenness   Captain of the *Aroostook* and guardian of Lydia Blood while she is aboard in William Dean Howells's *The Lady of the Aroostook*.

Jabe Jenney   Farmer and friend of Austen Vane in Winston Churchill's *Mr. Crewe's Career*.

Betsey Jennings   Liverpool woman who starves to death with her three children in Herman Melville's *Redburn*.

W. B. Jennings   Newspaper reporter and writer of boys' adventure books; outside observer of events at Tom Scanlon's ninetieth birthday in Wright Morris's *Ceremony in Lone Tree*.

Myrtle Jennison   Tim Noonan's lover who inspires Whisper Thaler's jealousy in Dashiell Hammett's *Red Harvest*.

Jenny   See Virginia Du Pre and Genevieve Steinbauer.

Jenny   Boyhood sweetheart of Israel Potter; marries Sergeant Singles in Herman Melville's *Israel Potter*.

Jenny   Prostitute working in the Chicago hotel where Cross Damon stays before leaving for New York; tries to convince Damon to take her with him in Richard Wright's *The Outsider*.

John Jermin   Chief mate of the *Julia* and nemesis of Captain Guy in Herman Melville's *Omoo*.

Jerry   Irish terrier pup "born to hate niggers" who travels with Van Horn to the British Solomons; must search for a white master after Van Horn is killed in Jack London's *Jerry of the Islands*.

Jerry   Carpenter and former slave of the Talbot family in Grace King's *The Pleasant Ways of St. Médard*.

Miss Jessel   Ghost of a governess and apparently a lover of Peter Quint in Henry James's *The Turn of the Screw*.

Cecilia (Sissy) Jessup   Younger daughter of Doremus Jessup; active in the New Underground in Sinclair Lewis's *It Can't Happen Here*.

Doremus Jessup   Editor of the Fort Beulah *Daily Informer* and later publisher of anti-government leaflets for the New Underground; after being beaten in a concentration camp, he escapes to Canada in Sinclair Lewis's *It Can't Happen Here*.

Emma Jessup   Solid, kindly wife of Doremus Jessup in Sinclair Lewis's *It Can't Happen Here*.

Leroy Jessup   Janitor at the Penmarks' apartment complex; murdered by Rhoda Penmark when she learns that he knows of her evil deeds in William March's *The Bad Seed*.

Mary Jessup   See Mary Jessup Greenhill.

Philip Jessup   Son of Doremus Jessup; attorney and later a Corporatist judge in Sinclair Lewis's *It Can't Happen Here*.

Jesting Squaw's Son   Devoted friend of Laughing Boy in Oliver La Farge's *Laughing Boy*.

Jethro (Ruel)   Mentor and father-in-law of Moses and father of Zipporah; Kenites priest with whom Moses lives for twenty years before accepting Jethro's challenge to deliver the Israelites from Egypt in Zora Neale Hurston's *Moses, Man of the Mountain*.

Jezebel   Ninety-five-year-old slave of Sapphira Dodderidge Colbert and the last of the African-born Colbert slaves in Willa Cather's *Sapphira and the Slave Girl*.

Jibbenainosay   See Nathan Slaughter.

Jiggs   Mechanic in William Faulkner's *Pylon*.

Jim   Personal slave of Peregrine Lacey Catlett and husband of Minna in Mary Lee Settle's *Know Nothing*.

Jim   Tahiti harbor pilot in Herman Melville's *Omoo*.

Jim   Free black man, husband of Mag Smith, and father of Frado in Harriet E. Wilson's *Our Nig*.

Jim   Runaway slave of Miss Watson in Samuel Langhorne Clemens's *Adventures of Huckleberry Finn*; accompanies Huck Finn and Tom Sawyer on a balloon trip across North Africa in *Tom Sawyer Abroad*.

Jesus Jiminez   I.W.W. organizer killed with Jack Gale in Louis Adamic's *Grandsons*.

Jimmy   Mercenary rover who escorts Toby to a whaling ship in Herman Melville's *Typee*.

William Hezekiah Jimson   Fundamentalist minister in Shelby Foote's *Follow Me Down*.

Madame Joachim   Creole neighbor of the Talbots in Grace King's *The Pleasant Ways of St. Médard*.

Al Joad   Brother of Tom Joad II; moves west with the family in John Steinbeck's *The Grapes of Wrath*.

John (Uncle John) Joad   Brother of Tom Joad I and uncle of Tom Joad II; helps the Joad family move west in John Steinbeck's *The Grapes of Wrath*.

Ma Joad   Mother of Tom II, Noah, Rose of Sharon, and Al Joad, among others; rejoices at Tom's release from prison, but worries about his involvement in rebellious activities at the California work farm in John Steinbeck's *The Grapes of Wrath*.

Noah Joad   Brother of Tom Joad II; moves west with the family in John Steinbeck's *The Grapes of Wrath*.

Rose of Sharon Joad   See Rose of Sharon Joad Rivers.

Tom (Pa) Joad (I)   Father of Tom Joad II; leads his family west to look for work and a new start in life in John Steinbeck's *The Grapes of Wrath*.

Tom (Tommy) Joad (II)   Young man who questions the injustices of Depression-era America while journeying west with his family in John Steinbeck's *The Grapes of Wrath*.

Joaquín   Member of El Sordo's partisan group in Ernest Hemingway's *For Whom the Bell Tolls*.

Joby   Sartoris slave and father of Loosh in William Faulkner's *Sartoris (Flags in the Dust)* and *The Unvanquished*.

Dame Jocelyn   Aged storyteller with whom George Washington possibly once flirted in Thomas Bailey Aldrich's *The Story of a Bad Boy*.

Jochebed   Wife of Amram and Hebrew mother of Aaron, Miriam, and a third child who may be Moses in Zora Neale Hurston's *Moses, Man of the Mountain*.

Joe   Killer of Kai-a in Edwin Corle's *Fig Tree John*.

Sergeant Joe (Jo–Jo)   American soldier who contracts syphilis in Naples in John Horne Burns's *The Gallery*.

Uncle Joe   See Uncle Joe Morgan.

Johansen   Cruel mate on the *Ghost* in Jack London's *The Sea-Wolf*.

Nikoline Johansen   Intellectual Norwegian friend of Peder Holm (Hansa); abandons America for Norway in O. E. Rölvaag's *Their Father's God*.

John   Dark-skinned black man who helps Emma Lou Morgan find a place to live and pay her rent; she refuses to continue their relationship because she feels his skin is too dark in Wallace Thurman's *The Blacker the Berry*.

John   Grounded British aviator in World War I who restlessly rides a bicycle around New York City; one of Sabina's lovers in Anaïs Nin's *A Spy in the House of Love*.

John   Sailor aboard the *Neversink* who precipitates the fighting that leads to the fighters' flogging in Herman Melville's *White-Jacket*.

Lady John   Noblewoman who is having an affair with Gilbert Long in Henry James's *The Sacred Fount*.

Johnny   Young man sodomized in William S. Burroughs's *Naked Lunch, Nova Express, The Soft Machine,* and *The Ticket That Exploded*.

Howard Johns   Gynecologist who examines Candy Christian in the men's room of a bar in Terry Southern and Mason Hoffenberg's *Candy*.

Johnson   Brutal, abusive father of Maggie and Jimmie Johnson in Stephen Crane's *Maggie*.

Johnson   British doctor on Tahiti in Herman Melville's *Omoo*.

Johnson   Servile black man who betrays other blacks as they attempt to become independent of the Cresswells; lynched by a mob led by Sheriff Colton in W. E. B. Du Bois's *The Quest of the Silver Fleece*.

Johnson (Yonson)   Crewman on the *Ghost* who drowns while attempting to escape the brutality on ship in Jack London's *The Sea-Wolf*.

Agnes Johnson   See Agnes Johnson Trent.

Barmy Johnson   Cellmate of Roy Earle; dies after having taught Earle how to deal with the loneliness of prison life in William Riley Burnett's *High Sierra*.

Bub Johnson   Eight-year-old son of Lutie Johnson in Ann Petry's *The Street*.

Clara Johnson   Twenty-six-year-old daughter of Margaret Johnson and her mother's traveling companion on a lengthy holiday in Italy, where Fabrizio Naccarelli falls hopelessly in love with her; has the mental acumen of a ten-year-old because of a childhood accident in Elizabeth Spencer's *The Light in the Piazza*.

Gertrude (Mrs. Sidney Bacon) Johnson   Southern novelist and would-be satirist; teaches writing for a semester at Benton College in Randall Jarrell's *Pictures from an Institution*.

Gwendolyn Johnson   Young friend of Emma Lou Morgan; marries Benson Brown in Wallace Thurman's *The Blacker the Berry*.

Jim Johnson   Estranged husband of Lutie Johnson in Ann Petry's *The Street*.

Jimmie Johnson   Brother of Maggie Johnson; a tough youth who is similar to his brutal father in Stephen Crane's *Maggie*.

Lutie Johnson   Determined young woman who hopes that hard work and sacrifice will enable her to leave Harlem and improve life for her young son, Bub Johnson; heroine of Ann Petry's *The Street*.

Maggie (Mag) Johnson   New Yorker who blossomed in a mud puddle; works in a sweatshop and is seduced and deserted by Pete; becomes a prostitute and commits suicide in Stephen Crane's *Maggie*; appears in *George's Mother*.

Margaret Johnson   Middle-aged American traveling abroad with her retarded daughter, with whom a young Italian falls in love, in Elizabeth Spencer's *The Light in the Piazza*.

Mary Johnson   Angry, violent mother of Maggie and Jimmie Johnson; rejects her daughter when Maggie tries to return home in Stephen Crane's *Maggie*.

Mary (Duchess of Uganda) Johnson   Satirical character and follower of Marcus Garvey in Countee Cullen's *One Way to Heaven*.

Mattie Johnson   Deeply religious maid of Constancia Brandon and innocent heroine duped into trusting and marrying Sam Lucas in Countee Cullen's *One Way to Heaven*.

Mr. Johnson   Man who charters Harry Morgan's boat for fishing, but does not pay for it, in Ernest Hemingway's *To Have and Have Not*.

Mrs. Johnson   Resident of the Diamond County Home for the Aged; tends the candy stand at the annual fair in John Updike's *The Poorhouse Fair*.

Noel Johnson   Cigarette industry executive who remains helplessly in the United States when his wife informs him from Italy that their retarded adult daughter is in love with a young Italian, and he with her, in Elizabeth Spencer's *The Light in the Piazza*.

Norman Johnson   Income tax official who pursues Honora Wapshot from St. Botolph's to Rome in John Cheever's *The Wapshot Scandal*.

Paul Johnson Southern mulatto whose attraction to a white fellow student, Bona Hale, emphasizes his ambivalence about racial identity in Jean Toomer's *Cane.*

Sister Sarah Johnson Friend of Aunt Hager Williams; claims white oppression made her leave home in Langston Hughes's *Not Without Laughter.*

Walter Johnson Cousin of Ralph Hartsook; studies medicine with Dr. Henry Small, but becomes a member of Small's band of robbers, in Edward Eggleston's *The Hoosier School-Master.*

Sir William Johnson British commander in James Kirke Paulding's *The Dutchman's Fireside.*

Sir William Johnson British administrator in North America and enemy of Major Robert Rogers in Kenneth Roberts's *Northwest Passage.*

Willie-Mae Johnson Granddaughter of Sarah Johnson and playmate of Sandy Rodgers in Langston Hughes's *Not Without Laughter.*

Joseph Eggleston Johnston Commander of the Confederate troops in the West when Vicksburg is lost; quarrels with and reprimanded by Jefferson Davis; asked to halt Sherman's march in Mary Johnston's *Cease Firing;* mentioned in *The Long Roll.*

Jo-Jo Actor, first husband of Ellen Thatcher in John Dos Passos's *Manhattan Transfer.*

Jones Envious preacher who attempts to undermine Zora's efforts to help his congregation free themselves from their sharecropping status in W. E. B. Du Bois's *The Quest of the Silver Fleece.*

Jones New Yorker who befriends Redburn in Herman Melville's *Redburn.*

Adelaide (Addy) Jones Daughter of Railroad Jones and lover of Abner Teeftallow; leaves Lane County, Tennessee, to join her missionary lover in India in T. S. Stribling's *Teeftallow.*

Alice Jones Gardener's daughter who plays often with Carolyn Bridge; because of her race, she is snubbed by the Bridge family in Evan Connell's *Mrs. Bridge* and *Mr. Bridge.*

Anna Jones Widowed mulatto and mother of Garvin Jones in Hamilton Basso's *The View from Pompey's Head.*

Barney Jones Lazy, loud-mouthed young black man from the Piney Woods of Texas; famous for his lies in Arna Wendell Bontemps's *God Sends Sunday.*

Brother John Jones Self-centered president of the Universal Mutual Insurance Company, at whose home Matthew Towns learns the identity of the woman who snubs him, in W. E. B. Du Bois's *Dark Princess.*

Charley (Charlie) Jones Jovial drinker who guides George Kelcey's descent into alcohol in Stephen Crane's *George's Mother.*

David (Railroad) Jones Crafty and unscrupulous entrepreneur who promotes the construction of a railroad through Lane County, Tennessee; murdered by James Sandage in T. S. Stribling's *Teeftallow.*

Easley Jones See Samuel Crouch.

Garwood B. Jones Former schoolmate of John Wickliff Shawnessy; opportunistic United States senator in Ross Lockridge, Jr.'s *Raintree County.*

Januarius Jones Obese sensualist in William Faulkner's *Soldiers' Pay.*

John Paul Jones Captain of the *Ranger, Bon Homme Richard,* and *Ariel;* befriends Israel Potter in Herman Melville's *Israel Potter.*

John Paul Jones Captain of the *Bonhomme Richard,* during whose victory over the *Serapis* Johnny Fraser is wounded, in James Boyd's *Drums.*

Joshua (Shine) Jones Ambitious moving van driver who falls in love with Linda Young in Rudolph Fisher's *The Walls of Jericho.*

Karl N. Jones Intended murder victim of Jasper Ammen in Conrad Aiken's *King Coffin.*

Lamont Quincy (L. Q.) Jones Marine radio operator killed at Saipan in Leon Uris's *Battle Cry.*

Love Jones Provocative black woman over whom Willie Copeland fights Junebug in Carson McCullers's *The Heart Is a Lonely Hunter.*

Marjorie Jones Object of Penrod Schofield's affections in Booth Tarkington's *Penrod, Penrod and Sam,* and *Penrod Jashber.*

Milly Jones Mother, by Thomas Sutpen, of a daughter; her grandfather, Wash Jones, kills her, Sutpen, and the baby in William Faulkner's *Absalom, Absalom!*

Mitchell (Mitchy-Mitch) Jones Brother of Marjorie Jones; frequently interrupts Penrod Schofield's attempts to gain Marjorie's attention in Booth Tarkington's *Penrod.*

Nevada Jones Showgirl, ex-prostitute, who marries Congo in John Dos Passos's *Manhattan Transfer.*

Olin Jones Harelipped northern drifter and consummate panhandler who passes on his skill to Cass McKay in Nelson Algren's *Somebody in Boots.*

Lieutenant Oliver Cromwell Jones See Rau-Ru.

Peter (Pete) Jones   Corrupt county commissioner and father of seven schoolchildren in Edward Eggleston's *The Hoosier School-Master.*

Richard (Dickon) Jones   Templeton architect and sheriff who imprisons Natty Bumppo for hunting out of season in James Fenimore Cooper's *The Pioneers.*

Simolean (Sim) Jones   Friend of Steven Grendon in August Derleth's *The Shield of the Valiant;* also appears in *Evening in Spring.*

Theophilus Jones   Abolitionist preacher beaten by a mob during a meeting at Flat Rock; blames Nathaniel Hyman for directing the mob to the meeting, but provides protection and patronage for Jesse Hyman, in Albion W. Tourgee's *A Fool's Errand.*

Wash Jones   Grandfather of Milly Jones; kills her, her baby, and the baby's father, Thomas Sutpen, in William Faulkner's *Absalom, Absalom!*

William (Super) Jones   Mentally unbalanced superintendent of the apartment building where Lutie Johnson lives; gets Bub Johnson in trouble with the law after Lutie rejects Jones's advances in Ann Petry's *The Street.*

Wissey Jones   Executive of the United Lymphomilloid Company and "Child Buyer" who comes to the town of Pequot to purchase a specimen for his company's experimental research in John Hersey's *The Child Buyer.*

Major Victor Joppolo   Allied Occupation officer in Adano who seeks advice from townspeople, shows them respect, and secures the town a bell in John Hersey's *A Bell for Adano.*

Jordan   English printer who encourages Thomas Paine and who is jailed for publishing Paine's *The Rights of Man* in Howard Fast's *Citizen Tom Paine.*

Daniel (Dan, Smoke) Jordan   Black drummer who meets Rick Martin in a bowling alley; member of Jeff Williams's band in Dorothy Baker's *Young Man with a Horn.*

Rachel Jordan   See Rachel Jordan Beaumont.

Robert (Inglés, Roberto) Jordan   American volunteer with the Spanish Republican Army whose mission is to blow up a bridge in Ernest Hemingway's *For Whom the Bell Tolls.*

Zeke (Zeki-O) Jordan   Friend of Fish Tucker; enlists in the army and is sent to France in Richard Wright's *The Long Dream.*

Christian Jorgensen (Sidney Kelterman)   Conniving second husband of Mimi Jorgensen in Dashiell Hammett's *The Thin Man.*

Mimi Jorgensen   Money-hungry former wife of Clyde Wynant in Dashiell Hammett's *The Thin Man.*

Jose   Mexican worker who befriends Johnny Mack and sells him a Ford car in Edwin Corle's *Fig Tree John.*

Joseph   Volatile, interpretive intellectual and fumbler with his own freedom; dangler and diarist-narrator of Saul Bellow's *Dangling Man.*

Moredecai (Reb Mordecai) Joseph   Cabalist and one-time foe of Rabbi Benish Ashkenazi; beguiled but ultimately disillusioned by the messianic claims of Sabbatai Zevi; exorcises the demon from Rechele Babad's body in Isaac Bashevis Singer's *Satan in Goray.*

Joshua   Confidant and adopted son of Moses and leader of the Israelite army in Zora Neale Hurston's *Moses, Man of the Mountain.*

Mme. Joubert   Kindly but sad Frenchwoman in whose home Claude Wheeler and David Gerhardt stay when they are not fighting on the front in Willa Cather's *One of Ours.*

Jourdonnais   French sidekick of Boone Caudill and Dick Summers; killed in an Indian raid in A. B. Guthrie's *The Big Sky.*

Joy   Elderly, lame labor organizer who is killed during the strike in John Steinbeck's *In Dubious Battle.*

Edward Joyner   Only son of Robert Joyner in Thomas Wolfe's *The Hills Beyond.*

Emily Drumgoole Joyner   Wife of Theodore Joyner and mother of Gustavus Adolphus Joyner in Thomas Wolfe's *The Hills Beyond.*

Gustavus Adolphus (Dolph, Silk) Joyner   Younger son of Theodore and Emily Joyner; becomes a lawyer and goes West in Thomas Wolfe's *The Hills Beyond.*

Mag Joyner   Hypochondriac who exploits and dominates her husband, Mark Joyner, and is disliked by her nephew George Webber in Thomas Wolfe's *You Can't Go Home Again* and *The Web and the Rock.*

Mark Joyner   Maternal uncle of George Webber in Thomas Wolfe's *You Can't Go Home Again* and *The Web and the Rock.*

Maw Joyner   Spinster aunt who rears George Webber after the death of his long-suffering mother in Thomas Wolfe's *You Can't Go Home Again* and *The Web and the Rock.*

Robert Joyner   Brother of Zachariah Joyner; lawyer with a reputation for honesty in Thomas Wolfe's *The Hills Beyond.*

Theodore Joyner   Youngest son of William Joyner; founds the first school of higher learning in Libya Hill and later becomes a Confederate colonel in the Civil War in Thomas Wolfe's *The Hills Beyond.*

William (Bear) Joyner   Founder of the Joyner clan, father of Zachariah Joyner, and ancestor of George Webber in Thomas Wolfe's *The Hills Beyond.*

Zachariah (Zack) Joyner   Son of William Joyner; governor of the state of Catawba and later a United States senator in Thomas Wolfe's *The Hills Beyond*.

Juana   Slave of Lafitte; tends to Constanza Velasquez in Joseph Holt Ingraham's *Lafitte*.

Juana   Wife of Kino; attempts to persuade her husband to return the pearl to the sea, once she sees that the pearl will bring them grief and danger, in John Steinbeck's *The Pearl*.

Juan Tomás   Brother of Kino; hides his brother and Kino's family after their home is burned and after Kino kills a thief in John Steinbeck's *The Pearl*.

Juba   Teenaged paramour and confidante of Gabriel Prosser in Arna Wendell Bontemps's *Black Thunder*.

Tanis Judique   Attractive widow who rents an apartment from George Babbitt and becomes his mistress in Sinclair Lewis's *Babbitt*.

Judith   Maid of Clara Wieland; Carwin uses her to familiarize himself with Clara's habits in Charles Brockden Brown's *Wieland*.

James (Fatso) Judson   Sadistic chief guard at the Schofield Barracks Post Stockade who persecutes Angelo Maggio and oversees the fatal beating of Blues Berry; killed by Robert E. Lee Prewitt to avenge Berry's death in James Jones's *From Here to Eternity*.

Mrs. Judson   Housekeeper who helps Marmaduke Ruggles with his new restaurant and eventually marries him in Harry Leon Wilson's *Ruggles of Red Gap*.

Jug   Newspaper photographer in William Faulkner's *Pylon*.

Jule (Big Jule)   Renegade lover of Ollie and father out of wedlock of their son, Jule Jackson, in George Wylie Henderson's *Ollie Miss and Jule*.

Julia   Secretary of Walter Bridge in Evan Connell's *Mrs. Bridge* and *Mr. Bridge*.

Cousin Julia   Sophisticated British writer and relative of the narrator of Aline Bernstein's *The Journey Down*.

Lady Julia   Deceased mother of Mrs. Brookenham and friend of Mr. Longdon in Henry James's *The Awkward Age*.

Junebug   Rival wounded by Willie Copeland in a knife fight over Love Jones in Carson McCullers's *The Heart Is a Lonely Hunter*.

Heinrich Jung   Nazi friend of Lanny Budd in Upton Sinclair's *Dragon's Teeth*.

Brother Juniper   Red-haired Franciscan monk who witnesses the fall of the bridge and decides to document the lives of those who died; as a result of his research, he and his book are burned in Thornton Wilder's *The Bridge of San Luis Rey*.

Mr. (Old Man Junto) Junto   White owner of bars, whorehouses, and dance halls in Harlem; lusts after Lutie Johnson and inadvertently helps destroy her life in Ann Petry's *The Street*.

Jurgen   Middle-aged pawnbroker and failed poet who through flattery regains his youth for one year in James Branch Cabell's *Jurgen*.

Jutta   Younger sister of Stella Snow and mistress of Zizendorf; mother of the child cannibalized in John Hawkes's *The Cannibal*.

Céleste Juvet   Pretty fifteen-year-old daughter of Hugo Juvet and granddaughter of Mme. Jacques Juvet; eventually wins the heart of Diron Desautels in Arna Wendell Bontemps's *Drums at Dusk*.

Hugo Juvet   Drunken, nomadic son of Mme. Juvet and natural father of Céleste Juvet in Arna Wendell Bontemps's *Drums at Dusk*.

Mme. Jacques Juvet   Ugly former house servant at Bréda; matron in her fifties thought by the plantation's slaves to be a witch in Arna Wendell Bontemps's *Drums at Dusk*.

Ralph Kabnis   Northern black professor and poet who goes south to educate underprivileged blacks; his fear of racial violence renders him ineffective as an educator in Tean Toomer's *Cane.*

Peter Kaden   German immigrant and farmer; driven to suicide by Augustus M. Barr in Oscar Micheaux's *The Homesteader.*

Nathan Kadish   Childhood friend of Sonia Marburg, later loved by Marburg for the deformity caused by a large birthmark on his face; leaves Boston to study in Paris in Jean Stafford's *Boston Adventure.*

Edwin L. Kaffrath   Director of the Chicago natural gas company in Theodore Dreiser's *The Titan.*

Kitty Kahl   Marine corporal and former lightweight boxer; killed in France during World War I in Thomas Boyd's *Through the Wheat.*

Paul (Paula) Kahler   Transsexual and psychotic killer; understood by Dr. Leopold Lehmann as a symbol of the possibilities of transformation in Wright Morris's *The Field of Vision.*

Kai-a (Bi-Tli-Kai, Nalin, White Deer's Daughter)   Apache Indian wife of Agocho and mother of Johnny Mack; murdered, raped, and burned by Joe in Edwin Corle's *Fig Tree John.*

Don (Doc) Kaiser   Psychiatrist and flight surgeon for the 918th Bomb Group in Beirne Lay, Jr., and Sy Bartlett's *Twelve O'Clock High!*

Kid Kamm   Contestant in the dance marathon; partnered with Jackie Miller after his original partner, Mattie Barnes, collapses in Horace McCoy's *They Shoot Horses, Don't They?*

Archibald Kane   Wealthy manufacturer and father of Lester Kane; stipulates in his will that Lester must either marry or leave Jennie Gerhardt in order to receive his inheritance in Theodore Dreiser's *Jennie Gerhardt.*

Lester Kane   Son of Archibald Kane; loves Jennie Gerhardt, but leaves her in order to inherit his father's money; marries Letty Pace Gerald, but cannot love her as he loves Gerhardt in Theodore Dreiser's *Jennie Gerhardt.*

Letty Pace Gerald Kane   See Letty Pace Gerald.

Robert Kane   Older brother of Lester Kane, whose relationship with Jennie Gerhardt Robert opposes in Theodore Dreiser's *Jennie Gerhardt.*

Willard Kane   New York painter and lover of Etta Barnes in Theodore Dreiser's *The Bulwark.*

Sulo Kangas   Jailer in Robert Traver's *Anatomy of a Murder.*

Dominie Kanttwell   Village clergyman in James Kirke Paulding's *Koningsmarke.*

Stanislas Kapp   Heir to a brewery; quarrels with Valentin de Bellegarde about Noémie Nioche in Henry James's *The American.*

Karakoee   Former shipmate of Tommo; helps Tommo escape from the Typees in Herman Melville's *Typee.*

Karintha   Beautiful black woman warped by a premature sexual experience in Jean Toomer's *Cane.*

Karkov   Russian journalist who is a friend of Robert Jordan in Ernest Hemingway's *For Whom the Bell Tolls.*

Karky   Typean tattoo artist in Herman Melville's *Typee*.

Julius Karp   Proprietor of a wine and liquor store near Morris Bober's grocery store in Bernard Malamud's *The Assistant*.

Louis Karp   Son of Julius Karp and would-be suitor of Helen Bober in Bernard Malamud's *The Assistant*.

Kate-Careless   Lover of Wendell Ryder and mother of three in Djuna Barnes's *Ryder*.

Katie   High-class prostitute who wants to marry Bruce Pearson for his insurance money in Mark Harris's *Bang the Drum Slowly*.

Aunt Katy   Slave housekeeper of Canema plantation; owned by Nina Gordon in Harriet Beecher Stowe's *Dred*.

Katya   See Katya Cronstadt.

Katz   Crooked lawyer who defends Frank Chambers; cheats Chambers and gets the insurance money and Nick Papadakis's restaurant in James M. Cain's *The Postman Always Rings Twice*.

Julius Kauffman   Brother of Eva Wiseman; attends the yacht party in William Faulkner's *Mosquitoes*.

Kauka   Manukuran who survives the hurricane in Charles Nordhoff and James Norman Hall's *The Hurricane*.

Princess Kautilya (Dark Princess, Maharanee of Bwodpur)   Young princess concerned for the uniting of the colored races of the world against racism; marries Matthew Towns and bears their child, the future Maharajah of Bwodpur, in W. E. B. Du Bois's *Dark Princess*.

Arthur Kavanagh   Minister who marries Cecilia Vaughan in Henry Wadsworth Longfellow's *Kavanagh*.

Julia Kaye   Strong-willed Englishwoman seeking power through marriage to an influential man, such as John Gwynne, in Gertrude Atherton's *Ancestors*.

Kaysinata   Shawnee Indian who serves as Salathiel Albine's adoptive father in Hervey Allen's *The Forest and the Fort*.

Kazak   Time-traveling dog of Winston Niles Rumfoord in Kurt Vonnegut's *The Sirens of Titan*; Doberman guard dog in *Breakfast of Champions*.

Johnny Kazarakis   Talented athlete and track teammate of Jack Duluoz in Jack Kerouac's *Maggie Cassidy*.

Doctor Kearsley   Physician who nurses Thomas Paine back to health when Paine first arrives in America in Howard Fast's *Citizen Tom Paine*.

Peter (Petey) Keating   Ambitious architect; compromises self-esteem and happiness for shallow accolades in Ayn Rand's *The Fountainhead*.

Roland Keefer   Son of a politician, military school graduate, and friend of Willie Keith in Herman Wouk's *The Caine Mutiny*.

Thomas (Tom) Keefer   Half brother of Roland Keefer; communications officer on the USS *Caine* who plants seeds of mutiny and becomes captain of the *Caine* in Herman Wouk's *The Caine Mutiny*.

Keekee   See Zeke.

Azariah Keel   Frontiersman who calls Johnny Lacey a Tuckahoe and a turncoat, nearly starting a fight with Solomon McKarkle, in Mary Lee Settle's *O Beulah Land*.

Doctor Charlie Keene   Physician friend of Joseph Frowenfeld; loves Aurora Nancanou in George Washington Cable's *The Grandissimes*.

Fred Kegerise   Former burgess of Andrews; brings his eight-year-old grandson to the fair in John Updike's *The Poorhouse Fair*.

Edwin (Ed, Eddy, Keggsy) Keggs   Former high school algebra teacher who joins the navy and is assigned to a minesweeper-destroyer; friend of Willie Keith in Herman Wouk's *The Caine Mutiny*.

Compton J. Keith   Wealthy coal mine owner infatuated with Delia Poole; eventually marries Mercy Wellington in Janet Manner's *The Cubical City*.

Ensign James L. (Jim) Keith   Green officer who tries to follow navy regulations until he gets drunk with some enlisted men; provides comic relief in Thomas Heggen's *Mister Roberts*.

Mrs. Keith   Mother of Willie Keith in Herman Wouk's *The Caine Mutiny*.

Willis Seward (Keither, Willie) Keith   Princeton graduate and former nightclub pianist who supports the mutiny and serves as the last captain of the USS *Caine* in Herman Wouk's *The Caine Mutiny*.

George (Georgie, Kel') Kelcey   Young slum resident who learns to drink, fight, and swear in front of his long-suffering mother in Stephen Crane's *George's Mother*.

Gerry Kells   Los Angeles gangster who tries to benefit financially from being caught in a power struggle in Paul Cain's *Fast One*.

Bill Kelly   Oldest brother of Mick Kelly in Carson McCullers's *The Heart Is a Lonely Hunter*.

Etta Kelly   Older sister of Mick Kelly; Etta's illness forces Mick to quit school and go to work in Carson McCullers's *The Heart Is a Lonely Hunter*.

George (Baby-Killer, Bubber) Kelly Younger brother of Mick Kelly; accidentally shoots and wounds four-year-old Baby Wilson in Carson McCullers's *The Heart Is a Lonely Hunter.*

Hazel Kelly Oldest sister of Mick Kelly in Carson McCullers's *The Heart Is a Lonely Hunter.*

Knute Kelly Sharecropper who works on a fifty-fifty basis with Uncle Alex in George Wylie Henderson's *Ollie Miss.*

Mick Kelly Adolescent girl trapped by her family's poverty; abandons her dreams of musical fame to drop out of school and take a job at Woolworth's in Carson McCullers's *The Heart Is a Lonely Hunter.*

Ralph Kelly Baby brother of Mick Kelly in Carson McCullers's *The Heart Is a Lonely Hunter.*

Wilbur Kelly Disabled father of Mick Kelly and Mick's five brothers and sisters; tries to work as a watch repairman in Carson McCullers's *The Heart Is a Lonely Hunter.*

Dessie Kelsey Black midwife, laundress, and helpmate to the Meserves; wife of Joe Kelsey in Zora Neale Hurston's *Seraph on the Suwanee.*

Hiram (Hi) Kelsey Young, handsome, and intense preacher whose faith is severely tried by the mountaineers he serves; dies under ironic circumstances in Mary Noailles Murfree's *The Prophet of the Great Smoky Mountains.*

Joe Kelsey Black friend, confidant, and hired hand of Jim Meserve and blues-picking musician who teaches Kenny Meserve to play the guitar; husband of Dessie Kelsey in Zora Neale Hurston's *Seraph on the Suwanee.*

Rob't Kelsey Kentucky wagon driver who drowns crossing the Snake River in Emerson Hough's *The Covered Wagon.*

Georgia Kelterman Wife of Christian Jorgensen (Sidney Kelterman), whom he failed to divorce before marrying Mimi Wynant Jorgensen, in Dashiell Hammett's *The Thin Man.*

Ellen Kendall Aunt of Joel Harrison Knox; takes care of him after his mother's death but is deceived into sending him to stay at Skully's Landing in Truman Capote's *Other Voices, Other Rooms.*

Major Kendall Companion of William Demarest; pursues Peggy Davis in Conrad Aiken's *Blue Voyage.*

Henley Kendrick Brother of Gertie Nevels; killed in World War II in Harriette Arnow's *The Dollmaker.*

Mrs. Kendrick Mother of Gertie Nevels; persuades John Ballew not to sell the Tipton Place to Gertie so Gertie will join her husband in Detroit in Harriette Arnow's *The Dollmaker.*

Bob Kendry Alcoholic father of Clare Kendry and impoverished college-educated janitor of a Chicago apartment building; killed in a saloon fight in Nella Larsen's *Passing.*

Clare Kendry Daughter of Bob Kendry; passes for white and marries John Bellew, who doesn't know she is black; dies in a fall from a Harlem apartment after a confrontation with Bellew in Nella Larsen's *Passing.*

Frank Kennedy Second husband of Scarlett O'Hara; killed by Union soldiers while involved in a Ku Klux Klan raid in Margaret Mitchell's *Gone with the Wind.*

Hart Kennedy Denver jazz fan and philanderer in John Clellon Holmes's *Go.*

Ray H. Kennedy Freethinking railroad conductor; admires Thea Kronborg and leaves money for her musical studies in Willa Cather's *The Song of the Lark.*

Watt Kennedy Sheriff in William Faulkner's *Light in August.*

Kate Kenner Leader of the Red Gap Bohemian set; marries Nevil Vane-Basingwell in Harry Leon Wilson's *Ruggles of Red Gap.*

Carol Milford (Carrie) Kennicott Librarian from St. Paul who marries Will Kennicott and moves to his home in Gopher Prairie, Minnesota, in Sinclair Lewis's *Main Street.*

Dr. Will Kennicott Doctor who marries Carol Milford; cannot understand why his wife is unhappy living in Gopher Prairie in Sinclair Lewis's *Main Street.*

Ruby (Rube) Kenny Model and lover of Eugene Witla in Theodore Dreiser's *The "Genius."*

Chick Kent Infant son of Ellen Chesser and Jasper Kent in Elizabeth Madox Roberts's *The Time of Man.*

Ellen Chesser Kent See Ellen Chesser.

Jasper Kent Tenant farmer and husband of Ellen Chesser; has an affair and is accused of barn burning in Elizabeth Madox Roberts's *The Time of Man.*

Kenyon American sculptor and friend of Miriam Schaefer; suspicious of her relationship with Brother Antonio; marries Hilda in Nathaniel Hawthorne's *The Marble Faun.*

Kepi Friend of Nanantatee; carries an address book listing the Paris brothels in Henry Miller's *Tropic of Cancer.*

Harley (Husband-Man) and Villa (Wife-Woman) Kerman White tourists on a cruise ship to which Jerry swims to escape Bashti in Jack London's *Jerry of the Islands.*

Patrick (Emerald Pat) Kerrigan Saloon owner and second ward boss in Theodore Dreiser's *The Titan.*

Kersaint Medical officer for the Tuamotu Group; tells his colleague Vernier about the hurricane in Charles Nordhoff and James Norman Hall's *The Hurricane*.

de Kersaint (I) Host of thirty relatives on the eve of the black emancipation in the West Indies; dies bravely in the fire at his house in Lafcadio Hearn's *Youma*.

de Kersaint (II) Son of de Kersaint I; incites the black rioters by shooting their leader Sylvain in Lafcadio Hearn's *Youma*.

Charles Kessler Millionaire father of the murdered Paulie Kessler in Meyer Levin's *Compulsion*.

Jonas Kessler Brother of Charles Kessler; discovers that Paulie Kessler has been killed in Meyer Levin's *Compulsion*.

Martha Kessler Wife of Charles Kessler and mother of the murdered Paulie Kessler in Meyer Levin's *Compulsion*.

Paulie Kessler Son of Charles and Martha Kessler; kidnapped and murdered by Artie Straus and Judd Steiner in Meyer Levin's *Compulsion*.

Arthur Ketcham Drinking friend of Paul Hobbes in John Clellon Holmes's *Go*.

Mr. Kettledrum Postman in Ellen Glasgow's *Barren Ground*.

Boykin Keye Lecherous white farmer who employs Jule Jackson as a farmhand and fights with him over Jackson's sixteen-year-old girlfriend, Bertha Mae, in George Wylie Henderson's *Jule*.

Evelyn Keyes Fiancée of Spider in Herbert Simmons's *Corner Boy*.

Keziah Obese great-aunt of Miranda in Katherine Anne Porter's *Old Mortality*.

Krishna (K. K.) Khaleel Indian ambassador to the United States and voice of the Third World with his constant concern for placating the USSR in Allen Drury's *Advise and Consent*.

Edwin Kibbler, Jr. Schoolmate who becomes a close friend of Cress Delahanty in Jessamyn West's *Cress Delahanty*.

Mrs. Edwin Kibbler Mother of Edwin Kibbler, Jr.; believes Cress Delahanty has purposely injured her son in Jessamyn West's *Cress Delahanty*.

Kiche Wolf; mate of One Eye and mother of White Fang in Jack London's *White Fang*.

Kid Nephew and companion of Dudley Osborn; narrator of Wright Morris's *My Uncle Dudley*.

The Kid Thug bodyguard of Bernie Despain in Wright Morris's *My Uncle Dudley*.

Annie Kilburn Only child of Judge Rufus Kilburn; wealthy spinster who tries to do good but discovers that charity alone is inadequate in William Dean Howells's *Annie Kilburn*.

Judge Rufus Kilburn Father of Annie Kilburn; dies in Italy in William Dean Howells's *Annie Kilburn*.

Logan Killicks Middle-aged farmer who becomes sixteen-year-old Janie Crawford's first husband in Zora Neale Hurston's *Their Eyes Were Watching God*.

Lucius (Dr. Mootry) Kimbell Sharecropper who works for Uncle Alex in George Wylie Henderson's *Jule*.

Abbey (Ab) King Four-year-old daughter of Austin and Martha King; eavesdrops on adult conversations, spends time in the kitchen with Rachel, and begins to adjust to the idea of a baby sister in William Maxwell's *Time Will Darken It*.

Austin King Lawyer whose perseverance wins the hand of Martha Hastings; pays off debts of foster relatives, though not legally obligated to do so; his kindness to his foster cousin, Nora Potter, causes gossip in William Maxwell's *Time Will Darken It*.

Belle King Nouveau riche sister of Phil Green; angered because her socialite friends think she is Jewish and will exclude her from their circle and their clubs in Laura Z. Hobson's *Gentleman's Agreement*.

Bill King Advertising agent and friend and classmate of Harry Pulham; becomes the lover of Kay Motsford Pulham in John P. Marquand's *H. M. Pulham, Esquire*.

Chad King Friend of Sal Paradise; works in a Denver library in Jack Kerouac's *On the Road*.

Edward King Father of Sarah King; feared by the people of Winesburg but befriended by Joe Welling in Sherwood Anderson's *Winesburg, Ohio*.

Martha Hastings King Wife of Austin King; defends her husband against rumors that he is unfaithful, though she is frustrated by the differences between them, in William Maxwell's *Time Will Darken it*.

Reginald (Reggie) King Wealthy yachtsman, travel writer, and friend of Alice Langham in Richard Harding Davis's *Soldiers of Fortune*.

Sarah King Daughter of Edward King; courted by Joe Welling in Sherwood Anderson's *Winesburg, Ohio*.

Tom King Son of Edward King; befriended by Joe Welling in Sherwood Anderson's *Winesburg, Ohio*.

King Devil Elusive fox that often leads Nunn Ballew to neglect his family in Harriette Arnow's *Hunter's Horn*.

Elizabeth (Biddy) Kingsblood Daughter of Neil and Vestal Kingsblood in Sinclair Lewis's *Kingsblood Royal.*

Faith Kingsblood Mother of Neil Kingsblood; learns that she is one-sixteenth black in Sinclair Lewis's *Kingsblood Royal.*

Dr. Kenneth M. Kingsblood Dentist and father of Neil Kingsblood; dies when he learns that his wife Faith is part black in Sinclair Lewis's *Kingsblood Royal.*

Neil Kingsblood Junior bank officer and family man who loses his standing in the community upon the discovery that he is one-thirty-second black in Sinclair Lewis's *Kingsblood Royal.*

Robert Kingsblood Brother of Neil Kingsblood in Sinclair Lewis's *Kingsblood Royal.*

Vestal Kingsblood Supportive wife of Neil Kingsblood; member of the Junior League in Sinclair Lewis's *Kingsblood Royal.*

Laurence Liam (Larry) Kinkaid Alleged murder victim of rustlers in Walter Van Tilburg Clark's *The Ox-Bow Incident.*

Kinney Storyteller whose work Bartley Hubbard sells without permission in William Dean Howells's *A Modern Instance.*

Kino Impoverished Indian fisherman who finds a giant pearl and dreams of becoming rich; becomes disillusioned when pearl dealers attempt to cheat him and when others attempt to deprive him of his pearl in John Steinbeck's *The Pearl.*

Kinosling New pastor of the Schofields' church; his brief flirtation with Margaret Schofield ends when her brother Penrod fills Kinosling's hat with tar in Booth Tarkington's *Penrod.*

Julia Kinship Girlfriend of Duff Conway in Shelby Foote's *Jordan County.*

Cass Kinsolving Alcoholic American painter on his way down; manipulated by Mason Flagg in William Styron's *Set This House on Fire.*

Poppy Kinsolving Wife of Cass Kinsolving in William Styron's *Set This House on Fire.*

Mrs. Gert Kipfer Owner of the brothel at which Alma Schmidt works in James Jones's *From Here to Eternity.*

Temperance Kipp Maid-servant at the New England Owen farm who has money of her own; stays on with the Owens more as an equal than as a servant because she has always been with the family in Sarah Orne Jewett's *A Marsh Island.*

Kirby Callous scion of a mill owner in Rebecca Harding Davis's *Life in the Iron Mills.*

Morissa (Issy) Kirk Stepdaughter of Robin Thomas; flees the charge of being an illegitimate child by going west; doctor unable to save her husband, Eddie Ellis, from disgrace and death in Mari Sandoz's *Miss Morissa.*

Ralph Kirkwood Ku Klux Klan member who guides the raiding party to Jerry Hunt's house; in confessing to Comfort Servosse and Thomas Denton, Kirkwood reveals the names of many Klan leaders in Albion W. Tourgee's *A Fool's Errand.*

Mary Randolph (Rannie) Kirsted New neighbor of the Baxters; a ten-year-old who incites Jane Baxter to help Jane's brother, William, make a fool of himself at Miss Lola Pratt's departure in Booth Tarkington's *Seventeen.*

Flossie Kiskadden Daughter of a minister; has a romantic but somber love for a Confederate soldier in Hervey Allen's *Action at Aquila.*

Captain Alvinza Kitchell Piratical captain of the *Bertha Millner* who shanghaies the dandified Ross Wilbur in San Francisco in Frank Norris's *Moran of the Lady Letty.*

Campbell Kitchen Retired white author who promotes interest in black cultural and social life in Harlem; employs Emma Lou Morgan as a personal maid for his wife in Wallace Thurman's *The Blacker the Berry.*

K.K. See Krishna Khaleel.

Abner Klang Unlettered literary agent of Lee Youngdahl in Mark Harris's *Wake Up, Stupid.*

Don Klausmeyer Employee of Janoth Enterprises who brings Louise Patterson to the Crimeways office to identify the missing witness in Kenneth Fearing's *The Big Clock.*

Solly Klein Cynical teacher at North Manual Trades High School in Evan Hunter's *The Blackboard Jungle.*

Klinker See William Lee.

Ewing Klipspringer Frequent guest at Jay Gatsby's house in F. Scott Fitzgerald's *The Great Gatsby.*

Jotham Klore Lover of Molly Larkins and bully of the canal; eventually beaten in a fight by Daniel Harrow in Walter D. Edmonds's *Rome Haul.*

Neil Klugnian Librarian and lover of Brenda Patimkin; narrator of Philip Roth's *Goodbye, Columbus.*

Sebastian Knight Russian-born English writer whose elusive past becomes the obsession of his half brother and biographer, V., in Vladimir Nabokov's *The Real Life of Sebastian Knight.*

Virginia Knight English mother of Sebastian Knight, who adopts her maiden name; abandons her family for another man in Vladimir Nabokov's *The Real Life of Sebastian Knight.*

Lady Catharine (Lady Kitty) Knollys Love interest of John Law in Emerson Hough's *The Mississippi Bubble.*

Henry Knox Senior partner in Sheffield, Knox law firm; mentor and father figure to Timothy Colt in Louis Auchincloss's *The Great World and Timothy Colt*.

Joel Harrison Knox Thirteen-year-old boy who goes to live with his paralyzed father, his stepmother, and her cousin at Skully's Landing, where he learns about homosexuality, in Truman Capote's *Other Voices, Other Rooms*.

Orrin Knox Senior senator from Illinois, two-time loser of his party's presidential nomination, and best friend of Senator Brigham Anderson; leads the fight against the nomination of Robert Leffingwell for Secretary of State after the suicide of Brigham Anderson in Allen Drury's *Advise and Consent*.

Fireball Kodadek Henchman of Bonifacy Konstantine and adversary of Bruno (Lefty) Bicek; rapes Bicek's girlfriend Steffi Rostenkowski in Nelson Algren's *Never Come Morning*.

Franz Koenig Nazi supporter and colleague of Paul Bronski in Leon Uris's *Mila 18*.

Barton Kohl Husband of Linda Snopes in William Faulkner's *The Mansion*.

Linda Snopes Kohl Illegitimate daughter of Eula Varner Snopes and Hoake McCarron in William Faulkner's *The Town*; wife of Barton Kohl in *The Mansion*.

Else von Kohler German woman with whom George Webber becomes involved in Thomas Wolfe's *You Can't Go Home Again*.

Stephani Kolhoff Estranged wife of Hamm Rufe; labor activist in Mari Sandoz's *Capital City*.

Kolory Lord primate of Typee in Herman Melville's *Typee*.

Koningsmarke (Long Finne) Young hero in James Kirke Paulding's *Koningsmarke*.

Bonifacy (The Barber) Konstantine Polish barber, brothel owner, and leader of a group of neighborhood Polish hoods in Nelson Algren's *Never Come Morning*.

Kooloo Tahitian who befriends and then deserts Typee in Herman Melville's *Omoo*.

Odis Korby Undertaker in Jessamyn West's *The Witch Diggers*.

Bud Korpenning Drifter who murders his father in a fit of anger and is so haunted by guilt that he jumps off the Brooklyn Bridge in John Dos Passos's *Manhattan Transfer*.

Kory-Kory Servitor to Tommo in Herman Melville's *Typee*.

Koshchei the Deathless Changeling god and creator, of things as they are; sets Jurgen on the road that leads him through a year of regained youth in James Branch Cabell's *Jurgen*.

Violet Koskozka Lusty woman whose boyfriend lives with her and her husband in Nelson Algren's *The Man with the Golden Arm*.

Grant Koven Hired hand of Arnold Haldmarne; experiences unrequited love for Merle Haldmarne in Josephine Johnson's *Now in November*.

Yozhé Kozak Slovenian artist employed to develop Rudolf Stanka's artistic talents in Louis Adamic's *Cradle of Life*.

Peter Krajiek Bohemian immigrant who sells the Shimerdas a house at an unfair price; feels guilt at Shimerda's suicide in Willa Cather's *My Ántonia*.

Kramner Corrupt vice squad lieutenant who is killed by Roy Earle in William Riley Burnett's *High Sierra*.

Doctor Irving Krankeit See Irving Semite.

Marc Krantz Junior partner at Glymmer, Read who decides to become a writer in Paris when the firm goes bankrupt in Nathan Asch's *The Office*.

Brandon Kregg Wealthy proprietor of Albion, devout Presbyterian, and husband of Sally Crawford Lacey's oldest sister; refuses a loan to Brandon and Sally Lacey in Mary Lee Settle's *Know Nothing*.

Crawford (Fish) Kregg Son of Brandon Kregg, roommate of Johnny Catlett at the University of Virginia, and one of the wealthiest young men in Virginia; marries Melinda Lacey, compromises his principles for a political career, hates Johnny Catlett because he knows Melinda always loved Johnny and bore his child, and finally joins the Confederate army hoping to be killed in Mary Lee Settle's *Know Nothing*.

Lacey Kregg Daughter of Melinda Kregg and, supposedly, Crawford Kregg; her natural father is Johnny Catlett in Mary Lee Settle's *Know Nothing*.

Melinda Lacey Kregg Granddaughter of Peregrine Lacey and ward of Peregrine Lacey Catlett; loved by Lewis and Johnny Catlett but marries Crawford Kregg for security; bears two children by Crawford and one child by Johnny before she dies of a broken spirit in Mary Lee Settle's *Know Nothing*.

Moses Kregg Bachelor lawyer, storekeeper, justice of the peace in Fluvanna County, and friend of Johnny Lacey in Mary Lee Settle's *O Beulah Land*.

Dr. Noah Kregg Cousin of Crawford Kregg and physician who attends Melinda Lacey Kregg in her final illness in Mary Lee Settle's *Know Nothing*.

Sanhedron Kregg Keeper of the land office of Fluvanna County and friend of Johnny Lacey; with his three brothers, controls the settlement at Kreggs' Crossing in Mary Lee Settle's *O Beulah Land*.

Mr. and Mrs. Peter Kronborg   Parents of Thea Kronborg; he is a small-town Methodist minister in Willa Cather's *The Song of the Lark.*

Thea Kronborg   Daughter of a small-town minister; studies voice in Chicago and New York and becomes a leading opera singer in Willa Cather's *The Song of the Lark.*

Professor Adam (Adamka, Adam the Ninth, Mugakrad, Gumakrad) Krug   Influential philosopher, husband of Olga Krug, and father of David Krug; the government unsuccessfully tries to persuade him to accept the new regime by arresting his friends and relatives and even torturing and murdering his son; goes mad before he is killed in Vladmir Nobokov's *Bend Sinister.*

David Krug   Eight-year-old son of Adam and Olga Krug kidnapped by the government to force his father to accept the new regime; through apparent bungling on the part of government thugs, he dies after being tortured in Vladimir Nabokov's *Bend Sinister.*

Olga Krug   Beloved wife of Adam Krug and mother of David Krug; dies following a kidney operation; persecution of her husband begins the day after her death in Vladimir Nabokov's *Bend Sinister.*

Kruger   Artist and sculptor who lends money to Henry Miller and permits Miller to live in his studio in Henry Miller's *Tropic of Cancer.*

Fritz Kruppenbach   Lutheran minister who refuses to intervene in Rabbit Angstrom's marital problems in John Updike's *Rabbit, Run.*

Stepan Krylenko   Russian friend of the Shanes who becomes an international communist leader in Louis Bromfield's *The Green Bay Tree.*

Alexandr Petrovich (Al Cook) Kukolnikov   Americanized Russian émigré and husband of Susan Kukolnikov; during alternate summers opens his New England country home to other Russian émigré friends in Vladimir Nabokov's *Pnin.*

Susan Marshall (Susanna Karlovna) Kukolnikov   American wife of Alexandr Petrovich Kukolnikov and gracious hostess to Russian and American friends at The Pines, a country home inherited from her father, in Vladimir Nabokov's *Pnin.*

Kuno   See Kuno Hillentafel.

Abe Kusich   Dwarf who befriends Tod Hackett in Nathanael West's *The Day of the Locust.*

Cousin Kvorka   Neighborhood police sergeant who warns Frankie Machine of his imminent arrest in Nelson Algren's *The Man with the Golden Arm.*

L Slovenian immigrant worker-writer and eventual author of Peter Gale's proposed novel "Grandsons"; narrator of Louis Adamic's *Grandsons.*

Eugene de Laage French colonial administrator of the Tuamotu Group who attempts unsuccessfully to capture Terangi in Charles Nordhoff and James Norman Hall's *The Hurricane.*

Germaine Anne Marie de Laage Wife of Eugene de Laage; rescued by Terangi during the hurricane; later helps him escape in Charles Nordhoff and James Norman Hall's *The Hurricane.*

General Labonne Frenchman whom Mary Douglas convinces to accompany Lord Balham in his attempt to help the German and Austrian refugees in Martha Gellhorn's *A Stricken Field.*

Labove Teacher who attempts to seduce Eula Varner in William Faulkner's *The Hamlet.*

Julien Raymond (Papa Zulien) La Brierre New Orleans doctor brought, by chance, to Viosca's Point eleven years after the supposed drowning of his daughter Chita Viosca in Lafcadio Hearn's *Chita.*

Robert W. Lacaud Persistent prospector who follows Curtin to the gold mine and causes dissent among the other miners in B. Traven's *The Treasure of the Sierra Madre.*

A. Gray Lacefield Son of Caruthers Lacefield, brother of Drusilla Lacefield, and betrothed of Marcia Vaiden; plantation aristocrat who becomes editor of a newspaper in Florence, Alabama; appears in T. S. Stribling's *The Forge* and *The Store.*

Caruthers Lacefield Landed aristocrat and slave owner; patriarch of Lacefield Manor and father of A. Gray and Drusilla Lacefield in T. S. Stribling's *The Forge.*

Drusilla Lacefield See Drusilla Lacefield Crowninshield.

Lucy Lacefield See Lucy Lacefield Vaiden.

Brandon Lacey Great-grandson of Montague Lacey, proprietor of Crawford's Landing plantation, and husband of Sally Crawford Lacey; bankrupted by the Panic of 1837 in Mary Lee Settle's *Know Nothing.*

Jonathan (Johnny) Lacey Provincial captain and survivor of Braddock's army, frontier landholder, and member of the Virginia House of Burgesses; descendant of Johnny Church and husband of Sally Sawyer Lacey in Mary Lee Settle's *O Beulah Land.*

Katherine (Kathy) Lacey Divorced teacher who falls in love with Phil Green and finds she is more concerned about appearances than about individuals in Laura Z. Hobson's *Gentleman's Agreement.*

Melinda Lacey See Melinda Lacey Kregg.

Montague Crawford Bacchus Lacey Eldest son of Johnny and Sally Lacey; marries Brandon Crawford's daughter and becomes his heir in Mary Lee Settle's *O Beulah Land.*

Peregrine Lacey Son of Johnny and Sally Lacey; shares his mother's disdain for frontier settlers, hates his father for bringing him to the frontier, and is disinherited for his part in the massacre of Shawnee Indians in Mary Lee Settle's *O Beulah Land;* returns to Beulah.

Sally Crawford (Sal) Lacey Frivolous wife of Brandon Lacey, niece of Mamie Brandon Catlett, and mother-in-law of Lewis Catlett in Mary Lee Settle's *Know Nothing.*

Sally Sawyer (Sal) Lacey   Shallow, blonde wife of Johnny Lacey; considers the frontier settlers her inferiors and so is never satisfied or accepted at Beulah; eventually has her hair forcibly cut off because of her aristocratic pretensions and goes mad as a result in Mary Lee Settle's *O Beulah Land*.

Sara Lacey   See Sara Lacey (Mrs. Ezekiel) Catlett and Sara Lacey (Mrs. Lewis) Catlett.

Lafayette   French nobleman who fights in the American Revolution and later supports Thomas Paine's efforts in the French Revolution in Howard Fast's *Citizen Tom Paine*.

Lafe   Father of Dewey Dell Bundren's unborn child in William Faulkner's *As I Lay Dying*.

Lafitte (Achille)   Twin brother of Count Alphonse D'Oyley, impulsive pirate, and patriotic hero-villain in Joseph Holt Ingraham's *Lafitte*.

Lafon   French nobleman and father of the twins Lafitte and Count Alphonse D'Oyley in Joseph Holt Ingraham's *Lafitte*.

Rosemarie de Laframboise   Long Island socialite living in Rome as the mistress of Mason Flagg in William Styron's *Set This House on Fire*.

Roger Burns Lakeside   Mortician presiding over the funeral of Grandmother Herkimer in Wright Morris's *The Man Who Was There*.

Lallemont   General and corps commander in William Faulkner's *A Fable*.

Lamai   Island boy who finds Jerry in the sea after the Arangi is destroyed in Jack London's *Jerry of the Islands*.

Ruby Lamar   Common-law wife of Lee Goodwin in William Faulkner's *Sanctuary*.

J. A. Lamb   Head of a wholesale drug firm; employer of Virgil Adams until Adams takes a formula for glue and starts his own factory; eventually buys out Adams's company in Booth Tarkington's *Alice Adams*.

Letitia (Letty) Lamb   Close friend of Harriet Alden in George Santayana's *The Last Puritan*.

Mary Lambert   Wife of Thomas Paine; dies of a fever in England, leaving Paine alone and emotionally drained before he immigrates to America, in Howard Fast's *Citizen Tom Paine*.

Tom Lambert   American journalist and colleague of Mary Douglas in Martha Gellhorn's *A Stricken Field*.

Rose Lampkin   Suspected mistress of Gilbert Blount in Richard Wright's *The Outsider*.

Hattie Lampson   Dead mother of Luke and Mulge Lampson and mother-in-law of Ma Lampson; buried on the side of the dam overlooking the area where Mulge died in John Hawkes's *The Beetle Leg*.

Luke (Cowboy) Lampson   Younger son of Hattie Lampson and Cap Leecher; while fishing by the dam, he snares a human fetus, which he throws back; lives with Ma Lampson and Maverick in John Hawkes's *The Beetle Leg*.

Ma Lampson   Widow of Mulge Lampson, sister-in-law of Luke Lampson, and daughter-in-law of Hattie Lampson; lives with Luke Lampson and Maverick and searches for Mulge's grave with a divining rod in John Hawkes's *The Beetle Leg*.

Gerald Lamson   English novelist with whom Lorelei Lee takes up when Gus Eisman is out of town, using him to gain leverage with Gus, in Anita Loos's *Gentlemen Prefer Blondes*.

Caesar Lanark   Minnesota landowner and fur trader; father of Selene Lanark in Sinclair Lewis's *The God Seeker*.

Selene (Princess) Lanark   Half-Sioux daughter of Caesar Lanark; wife of Aaron Gadd in Sinclair Lewis's *The God-Seeker*.

Albert Lancaster   Chicago socialite and husband of Muriel Lester Lancaster in Margaret Ayer Barnes's *Years of Grace*.

Cicily Carver Bridges Lancaster   Daughter of Stephen and Jane Ward Carver in Margaret Ayer Barnes's *Years of Grace*; independent woman who defies convention and divorces Jack Bridges to marry Albert Lancaster, Jr.; comes to terms with Lancaster's infidelity in *Wisdom's Gate*.

Muriel Lester Lancaster   Schoolmate of Jane Ward, wife of Albert Lancaster, and mother of Albert Lancaster, Jr.; marries Ed Brown after Albert Lancaster's death in Margaret Ayer Barnes's *Years of Grace*; also appears in *Wisdom's Gate*.

Valerie (Val) Land   Niece of George Atkinson, daughter of an aspiring but unsuccessful painter, and lover and eventual wife of Saint Wentworth in DuBose Heyward's *Mamba's Daughters*.

Dov Landau   Survivor of the Warsaw Ghetto Revolt and Auschwitz; a runner and forger in the Warsaw ghetto; lover of Karen Clement in Leon Uris's *Exodus*.

Landers   Republican postmaster and proponent of justice and equality for blacks; opposed to mob violence but unable to prevent the lynching of Toussaint Vaiden in T. S. Stribling's *The Store*.

Mavis Landour   London society woman and lover of Freddie Ransome in H. D.'s *Palimpsest*.

Adele Landry   Wife of Al Landry and stepmother of Annie Landry in Shirley Ann Grau's *The Hard Blue Sky*.

Alistair (Al) Landry   Widowed father of Annie Landry; makes his daughter jealous when he marries Adele Landry in Shirley Ann Grau's *The Hard Blue Sky*.

Annie Landry   Bored sixteen-year-old who falls in love with Inky D'Alfonso and marries him in Shirley Ann Grau's *The Hard Blue Sky*.

Asshur Lane   Unconventional but faithful friend and eventual mate of Melissa Paul in Jessie Redmon Fauset's *The Chinaberry Tree*.

Jimmy (Jimmie) Lane   Friend and playmate of Sandy Rodgers; his mother dies and he quits school to become a bellhop in Langston Hughes's *Not Without Laughter*.

Lionel Lane   See Cross Damon.

Alison Langdon   Frail wife of Major Morris Langdon and employer of Anacleto; loses her baby daughter and dies shortly after being institutionalized for mental problems in Carson McCullers's *Reflections in a Golden Eye*.

Fred Langdon   Boyhood friend of Tom Bailey; captured in the snowball fight; becomes a California vintner in Thomas Bailey Aldrich's *The Story of a Bad Boy*.

Major Morris (The Buffalo) Langdon   Unfaithful husband of Alison Langdon and lover of Leonora Penderton; feels guilt and remorse at the death of his wife in Carson McCullers's *Reflections in a Golden Eye*.

Wolfgang Langfanger   Potter and councilman in James Kirke Paulding's *Koningsmarke*.

Alice Langham   Elder daughter of Andrew Langham; socialite who fascinates Robert Clay in Richard Harding Davis's *Soldiers of Fortune*.

Andrew Langham   Eastern tycoon who finances the Olancho Mining Company in Richard Harding Davis's *Soldiers of Fortune*.

Hope Langham   Younger daughter of Andrew Langham; falls in love with Robert Clay in Richard Harding Davis's *Soldiers of Fortune*.

Theodore Langham   Son of Andrew Langham; college student sent to Olancho to oversee his father's mining interests in Richard Harding Davis's *Soldiers of Fortune*.

Lady Aurora Langrish   Spinster philanthropist who ministers to the poor and admires the revolutionary Paul Muniment in Henry James's *The Princess Casamassima*.

Ellen Langton   Ward of the Melmoths; abducted by Butler and rescued by Fanshawe; marries Edward Walcott in Nathaniel Hawthorne's *Fanshawe*.

John Langton   Evil rival for power with George Posey; captain of a company of Confederate soldiers; killed by Posey in Allen Tate's *The Fathers*.

John Langton   Father of Ellen Langton; presumed lost at sea in Nathaniel Hawthorne's *Fanshawe*.

Gertrude Langueville   Frenchwoman who inspires love and murder in Joseph Holt Ingraham's *Lafitte*.

Joyce Lanyon   Unhappily married second wife of Martin Arrowsmith in Sinclair Lewis's *Arrowsmith*.

Irene Lapham   Daughter of Silas and Persis Lapham; falls in love with Tom Corey in William Dean Howells's *The Rise of Silas Lapham*.

Penelope (Pen) Lapham   Daughter of Silas and Persis Lapham; marries Tom Corey in William Dean Howells's *The Rise of Silas Lapham*.

Persis (Pert) Lapham   Wife of Silas Lapham; former country schoolteacher who is uneasy in Boston society in William Dean Howells's *The Rise of Silas Lapham*.

Silas Lapham   Wealthy businessman without social background; loses his fortune when he refuses to enter into an unethical business deal in William Dean Howells's *The Rise of Silas Lapham*.

Lapin   Thief executed with Stefan in William Faulkner's *A Fable*.

Volida La Porte   Friend of Etta Barnes, whom La Porte encourages to attend the University of Wisconsin, in Theodore Dreiser's *The Bulwark*.

Alexander (Aleck) Larkin   Nephew of Obed Larkin; lawyer in partnership with his brother Horace until Aleck discovers that Horace is using the firm to advance his political ambitions; idealist who quests for the meaning of life and marries Gertrude Larkin in Hjalmar Hjorth Boyesen's *The Mammon of Unrighteousness*.

Bobby Larkin   Friend of Diana Deacon, with whom he plans to elope until dissuaded by Lulu Bett, in Zona Gale's *Miss Lulu Bett*.

Gertrude (Gertie) Larkin   Adopted daughter of Obed Larkin; an aspiring sculptress; engaged to Dr. Archibald Hawk until she discovers that he wants her money; marries Aleck Larkin in Hjalmar Hjorth Boyesen's *The Mammon of Unrighteousness*.

Horace Larkin   Nephew of Obed Larkin; lawyer and politician who marries Kate Van Schaak and, because of her, establishes a career in diplomacy in Hjalmar Hjorth Boyesen's *The Mammon of Unrighteousness*.

Obed Larkin   Uncle and adoptive father of Aleck and Horace Larkin and adoptive father of Gertrude Larkin; philanthropist and founder of Larkin University in Hjalmar Hjorth Boyesen's *The Mammon of Unrighteousness*.

Molly Larkins   Lover of Daniel Harrow in Walter D. Edmonds's *Rome Haul.*

Laroussel   Creole traveling with Captain Harris; interrogates Chita Viosca and discovers her Creole background in Lafcadio Hearn's *Chita.*

Larry   Anticivilization sailor aboard the *Highlander* in Herman Melville's *Redburn.*

Larry   Husband of Lillian in Anaïs Nin's *Ladders to Fire* and *Seduction of the Minotaur.*

Death Larsen   Brother of Wolf Larsen and captain of the *Macedonia* in Jack London's *The Sea-Wolf.*

Wolf Larsen   Brutal captain of the *Ghost* in Jack London's *The Sea-Wolf.*

Gummy Larson   Contractor to whom Willie Stark gives the hospital contract in exchange for political support in Robert Penn Warren's *All the King's Men.*

Mademoiselle La Rue (Mrs. Crayton)   Teacher at Charlotte Temple's school who aids Jack Montraville in Charlotte's seduction; briefly she is the romantic interest of Belcour, only to abandon him for marriage to Colonel Crayton, whom she meets on her journey from England to the United States in Susanna Rowson's *Charlotte.*

Mrs. Larue   Sister-in-law of Dr. Ravenel; her rank opportunism and amoral behavior lead her to an affair with John Carter, despite his marriage to her niece, in John William De-Forest's *Miss Ravenel's Conversion from Secession to Loyalty.*

Reverend James J. Lasher   Spiritual leader of the Ghost Shirt Society's revolt in Kurt Vonnegut's *Player Piano.*

John Laskell   Young liberal searching for the middle ground between conflicting absolutist ideologies in Lionel Trilling's *The Middle of the Journey.*

Charles (Spud) Latham   Son of Evans Latham and Mrs. Latham and best friend of Lymie Peters; loves Sally Forbes in William Maxwell's *The Folded Leaf.*

Deacon Latham   Father of Maria Latham and grandfather of Lydia Blood in William Dean Howells's *The Lady of the Aroostook.*

Evans Latham   Father of Helen and Spud Latham in William Maxwell's *The Folded Leaf.*

Helen Latham   Sister of Spud Latham in William Maxwell's *The Folded Leaf.*

Maria Latham   Aunt and guardian of Lydia Blood in William Dean Howells's *The Lady of the Aroostook.*

Mildred Latham   Woman with a mysterious past who loves Sidney Wyeth, sells his book, and eventually marries him in Oscar Micheaux's *The Forged Note.*

Mrs. Latham   Mother of Helen and Spud Latham in William Maxwell's *The Folded Leaf.*

Phil Latham   Wrestling coach at Devon School in John Knowles's *A Separate Peace.*

Latnah   Woman who supports the black expatriates in Marseilles in Claude McKay's *Banjo.*

Clarence Latouche   Murderer of Asa Stryker in Edmund Wilson's *Memoirs of Hecate County.*

Jean Marie Latour   French missionary appointed vicar apostolic of New Mexico and later archbishop; oversees reforms in the New Mexico church and builds a cathedral in Santa Fe in Willa Cather's *Death Comes for the Archbishop.*

Ephemia (Effie) Lattimore   Homemaker sister of Olivia and Forester Lattimore in Mary Austin's *A Woman of Genius.*

Forester (Forrie) Lattimore   Brother of Olivia and Effie Lattimore and the favored child of the widowed Sally Lattimore; small-town shopkeeper in Mary Austin's *A Woman of Genius.*

Olivia May Lattimore   Sister of Effie and Forester Lattimore; widow of Tommy Bettersworth, lover of Helmeth Garrett, and longtime friend and probable future wife of Gerald McDermott; gifted and successful actress hampered by roles traditionally imposed on women; narrator of Mary Austin's *A Woman of Genius.*

Sally Lattimore   Widowed mother of Olivia, Forester, and Effie Lattimore in Mary Austin's *A Woman of Genius.*

Hymie Laubscher   Assistant to Henry Miller at the telegraph company; frequently lends him money in Henry Miller's *Tropic of Capricorn.*

Laughing Boy (Blind Eyes, Horse Trader, My Slayer of Enemy Gods, Sings Before Spears, Turns His Back, Went Away)   Skilled horseman and artisan of silver jewelry who makes bowguards and is married to Slim Girl in Oliver La Farge's *Laughing Boy.*

Peter Laughlin   Speculator and member of the Chicago Board of Trade; business partner of Frank Cowperwood in Theodore Dreiser's *The Titan.*

Amy March Laurence   See Amy Curtis March.

Bess Laurence   Daughter of Amy March and Theodore Laurence; stays briefly at Plumfield in Louisa May Alcott's *Little Men.*

James Laurence   Wealthy, elderly grandfather of Theodore Laurence in Louisa May Alcott's *Little Women.*

Theodore (Laurie, Teddy) Laurence Wealthy grandson of James Laurence; proposes marriage to Jo March, but ultimately marries Amy March in Louisa May Alcott's *Little Women;* also appears in *Little Men.*

Laurent Young helper in Creuzot's print shop; harassed by Virginians, who pejoratively label him a Jacobin, in Arna Wendell Bontemps's *Black Thunder.*

Phillip Laurie Fiancée of Daisy Cowan; smug, eager business-man in Nathan Asch's *Pay Day.*

Grandma Lausch Imperious ruler of the March household until she is consigned to an institution for the elderly, where she dies, in Saul Bellow's *The Adventures of Augie March.*

Albert (Kid Lousy, Louse, Kid Louso, Lousy) Lauzon Boy-hood friend and companion of Jack Duluoz in Jack Kerouac's *Doctor Sax, Maggie Cassidy,* and *Book of Dreams.*

Arial Lavalina Handsome young novelist introduced to Frank Carmody by Leo Percepied in Jack Kerouac's *The Subter-raneans.*

Lavender Mulatto steward aboard the *Highlander* in Herman Melville's *Redburn.*

Jay Laverick Playboy friend of Cass and Jinny Timberlane in Sinclair Lewis's *Cass Timberlane.*

Lenore La Verne See Elly Chipley.

Catharine Law Illegitimate daughter of John Law and Mary Cormynge in Emerson Hough's *The Mississippi Bubble.*

John (Beau, Jack, Jean L'as, Jessamy) Law Precocious, ar-rogant gambler and financial wizard in Emerson Hough's *The Mississippi Bubble.*

Will (Guillaume Las) Law Brother of John Law in Emerson Hough's *The Mississippi Bubble.*

Lawrence Eccentric window dresser and friend who paints Djuna's apartment with phosphorescent paint in Anaïs Nin's *Children of the Albatross.*

Amy Lawrence Girlfriend of Tom Sawyer until Becky Thatcher comes to town in Samuel Langhorne Clemens's *The Adventures of Tom Sawyer.*

Major Billy Lawrence Second-in-command to Colonel Templeton on the thirty-six-mile hike in William Styron's *The Long March.*

Charles Gans Lawrence Wealthy college tennis star with a magnetic personality and a habit of perfection; gored in an am-ateur bullfight and later kills himself in Wright Morris's *The Huge Season.*

Leon (Griffin) Lawrence Actor who seduces and later mar-ries Sarah Croyden; as Leon Griffin, he is the friend and would-be lover of Olivia Lattimore in Mary Austin's *A Woman of Genius.*

Maureen Fairchild (Great-Aunt Mac) Laws Widowed aunt of Battle Fairchild; lives at Shellmound plantation in Eudora Welty's *Delta Wedding.*

Berry Lawson Former slave who moves to the Red Wing set-tlement; flees with Nimbus after the battle with the Ku Klux Klan, but reappears years later as a settler in Eupolia, Kansas, in Albion W. Tourgée's *Bricks Without Straw.*

Jack Lawson Best friend of Henry Miller; remains ill for a year and dies; Miller claims to have forgotten him immediately after his death in Henry Miller's *Tropic of Capricorn.*

Sally Ann Lawson Wife of Berry Lawson, with whom she moves to Red Wing and flees following the Ku Klux Klan at-tack; returns with their children to Red Wing, and is resettled, by Mollie Ainslie, in Kansas, in Albion W. Tourgée's *Bricks Without Straw.*

Captain John (Jack) Lawton Fearless captain of the Virginia dragoons who tries to track down Harvey Birch; fatally wounded toward the end of the Revolutionary War in James Fenimore Cooper's *The Spy.*

Mrs. Layden Wealthy observer of the dance marathon who chooses Robert Syverten and Gloria Beatty as her favorite cou-ple; accidentally killed in the shooting in the Palm Garden in Horace McCoy's *They Shoot Horses, Don't They?*

Edgar Laydon Teacher of literature and first love of Hagar Ashendyne in Mary Johnston's *Hagar.*

Solace Layfield False prophet hired by Hoover Shoats as Hazel Motes's double; Motes kills him by running over him with a rat-colored Essex in Flannery O'Connor's *Wise Blood.*

George Leach Former cabin boy who attempts to murder the captain and cook aboard the *Ghost* in Jack London's *The Sea-Wolf.*

Leah Older sister of Augie; rears him after the death of their mother in Arna Wendell Bontemps's *God Sends Sunday.*

Veronica Leary Army nurse and romantic love interest of Carlo Reinhart in Thomas Berger's *Crazy in Berlin.*

Anna Leath Wealthy American woman living in France after her marriage to Fraser Leath; widowed and pained by her reti-cence and inability to experience passion, she renews a relation-ship with George Darrow, a former suitor who has recently had an affair with Sophy Viner, governess to Anna's daughter, in Edith Wharton's *The Reef.*

Effie Leath Daughter of Anna and Fraser Leath in Edith Wharton's *The Reef.*

Fraser Leath   Deceased husband of Anna Leath; cosmopolitan man who collected enameled snuffboxes and painted in watercolors in Edith Wharton's *The Reef*.

Owen Leath   Stepson of Anna Leath; his wish to marry Sophy Viner eventually causes George Darrow, Anna's fiancé, to reveal his affair with Sophy in Edith Wharton's *The Reef*.

Leather-stocking   See Nathaniel Bumppo.

Bill Leatherwood   Leader of a band of ruthless, fortune-seeking marauders in T. S. Stribling's *The Forge*.

Eleanore Leavenworth   Cousin of Mary Leavenworth; niece of Horatio Leavenworth, whom she is suspected of having murdered, in Anna Katharine Green's *The Leavenworth Case*.

Horatio Leavenworth   Wealthy man found murdered in his library in Anna Katharine Green's *The Leavenworth Case*.

Mary Leavenworth   Cousin of Eleanore Leavenworth; sole heir of her uncle Horatio Leavenworth, until he discovers her secret marriage to Henry Clavering, an Englishman, in Anna Katharine Green's *The Leavenworth Case*.

Mr. Leavenworth   Rich American widower traveling in Europe who becomes engaged to Augusta Blanchard; commissions Roderick Hudson to sculpt a representation of Intellectual Refinement in Henry James's *Roderick Hudson*.

Le Balafré   Venerable Sioux leader, father of Tachechana, and father-in-law of Mahtoree; offers to adopt and thereby save Mahtoree's captive, Hard Heart, in James Fenimore Cooper's *The Prairie*.

Madame Lebrun   Owner of an island resort where the Pontelliers, the Ratignolles, and Mademoiselle Reisz vacation; mother of Robert Lebrun in Kate Chopin's *The Awakening*.

Robert Lebrun   Young man with whom Edna Pontellier falls in love; son of Madame Lebrun in Kate Chopin's *The Awakening*.

Madame Lecerf   See Nina Toorovetz de Rechnoy.

Dr. Ledsmar   Scientist and student of Darwinian theory consulted by Theron Ware; Ledsmar derisively names a lizard after Ware in Harold Frederic's *The Damnation of Theron Ware*.

Oscar (Shad) Ledue   Surly peasant, hired man of Doremus Jessup, and captain of the local Minute Men; caught embezzling funds, he is sent to a concentration camp, where he is killed by people he sent there, in Sinclair Lewis's *It Can't Happen Here*.

Thomas Ledward   Acting surgeon aboard HMS *Bounty* in Charles Nordhoff and James Norman Hall's *Mutiny on the Bounty*; set adrift with Captain Bligh; narrator of *Men against the Sea*.

Lee (Ching Chong)   Wise Chinese servant in the Trask household; helps to rear the twins Caleb and Aron Trask and acts as friend and adviser to Adam Trask in John Steinbeck's *East of Eden*.

Lee Buck Cal   See Lee Buck Calhoun.

Lee the Agent   See William Lee.

Buddy Lee   Sensitive twin whose brother died of cancer at age fifteen; works for Stephen Conner as secretary and confidant in John Updike's *The Poorhouse Fair*.

Dixie Lee   Pioneer who becomes a brothel madam and later an oil baron in Edna Ferber's *Cimarron*.

Inspector J. Lee   See William Lee.

Lorelei Lee   Blonde diarist and intercontinental adventuress who, accompanied by Dorothy Shaw, collects amours and diamonds; her diary constitutes Anita Loos's *Gentlemen Prefer Blondes;* chronicles further adventures and the life of Dorothy in *But Gentlemen Marry Brunettes*.

Madeleine Ross (Mrs. Lightfoot Lee) Lee   Young widow who moves to Washington to observe democracy in action and starts a salon where various personalities meet for lively conversation; accepts the marriage proposal of Senator Ratcliffe, then rejects it after learning of his improper political dealings, in Henry Adam's *Democracy*.

William (Bill, Billy, Lee the Agent, El Hombre Invisible, Inspector J. Lee, Klinker, William Seward) Lee   Heroin addict and petty criminal in New York, New Orleans, Texas, and eventually Mexico City; narrator of William S. Burroughs's *Junkie;* appears also in *Naked Lunch, Nova Express, The Soft Machine, The Ticket That Exploded,* and *Exterminator!*

Cap Leech   Father of Luke and Mulge Lampson; lives with the Indians and practices irregular and illegal medicine; delivers Harry Bohn from the body of the infant's dead mother in John Hawkes's *The Beetle Leg*.

George (Grig) Leeds   Abyssinian piano player with whom Malcolm shares a room in the house of Eloisa and Jerome Brace in James Purdy's *Malcolm*.

Leete   Twenty-first century doctor and father of Edith Leete; discusses the advances of society in the time Julian West has been asleep in Edward Bellamy's *Looking Backward*.

Edith Leete   Daughter of Doctor Leete and descendant of Edith Bartlett; loves Julian West in Edward Bellamy's *Looking Backward*.

Leevey   American military overseer of a partitioned Germany; pursued by Zizendorf in John Hawkes's *The Cannibal*.

Jim Lefferts   College roommate and close friend of Elmer Gantry; they drift apart when Gantry decides to enter the ministry in Sinclair Lewis's *Elmer Gantry*.

Lawrence Lefferts   Member of the old New York social set; known as the authority on correct form in Edith Wharton's *The Age of Innocence*.

Robert A. (Bob) Leffingwell   Highly controversial presidential nominee for Secretary of State in Allen Drury's *Advise and Consent*.

Will Legate   Hunter in William Faulkner's *Go Down, Moses* and protector of Lucas Beauchamp in *Intruder in the Dust*.

Dr. Leggett   Marine biologist on the *Sea Beast;* student of the primeval ooze of life in Wright Morris's *Love Among the Cannibals*.

Peter Legrand   Mill owner and moneylender; spends half a lifetime longing for Julia Cropleigh Cree and the child he thinks is his own in Andrew Lytle's *The Velvet Horn*.

Julian Legree   Matinee idol and frequent drinker in Henry Miller's *Black Spring*.

Simon Legree   Final owner of Uncle Tom, whom he tortures to death in an effort to make Tom reveal the whereabouts of two escaped female slaves, in Harriet Beecher Stowe's *Uncle Tom's Cabin*.

Simon Legree   Cruel, opportunistic former slave owner who gains political power during Reconstruction in Thomas Dixon's *The Leopard's Spots*.

Legs (Red)   Gambler and bootlegger; shares a room with Sidney Wyeth in Oscar Micheaux's *The Forged Note*.

Dr. Leopold Lehmann   Pseudo-psychiatrist specializing in cases of human transformation; guardian of Paula Kahler in Wright Morris's *The Field of Vision*.

Annabel Leigh   First love of Humbert Humbert and source of his passion for Dolores Haze; dies of typhus four months after her Riviera summer with him in Vladimir Nabokov's *Lolita*.

Alma Leighton   Artist romantically interested in Angus Beaton in William Dean Howells's *A Hazard of New Fortunes*.

Patricia (Pat) Leighton   New York advertising agent and lover of Jim Calder; attempts to free Calder from his attachment to the Brills and Wickford Point in John P. Marquand's *Wickford Point*.

Le Loup Cervier   Indian brave who gives Natty Bumppo the name Hawkeye; first man killed by Bumppo in James Fenimore Cooper's *The Deerslayer*.

Iris Lemon   Woman who brings Roy Hobbs out of his batting slump and to whom he goes after being sold out by Memo Paris in Bernard Malamud's *The Natural*.

Mr. Lemon   Caretaker of the trailer park where the Manions live; Frederic Manion turns himself in to Lemon, a deputy sheriff, after shooting Barney Quill in Robert Traver's *Anatomy of a Murder*.

Casaubon Le Moyne   Father of Hesden Le Moyne; Unionist who is the only Whig to have represented Horsford County in the North Carolina legislature in Albion W. Tourgee's *Bricks Without Straw*.

Hesden Le Moyne   Southern gentleman and Unionist whose code of honor leads him to enlist as a private in the Confederate army; befriends Eliab Hill and Nimbus; repudiates the racial prejudice of his Southern neighbors; marries Mollie Ainslie in Albion W. Tourgee's *Bricks Without Straw*.

Hester Richards Le Moyne   Granddaughter of Black Jim Richards, from whom she inherits Mulberry Hill plantation, and mother of Hesden Le Moyne; treats Mollie Ainslie as her social inferior until Mollie shames her by demonstrating a rigorous code of personal honor in Albion W. Tourgee's *Bricks Without Straw*.

Hildreth Le Moyne   Son of Hesden and Julia Lomax Le Moyne; dies of yellow fever, despite the nursing of Mollie Ainslie, whom he loves from the moment they meet, in Albion W. Tourgee's *Bricks Without Straw*.

Julia Lomax Le Moyne   First wife of Hesden Le Moyne; dies while giving birth to Hildreth Le Moyne in Albion W. Tourgee's *Bricks Without Straw*.

Lemsford   Poet friend of White-Jacket in Herman Melville's *White-Jacket*.

Anna Lenihan (Lenihanova)   Impoverished dance-hall hostess and then a waitress who is one of the narrator's mistresses in Edmund Wilson's *Memoirs of Hecate County*.

Sylvia Lennox   Wealthy and spoiled Los Angeles socialite; wife of Terry Lennox; Philip Marlowe investigates her murder in Raymond Chandler's *The Long Goodbye*.

Terry Lennox   War hero and drunken husband of wealthy socialite and murder victim Sylvia Lennox; suspected by police in wife's death; flees to Mexico and is pursued by Philip Marlowe in Raymond Chandler's *The Long Goodbye*.

Alexander (Uncle Aleck) Lenoir   Simpleminded former slave of Jeannie Campbell Lenoir; elected to the state legislature in Thomas Dixon's *The Clansman*.

Capitola (Cap Black) Le Noir   Feisty heroine who first appears disguised as a newsboy and continues her adventures as a damsel errant, fighting duels, capturing bandits, and rescuing damsels in distress, in E.D.E.N. Southworth's *The Hidden Hand*.

Craven Le Noir   Bumbling son of Gabriel Le Noir; falls in love with Capitola Le Noir in E.D.E.N. Southworth's *The Hidden Hand*.

Gabriel Le Noir   Villainous uncle of Capitola Le Noir; conspires to obtain her fortune and that of Clara Day in E.D.E.N. Southworth's *The Hidden Hand*.

Jeannie Campbell Lenoir   Widow and mother of Marion Lenoir; commits suicide with her daughter after Marion is raped in Thomas Dixon's *The Clansman*.

Marion Lenoir   Sweetheart of Ben Cameron; commits suicide after being raped by Augustus Caesar in Thomas Dixon's *The Clansman*.

Susan (Loma Sackville, Susie) Lenox   Mistress of Rod Spenser and of Freddie Palmer; factory worker and prostitute in Cincinnati and New York before becoming an acclaimed actress in David Graham Phillips's *Susan Lenox*.

Foscoe Leonard   Homesteader and minister who is killed when a posse overtakes Wade Shiveley; his death helps cause Shiveley's hanging in H. L. Davis's *Honey in the Horn*.

Margaret Leonard   Consumptive woman who befriends Eugene Gant in Thomas Wolfe's *Look Homeward, Angel*.

Ruth Leonard   Lover of Rabbit Angstrom; becomes pregnant by him in John Updike's *Rabbit, Run*.

Leopard   Greedy and fierce robber chief killed by Wang the Tiger in Pearl Buck's *Sons*.

Elwin (Leper) Lepellier   Clumsy schoolmate of Gene Forrester and Finny; suffers a mental breakdown after joining the Ski Patrol and receives a dishonorable discharge in John Knowles's *A Separate Peace*.

Leslie   Republican judge who teaches democracy and American politics to John Gwynne in Gertrude Atherton's *Ancestors*.

Faith Leslie   Sister of Hope Leslie; captured by Indians and married to the Pequod Oneco in Catharine Maria Sedgwick's *Hope Leslie*.

Hope Leslie   Savior of the Indians Nelema and Magawisca; betrothed of Everell Fletcher in Catharine Maria Sedgwick's *Hope Leslie*.

Dr. John Leslie   Widowed New England country doctor who has avoided the cities and great hospitals to minister instead to country folk; guardian of Nan Prince in Sarah Orne Jewett's *A Country Doctor*.

Lester   Saxophonist whom Dorothy Shaw marries despite his ugliness and, as it turns out, homosexuality; bribed by Charlie Breene's parents to prevent a divorce, then murdered at their instigation in Anita Loos's *But Gentlemen Marry Brunettes*.

Ada Lester   Mother of seventeen children, not all by her husband Jeeter Lester; longs to be buried in a new dress in Erskine Caldwell's *Tobacco Road*.

Dan Lester   Young New England farmer-blacksmith who almost loses his lifelong love, Doris Owen, to Dick Dale, but finally marries her, in Sarah Orne Jewett's *A Marsh Island*.

Dude Lester   Sixteen-year-old who marries Bessie Rice an itinerant preacher, in Erskine Caldwell's *Tobacco Road*.

Ellie May Lester   Harelipped daughter of Jeeter and Ada Lester; leaves her parents to become the mate of Lov Bensey, a man her younger sister Pearl Lester deserted, in Erskine Caldwell's *Tobacco Road*.

Howard Lester   Judge who presides over Frederick Eichner's grand jury hearing in Terry Southern's *Flash and Filigree*.

Jeeter Lester   Georgia tenant farmer whose obsession with the soil causes him to reject the financial security of the cotton mills in Erskine Caldwell's *Tobacco Road*.

Mother Lester   Half-starved grandmother of the Lester children; run over by an automobile driven by her grandson Dude Lester and buried in a field before she is dead in Erskine Caldwell's *Tobacco Road*.

Muriel Lester   See Muriel Lester Lancaster.

Asa Leventhal   Middle-aged New York Jew and trade-journal editor who must cope with his fears of loneliness, anti-Semitism, displacement, and death in order to strike an informed balance between what he owes to others and what he owes to himself in Saul Bellow's *The Victim*.

Peter Charles Leverett   Young attorney from Virginia and childhood friend of Mason Flagg; narrator of William Styron's *Set This House on Fire*.

Jake Levin   Jewish marine radio operator and friend of Mortimer Gray; killed on Tarawa in Leon Uris's *Battle Cry*.

Gerald David Levine   R.A.F. pilot who commits suicide in William Faulkner's *A Fable*.

Noach Levinson   Recordkeeper for the Judenrat (a Nazi-controlled governing body) and principal narrator of an account of the Nazi occupation of Poland and the Jewish resistance movement in a Warsaw ghetto in John Hersey's *The Wall*.

Matt Levitt   Mechanic enamored of Linda Snopes in William Faulkner's *The Town*.

Jacob (Jake, Jawn) Levy   Jewish Jeep driver for Lieutenant Colonel John Dawson Smithers; lover and fiancé of Kathe Limpert; deliberately runs over three Germans after visiting Dachau in Martha Gellhorn's *Wine of Astonishment*.

Maurice Levy   Rival of Penrod Schofield for the attention of Marjorie Jones; alternates between being Penrod's bitter foe and one of his regular playmates in Booth Tarkington's *Penrod, Penrod and Sam*, and *Penrod Jashber*.

Sol Levy   Osage, Oklahoma, Jew who rises from street peddler to prosperous and respected businessman in Edna Ferber's *Cimarron*.

John Lewis   Numbers runner who fails to pay off Hubert Cooley's $7.00 bet on 417 in Julian Mayfield's *The Hit*.

Spotteswood Lewis   Tuckahoe gentleman and provincial officer in charge of Fort Young; snubbed by Sally Lacey because he lives with an Indian squaw in Mary Lee Settle's *O Beulah Land*.

Stanley Lewis   Elihu Willsson's secretary in Dashiell Hammett's *Red Harvest*.

Lu Libble   Football coach of Jack Duluoz at Columbia University in Jack Kerouac's *Maggie Cassidy;* appears as Lou Little in *Visions of Cody*.

Bayou de Libertas   Overseer of the plantation at Bréda known for his kind treatment of slaves; friend of Captain Frounier in Arna Wendell Bontemps's *Drums at Dusk*.

Ernest Lieberman   Psychiatrist at Gan Dafna kibbutz who works with concentration camp survivors in Leon Uris's *Exodus*.

The Lie Detector   Man who assumes that Sabina is guilty and follows her and other artists, extracting confessions from them, in Anaïs Nin's *A Spy in the House of Love* and *Seduction of the Minotaur*.

Emily Liggett   Wife of Weston Liggett; does not suspect her husband's infidelity in John O'Hara's *Butterfield 8*.

Weston Liggett   Wealthy, Yale-educated husband of Emily Liggett and lover of Gloria Wandrous; his double life finally is exposed when he returns home beaten up and drunk in John O'Hara's *Butterfield 8*.

Christina (Princess Casamassima) Light   Beautiful, illegitimate daughter of Mrs. Light and the Cavaliere Giacosa; loved by Roderick Hudson, but marries Prince Casamassima, in Henry James's *Roderick Hudson;* leaves her husband to pursue revolutionary activity in *The Princess Casamassima*.

Gracie Light   See Gracie Vaiden.

Mrs. Light   Widowed mother, by the Cavaliere Giacosa, of Christina Light; obsessed with making a great fortune by marriage for her daughter in Henry James's *Roderick Hudson*.

Amanda Lightfoot   Feminine ideal of the young Gamaliel Bland Honeywell; remains faithful to her brief engagement to him in Ellen Glasgow's *The Romantic Comedians*.

Maria Lightfoot   Mulatto grandmother of Emma Lou Morgan in Wallace Thurman's *The Blacker the Berry*.

Samuel Lightfoot   Mulatto grandfather of Emma Lou Morgan in Wallace Thurman's *The Blacker the Berry*.

Shining Lighttower   Marine radio operator wounded at Saipan in Leon Uris's *Battle Cry*.

Lillian   See Lillian Beye.

Kathe Limpert   Catholic waitress in Luxembourg; lover and intended wife of Jacob Levy in Martha Gellhorn's *Wine of Astonishment*.

Abraham Lincoln   President of the United States who pardons Ben Cameron and whose assassination leads to the radical Republican policies of Reconstruction in Thomas Dixon's *The Clansman*.

Berthold Lindau   German-born American socialist who is the editor of *Every Other Week* and is fired by Jacob Dryfoos; killed by the police during a streetcar workers' strike in William Dean Howells's *A Hazard of New Fortunes*.

Evan Lindley   Progress-minded attorney; learns prudence from his wife Serena Lindley after suffering financial reverses in Mary Austin's *Santa Lucia*.

Serena Haven Lindley   Wife of Evan Lindley; frustrated by exclusion from her husband's business affairs until financial reverses force an end to his protectiveness in Mary Austin's *Santa Lucia*.

Mrs. Lindow   Plump and pleasant grandmotherly housekeeper who prepares meals for the narrator and her young writer-lover during their stay at Ambleside in Aline Bernstein's *The Journey Down*.

Henry Lindsay   Son of Philip Lindsay, brother of Mildred Lindsay, and friend of Stephen Foster; visits Cornwallis to assure Arthur Butler's fair treatment in John Pendleton Kennedy's *Horse-Shoe Robinson*.

Mildred Lindsay   Daughter of Philip Lindsay, sister of Henry Lindsay, and wife of Arthur Butler; visits Cornwallis to assure her husband's fair treatment; reunited with Butler at King's Mountain in John Pendleton Kennedy's *Horse-Shoe Robinson*.

Mr. Lindsay   Scottish uncle of Ellen Montgomery; supervises her training and education while she lives in Scotland in Susan Warner's *The Wide, Wide World*.

Mrs. Lindsay   Scottish grandmother of Ellen Montgomery; disowned Ellen's mother after she married an American, but rears Ellen as a teenager in Susan Warner's *The Wide, Wide World*.

Philip Lindsay   Father of Henry and Mildred Lindsay; master of Dove Cote; dies in a misdirected effort to pursue his daughter and join the British and Tory forces at King's Mountain in John Pendleton Kennedy's *Horse-Shoe Robinson*.

Mickey Linehan   Continental Detective Agency operative who answers the Continental Op's call for assistance in Dashiell Hammett's *Red Harvest*.

Lena Lingard   Jim Burden's girlfriend while he is in college in Willa Cather's *My Ántonia*.

Byron Linkhorn   Brother of Dove Linkhorn; his death causes the passion to go out of his father's sermons in Nelson Algren's *A Walk on the Wild Side*.

Dove Linkhorn   Innocent involved in numerous shady schemes in Nelson Algren's *A Walk on the Wild Side*.

Fitz Linkhorn   Father of Byron and Dove Linkhorn; drunken fire-and-brimstone preacher in Nelson Algren's *A Walk on the Wild Side*.

Carl Linstrum   Childhood friend of Alexandra Bergson, whom he marries, in Willa Cather's *O Pioneers!*

Lion   Dog in William Faulkner's *Go Down, Moses* (where he helps capture Old Ben) and *The Town*.

Private Lipido   Defender of Mother Ormsby; companion to Warren K. Ormsby in ceremonies dedicating the USS *Ormsby* in Wright Morris's *Man and Boy*.

Lip-lip   Dog of Gray Beaver; killed by White Fang in Jack London's *White Fang*.

Mabel Blitch Lipscomb   Childhood friend of Undine Spragg; divorces and remarries to enhance her social status in Edith Wharton's *The Custom of the Country*.

Dame Lisa (Adelais)   Shrewish wife of Jurgen in James Branch Cabell's *Jurgen*.

Lissus   Opponent wounded with a machete during a fight with Augie in Arna Wendell Bontemps's *God Sends Sunday*.

Lou Little   See Lu Libble.

Eunice Littlefield   Daughter of Howard Littlefield and neighbor of the Babbitts; elopes with Theodore Babbitt in Sinclair Lewis's *Babbitt*.

Howard Littlefield   Father of Eunice Littlefield and neighbor of George Babbitt; employment manager of the Zenith Street Traction Company in Sinclair Lewis's *Babbitt*.

Joe Little Fox   Indian boatbuilder for Backwater Brandon and lover of Lyddy; burned to death by the Kreggs when they hear that the land beyond the mountains is reserved for the Indians in Mary Lee Settle's *O Beulah Land*.

Little Harp   Bandit who discovers that Jamie Lockhart is both a robber and a gentleman in Eudora Welty's *The Robber Bridegroom*.

Mary Little John   New friend of Frankie Addams; her arrival allows Frankie to ignore the death of John Henry West in Carson McCullers's *The Member of the Wedding*.

Mrs. Little John   Boardinghouse owner in William Faulkner's *The Hamlet* and *The Town*.

Ulysses Little John   Spendthrift companion of Cuthbert Dangerfield in James Kirke Paulding's *Westward Ho!*

Little Luke   See Luther.

Agatha (Aunt Agatha) Littlepage   Aunt of Virginius Littlepage; condemned to her third-story back bedroom because of an early indiscretion with Colonel Bletheram in Ellen Glasgow's *They Stooped to Folly*.

Captain Littlepage   Stately and refined retired sea captain and lover of the poets Shakespeare and Milton; haunted by a story about a city of ghosts near the North Pole in Sarah Orne Jewett's *The Country of the Pointed Firs*.

Curle Littlepage   Popular, vulgar, and naively optimistic son of Victoria and Virginius Littlepage in Ellen Glasgow's *They Stooped to Folly*.

Duncan Littlepage   Spoiled son of Victoria and Virginius Littlepage; demoralized by World War I in Ellen Glasgow's *They Stooped to Folly*.

Marmaduke Littlepage   Byronic older brother of Virginius Littlepage; modernist painter and opponent of Victorian psychology in Ellen Glasgow's *They Stooped to Folly*.

Mary Victoria Littlepage   See Mary Victoria Littlepage Welding.

Victoria Brooke Littlepage   Wealthy and orderly wife of Virginius Littlepage in Ellen Glasgow's *They Stooped to Folly*.

Virginius Curle Littlepage   Pillar of society who, as he is attracted to Amy Dalrymple, begins to find his happy marriage monotonous in Ellen Glasgow's *They Stooped to Folly*.

Mortimer Lonzo Littlepaugh   Counsel for the American Electric Power Company; commits suicide when replaced as counsel by Judge Irwin in Robert Penn Warren's *All the King's Men*.

Little Rock   Night-crew hoist man at the Past Bay Manufacturing Company factory killed during the power outage in Robert Cantwell's *The Land of Plenty*.

Little Sunshine   Hermit figure who lives at the Cloud Hotel on Drownin Pond; maker of charms in Truman Capote's *Other Voices, Other Rooms*.

Mark Littleton   New Yorker who visits his cousin and friend Ned Hazard in Virginia; narrator of John Pendleton Kennedy's *Swallow Barn*.

Henry Livaudais   Eighteen-year-old resident of Isle aux Chiens; runs away with a young woman from a neighboring island but is believed to be dead in Shirley Ann Grau's *The Hard Blue Sky*.

Pete Livaudais   Brother of Henry Livaudais; sets fire to several buildings on a rival island, Terre Haute, exacerbating a feud in Shirley Ann Grau's *The Hard Blue Sky.*

Lieutenant Crofts Livingston   Officer in charge of harbor facilities who aids Major Joppolo in securing a bell for the town in John Hersey's *A Bell for Adano.*

Richard Olney (Dickie) Livingston III   Language tutor and playboy; brings to an anniversary gathering the gun that killed Charles Lawrence in Wright Morris's *The Huge Season.*

Aunt Llanyllyn   Aunt of Lucy Tartan in Herman Melville's *Pierre.*

Loady   Personal slave of Mamie Brandon Catlett; mother of the slave sold to pay for the Catletts' trip to Egeria Springs in Mary Lee Settle's *Know Nothing.*

Major Clyde Lockert   Cocoa grower from British Guiana; friend of Fran and Sam Dodsworth in Europe in Sinclair Lewis's *Dodsworth.*

Anastasie (Taisie) Lockhart   Owner of Texas cattle; accompanies the trail herd to Abilene in Emerson Hough's *North of 36.*

Gertrude (Dirty Gertie) Lockhart   Promiscuous housewife in Proxmire Manor repeatedly thwarted by modern appliances and plumbing; eventually commits suicide in John Cheever's *The Wapshot Scandal.*

Jamie Lockhart   Bandit who becomes the robber bridegroom and hides his identity from his bride, Rosamond Musgrove, in Eudora Welty's *The Robber Bridegroom.*

Rosamond Musgrove Lockhart   Daughter of Clement Musgrove; lover and wife of the robber bridegroom, Jamie Lockhart, in Eudora Welty's *The Robber Bridegroom.*

Mitch Lodwick   District attorney prosecuting Frederic Manion; longtime rival of Paul Biegler in Robert Traver's *Anatomy of a Murder.*

Ann (Annie) Loeb   Young film editor; Manley Halliday's companion, nurse, confidante, and lover in Budd Schulberg's *The Disenchanted.*

Helen Peyton Loftis   Mother of Peyton and Maudie Loftis and wife of Milton Loftis in William Styron's *Lie Down in Darkness.*

Maudie (Maudie-poo) Loftis   Second child of Helen and Milton Loftis and younger sister of Peyton Loftis; dies after a childhood accident in William Styron's *Lie Down in Darkness.*

Milton (Bunny, Cap'n Milton, Milt) Loftis   Father of Peyton and Maudie Loftis, husband of Helen Loftis, and lover of Dolly Bonner in William Styron's *Lie Down in Darkness.*

Peyton Loftis   Twenty-two-year-old daughter of Milton and Helen Loftis; a suicide whose funeral is being conducted in William Styron's *Lie Down in Darkness.*

Rosemary Loftis   Dance-marathon contestant who lures Robert Syverten into a sexual liaison under the bandstand in Horace McCoy's *They Shoot Horses, Don't They?*

Sonny Loftus   Army lieutenant whose attention to Mary Pilant makes Barney Quill jealous in Robert Traver's *Anatomy of a Murder.*

Adah Elwood (Cousin Adah) Logan   Vivacious midwestern socialite; wife of Joe Logan and second cousin of Judd Rankin in Susan Glaspell's *Judd Rankin's Daughter.*

Joe Logan   Wealthy inventor and husband of Adah Elwood Logan in Susan Glaspell's *Judd Rankin's Daughter.*

Tom Loker   Slave catcher who pursues Eliza Harris and her family; gives up his trade after being wounded and then cared for by the Quakers in Harriet Beecher Stowe's *Uncle Tom's Cabin.*

Lolita   See Dolores Haze.

Hetty Lomax   Sister of Julia Lomax Le Moyne and cousin of Hester Le Moyne, who wills Hetty a half interest in Mulberry Hill plantation, in Albion W. Tourgee's *Bricks Without Straw.*

Lombardo   Author of Koztanza, a masterpiece admired by Babbalan Ja, in Herman Melville's *Mardi.*

Caesar Lomellini   Commanding general of the Brotherhood of Destruction who leads a revolution against the Oligarchy; murdered by his own followers in Ignatius Donnelly's *Caesar's Column.*

Royal (Roy) Lommax   American army cook in Luxembourg; wounded in the stomach by a shell fragment from a tank cannon in Martha Gellhorn's *Wine of Astonishment.*

London   Leader of the migrant workers who strike during apple picking in John Steinbeck's *In Dubious Battle.*

Miss Lonelyhearts   Male advice columnist burdened by his inability to assist those who write for help in Nathanael West's *Miss Lonelyhearts.*

Lonesome Blue   Friend of Banjo and Ray; deported from France in Claude McKay's *Banjo.*

Gertrude Long   Hotel cigar counter clerk, then second wife of Will Brady in Wright Morris's *The Works of Love.*

Gilbert Long   Young gentleman who is having an affair with Lady John in Henry James's *The Sacred Fount.*

Mr. Longdon   Wealthy friend of Lady Julia and Mrs. Brookenham in Henry James's *The Awkward Age.*

Long Ghost (Long Doctor, Peter)   Doctor aboard the *Julia* and Typee's companion in Herman Melville's *Omoo*.

la Longue Carabine   See Nathaniel Bumppo.

Frances (Fran, Frances Dowson) Lonigan   Sister of Studs Lonigan in James T. Farrell's *Young Lonigan;* appears in *The Young Manhood of Studs Lonigan;* happily married, as Frances Dowson, in *Judgment Day.*

Loretta (Fritzie) Lonigan   Sister of Studs Lonigan in James T. Farrell's *Young Lonigan;* girlfriend of Phillip Rolfe in *The Young Manhood of Studs Lonigan;* happily married to Rolfe in *Judgment Day.*

Mary Lonigan   Mother of Studs Lonigan; envisions her son as a priest in James T. Farrell's *Young Lonigan;* also appears in *The Young Manhood of Studs Lonigan* and *Judgment Day.*

Patrick J. (Paddy, Pat) Lonigan   Father of Studs Lonigan in James T. Farrell's *Young Lonigan;* gets successful contracts by paying kickbacks in *The Young Manhood of Studs Lonigan;* loses most of his money in the Great Depression in *Judgment Day.*

William (Bill, Studs) Lonigan   South Chicago grammar school graduate who spends an aimless summer hanging out and daydreaming in James T. Farrell's *Young Lonigan;* works for his father and frequents poolrooms and brothels in *The Young Manhood of Studs Lonigan;* engaged to marry Catherine Banahan.

Loo   Daughter of Arfretee and Deacon Ereemear Po-Po; fends off Long Ghost's advances in Herman Melville's *Omoo.*

Imogen Loomis   Crippled young married woman seduced by the narrator in Edmund Wilson's *Memoirs of Hecate County.*

Loosh   See Lucius.

Lop-Ear   Friend of Big-Tooth; after learning to paddle a log, he travels away from the tribe in Jack London's *Before Adam.*

Bradley Lord   Sycophantic team secretary of the New York Mammoths in Mark Harris's *The Southpaw.*

Lorency   Cook at Knapp-of-Reeds plantation and mother of Nimbus; traded south following Nimbus's marriage; dies in Louisiana during a journey back to North Carolina in Albion W. Tourgee's *Bricks Without Straw.*

Reuben (Mink) Lorey   Troublesome woodsman who, if he is responsible for destroying Gus Griff's mill, is responsible for Tad's presumed death in Mary Noailles Murfree's *In the Clouds.*

Euphemia Wiatte Lorimer   Benefactress of Clithero Edny; aunt of Clarice Wiatte Lorimer, to whom Edny is engaged; sister of Arthur Wiatte, who drives away her lover, Sarsefield, whom she ultimately marries; victim of attempted murder by Clithero Edny in Charles Brockden Brown's *Edgar Huntly.*

Linda Loring   Sister of Sylvia Lennox; Philip Marlowe's lover in Raymond Chandler's *The Long Goodbye.*

Lotus (Lotus Flower)   Teahouse prostitute bought as a concubine by Wang Lung, whose son she also attracts, in Pearl Buck's *The Good Earth.*

Louella   Volunteer Red Cross worker in Naples and comforter to all lost American soldiers in John Horne Burns's *The Gallery.*

Louie   Bus driver who becomes so attracted to Camille Oaks that he reserves a seat behind his in an attempt to make a date with her, despite the protests of an elderly passenger who desires to sit in the reserved seat, in John Steinbeck's *The Wayward Bus.*

Louie   Hospital chemist living at Queenie's boardinghouse in Thornton Wilder's *Heaven's My Destination.*

Louis   Crew member on the *Ghost* who is kind to Hump Van Weyden in Jack London's *The Sea-Wolf.*

Louisa   Southern black woman desired by both Tom Burwell, a black laborer, and Bob Stone, son of her white employer, in Jean Toomer's *Cane.*

Louisa   Woolworth floorwalker in William Goyen's *In a Farther Country.*

Louvinia   Wife of Joby's; Ringo's grandmother in William Faulkner's *Sartoris (Flags in the Dust)* and *The Unvanquished.*

Colonel Richard Lovelace   English governor in James Kirke Paulding's *Koningsmarke.*

Sally Lovelace   Well-to-do third wife of John Buddy Pearson in Zora Neale Hurston's *Jonah's Gourd Vine.*

Charlotte (Chatty) Lovell   Poor cousin of Delia Ralston; mother of Clementina Ralston by Delia's former suitor, Clement Spender; the old maid of Edith Wharton's *The Old Maid.*

Clementina Lovell   See Clementina Lovell Ralston.

Jessica (Jessie) Lovell   Member of the Clyde upper class; discouraged by her father from marrying her first love, Charles Gray; marries Jackie Mason in John P. Marquand's *Point of No Return.*

Laurence Lovell   Father of Jessica Lovell; opposes his daughter's marriage to Charles Gray in John P. Marquand's *Point of No Return.*

Vee Lovell   Dance partner of Mary Hawley; agrees to marry Mary during the marathon as a publicity ploy in Horace McCoy's *They Shoot Horses, Don't They?*

Lord Lovely   Elegant man in Liverpool whom Harry Bolton avoids in Herman Melville's *Redburn.*

Michael (Mike) Lovett   Amnesia victim, retainer of William McLeod's black box, and narrator of Norman Mailer's *Barbary Shore.*

Maud Lowder   Aunt of Kate Croy; opposes Croy's engagement to Merton Densher because he has no money in Henry James's *The Wings of the Dove.*

Geneve Lowe   First mistress of Frank Hirsh and ambitious buyer for the Mode Shop in James Jones's *Some Came Running.*

Julian Lowe   Flight cadet in William Faulkner's *Soldiers' Pay.*

Everett Lowell   Boston congressman who supports political equality for blacks but opposes social integration in Thomas Dixon's *The Leopard's Spots.*

Ella Lowry   See Ella Lowry Sturgis.

George R. Lucas   Resident and pig-tender at the Diamond County Home for the Aged; husband of Martha Lucas; former truck farmer whose land was requisitioned by the Federal Department of Conservation; brings bottles of rye to the fair and participates in the stoning of Stephen Connor in John Updike's *The Poorhouse Fair.*

Martha (Marty) Lucas   Resident of the Diamond County Home for the Aged and wife of George Lucas; complaining woman with bad legs and a love for her pet parakeet in John Updike's *The Poorhouse Fair.*

Mattie Johnson Lucas   See Mattie Johnson.

Sam Lucas   Con man who marries and betrays Harlem innocent Mattie Johnson; redeems himself at the conclusion of Countee Cullen's *One Way to Heaven.*

Carl Luce   Columbia University student and former adviser of Holden Caulfield at the Whooton School; meets Holden at the Wicker Bar for a drink and a conversation about sex in J. D. Salinger's *The Catcher in the Rye.*

Marino Lucero   Poor priest of Arroyo Hondo who accumulates great wealth and fears that it will be stolen in Willa Cather's *Death Comes for the Archbishop.*

Lucius (Loosh)   Son of Joby; Sartoris slave in William Faulkner's *The Unvanquished.*

Achsa Luckett   Daughter of Worth and Jary Luckett; steals Louie Scurrah from her sister Genny Luckett and runs off with him to the western territory in Conrad Richter's *The Trees;* after Scurrah's death, she lives with another man in *The Fields.*

Genny (Ginny) Luckett   Beautiful sister of Sayward Luckett; after her husband Louie Scurrah deserts her, she is so frightened by a panther that for a time she becomes deranged; eventually hires out for work with a nearby family in Conrad Richter's *The Trees;* continues in this position until she marries a boatyard owner in *The Fields;* dies in *The Town.*

Jary Luckett   Wife of Worth Luckett; distressed to leave her Pennsylvania birthplace and settle in the Ohio territory; rears five children and dies of a fever in Conrad Richter's *The Trees.*

Sayward (Saird) Luckett   Oldest daughter of Worth and Jary Luckett; marries Portius Wheeler and becomes a heroic, energetic, capable homemaker; watches as the forest area grows toward civilization; has nine living children; performs herculean tasks under primitive conditions, but when the family becomes prosperous she acquiesces to having a large home built in Americus, Ohio, where she lives; principal character in Conrad Richter's *The Fields, The Town,* and *The Trees.*

Sulie Luckett   Youngest child of Worth and Jary Luckett; disappears in the woods in Conrad Richter's *The Trees;* marries an Indian and wants no contact with her white family in *The Town.*

T. P. Luckett   Chicken egg entrepreneur; model of success to Will Brady in Wright Morris's *The Works of Love.*

Worth Luckett   Head of a pioneer family that travels into the Ohio territory and builds a home there; after his wife's death, he eventually leaves his family in the charge of his eldest daughter, Sayward Luckett, and travels further into the midwestern wilderness in Conrad Richter's *The Trees;* returns to what is now a thriving town and lives primitively there until his death in *The Town.*

Wyitt Luckett   Son of Worth and Jary Luckett; in his eagerness to hunt and be a woodsman he takes after his father in Conrad Richter's *The Trees;* strikes out for the distant western territory in *The Fields;* the family wonders about his fate in *The Town.*

Lucy   Maid of the Churchills; her unhappy relationship with a foreign bootmaker leads to her suicide in Henry Wadsworth Longfellow's *Kavanagh.*

Lucy   Widowed slave who goes mad awaiting the return of her drowned son Abe in John Pendleton Kennedy's *Swallow Barn.*

Luff   See Wymontoo-Hee.

Lugena   Wife of Nimbus; refuses to tell the Ku Klux Klan the whereabouts of Eliab Hill; resettles with her children in Kansas on land purchased for her by Mollie Ainslie in Albion W. Tourgee's *Bricks Without Straw.*

Luluque   Soldier in William Faulkner's *A Fable.*

Lumen   Professor and advocate of social Darwinism in William Dean Howells's *A Traveler from Altruria.*

Captain Enoch (Nuck) Lumsden   Large landholder whose manipulative, controlling, and acquisitive nature causes his estrangement from his daughter, Patty Lumsden, and from his nephew, Kike Lumsden, in Edward Eggleston's *The Circuit Rider.*

Hezekiah (Kike) Lumsden   Delicate youth who converts to Methodism and becomes a zealous circuit rider, endangering his already frail health, in Edward Eggleston's *The Circuit Rider.*

Patty Lumsden   Beautiful and aristocratic daughter of Enoch Lumsden; refuses to see Morton Goodwin following his conversion to Methodism, although she herself eventually converts, in Edward Eggleston's *The Circuit Rider*.

Adeline Luna   Worldly sister of Oliver Chancellor; takes an interest in Basil Ransom in Henry James's *The Bostonians*.

Isaac Lund   Son of a homesteader; shot by Clay Calvert while trying to rob Calvert's wagon in H. L. Davis's *Honey in the Horn*.

Captain Adam Lundy   Union officer who burns Isaac Jameson's home in Shelby Foote's *Jordan County*.

Luster   Servant or stable worker in William Faulkner's *The Sound and the Fury; Absalom, Absalom!;* and *The Reivers*.

Dotty and Kitty Lutch   American friends of Maggie Verver in Henry James's *The Golden Bowl*.

Luter   Foreman at a print shop who tries to seduce Genya Schearl in Henry Roth's *Call It Sleep*.

Luther (Fort)   Transient from Fort Meyers, Florida, who likes chocolate ice in Nelson Algren's *A Walk on the Wild Side*.

Luther (Little Luke)   Transient who leads Dove Linkhorn into fraudulent sales pitches in Nelson Algren's *A Walk on the Wild Side*.

Lutte   Beautiful German model who dances with Charles Upton at a Berlin cabaret in Katherine Anne Porter's *The Leaning Tower*.

Grandma Luttrell   Herb doctor and adventurer in H. L. Davis's *Beulah Land*.

Henry van der Luyden   Husband of Louisa van der Luyden; one of the last remaining members of an aristocratic New York family and so considered a source of social wisdom in Edith Wharton's *The Age of Innocence;* mentioned in *The Old Maid*.

Louisa Dagonet van der Luyden   Wealthy New York aristocrat revered by other old New York families; wife of Henry van der Luyden in Edith Wharton's *The Age of Innocence;* mentioned in *The Old Maid*.

Luz (Luce)   Daughter of a horse trader; love of Clay Calvert and his guide to an understanding and acceptance of the necessary evil in human nature in H. L. Davis's *Honey in the Horn*.

Lydia (Lyddy)   Mulatto slave and daughter of Backwater Brandon and lover of Joe Little Fox; loves Johnny Lacey, who buys her after Brandon's death and brings her to Beulah, in Mary Lee Settle's *O Beulah Land*.

Eric Lyle   Thief who travels with his mother in Paul Bowles's *The Sheltering Sky*.

Mrs. Lyle   Australian travel writer and mother of Eric Lyle in Paul Bowles's *The Sheltering Sky*.

Lyman   Judge and anti-temperance congressman who is beaten up by a mob angry over the death of Willy Hammond in T. S. Arthur's *Ten Nights in a Bar-Room*.

Andrew Lynch   Painter; brother of Mary Follet and uncle of Rufus Follet; sent to the scene of Jay Follet's automobile accident, he confirms Jay's death to his waiting family; describes Jay's funeral to Rufus in James Agee's *A Death in the Family*.

Catherine Lynch   Mother of Mary Follet and grandmother of Rufus Follet in James Agee's *A Death in the Family*.

Hannah Lynch   Aunt of Mary Follet and great aunt of Rufus Follet; comforts Mary, whose husband has died in an automobile accident in James Agee's *A Death in the Family*.

Joel Lynch   Father of Mary Follet and grandfather of Rufus Follet in James Agee's *A Death in the Family*.

Silas Lynch   Black lieutenant governor of South Carolina in Thomas Dixon's *The Clansman*.

Polk Lynde   Wealthy playboy and lover of Aileen Cowperwood in Theodore Dreiser's *The Titan*.

Buddy van der Lynn   Romantic leading man in Ludwig Bemelmans's *Dirty Eddie*.

Mac   Marine sergeant in and narrator of Leon Uris's *Battle Cry*.

Mac   See Fenian McCreary.

Mrs. Macallister   Flirtatious acquaintance of Bartley Hubbard in William Dean Howells's *A Modern Instance*.

Maria Miranda Macapa   Psychologically peculiar cleaning woman who marries Zerkow; murdered by Zerkow in Frank Norris's *McTeague*.

Herbert Macaulay   Attorney who administers the affairs of Clyde Wynant in Dashiell Hammett's *The Thin Man*.

Homer Macauley   Fourteen-year-old night messenger for Western Union whose job brings him into contact with various aspects of life in Ithaca, California, in William Saroyan's *The Human Comedy*.

Marcus Macauley   Brother of Homer and Ulysses Macauley; killed in World War II in William Saroyan's *The Human Comedy*.

Ulysses Macauley   Four-year-old brother of Homer and Marcus Macauley; curious about everything around him in William Saroyan's *The Human Comedy*.

Doctor (Mac) MacDonald   Son-in-law of Professor Ball and leader of the Bardsville raid on tobacco buyers' warehouses in Robert Penn Warren's *Night Rider*.

General MacDonald   Editor of the *Chicago Inquirer* in Theodore Dreiser's *The Titan*.

Truman Leslie MacDonald   Son of General MacDonald; demands railway stock in exchange for supporting Frank Cowperwood's streetcar plans in Theodore Dreiser's *The Titan*.

Thomas Harold MacDougal   Artisan in stone and plaster of Paris, and owner of Artifacts of Spain; husband of Marietta McGee-Chavéz in William Goyen's *In a Farther Country*.

Don Joaquin MacGillivray   American boatman and trader who kidnaps Commodore Robinette in H. L. Davis's *Harp of a Thousand Strings*.

Hector Macgoblin   Secretary of State under Lee Sarason; flees to Cuba after shooting Sarason in Sinclair Lewis's *It Can't Happen Here*.

MacGregor   Friend of Henry Miller; drinks in bars without having money to pay his tab; brings his girlfriends home to spend the night and asks his mother to serve them breakfast in bed in Henry Miller's *Tropic of Capricorn*.

Irwin K. (Mac) Macgregor   Writer of popular music and partner of Earl Horter; marries Billie Harcum in Wright Morris's *Love Among the Cannibals*.

Macha   Former Russian princess who moves in with Fillmore; spends her time in bed reading Russian newspapers and avoiding Fillmore's advances in Henry Miller's *Tropic of Cancer*.

James Duncan MacHardie   Wealthy and powerful New York financier who hires Alfred Eaton after Eaton rescues MacHardie's young grandson, who had fallen through the ice while skating, in John O'Hara's *From the Terrace*.

Frankie Machine   See Francis Majcinek.

Balliol (Jones, Mac, James Watson) MacJones   Successful chronicler of the beat generation and literary rival of Leo Percepied in Jack Kerouac's *The Subterraneans;* also appears in *Book of Dreams*.

Mack　Leader of the group of vagrant men who frequent Lee Chong's grocery; convinces Chong to appoint him and the others guardians of the building Chong received from Horace Abbeville; names the building the Palace Flophouse and Grill in John Steinbeck's *Cannery Row.*

George Mack　Ranch owner who employs Johnny Mack (who takes George's surname) and Jose in Edwin Corle's *Fig Tree John.*

Johnny (Fig Tree Junior, Great Spirits, Juanito Fig Tree, N'Chai Chidn) Mack　Apache son of Agocho and Kaia; marries the Mexican Maria and gradually loses his Indian heritage in Edwin Corle's *Fig Tree John.*

Barney MacKean　Playmate rejected by Frankie Addams after they commit a secret and unknown sin in Carson McCullers's *The Member of the Wedding.*

Allison MacKenzie　Daughter of Constance MacKenzie; aspiring writer who looks upon the scandal and social injustice of her hometown as material for a novel in Grace Metalious's *Peyton Place.*

Constance (Connie, Constance Standish) MacKenzie　Mother of Allison MacKenzie; assumes the name of her married lover after bearing their illegitimate daughter and moves to the small town where she opens a dress shop and passes herself off as a widow; later marries Tomas Makris in Grace Metalious's *Peyton Place.*

Shreve MacKenzie　Harvard roommate of Quentin Compson I in William Faulkner's *The Sound and the Fury.* See also Shrevlin McCannon.

Ida May Mackerel　Late wife of Andrew Mackerel; founder of a clinic ("She was crazy about mental health.") and memorial dedicatee of the Ida May Mackerel Plaza and shopping center in Peter De Vries's *The Mackerel Plaza.*

Reverend Andrew Mackerel　Widowed pastor of the People's Liberal Church in Avalon, Connecticut; narrator of Peter De Vries's *The Mackerel Plaza.*

Mary Lamar Mackey　Best friend of Dabney Fairchild; plays the piano at Dabney's wedding in Eudora Welty's *Delta Wedding.*

Mack MacLeod　Alcoholic owner of an Alabama plantation in George Wylie Henderson's *Ollie Miss.*

Charles (Mac) MacMahon　Father of Rose MacMahon and manager of the Past By Manufacturing Company factory in Robert Cantwell's *The Land of Plenty.*

Rose (Kitten, Kitty) MacMahon　Daughter of Charles MacMahon; while possibly pregnant by Roger Schwartz, she begins a relationship with Walt Connor in Robert Cantwell's *The Land of Plenty.*

Cassie Beal MacMurtrie　Wife of Scott MacMurtrie, whose infidelity leads Cassie to suicide in Elizabeth Madox Roberts's *The Time of Man.*

Scott MacMurtrie　Husband of Cassie Beal MacMurtrie and lover of Amanda Cain in Elizabeth Madox Roberts's *The Time of Man.*

Adèle Macomb　Rich, popular bully who marries James March and is Leda March's nemesis in Nancy Hale's *The Prodigal Women.*

Bob MacSwain　One-time detective in the Personville Police Department fired by Chief Noonan for suspicion of covering up Tim Noonan's murder in Dashiell Hammett's *Red Harvest.*

Mr. Mactabb　Creditor of Cuthbert Dangerfield in James Kirke Paulding's *Westward Ho!*

John MacWalsey (McWalsey)　Professor vacationing in the Florida Keys who becomes involved with Helen Gordon in Ernest Hemingway's *To Have and Have Not.*

MacWilliams　Civil engineer and Robert Clay's ablest assistant in Richard Harding Davis's *Soldiers of Fortune.*

Mad Jack　Brandy-drinking lieutenant who defies the captain to save the *Neversink* during a gale off Cape Horn and who puts down a mutiny aboard the same ship in Herman Melville's *White-Jacket.*

Maddalena　Cook of Evalina Bowen; sings to Effie Bowen in William Dean Howells's *Indian Summer.*

Celia Madden　Voluptuous church organist and freethinker; Theron Ware mistakes her avowal of women's independence for sexual license in Harold Frederic's *The Damnation of Theron Ware.*

Jeremiah (Jerry) Madden　Wealthy but unpretentious sawmill owner; father of Celia, Michael, and Theodore Madden in Harold Frederic's *The Damnation of Theron Ware.*

Michael Madden　Consumptive brother of Celia Madden; advises Theron Ware to stop meddling, but Ware ignores the advice in Harold Frederic's *The Damnation of Theron Ware.*

Terence (Theodore) Madden　Dissolute younger brother of Celia Madden; Celia's trip to New York to aid him is misinterpreted by Theron Ware in Harold Frederic's *The Damnation of Theron Ware.*

Lannie Madison　Disturbed young woman whose testimony erodes William McLeod's resistance in Norman Mailer's *Barbary Shore.*

Opal Madvig　Daughter of Paul Madvig; enamored of Taylor Henry, the man her father is accused of murdering, in Dashiell Hammett's *The Glass Key.*

Paul Madvig   Political boss who is accused of murdering the son of a U.S. senator in Dashiell Hammett's *The Glass Key*.

Emory Mafferson   Employee of Janoth Enterprises who covers the police investigation of the murder of Pauline Delos and reports privately to George Stroud; a narrator of Kenneth Fearing's *The Big Clock*.

Magawisca   Daughter of the Pequod chief Mononotto and sister of Oneco; risks her life to save Everell Fletcher from execution in Catharine Maria Sedgwick's *Hope Leslie*.

Magdalena (Ma)   Fruit store operator who serves as Rico Bandello's fence in William Riley Burnett's *Little Caesar*.

Tia Magdalena   Housekeeper for Bob Webster; feared and respected by the townspeople because she is a witch in Josefina Niggli's *Mexican Village*.

Teacake Magee   See Teacake Sistrunk Magee Ponder.

Maggie   See Margaret Stevens Mallison.

Angelo Maggio   Gambling, sarcastic private in G Company who befriends Robert E. Lee Prewitt; discharged with a Section 8 after being persecuted by Fatso Judson in the stockade in James Jones's *From Here to Eternity*.

Mr. Magruder   Methodist circuit rider and elder who supervises and advises Morton Goodwin in Edward Eggleston's *The Circuit Rider*.

Magua (le Renard Subtil)   Indian guide who, seeking revenge against Colonel Munro, leads Duncan Heyward into dangerous territory and later abducts Cora Munro to be Magua's wife in James Fenimore Cooper's *The Last of the Mohicans*.

Mahailey   Faithful servant to the Wheeler family in Willa Cather's *One of Ours*.

Clarabelle Mahon   Teacher who tries to make her immigrant students into homogeneous Americans, but suffers disenchantment and a breakdown, in O. E. Rölvaag's *Peder Victorious*.

Donald Mahon   Disfigured American R.A.F. pilot who returns to Georgia and marries Margaret Powers in William Faulkner's *Soldiers' Pay*.

Margaret Powers Mahon   Widow of Richard Powers and wife of Donald Mahon in William Faulkner's *Soldiers' Pay*.

The Reverend (Uncle Joe) Mahon   Episcopalian minister and father of Donald Mahon in William Faulkner's *Soldiers' Pay*.

Mahtoree   Treacherous Sioux chieftain; villainous but courageous opponent slain by the noble Hard Heart in single combat in James Fenimore Cooper's *The Prairie*.

Maida   Secretary to Paul Biegler in Robert Traver's *Anatomy of a Murder*.

Maimiti   Strong-willed Tahitian who marries Fletcher Christian in Charles Nordhoff and James Norman Hall's *Mutiny on the Bounty*; Joins Christian in attempting to establish a democracy on an isolated island, where she provides strong leadership for the women and children when violence erupts, in *Pitcairn's Island*.

Honora Tremont Mairs   Adopted orphan cousin of Beverly Peele whom Mairs murders out of jealousy in Gertrude Atherton's *Patience Sparhawk and Her Times*.

Francis (Automatic, Frankie Machine) Majcinek   Card hustler and morphine addict who cannot break his habit in Nelson Algren's *The Man with the Golden Arm*.

Sophie (Zoschka, Zosh) Majcinek   Wheelchair-bound and shrewish wife of Frankie Machine in Nelson Algren's *The Man with the Golden Arm*.

Mrs. Makely   Society woman who believes that Homos is an American posing as an Altrurian in William Dean Howells's *A Traveler from Altruria*.

Mako   Son of Tavi and Marunga and altar boy and servant to Father Paul; reveals Terangi's hiding place to Eugene de Laage shortly before the hurricane, which Mako fails to survive, in Charles Nordhoff and James Norman Hall's *The Hurricane*.

Constance Makris   See Constance MacKenzie.

Tomas (Tom, Michael Rossi) Makris   Greek man from New York hired as a small-town school principal; lover and later husband of Constance MacKenzie in Grace Metalious's *Peyton Place*.

Malcolm   Fifteen-year-old in search of his father; through the auspices of Mr. Cox, begins an adventure through the stages of life in James Purdy's *Malcolm*.

Black Jack Mallard   Highwayman who saves Amber St. Clare by taking her with him when he escapes from Newgate Prison; instructs her in survival by crime in Kathleen Winsor's *Forever Amber*.

Rowland Mallet   Wealthy American art lover traveling in Europe; patron of Roderick Hudson and in love with Hudson's fiancée, Mary Garland, in Henry James's *Roderick Hudson*.

Mary (Marie de Sabrevois) Mallinson   Childhood love of Steven Nason; abducted by Guerlac: in Kenneth Roberts's *Arundel*.

Charles Mallison   Husband of Margaret Stevens and father of Chick Mallison in William Faulkner's *Intruder in the Dust*, *The Town*, and *The Mansion*.

Charles (Chick) Mallison   Son of Charles and Margaret Stevens Mallison in William Faulkner's *Intruder in the Dust*, *The Town*, and *The Mansion*.

Margaret Stevens (Maggie) Mallison   Sister of Gavin Stevens, wife of Charles Mallison, and mother of Chick Mallison in William Faulkner's *Intruder in the Dust, Requiem for a Nun, The Town,* and *The Mansion.*

Pamela (Pam) Mallory   Flight lieutenant and girlfriend of Frank Savage in Beirne Lay, Jr., and Sy Bartlett's *Twelve O'Clock High!*

Steven (Steve) Mallory   Sculptor whose work reflects the heroic in man in Ayn Rand's *The Fountainhead.*

Jimmy Malloy   Alcoholic newspaper reporter who meets Eddie Brunner at a jam session and later tries to find out about Gloria Wandrous from him in John O'Hara's *Butterfield 8.*

John J. (Jack) Malloy   Former I.W.W. member and stockade prisoner who attempts to teach Robert E. Lee Prewitt the value of passive resistance; escapes from the stockade in James Jones's *From Here to Eternity.*

Moose Malloy   Ex-convict who hires Philip Marlowe to find his lost love, Velma Valento—who murders him—in Raymond Chandler's *Farewell, My Lovely.*

Frances Xavier (Frankie) Malone   Son of Nora and Patrick Malone, ambitious messenger boy for a Wall Street brokerage firm, and first boyfriend and later husband of Margy Shannon in Betty Smith's *Tomorrow Will Be Better.*

Margy Malone   See Margaret Shannon.

Nora Malone   Wife of Patrick Malone and possessive mother of Frankie Malone in Betty Smith's *Tomorrow Will Be Better.*

Patrick (Patsy) Malone   Joker and Brooklyn police officer; correspondence student of embalming, a profession for his retirement; husband of Nora Malone and father of Frankie Malone in Betty Smith's *Tomorrow Will Be Better.*

Maloney the Areopagite   Catholic mystic and biographer of Saint Puce, a holy flea, in Nathanael West's *The Dream Life of Balso Snell.*

Malty   See Buchanan Malt Avis.

Tootsie Maltz   Radical whom Harry Bogen uses to start a strike of shipping clerks in the women's garment industry; becomes Bogen's partner in a delivery service, and then becomes sole owner of the service, in Jerome Weidman's *I Can Get It for You Wholesale.*

Mamba   Grandmother of Lissa Atkinson and mother of Hagar; domestic servant of the Wentworths and later of the Atkinsons in DuBose Heyward's *Mamba's Daughters.*

Mambo   Black Caribbean musician and nightclub singer; one of Sabina's lovers in Anaïs Nin's *A Spy in the House of Love.*

Aunt Mamie   Boardinghouse proprietor who offers bountiful meals, chaos, and love to the narrator of Aline Bernstein's *The Journey Down.*

Mammy   Personal slave of Marie St. Clare and mother figure to Eva St. Clare in Harriet Beecher Stowe's *Uncle Tom's Cabin.*

Mammy   Slave who is Scarlett O'Hara's nanny in Margaret Mitchell's *Gone with the Wind.*

Sally Manchester   Friend of Alice Archer; tends to Alice's mother and rejects men following a broken engagement in Henry Wadsworth Longfellow's *Kavanagh.*

Charlie Mandarin   Cousin of Honoré Grandissime; attempts to lynch Clemence in George Washington Cable's *The Grandissimes.*

Dr. Mandelet   Physician who perceives Edna Pontellier's awakening to individuality and sensuality in Kate Chopin's *The Awakening.*

Agnes Mandeville   Foster mother of Margo Dowling who takes the child after her father disappears in John Dos Passos's *U.S.A.* trilogy.

Frank Mandeville   Vaudevillian who introduces his foster daughter, Margo Dowling, to show business; she elopes after he rapes her in John Dos Passos's *U.S.A.* trilogy.

Mandy   Mixed-blood washerwoman fired by Belinda Treadwell a month before Mandy's white son is born of her union with Cyrus Treadwell in Ellen Glasgow's *Virginia.*

Aunt Mandy   Wise, matriarchal protector of Mattie Johnson in Countee Cullen's *One Way to Heaven.*

Al Manheim   Drama critic turned screenwriter; narrator of Budd Schulberg's *What Makes Sammy Run?*

Frederic (Manny) Manion   Army lieutenant whose wife, Laura Manion, Barney Quill allegedly rapes; pleads temporary insanity to the charge of murdering Quill in Robert Traver's *Anatomy of a Murder.*

Laura Manion   Wife of Frederic Manion; allegedly raped by Barney Quill in Robert Traver's *Anatomy of a Murder.*

Dorothy (Dolly) Manners   Frivolous, socially ambitious young woman who matures and becomes the worthy wife of Richard Carvel in Winston Churchill's *Richard Carvel.*

Margaret Manners   Wife of Marmaduke Manners and mother of Dorothy Manners in Winston Churchill's *Richard Carvel.*

Marmaduke Manners   Devious, social-climbing fop; husband of Margaret Manners and father of Dorothy Manners in Winston Churchill's *Richard Carvel.*

Nancy Mannigoe   Maid of Gowan and Temple Drake Stevens; hanged for murdering the Stevenses' baby daughter in William Faulkner's *Requiem for a Nun.*

Captain Al Mannix   Jewish Marine from Brooklyn and closest friend of Lieutenant Culver; scorns the Marine Corps and openly hates Colonel Templeton in William Styron's *The Long March.*

Mannock   British pilot in William Faulkner's *A Fable.*

Manolin   Young Cuban friend of Santiago in Ernest Hemingway's *The Old Man and the Sea.*

Senator Aaron Mansfield   Presiding member of the committee investigating the attempted purchase of Barry Rudd; tries unsuccessfully to make sense of circuitous and conflicting testimony in John Hersey's *The Child Buyer.*

Marchioness Medora Manson   Eccentric aunt who takes charge of Ellen Olenska after the death of Ellen's parents in Edith Wharton's *The Age of Innocence.*

Mañuel   Twin brother of Esteban; falls in love with Camila Perichole and dies from an accident in Thornton Wilder's *The Bridge of San Luis Rey.*

Ezra Maple   Proprietor of the Hard Times general store, which Clay Turner burns; helps Blue bury the dead and then leaves town in E. L. Doctorow's *Welcome to Hard Times.*

Isaac Maple   Brother of Ezra Maple; rebuilds his brother's store and cares for Helga Bergenstrohm; financially ruined in E. L. Doctorow's *Welcome to Hard Times.*

Father Mapple   New Bedford preacher who delivers a sermon about Jonah in Herman Melville's *Moby-Dick.*

Marama   Daughter of Fakahau and Mata, sister of Arai, and wife of Terangi; faithfully waits for her husband while he is in jail, helps him rescue Madame de Laage during the hurricane, and escapes with him after the storm in Charles Nordhoff and James Norman Hall's *The Hurricane.*

Jerry Marble   Fat church deacon who, despite the scolding of his late wife, is inordinately fond of jokes and laughter in Henry Ward Beecher's *Norwood.*

Marbonna   Marquesan nurse of Queen Pomaree's children in Herman Melville's *Omoo.*

Hermann Marburg   German-born father of Sonia and Ivan Marburg and husband of Shura Korf Marburg; deserts his family before Ivan's birth in Jean Stafford's *Boston Adventure.*

Ivan Marburg   Brother of Sonia Marburg; dies in childhood and is given a pauper's burial in Jean Stafford's *Boston Adventure.*

Shura Korf Marburg   Mentally deranged Russian-born mother of Sonia and Ivan Marburg and wife abandoned by Hermann Marburg in Jean Stafford's *Boston Adventure.*

Sonia (Sonie) Marburg   Daughter of impoverished immigrant parents; realizes her childhood dream when she becomes secretary to Miss Pride; narrator of Jean Stafford's *Boston Adventure.*

March   Highminded, impecunious father of Meg, Jo, Beth, and Amy March; his war service keeps him away from home in Louisa May Alcott's *Little Women.*

Amy Curtis (Mrs. Theodore Laurence) March   Artistic and sensitive but vain and self-centered youngest sister of Meg, Jo, and Beth March; and ultimately marries Theodore Laurence in Louisa May Alcott's *Little Women;* also appears in *Little Men.*

Augie (Bolingbroke) March   Picaresque hero and quester after a worthwhile fate through adventures in Chicago, Canada, Mexico, the African Sea, and Paris; marries Stella Chesney and plans to establish a home for orphans; narrator of Saul Bellow's *The Adventures of Augie March.*

Aunt March   Wealthy, prim aunt of Meg, Jo, Beth, and Amy March; leaves her home to Jo March in Louisa May Alcott's *Little Women.*

Basil March   Husband of Isabel March; travels across New York and Canada on their honeymoon in William Dean Howells's *Their Wedding Journey;* leaves a dull insurance job in Boston to edit a literary magazine in New York in *A Hazard of New Fortunes;* narrator of *The Shadow.*

Elizabeth (Beth) March   Quiet, gentle, domestic sister of Meg, Jo, and Amy March; dies after being weakened by scarlet fever in Louisa May Alcott's *Little Women.*

Georgie March   Mentally retarded but gentle younger brother of Augie March; institutionalized by Grandma Lausch and becomes a competent and content shoe repairman in Saul Bellow's *The Adventures of Augie March.*

Henry (Hurry Harry) March   Untrustworthy and careless woodsman who wants to marry Judith Hutter in James Fenimore Cooper's *The Deerslayer.*

Isabel March   Wife of Basil March; travels across New York and Canada on their honeymoon in William Dean Howells's *Their Wedding Journey;* makes an uneasy adjustment to New York City in *A Hazard of New Fortunes;* appears in *The Shadow of a Dream.*

James March   Doctor and first cousin of Leda March; marries Leda and then Adée Macomb in Nancy Hale's *The Prodigal Women.*

Jo (Mrs. Friedrich Bhaer) March   Awkward, straightforward tomboy who aspires to be a writer and who ultimately marries

Friedrich Bhaer in Louisa May Alcott's *Little Women;* also appears in *Little Men.*

Leda March　Awkward girl who grows into a great beauty but remains insecure; wife of James March, mother of Treat March, and lover of Lambert Rudd in Nancy Hale's *The Prodigal Women.*

Mama March　Simpleminded mother of Simon, Augie, and Georgie March; placed in a nursing home when the boys grow up in Saul Bellow's *The Adventures of Augie March.*

Margaret (Meg, Mrs. John Brooke) March　Eldest sister of Jo, Beth, and Amy March; becomes a governess and ultimately marries John Brooke in Louisa May Alcott's *Little Women;* also appears in *Little Men.*

Miss March　Compassionate teacher who befriends Frado; lectures the class against prejudice in Harriet E. Wilson's *Our Nig.*

Mrs. (Marmee) March　Wise and understanding mother of Meg, Jo, Beth, and Amy March in Louisa May Alcott's *Little Women.*

Treat March　Son of Leda and James March and friend of Betsy Jekyll in Nancy Hale's *The Prodigal Women.*

Dr. Oliver Marchand　Physician who treats Caribbean victims of the plague in Sinclair Lewis's *Arrowsmith.*

Morton Marcher　Rich planter and maternal grandfather of Jeremiah Beaumont in Robert Penn Warren's *World Enough and Time.*

Julia Marcia　Aunt of Caesar; has great political insight and influence in Thornton Wilder's *The Ides of March.*

Kate Marcy　Lover of Preston Parr; driven to alcoholism and prostitution by Eldon Parr in Winston Churchill's *The Inside of the Cup.*

Charley Marden　Boyhood friend of Tom Bailey in Thomas Bailey Aldrich's *The Story of a Bad Boy.*

Marengo (Ringo)　Boyhood friend of Bayard Sartoris II in William Faulkner's *The Unvanquished.*

Margie　Unfaithful mistress of Quincy Boardman and resident of the Glen Cove Apartments in Albert Halper's *Union Square.*

Margo　Ticket seller at The Go Hole in John Clellon Holmes's *Go.*

Marheyo　Father of Kory-Kory in Herman Melville's *Typee.*

Maria　Mexican servant who marries Johnny Mack; raped by Agocho, her father-in-law, in Edwin Corle's *Fig Tree John.*

Maria　Older sister of Miranda in Katherine Anne Porter's *Old Mortality.*

Maria　Aged black proprietor of a Catfish Row cook shop; formidable foe of disruptive and debilitating influences, such as Sportin' Life, in DuBose Heyward's *Porgy.*

Maria　Member of Pablo's partisan group who is raped and becomes the lover of Robert Jordan in Ernest Hemingway's *For Whom the Bell Tolls.*

Maria (Rachel)　Slave who accompanies Sally and Brandon Lacey on their visit to Beulah; renamed by Sally after visiting France in Mary Lee Settle's *Know Nothing.*

Arthur Marion　Planter, owner of Roseland and Bellevue plantations, and husband of Cornelia Wilton Marion; badly burned while rescuing slaves and other property from a fire in Caroline Gilman's *Recollections of a Southern Matron.*

Cornelia Wilton Marion　See Cornelia Wilton.

Francis (The Swamp Fox) Marion　Colonel of the partisan cavalry who offers his services to Horatio Gates for the Battle of Camden in William Gilmore Simms's *The Partisan.*

Lorna Maris　Dancer and mistress of Frank Cowperwood in Theodore Dreiser's *The Stoic.*

Maritze　White tenant of Silla Boyce; despises the fact that she must rent from a black person in Paule Marshall's *Brown Girl, Brownstones.*

Marius　Roman officer and lover of Hipparchia in H. D.'s *Palimpsest.*

Mark　Middle-aged sailor flogged for fighting aboard the *Neversink* in Herman Melville's *White-Jacket.*

Lord Mark　English gentleman who, after being rejected by Mildred Theale, tells her about Kate Croy and Merton Densher's plot in Henry James's *The Wings of the Dove.*

Frau Markheim　Swedish wife of a Jewish Czechoslovakian doctor; solicits the aid of Mary Douglas in escaping the Nazi occupation of Czechoslovakia in Martha Gellhorn's *A Stricken Field.*

Marlowe　Alcoholic reviewer and translator who can articulate only one phrase, "You pay"; asks Henry Miller and Carl to review for him while he is in San Francisco in Henry Miller's *Tropic of Cancer.*

Philip Marlowe　Tough, cynical, independent forty-two-year-old Los Angeles private detective who has close encounters with thugs while investigating the murder of Terry Lennox's wealthy socialite wife, Sylvia, in Raymond Chandler's *The Long Goodbye.* Marlowe is the hero in all of Raymond Chandler's novels: *The Big Sleep; Farewell, My Lovely; The High Window; The Lady in the Lake; The Little Sister, The Long Goodbye;* and *Playback.*

Marnoo　English-speaking native who helps Tommo escape from the Typees in Herman Melville's *Typee.*

Marquis de Marnessie   French emigrant who hosts Captain John Farrago and Duncan Ferguson in Hugh Henry Brackenridge's *Modern Chivalry*.

Marquis of Tempo-Rubato   Freethinking Italian son of the Duke of Largo and friend of Count-Fin-de-Siècle; gives a rare, perfect bloom from his conservatory in tribute to the Chatelaine in Henry Blake Fuller's *The Chatelaine of La Trinité*.

Lindsay Marriott   Blackmailer who is murdered in Raymond Chandler's *Farewell, My Lovely*.

Eddie Mars   Racketeer in Raymond Chandler's *The Big Sleep*.

Mona Mars   Wife of Eddie Mars; she helps Philip Marlowe escape from her husband in Raymond Chandler's *The Big Sleep*.

James T. (Jimmy) Marsala   Italian-American brother-in-arms to Carlo Reinhart in Thomas Berger's *Crazy in Berlin*.

President Donald Marsh   President of Lincoln College and critic of local politics in Charles M. Sheldon's *In His Steps*.

Hattie (Puss) Marsh   Daughter of Rachael Marsh; attracted to Berkeley, whom she knows as Howard Tracy, in Samuel Langhorne Clemens's *The American Claimant*.

Rachael Marsh   Landlady of Berkeley, whom she knows as Howard Tracy, in Samuel Langhorne Clemens's *The American Claimant*.

Verena Marsh   Deaf housekeeper hired to cook for Charity Royall and her guardian, Lawyer Royall, after he makes sexual advances toward Charity in the doorway of her bedroom in Edith Wharton's *Summer*.

David Marshall   Husband of Eliza Marshall and father of Jane, Rosamund, Roger, and Truesdale Marshall; wealthy Chicago wholesale grocer in Henry Blake Fuller's *With the Procession*.

Eddie (Eddy) Marshall   Alcoholic friend and boat's helper of Harry Morgan in Ernest Hemingway's *To Have and Have Not*.

Eliza Marshall   Wife of David Marshall and mother of Jane, Rosamund, Roger, and Truesdale Marshall in Henry Blake Fuller's *With the Procession*.

Jane Marshall   Daughter of Eliza and David Marshall; attempts to restore her family's lost social standing; establishes a club for working women; falls in love with Theodore Brower in Henry Blake Fuller's *With the Procession*.

Joanna (Janna) Marshall   Young dancer battling racial prejudice who eventually chooses marriage to Peter Bye over her career in Jessie Redmon Fauset's *There Is Confusion*.

Joel Marshall   Inspirational father of Joanna Marshall in Jessie Redmon Fauset's *There Is Confusion*.

Philip Marshall   Brother of Joanna Marshall working with interracial organizations; second husband of Maggie Ellersley in Jessie Redmon Fauset's *There Is Confusion*.

Richard Truesdale (Dick) Marshall   Son of Eliza and David Marshall; dilettante artist called home to Chicago from Europe in Henry Blake Fuller's *With the Procession*.

Roger Marshall   Son of Eliza and David Marshall; lawyer and real estate speculator who manages his father's interests in Henry Blake Fuller's *With the Procession*.

Rosamund (Rosy) Marshall   Daughter of Eliza and David Marshall; leaves Chicago for England, where she lives with her husband, in Henry Blake Fuller's *With the Procession*.

Susan Marshall   See Susan Marshall Kukolnikov.

Sylvia Marshall   Domestic sister of Joanna Marshall in Jessie Redmon Fauset's *There Is Confusion*.

Virginia (Jinny) Marshland   See Virginia Marshland Timberlane.

Uncle Peepee (George Humbolt) Marshmallow   Eccentric and village exhibitionist in John Cheever's *The Wapshot Chronicle*.

George Marshman   Kindly gentleman who befriends Ellen Montgomery on her lonely trip to Thirlwall; later she learns he is of the Marshman family of Ventnor in Susan Warner's *The Wide, Wide World*.

Mr. Marshman   Country gentleman who befriends Ellen Montgomery at his Christmas party; proprietor of Ventnor in Susan Warner's *The Wide, Wide World*.

Marthe (Magda)   See Marthe Demont.

Abby (Queen's Twin) Martin   Lonely widow who collects memorabilia about Queen Victoria, who was born on the same day as Abby, in Sarah Orne Jewett's *The Country of the Pointed Firs*.

Alma Martin   Second-year student at the University of Southern California in Wallace Thurman's *The Blacker the Berry*.

Bob Martin   Thrifty and industrious freedman blacksmith who refuses to work for white men who owe him money; achieves no legal redress for his whipping or for his wife and daughter's abuse in Albion W. Tourgee's *A Fool's Errand*.

Donald Martin   Rancher hanged by the lynch mob because he cannot produce a bill of sale for the cattle he bought from Harley Drew and because Larry Kinkaid's pistol is found in the possession of Juan Martinez, Martin's employee, in Walter Van Tilburg Clark's *The Ox-Bow Incident*.

Edward Richard (Rick) Martin   Musician who rises to stardom as a jazz trumpeter, but dies at a young age because of alcohol and drug abuse, in Dorothy Baker's *Young Man with a Horn*.

Elizabeth Martin   Daughter of Herb Martin, who, before he dies, gives her to George Brush, in Thornton Wilder's *Heaven's My Destination.*

Gertrude Martin   Light-skinned black woman who can pass for white; grows up on the south side of Chicago with Clare Kendry; marries a white butcher who accepts her being black in Nella Larsen's *Passing.*

Gilbert (Gil) Martin   Young settler in Deerfield who fights as an American militiaman against the Indians and irregulars in Walter D. Edmonds's *Drums along the Mohawk.*

Herbert (Herb) Martin   Newspaperman living at Queenie's Boarding House; before dying, he gives his daughter, Elizabeth Martin, to George Brush in Thornton Wilder's *Heaven's My Destination.*

Lucinda Martin   See Lucinda Martin Stone.

Magdelana Borst (Lana) Martin   Wife of Gilbert Martin; miscarries their first child but bears two other children in Walter D. Edmonds's *Drums along the Mohawk.*

Mr. Martin   Seducer of Ophelia Shepherd, his wife's sister, in William Hill Brown's *The Power of Sympathy.*

Mrs. Martin   Rhode Island cousin of Mrs. Francis in William Hill Brown's *The Power of Sympathy.*

Sponge Martin   Coworker and friend of Bruce Dudley in Old Harbor, Indiana; freespirited man who foresees the attraction between Aline Grey and Dudley in Sherwood Anderson's *Dark Laughter.*

Betty Martindale   Childhood friend and later the sympathetic and levelheaded confidante of Grace Caldwell Tate in John O'Hara's *A Rage to Live.*

Antonio José Martinez   Wealthy priest in Taos who ignores his celibacy vows in Willa Cather's *Death Comes for the Archbishop.*

Juan (Francisco Morez) Martinez   Mysterious Mexican employee of Donald Martin; his possession of Larry Kinkaid's pistol convinces the mob that he is one of Kinkaid's murderers; hanged with Alva Hardwick and Martin in Walter Van Tilburg Clark's *The Ox-Bow Incident.*

Sergeant Julio Martinez   Mexican-American soldier who helps Sergeant Croft arrange the death of Lieutenant Hearn in Norman Mailer's *The Naked and the Dead.*

André Marty   Commissar who detains Andres and Captain Rogelio Gomez in Ernest Hemingway's *For Whom the Bell Tolls.*

Maruca   Quadroon former slave and wife of Perrault in H. L. Davis's *Beulah Land.*

Marunga   Wife of Tavi and mother of Hitia and Mako; survives the hurricane in Charles Nordhoff and James Norman Hall's *The Hurricane.*

Athene Marvell   Graduate student with Vridar Hunter in Vardis Fisher's *We Are Betrayed;* Hunter's second wife in *No Villain Need Be;* divorced from Hunter in *Orphans in Gethsemane.*

Mrs. Marvell   Widowed mother of Ralph Marvell and member of the prestigious New York Marvell and Dagonet families in Edith Wharton's *The Custom of the Country.*

Paul Marvell   Son of Ralph Marvell and Undine Spragg; after divorcing Ralph, Undine uses Paul to blackmail him in Edith Wharton's *The Custom of the Country.*

Ralph Marvell   Reserved husband of Undine Spragg; writes poetry and hopes to rescue her from the influence of unprincipled social flatterers; commits suicide after Undine tries to blackmail him in Edith Wharton's *The Custom of the Country.*

Undine Marvell   See Undine Spragg.

General Marvin   Officer regarded by his subordinates as callous and arbitrary; transfers Major Joppolo to Algiers for countermanding an order banning carts in Adano in John Hersey's *A Bell for Adano.*

Phoebe Marvin   Tomboy who sails a sloop and accompanies Benedict Arnold's army to Quebec; marries Steven Nason in Kenneth Roberts's *Arundel.*

Carlo Marx   Sorrowful, poetic con man; friend of Sal Paradise and Dean Moriarty in Jack Kerouac's *On the Road.*

Mary   Youngest of the orphaned girls in the care of Rachel Cooper in Davis Grubb's *The Night of the Hunter.*

Handsome Mary   English wife of Danby and proprietor of the Baltimore Clipper boardinghouse in Liverpool in Herman Melville's *Redburn.*

Miss Mary   Dying senile tenant of Silla Boyce; mother of Maritze and friend of Selina Boyce in Paule Marshall's *Brown Girl, Brownstones.*

Marya   Sister of Marthe and half sister of Stefan in William Faulkner's *A Fable.*

Lieutenant Stephen (Steve) Maryk   Executive officer who seizes control of the USS *Caine* from Captain Queeg during a typhoon in Herman Wouk's *The Caine Mutiny.*

Marylou   First wife of Dean Moriarty in Jack Kerouac's *On the Road.*

Mrs. Mash   Caseworker for Crib adoption agency in Peter De Vries's *The Tunnel of Love.*

Bruce Mason   Younger son of Elsa and Bo Mason; resents his intimidating father; interrupts law school to be with his dying mother; after his mother's death he is estranged from his father, whom he views as ineffectual, exploitative, and self-indulgent, in Wallace Stegner's *The Big Rock Candy Mountain.*

Chester (Chet) Mason   Eldest son of Elsa and Bo Mason; relinquishes a chance at a baseball career after a humiliating arrest due to his father's bootlegging activities; precipitously marries his high school sweetheart; dies of pneumonia as a young man who had already become discouraged about his future in Wallace Stegner's *The Big Rock Candy Mountain.*

Elsa Norgaard Mason   Devoted long-suffering wife of Bo Mason and daughter of Nels Norgaard; leaves her Minnesota home as a young woman after her father marries her friend Sarah; goes to live with her uncle in North Dakota, where she meets her future husband; dies of cancer, leaving her husband bereft, in Wallace Stegner's *The Big Rock Candy Mountain.*

Gloria Mason   Girlfriend of Tyree Tucker; possesses canceled bribery checks written by Tyree Tucker to Gerald Cantley in Richard Wright's *The Long Dream.*

Harry G. (Bo) Mason   Peripatetic opportunist who moves his family from place to place in the West in search of elusive prosperity and lasting security; murders Elaine Nesbitt, with whom he had an extramarital affair, and commits suicide when his last years find him living in poverty and despair in Wallace Stegner's *The Big Rock Candy Mountain.*

Hazel Mason   Black student from Texas who flunks out of college; disliked by Emma Lou Morgan because of her "Negro mannerisms" in Wallace Thurman's *The Blacker the Berry.*

Jack (Jackie) Mason   Upper-middle-class boyhood friend of Charles Gray; becomes successful in Clyde and marries Jessica Lovell in John P. Marquand's *Point of No Return.*

Jessica Lovell Mason   See Jessica Lovell.

Laura Mason   High school sweetheart of Chet Mason; later marries him, a decision which meets with the disapproval of Chet's parents; becomes a young widow after Chet's untimely death from pneumonia in Wallace Stegner's *The Big Rock Candy Mountain.*

Mr. Mason   Second mate aboard the *Aroostook* in William Dean Howells's *The Lady of the Aroostook.*

Opal Mason   Prostitute who laughs at Will Brady's offer of marriage in Wright Morris's *The Works of Love.*

Rose Dutcher Mason   See Rose Dutcher.

Mrs. Stacy McAndrews Mason   Aunt of Sally Lacey; sees her first husband tortured and scalped by Indians but survives to remarry and raise a total of nine children in Mary Lee Settle's *O Beulah Land.*

Warren Mason   Newspaperman and aspiring novelist; proposes marriage apologetically to Rose Dutcher, who accepts his liberal conditions, in Hamlin Garland's *Rose of Dutcher's Coolly.*

Joe (Gentleman Joe) Massara   Handsome and debonair member of the Vettori gang who wishes to leave it in order to pursue a dancing career in William Riley Burnett's *Little Caesar.*

Richard Mast   Army private who struggles to maintain possession of a pistol he believes will someday save him from a Japanese major with a Samurai saber in James Jones's *The Pistol.*

Cass Mastern   Maternal uncle of Ellis Burden; his letters during the Civil War serve as a basis for Jack Burden's doctoral dissertation in Robert Penn Warren's *All the King's Men.*

Mat   See Mat Moss.

Mata   Wife of Fakahau and mother of Marama and Arai; dies during the hurricane in Charles Nordhoff and James Norman Hall's *The Hurricane.*

Matches   Black hobo arrested in El Paso with Cass McKay in Nelson Algren's *Somebody in Boots.*

Mateo   English-speaking employee of Feliu Viosca, for whom Mateo acts as an interpreter, in Lafcadio Hearn's *Chita.*

Itche (Gelding, Reb Itche) Mates   Ascetic packman and follower of Sabbatai Zevi; weds Rechele Babad but never consummates the marriage; travels to foreign places with Reb Mordecai Joseph bearing the good news of the Messiah's advent in the person of Sabbatai Zevi, but returns to Goray disillusioned in Isaac Bashevis Singer's *Satan in Goray.*

Hopestill (Hope) Mather   Rebellious niece and ward of Miss Pride; marries Dr. Philip McAllister after being impregnated by Harry Morgan; dies in a riding accident in Jean Stafford's *Boston Adventure.*

Matilda (Mat)   Worker at Hosea Ortman's farm and lover of Paul Hardin; causes the quarrel that leads to Smoke's lynching in Brand Whitlock's *J. Hardin & Son.*

Matilda   Small crazy woman who sits on benches near the river for twenty years waiting for her lover to return in Anaïs Nin's *Children of the Albatross.*

Matt   Dogmusher who helps Weedon Scott tame White Fang in Jack London's *White Fang.*

Eloise Matthews   Wife of H. K. Matthews who makes a pass at Ned Beaumont on the evening of her husband's suicide in Dashiell Hammett's *The Glass Key.*

H. K. Matthews   Publisher of the *Observer* who attempts to use his influence to get Paul Madvig indicted for the murder of Senator Henry in Dashiell Hammett's *The Glass Key.*

Lady Kitty Maudulayne   Wife of Lord Claude Maudulayne in Allen Drury's *Advise and Consent*.

Lord Claude Maudulayne   British ambassador to the United States; with French ambassador Raoul Barre, presents the view of the NATO countries in Allen Drury's *Advise and Consent*.

Matthew Maule (I)   Father of Thomas Maule; hanged for witchcraft; curses the Pyncheon family in Nathaniel Hawthorne's *The House of the Seven Gables*.

Matthew Maule (II)   Son of Thomas Maule; hypnotizes Alice Pyncheon in Nathaniel Hawthorne's *The House of the Seven Gables*.

Thomas Maule   Son of Matthew Maule I; architect and builder of the Pyncheon house; hides the Pyncheon land deed in Nathaniel Hawthorne's *The House of the Seven Gables*.

Maum Netta (Mauma)   Old mulatto servant of the Wentworths in DuBose Heyward's *Mamba's Daughters*.

Patricia Maurier   Wealthy widow who hosts the yacht party in William Faulkner's *Mosquitoes*.

Maverick   Mandan Indian woman who lives with Luke and Ma Lampson in John Hawkes's *The Beetle Leg*.

Mawakis   Shawnee Indian who serves as Salathiel Albine's adoptive mother in Hervey Allen's *The Forest and the Fort*.

Max   Attorney secured by Jan Erlone to defend Bigger Thomas against the charge of murdering Mary Dalton in Richard Wright's *Native Son*.

Max   Machinist and cold husband of Christine in John Clellon Holmes's *Go*.

Max (Red Max)   Hot-tempered sailor with two wives, who befriends Redburn in Herman Melville's *Redburn*.

Captain Harris Maxey   First officer of B Company and Claude Wheeler's captain in Willa Cather's *One of Ours*.

Gifford (Giff) Maxim   Political revolutionary disowned by the Party in Lionel Trilling's *The Middle of the Journey*.

Maximov   Husband of Anna Petrovna Maximov; arrested with her while Adam Krug and Krug's son stay with them at their country home in Vladimir Nabokov's *Bend Sinister*.

Anna Petrovna Maximov   Kind old woman and wife of Maximov; arrested while caring for David Krug in Vladimir Nabokov's *Bend Sinister*.

Henry Maxwell   Minister of the First Church of Raymond, Kansas, who asks his parishioners to ask themselves "What would Jesus do?" in Charles M. Sheldon's *In His Steps*.

John Maxwell   Advertising manager for Jonathan Beer, the company that, at Mrs. Layden's suggestion, sponsors Robert Syverten and Gloria Beatty in the dance marathon in Horace McCoy's *They Shoot Horses, Don't They?*

May (Aunt May)   Daughter of Grandfather Adams and aunt of Stephen Grendon; meddler who opposes Grendon's dating of Margery Estabrook in August Derleth's *Evening in Spring*.

May   Neighbor of Daniel Verger; moves in with Bill Agatson, who throws her out three days before he is killed, in John Clellon Holmes's *Go*.

John May   Physician and would-be philanthropist in Rebecca Harding Davis's *Life in the Iron Mills*.

Kate Maybone   Mother who charges Duncan Ferguson with bastardy in Hugh Henry Brackenridge's *Modern Chivalry*.

Julia Maybury   Socialite wife of Antrim Stairs; driven to suicide by his refusal to divorce her so she can marry Jim Halford in Mary Austin's *Santa Lucia*.

Mayhew   Florence, Alabama, peace officer who conspires with John Handback to find the money Miltiades Vaiden stole from Handback in T. S. Stribling's *The Store*.

Jessie Mayhew   College student working at Camp Morgan who attracts George Brush's interest until he learns that she believes in evolution in Thornton Wilder's *Heaven's My Destination*.

Mayotte   Daughter of Aimée Peyronnette and Louis Desrivières; nurtured by her beloved foster mother Youma in Lafcadio Hearn's *Youma*.

Esther Mazur   Devoted wife of Yasha Mazur, despite his lechery; unable to bear children, she spends her days as a head seamstress, meticulously abiding by Jewish customs, in Isaac Bashevis Singer's *The Magician of Lublin*.

Rutka Mazur   Member of a Zionist youth movement; joins Jewish resistance fighters in Warsaw and, hiding in a bunker from Nazi soldiers walking overhead, endures a comrade's putting to death her incessantly crying baby in John Hersey's *The Wall*.

Yasha (Magician of Lublin, Reb Jacob the Penitent) Mazur   Adulterous husband of Esther Mazur and itinerant magician; lover of Magda Zbarski and Zeftel and would be husband of Emilia Chrabotzky; after Magda's death, he repents, changes his name, lives hermetically, and becomes famous for his piety and healing powers in Isaac Bashevis Singer's *The Magician of Lublin*.

Dr. Philip (Perly) McAllister   Aristocratic Boston physician secretly loved by Sonia Marburg; marries Hopestill Mather in Jean Stafford's *Boston Adventure*.

Reverend Charles McAndrews   Virginia gentleman who becomes a fundamentalist preacher and abolitionist, and eventually dies in Kansas for his beliefs, in Mary Lee Settle's *Know Nothing*.

James McArdle   Fanatical evangelist; appears in Hervey Allen's *Bedford Village* and *The Forest and the Fort*.

Dirk McArthur   Self-centered playboy whom Eveline Hutchins meets aboard ship and with whom she has an affair that ends because of his drunkenness in John Dos Passos's *U.S.A.* trilogy.

Terry McBain   Aspiring woman writer involved in a flirtation with the narrator of Peter De Vries's *The Tunnel of Love*.

Mrs. McBales   See Mrs. McKeckeran.

Henry (Hank) McBee   Stingy, noaccount plebeian for the captain of the wagon train in A. B. Guthrie's *The Way West*.

Mercy McBee   Sensual daughter of Hank McBee; lover of Curtis Mack, by whom she has a child; wife of Brownie Evans in A. B. Guthrie's *The Way West*.

Ada Fincastle McBride   See Ada Fincastle.

Mrs. McBride   Strict mother of Ralph McBride; product of curdled Calvinism, her values are based on hatred; consigns her son to a forced marriage to Janet Rowan and military service in Ellen Glasgow's *Vein of Iron*.

Ralph McBride   Brilliant and headstrong man trapped by the forces of morality and money into marrying Janet Rowan; later marries Ada Fincastle in Ellen Glasgow's *Vein of Iron*.

Ranny McBride   Handsome, intelligent, and illegitimate son of Ada Fincastle and Ralph McBride; insists on social change in Ellen Glasgow's *Vein of Iron*.

Anse McCallum   Son of Buddy McCallum; fights Matt Levitt in William Faulkner's *The Town*.

Buddy McCallum   Father of Anse McCallum in William Faulkner's *Intruder in the Dust* and *The Town*.

Lafe McCallum   See Lafe.

Bridget McCandliss   Girl whose parents are lost in an Indian raid and who is returning to relatives in Carlisle, Pennsylvania, in Hervey Allen's *Toward the Morning*.

Shrevlin (Shreve) McCannon   Harvard roommate of Quentin Compson I and one of the narrators of William Faulkner's *Absalom, Absalom!* See also Shreve MacKenzie.

Hoake McCarron   Tennesseean who fathers Eula Varner's daughter Linda Snopes; appears in William Faulkner's *The Hamlet, The Town*, and *The Mansion*.

Mike McCarthy   Irish idler admired by young Sam McPherson in Sherwood Anderson's *Windy McPherson's Son*.

Newton Justine (Brother McCarthy, Colonel, Judge, Mac, Newt, N. J., Papa, Prince of Evil) McCarthy   Unscrupulous minister; turns his daughter Orlean against Jean Baptiste and is murdered by her in Oscar Micheaux's *The Homesteader*.

Orlean E. McCarthy   Wife of Jean Baptiste and daughter of Newton Justine McCarthy; kills her father and herself in Oscar Micheaux's *The Homesteader*.

Parnell Emmett Joseph (Parn) McCarthy   Alcoholic lawyer who makes a comeback by assisting Paul Biegler in defending Frederic Manion in Robert Traver's *Anatomy of a Murder*.

Amodeus (Uncle Buddy) McCaslin   Son of Carothers McCaslin and twin of Theophilus (Uncle Buck) McCaslin; appears in William Faulkner's *The Unvanquished* and *Go Down, Moses*.

Carothers McCaslin   See Lucius Quintus Carothers McCaslin.

Isaac (Ike) McCaslin   Son of Theophilus (Buck) and Sophonsiba Beauchamp McCaslin; renounces his birthright; appears in William Faulkner's *The Hamlet; Go Down, Moses; Intruder in the Dust; The Town; The Mansion;* and *The Reivers*.

Lucius Quintus Carothers (Old Carothers) McCaslin   Father of Amodeus (Buddy) McCaslin, Theophilus (Buck) McCaslin, a daughter, and, by the slave Tomasina, Tomey's Turl; appears in William Faulkner's *Go Down, Moses; Intruder in the Dust;* and *The Reivers*.

Sophonsiba Beauchamp McCaslin   Wife of Theophilus (Buck) McCaslin, and mother of Ike McCaslin in William Faulkner's *Go Down, Moses*.

Theophilus (Uncle Buck) McCaslin   Son of Carothers McCaslin, husband of Sophonsiba Beauchamp McCaslin, and the father of Ike McCaslin; appears in William Faulkner's *Absalom, Absalom!; The Unvanquished; The Hamlet; Go Down, Moses;* and *The Reivers*.

Polly Ann Ripley McChesney   See Polly Ann Ripley.

Thomas (Tom) McChesney   Strong and faithful Kentucky pioneer; husband of Polly Ann Ripley and friend of David Ritchie in Winston Churchill's *The Crossing*.

Clarisse McClellan   Young neighbor of Guy Montag; her unconventional ideas inspire Montag to rebel against the antiliterate society in Ray Bradbury's *Fahrenheit 451*.

A. M. (Forenoon) McClintock   Hedonistic college roommate of Vridar Hunter in Vardis Fisher's *Passions Spin the Plot*.

Father McConagha   Catholic priest at St. Dominick's church in Chicago in William Riley Burnett's *Little Caesar*.

McCord   Newspaperman in William Faulkner's *The Wild Palms*.

Pat McCormick   Oil camp contractor who employs Dobbs and Curtin; pays his employees only when threatened with death in B. Traven's *The Treasure of the Sierra Madre*.

Mrs. Margie (Marge) McCoy   Companion of Doremus Blodgett; finds George Brush's ideas ludicrous and is the first of many people to call him nuts in Thornton Wilder's *Heaven's My Destination*.

William McCoy   Dour Scottish seaman who is a leader of the rebellion aboard HMS *Bounty* in Charles Nordhoff and James Norman Hall's *Mutiny on the Bounty*; his love of alcohol precipitates the final violence between the Tahitians and the whites and leads to his suicide in *Pitcairn's Island*.

Joe McCoyne   President of the Abilene stockyards who buys the cattle driven there from Texas in Emerson Hough's *North of 36*.

Reverend Mister McCrae   Assistant to the Reverend Hodder in Winston Churchill's *The Inside of the CUP*.

Fenian Fainy McCreary (Mac)   Itinerant radical who forsakes all, most notably his wife and family, to labor for the working-man in John Dos Passos's *U.S.A.* trilogy.

McCudden   British pilot in William Faulkner's *A Fable*.

Gerald (Jerry) McDermott   Playwright who is the longtime friend and probable future husband of Olivia Lattimore in Mary Austin's *A Woman of Genius*.

Mrs. Simon McEachern   Wife of Simon McEachern; with her husband, adopts Joe Christmas, who eventually steals her money, in William Faulkner's *Light in August*.

Simon McEachern   Farmer who, with his wife, adopts Joe Christmas, who possibly murders McEachern, in William Faulkner's *Light in August*.

Angus Mcellhenny   Old miner and prospector who identifies Clay Turner as the Bad Man in E. L. Doctorow's *Welcome to Hard Times*.

Jim McGarrity   Kindly saloonkeeper and friend of the Nolans in Betty Smith's *A Tree Grows in Brooklyn*.

Marietta McGee–Chavéz   Wife of Thomas Harold MacDougal; yearns to restore a wholeness to herself through artifacts and fantasy of Spain in William Goyen's *In a Farther Country*.

Mary McGeeney   Biographer who teaches John Gilson and who is Balso Snell's childhood sweetheart in Nathanael West's *The Dream Life of Balso Snell*.

Agnes Bedford McGehee   Sister of Malcolm Bedford, wife of Hugh McGehee, and mother of Edward and Lucinda McGehee; travels from Natchez to Shiloh to find and bring home her dead son in Stark Young's *So Red the Rose*.

Edward McGehee   Son of Hugh and Agnes McGehee and admirer of Jefferson Davis; enlists in the Confederate army and dies at Shiloh in Stark Young's *So Red the Rose*.

Hugh McGehee   Husband of Agnes McGehee and father of Edward and Lucinda McGehee; opposes slavery and secession; owner of Montrose plantation, which is looted and burned by Union soldiers, in Stark Young's *So Red the Rose*.

Lucinda (Lucy) McGehee   Daughter of Hugh and Agnes McGehee; loves her cousin Charlie Taliaferro, who is killed at Shiloh, in Stark Young's *So Red the Rose*.

Theresa McGoun   Swift and pretty stenographer for the Babbitt Thompson Realty Company in Sinclair Lewis's *Babbitt*.

McGovern   One of Henry Miller's assistants at the telegraph company in Henry Miller's *Tropic of Capricorn*.

Terence McGuffy   Night-beat policeman in Albert Halper's *Union Square*.

Hugh McGuire   Altamont doctor and friend of the Gant family in Thomas Wolfe's *Look Homeward, Angel* and *Of Time and the River*.

Ross McGurk   Founder of the McGurk Institute of Biology in Sinclair Lewis's *Arrowsmith*.

Lloyd McHarg   Well-known American novelist and close friend of George Webber in Thomas Wolfe's *You Can't Go Home Again*.

Arthur McHenry   Law partner and trusted friend of Joe Chapin I in John O'Hara's *Ten North Frederick*; Lockwood family lawyer in *The Lockwood Concern*.

Watts McHurdie   Civil War veteran; poet, philosopher, and harness maker in William Allen White's *A Certain Rich Man*.

Sergeant McIllhenny   Amorous sergeant who is three times reduced in rank to private; member of the 918th Bomb Group killed in battle in Beirne Lay, Jr., and Sy Bartlett's *Twelve O'Clock High*.

Bobby McIlvaine   Avant-garde theatrical designer in Edmund Wilson's *I Thought of Daisy*.

Henry (Big Henry) McIntosh   Boyfriend of Dessie; boyhood playmate then houseboy of Tracy Deen; lynch mob victim when he is mistakenly identified as Deen's murderer in Lillian Smith's *Strange Fruit*.

Alice McIntyre   College friend and later New York roommate of Derrick Thornton in Helen Hooven Santmyer's *Herbs and Apples*.

Ben McKarkle Son of Solomon McKarkle; avenges Sally Lacey's insult to his father by leading the group of young men who crop her hair in Mary Lee Settle's *O Beulah Land.*

Gideon McKarkle Son of Peregrine Lacey Catlett's former overseer; hunting companion and trusted friend of Johnny Catlett; joins Johnny's Confederate army unit because his father told him to keep the Union troops out of Virginia in Mary Lee Settle's *Know Nothing.*

Jeb McKarkle Inefficient brother of Gideon McKarkle in Mary Lee Settle's *Know Nothing.*

Mr. McKarkle Overseer of Beulah and manager of the inn; moves to western Virginia to farm on his own; father of Gideon and Jeb McKarkle in Mary Lee Settle's *Know Nothing.*

Solomon McKarkle Former hat maker driven out of business by British trade laws; settles at Beulah, defends Johnny Lacey, but is insulted when Sally Lacey does not really like the thimble bed he has made for Sara Lacey Catlett and so is indirectly responsible for the retaliatory cropping of Sally Lacey's hair in Mary Lee Settle's *O Beulah Land.*

Tad McKarkle Son of Solomon McKarkle; marries the granddaughter of Mother Carver in Mary Lee Settle's *O Beulah Land.*

Bryan McKay Brother of Cass McKay and drunken veteran of World War I in Nelson Algren's *Somebody in Boots.*

Cass McKay Ignorant, dirt-poor Texas drifter who becomes a petty criminal in Chicago in Nelson Algren's *Somebody in Boots.*

Nancy McKay Sister of Cass McKay; becomes a prostitute in Nelson Algren's *Somebody in Boots.*

Stuart (Stub, Stubby) McKay Brutal father of Cass and Nancy McKay; his treatment of Cass causes Nancy to leave home in Nelson Algren's *Somebody in Boots.*

Mrs. McKeckeran (Mrs. McBales) Wife of a factory executive; as a gospel worker, visits the housing development where Gertie and Clovis Nevels live; later wants carved dolls for a Christmas bazaar in Harriette Arnow's *The Dollmaker.*

Calvin McKee Grandson of Walter and Lois McKee; elopes with Etoile Momeyer; organizes the western ritual enacted on Tom Scanlon's ninetieth birthday in Wright Morris's *Ceremony in Lone Tree.*

Eileen McKee Daughter-in-law of Walter and Lois McKee and mother of Calvin and Gordon McKee in Wright Morris's *Ceremony in Lone Tree.*

Emily Dodsworth McKee Civic-minded daughter of Fran and Sam Dodsworth and wife of Harry McKee in Sinclair Lewis's *Dodsworth.*

Gordon Scanlon McKee Five-year-old grandson of Walter and Lois McKee; falls under the influence of Gordon Boyd in Wright Morris's *The Field of Vision* and *Ceremony in Lone Tree.*

Harry McKee Husband of Emily Dodsworth McKee and assistant general manager of the Vandering Bolt and Nut Company in Zenith in Sinclair Lewis's *Dodsworth.*

Lois Scanlon McKee Wife of Walter McKee; still influenced by an adolescent kiss from Gordon Boyd in Wright Morris's *The Field of Vision;* frantically opposes male authority and fires a precipitating gunshot in *Ceremony in Lone Tree.*

Walter McKee Proponent of typical middle-class values; avatar of the average in Wright Morris's *The Field of Vision* and *Ceremony in Lone Tree.*

Albert McKisco Novelist who fights a duel with Tommy Barban in F. Scott Fitzgerald's *Tender Is the Night.*

Sarah McKlennar Motherly widow of a British officer; hires Gil Martin to farm for her during the Mohawk Valley campaign in Walter D. Edmonds's *Drums along the Mohawk.*

Andrew (Andy) McLane Lover of Christina Goering until she leaves him for a gangster in Jane Bowles's *Two Serious Ladies.*

Red McLaughlin Boyfriend of Marsan Vaiden, whom he impregnates, in T. S. Stribling's *Unfinished Cathedral.*

McLeod (Mac) Experienced labor organizer and mentor of Jim Nolan; instigates the strike among the fruit pickers in John Steinbeck's *In Dubious Battle.*

Allan McLeod Orphan reared by Mrs. John Durham; rises to political power during Reconstruction in Thomas Dixon's *The Leopard's Spots.*

Beverly Guinevere McLeod Landlady of the boardinghouse, wife of William McLeod, mother of Monina, and lover of Leroy Hollingsworth in Norman Mailer's *Barbary Shore.*

William (Bill) McLeod Former communist revolutionary who has stolen a mysterious black box from the U.S. government; pursued by Leroy Hollingsworth, befriended by Michael Lovett, and married to Beverly Guinevere McLeod in Norman Mailer's *Barbary Shore.*

Eva McLoch See Christine Monahan.

Kevin McLoch See Sean Monahan.

Casey McMahon Handsome, superficial man who is Betsy Allbright's fourth husband in Ludwig Bemelmans's *Dirty Eddie.*

Mrs. Ella McManus Fort Worth medium whom George Brush visits but refuses to pay because he learns that she is a fraud in Thornton Wilder's *Heaven's My Destination.*

Daniel (Dan) McMasters   Texas Ranger and sheriff who is responsible for the success of the cattle drive in Emerson Hough's *North of 36*.

William (Sandy) McNab   Employee of John Bonnyfeather and friend of Anthony Adverse in Hervey Allen's *Anthony Adverse*.

Cornelia McNabb   See Cornelia McNabb Tillinghast Brainard.

Gus McNiel   Milkman represented in a personal injury suit by the ambulance-chasing attorney George Baldwin in John Dos Passos's *Manhattan Transfer*.

Nellie McNiel   Wife of Gus McNeil seduced by George Baldwin while he is representing her husband in a personal injury suit in John Dos Passos's *Manhattan Transfer*.

Princess McNott   Yankton Indian wife of Sergeant Rob't McNott in Kenneth Roberts's *Northwest Passage*.

Sergeant Rob't (Mac) McNott   Soldier and trader who searches for a route to the Pacific Ocean; friend of Major Robert Rogers in Kenneth Roberts's *Northwest Passage*.

Jane McPherson   Wife of John (Windy) McPherson and mother of Sam McPherson in Sherwood Anderson's *Windy McPherson's Son*.

John (Windy) McPherson   Civil War veteran and house painter who is the drunken father of Sam and Kate McPherson in Sherwood Anderson's *Windy McPherson's Son*.

Kate McPherson   Daughter of John (Windy) McPherson and sister of Sam McPherson in Sherwood Anderson's *Windy McPherson's Son*.

Sam McPherson   Son of John (Windy) McPherson; newspaperboy who becomes a business giant and then wanders off in search of truth; loves Janet Eberly and marries Sue Rainey in Sherwood Anderson's *Windy McPherson's Son*.

Sue Rainey McPherson   See Sue Rainey.

Rev. Alex McPhule   White fundamentalist preacher, founder of True Faith Christ Lovers' Church, and leader of a lynch mob in George S. Schuyler's *Black No More*.

Laura McRaven   Nine-year-old only cousin of India Fairchild; leaves Jackson, Mississippi, after her mother's death to attend Dabney Fairchild's wedding at Shellmound plantation in Eudora Welty's *Delta Wedding*.

Malcolm M'Crea   Proprietor of the house in which Constantia and Stephen Dudley live after their financial ruin; sells a locket belonging to Constantia in Charles Brockden Brown's *Ormond*.

Sergeant Michael McShane   Brooklyn police officer and loving second husband of Katie Nolan in Betty Smith's *A Tree Grows in Brooklyn*.

McTeague (Mac)   Dentist who degenerates to a brutish condition, murders his wife and steals her savings, and is last seen handcuffed to the corpse of his pursuer, Marcus Schouler, in Frank Norris's *McTeague*.

Trina Sieppe McTeague   First wife of McTeague; develops pathologically miserly traits, thus hastening McTeague's degeneration and precipitating his murdering her, in Frank Norris's *McTeague*.

Anne McVey   See Anne Sparrow.

Clara Butterworth McVey   See Clara Butterworth.

Hugh McVey   Young Missourian of poor white background who seeks to improve himself through education; becomes a railway station master and later a successful inventor of labor-saving machinery; marries Clara Butterworth in Sherwood Anderson's *Poor White*.

John Endicott (Johnny) McVey   First husband of Anne Sparrow; business failure who moves to California, where he dies of cholera, in Joseph Kirkland's *Zury*.

Margaret (Meg) McVey   Illegitimate daughter of Anne Sparrow and Zury Prouder in Joseph Kirkland's *Zury*.

Philip (Phil) McVey   Illegitimate son of Anne Sparrow and Zury Prouder in Joseph Kirkland's *Zury*.

Harvey McWilliams   Attorney who offers to defend Tyree Tucker and Dr. Bruce against possible charges of negligence resulting in the fire at the Grove; defends Fish Tucker against a charge of attempted rape in Richard Wright's *The Long Dream*.

M'Donald   Scottish gentleman who provides cynical commentary on the observations of Captain John Farrago in Hugh Henry Brackenridge's *Modern Chivalry*.

Ann Eliza Meacham   Pretty and apparently devout Methodist renowned for her prayers; seeks to marry Morton Goodwin in Edward Eggleston's *The Circuit Rider*.

Zebulun (Zeb) Meader   First and most important client of Austen Vane in Winston Churchill's *Mr. Crewe's Career*.

Essie Meadowfill   See Essie Meadowfill Smith.

George Means   Refined young friend of Aunt Abby; falls in love with Jane Bellmont and with her defies Mrs. Bellmont's demands that Jane marry Henry Reed in Harriet E. Wilson's *Our Nig*.

Israel W. (Bud) Means   Twenty-year-old son of Jack Means and a leader among the schoolboys; won over by Ralph Hartsook in Edward Eggleston's *The Hoosier School-Master*.

Jack Means   Farmer and influential trustee of the Flat Creek school district in Edward Eggleston's *The Hoosier School-Master.*

Sophronie Meanwell   Neighbor of Gertie and Clovis Nevels, factory worker, and wife of Whit Meanwell in Harriette Arnow's *The Dollmaker.*

Whit Meanwell   Fellow worker of Clovis Nevels and husband of Sophronie Meanwell; Joins Clovis in his union activities and aids him in taking revenge against an attacker in Harriette Arnow's *The Dollmaker.*

Bessie Mears   Girlfriend of Bigger Thomas, who bashes in her skull and throws her body down an elevator shaft, in Richard Wright's *Native Son.*

Media   King of Odo and Taji's companion in Herman Melville's *Mardi.*

Caroline (Carrie Madenda, Sister Carrie, Mrs. Wheeler) Meeber   Woman from Wisconsin who moves to Chicago to find work; runs away with George Hurstwood to New York, where she becomes a successful actress, in Theodore Dreiser's *Sister Carrie.*

Mr. Meeks   Rivermouth apothecary in Thomas Bailey Aldrich's *The Story of a Bad Boy.*

Mr. Meeks   Traveling copper flue salesman who gives Francis Marion Tarwater a ride to the city and hopes to hire him at minimal cost to help with his business in Flannery O'Connor's *The Violent Bear It Away.*

Arthur (Henry, Junior) Meesum   Sixty-two-year-old son of Joseph Meesum; mayor of Avalon, Connecticut, and part of the new blood at the Stilton Club in Peter De Vries's *The Mackerel Plaza.*

Joseph Meesum   Patriarch of the Stilton Club in Peter De Vries's *The Mackerel Plaza.*

Ludus Meggs   Murderer of Pammy Lee Sparkman in T. S. Stribling's *Unfinished Cathedral.*

Mehevi   Chief of the Typees in Herman Melville's *Typee.*

Daisy Meissner   See Daisy Meissner Coleman.

Kurt Meissner   Composer, former lover of Mabel Dingle, and Nazi supporter in Upton Sinclair's *Dragon's Teeth.*

Melba   Singer who falls in love with Malcolm immediately after meeting him; weds Malcolm but runs off with a Cuban valet in James Purdy's *Malcolm.*

Mr. Melbourne   Friend of Stephen Dudley; judge who supports the Dudleys in order to alleviate their poverty in Charles Brockden Brown's *Ormond.*

Paul Melia   Husband of Tante Melia; hangs himself in Henry Miller's *Black Spring.*

Tante Melia   Manager, with her husband Paul Melia, of a saloon; committed to an insane asylum in Henry Miller's *Black Spring.*

Dr. and Sarah Melmoth   Guardians of Ellen Langton; he is the president of Harley College in Nathaniel Hawthorne's *Fanshawe.*

Melody   Apricot-colored mulatto known as a white man's woman; Juba fears Melody's beauty will attract Gabriel Prosser in Arna Wendell Bontemps's *Black Thunder.*

Melody   See Melody Moss.

Dorothy and Robert Melville   Childless farm couple with whom Mary Fowler stays while Jerry Fowler works on the canal and in whose home Mary bears a child in Walter D. Edmonds's *Erie Water.*

Memoria   Pretty, nearly white woman who, when she was three, was saved from a burning house by George Birdsong; continues as Birdsong's lover following his marriage in Ellen Glasgow's *The Sheltered Life.*

Mendelssohn   Deceased superintendent of the Diamond County Home for the Aged; notorious alcoholic who often ignored the needs of the residents, who now glorify him, in John Updike's *The Poorhouse Fair.*

General Mendoza   Treacherous general and leader of the Opposition in the Olancho Senate who overthrows the government in Richard Harding Davis's *Soldiers of Fortune.*

Louis Mendoza   Mexican criminal who informs the police about Roy Earle and Marie Garson in William Riley Burnett's *High Sierra.*

Menelaos   Brother of Agamemnon and husband of Helen; refuses to kill Helen; professes traditional views of love and morality but acts according to Helen's wishes in John Erskine's *The Private Life of Helen of Troy.*

Roberto Ortega Menéndez y Castillo   See Robert Webster.

Mendy Menendez   Racketeer friend of Terry Lennox in Raymond Chandler's *The Long Goodbye.*

Herbert Menti   Communist party member who murders Lionel Lane in Richard Wright's *The Outsider.*

Mentu   Old stableman at Pharoah's castle; companion, friend, and mentor of Moses; inventor of stories and bearer of legends in Zora Neale Hurston's *Moses, Man of the Mountain.*

Rachel Menzies   Jewish university student and aspiring social worker who marries Bunny Ross and helps him plan his labor college in Upton Sinclair's *Oil!*

Professor Mephesto Lecherous professor who seduces Candy Christian in Terry Southern and Mason Hoffenberg's *Candy.*

Merchant of Sex See A. J.

Miss Mergan Librarian and member of the school board who dies of lung cancer in August Derleth's *The Shield of the Valiant.*

James Merivale Son of Jefferson Merivale who prospers in business with his father in John Dos Passos's *Manhattan Transfer.*

Jefferson Merivale Successful banker, uncle of Jimmy Herf who offers his nephew a job and is turned down in John Dos Passos's *Manhattan Transfer.*

Francis (Frank) Meriwether Cousin of Mark Littleton and husband of Lucretia Hazard Meriwether; Southern gentleman and master of Swallow Barn who graciously permits his neighbor Isaac Tracy to win an old lawsuit over a worthless piece of land in John Pendleton Kennedy's *Swallow Barn.*

Lucretia Hazard Meriwether Sister of Ned Hazard and wife of Frank Meriwether; vigilant nurse to both white and black children in John Pendleton Kennedy's *Swallow Barn.*

Lucy Meriwether Daughter of Frank and Lucretia Meriwether in John Pendleton Kennedy's *Swallow Barn.*

Philip (Rip) Meriwether Son of Frank and Lucretia Meriwether in John Pendleton Kennedy's *Swallow Barn.*

Prudence (Pru) Meriwether Spinster sister of Frank Meriwether; devoted to poetry, Virginia's past glories, elegant dress, and temperance in John Pendleton Kennedy's *Swallow Barn.*

Victorine Meriwether Daughter of Frank and Lucretia Meriwether in John Pendleton Kennedy's *Swallow Barn.*

Dr. Merkle Abortionist whom Charity Royall consults to confirm her pregnancy in Edith Wharton's *Summer.*

Madame Serena Merle Mother, by her lover Gilbert Osmond, of Pansy Osmond; nemesis of Isabel Archer in Henry James's *The Portrait of a Lady.*

Merlin Camelot wizard who is bested by Hank Morgan's nineteenth-century tricks in Samuel Langhorne Clemens's *A Connecticut Yankee in King Arthur's Court.*

Jane Merrill Sister of Susan Merrill; pampered but devoted friend of Cynthia Wetherell in Winston Churchill's *Coniston.*

Stephen (Steve) Merrill Father of Susan and Jane Merrill; mildly ethical railroad executive in Winston Churchill's *Coniston.*

Susan Merrill Sister of Jane Merrill; pampered but devoted friend of Cynthia Wetherell in Winston Churchill's *Coniston.*

Sally Merrillee Neighbor and girlhood sweetheart of Johnny Fraser in James Boyd's *Drums.*

Fred Merrit Embittered half-black and half-white lawyer who moves into a white neighborhood in Rudolph Fisher's *The Walls of Jericho.*

Arthur Mervyn Bumpkin narrator who relates his coming-of-age in 1793 Philadelphia in Charles Brockden Brown's *Arthur Mervyn.*

Angeline Meserve Second child of Arvay and Jim Meserve, wife of Hatton Howland, and socialite in Citrabelle, Florida, in Zora Neale Hurston's *Seraph on the Suwanee.*

Arvay Meserve See Arvay Henson.

Earl David Meserve Eldest child and handicapped son of Arvay and Jim Meserve; shot and killed by a posse of men that includes his father in Zora Neale Hurston's *Seraph on the Suwanee.*

James Kenneth (Kenny) Meserve Third child of Arvay and Jim Meserve; blues musician first instructed by Joe Kelsey in Zora Neale Hurston's *Seraph on the Suwanee.*

Jim Meserve Entrepreneurial hero, husband of Arvay Henson, and father of Earl, Angeline, and Kenny Meserve in Zora Neale Hurston's *Seraph on the Suwanee.*

Messala Haughty young Roman who rejects his childhood Jewish friend, Judah Ben-Hur; strong with classical Roman good looks; has the Hur family imprisoned and Judah enslaved after a misfortunate accident; years later, after he discovers that Ben-Hur has escaped slavery and has inherited the fortunes of a Roman tribune-turned-duumvir, conspires to brutally defeat him in a chariot race; is himself defeated in the race and, in an accident, loses his ability to walk; is eventually killed by his mistress, Iras, who was once the mistress of Judah in Lew Wallace's *Ben-Hur: A Tale of the Christ.*

Lt. Palmer Metcalf Staff officer from New Orleans; narrates part of Shelby Foote's *Shiloh.*

Metro (Met) Tenor saxophonist with a crude sound who idolizes Edgar Pool in John Clellon Holmes's *The Horn.*

Tadeusz Mey Polish pianist; roomer at Rosa Reichl's boardinghouse in Katherine Anne Porter's *The Leaning Tower.*

Meyers American gambler; gives tips about crooked horse races to Frederic Henry and Catherine Barkley in Milan in Ernest Hemingway's *A Farewell to Arms.*

Lulu Meyers Rising actress who has an affair with Sergius O'Shaugnessy and later with Charles Eitel in Norman Mailer's *The Deer Park.*

Mrs. Meyers   Effusive wife of Meyers; brings gifts to wounded soldiers in the American hospital in Milan in Ernest Hemingway's *A Farewell to Arms*.

Big Mac M'Gann   Famous fixer and fence who buys Roy Earle's pardon; dies in his sleep before he can fence a half-million dollars in stolen jewelry in William Riley Burnett's *High Sierra*.

Michael   College student, lover of Donald, and failed lover of Djuna in Anaïs Nin's *Children of the Albatross*.

Michael   Irish terrier pup; brother of Jerry in Jack London's *Jerry of the Islands*.

Roger Michael   Pen name of an Englishwoman author; Fabian socialist who enlightens young Hagar Ashendyne about a larger role in life for women in Mary Johnston's *Hagar*.

Lou Michaelson   Rich fiancé of Marsha Zelenko in Herman Wouk's *Marjorie Morningstar*.

Lawrence (Larry) Mickler   Advertising man and Dostoyevski aficionado in Edmund Wilson's *I Thought of Daisy*.

Middleton   American captain in William Faulkner's *A Fable*.

Carl Middleton   Pastor of Day Spring Baptist Church; husband of Larraine Henson but admirer of her sister, Arvay Henson, in Zora Neale Hurston's *Seraph on the Suwanee*.

Duncan Uncas Middleton   Grandson of Duncan Heyward and Alice Munro; military officer who pursues his kidnapped bride, Inez de Certavallos, onto the prairie and rescues her with the help of Natty Bumppo in James Fenimore Cooper's *The Prairie*.

Larraine (Raine) Henson Middleton   Sister of Arvay Henson and wife of Carl Middleton in Zora Neale Hurston's *Seraph on the Suwanee*.

Luigi Migliore   Italian policeman, Fascist, and student of humanistic philosophy; lectures Cass Kinsolving about Cass's self-destructive behavior in William Styron's *Set This House on Fire*.

Miguel   Leader of a band of thieves who waylay Dobbs and his gold dust on the road to Durango in B. Traven's *The Treasure of the Sierra Madre*.

Miguel   Mexican gamecock fighter in Nathanael West's *The Day of the Locust*.

Miguel   Employee of Feliu Viosca; assists in rescuing the baby Conchita in Lafcadio Hearn's *Chita*.

Jenny Wheelwright Milbury   Friend of Evalina Bowen; as a young woman, jilts Theodore Colville in William Dean Howells's *Indian Summer*.

Miles   Brother of Flora; apparently dies when confronted by the governess about the ghosts in Henry James's *The Turn of the Screw*.

Enoch Miles   Hired man of Jess and Eliza Birdwell in Jessamyn West's *The Friendly Persuasion* and *Except for Me and Thee*.

Mr. Miles   Episcopal minister who officiates at the burial of Mary Hyatt in Edith Wharton's *Summer*.

Shannon Fairchild (Great Aunt Shannon) Miles   Widowed aunt of Battle Fairchild; lives with the Fairchild family at Shellmound plantation in Eudora Welty's *Delta Wedding*.

Carol Milford   See Carol Milford Kennicott.

Victor Milgrim   Motion-picture producer who affects an air of refinement and literary taste; employs Manley Halliday as a screenwriter in order to increase his own prestige in Budd Schulberg's *The Disenchanted*.

Warren Milholland   English professor turned manager of a commercially successful book club, the Readers' Circle, in Edmund Wilson's *Memoirs of Hecate County*.

Rosa (Granny) Millard   Mother-in-law of John Sartoris and grandmother of Bayard Sartoris II; killed by Major Grumby; appears in William Faulkner's *The Unvanquished* and *The Hamlet*.

Jack Millay   One-armed man who dies in the fire at the Silver Sun in E. L. Doctorow's *Welcome to Hard Times*.

Annie P. (Daisy) Miller   Innocent and audacious American traveling in Europe with her mother and brother; dies of malaria in Henry James's *Daisy Miller*.

Daisy Miller   See Annie P. Miller.

Dr. William Miller   Afro-American surgeon educated in Vienna; adversary of Major Philip Carteret in Charles W. Chesnutt's *The Marrow of Tradition*.

Duane (Duke) Miller   Prisoner and surprise witness for the prosecution in Robert Traver's *Anatomy of a Murder*.

Gregory (Greg) Miller   Black problem student who eventually respects his teacher Richard Dadier in Evan Hunter's *The Blackboard Jungle*.

Henry V. (Joe) Miller   Narrator who tells of his experiences in Paris in Henry Miller's *Tropic of Cancer*; narrator who describes the customers in his father's Brooklyn tailor shop in *Black Spring*; employee of the Cosmodemonic Telegraph Company and narrator of *Tropic of Capricorn*.

Hugh Miller   Attorney general under Willie Stark; resigns because of a real estate scandal in Stark's administration in Robert Penn Warren's *All the King's Men*.

Jackie Miller   Dance-marathon partner of Mario Petrone; after Petrone's arrest, she is partnered with Kid Kamm in Horace McCoy's *They Shoot Horses, Don't They?*

Lulu (L. L.) Miller　Married woman who befriends the adolescent Felix Fay and takes him to sophisticated parties in Floyd Dell's *Moon-Calf*.

Mrs. Miller　Nervous woman traveling in Europe with her children Daisy and Randolph Miller in Henry James's *Daisy Miller*.

Randolph Miller　Brother of Daisy Miller; an uncontrollable brat who hates being in Europe in Henry James's *Daisy Miller*.

John Millet　English knight who hires and befriends Israel Potter in Herman Melville's *Israel Potter*.

Sergeant Millhouse　Devoted adherent of Captain Porgy and overseer of Glen-Eberley in William Gilmore Simms's *Woodcraft*.

Henry Mills　Chicago attorney and husband of Pauline Mills; offers Olivia Lattimore financial help, which she refuses, in return for her silence to his wife about his attentions to actresses in Mary Austin's *A Woman of Genius*.

Ernest (Putsi) Mills　Television director who directs Isolde Poole and Dick in P.T.A. entertainment in Peter De Vries's *The Tunnel of Love*.

Martha Mills　Actress and singer who is the girlfriend of Harry Bogen in Jerome Weidman's *I Can Get It for You Wholesale*; becomes the mistress of Theodore Ast and runs off with Bogen's money in *What's in It for Me?*

Pauline Allingham Mills　Wife of Henry Mills and longtime friend of Olivia Lattimore; moralizes instead of helping Olivia financially in Mary Austin's *A Woman of Genius*.

Lafayette (Lafe) Millspaugh　Neighbor of the Birdwells; has a longstanding aversion to bathing in Jessamyn West's *The Friendly Persuasion*.

Charles (Charlie) Millthorpe　Poor boyhood friend of Pierre Glendinning III; tries too late to help the imprisoned Glendinning in Herman Melville's *Pierre*.

Milly　Slave of Loo Nesbit; works as a housekeeper to help the ailing finances of Canema plantation but is shot by her employer; eventually flees to New York, where she rears orphan children, in Harriet Beecher Stowe's *Dred*.

Arnold Francis (Babe) Milnik　Inexperienced criminal who is killed in a car crash in William Riley Burnett's *High Sierra*.

George Milton　Wandering ranch hand who is the traveling companion, caretaker, and executioner of Lennie Small in John Steinbeck's *Of Mice and Men*.

Rytza Miltz　Sister of Herman; offers refuge to Zeftel and later manages Herman's prostitution operation in Isaac Bashevis Singer's *The Magician of Lublin*.

Mimi (Turtle Dove)　Indian mother in James Kirke Paulding's *Koningsmarke*.

Min　Middle-aged woman who lives with William Jones in Ann Petry's *The Street*.

Fanny Minafer　Sister of Wilbur Minafer; middle-aged spinster secretly in love with Eugene Morgan, who loves Isabel Amberson Minafer, in Booth Tarkington's *The Magnificent Ambersons*.

George Amberson (Georgie) Minafer　Son of Isabel and Wilbur Minafer; proud and arrogant heir to Major Amberson's dwindling wealth in Booth Tarkington's *The Magnificent Ambersons*.

Isabel Amberson Minafer　Daughter of Major Amberson and widow of Wilbur Minafer; stopped by her son George Amberson Minafer from marrying Eugene Morgan in Booth Tarkington's *The Magnificent Ambersons*.

Wilbur Minafer　Quiet businessman and husband of Isabel Amberson Minafer; ignored by his son George Amberson Minafer in Booth Tarkington's *The Magnificent Ambersons*.

Minarii　Tahitian chieftain who joins Fletcher Christian in attempting to establish a democracy; killed by Matthew Quintal in Charles Nordhoff and James Norman Hall's *Pitcairn's Island*.

Steve Minetta　Italian-American soldier who fakes insanity but fails to get a discharge in Norman Mailer's *The Naked and the Dead*.

Minette　See Henrietta Anne Stuart.

Mingo　Boyfriend of Harriett Williams; his insistence on going to a dance leads Sandy Rodgers to his first encounter with the secular world in Langston Hughes's *Not Without Laughter*.

Mingo　Freedman and saddlemaker; friend to the rebelling slaves; often reads aloud to the slaves from the Bible and other books in Arna Wendell Bontemps's *Black Thunder*.

Catherine Spicer (Mrs. Manson Mingott) Mingott　Obese matriarch of the Mingott family; instrumental in preventing her granddaughter, Ellen Olenska, from having to return to a cruel husband in Edith Wharton's *The Age of Innocence*; mentioned in *The Old Maid*.

Mrs. Lovell Mingott　Member of the old New York Mingott family by marriage; sister-in-law of Augusta Welland and daughter-in-law of Catherine Mingott in Edith Wharton's *The Age of Innocence*.

John Minify　Vital editor in chief of a weekly magazine who hires Phil Green and becomes his friend and mentor in Laura Z. Hobson's *Gentleman's Agreement*.

Minna   Catlett slave, wife of Jim, mother of Toey, mistress of Peregrine Lacey Catlett, and mammy to the Catlett children in Mary Lee Settle's *Know Nothing.*

Minnie   Maid of Reba Rivers in William Faulkner's *Sanctuary, The Mansion,* and *The Reivers.*

Minnie   Part-time maid of Erskine Fowler in Richard Wright's *Savage Holiday.*

Ward Minogue   Crook who robs Morris Bober, blackmails Frank Alpine, attempts to assault Helen Bober, and dies setting a fire in Julius Karp's store in Bernard Malamud's *The Assistant.*

Marie Minotti   See May Wynn.

Harry Minowitz   Neighbor and first sexual partner of Mick Kelly in Carson McCullers's *The Heart Is a Lonely Hunter.*

Barbara (Babs) Mintner   Nurse at the Hauptman Clinic who is seduced by Ralph Edwards in Terry Southern's *Flash and Filigree.*

Harold Mintouchian   Sybaritic Armenian lawyer who tries to teach Augie March by precept but not by example to accept himself and his fate in Saul Bellow's *The Adventures of Augie March.*

Count Mippipopolous   Count who lavishly entertains Lady Brett Ashley and Jake Barnes in Ernest Hemingway's *The Sun Also Rises.*

Miranda   Drama critic for the *Blue Mountain News* who, after nearly dying of influenza, awakens to what she perceives as an unsatisfactory world in Katherine Anne Porter's *Pale Horse, Pale Rider;* Catholic woman who elopes at age eighteen; rebels against Southern society only to question her unromantic reality and alienation from her family in *Old Mortality.*

Miriam   See Miriam Schaefer.

Miriam   Sister of Aaron and perhaps of Moses; daughter of Amram and Jochebed; prophetess and first high priestess of the Hebrews in Zora Neale Hurston's *Moses, Man of the Mountain.*

Miss Wisteria   Midget in a traveling show; young Idabel Thompkins falls in love with her in Truman Capote's *Other Voices, Other Rooms.*

Mitchell   Gentleman who sympathizes with Hugh Wolfe but prosecutes him for grand larceny in Rebecca Harding Davis's *Life in the Iron Mills.*

Eddie Mitchell   Friend of Jim Cowan; takes Helen from Cowan in Nathan Asch's *Pay Day.*

Frances Rankin Mitchell   Iowa native who is the daughter of Judd Rankin, the wife of Leonard Mitchell, and the mother of Judson and Madeleine Mitchell; searches for the meaning of life in Susan Glaspell's *Judd Rankin's Daughter.*

Harry Mitchell   First husband of Belle Mitchell Benbow and father of Titania Mitchell in William Faulkner's *Sartoris (Flags in the Dust)* and *Sanctuary.*

Judson Mitchell   Son of Frances and Leonard Mitchell and grandson of Judd Rankin; soldier who has a breakdown during World War II in Susan Glaspell's *Judd Rankin's Daughter.*

Leonard (Len) Mitchell   Husband of Frances Mitchell, father of Judson and Madeleine Mitchell, and son-in-law of Judd Rankin; literary critic who reviews Rankin's book in Susan Glaspell's *Judd Rankin's Daughter.*

Madeleine (Maddie) Mitchell   Daughter of Frances and Leonard Mitchell and granddaughter of Judd Rankin in Susan Glaspell's *Judd Rankin's Daughter.*

Titania (Little Belle) Mitchell   Daughter of Harry and Belle Mitchell in William Faulkner's *Sartoris (Flags in the Dust)* and *Sanctuary.*

Mitchy Mitchett   Friend of Mrs. Brookenham and potential husband of Nanda Brookenham in Henry James's *The Awkward Age.*

Herr Mittelburger   German immigrant whose family accompanies the Laceys to Beulah in Mary Lee Settle's *O Beulah Land.*

M'Kewn   Sinister, cunning, and unscrupulous mercenary in William Gilmore Simms's *Woodcraft.*

Moby-Dick   White whale pursued by Captain Ahab in Herman Melville's *Moby-Dick.*

Moddle   Manhandled nurse of Maisie Farange's nursery days with Beale Farange in Henry James's *What Maisie Knew.*

Elmer Moffatt   Swaggering Wall Street speculator; as a shiftless outcast in Apex City, he was Undine Spragg's first husband; later, a wealthy railroad magnate, he becomes her fourth husband in Edith Wharton's *The Custom of the County.*

Tom Moffatt   True aristocrat, according to some, because he never questions prices at the tailor shop, because he never pays his bills, in Henry Miller's *Black Spring.*

Undine Moffatt   See Undine Spragg.

Alf Moffet   Fun-loving stagecoach driver who tells Blue about the destruction of Kingsville, Kansas, in E. L. Doctorow's *Welcome to Hard Times.*

Mohi (Braid-Beard)   Historian from Odo and Taji's companion in Herman Melville's *Mardi.*

Moldorf   Friend of Henry Miller; has a wife and two children in the United States, but claims to be falling in love with Tania in Henry Miller's *Tropic of Cancer.*

Henry A. Mollenhauer   Philadelphia politician who helps ruin Frank Cowperwood in Theodore Dreiser's *The Financier*.

Bud Momeyer   Husband of Maxine Momeyer, father of Etoile Momeyer, and brother-in-law of Walter McKee; postman and archery enthusiast in Wright Morris's *Ceremony in Lone Tree*.

Etoile Momeyer   Audacious daughter of Bud and Maxine Momeyer; elopes with Calvin McKee; stars as the Girl of the Golden West in the ritual for Tom Scanlon's ninetieth birthday in Wright Morris's *Ceremony in Lone Tree*.

Lee Roy Momeyer   Nephew of Bud Momeyer; protests high school bullying by running over three of his tormenters with his car in Wright Morris's *Ceremony in Lone Tree*.

Maxine Momeyer   Wife of Bud Momeyer, sister of Lois McKee, and mother of Etoile Momeyer in Wright Morris's *Ceremony in Lone Tree*.

Mona   New York girlfriend of Henry Miller; promises to come to Paris in Henry Miller's *Tropic of Cancer*.

Christine (Eva McLoch) Monahan   Placid and hospitable wife of Sean Monahan in Jack Kerouac's *The Dharma Bums*; also appears in *Desolation Angels*.

Mary Monahan   Boston Irish woman who is George Apley's first love; rejected by Apley's family as an unsuitable wife for Apley in John P. Marquand's *The Late George Apley*.

Sean (Kevin McLoch) Monahan   Carpenter and Buddhist; husband of Christine Monahan and host of Japhy Ryder and Ray Smith in Jack Kerouac's *The Dharma Bums*; also appears in *Desolation Angels*.

Monee   Factotum of Deacon Ereemear PoPo in Herman Melville's *Omoo*.

Shadrach Moneypenny   Emissary from William Penn in James Kirke Paulding's *Koningsmarke*.

Monica   Lover, briefly, of Henry Miller; her hands smell of grease from working in a restaurant in Henry Miller's *Tropic of Capricorn*.

Sister Monica   See Irene Shane.

Monina   Daughter whom Beverly Guinevere would like to make into a movie star in Norman Mailer's *Barbary Shore*.

Monk   White drug pusher for whom Jake Adams works in St. Louis's black community in Herbert Simmons's *Corner Boy*.

Monk   Gunman in the Palm Garden whose gunfire kills Mrs. Layden in Horace McCoy's *They Shoot Horses, Don't They?*

Mononotto   Pequod chief and father of Magawisca and Oneco; perpetrator of the massacre at the Fletcher homestead in Catharine Maria Sedgwick's *Hope Leslie*.

Ursula Monrose   See Martinette de Beauvais.

Guy Montag   Fireman whose job is to burn books; rebels against the antiliterate society in Ray Bradbury's *Fahrenheit 451*.

Mildred Montag   Suicidal housewife who reports her husband Guy Montag to authorities for owning books in Ray Bradbury's *Fahrenheit 451*.

Dr. John Montague   Anthropologist interested in supernatural phenomena who plans to investigate the spectral occurrences at Hill House; Eleanor Vance and Theodora come to Hill House at his invitation in Shirley Jackson's *The Haunting of Hill House*.

Mrs. Montague   Wife of Dr. John Montague; rabid but unscientific detective of paranormal phenomena; dominates her husband and takes over his investigation of Hill House in Shirley Jackson's *The Haunting of Hill House*.

Sarah Nevada (Flips) Montague   Actress and stunt performer who assists Merton Gill in Hollywood and introduces him to Jeff Baird, who makes Gill a star, in Harry Leon Wilson's *Merton of the Movies*.

Pete Montana   Chicago crime boss who tries to make peace with Rico Bandello in William Riley Burnett's *Little Caesar*.

Montana Slim   Sardonic hitchhiker and slaphappy drunk who befriends Sal Paradise in Jack Kerouac's *On the Road*.

Montcalm (Louis de Saint Véran, Marquis of Montcalm)   French commander who captures Fort William Henry and unwittingly sends his prisoners into an Indian massacre in James Fenimore Cooper's *The Last of the Mohicans*.

Doña Clara de Montemayor   Daughter of Doña Maria de Montemayor; moves from Peru to Spain to escape her mother; Doña Maria's letters to Doña Clara become famous in Thornton Wilder's *The Bridge of San Luis Rey*.

Doña Maria (Marquesa de Montemayor) de Montemayor   Wealthy but ugly native of Lima, Peru, who clings desperately to her daughter, Doña Clara de Montemayor; her letters to her daughter become famous; dies in the fall of the bridge in Thornton Wilder's *The Bridge of San Luis Rey*.

Anne Montgomery   Friend of Isabel Otis; forced by her family's attitude toward women to sacrifice a musical career and to become a caterer in Gertrude Atherton's *Ancestors*.

Ellen (Ellie) Montgomery   Young heroine who learns to make her way in the world when her parents leave her with her aunt, Fortune Emerson; becomes a devout Christian who submits to others in Susan Warner's *The Wide, Wide World*.

Jake Montgomery   Lumberman murdered by Crawford Gowrie in William Faulkner's *Intruder in the Dust*.

Captain Morgan Montgomery   Father of Ellen Montgomery; dies on his return passage to America in the ship *Duc d'Orleans* in Susan Warner's *The Wide, Wide World*.

Mrs. Montgomery   Widowed sister of Morris Townsend; warns Dr. Sloper not to let her brother marry Catherine Sloper in Henry James's *Washington Square*.

Mrs. Montgomery   Invalid mother of Ellen Montgomery; dies abroad where she had traveled with her husband in hope of curing her disease in Susan Warner's *The Wide, Wide World*.

Christopher (Chris) de Monti (De Monti)   Friend of Andrei Androfski and lover of Deborah Bronski; American journalist who publicizes the story of extermination centers in Poland and Germany; author of the final entry in Alexander Brandel's journal in Leon Uris's *Mila 18*.

Charles Edward Montmorency   See Squire Raglan.

Baltazar Montoya   Early eighteenth-century friar and missionary at Acoma who kills an Indian serving boy and who is thrown off a cliff by the Indians in Willa Cather's *Death Comes for the Archbishop*.

Jack Montraville   Seducer of Charlotte Temple; convinced by Belcour that Charlotte has become sexually promiscuous, he abandons her, only to learn too late that he has been deceived; he then kills Belcour and, filled with remorse by his treatment of Charlotte, visits her grave regularly in Susanna Rowson's *Charlotte*.

Julia Franklin Montraville   See Julia Franklin.

Gilbertson Montrose   Scenario writer in whose movie on the sex life of Dolly Madison Lorelei Lee wishes to appear in Anita Loos's *Gentlemen Prefer Blondes*.

Monuna   Owner of a bar in Naples frequented by homosexual soldiers in John Horne Burns's *The Gallery*.

Moodie (Old Moodie, Faunderoy)   Father of Zenobia and Priscilla, by different women, in Nathaniel Hawthorne's *The Blithedale Romance*.

Fluvanna Moody   Granddaughter of Aunt Mehitable Green and companion of Dorinda Oakley in Ellen Glasgow's *Barren Ground*.

Ralph Moody   Mortician in charge of the funeral of Caddy Hibbard in Wright Morris's *The World in the Attic*.

Mook   Halfwit who lives on the farm formerly owned by Ebenezer Cowley in Sherwood Anderson's *Winesburg, Ohio*.

Adam Moorad   Beat poet; friend and host of Leo Percepied in Jack Kerouac's *The Subterraneans*.

Denis Moore   Father, by Maria Bonnyfeather, of Anthony Adverse in Hervey Allen's *Anthony Adverse*.

Dennis Patrick (Denny) Moore   Cause of his mother's death in childbirth, younger brother reared by Maggie Moore, and husband of Tessie Vernacht in Betty Smith's *Maggie-Now*.

John Moore   Gambler and pious thief; runs a rooming house where Sidney Wyeth stays in Oscar Micheaux's *The Forged Note*.

Kathleen Moore   Englishwoman who is the former mistress of a king; Monroe Stahr's lover in F. Scott Fitzgerald's *The Last Tycoon*.

Margaret Rose (Maggie, Maggie-Now) Moore   Only child of Mary Moriarity and Patrick Dennis Moore; mother to Brooklyn orphans and her little brother, Denny Moore; housekeeper for her widowed father; and loyal wife of Claude Bassett in Betty Smith's *Maggie-Now*.

Mrs. Moore   First employer of Frado after her indenture to the Bellmont family in Harriet E. Wilson's *Our Nig*.

Nat Moore   Rubber worker and companion of Larry Donovan and Jasper Collins in Jack Conroy's *The Disinherited*.

Patrick Dennis (Deef Pat, Patsy) Moore   Spoiled son of an Irish widow, immigrant to New York, stable boy for Mike Moriarity, husband of Mary Moriarity, and rascal father of Maggie Moore; later husband of Mary O'Crawley and the one who scatters Claude Bassett's ashes from the Statue of Liberty in Betty Smith's *Maggie-Now*.

Ginnie Moorehead   Town whore and brassiere factory worker who marries Dave Hirsh after the annulment of her marriage to an ex-marine in James Jones's *Some Came Running*.

Jabez Moorhouse   Hired hand and elderly confidant of Judith Blackford in Edith Summers *Kelley's Weeds*.

Patricia Moors   Wealthy, glittering society woman and owner of the New York Mammoths baseball team in Mark Harris's *The Southpaw*, *Bang the Drum Slowly*, *A Ticket for a Seamstitch*, and *It Looked Like For Ever*.

Dr. Mootry   See Lucius Kimbell.

Captain Mora   Leader of the Fascist group that attacks El Sordo's men in Ernest Hemingway's *For Whom the Bell Tolls*.

Morache   French soldier in William Faulkner's *A Fable*.

José Morales   Mexican Communist, lover of Helen Jackson, and resident of Twenty-Door City in Albert Halper's *Union Square*.

John Moredock   Colonel who hates Indians yet has a loving heart in Herman Melville's *The Confidence-Man*.

Morehouse   Catholic bishop who sells his possessions and works for the poor; killed during the Chicago Commune labor riots in Jack London's *The Iron Heel*.

J. Ward Morehouse   Ambitious journalist and advertising man who sees the need for public relations and forges a very successful career in that field in John Dos Passos's *U.S.A.* trilogy.

Shep Morelli   Thuggish former boyfriend of Julia Wolf who feels he is a suspect in her murder and asks Nick Charles to help avoid charges in Dashiell Hammett's *The Thin Man.*

Katherine (Kit) Moresby   Wife of Porter Moresby; heroine of Paul Bowles's *The Sheltering Sky.*

Porter (Port) Moresby   Traveler and disillusioned writer; hero of Paul Bowles's *The Sheltering Sky.*

Ettore Moretti   Thrice-wounded Italian from San Francisco serving in the Italian army in Ernest Hemingway's *A Farewell to Arms.*

Francisco Morez   See Juan Martinez.

Mademoiselle Marie-Astrése-Luce de Morfontaine   Member of the Cabala; Second Century Christian who is obsessed with seeing the throne of France restored to the Bourbons and with restoring the divine right of kings to church dogma; her simple faith is destroyed by Cardinal Vaini's intellectual games in Thorton Wilder's *The Cabala.*

Constance Morgan   Childlike innocent and protégée of the narrator in Randall Jarrell's *Pictures from an Institution.*

Dr. Morgan   Kindly, retired Presbyterian minister who practices medicine and cares for Kike Lumsden in Edward Eggleston's *The Circuit Rider.*

Eugene Morgan   Widower who courts Isabel Amberson Minafer; pioneer in the automobile industry whose name replaces Amberson as the most significant family name in Booth Tarkington's *The Magnificent Ambersons.*

Frederick Morgan   Actor with whom Dorothy Shaw sleeps after resisting the advances of the deputy sheriff; she joins his acting company in Anita Loos's *But Gentlemen Marry Brunettes.*

Hank (The Boss) Morgan   Nineteenth-century man who, after being hit on the head, awakens in sixth-century England; introduces nineteenth-century ideas to Camelot; author of the manuscript "Tales of the Lost Land" in Samuel Langhorne Clemens's *A Connecticut Yankee in King Arthur's Court.*

Harry Morgan   Millionaire from Long Island who is shunned by Boston society; fathers a child by Hopestill Mather in Jean Stafford's *Boston Adventure.*

Harry Morgan   Boat owner engaged in various illegal activities; a narrator of and central character in Ernest Hemingway's *To Have and Have Not.*

Henrietta (Nettie) Morgan   Spirited daughter of Dr. Morgan; falls in love with Kike Lumsden while he is recuperating in the Morgan home in Edward Eggleston's *The Circuit Rider.*

Jane Lightfoot Morgan   Mother of Emma Lou Morgan in Wallace Thurman's *The Blacker the Berry.*

Jim Morgan   Father of Emma Lou Morgan in Wallace Thurman's *The Blacker the Berry.*

Joe Morgan   Father of Mary Morgan; drunken pauper who becomes successful after giving up alcohol in T. S. Arthur's *Ten Nights in a Bar-Room.*

Uncle Joe Morgan   Uncle of Emma Lou Morgan; sends her to the University of Southern California and attempts to discourage her preoccupation with skin color in Wallace Thurman's *The Blacker the Berry.*

Lucy Morgan   Daughter of Eugene Morgan; loves the arrogant George Minafer in Booth Tarkington's *The Magnificent Ambersons.*

Marie Morgan   Wife of Harry Morgan in Ernest Hemingway's *To Have and Have Not.*

Mary Morgan   Brave daughter of Joe Morgan; her dying request is that her father give up alcohol in T. S. Arthur's *Ten Nights in a Bar-Room.*

O'Reilly Morgan   Morning servant of Kermit Raphaelson; walks through the house either unclad or in a kimono in James Purdy's *Malcolm.*

Capt. Rex Morgan   Officer of the Royal Guard and devoted lover of Amber St. Clare; killed in a duel over her with Bruce Carlton in Kathleen Winsor's *Forever Amber.*

Morgan le Fay   Ruthless sister of Arthur in Samuel Langhorne Clemens's *A Connecticut Yankee in King Arthur's Court.*

Adolph Morgenroth   Farmer whose injured arm Will Kennicott amputates in Sinclair Lewis's *Main Street.*

Arnold Morgenstern   Father of Marjorie Morningstar and part owner of a feather-importing business in Herman Wouk's *Marjorie Morningstar.*

Marjorie (Marjorie Morningstar) Morgenstern   Young Jewish woman who aspires to become an actress; lives with her parents in New York City in the 1930s in Herman Wouk's *Marjorie Morningstar.*

Rose Kupperberg Morgenstern   Mother of Seth Morgenstern and Marjorie Morningstar in Herman Wouk's *Marjorie Morningstar.*

Seth Morgenstern   Brother of Marjorie Morningstar in Herman Wouk's *Marjorie Morningstar.*

Mary Moriarity   Only child of Mike and Molly Moriarity, kindly but determined spinster schoolteacher, wife of immigrant

Patrick Dennis Moore, and mother of Maggie and Denny Moore in Betty Smith's *Maggie-Now.*

Mike (The Boss) Moriarity Tammany ward heeler indicted for graft and corruption but killed by a stroke before his trial; husband of Molly Moriarity and father of Mary Moriarity in Betty Smith's *Maggie-Now.*

Molly (The Missus) Moriarity Wife of Mike Moriarity and mother of Mary Moriarity; beloved by her son-in-law, Patrick Dennis Moore, until she takes off for Boston with her dead husband's insurance money in Betty Smith's *Maggie-Now.*

Dean Moriarty Reform school veteran and free-spirited hipster philosopher; friend and cross-country traveling companion of Sal Paradise in Jack Kerouac's *On the Road.*

Elizabeth Blaney (Bess) Morison Wife of James Morison and mother of Robert and Peter Morison; dies of pneumonia, a complication of flu contracted during the 1918 epidemic, soon after giving birth to her third son in William Maxwell's *They Came Like Swallows.*

James B. Morison Father of Robert and Peter Morison and an unnamed newborn son; seen primarily presiding at meals, playing solitaire, and reading the paper, until the death of his wife, Elizabeth Morison, in William Maxwell's *They Came Like Swallows.*

Peter (Bunny) Morison Introverted eight-year-old who dislikes being outside, preferring to construct elaborate stories, have his mother read to him, and eavesdrop on conversations between his mother and her sister, in William Maxwell's *They Came Like Swallows.*

Robert Morison Thirteen-year-old who as a young child lost one leg in an accident; enjoys rough games and alternately bullies and protects his younger brother, Peter Morison, in William Maxwell's *They Came Like Swallows.*

Morley (Molly) Timid assistant to Carl Belcher in Robert Cantwell's *The Land of Plenty.*

Henry (Morl) Morley Librarian and skilled mountain climber; accompanies Japhy Ryder and Ray Smith in their ascent of Matterhorn mountain in Jack Kerouac's *The Dharma Bums.*

Marjorie Morningstar See Marjorie Morgenstern.

James Morrell Friend of Ellen and Ralph Putney; friend and admirer of Annie Kilburn in William Dean Howells's *Annie Kilburn.*

Morris (Q) Detective who discovers the location of the missing maid Hannah Chester in Anna Katharine Green's *The Leavenworth Case.*

Julian Morris See Louis Eugene Dupont.

Syra Morris Book editor at the Denver Call who encourages Homer Zigler's literary ambitions in Clyde Brion Davis's *The Great American Novel.*

Hannah Morrison Daughter of a drunkard; blames her troubles on Bartley Hubbard in William Dean Howells's *A Modern Instance.*

Mistress Morrison Housekeeper at Dove Cote in John Pendleton Kennedy's *Horse-Shoe Robinson.*

Mrs. Morrow Mother of Holden Caulfield's schoolmate Ernest Morrow; charms Holden when he meets her on the train to New York City in J. D. Salinger's *The Catcher in the Rye.*

Ruth Morse Society woman who inspires Martin Eden to become a writer, but who loves him only for the fame his writing brings in Jack London's *Martin Eden.*

Victor Morse American ace aviator from Crystal Lake, Nebraska, who goes to Canada to enlist in the British army in Willa Cather's *One of Ours.*

Edmund Mortimer (Radclyffe) Conniving nobleman and third husband of Amber St. Clare; unknown to her, the jilted fiancé of her mother; almost succeeds in poisoning Amber, but she abets his murder during the London Fire in Kathleen Winsor's *Forever Amber.*

Amelia (Amy) Mortis Short, balding woman in her eighties with a goiter; resident of the Diamond County Home for the Aged; makes quilts to sell at the annual fair in John Updike's *The Poorhouse Fair.*

Captain Morton Petty antagonist of Mr. Roberts and more of an enemy to his crew than are the Japanese in Thomas Heggen's *Mister Roberts.*

Mr. Morton Clergyman who is a friend of Evalina Bowen and suitor of Imogene Graham in William Dean Howells's *Indian Summer.*

Mrs. Morgan Morton See Mrs. Herman Muller.

Angèle Mory See Angela Murray.

Moses Son of Princess Royal, grandson of Pharaoh, nephew of Ta-Phar, and commander in chief of the Egyptian armies; adopted son and later son-in-law of Jethro, husband of Zipporah, and emancipator of the Hebrews in Zora Neale Hurston's *Moses, Man of the Mountain.*

Adam Moss Nature-loving recluse who falls in love with Georgiana Cobb; narrator of James Lane Allen's *A Kentucky Cardinal;* marries Georgiana in *Aftermath.*

Chinatown (China) Moss Innocently hedonistic half brother of Mat and Melody Moss; blinded in an industrial holocaust in William Attaway's *Blood on the Forge.*

Georgiana Cobb Moss　See Georgiana Cobb.

Mat (Big Mat) Moss　Devoutly religious eldest of three half brothers who are collectively the protagonists of William Attaway's *Blood on the Forge*.

Melody Moss　Black sharecropper and musician whose move to the steel mills of Pennsylvania with his half brothers, and their subsequent destruction, are at the center of William Attaway's *Blood on the Forge*.

Serphin Moss　Sheepherder in H. L. Davis's *Honey in the Horn*.

Mostro　Prisoner of Il Gufo; all the fathers of Sasso Fetore desire his release so he can marry their daughters; after killing the village's four ganders, he escapes but is recaptured and hanged in John Hawkes's *The Owl*.

Hazel (Haze) Motes　Young man trying to evade redemption by sinning, owning a car, and preaching a Church Without Christ; blinds himself and adopts other severe penitential practices which lead to his death in Flannery O'Connor's *Wise Blood*.

Major Motes　Pompous censorship officer from Virginia who thinks reading letters is more important than fighting in John Horne Burns's *The Gallery*.

Mother Red-Cap　Leader of London criminals in the White-friars district; protects Amber St. Clare during Amber's first childbirth but expects to be repaid in Kathleen Winsor's *Forever Amber*.

Wesley Mouch　Washington lobbyist for Henry Rearden; betrays him to become economic director of the nation in Ayn Rand's *Atlas Shrugged*.

Mowanna　King of Nukuheva in Herman Melville's *Typee*.

Colonel Mowbray　Befuddled executive officer for General Ira N. Beal; cannot handle administrative difficulties in James Gould Cozzens's *Guard of Honor*.

Lump Mowbray　Former slave assaulted by Polycarp Vaiden; attempts to persuade other former slaves to leave their plantations after the Civil War in T. S. Stribling's *The Force* and *The Store*.

Mow-Mow　One-eyed Typean chief in Herman Melville's *Typee*.

Mowree　See Bembo.

M. T.　Reader of Hank Morgan's manuscript in Samuel Langhorne Clemens's *A Connecticut Yankee in King Arthur's Court*.

Mtalba　Fat, pampered royal sister of Queen Willatale; offers herself in marriage to Eugene Henderson with presents and a ritual dance in Saul Bellow's *Henderson the Rain King*.

Thomas (Cooky Tommy) Mugridge　Cook aboard the *Ghost* who abuses Hump Van Weyden; George Leach tries to kill him in Jack London's *The Sea-Wolf*.

David (Davy) Muir　Traitorous British quartermaster killed by Arrowhead in James Fenimore Cooper's *The Pathfinder*.

Diony Hall Jarvis Muir　See Diony Hall Jarvis.

Evan Muir　Provider for and second husband of Diony Hall Jarvis; loses Diony when Berk Jarvis, her first husband, returns from Indian captivity in Elizabeth Madox Roberts's *The Great Meadow*.

Norah Muldoon　Irish nursemaid to Patrick Dennis in Patrick Dennis's *Auntie Mame*.

Gottlieb Leberecht Müller　Name used by Henry Miller when he is born anew and assumes a new identity in Henry Miller's *Tropic of Capricorn*.

Mrs. Herman (Miss Idell, Mrs. Morgan Morton, Mrs. Seth Parton) Muller　Lover of Aaron Starr and wife of Seth Parton; poses as a colonel's wife during the Civil War and befriends Amantha Starr in Robert Penn Warren's *Band of Angels*.

Margaret (Duchess of Müller, Mag, Maggie) Müller　Opportunistic and materialistic mother of Kenyon Adams; marries Henry Fenn, but divorces him to marry Thomas Van Dorn in William Allen White's *In the Heart of a Fool*.

Hannah Mullett　Faithful servant of the March family in Louisa May Alcott's *Little Women*.

Fern Mullins　Gopher Prairie teacher who is fired for having attended a party at which alcohol was served in Sinclair Lewis's *Main Street*.

Michael J. (Mike) Mulrooney　Kindly manager of the minor-league team on which Henry Wiggen first played in Mark Harris's *The Southpaw*.

Bennie Mulry　Friend of Jimmie Vaiden; itinerant Methodist preacher and proslavery advocate who foretells the fall of Fort Sumter in T. S. Stribling's *The Forge*.

Ludlow Mumm　Inept, politically liberal screenwriter for Olympia Studios in Ludwig Bemelmans's *Dirty Eddie*.

Bobby (Will) Muncy　City-born son of Clyde Muncy in Wright Morris's *The Home Place* and *The World in the Attic*.

Clara Cropper Muncy　Rural Nebraska aunt of Clyde Muncy and wife of Harry Muncy; staunch believer in country virtues in Wright Morris's *The Home Place*.

Clyde Muncy　Returned Nebraska native forced to decide between country and city living; narrator of Wright Morris's *The Home Place*; ponders the nature of small-town nostalgia in *The World in the Attic*.

Harry (Uncle Harry) Muncy　Husband of Clara Muncy and uncle of Clyde Muncy in Wright Morris's *The Home Place*.

Peg Muncy   City-bred wife of Clyde Muncy in Wright Morris's *The Home Place* and *The World in the Attic*.

Peggy Muncy   Daughter of Clyde and Peg Muncy in Wright Morris's *The Home Place* and *The World in the Attic*.

Charlie Munger   Mass murderer in Wright Morris's *Ceremony in Lone Tree*.

Mrs. Munger   Socialite who instigates the Social Union scheme in William Dean Howells's *Annie Kilburn*.

Paul Muniment   Subversive deeply involved in revolutionary work; initiates Hyacinth Robinson into socialist activities in Henry James's *The Princess Casamassima*.

Munn   Grizzled Civil War major who calls Molly Riordan daughter; dies of a stroke, whereupon his body is eaten by buzzards, in E. L. Doctorow's *Welcome to Hard Times*.

May Cox Munn   Wife of Percy Munn in Robert Penn Warren's *Night Rider*.

Percy (Barclay, Perse) Munn   Lawyer who becomes involved with the Association of Growers of Dark Fired Tobacco and with its violent arm, the Free Farmers' Brotherhood of Protection and Control, the night riders; lover of Sukie Christian in Robert Penn Warren's *Night Rider*.

Alice Munro   Daughter of Colonel Munro; loves Duncan Heyward in James Fenimore Cooper's *The Last of the Mohicans*.

Colonel Munro   Commander of Fort William Henry and father of Cora and Alice Munro in James Fenimore Cooper's *The Last of the Mohicans*.

Cora Munro   Daughter of Colonel Munro; loved by Uncas and desired as a wife by Magua; killed when she refuses to marry Magua in James Fenimore Cooper's *The Last of the Mohicans*.

Sally Munro   See Sally Munro Tallant.

Carlyle (Collie) Munshin   Movie producer known for pirating scripts in Norman Mailer's *The Deer Park*.

Buford Munson   Black neighbor of the Tarwaters in Powderhead; buries Mason Tarwater, marks his grave with a cross, and plows his field after Francis Marion Tarwater has gotten drunk, burned the house down, and run away to the city in Flannery O'Connor's *The Violent Bear It Away*.

Robert Durham (Bob) Munson   Senior senator from Michigan and Senate Majority Leader who eventually supports the Senate and House of Representatives even above his party's president in the controversial nomination of Robert Leffingwell for Secretary of State in Allen Drury's *Advise and Consent*.

Baroness Eugenia-Camilla-Dolores Münster   Complex baroness of the German province of Silberstadt-Schreckenstein who comes to the United States to seek her fortune; courted by Robert Acton, whom she rejects, in Henry James's *The Europeans*.

Anthony Joseph (Tony) Murascho   See Al Grecco.

Bogan Murdock   Unscrupulous developer and entrepreneur who manages to bilk the legislature on a land deal in Robert Penn Warren's *At Heaven's Gate*.

Sue Murdock   Daughter of Bogan Murdock and fiancée of Jerry Calhoun; breaks the engagement and enters relationships with Slim Sarrett and then Jason Sweetwater; killed by Sarrett in Robert Penn Warren's *At Heaven's Gate*.

Father Murphy   Irish priest on Tahiti in Herman Melville's *Omoo*.

Angela Murray (Angéle Mory)   Young painter from a modest Philadelphia home who passes for white in New York City until she sees the error of her ways in Jessie Redmon Fauset's *Plum Bun*.

Junius Murray   Dark-skinned black father of Angela Murray in Jessie Redmon Fauset's *Plum Bun*.

Mattie Murray   Light-skinned black mother of Angela Murray in Jessie Redmon Fauset's *Plum Bun*.

Virginia (Jinny) Murray   Teacher; kind-hearted, dark-skinned sister of Angela Murray in Jessie Redmon Fauset's *Plum Bun*.

Mrs. Murrett   Rich American woman of doubtful reputation to whom Sophy Viner is an assistant in Edith Wharton's *The Reef*.

Allen Musgrove   Father of Mary Musgrove; Tory partisans burn his farm in John Pendleton Kennedy's *Horse-Shoe Robinson*.

Amalie Musgrove   Virginia-born first wife of Clement Musgrove; dies when she is forced to watch Indians boil her son in burning oil in Eudora Welty's *The Robber Bridegroom*.

Ann Chapin Musgrove   See Ann Chapin.

Clement Musgrove   Planter whose plantation is near Rodney's Landing on the Mississippi River; father of Rosamond Musgrove; unwittingly promises to reward Jamie Lockhart with Rosamond's hand in marriage if he kills the bandit who stole her clothes—Lockhart himself—in Eudora Welty's *The Robber Bridegroom*.

Mary Musgrove   Daughter of Allen Musgrove; warns Arthur Butler of Wat Adair's plot to betray him; accompanies the Lindsays on their trip to see Cornwallis in John Pendleton Kennedy's *Horse-Shoe Robinson*.

Rosamond Musgrove   See Rosamond Musgrove Lockhart.

Salome Thomas Musgrove　Second wife of Clement Musgrove; marries him after they are released by Indians who have killed their spouses in Eudora Welty's *The Robber Bridegroom.*

Musso　Army supply clerk who eventually reclaims the pistol in the possession of Richard Mast in James Jones's *The Pistol.*

Mutchkin　Grocer whose daughter is courted by Teague Oregan in Hugh Henry Brackenridge's *Modern Chivalry.*

M'Whorter　Young clergyman deranged because of Teague Oregan in Hugh Henry Brackenridge's *Modern Chivalry.*

Adolph Myers　See Wing Biddlebaum.

Marvin Myles　Self-made New York career woman and lover of Harry Pulham; marries a wealthy classmate of Pulham in John P. Marquand's *H. M. Pulham, Esquire.*

Mysis　Servant of Chrysis and special companion of Glycerium in Thornton Wilder's *The Woman of Andros.*

Jim Nabours Foreman of the Laguna del Sol ranch and adviser to Taisie Lockhart in Emerson Hough's *North of 36*.

Fabrizio Naccarelli Handsome young Florentine who falls desperately in love with a retarded American girl, Clara Johnson, whose childlike innocence bewitches him in Elizabeth Spencer's *The Light in the Piazza*.

Signor Naccarelli Father of the young Italian in love with an American girl whose mental retardation the Signor may or may not be aware of; his designs are on the girl's mother in Elizabeth Spencer's *The Light in the Piazza*.

President Harmon Nagel College president afraid of the alumni and clever bargainer for Raymond Blent's right to play football in Howard Nemerov's *The Homecoming Game*.

George Nagle Captain of the Katopua; treats Terangi as a son, does not help him escape, sees him pardoned, leaves the Katopua to him, and dies shortly after the hurricane in Charles Nordhoff and James Norman Hall's *The Hurricane*.

Matilda Nagy Zagreb midwife assisting at the birth of Rudolf Stanka; charged with being a liaison between Stanka's mother and the Dug family in Louis Adamic's *Cradle of Life*.

Nana (Mrs. Greenfield, Ray) Beautiful, elegant, and influential aunt of the narrator of Aline Bernstein's *The Journey Down*.

Nanantatee Hindu representing himself as a wealthy merchant; lives in poverty and has not worked in five years in Henry Miller's *Tropic of Cancer*.

Aurore De Grapion Nancanou Young Creole widow who marries Honoré Grandissime in George Washington Cable's *The Grandissimes*.

Clotilde De Grapion Nancanou Daughter of Aurora Nancanou; marries Joseph Frowenfeld in George Washington Cable's *The Grandissimes*.

Nancy Cook for Clarissa and Edward Packard; fired for rudeness in Caroline Gilman's *Recollections of a Housekeeper*.

Nancy Daughter of Till and an unknown white man; mulatto slave of Sapphira Dodderidge Colbert; runs away to Canada to avoid the sexual advances of Martin Colbert in Willa Cather's *Sapphira and the Slave Girl*.

Nanny Grandmother who arranges Janie Crawford's marriage to Logan Killicks in Zora Neale Hurston's *Their Eyes Were Watching God*.

Nanny Old nurse of Lillian's children and chief protector of familial harmony in Lillian's home in Anaïs Nin's *Ladders to Fire*.

Napoleon Slave of Sally and Brandon Lacey; carriage driver on their visit to Beulah in Mary Lee Settle's *Know Nothing*.

Narciss Black housekeeper for Sam and Daniel Ponder in Eudora Welty's *The Ponder Heart*.

Gabriel Nash Talkative friend of Nick Dormer in Henry James's *The Tragic Muse*.

Phoebe Marvin Nason See Phoebe Marvin.

Steven (Stevie) Nason Maine woodsman who accompanies Benedict Arnold to Quebec to rescue Mary Mallinson; marries Phoebe Marvin in Kenneth Roberts's *Arundel*.

Mayor Nasta Fascist collaborator given an opportunity to perform penitential service for Adano; circulates rumors about

German advances and is banished from the town in John Hersey's *A Bell for Adano.*

Natanis   Abenaki Indian friend of Steven Nason; helps Benedict Arnold's army in Kenneth Roberts's *Arundel.*

Nathan   Young rabbi who creates a substitute home for Felix Fay before Fay becomes a reporter in Floyd Dell's *Moon-Calf.*

Dame (Aunt) Nauntje   Black servant to the Vancours in James Kirke Paulding's *The Dutchman's Fireside.*

Floyd Naylor   Farmer who, after marrying his cousin Lulu Bains, moves with his wife to Zenith in Sinclair Lewis's *Elmer Gantry.*

Henderson Neal   First husband of Maggie Ellersley; gambler and eventual suicide in Jessie Redmon Fauset's *There Is Confusion.*

Ned   Servant of the Glendinnings; seduces Delly Ulver in Herman Melville's *Pierre.*

Uncle Ned   Relative of Henry Miller; goes on a three-day drinking binge and dies from a head injury in Henry Miller's *Tropic of Capricorn.*

Annie Brandon Neill   See Annie Brandon O'Neill.

Dan Neill   Son of Big Dan O'Neill, husband of Lydia Catlett, owner of a livery stable, and politican advocating the separation of the wealthier western Virginia from the bankrupt eastern Virginia in Mary Lee Settle's *Know Nothing.*

James Peregrine Neill   Infant son of Dan and Lydia Catlett Neill in Mary Lee Settle's *Know Nothing.*

Lydia Catlett (Liddy, Liddy Boo) Neill   Daughter of Leah and Peregrine Lacey Catlett and sister of Lewis and Johnny Catlett; marries Dan Neill after her father's death and finances his ventures with her inheritance in Mary Lee Settle's *Know Nothing.*

Nelema   Aged Indian woman accused of witchcraft in Catharine Maria Sedgwick's *Hope Leslie.*

Nellie   Flirtatious former lover of Pete in Stephen Crane's *Maggie.*

Nelse   See Nelson Gaston.

David Nelson   Botanist aboard HMS *Bounty* whose job is to collect Tahitian breadfruit in Charles Nordhoff and James Norman Hall's *Mutiny on the Bounty;* set adrift with Captain Bligh, whom Nelson assists with his scientific knowledge, in *Men against the Sea.*

David Nelson   Dedicated Union man who considers moving west, but decides to remain in the South because such men as Comfort Servosse give him hope for a more tolerant Southern attitude, in Albion W. Tourgee's *A Fool's Errand.*

George Nelson   Brother-in-law of Elsa Mason; Minneapolis attorney in Wallace Stegner's *The Big Rock Candy Mountain.*

Kristin Norgaard Nelson   Sister of Elsa Norgaard Mason; wife of George Nelson in Wallace Stegner's *The Big Rock Candy Mountain.*

Cornelius Nepos   Roman historian and biographer who keeps a commonplace book in Thornton Wilder's *The Ides of March.*

Bedelia Satterthwaite Nesbit   Wife of James Nesbit and mother of Laura Nesbit; helps care for young Kenyon Adams following Mary Adams's death in William Allen White's *In the Heart of a Fool.*

James Nesbit   Medical doctor and father of Laura Nesbit; his moral voice counterpoints Thomas Van Dorn's materialism in William Allen White's *In the Heart of a Fool.*

Louisa (Aunt Loo) Nesbit   Widowed aunt and companion of Nina Gordon; selfish devotee of comfortable Christianity in Harriet Beecher Stowe's *Dred.*

Milly Nesbit   See Milly.

Tomtit Nesbit   See Tomtit.

Elaine Nesbitt   Woman who has an affair with Bo Mason; Mason kills her before he commits suicide in Wallace Stegner's *The Big Rock Candy Mountain.*

Nessus   Young centaur who sets Jurgen on the road that will lead him to Koshchei the Deathless; gives Jurgen his multicolored shirt to wear on his journey in James Branch Cabell's *Jurgen.*

Amos Nevels   Youngest son of Gertie and Clovis Nevels; his mother urges an army officer and his driver to take him to a Kentucky village doctor when he is critically ill with diptheria in Harriette Arnow's *The Dollmaker.*

Cassie Marie Nevels   Youngest daughter of Gertie and Clovis Nevels; killed by a train when she is distracted by playing with her imaginary playmate in Harriette Arnow's *The Dollmaker.*

Clovis Nevels   Husband of Gertie Nevels; mechanic who works as a repairman in a Detroit factory during World War II; driven to murder to revenge himself upon a young man hired to beat him up because of his union activities in Harriette Arnow's *The Dollmaker.*

Clytie Nevels   Oldest daughter of Gertie and Clovis Nevels in Harriette Arnow's *The Dollmaker.*

Enoch Nevels   Middle son of Gertie and Clovis Nevels in Harriette Arnow's *The Dollmaker.*

Gertie Kendrick Nevels   Dollmaker who leaves a Kentucky farm to join her husband, Clovis Nevels, who has gone to Detroit to work in a factory during World War II; destroys a statue of Christ she carved in order to use the wood to make dolls to help support her family in Harriette Arnow's *The Dollmaker;* also appears in *The Weed-Killer's Daughter.*

Reuben Nevels   Oldest son of Gertie and Clovis Nevels; returns to Kentucky because of his dislike for Detroit in Harriette Arnow's *The Dollmaker.*

Augusta (Gussie) Newcomb   Landlady and heir of Agee Ward; falls under Ward's mystical influence in Wright Morris's *The Man Who Was There.*

Susan Newell   Eight-year-old daughter of Renie and Claud Newell; allegedly raped by Dr. Mark Channing in Lillian Smith's *One Hour.*

Christopher Newman   American millionaire who loses interest in business and visits Europe to increase his aesthetic sense; loves Claire de Cintré against her family's wishes in Henry James's *The American.*

Chadwick (Chad) Newsome   American expatriate living in Paris who remains in Europe against the wishes of his family; lover of Madame de Vionnet and friend of Lambert Strether in Henry James's *The Ambassadors.*

Mrs. Newsome   Rich, widowed mother of Chad Newsome; sends her fiancé, Lambert Strether, to Europe to disentangle her son from an involvement with Madame de Vionnet and bring him home to take over the family business in Woollett, Massachusetts, in Henry James's *The Ambassadors.*

Niceratus   Youthful guest at Chrysis's dinners; asks Chrysis to predict what life would be like in 2,000 years in Thornton Wilder's *The Woman of Andros.*

Brigadier General (J. J., Jo-Jo) Nichols   Intuitive Chief of Air Staff whose almost preternatural intelligence manifests "an undeceived apprehension, a stern, wakeful grasp of the nature of things" in James Gould Cozzens's *Guard of Honor.*

James Nicholson   Eccentric printer who distributes cards and flyers containing gnomic messages in Albert Halper's *Union Square.*

Nick of the Woods   See Nathan Slaughter.

Lola Niessen   First piano teacher of Henry Miller; he seduces her because he is fascinated by her sallow complexion and abundance of body hair in Henry Miller's *Tropic of Capricorn.*

Nigger   Lower East Side gang leader and later a gangster; Michael Gold's boyhood Jewish mentor in Michael Gold's *Jews without Money.*

Nigger Ed (Negro Ed)   Town crier, drunkard, and buffoon who becomes the hero of Paul Laurence Dunbar's *The Fanatics.*

Night Shadow   Young Indian warrior in James Kirke Paulding's *Koningsmarke.*

Tug Nightingale   Painter and soldier in William Faulkner's *The Mansion.*

Arthur Nightwine   Thief turned Hollywood servant in Ludwig Bemelmans's *Dirty Eddie.*

Peter Nilssen   Uncle of Helga Crane who pays for her education, disowns her after his marriage, but sends her $5,000 with the suggestion she go to Denmark in Nella Larsen's *Quicksand.*

Nimbus (George Nimbus, Nimbus Desmit, Nimbus Ware)   Industrious black slave who flees his owner (Potem Desmit); enlists in the Union army (where he is given the name George Nimbus); returns to Horsford County and, as Nimbus Desmit, registers his marriage to Lugena; enrolls as a voter as Nimbus Ware; buys the Red Wing plantation, establishes a successful tobacco farm and freedmen's community, is forced to flee the Ku Klux Klan, returns to Horsford County, and eventually moves to Kansas to rejoin his family in Albion W. Tourgee's *Bricks Without Straw.*

Nimni   Major Taparian on Pimminee and husband of Ohiro-Moldona-Fivona in Herman Melville's *Mardi.*

Nino   Wounded soldier who recovers in Castiglione and befriends Adeppi; friend of Edouard and Dolce in John Hawkes's *The Goose on the Grave.*

Nioche   Father of Noémie Nioche; businessman who has experienced substantial losses and lives off Noémie, about whom he worries, in Henry James's *The American.*

Noémie Nioche   Heartless and calculating woman who wishes to become the mistress of a wealthy man; delighted when Valentin de Bellegarde and Stanislas Kapp fight a duel over her in Henry James's *The American.*

Leonard (Lenny) Nissem   Owner of a finance company that lends money to Harry Bogen on the basis of fraudulent dress orders in Jerome Weidman's *What's in It for Me?*

Charles Arnold (Charlie) Noble   Stranger who tells Frank Goodman about John Moredock; accused of being a Mississippi operator in Herman Melville's *The Confidence-Man.*

Maury Noble   Disloyal friend of Anthony Patch in F. Scott Fitzgerald's *The Beautiful and Damned.*

Mrs. Noble   Nursemaid for the Principino in Henry James's *The Golden Bowl.*

N'Ogo   Relative and servant of N'Gana Frimbo in Rudolph Fisher's *The Conjure-Man Dies.*

Annie Laurie Nolan   Third child of Johnny and Katie Nolan; born after her father's death in Betty Smith's *A Tree Grows in Brooklyn.*

Cornelius John (Neeley) Nolan　Second child of Johnny and Katie Nolan; adored brother and friend of Francie Nolan in Betty Smith's *A Tree Grows in Brooklyn*.

Jim Nolan　Young man who, as a result of his father's killing during a labor dispute, becomes a Communist organizer among migrant workers and is killed during the strike in John Steinbeck's *In Dubious Battle*.

John (Johnny) Nolan　Handsome, lovable son of Irish immigrants; poverty-ridden alcoholic dreamer and singing waiter; husband of Katie Nolan and father of Francie Nolan in Betty Smith's *A Tree Grows in Brooklyn*.

Katherine (Katie) Rommely Nolan　Child of Austrian immigrants, impoverished janitress, and loving wife of Johnny Nolan and mother of Francie Nolan; firm believer in education and role model for her daughter in Betty Smith's *A Tree Grows in Brooklyn*.

Mary Frances (Francie) Katherine Nolan　Brooklyn tenement child in the early 1900s, avid reader with a passion for beauty, first child of Johnny and Katie Nolan, and devoted big sister of Neeley and Annie Laurie Nolan; victim of near rape and determined heroine of Betty Smith's *A Tree Grows in Brooklyn*.

Vincent (Vinc) Nolte　Successful banker and friend of Anthony Adverse; advises Adverse to invest in silver mines in Hervey Allen's *Anthony Adverse*.

Noomai　King of Hannamanoo in Herman Melville's *Omoo*.

Noonan　Chief of police and one of the four criminal bosses in Personville in Dashiell Hammett's *Red Harvest*.

Tim Noonan　Brother of the police chief; apparent suicide murdered by Bob MacSwain in Dashiell Hammett's *Red Harvest*.

Nord　Maintopman with a mysterious past aboard *the Neversink* in Herman Melville's *White-Jacket*.

Karl Norgaard　Uncle of Elsa Norgaard Mason; store owner in North Dakota with whom Elsa goes to live as young woman; disapproves of her marriage to Bo Mason in Wallace Stegner's *The Big Rock Candy Mountain*.

Nels Norgaard　Father of Elsa Norgaard Mason; marries Elsa's girlhood friend, prompting Elsa to move away from home, in Wallace Stegner's *The Big Rock Candy Mountain*.

Sarah Norgaard　Wife of Nels Norgaard; girlhood friend of Elsa Norgaard Mason; her marriage to Elsa's father prompts Elsa to move away from home in Wallace Stegner's *The Big Rock Candy Mountain*.

Norma　Shy young woman hired by Alice Chicoy to help at the diner; writes long, passionate letters to Clark Gable and fantasizes about getting a glamorous job in Hollywood; leaves on Juan Chicoy's bus in order to find a life away from the diner in John Steinbeck's *The Wayward Bus*.

Edward Norman　Christian journalist who excludes whiskey and tobacco advertising from the Raymond *Daily News* in Charles M. Sheldon's *In His Steps*.

Hose Norman　Son-in-law of Tom Camp; joins the Ku Klux Klan following his wife's murder in Thomas Dixon's *The Leopard's Spots*.

Abraham (Abe) North　Alcoholic composer and close friend of Dick and Nicole Diver in F. Scott Fitzgerald's *Tender Is the Night*.

Amy (Doctor) North　Unbalanced woman who marries Rick Martin in Dorothy Baker's *Young Man with a Horn*.

Frank North　Young black portrait painter who is a graduate of a New York art school and a member of the Charleston black artistic set; suitor of Lissa Atkinson in DuBose Heyward's *Mamba's Daughters*.

Mary North (Contessa di Minghetti)　Wife, then widow, of Abe North; turns against Dick Diver after her marriage to a foreign potentate in F. Scott Fitzgerald's *Tender Is the Night*.

Perry Northcutt　Brother of Roxie Biggers; bank cashier who is a hypocritical zealot and avowed fundamentalist; chief instigator of a revival by the Reverend Blackman to effect moral reform in T. S. Stribling's *Teeftallow*.

Norton　White trustee of a black college who is shocked by his experience with Jim Trueblood and the black veterans at the Golden Day bar in Ralph Ellison's *Invisible Man*.

John Norton　Quartermaster aboard the HMS *Bounty* who is set adrift with Captain Bligh in Charles Nordhoff and James Norman Hall's *Mutiny on the Bounty*; the only person to die on the difficult journey to Timor in *Men Against the Sea*.

Henry Novak　North Dakota farmer whose daughter dies from an allergic reaction to medicine administered by Martin Arrowsmith in Sinclair Lewis's *Arrowsmith*.

Molly (Molly N., Molly-O) Novotny　Lover of Frankie Machine in Nelson Algren's *The Man with the Golden Arm*.

Antoinette Nowak　Private secretary to and mistress of Frank Cowperwood in Theodore Dreiser's *The Titan*.

Parker Nowell　Lawyer for the defense and narrator of Shelby Foote's *Follow Me Down* and *Jordan County*.

Catfoot Nowogrodski　Henchman of Bonifacy Konstantine; helps set up Bruno (Lefty) Bicek for arrest for murder in Nelson Algren's *Never Come Morning*.

Nung En (Elder, Wang the Eldest, Wang the Landlord)　Pleasure-loving weakling married into a prosperous family in

Pearl Buck's *The Good Earth;* moves with his wife to a big city because of their local unpopularity as grasping landlords in *Sons;* his sybaritic, parasitic ways continue in *A House Divided.*

Nung Wen (Wang the Second, Wang the Merchant) Grasping and tight-fisted mercantilist in Pearl Buck's *The Good Earth;* his successful business activities continue in *Buck's Sons* and *A House Divided.*

Arthur Nunheim (Albert Norman)   Petty crook, stool pigeon, associate of Julia Wolfe's, and murder victim in Dashiell Hammett's *The Thin Man.*

Miriam Nunheim   Volatile wife of Arthur Nunheim in Dashiell Hammett's *The Thin Man.*

Cedric Nunnery   Youth whose disappearance leads to Eck Snopes's death in William Faulkner's *The Town.*

Nu-Nu   Member of the savage tribe that massacres the crew of the *Jane Guy;* captured by Arthur Gordon Pym and Dirk Peters in their escape from the island of Tsalal and subsequently dies of fright as the party nears the South Pole in Edgar Allan Poe's *The Narrative of Arthur Gordon Pym.*

Miss Abigail Nutter   Maiden sister of Grandfather Nutter and manager of the Nutter household in Thomas Bailey Aldrich's *The Story of a Bad Boy.*

Grandfather (Captain) Nutter   Soldier injured in the War of 1812; grandfather of Tom Bailey in Thomas Bailey Aldrich's *The Story of a Bad Boy.*

Nymwha   Shawnee Indian medicine man who serves as Salathiel Albine's mentor in Hervey Allen's *The Forest and the Fort.*

O See Lila Swallow.

O Daughter of Nimni and Ohiro-Moldona-Fivona in Herman Melville's *Mardi*.

Dr. Oakenburg (Oakenburger) Root doctor traveling with Lieutenant Porgy to join Francis Marion in William Gilmore Simms's *The Partisan*.

Dorinda (Dorindy, Dorrie) Oakley Strong-willed woman seduced, impregnated, and abandoned by Jason Greylock; struggles for revenge by succeeding as a dairy farmer; marries Nathan Pedlar in Ellen Glasgow's *Barren Ground*.

Eudora Abernethy Oakley Mother of Dorinda, Josiah, and Rufus Oakley; following the death of her missionary lover, marries into a life of hard, monotonous work and crazed African dreams in Ellen Glasgow's *Barren Ground*.

Francis (Frank) Oakley Wastrel and half brother of Maurice Oakley; falsely accuses Berry Hamilton of stealing in Paul Laurence Dunbar's *The Sport of the Gods*.

Joshua Oakley Father of Dorinda, Josiah, and Rufus Oakley; looks like John the Baptist; poor, humble, slow-witted man who lives as a slave of the land and is distant from his daughter in Ellen Glasgow's *Barren Ground*.

Josiah Oakley Elder brother of Dorinda Oakley in Ellen Glasgow's *Barren Ground*.

Col. Maurice Oakley Genteel southern landowner and employer of Berry Hamilton; believes the lie of his half brother that Hamilton stole money in Paul Laurence Dunbar's *The Sport of the Gods*.

Phoebe Thynne Oakley Daughter of Mortimer Thynne; marries Tom Oakley in Australia; leaves her husband and their child and returns to England in Charles Nordhoff and James Norman Hall's *Botany Bay*.

Rufus Oakley Handsome, spoiled younger brother of Dorinda Oakley; kills a man over a game of cards in Ellen Glasgow's *Barren Ground*.

Tom Oakley English highwayman imprisoned in Australia; escapes from the penal colony and returns to England, but is caught and hanged when he resumes his old ways in Charles Nordhoff and James Norman Hall's *Botany Bay*.

Camille Oaks Sexy, gorgeous blonde who works as a stripper in men's clubs and who, as a passenger on Juan Chicoy's bus, instantly becomes the center of attention of some men on the bus, to her dismay, in John Steinbeck's *The Wayward Bus*.

Kayo Obermark Slovenly but bright student who instructs Augie March about the bitterness in the chosen thing in Saul Bellow's *The Adventures of Augie March*.

Count Kurt von Obersdorf Austrian count and banker; lover of Fran Dodsworth in Sinclair Lewis's *Dodsworth*.

Ford Obert Painter and social observer in Henry James's *The Sacred Fount*.

O'Brien One of the soldiers who tries to buy or steal the pistol in the possession of Richard Mast in James Jones's *The Pistol*.

Bernice (Mrs. W. B.) O'Brien Favorite correspondent of Annabel Williams; mother of Echo O'Brien in James Leo Herlihy's *All Fall Down*.

Echo Malvina O'Brien Daughter of Bernice O'Brien and lover of Berry-berry Williams; dies in an automobile accident in James Leo Herlihy's *All Fall Down.*

Harvey O'Brien Rival of Homer Zigler on the staff of the *Denver Call* in Clyde Brion Davis's *The Great American Novel.*

Mackate (Black Gown) Ockola Indian conjurer in James Kirke Paulding's *Koningsmarke.*

Dr. Matthew O'Connor Family physician to the Ryders and lover of Molly Dance in Djuna Barnes's *Ryder.*

Dr. Matthew O'Connor Transvestite Irishman from San Francisco who narrates much of Djuna Barnes's *Nightwood.*

Florinda (Splutter) O'Connor Artist's model in love with Billie Hawker in Stephen Crane's *The Third Violet.*

Mary O'Crawley Twice-widowed boardinghouse proprietor and second wife of Patrick Dennis Moore in Betty Smith's *Maggie-Now.*

Octavius Nephew and later the adopted son of Caesar in Thornton Wilder's *The Ides of March.*

O'Daddy See Rhino Gross.

Harry O'Dell Owner of the Friendly Hearth Wood Yard and uncle of Lorena Hessenwinkle in Josephine Pinckney's *Three O'Clock Dinner.*

Marcia Mae Hunt O'Donnell Older widowed daughter of Nan and Jason Hunt and former fiancée of Duncan Harper, whom she jilted although she still loved him, in Elizabeth Spencer's *The Voice at the Back Door.*

James Michael (Big Boy) O'Doul Powerful Chicago criminal in William Riley Burnett's *Little Caesar.*

Patsy O'Dowd Bowery bartender famous for insulting wealthy patrons in Henry Miller's *Black Spring.*

Irene (Reenie) O'Farron Best friend and coworker of Margy Shannon; wife of Salvatore De Muccio in Betty Smith's *Tomorrow Will Be Better.*

Maizie O'Farron Loving but difficult mother of Reenie O'Farron in Betty Smith's *Tomorrow Will Be Better.*

Dorothea O'Faye Mother of Marion Faye; holds court at The Hangover in Norman Mailer's *The Deer Park.*

Peggy O'Flagherty Housekeeper for the Dalton family in Richard Wright's *Native Son.*

Constance Ogden Pretty, spoiled daughter of wealthy parents; infatuated with Frank Ellinger, whom she eventually marries, in Willa Cather's *A Lost Lady.*

George Ogden Bank cashier who marries Abbie Brainard after the death of his first wife, Jessie Bradley, in Henry Blake Fuller's *The Cliff-Dwellers.*

Mary Ogden See Countess Marie Zattiany.

James (Jim) Oglethorpe Son of Jane Oglethorpe and father of Janet Oglethorpe; advised by Lee Clavering to educate Janet about the real world in Gertrude Atherton's *Black Oxen.*

Jane Oglethorpe Girlhood friend of Mary Ogden and self-sacrificing sexagenarian in Gertrude Atherton's *Black Oxen.*

Janet Oglethorpe Self-assured but shallow flapper and granddaughter of Jane Oglethorpe; youthful rival of Mary Ogden for the love of Lee Clavering in Gertrude Atherton's *Black Oxen.*

Jem Oglethorpe Wealthy rival of Billie Hawker for the affection of Grace Fanhall in Stephen Crane's *The Third Violet.*

Violet Ogure Prostitute who refuses to move to Wahiawa with Robert E. Lee Prewitt after his transfer to G Company in James Jones's *From Here to Eternity.*

Gerald O'Hara Irish immigrant who acquires the Georgia plantation Tara in a poker game; father of Scarlett O'Hara in Margaret Mitchell's *Gone with the Wind.*

Larry (Danny Richman) O'Hara San Francisco bookstore owner and drinking buddy of Leo Percepied in Jack Kerouac's *The Subterraneans;* mentioned in *Book of Dreams.*

Scarlett O'Hara Heroine married first to Charles Hamilton, then to Frank Kennedy, and finally to Rhett Butler; struggles to survive the horrors of Reconstruction in Margaret Mitchell's *Gone with the Wind.*

Tim O'Hara Printer uncle of Mac who takes him to Chicago as a boy, teaches him the printing trade, and encourages his development as a radical in John Dos Passos's *U.S.A.* trilogy.

Ohiro-Moldona-Fivona Wife of Nimni in Herman Melville's *Mardi.*

Bernie Ohls Sheriff's deputy in Raymond Chandler's *The Long Goodbye.*

Oh-Oh Ugly antiquarian on Padulla in Herman Melville's *Mardi.*

Mary Martha O'Keefe Common-law wife of Jarcey Pentacost; rescues Jarcey when the Kreggs try to burn him out, moves with him to Beulah, but later leaves with a land agent in Mary Lee Settle's *O Beulah Land.*

O-lan Wife of Wang Lung; achieves her greatest satisfaction from having borne children and from living to witness the marriage of her oldest son in Pearl Buck's *The Good Earth.*

Old Ben   Venerable bear in William Faulkner's *Go Down, Moses.*

Old Hundred (John)   Coachman at Canema plantation; first person to die in the cholera epidemic in Harriet Beecher Stowe's *Dred.*

Old Hurricane   See Major Ira Warfield.

Old Lord   See Lord Hwang.

Old Man   The Mississippi River in William Faulkner's *The Wild Palms.*

Old Running Water   Proprietor of the Lafayette Street warehouse who fires Hank Austin in Albert Halper's *Union Square.*

Master Oldale   Tavern keeper in James Kirke Paulding's *Koningsmarke.*

Sally Oldham   See Sally Oldham Collier.

Old Mammy Phillis   Black housekeeper in James Kirke Paulding's *Westward Ho!*

Salvador Hassan (After Birth Tycoon, K. Y. Ahmed, Pepe El Culito, Hassan, Placenta Juan) O'Leary   Liquefactionist and possible secret Sender engaged in numerous international schemes; uses various aliases in William S. Burroughs's *Naked Lunch.*

Sergeant O'Leary   Soldier on the thirty-six-mile hike who annoys Lieutenant Culver by defending Colonel Templeton in William Styron's *The Long March.*

Countess Ellen Olenska   Granddaughter of Catherine Mingott and cousin of May Welland; leaves her abusive Polish husband and returns to her family in New York, where she falls in love with Newland Archer, her cousin's fiancé, in Edith Wharton's *The Age of Innocence.*

Olga   Russian shoemaker; provides free meals for Henry Miller that always begin with soup in Henry Miller's *Tropic of Cancer.*

Antonio Olivares   Wealthy don who contributes to Bishop Latour's cathedral fund in Willa Cather's *Death Comes for the Archbishop.*

Isabella Olivares   Wife of Antonio Olivares; forced to reveal her age in order to keep her husband's estate in Willa Cather's *Death Comes for the Archbishop.*

Olivia   Lover of Marius and rival to Hipparchia in H. D.'s *Palimpsest.*

Ollentangi   Aged warrior and sage in James Kirke Paulding's *Koningsmarke.*

Ollie (Ollie Miss)   Farmhand employed by Uncle Alex, lover of Jule, and mother out of wedlock of Jule Jackson in George Wylie Henderson's *Ollie Miss* and *Jule.*

Hans Olsa   Immigrant Norwegian farmer and friend of Per Hansa; his deathbed wish for a minister causes the death of his friend Per in O. E. Rölvaag's *Giants in the Earth.*

Sörine (Sörinna) Olsa   Wife and then widow of Hans Olsa in O. E. Rölvaag's *Giants in the Earth;* neighbor and confessor to the Norwegian community in *Peder Victorious;* appears in *Their Father's God.*

Axel Olsen   Copenhagen artist who paints a portrait of Helga Crane and proposes to her, but is rejected, in Nella Larsen's *Quicksand.*

Anita O'Malley   Tragic widow of a general and lover of a goatherd, both of whom died because of their love for her; forced by her father to go on the stage, she becomes famous for her coldness and self-isolation in Josefina Niggli's *Mexican Village.*

O'Mara   Friend and chief assistant of Henry Miller at the telegraph company; recently returned from the Philippines in Henry Miller's *Tropic of Capricorn.*

Dallas O'Mara   Artist and friend of Dirk DeJong in Edna Ferber's *So Big.*

One-armed Pete   Western bank robber whose clothes Berkeley steals during a hotel fire in Samuel Langhorne Clemens's *The American Claimant.*

Oneco   Son of the Pequod chief Mononotto, brother of Magawisca, and husband of the Puritan Faith Leslie in Catharine Maria Sedgwick's *Hope Leslie.*

One Eye   Dog; mate of Kiche and father of White Fang in Jack London's *White Fang.*

Louis One Eye   Gangster, Tammany Hall employee, and pigeon fancier in Michael Gold's *Jews without Money.*

Annie Brandon O'Neill (Neill)   Daughter of Stuart Brandon and niece of Mamie Brandon; comes to Beulah as an impoverished orphan with the hope of marrying Peregrine Lacey Catlett; remains there as a neurotic spinster, having an affair with Big Dan O'Neill (whom she ostensibly scorns); marries O'Neill after his wife has died and she has spent a year in Cincinnati "for her Brandon nerves" in Mary Lee Settle's *Know Nothing.*

Big Dan O'Neill (Neill)   Irish lifter at Peregrine Lacey Catlett's salt furnace; marries Annie Brandon, becomes a respectable innkeeper, and changes his name to satisfy Annie and their son, Dan Neill, in Mary Lee Settle's *Know Nothing.*

Little Dan O'Neill   See Dan Neill.

Danny O'Neill   Boy who hangs around and admires Studs Lonigan in James T. Farrell's *Young Lonigan;* attends the University of Chicago and escapes the old neighborhood in *The Young Manhood of Studs Lonigan.*

Marie O'Neill   See Belinda.

Molly O'Neill   Younger sister of Dan Neill in Mary Lee Settle's *Know Nothing.*

Nubby O'Neill   Criminal who introduces Cass McKay to the criminal life and shares a cell with him in El Paso in Nelson Algren's *Somebody in Boots.*

Teeny O'Neill   Younger sister of Dan Neill and first sexual partner of Johnny Catlett in Mary Lee Settle's *Know Nothing.*

Fospe and Terese Ontstout   Impoverished citizens in James Kirke Paulding's *Koningsmarke.*

Orchis (Doleful Dumps)   Shoemaker who wins a lottery and forces China Aster to accept a loan in Herman Melville's *The Confidence-Man.*

Matt Ord   Airplane builder in William Faulkner's *Pylon.*

Teague Oregan (O'Regan)   Ambitious and ignorant servant of Captain John Farrago; follows afoot behind Farrago's horse as he and his master tour the country; becomes involved in numerous careers, to his master's embarrassment, in Hugh Henry Brackenridge's *Modern Chivalry.*

O'Reilly   Irish lawyer and politician; relative of Mary Monahan; attempts to blackmail George Apley in John P. Marquand's *The Late George Apley.*

Orestes   Son of Agamemnon and Clytemnestra; in the name of duty, avenges his father's murder by killing Clytemnestra and her lover Aegisthus; violates the law of hospitality by killing Pyrrhus; runs off with Hermione in John Erskine's *The Private Life of Helen of Troy.*

Jose O'Riely   Married Spanish artist with whom Eveline Hutchins has an affair in John Dos Passos's *U.S.A.* trilogy.

Oris   Sun-colored Englishwoman who tries to bring poetry into Marietta McGee-Chavéz's Spain in William Goyen's *In a Farther Country.*

Edward (Ed) Orlin   Employee of Janoth Enterprises who is assigned by George Stroud to stake out Gil's Tavern in the search for the unidentified witness to Pauline Delos's murder; a narrator of Kenneth Fearing's *The Big Clock.*

Captain Robert Orme   Arrogant aide de camp to General Braddock; injured but survives the expedition to Fort Duquesne in Mary Lee Settle's *O Beulah Land.*

Ormond   Mysterious figure whose designs on Constantia Dudley lead him first to aid the Dudley family and then to instigate the murder of Stephen Dudley; killed by Constantia in Charles Brockden Brown's *Ormond.*

Violet Ames (Mother) Ormsby   Audacious representative of American Motherhood; asked by the navy to dedicate the USS *Ormsby* in Wright Morris's *Man and Boy.*

Virgil Ormsby   Son of Violet Ames and Warren K. Ormsby killed in World War II; the USS *Ormsby* is named after him in Wright Morris's *Man and Boy.*

Warren K. Ormsby   Husband of Violet Ames Ormsby and father of Virgil Ormsby in Wright Morris's *Man and Boy.*

Shad O'Rory   Politically powerful mobster who opposes Paul Madvig for control of the city in Dashiell Hammett's *The Glass Key.*

O'Rourke   Company detective at the Cosmodemonic Telegraph Company in Henry Miller's *Tropic of Capricorn.*

Pedro Ortega   Dance partner of Lillian Bacon; assaults Bacon and Rocky Gravo when he learns that Rocky attempted to seduce Bacon in Horace McCoy's *They Shoot Horses, Don't They?*

Hosea Ortman   Farm owner in Brand Whitlock's *J. Hardin & Son.*

Dudley (Uncle Dudley) Osborn   American picaro seeking a definition of bravery in Wright Morris's *My Uncle Dudley.*

Grace Osborn   Mother of the protagonists in Wright Morris's *The Man Who Was There, The Home Place, The World in the Attic,* and *Cause for Wonder.*

Hank Osborne   Failed novelist and onetime friend of Manley Halliday; teaches at Webster, an Ivy League college; Halliday resents Osborne's ability to pass gracefully from youth to middle age in Budd Schulberg's *The Disenchanted.*

Helen Osborne   Sister of Mildred Osborne in Paul Laurence Dunbar's *The Love of Landry.*

John Osborne   Father of Mildred and Helen Osborne in Paul Laurence Dunbar's *The Love of Landry.*

Mildred Osborne   Daughter of wealthy easterners; goes west to regain her health and falls in love with Landry Thayer, a cowboy who saves her life during a cattle stampede, in Paul Laurence Dunbar's *The Love of Landry.*

Oscar   Lion that is the major attraction in Huguenine's circus; exhibited in five towns after he dies in Walter D. Edmonds's *Chad Hanna.*

Brigid O'Shaughnessy (Miss Wonderly)   Duplicitous temptress who hires Spade & Archer first, ostensibly, to help find a missing sister and who, after Archer's murder, hires Spade to help find the jewel-encrusted statuette in Dashiell Hammett's *The Maltese Falcon.*

Sergius (Gus, Mac, Slim, Spike) O'Shaugnessy   Air force veteran and narrator of Norman Mailer's *The Deer Park.*

Terry O'Shawn   Governor of Alabama and staunch advocate of white supremacy in T. S. Stribling's *The Store.*

Robert O'Sheean   See Sugar-Boy.

Dr. Charles Osman   History professor who fails star football player Raymond Bent; loves Bent's girlfriend, Lily Sayre, in Howard Nemerov's *The Homecoming Game.*

Gilbert Osmond   Calculating dilettante and father, by his lover Madame Merle, of Pansy Osmond; marries Isabel Archer in Henry James's *The Portrait of a Lady.*

Pansy Osmond   Illegitimate daughter of Gilbert Osmond and Madame Merle; befriended by Isabel Archer in Henry James's *The Portrait of a Lady.*

Osterman   Wheat grower in the San Joaquin Valley who fails to influence the state commission regulating railroad shipping rates and who dies during a gunfight with the railroad's agents in Frank Norris's *The Octopus.*

Ramón (The Greek) Otero   Mexican member of the Vettori gang dedicated to Rico Bandello; killed by the police in William Riley Burnett's *Little Caesar.*

Isabel Otis   Californian who manages a chicken ranch and who is forced to choose between independence and marriage to John Gwynne in Gertrude Atherton's *Ancestors.*

Frances Melissa O'Toole   Irish immigrant lover of Salathiel Albine, by whom she has a child in Hervey Allen's *Toward the Morning.*

Philip Frederick Ottenburg   Son of a wealthy Chicago family; married to an heiress and later to Thea Kronborg in Willa Cather's *The Song of the Lark.*

Ottima   One of three sisters operating a wine shop; hired to be Samuele's maid in Thornton Wilder's *The Cabala.*

Dr. Elvin R. Outerbridge   Kindly, wise elderly professor who tries to advise Lee Youngdahl in Mark Harris's *Wake Up, Stupid.*

Archy Outlaw   Son of a colonial North Carolina farmer; follows his fugitive brother Rion Outlaw to Tennessee, where Archy is captured by the Cherokee Indians and joins their tribe, in Caroline Gordon's *Green Centuries.*

Jocasta Dawson (Cassy) Outlaw   Sister of Francis Dawson and wife of Rion Outlaw; settles in Tennessee in Caroline Gordon's *Green Centuries.*

Orion (Rion) Outlaw   Son of a colonial North Carolina farmer; revolutionary who avoids hanging by settling in Tennessee in Caroline Gordon's *Green Centuries.*

Ouvrard   French banker and political manipulator in H. L. Davis's *Harp of a Thousand Strings.*

Miss Overmore   See Mrs. Beale Farange.

Doris Owen   Beautiful daughter of Israel and Martha Owen; temporarily attracted to the New York artist Dick Dale, but realizes that country ways suit her best and marries Dan Lester, her lifelong country suitor, in Sarah Orne Jewett's *A Marsh Island.*

Frederick Owen   New rector of St. John's Episcopal Church, eligible bachelor, and suitor of Sara Carroll in Constance Fenimore Woolson's *For the Major.*

Israel Owen (I)   Elderly New England farmer who is the husband of Martha Owen and the father of Doris Owen and Israel Owen II; fights to maintain the farm and his own equanimity despite his grief over the death of his son in Sarah Orne Jewett's *A Marsh Island.*

Israel Owen (II)   Son of Israel Owen I and Martha Owen; killed in the Civil War in Sarah Orne Jewett's *A Marsh Island.*

Martha (Marthy) Owen   Wife of Israel Owen I and mother of Doris Owen and Israel Owen II; yearned for an exciting life, but learns to accept the life of the farm, in Sarah Orne Jewett's *A Marsh Island.*

Barclay (Julius Caesar) Owens   American army captain fascinated with the ruins of Julius Caesar's camps, one of which he discovered, in Willa Cather's *One of Ours.*

Owl Eyes   Alcoholic guest at Jay Gatsby's parties in F. Scott Fitzgerald's *The Great Gatsby.*

Willy (Owlie) Owls   Manager of Curny Finnley in John Clellon Holmes's *The Horn.*

Widow Paarlenberg   Neighbor of Pervus and Selina Dejong; marries Klaas Pool in Edna Ferber's *So Big*.

Pablo   Leader of a partisan group that Robert Jordan leads in bridge blowing in Ernest Hemingway's *For Whom the Bell Tolls*.

Walter Pach   Translator of *History of Art* in Henry Miller's *Tropic of Cancer*.

Pacifica   Young Spanish prostitute from Panama who becomes the intimate friend and companion of Frieda Copperfield in Jane Bowles's *Two Serious Ladies*.

Clarissa Gray (Clara) Packard   Wife of Edward Packard; advocates women's relief from homemaking duties; narrator of Caroline Gilman's *Recollections of a Housekeeper*.

Edward Packard   Husband of Clarissa Packard; attorney who sympathizes with his wife's domestic problems in Caroline Gilman's *Recollections of a Housekeeper*.

Judith Paddock   Meddling wife of Zeno Paddock in James Kirke Paulding's *Westward Ho!*

Zeno Paddock   Busybody schoolmaster and editor in James Kirke Paulding's *Westward Ho!*

Paddy   Speakeasy proprietor in Nathan Asch's *Pay Day*.

Manny Padilla   Skinny Mexican who attends Crane College with Augie March; employs Augie as a textbook thief and helps him rescue Mimi Villars from near death after her visit to an abortionist in Saul Bellow's *The Adventures of Augie March*.

Paduk (Toad, Leader)   Former schoolmate and adversary of Adam Krug; ruler of the totalitarian nightmare state and head of the Ekwilist party who tries to force Krug to accept the regime publicly, but fails in Vladimir Nabokov's *Bend Sinister*.

Anson Page   Lawyer for a New York publishing company who must solve a complicated puzzle of missing royalties when he returns home to Pompey's Head, South Carolina, in Hamilton Basso's *The View from Pompey's Head*.

Clara Page   Widowed cousin of Amory Blaine in F. Scott Fitzgerald's *This Side of Paradise*.

Evelyn Page   Widowed, overprotective mother of Norman Page, whom she dominates and stifles, in Grace Metalious's *Peyton Place*.

Meg Page   Wife of Anson Page in Hamilton Basso's *The View from Pompey's Head*.

Norman Page   Shy and sheltered only son of Evelyn Page; childhood sweetheart of Allison MacKenzie in Grace Metalious's *Peyton Place*.

Rollin Page   Brother of Virginia Page and idle young clubman recently converted to Christianity in Charles M. Sheldon's *In His Steps*.

Virginia Page   Local heiress who finances a settlement house in Charles M. Sheldon's *In His Steps*.

Aristide Pailleron   Money-hungry white French professor who marries Teresa Cary in Jessie Redmon Fauset's *Comedy, American Style*.

Nerissa Paine   Night-nurse for John Laskell in Lionel Trilling's *The Middle of the Journey*.

Thomas Paine   English craftsman who migrates to America, where his passion for liberty and freedom for all men forces him to write such inflammatory works as *Common Sense, The Rights of Man,* and *The Age of Reason,* which aid the revolutionary cause, in Howard Fast's *Citizen Tom Paine.*

Adelaide Painter   American woman living in Paris for thirty years who remains avidly hostile to Gallic culture in Edith Wharton's *The Reef.*

Clara Morison Paisley   Aunt of Robert and Peter Morison; James Morison briefly considers allowing her to rear his sons upon the death of his wife in William Maxwell's *They Came Like Swallows.*

Palalakonuh   See Great World Snake.

Faith Paleologus   Housekeeper for John Bonnyfeather; seduces Anthony Adverse; lover of Marquis da Vincitata in Hervey Allen's *Anthony Adverse.*

Annie Palmer   Teacher who sells books for Sidney Wyeth and falls in love with him in Oscar Micheaux's *The Forged Note.*

Barbara Palmer, Lady Castlemaine   Cousin of the Duke of Buckingham and magnificently cunning mistress of Charles II; uses her influence and her beauty to attack her enemies and defend her position at Court in Kathleen Winsor's *Forever Amber.*

Freddie Palmer   New York hoodlum and pimp and later a wealthy politician; takes Susan Lenox to Europe as his consort; out of jealousy he causes the death of his friend and Lenox's mentor, Robert Brent, in David Graham Phillips's *Susan Lenox.*

Mildred Palmer   Upper-class woman whom Alice Adams believes to be her closest friend; breaks the friendship because Alice is too affected in Booth Tarkington's *Alice Adams.*

Palmyre (Madame Inconnue) la Philosophe   Quadroon freed slave and widow of Bras-Coupé; uses voodoo to seek revenge on Agricola Fusilier in George Washington Cable's *The Grandissimes.*

Pamphilus   Son of Simo and Sostrata; supposed to marry Philumena, but falls under the influence of Chrysis and in love with Glycerium; his introspective nature marks him as a Christian in a pre-Christian era in Thornton Wilder's *The Woman of Andros.*

Alexis Pan   Outrageous futurist poet with whom Sebastian Knight travels on a poetry-reading tour in Vladimir Nabokov's *The Real Life of Sebastian Knight.*

Pancras   Homosexual superior at Remsen Park whose attempt to seduce Coverly Wapshot leads to Wapshot's doubts about his own sexual identity in John Cheever's *The Wapshot Chronicle.*

Pani   Blind guide on Maramma in Herman Melville's *Mardi.*

Reb Yidel Pankower   Rabbi who discovers David Schearl's intellect in Henry Roth's *Call It Sleep.*

Paoli   Sergeant who turns in Richard Mast for the pistol Mast possesses in James Jones's *The Pistol.*

Paolo   Narcissistic gigolo who claims he loves Mrs. Karen Stone but runs off with an American film actress in Tennessee Williams's *The Roman Spring of Mrs. Stone.*

Paolo   Italian servant of Theodore Colville in William Dean Howells's *Indian Summer.*

Cora Smith Papadakis   Seductive wife of Nick Papadakis and lover of Frank Chambers, who helps Cora murder Nick; dies in an automobile accident in James M. Cain's *The Postman Always Rings Twice.*

Nick (the Greek) Papadakis   Restaurant owner murdered by his wife Cora and her lover Frank Chambers in James M. Cain's *The Postman Always Rings Twice.*

Nicholas (Nick, Pappy, the Greek) Papadoupalous   Restaurant owner whose scruples are questionable but who shows compassion for his ailing wife and for the Reverend MacCarland Sumpter in Robert Penn Warren's *The Cave.*

Alphonse (Al) Paquette   Bartender at the Thunder Bay Inn who sees Frederic Manion shoot Barney Quill; although he testifies for the prosecution, his testimony helps Manion in Robert Traver's *Anatomy of a Murder.*

Sal Paradise   Disenchanted writer whose idealism and dreams of travel are rekindled by Dean Moriarty; narrator of Jack Kerouac's *On the Road.*

May Parcher   Daughter of Mr. Parcher; hosts Miss Lola Pratt for a summer; encourages her male acquaintances in their pursuit of Miss Pratt in Booth Tarkington's *Seventeen.*

Mr. Parcher   Father of May Parcher; his peaceful home life is shattered by the arrival of the simpering Miss Lola Pratt in Booth Tarkington's *Seventeen.*

Doctor Parcival   Slovenly physician whose affected contempt for humanity leads him to disregard the young victim of a carriage accident in Sherwood Anderson's *Winesburg, Ohio.*

Theron Pardee   Former Union military captain who settles and establishes a law practice near Horsford County; belongs to the board that registers freedmen as voters, advises the Red Wing settlement, and serves as Hesden Le Moyne's agent in searching for the rightful owner of Mulberry Hill plantation in Albion W. Tourgee's *Bricks Without Straw.*

Matthias Pardon   Journalist who proposes marriage to Verena Tarrant in Henry James's *The Bostonians.*

Paris   Lover of Helen; killed in the Trojan War in John Erskine's *The Private Life of Helen of Troy*.

Memo Paris   Niece of Pop Fisher, lover of Bump Baily, and lover who sells out Roy Hobbs to Judge Banner in Bernard Malamud's *The Natural*.

Florence Udney Parish   Early love of Anthony Adverse; after being widowed, becomes Adverse's first wife; dies in a fire in Hervey Allen's *Anthony Adverse*.

Walter Parish   Retired New England sea captain; cousin and close friend of Miss Anna Prince in Sarah Orne Jewett's *A Country Doctor*.

A. Hopkins Parker   Former student at Devon School who set a school swimming record that Finny later breaks unofficially in John Knowles's *A Separate Peace*.

Charles Parker   Cousin who commits Spiros Antonapoulos to an insane asylum in Carson McCullers's *The Heart Is a Lonely Hunter*.

Doc Parker   Operator of a health institute racket who helps his friend Roy Earle arrange for an operation on Velma Goodhue's clubfoot in William Riley Burnett's *High Sierra*.

Mark Parker   American journalist friend of Kitty Fremont and David Ben Ami; brakes the story of children escaping to Israel on the *Exodus* in Leon Uris's *Exodus*.

Richard Parker   Mutineer who is spared when Arthur Gordon Pym, Augustus Barnard, and Dirk Peters retake the *Grampus;* when the group is adrift on the foundering vessel, he is cannibalized by his companions in Edgar Allan Poe's *The Narrative of Arthur Gordon Pym*.

Alison Parr   Estranged daughter of Eldon Parr and wife of John Hodder; independent and spirited architect in Winston Churchill's *The Inside of the Cup*.

Burt Parr   Filling station attendant and husband of Mollie Tyndale, until the marriage is annulled; tied to a tree and severely beaten in Mari Sandoz's *Capital City*.

Eldon Parr   Hypocritical church layman and rapacious businessman; father of Alison and Preston Parr in Winston Churchill's *The Inside of the Cup*.

Preston Parr   Sensitive son of Eldon Parr; driven to alcoholism and death by his father in Winston Churchill's *The Inside of the Cup*.

Eva Parrington   Spinster cousin of Harry and Amy; Latin teacher devoted to women's suffrage in Katherine Anne Porter's *Old Mortality*.

Zed Parrum   Rustic hillman and close friend of Abner Teeftallow in T. S. Stribling's *Teeftallow*.

Parthenia (Partheny)   Black nurse to the Fairchild children; invited to attend Dabney Fairchild's wedding in Eudora Welty's *Delta Wedding*.

Parthenia   Large yellow woman in a San Antonio red-light district and Augie's first date in Arna Wendell Bontemps's *God Sends Sunday*.

Seth Parton   Union officer and friend of Tobias Sears; Amantha Starr falls in love with him before she marries Sears, but Parton rejects her in Robert Penn Warren's *Band of Angels*.

Mrs. Seth Parton   See Mrs. Herman Muller.

Karl Pascal   Car mechanic and Communist; shares a concentration camp jail cell with Doremus Jessup in Sinclair Lewis's *It Can't Happen Here*.

Eugénie Pasdenion   Aging Parisian actress snubbed by the Chatelaine in Henry Blake Fuller's *The Chatelaine of La Trinité*.

Paskingoe (One-eye)   Mohawk chief in James Kirke Paulding's *The Dutchman's Fireside*.

Tony (Antonio Passalacqua) Passa   Youthful member of the Vettori mob who drives for holdups; killed by Rico Bandello in William Riley Burnett's *Little Caesar*.

Gene Pasternak   Writer who impregnates Christine and has an affair with Kathryn Hobbes in John Clellon Holmes's *Go*.

Father Pasziewski   Priest of Queenie Craven; prays on Fridays for George Brush; following Pasziewski's death, Brush receives a silver spoon from him in the mail in Thornton Wilder's *Heaven's My Destination*.

Pat   Friend and heroin connection of William Lee in New Orleans in William S. Burroughs's *Junkie*.

Adam J. Patch   Multimillionaire reformist grandfather of Anthony Patch; disinherits Anthony in F. Scott Fitzgerald's *The Beautiful and Damned*.

Anthony Patch   Alcoholic dilettante who undergoes a process of deterioration while waiting for his inheritance in F. Scott Fitzgerald's *The Beautiful and Damned*.

Gloria Gilbert Patch   Pleasure-seeking wife of Anthony Patch in F. Scott Fitzgerald's *The Beautiful and Damned*.

Mr. Patch-Withers   Substitute headmaster for the special summer session at Devon School in John Knowles's *A Separate Peace*.

Pathfinder   See Nathaniel Bumppo.

Ben Patimkin   Prosperous businessman and indulgent father of Brenda, Ron, and Julie Patimkin in Philip Roth's *Goodbye, Columbus*.

Brenda (Bren, Buck) Patimkin   Radcliffe student and lover of Neil Klugman; their affair ends when her parents discover her diaphragm in Philip Roth's *Goodbye, Columbus.*

Julie Patimkin   Spoiled younger sister of Brenda Patimkin in Philip Roth's *Goodbye, Columbus.*

Leo A. Patimkin   Lightbulb salesman and half brother of Ben Patimkin; confides in Neil Klugman in Philip Roth's *Goodbye, Columbus.*

Ronald (Ron) Patimkin   Athletic older brother of Brenda Patimkin; marries Harriet Ehrlich in Philip Roth's *Goodbye, Columbus.*

Henry (Pat) Patmore   Owner of a pool parlor and saloon who deals in illegal gambling and bootlegging in Rudolph Fisher's *The Walls of Jericho;* also appears in *The Conjure-Man Dies.*

Michael Patrick   Lost, wandering soldier who attends a performance of La Bohème and searches for love in John Horne Burns's *The Gallery.*

Ferd Pattee   Salesman and frequent drinker in Henry Miller's *Black Spring.*

Louise Patterson   Artist who is admired and collected by George Stroud and who can identify Stroud as the missing witness; a narrator of Kenneth Fearing's *The Big Clock.*

Paul   Seventeen-year-old boy who is trapped by his parents; becomes the lover of Djuna in Anaïs Nin's *Children of the Albatross* and *The Four-Chambered Heart.*

Paul   See Paul Melia.

Paul   See Typee.

Paul   Son of Lillian in Anaïs Nin's *Ladders to Fire.*

Paul   Ranch owner who employs his neighbor Johnny Mack in Edwin Corle's *Fig Tree John.*

Father Paul   French Catholic missionary on Manukura who shelters Terangi; dies in his church during the hurricane before learning that he has been ordered back to France in Charles Nordhoff and James Norman Hall's *The Hurricane.*

Melissa Paul   Illegitimate cousin of Laurentine Strange; does not know she is the half sister of her boyfriend Malory Forten in Jessie Redmon Fauset's *The Chinaberry Tree.*

Lieutenant (jg) Ed Pauley   Special friend who shares Mr. Roberts's dislike of Captain Morton in Thomas Heggen's *Mister Roberts.*

Pavel and Peter   Immigrants who left Russia in shame for having sacrificed a bride, bridegroom, and other friends to wolves in order to save themselves in Willa Cather's *My Ántonia.*

Katherine Lacey Pawling   See Katherine Lacey.

Ensign Paynter   Assistant communications officer on the USS *Caine* in Herman Wouk's *The Caine Mutiny.*

Lucius Quintus Peabody   Physician in William Faulkner's *Sartoris (Flags in the Dust), The Sound and the Fury, As I Lay Dying, The Hamlet, The Town,* and *The Reivers.*

Simeon Peake   Father of Selina Peake Dejong; gambler who is killed by a woman who intends to kill another man in Edna Ferber's *So Big.*

Pearl   Illegitimate daughter of Hester Prynne and Arthur Dimmesdale in Nathaniel Hawthorne's *The Scarlet Letter.*

Alf Pearson   White plantation owner and reputed real father of John Buddy Pearson in Zora Neale Hurston's *Jonah's Gourd Vine.*

Bruce William Pearson, Jr.   Third-string catcher for the New York Mammoths and roommate of Henry Wiggen; learns he is dying of Hodgkin's disease in Mark Harris's *Bang the Drum Slowly.*

Captain Pearson   Captain of the Serapis who surrenders to John Paul Jones in order to stop the carnage in Herman Melville's *Israel Potter.*

Hattie Pearson   See Hattie Tyson.

John Pearson   Elderly one-legged basketmaker and veteran of the War of 1812 who houses Shocky Thomson rather than see him bound over to a cruel master; falsely accused of aiding robbers in Edward Eggleston's *The Hoosier School-Master.*

John Buddy Pearson   Baptist preacher, carpenter, mayor of Eatonville, Florida, philandering husband of Lucy Potts, and hero of Zora Neale Hurston's *Jonah's Gourd Vine.*

Lucy Pearson   See Lucy Ann Potts.

Ray Pearson   Winesburg farmhand who is forced to evaluate the frustrated goals of his life when a younger worker asks him for advice in Sherwood Anderson's *Winesburg, Ohio.*

Thomas J. (Tub) Pearson   President of the Centaur State Bank and best friend of Sam Dodsworth in Sinclair Lewis's *Dodsworth.*

Idella Peck   Infant daughter of Rev. Julius W. Peck; adopted by Annie Kilburn following her father's death in William Dean Howells's *Annie Kilburn.*

Rev. Julius W. Peck   Liberal minister who stirs up the community and precipitates Annie Kilburn's social and moral awakening in William Dean Howells's *Annie Kilburn.*

Peckover   Man who works for a newspaper and part time in a dentist's office to pay for his false teeth; saves cigarette butts to smoke in his pipe in Henry Miller's *Tropic of Cancer.*

Samanthetie Pedigo   Wild young girl whom other children view with suspicion; occasional student of Louisa Sheridan in Harriette Simpson Arnow's *Mountain Path*.

John Abner Pedlar   Clubfooted son of Nathan Pedlar in Ellen Glasgow's *Barren Ground*.

Lena Pedlar   Daughter of Nathan Pedlar; appears to be over-sexed and weak-minded in Ellen Glasgow's *Barren Ground*.

Nathan Pedlar   Tall, homely man who reminds Dorinda Oakley of her father; becomes Dorinda's partner and husband in Ellen Glasgow's *Barren Ground*.

Rose Emily Milford Pedlar   First wife of Nathan Pedlar and teacher of Dorinda Oakley; faces death with illusions in Ellen Glasgow's *Barren Ground*.

Hester Pedlock   Sister-in-law and housekeeper for Andrew Mackerel; successful rival of Molly Calico for his hand in marriage in Peter De Vries's *The Mackerel Plaza*.

John Peel   Tutor of Sophia Grieve Ryder whom he impregnates and marries; father of Wendell Ryder in Djuna Barnes's *Ryder*.

Beverly Peele   Lover and then husband of Patience Sparhawk; dies from an overdose of morphine in Gertrude Atherton's *Patience Sparhawk and Her Times*.

Harriet (Hal) Peele   Sister of Beverly Peele and friend and sister-in-law of Patience Sparhawk in Gertrude Atherton's *Patience Sparhawk and Her Times*.

Patience Sparhawk Peele   See Patience Sparhawk.

Peepi   Boy ruler of Valapee in Herman Melville's *Mardi*.

Father Peitsch   Catholic priest who is critical of Preston Robinson's method of teaching in August Derleth's *The Shield of the Valiant*.

Peleg   An owner of the *Pequod* in Herman Melville's *Moby-Dick*.

Pelican   Assistant surgeon aboard the *Neversink* in Herman Melville's *White-Jacket*.

Dorothy (Doll) Pelky   Woman devoted to Dix Handley in William Riley Burnett's *The Asphalt Jungle*.

Master Sergeant Dominic (Danny) Pellerino   Crew chief for General Ira N. Beal; a seasoned enlisted veteran in James Gould Cozzens's *Guard of Honor*.

Dorothea O'Faye Pelley   See Dorothea O'Faye.

Sir Arthur (Pem) Pembroke   Rival of John Law for the love of Lady Catharine Knollys; killed by Indians in Emerson Hough's *The Mississippi Bubble*.

Pender   Sergeant who allows Richard Mast to keep the pistol he possesses in James Jones's *The Pistol*.

Garrett Pendergass (Pendergrass)   Owner of a frontier tavern and store who befriends Salathiel Albine; appears in Hervey Allen's *The Forest and the Fort* and *Bedford Village*.

Rose Pendergass   Wife of Garrett Pendergass in Hervey Allen's *The Forest and the Fort* and *Bedford Village*.

Leonora (The Lady) Penderton   Nominal wife of Captain Weldon Penderton and lover of Major Morris Langdon; bored with military life in Carson McCullers's *Reflections in a Golden Eye*.

Capt. Weldon (Captain Flap-Fanny) Penderton   Androgynous, self-tortured husband of Leonora Penderton; both attracted to and fearful of the handsome Private Ellgee Williams in Carson McCullers's *Reflections in a Golden Eye*.

Mr. Pendexter   Retired minister who questions the orthodoxy of Arthur Kavanagh in Henry Wadsworth Longfellow's *Kavanagh*.

Gabriel Pendleton   Former Confederate soldier and father of Virginia Pendleton; mild-mannered preacher who dies while trying to stop a lynching in Ellen Glasgow's *Virginia*.

Jig Pendleton   Superstitiously religious fisherman and drinking partner of Burley Coulter; his life on a shanty boat in the Kentucky River provides low comedy in Wendell Berry's *Nathan Coulter*.

Lucy Pendleton   Mother of Virginia Pendleton; naive idealist who lives in dignified poverty in Ellen Glasgow's *Virginia*.

Virginia (Jinny) Pendleton   Sentimental, loving, and provincial woman who marries Oliver Treadwell in Ellen Glasgow's *Virginia*.

Julia Peniston   Wealthy widow and paternal aunt with whom Lily Bart lives in Edith Wharton's *The House of Mirth*.

Christine Penmark   Mother of Rhoda Penmark; after discovering that she herself was an adopted child and that her natural mother was a mass murderer, she feels responsible for implanting the bad seed in Rhoda; plans Rhoda's murder and commits suicide in William March's *The Bad Seed*.

Kenneth Penmark   Husband of Christine Penmark and father of Rhoda Penmark; devastated when he returns from South America to find that his wife committed suicide and tried to kill their daughter in William March's *The Bad Seed*.

Rhoda Penmark   Remorseless eight-year-old who murders people in order to gain possessions that she thinks are rightly hers in William March's *The Bad Seed*.

Lavinia Sloper Penniman   Widowed sister of Austin Sloper and romantic, foolish aunt of Catherine Sloper; secretly encourages Morris Townsend's suit of Catherine in Henry James's *Washington Square*.

Lucretia Penniman   Author, teacher, and crusader for women's rights; friend of Cynthia Wetherell in Winston Churchill's *Coniston*.

Rose Timberlane Pennloss   Sister of Cass Timberlane in Sinclair Lewis's *Cass Timberlane*.

Pennoyer (Penny)   Penniless artist; shares an apartment with Billie Hawker in Stephen Crane's *The Third Violet*.

John Penny   Gruff city editor of the *Morning Journal* who gives Homer Zigler his first newspaper job in Clyde Brion Davis's *The Great American Novel*.

Julius Penrose   Coldly rational lawyer crippled by polio; partner and friend of Arthur Winner in James Gould Cozzens's *By Love Possessed*.

Marjorie Penrose   Alcoholic, emotional woman of disturbing sexuality; wife of Julius Penrose; has had an affair with Arthur Winner and intends to convert to Catholicism in James Gould Cozzens's *By Love Possessed*.

Jarcey Pentacost   Quaker, printer, and friend of Johnny Lacey; transported to Virginia as a felon and there begins to publish a newspaper; moves to Beulah as settler, schoolteacher, and second in command after being burned out by the Kreggs for supporting the proclamation closing Indian lands to settlers in Mary Lee Settle's *O Beulah Land*.

Mary Martha O'Keefe Pentacost   See Mary Martha O'Keefe.

Bascom Pentland   Scholar, retired preacher, and uncle of Eugene Gant in Thomas Wolfe's *Of Time and the River*.

Pepita   Orphan in the Convent of Santa Maria Rosa de las Rosas; sent by Maria del Pilar to live with Doña Maria de Montemayor; dies in the fall of the bridge in Thornton Wilder's *The Bridge of San Luis Rey*.

Leo (Ti Leo) Percepied   Alcoholic writer and lover of Mardou Fox; narrator of Jack Kerouac's *The Subterraneans*.

Camila (Micaela Villegas) Perichole   Great actress who becomes the mistress of Don Andres de Ribera, by whom she has three children; becomes a recluse after having smallpox in Thornton Wilder's *The Bridge of San Luis Rey*.

Miguel Perigua   Wild and impulsive leader of a group for the union of Pan-Africa and Pan-Asia; plots to wreck a train filled with Ku Klux Klansmen in W. E. B. Du Bois's *Dark Princess*.

Effie Perine   Secretary of Sam Spade in Dashiell Hammett's *The Maltese Falcon*.

Frederick Perkins   American tourist from Detroit who tries to use Samuele to secure entrance to private villas and sites; when he jumps over the wall at the Villa Colonna, he discovers the body of Marcantonio d'Aquilanera in Thornton Wilder's *The Cabala*.

Orville (Flash) Perkins   Uneducated friend of John Wickliff Shawnessy; dies in the Civil War in Ross Lockridge, Jr.'s *Raintree County*.

Peter Perkins   See Israel Potter.

Perrault   Elderly Frenchman who makes deceptive card boxes for faro dealers in H. L. Davis's *Beulah Land*.

Mr. Perriam   Odious millionaire lover of Ida Farange during her marriage to Sir Claude in Henry James's *What Maisie Knew*.

Charity M. Perrin   Teacher of Barry Rudd who resists the sale of the boy to the United Lymphomilloid Company; harassed by the Committee on Education, Welfare, and Public Morality for her participation in a teachers' strike years before in John Hersey's *The Child Buyer*.

Yolande Perrotti   Schoolmate of Cress Delahanty and house party participant in Jessamyn West's *Cress Delahanty*.

Nathan Perry   Superintendent of an independent mine; supporter of Grant Adams's reforms in William Allen White's *In the Heart of a Fool*.

Dr. Sam Perry   Physician to Colored Town in Maxwell, Georgia; saves Ed Anderson from a lynch mob and is willing to marry Nonnie Anderson after the death of Tracy Deen in Lillian Smith's *Strange Fruit*.

Perth   Blacksmith aboard the *Pequod* in Herman Melville's *Moby-Dick*.

Pete   Brother of Red and blackmailer/lover of Temple Drake in William Faulkner's *Requiem for a Nun*.

Pete   Bartender who seduces and deserts Maggie Johnson in Stephen Crane's *Maggie*.

Peter   See Long Ghost.

Peter   Handsome sailor aboard the *Neversink* who is flogged for fighting in Herman Melville's *White-Jacket*.

Peter   See Pavel and Peter.

Peter   Aged black carriage driver and friend of Porgy; falsely accused of murdering Robbins, until the real murderer is revealed, in DuBose Heyward's *Porgy*.

Dirk Peters   Half-breed sailor who befriends Augustus Barnard and Arthur Gordon Pym after the mutiny on the *Grampus*; accompanies Pym on the last half of his journey in Edgar Allan Poe's *The Narrative of Arthur Gordon Pym*.

Ivy (Poison Ivy) Peters   Cruel, arrogant, and unethical lawyer who uses his relationship with Marian Forrester to advance himself in Willa Cather's *A Lost Lady*.

Lymie Peters   Son of Lymon Peters and best friend of Spud Latham; attempts suicide in William Maxwell's *The Folded Leaf*.

Lymon Peters   Father of Lymie Peters; turns to drink and a transient way of life after the death of his wife and infant daughter in William Maxwell's *The Folded Leaf*.

Rollo Peters   Floor judge for the dance marathon in Horace McCoy's *They Shoot Horses, Don't They?*

Carl Peterson   Man whom Dr. Benway turns into a homosexual in William S. Burroughs's *Naked Lunch;* transformed into a woman in *The Soft Machine;* mentioned in *The Ticket That Exploded*.

Pete the Finn   Bootlegger and one of the four criminal bosses in Personville in Dashiell Hammett's *Red Harvest*.

Jenny Petherbridge   Middle-aged American widow who takes Robin Vote from Nora Flood, becomes Robin's lover, and then loses her in Djuna Barnes's *Nightwood*.

Maximilian (Arthur Phillips) Petion   Husband of Christina Jansen; leader in the Brotherhood of Destruction who serves as Gabriel Weltstein's guide to America under the Oligarchy in Ignatius Donnelly's *Caesar's Column*.

Junior Petman   Son of Marvin Petman and adolescent clairvoyant in T. S. Stribling's *Unfinished Cathedral*.

Marvin Petman   Realtor and father of Junior Petman in T. S. Stribling's *Unfinished Cathedral*.

J. Adlee Petrie   Liberal high school science teacher and cynic; marries his student Marsan Vaiden and becomes a beneficiary of the Vaiden fortune in T. S. Stribling's *Unfinished Cathedral*.

Mario (Giuseppe Lodi) Petrone   Convicted murderer who participates in the dance marathon under an assumed name; apprehended by policemen who come to watch the contest in Horace McCoy's *They Shoot Horses, Don't They?*

Petterman   Shopkeeper and deputy sheriff who trades with Agocho in Edwin Corle's *Fig Tree John*.

Pettibone   Virginia plantation owner who indirectly insults Thomas Sutpen in William Faulkner's *Absalom, Absalom!*

Pettingil   Owner of a bar and a confectionery store in Thomas Bailey Aldrich's *The Story of a Bad Boy*.

Adolphus (Dolly) Pettingill   Stutterer in Louisa May Alcott's *Little Men*.

Letitia (Litt) Pettingill   Mountaineer loved inordinately by Fee Guthrie in Mary Noailles Murfree's *In the "Stranger People's" Country*.

Adélaïde-Hortense-Aimée Peyronnette   Daughter of Madame Léonie Peyronnette and mother of Mayotte; contracts pleurisy and dies two years after her marriage to Louis Desrivières in Lafcadio Hearn's *Youma*.

Léonie Peyronnette   Mother of Aimée Peyronnette and grandmother of Mayotte; discourages the romance between her slave Youma and Gabriel in Lafcadio Hearn's *Youma*.

Bena Peyton   Plump and valuable friend of Jenny Blair Archbald; brags about her wealth and is curious about sexual matters in Ellen Glasgow's *The Sheltered Life*.

Jeanette Peyton   Cousin of Peyton Dunwoodie and maiden aunt of Frances, Henry, and Sarah Wharton in James Fenimore Cooper's *The Spy*.

Tiff (Old Tiff) Peyton   Slave of Sue Peyton Cripps; protects Cripps's children from their depraved father after Cripps's death by securing a Christian education for them and by fleeing with them to Dred Vesey's camp and then to New England in Harriet Beecher Stowe's *Dred*.

Fatty Pfaff   Medical school classmate of Martin Arrowsmith; becomes an obstetrician in Sinclair Lewis's *Arrowsmith*.

Othman Pfegel   Councilman in James Kirke Paulding's *Koningsmarke*.

Pharaoh   Egyptian ruler, grandfather of Moses, and enslaver of the Hebrews in Zora Neale Hurston's *Moses, Man of the Mountain*.

Pharoah   Slave on the Trosser plantation in Arna Wendell Bontemps's *Black Thunder*.

Benny Phelps   Daughter of Silas and Sally Phelps; courted by Brace Dunlap against her parents' wishes in Samuel Langhorne Clemens's *Tom Sawyer, Detective*.

Philadelphy   Sartoris servant and wife of Loosh in William Faulkner's *The Unvanquished*.

Père Philéas   Hardworking priest of St. Médard parish; rears the young orphan Cribiche in Grace King's *The Pleasant Ways of St. Médard*.

Philemon   Female slave belonging to Sally Lacey; accompanies the Laceys to Beulah and finally back to the Tidewater in Mary Lee Settle's *O Beulah Land*.

Philip   German who sings "Tristan and Isolde" on the Provincetown beach; one of Sabina's lovers in Anaïs Nin's *A Spy in the House of Love*.

Philip Brother of Hipparchia; killed by Romans in H. D.'s *Palimpsest*.

Uncle Philip Witness to all family events in Anaïs Nin's *Children of the Albatross*.

Philippe of Orléans (Duke of Orléans, Grace Philippe) Regent of France whose greed destroys the banking system in Emerson Hough's *The Mississippi Bubble*.

Mrs. Philipson Cook for Clarissa and Edward Packard; fired for dishonesty in Caroline Gilman's *Recollections of a Housekeeper*.

Arthur Phillip Royal navy captain who becomes the first governor of the Australian penal colony; revered by the convicts for treating them as humanely as possible in Charles Nordhoff and James Norman Hall's *Botany Bay*.

Arthur Phillips See Maximilian Petion.

Philocles Aged and insane sea captain and friend of Chrysis, who provides for his support, in Thornton Wilder's *The Woman of Andros*.

Philumena Daughter of Chremes; supposed to marry Pamphilus in Thornton Wilder's *The Woman of Andros*.

Phineas (Finny) Outstanding natural athlete who breaks his leg in a fall from a tree; dies during surgery when his leg is being set after a second break in John Knowles's *A Separate Peace*.

Phoebe (Fibby) Wife of Roscius and mother of Thucydides in William Faulkner's *Go Down, Moses*.

Luigi Piani Italian ambulance driver who remains with Frederic Henry during the retreat from Caporetto in Ernest Hemingway's *A Farewell to Arms*.

Dr. Almus Pickerbaugh Director of Public Health in Nautilus, Iowa, who employs Martin Arrowsmith and is later elected to Congress in Sinclair Lewis's *Arrowsmith*.

Picklock French soldier in William Faulkner's *A Fable*.

Herbert (Bert) Pierce Formerly successful developer who loses his money in the depression; first husband of Mildred Pierce; remarries Mildred following her divorce from Monty Beragon in James M. Cain's *Mildred Pierce*.

Loren Pierce Wealthy businessman and tightfisted church trustee who conspires with Erastus Winch against Levi Gorringe in Harold Frederic's *The Damnation of Theron Ware*.

Mildred Pierce Divorced woman who works her way to success, only to have her money drained away by the men in her life and by her demanding daughter Veda Pierce in James M. Cain's *Mildred Pierce*.

Moire (Ray) Pierce Daughter of Herbert and Mildred Pierce; dies in James M. Cain's *Mildred Pierce*.

Veda Pierce Snobbish, social-climbing daughter of Herbert and Mildred Pierce; ashamed of her mother's working-class background; becomes a famous singer and betrays her mother by sleeping with Mildred's husband, Monty Beragon, in James M. Cain's *Mildred Pierce*.

Blind Pig (Piggy-O) Blind, filthy drug deliverer and later drug dealer in Nelson Algren's *The Man with the Golden Arm*.

Pig Butcher Devoted follower of Wang the Tiger in Pearl Buck's *Sons* and *A House Divided*.

Pigg-O See Blind Pig.

Lorinda (Linda, Lindy) Pike Tavernkeeper, suffragist, pacifist, and mistress of Doremus Jessup in Sinclair Lewis's *It Can't Happen Here*.

Piko Joint king, with Hello, of Diranda; they control the population size by holding deadly games in Herman Melville's *Mardi*.

Mary Pilant Former hostess at the Thunder Bay Inn, girlfriend of Barney Quill, and proprietor of the inn after Quill's death in Robert Traver's *Anatomy of a Murder*.

Pilar Former mistress of matadors; gypsy woman and leader of partisan band in Ernest Hemingway's *For Whom the Bell Tolls*.

Madre Maria del Pilar Abbess at the Convent of Santa Maria Rosa de las Rosas, where she has watched Pepita, Manuel, and Esteban grow up; becomes a comforter for Camila Perichole and Doña Clara de Montemayor after their losses in Thornton Wilder's *The Bridge of San Luis Rey*.

Pills Surgeon's steward aboard the *Neversink* in Herman Melville's *White-Jacket*.

Pilon Penniless, opportunistic friend of Danny; rents one of Danny's houses without really paying rent; his chief interest in life is obtaining liquor in John Steinbeck's *Tortilla Flat*.

July Pinesett Gambler who is the fun-loving twin of June Pinesett, husband of Mary Pinesett, father of Unexpected Pinesett, and conjured lover of Cinder in Julia Peterkin's *Scarlet Sister Mary*.

June Pinesett Hardworking twin of July Pinesett and father, by Mary Pinesett, of Seraphine Pinesett in Julia Peterkin's *Scarlet Sister Mary*.

Mary (Sister Mary) Pinesett Ward of Maum Hannah, wife of July Pinesett, rival of Doll and Cinder, and lover of June Pinesett and others; excommunicated from Heaven's Gate Church for sexual indiscretions, but later rebaptized, in Julia Peterkin's *Scarlet Sister Mary*.

Seraphine Pinesett Illegitimate daughter of Mary Pinesett and June Pinesett in Julia Peterkin's *Scarlet Sister Mary.*

Unexpected (Unex) Pinesett Son of Mary and July Pinesett; dies in childhood in Julia Peterkin's *Scarlet Sister Mary.*

Mimi Pinseau (Pinson) Spinster who runs a small school in her home to support herself and her widowed father in Grace King's *The Pleasant Ways of St. Médard.*

Uncle Pio Discoverer of Camila Perichole, whom he trained to become one of the world's great actresses; trains her son Don Jaime de Ribera; dies in the fall of the bridge in Thornton Wilder's *The Bridge of San Luis Rey.*

Piotr (Pierre Bouc, Zsetflani) Soldier in William Faulkner's *A Fable.*

Pip (Pippin) Alabama black man who becomes insane and who is befriended by Ahab in Herman Melville's *Moby-Dick.*

Hans (I Drink, Minikoue) Pipe Drunken, trouble-making Indian in James Kirke Paulding's *The Dutchman's Fireside.*

Christina Piper Daughter of Heer Peter Piper and beloved of Koningsmarke in James Kirke Paulding's *Koningsmarke.*

Edith Piper Shrewish sister of Heer Peter Piper in James Kirke Paulding's *Koningsmarke.*

Heer Peter (Pepper Pot Peter) Piper Governor of Elsingburgh, New Sweden, in James Kirke Paulding's *Koningsmarke.*

Pipistrello Blind husband of Arsella; killed by a falling boulder during a walk with Adeppi in John Hawkes's *The Goose on the Grave.*

Annie and Bill Pippinger Parents of Judith, Lizzie May, and Luella Pippinger in Edith Summers Kelley's *Weeds.*

Judith Pippinger See Judith Pippinger Blackford.

Lizzie May and Luella Pippinger Twin daughters of Annie and Bill Pippinger and sisters of Judith Pippinger in Edith Summers Kelley's *Weeds.*

Pirate Huge, broad, bearded wood seller who lived in a deserted chicken house with his five dogs before Pilon persuaded him to live in Danny's house in an attempt by Pilon to acquire Pirate's stashed money in John Steinbeck's *Tortilla Flat.*

Pitch (Coonskins) Bachelor backwoodsman who buys a boy worker in Herman Melville's *The Confidence-Man.*

Lemuel Pitkin Teenaged Vermonter who, in trying to make his fortune, is victimized by almost everyone in Nathanael West's *A Cool Million.*

James Elmo (Dummy) Pitts Deaf-mute witness in the trial of Luther Eustis; narrates part of Shelby Foote's *Follow Me Down.*

Miz Pitts Homesteader on an island in the Mississippi River; mother of Dummy Pitts in Shelby Foote's *Follow Me Down.*

Otto (Gordon) Pivner Aspiring playwright who takes up with Esther Gwyon in William Gaddis's *The Recognitions.*

Placenta Juan See Salvador Hassan O'Leary.

Mars Plasair Tubercular old slave on the plantation at Bréda in Arna Wendell Bontemps's *Drums at Dusk.*

Stephanie Platow Actress and lover of Forbes Gurney and Frank Cowperwood in Theodore Dreiser's *The Titan.*

Leo Platt Dumur County locator and suitor of Libby Slogum in Mari Sandoz's *Slogum House.*

Catharine Pleyel See Catharine Pleyel Wieland.

Henry Pleyel Beloved of Clara Wieland; misled by Carwin to doubt Clara's purity, although he ultimately marries her in Charles Brockden Brown's *Wieland.*

Plotinus (Welsh) Plinlimmon Author of *Ei*, a volume of lectures that includes "Chronometricals and Horologicals," in Herman Melville's *Pierre.*

Manny Plinski Seventeen-year-old who puts turtles into Will Brady's pockets and assists Brady as Santa Claus's helper in Wright Morris's *The Works of Love.*

Hope Plowman Sincere and honest wife of Noah Ackerman; her positive influence furnishes his life with meaning and dedication to higher values in Irwin Shaw's *The Young Lions.*

Zeddy Plummer Buddy of Jake Brown and lover of Gin-head Susy in Claude McKay's *Home to Harlem.*

Liza Pnin See Dr. Elizaveta Innokentievna Bogolepov Pnin Wind.

Timofey (Timosha) Pavlovich Pnin Émigré professor of Russian at Waindell College; his trials in adjusting to life in America form the basis of Vladimir Nabokov's *Pnin.*

Pocahontas Indian princess deflowered by Captain John Smith in John Barth's *The Sot-Weed Factor.*

Jim Pocock Husband of Sarah Newsome Pocock; controls the Newsome business in Woollett, Massachusetts, during Chad Newsome's absence in Europe; sent to Europe to retrieve Chad in Henry James's *The Ambassadors.*

Mamie Pocock Sister of Jim Pocock; encouraged by Mrs. Newsome to marry Chad Newsome, whom she is sent to Paris to retrieve; becomes engaged to John Little Bilham in Henry James's *The Ambassadors.*

Sarah (Sally) Newsome Pocock   Sister of Chad Newsome and wife of Jim Pocock; sent to Paris to retrieve Chad in Henry James's *The Ambassadors.*

Arthur (Don Arturo) Poinsett   Handsome young man who tries to set wills and inheritances straight in Bret Harte's *Gabriel Conroy.*

Poky   Tahitian who befriends Typee in Herman Melville's *Omoo.*

Morris Polatkin   Manager of Olivia Lattimore in Mary Austin's *A Woman of Genius.*

Polchek   Soldier who betrays Stefan in William Faulkner's *A Fable.*

Tom Polhaus   Police detective who is investigating the murder of Miles Archer and Floyd Thursby in Dashiell Hammett's *The Maltese Falcon.*

Tris Polk   Cattleman and suitor of Morissa Kirk in Mari Sandoz's *Miss Morissa.*

Asinius Pollio   Confidential agent of Caesar; risks his life to defend Caesar in an early assassination attempt in Thornton Wilder's *The Ides of March.*

Guy Pollock   Gopher Prairie lawyer and intellectual in Sinclair Lewis's *Main Street.*

Polly   Scullery maid for Clarissa and Edward Packard; led into dishonesty by Mrs. Philipson in Caroline Gilman's *Recollections of a Housekeeper.*

Aunt Polly   Gullible guardian of Tom Sawyer in Samuel Langhorn Clemens's *The Adventures of Tom Sawyer, Adventures of Huckleberry Finn, Tom Sawyer Abroad,* and *Tom Sawyer, Detective.*

Sergeant Jefferson Polly   Confederate cavalry scout; narrates part of Shelby Foote's *Shiloh.*

Pomaree-Tanee   See Tanee.

Pomaree Vahinee I (Aimata)   Queen of Tahiti in Herman Melville's *Omoo.*

Alice Pomfret   Daughter of Fanny Pomfret; marries Humphrey Crewe in Winston Churchill's *Mr. Crewe's Career.*

Fanny Pomfret   Rich, snobby mother of Alice Pomfret; wants American politics to emulate English politics in Winston Churchill's *Mr. Crewe's Career.*

Judge Pommeroy   Uncle of Niel Herbert and close friend of and counsel to Daniel Forrester in Willa Cather's *A Lost Lady.*

Pompeia   Wife of Caesar; replaced as his wife by Calpurnia following the scandalous events at the Ceremonies of the Good Goddess in Thornton Wilder's *The Ides of March.*

Pompey the Little   Grandson of Pompey Ducklegs; jockey for Cuthbert Dangerfield in James Kirke Paulding's *Westward Ho!*

Bonnie Dee Peacock Ponder   Seventeen-year-old second wife of Daniel Ponder; leaves him after five years of marriage, then returns to oust him from his home; dies laughing when Daniel tickles her in Eudora Welty's *The Ponder Heart.*

Daniel Ponder   Youngest child of Sam Ponder; gives the Beulah Hotel to his niece and contemporary, Edna Earle Ponder; acquitted of the charge of murdering his second wife, Bonnie Dee Ponder, in Eudora Welty's *The Ponder Heart.*

Edna Earle Ponder   Unmarried manager of the Beulah Hotel in Clay, Mississippi; granddaughter of Sam Ponder and narrator of Eudora Welty's *The Ponder Heart.*

Sam Ponder   Original owner of the Beulah Hotel, his wife's inheritance; father of Daniel Ponder and grandfather of Edna Earle Ponder in Eudora Welty's *The Ponder Heart.*

Teacake (Miss Teacake) Sistrunk Magee Ponder   First wife of Daniel Ponder, whom she marries and divorces in 1944, in Eudora Welty's *The Ponder Heart.*

Phineas Delfase Ponniman   Eminent New York attorney and avowed agnostic who defends six black men accused of raping a white woman in T. S. Stribling's *Unfinished Cathedral.*

John Ponta   Brutal boxer who kills Joe Fleming in a boxing match in Jack London's *The Game.*

Edna Pontellier   Wife of Léonce Pontellier and mother of Etienne and Raoul Pontellier; artist and outsider in Creole society, who, during an infatuation with Robert Lebrun, awakens to her individuality and sensuality; walks into the ocean to her death at the end of Kate Chopin's *The Awakening.*

Etienne Pontellier   Four-year-old son of Edna and Léonce Pontellier in Kate Chopin's *The Awakening.*

Léonce Pontellier   Possessive Creole husband of Edna Pontellier and father of Etienne and Raoul Pontellier; New Orleans cotton merchant in Kate Chopin's *The Awakening.*

Raoul Pontellier   Five-year-old son of Edna and Léonce Pontellier in Kate Chopin's *The Awakening.*

Edgar (Eddie, Horn) Pool   Superlative saxophonist fallen on hard times in John Clellon Holmes's *The Horn.*

Klaas Pool   Truck farmer who marries Widow Paarlenberg following the death of his first wife Maartje in Edna Ferber's *So Big.*

Maartje Pool   Wife of Klaas Pool and mother of Roelf Pool; dies during childbirth in Edna Ferber's *So Big*.

Roelf Pool   Famous sculptor in Edna Ferber's *So Big*.

Agatha Poole   Mother of Delia Poole; moves from Excelsior, Ohio, to live with her daughter after the suicide of James Poole in Janet Flanner's *The Cubical City*.

Augie Poole   Unsuccessful cartoonist in whom a first-rate gagman was trying to claw his way out; husband of Isolde Poole; philanderer who unwittingly adopts his own bastard in Peter De Vries's *The Tunnel of Love*.

Delia Poole   New York City costume designer employed by Goldstein; heroine of Janet Flanner's *The Cubical City*.

Isolde Poole   Former actress, wife of Augie Poole, and aspiring parent who becomes pregnant after successful adoption in Peter De Vries's *The Tunnel of Love*.

James Poole   Father of Delia Poole; loses much of the family fortune and then kills himself in Janet Flanner's *The Cubical City*.

Pop   Father of Henry Wiggen in Mark Harris's *The Southpaw* and *Bang the Drum Slowly*.

Pop   Alcoholic father of Lutie Johnson; his only source of income is selling bootlegged liquor in Ann Petry's *The Street*.

Teddy (Mr. T) Pope   Homosexual actor who is forced to appear straight by movie industry executives in Norman Mailer's *The Deer Park*.

Popeye   See Popeye Vitelli.

Deacon Eeremear (Darer-of-Devils-in-the-Dark, Jeremiah, Jeremiah-in-the-Dark, Narmo-Nana) Po-Po   Native of Partoowye who hosts Typee and Long Ghost in Herman Melville's *Omoo*.

Clarence Popp   Hired hand and close friend of Otto Neumiller; helps Charles Neumiller (I) bury Otto in Larry Woiwode's *Beyond the Bedroom Wall*.

Claud Walsingham Popple   Society portrait painter who impresses Undine Spragg with his flattery and pomposity in Edith Wharton's *The Custom of the Country*.

Porcia   Wife of Brutus; suffers a miscarriage in Thornton Wilder's *The Ides of March*.

Peter Porcupine   Blackguard journalist in Pittsburgh whose pamphlet against the Jacobins brings to a head the issue of a free press in Hugh Henry Brackenridge's *Modern Chivalry*.

Porfirio   Woodcarver of Hidalgo known for his parsimony; tries to conduct a courtship on a budget in Josefina Niggli's *Mexican Village*.

Porgy   Crippled black beggar who takes Bess as a lover after Crown deserts her; kills Crown in self-defense in DuBose Heyward's *Porgy*.

Lieutenant Porgy   Officer under Francis Marion; fond of good food in William Gilmore Simms's *The Partisan;* as Captain Porgy, preoccupied with reclaiming his place and property as gentleman, cavalier, and master of Glen-Eberley plantation in Low Country South Carolina at the close of the American Revolution in *Woodcraft*.

Private Milt Porsum   Bank president and war hero duped by Bogan Murdock; helps reveal Murdock's swindle in Robert Penn Warren's *At Heaven's Gate*.

Big Joe Portagee   Army veteran and friend of Danny and Pilon; fond of living in jail, but when released, and upon hearing of Danny's good fortune, quickly becomes friendlier with Pilon and Danny in order to stay in Danny's home in John Steinbeck's *Tortilla Flat*.

Alexander Thornton (Lex) Porter   Closest friend of Alfred Eaton at Princeton and later his partner in an airplane manufacturing business in John O'Hara's *From the Terrace*.

Portia   Compassionate and free-spirited daughter of Benedict Mady Copeland; like his other children, she rebels against Copeland's teachings in Carson McCullers's *The Heart Is a Lonely Hunter*.

George (Brother George) Posey   Husband of Susan Posey and brother of Jane Posey; provides arms for a Confederate battalion; loner who kills his wife's brother and the slave who attacked his sister; drives his wife mad; afraid of death in Allen Tate's *The Fathers*.

Jane Posey   Sister of George Posey; agrees to marry Semmes Buchan but is assaulted by Yellow Jim and enters a nunnery in Allen Tate's *The Fathers*.

Aunt Jane Anne Posey   Mother of George Posey; concerned only with her personal health, has little concept of reality in Allen Tate's *The Fathers*.

Susan Buchan (Susie) Posey   Daughter of Major Lewis Buchan and wife of George Posey; instigates an assault on Jane Posey to stop Jane's marriage to Semmes Buchan; her hair turns white after the death of her brother Semmes in Allen Tate's *The Fathers*.

Sergeant-Major Postalozzi   Expectant father who loses his legs in combat in Martha Gellhorn's *Wine of Astonishment*.

Edward Postoak   Son of John Postoak; slave and butler of Isaac Jameson in Shelby Foote's *Jordan County*.

John (Chisahahoma) Postoak   Choctaw convert to Christianity; reports the Choctaws' ritual killing of two trappers in Shelby Foote's *Jordan County*.

Ann Potter   Daughter of Natty Potter, whom she accompanies to Michilimackinac; marries Langdon Towne in Kenneth Roberts's *Northwest Passage*.

Benjamin Potter   Last surviving child of Israel Potter and his wife; accompanies his aged father to the United States from England in Herman Melville's *Israel Potter*.

Harlan Potter   Powerful newspaper publisher; father of Sylvia Lennox and Linda Loring in Raymond Chandler's *The Long Goodbye*.

Israel (Peter Perkins, Yellow-hair) Potter   Farmer from the Berkshires who fights at Bunker Hill, talks with King George III, serves as courier to and for Benjamin Franklin, fights with John Paul Jones aboard the *Bon Homme Richard* against the Serapis, and sees Ethan Allen before spending most of the remainder of his life in unfortunate circumstances in London in Herman Melville's *Israel Potter*.

Joseph (Red) Potter   Young gang member who is killed in an automobile crash in William Riley Burnett's *High Sierra*.

J. Pennington Potter   Upper-class black advocate of social mixing of the races in Rudolph Fisher's *The Walls of Jericho*.

Muff Potter   Accomplice of Injun Joe; framed by Injun Joe for the murder of Dr. Robinson in Samuel Langhorne Clemens's *The Adventures of Tom Sawyer*.

Nathaniel (Natty) Potter   Alcoholic father of Ann Potter and secretary to Major Robert Rogers; accompanies Rogers to Michilimackinac in Kenneth Roberts's *Northwest Passage*.

Nora Potter   Foster cousin of Austin King; her romantic attachment to him causes complications in William Maxwell's *Time Will Darken It*.

Randolph Potter   Preening bachelor and brother of Nora Potter in William Maxwell's *Time Will Darken It*.

Reuben S. Potter   Foster relative of Austin King; entices some of King's friends into a fraudulent land scheme in William Maxwell's *Time Will Darken It*.

Senator Boyd Potter   United States senator who employs Hazel Stone; tries to take over the government by use of the atomic bomb in Mari Sandoz's *The Tom-Walker*.

Lucy Ann Potts   Wise and supportive wife of John Buddy Pearson and mother of their children in Zora Neale Hurston's *Jonah's Gourd Vine*.

Eustache Poupin   French exile, socialist, and bookbinder who befriends Hyacinth Robinson and takes him as an apprentice in Henry James's *The Princess Casamassima*.

Harry (Preacher) Powell   Psychotic murderer in search of Ben Harper's stolen money; marries Harper's widow, murders her, and pursues her children down the river; ultimately convicted of Willa Harper's murder in Davis Grubb's *The Night of the Hunter*.

Willa Harper Powell   See Willa Harper.

Alexander Powers   Superintendent of a railway maintenance shop who reports his discovery that the railway has been systematically violating regulations in Charles M. Sheldon's *In His Steps*.

Captain Powers   Former English professor serving as a Marine company commander in France during World War I and who is killed during an artillery barrage in Thomas Boyd's *Through the Wheat*.

Dorothy (Dot) Powers   Sixteen-year-old girlfriend of Cross Damon; becomes pregnant by Damon and tells his estranged wife of her intention to have him arrested for statutory rape in Richard Wright's *The Outsider*.

Mr. Powers   Hired man of Cress Delahanty's grandfather in Jessamyn West's *Cress Delahanty*.

Richard Powers   Husband of Margaret Powers; killed in World War I in William Faulkner's *Soldiers' Pay*.

Betty Prail   Girlfriend of Lemuel Pitkin; raped and sold into prostitution in Nathanael West's *A Cool Million*.

Doctor Mary J. Prance   Physician who attends Miss Birdseye in Henry James's *The Bostonians*.

Jonas W. Prather   First love and fiancé of Ellen Chesser, whom he abandons, in Elizabeth Madox Roberts's *The Time of Man*.

Helen Pratt   Good friend of Clare Bishop, acquaintance of Sebastian Knight, and typist for Mr. Goodman; helps V. in his quest for information about Knight in Vladimir Nabokov's *The Real Life of Sebastian Knight*.

Miss Lola Pratt   Lovely summer guest of the Parchers; drives the young men of the town into an adolescent frenzy, but her simpering ways disturb Mr. Parcher, in Booth Tarkington's *Seventeen*.

Polly Pratt   Gushing proselytizer for Catholicism whose emotional fervor governs her life in James Gould Cozzens's *By Love Possessed*.

Preacher   See Harry Powell.

Lon Preiser   Barrowville, Ohio, theater manager and boyfriend of Velma Goodhue in William Riley Burnett's *High Sierra*.

Mr. Prentiss   Owner of a card and printing shop where Sandy Rodgers works; his daughter allows Sandy to read literary classics in Langston Hughes's *Not Without Laughter*.

Wayne Prentiss   Head of the Employment Department at Margy Shannon's firm; attractive bachelor and devoted son to a demanding mother in Betty Smith's *Tomorrow Will Be Better*.

Ephraim (Eph) Prescott   Patronage seeker sponsored by Jethro Bass in Winston Churchill's *Coniston*.

The President   United States president and former governor of California; unscrupulous in using the powers of his office to secure his nomination of Robert Leffingwell for Secretary of State in Allen Drury's *Advise and Consent*.

Presley (Pres)   Would-be poet who fails to create the epical "Song of the West" he has attempted and who resorts to a species of transcendental philosophy to cope with the suffering that he has observed in the San Joaquin Valley in Frank Norris's *The Octopus*.

Tom Preston   Brother-in-law of Johnny Lacey; settles at Winchester and inspires Johnny to move west in Mary Lee Settle's *O Beulah Land*.

Robert E. Lee (Prew) Prewitt   Army private who transfers out of the Bugle Corps to G Company; wrongly imprisoned for assaulting Ike Galovitch; killed by sentries while trying to join the American defense against the Japanese at Pearl Harbor in James Jones's *From Here to Eternity*.

Miss Lucy Pride   Aristocratic Bostonian; guardian of Hopestill Mather and benefactress of Sonia Marburg in Jean Stafford's *Boston Adventure*.

Junius (June, Juny) Priest   Pianist influenced by Edgar Pool in John Clellon Holmes's *The Horn*.

Charles de Marigny Prieur-Denis   Kinsman of Hamish Bond included in Bond's coterie in Robert Penn Warren's *Band of Angels*.

Hester Prime   Strict Methodist spinster who adopts Frederick Brent after his father disappears and his mother dies of alcoholism; marries Eliphalet Hodges, who is less rigid religiously than she, in Paul Laurence Dunbar's *The Uncalled*.

Priming   Gunner's mate who blames White-Jacket for accidents and illnesses that have befallen members of their mess aboard the *Neversink* in Herman Melville's *White-Jacket*.

Primitivo   Member of Pablo's partisan band in Ernest Hemingway's *For Whom the Bell Tolls*.

Adeline Thacher (Addy) Prince   Daughter of old Mrs. Thacher; estranged from her family by her wildness and difficult temper; although dying of alcoholism and tuberculosis, she manages to get her child, Nan Prince, safely to Mrs. Thacher's New England farmhouse in Sarah Orne Jewett's *A Country Doctor*.

Anna (Nan) Prince   Orphaned ward of Dr. John Leslie; forgoes both marriage to George Gerry and inheritance from her rich aunt Nancy Prince to become a country doctor in Sarah Orne Jewett's *A Country Doctor*.

Anna (Nancy) Prince   Elderly, rich spinster aunt of the orphaned Nan Prince; decides too late to bequeath her house and wealth to her niece in Sarah Orne Jewett's *A Country Doctor*.

Miss Princip   Efficient secretary of Ludlow Mumm in Ludwig Bemelmans's *Dirty Eddie*.

Principino   Firstborn child of Maggie Verver and Prince Amerigo in Henry James's *The Golden Bowl*.

Priscilla (Veiled Lady)   Daughter of Moodie and half sister of Zenobia; controlled by Professor Westervelt; loves Hollingsworth and is loved by Miles Coverdale in Nathaniel Hawthorne's *The Blithedale Romance*.

Bernice Pritchard   Dainty, frigid, and headache-prone wife of Elliott Pritchard traveling to Mexico on Juan Chicoy's bus with her husband and their daughter Mildred Pritchard in John Steinbeck's *The Wayward Bus*.

Elliott Pritchard   Clannish, outwardly upright, and well-to-do businessman who, because he is taking his wife Bernice Pritchard and their daughter Mildred Pritchard on a vacation to Mexico, is a passenger on Juan Chicoy's bus in John Steinbeck's *The Wayward Bus*.

Mildred Pritchard   Daughter of Bernice and Elliott Pritchard; accompanies her parents on a vacation to Mexico; has a sexual encounter with Juan Chicoy after he leaves his stranded bus in John Steinbeck's *The Wayward Bus*.

Patrick (Pat) Pritchard   Major general at Pinetree in Beirne Lay, Jr., and Sy Bartlett's *Twelve O'Clock High!*

Gaston Probert   Frenchman who falls in love with Francie Dosson; must decide, after her interview appears in *The Reverberator*, whether to honor her or his family in Henry James's *The Reverberator*.

Jesse Lasky Proctor   Ineffectual political activist against fascism; under the influence of Charles Lawrence, shoots himself in the foot, defies Senator Joseph McCarthy, and nearly kills himself in Wright Morris's *The Huge Season*.

Major Proctor   Commander of the British garrison at Dorchester, South Carolina, in William Gilmore Simms's *The Partisan*.

Professor   Teacher aboard the *Neversink* in Herman Melville's *White-Jacket*.

Elias Proops   Veteran of the Revolutionary War, Chad Hanna's confidant and adviser, and porch sitter at the Yellow Bud Hotel in Walter D. Edmonds's *Chad Hanna*.

Gabriel (Gen'l Gabriel) Prosser   Stately young slave on the Prosser plantation; leads other slaves in a nearly successful revolt; protagonist of Arna Wendell Bontemps's *Black Thunder*.

Thomas (Marse Prosser) Prosser   Wealthy Virginia plantation owner in Arna Wendell Bontemps's *Black Thunder*.

Anita Proteus   Wife of Paul Proteus; leaves him for Lawson Shepherd in Kurt Vonnegut's *Player Piano*.

Paul Proteus   Husband of Anita Proteus and manager-engineer at Ilium Works; becomes the messiah of the revolutionary Ghost Shirt Society in Kurt Vormegut's *Player Piano*.

Anne Prouder   See Anne Sparrow.

Ephraim Prouder   Father of Zury Prouder; settles in frontier Illinois and, following the death of his wife and daughter, relinquishes his affairs to Zury in Joseph Kirkland's *Zury*.

Zury Prouder   Illinois dirt farmer whose hard character helps him become wealthy; learns humanity and compassion, finally finding happiness in marriage to Anne Sparrow, who had borne their illegitimate children, in Joseph Kirkland's *Zury*.

Willie (Man - with - hair - white - like - wind - on - water) Proudfit   Farmer who befriends and hides Barclay Munn after Munn is accused of killing a witness against Doctor MacDonald in Robert Penn Warren's *Night Rider*.

John William Prutt   President of the Second National Bank of Grand Republic in Sinclair Lewis's *Kingsblood Royal* and *Cass Timberlane*.

Hester Prynne   Wife of Roger Chillingworth, lover of Arthur Dimmesdale, and mother of Pearl; forced to wear the letter *A* to symbolize her adulterous behavior in Nathaniel Hawthorne's *The Scarlet Letter*.

Pucento   Ward of II Gufo; leads the band of soldiers escorting the prisoner into the village in John Hawkes's *The Owl*.

Jonathan Pue   Custom-house surveyor who wrote a manuscript about Hester Prynne in Nathaniel Hawthorne's *The Scarlet Letter*.

Jack Pugh   Illiterate Mississippi gambler and World War I marine private who befriends William Hicks in France in Thomas Boyd's *Through the Wheat*.

Clodia (Claudilla, Mousie) Pulcher   Intelligent socialite and gossip who attracts men, and especially Catullus; Caesar orders her out of Rome in Thornton Wilder's *The Ides of March*.

Publius Clodius Pulcher   Undisciplined troublemaker and brother of Clodia Pulcher; his sister introduces him as a votary at the all-female ceremony Mysteries of the Good Goddess, thus creating a city-wide disturbance, in Thornton Wilder's *The Ides of March*.

Henry Moulton (Harry, H. M.) Pulham   Boston aristocrat and investment counselor who adheres to the values of his social class; husband of Kay Motford Pulliam and lover of Marvin Myles; narrator of John P. Marquand's *H. M. Pulham, Esquire*.

Cornelia Motford (Kay) Pulliam   Boston aristocrat and wife of Harry Pulliam; commits adultery with Bill King in John P. Marquand's *H. M. Pulham, Esquire*.

Ensign Frank Pulver   Hero-worshipping friend decidedly influenced by Mr. Roberts's friendship, transfer, and death in Thomas Heggen's *Mister Roberts*.

Maurice (Mr. P.) Pulvermacher   Co-owner of Pulvermacher, Betschmann & Kalisch, manufacturers of Pulbetkal women's garments; first person to contract with Harry Bogen for delivery of garments during the strike Bogen has started in Jerome Weidman's *I Can Get It for You Wholesale*.

William Purcell   Surly carpenter aboard the HMS *Bounty* who thinks that Captain Bligh is responsible for the rebellion, but whose sense of duty requires him to follow Bligh in being cast adrift, in Charles Nordhoff and James Norman Hall's *Mutiny on the Bounty*; backs down from a duel with Bligh in *Men Against the Sea*.

Huldah Purdick   Teacher of Indian children at the Bois des Morts Mission; ends her engagement to Balthazar Harge in order to move to St. Paul in Sinclair Lewis's *The God-Seeker*.

Lemuel T. Purdy   Confidant of Clyde Muncy regarding the funeral of Caddy Hibbard in Wright Morris's *The World in the Attic*.

Paul Purdy   Wise and patient friend and colleague of Lee Youngdahl; wants to produce Youngdahl's play at the university in Mark Harris's *Wake Up, Stupid*.

Lord Frederick Purvis   Father of Hyacinth Robinson in Henry James's *The Princess Casamassima*.

Captain N. Purvis   American officer whose report results in Major Joppolo's reassignment to Algiers in John Hersey's *A Bell for Adano*.

Dorothy (Dot, Dottie) Pusey   Daughter of Pug Pusey; engaged to marry Tracy Deen when he is shot in Lillian Smith's *Strange Fruit*.

Pug Pusey   Father of Dorothy Pusey; owner of the Supply Store in Maxwell, Georgia, in Lillian Smith's *Strange Fruit*.

Ellen Putney   Long-suffering but loving wife of Ralph Putney; close friend of Annie Kilburn in William Dean Howells's *Annie Kilburn*.

Ralph Putney   Lawyer whose career is thwarted by his alcoholism; defends Julius W. Peck in William Dean Howells's *Annie Kilburn*.

Winthrop (Win) Putney   Invalid child of Ellen and Ralph Putney in William Dean Howells's *Annie Kilburn*.

Arthur Gordon Pym   Well-bred Nantucket youth; narrator of Edgar Allan Poe's *The Narrative of Arthur Gordon Pym.*

Alice Pyncheon   Daughter of Gervayse Pyncheon; plants posy seeds and plays the harpsichord in Nathaniel Hawthorne's *The House of the Seven Gables.*

Clifford Pyncheon   Brother of Hepzibah Pyncheon; unjustly imprisoned for the death of Jaffrey Pyncheon I in Nathaniel Hawthorne's *The House of the Seven Gables.*

Colonel Pyncheon   Patriarch of the Pyncheon family; claims the Maule land, after having Matthew Maule convicted of witchcraft; dies mysteriously in Nathaniel Hawthorne's *The House of the Seven Gables.*

Gervayse Pyncheon   Father of Alice Pyncheon in Nathaniel Hawthorne's *The House of the Seven Gables.*

Hepzibah Pyncheon   Cousin of Jaffrey Pyncheon II; runs a cent-shop in the Pyncheon house in Nathaniel Hawthorne's *The House of the Seven Gables.*

Jaffrey Pyncheon (I)   Uncle of Clifford Pyncheon and Jaffrey Pyncheon II; his death is mistakenly blamed on Clifford Pyncheon in Nathaniel Hawthorne's *The House of the Seven Gables.*

Judge Jaffrey Pyncheon (II)   Nephew of Jaffrey Pyncheon I; arranges evidence so as to convict Clifford Pyncheon of murdering Jaffrey Pyncheon I; owner of the Pyncheon house; dies mysteriously in Nathaniel Hawthorne's *The House of the Seven Gables.*

Phoebe Pyncheon   Cousin of Hepzibah and Clifford Pyncheon and of Jaffrey Pyncheon II; marries Holgrave in Nathaniel Hawthorne's *The House of the Seven Gables.*

Amanda (Pinnie) Pynsent   Poor dressmaker who is a friend of Florentine Vivier and the guardian of Hyacinth Robinson in Henry James's *The Princess Casamassima.*

Pyrrhus   Son of Achilles; killed by Orestes in John Erskine's *The Private Life of Helen of Troy.*

Cliff Quackenbush   Crew manager at Devon School in John Knowles's *A Separate Peace.*

Dr. Willoughby Quarles   President of Terwillinger College, which Elmer Gantry attends, in Sinclair Lewis's *Elmer Gantry.*

Lieutenant Commander Philip Francis Queeg   Tyrannical captain of the USS *Caine* who loses his command in a mutiny in Herman Wouk's *The Caine Mutiny.*

Queenie   Sister of Herman and Verman; her huge goiter attracts the neighborhood children, until she drives them away, in Booth Tarkington's *Penrod.*

Queen Mab (Old Deb)   Old, wise, and respected Indian woman; remains behind when other Indians depart for a more remote wilderness in Charles Brockden Brown's *Edgar Huntly.*

David (Davy) Queenslace   Anglican monk who believes that he is to write a new book of the Bible; drowns in a pond in Sinclair Lewis's *The God-Seeker.*

Queequeg (Quohog)   Cannibal who is Starbuck's harpooner and who is Ishmael's good friend; his coffin saves Ishmael's life in Herman Melville's *Moby-Dick.*

Waldo Quigley   Pump organ salesman in Jessamyn West's *The Friendly Persuasion.*

Barney Quill   Owner of the Thunder Bay Inn who is killed by Frederic Manion for allegedly having raped Manion's wife Laura in Robert Traver's *Anatomy of a Murder.*

Flora Quill   Englishwoman and proprietor of the Panamanian Hotel de las Palmas, frequented mainly by prostitutes; friend of Frieda Copperfield and Pacifica in Jane Bowles's *Two Serious Ladies.*

Geoffrey Quill   Cousin of Marjorie Morningstar; an author in Herman Wouk's *Marjorie Morningstar.*

Clare (Cue) Quilty   Famous playwright with whom Dolores Haze deceives Humbert Humbert and whom Humbert murders in Vladimir Nabokov's *Lolita.*

Jacob Quincy   Commander of the Oligarchy's air forces who sells out to the Brotherhood of Destruction and bombs the Oligarchy's army in Ignatius Donnelly's *Caesar's Column.*

Harrison Quinn   Philandering neighbor of the Charleses who romances Dorothy Wynant in Dashiell Hammett's *The Thin Man.*

Bill Quint   I.W.W. instigator sent to organize the mine workers in Personville in Dashiell Hammett's *Red Harvest.*

Peter Quint   Ghost who the governess believes influences Miles in Henry James's *The Turn of the Screw.*

Matthew Quintal   Largest and most obnoxious crewman aboard the HMS *Bounty* who, as a leader of the mutineers, nearly kills Captain Bligh before being persuaded to set him adrift in Charles Nordhoff and James Norman Hall's *Mutiny on the Bounty;* kills Minarii and is killed by Alexander Smith in *Pitcairn's Island.*

Quoin   Ill-natured quarter-gunner aboard the *Neversink* in Herman Melville's *White-Jacket.*

Rabbit   See Harry Angstrom.

Jascha Rabinowich   See Johannes Robin.

Rachel   Reliable maid of Austin and Martha King; leaves town to protect her daughter from sexual abuse but later returns to work for the Kings in William Maxwell's *Time Will Darken It.*

Rachel   See Maria.

Aunt Rachel   Elderly black woman who constantly pleads with powerful whites to keep her sons off the chain gang and to allow her to have food and shelter in W. E. B. Du Bois's *The Quest of the Silver Fleece.*

Radclyffe   See Edmund Mortimer.

Lady Radclyffe   See Amber St. Clare.

V. K. Radiff   Sewing machine salesman in William Faulkner's *The Hamlet, The Town,* and *The Mansion.* See also Suratt.

Arthur (Boo) Radley   Mysterious, reclusive neighbor and "mockingbird" who leaves gifts for Jem and Scout Finch; thwarts Bob Ewell's attempt to murder Scout and Jem in Harper Lee's *To Kill a Mockingbird.*

Radney   Mate aboard the *Town-Ho* who has an altercation with Steelkilt; killed by Moby-Dick in Herman Melville's *Moby-Dick.*

Rafael   Gypsy member of Pablo's partisan band in Ernest Hemingway's *For Whom the Bell Tolls.*

Andalous (Andy) Raffine   American painter in Paris who imagines encounters with various types of women; narrator of Lawrence Ferlinghetti's *Her.*

Captain Rafton   Former officer in the British army who befriends Helen Fairwood and gives her a tour of Karnak in H. D.'s *Palimpsest.*

Squire (Josiah Devotion, Charles Edward Montmorency) Raglan   Vicar's son turned London pickpocket; lover of Hannah Bridewell at Newgate Prison and father of the child she leaves with the Indians; transported to Virginia and bought by Peregrine Cockburn; steals Witcikti's English tomahawk as well as Peregrine's sash, horse, and silver-handled crop; becomes a frontier lawyer and is killed by Jeremiah Catlett in Mary Lee Settle's *O Beulah Land;* his grave is the basis for a local myth of tragic Indian lovers in *Know Nothing.*

Count (Rags) Ragsdale   Itinerant gambler and rival of Augie for the love of Florence Dessau in Arna Wendell Bontemps's *God Sends Sunday.*

Sue Rainey   Wealthy daughter of Colonel Tom Rainey; marries Sam McPherson, miscarries three times, and leaves her husband in Sherwood Anderson's *Windy McPherson's Son.*

Colonel Tom Rainey   President of the Rainey Arms Company who helps Sam McPherson succeed and then commits suicide in Sherwood Anderson's *Windy McPherson's Son.*

Dudley Rainsford   Temporarily insane, melancholy frontier hero in James Kirke Paulding's *Westward Ho!*

Gabriela (Gaby) Rak   Employee of the American Embassy in Warsaw who helps supply money and weapons to the Warsaw ghetto fighters; lover of Andrei Androfski in Leon Uris's *Mila 18.*

Clementina (Teeny, Tina) Lovell Ralston   Illegitimate daughter of Charlotte Lovell and Clement Spender; adopted by her aunt, Delia Ralston, when her mysterious origins prevent her from marrying a socially correct suitor in Edith Wharton's *The Old Maid*.

Delia Lovell Ralston   Wife of James Ralston and thus a member of one of the most conservative and wealthy families of old New York in Edith Wharton's *The Old Maid*.

James (Jim) Ralston   Wealthy and socially prominent husband of Delia Ralston in Edith Wharton's *The Old Maid*.

Joseph (Joe) Ralston   Cousin of Jim Ralston and fiance of Charlotte Lovell until the engagement is broken in Edith Wharton's *The Old Maid*.

Clarence (Crimson Rambler) Rambo   Class bully who is rousted by Edwin Kibbler, Jr., in Jessamyn West's *Cress Delahanty*.

Mary Rambo   Harlem woman who owns a boardinghouse where the narrator lives in Ralph Ellison's *Invisible Man*.

Arthur Ramirez   Police chief in Key Bonita, Florida, who looks after Clinton Williams in James Leo Herlihy's *All Fall Down*.

David Ramsay   Father of John Ramsay and neighbor of Allen Musgrove; Tory partisans burn his farm in John Pendleton Kennedy's *Horse-Shoe Robinson*.

John Ramsay (Ramsey)   Son of David Ramsay and beau of Mary Musgrove who helps Horse-Shoe Robinson free Arthur Butler; dies while protecting Butler from Tory marauders in John Pendleton Kennedy's *Horse-Shoe Robinson*.

Rob Ramsay   War veteran who commits suicide by walking off a pier in Henry Miller's *Black Spring*.

Mrs. Rance   American-born friend of Dotty and Kitty Lutch; travels in the Ververs' social circle in Henry James's *The Golden Bowl*.

Ben Rand   Circuit court clerk who narrates part of Shelby Foote's *Follow Me Down*.

Billie Rand   Aspiring starlet and companion of Al Manheim; becomes a prostitute in Budd Schulberg's *What Makes Sammy Run?*

Lewis Rand   Ambitious son of a tobacco roller; attorney and husband of Jacqueline Churchill; protégé of Thomas Jefferson and conspirator with Aaron Burr to rule Mexico; murders his magnanimous rival Ludwell Cary in Mary Johnston's *Lewis Rand*.

Dr. (Ran) Randall   Contentious druggist; discusses social problems with Sidney Wyeth in Oscar Micheaux's *The Forged Note*.

Elizabeth Thornwell Alvin (Betty) Randall   See Elizabeth Thornwell Alvin.

John Randolph, Earl of Almsbury   Cavalier, best friend of Bruce Carlton, and frequent companion and guide of Amber St. Clare in Kathleen Winsor's *Forever Amber*.

James Heyward (Jim) Randolph   College classmate idolized by George Webber in Thomas Wolfe's *The Web and the Rock*.

Rango   Self-destructive Guatemalan guitar player and nightclub singer; husband of Zora and lover of Djuna in Anaïs Nin's *The Four-Chambered Heart*.

Frances Rankin   See Frances Rankin Mitchell.

Judd (Juddie) Rankin   Homespun Iowa newspaper editor and author; father of Frances Rankin Mitchell, grandfather of Judson and Madeleine Mitchell, and second cousin of Adah Logan in Susan Glaspell's *Judd Rankin's Daughter*.

Basil Ransom   Cousin of Olive Chancellor; Mississippi gentleman who plans to marry Verena Tarrant in Henry James's *The Bostonians*.

Fred (Freddie) Ransome   British poet and soldier; lover of Mavis Landour and former husband of Raymonde Ransome in H. D.'s *Palimpsest*.

Raymonde Ransome   American poet living in London and formerly the wife of Freddie Ransome in H. D.'s *Palimpsest*.

Henryk Rapaport   Socialist who, despite political differences with many of those also trapped within the Warsaw ghetto, joins in the united effort to survive destruction at the hands of the Nazis in John Hersey's *The Wall*.

Kermit Raphaelson   Midget artist married to Laureen Raphaelson; Malcolm is exposed to the couple's marital problems soon after meeting them in James Purdy's *Malcolm*.

Laurel Raphaelson   Woman with a sordid past married to Kermit Raphaelson; leaves Kermit and marries Girard Girard in James Purdy's *Malcolm*.

Rartoo   Chief of Tamai in Herman Melville's *Omoo*.

Sona Rasmussen   Half-Japanese, half-Norwegian professor at Benton College and maker of welded sculpture in Randall Jarrell's *Pictures from an Institution*.

Ras the Exhorter (Ras the Destroyer)   Violent black nationalist who starts a riot in Ralph Ellison's *Invisible Man*.

Senator Silas P. Ratcliffe   Illinois senator, then Secretary of the Treasury; his, proposal of marriage to Madeleine Lee is rejected after she learns of his improper political dealings in Henry Adams's *Democracy*.

Henrietta Rathbone   Small-town dressmaker; loves Tommy Bettersworth, who turns to her when his wife, Olivia Lattimore, is away on acting engagements in Mary Austin's *A Woman of Genius*.

Adèle Ratignolle   Friend of Edna Pontellier and a "mother-woman" who bears a child every two years in Kate Chopin's *The Awakening*.

Rau-Ru (the k'la, Lieutenant Oliver Cromwell Jones)   Trusted black employee who turns against Hamish Bond in Robert Penn Warren's *Band of Angels*.

Dr. Rausch   Physician who treats Henry Miller's father and also lectures Miller on the evils of going against nature in Henry Miller's *Tropic of Capricorn*.

Gaylord Ravenal   Actor on the *Cotton Blossom* who is also a gambler; marries Magnolia Hawks in Edna Ferber's *Show Boat*.

Magnolia Hawks Ravenal   Daughter of Andy and Parthenia Ann Hawks; actress on the *Cotton Blossom* who later appears on the New York stage; marries Gaylord Ravenal, by whom she has a daughter, in Edna Ferber's *Show Boat*.

Doctor Ravenel   Father of Lillie Ravenel; his loyalty to the Union cause during the Civil War begins the process of Lillie's conversion to that cause in John William DeForest's *Miss Ravenel's Conversion from Secession to Loyalty*.

Lillie Ravenel   See Lillie Ravenel Carter.

Ravenspur   See Gerald Stanhope.

Lady Ravenspur   See Amber St. Clare.

Turner Ravis   Virtuous Victorian who breaks her engagement to Vandover when she discovers his seduction of Ida Wade and Wade's suicide in Frank Norris's *Vandover and the Brute*.

Harriet Ray   Conventional young woman who admires old New York society; seen by Mrs. Marvell as a marriage prospect for Ralph Marvell in Edith Wharton's *The Custom of the Country*.

John Ray, Jr.   Editor of the manuscript Humbert Humbert writes while in prison; author of the foreword to that published manuscript, which is Vladimir Nabokov's *Lolita*.

Bishop Rayber   Idiot child of Bernice Bishop and Mr. Rayber; inadvertently baptized by Francis Marion Tarwater in the act of drowning him in Flannery O'Connor's *The Violent Bear It Away*.

Mr. Rayber   Schoolteacher, husband of Bernice Bishop, father of Bishop Rayber, and uncle of Francis Marion Tarwater; fails in his attempt to reclaim Tarwater from the religious influence of Mason Tarwater; young Tarwater seeks out Rayber after Mason Tarwater's death in Flannery O'Connor's *The Violent Bear It Away*.

George Rayburn   Owner of the house the Tussies rent in Jesse Stuart's *Taps for Private Tussie*.

Dorothy Raycroft   Mistress of Anthony Patch when he is a soldier in World War I in F. Scott Fitzgerald's *The Beautiful and Damned*.

Raymond (Ray)   Railroad dining car waiter and intellectual who shares his knowledge with Jake Brown in Claude McKay's *Home to Harlem;* black American writer who plans to write about the expatriates living in Marseilles in *Banjo*.

Charles Raymond   White manager of the Phosphate Mining Company; former lover of Kate Wentworth, whose son, Saint Wentworth, Raymond employs, in DuBose Heyward's *Mamba's Daughters*.

Everett Raymond   Junior partner in the law firm of Veeley, Carr, and Raymond who, because he does not think that Eleanore Leavenworth killed her uncle, starts his own investigation of the case; narrator of Anna Katharine Green's *The Leavenworth Case*.

Helen Raymond   Librarian who helps Felix Fay continue his education after he drops out of high school in Floyd Dell's *Moon-Calf*.

Read   Womanizer and senior partner with Glymmer Read in Nathan Asch's *The Office*.

Christian Reagan   Private in the United States Army; a double for Agee Ward in Wright Morris's *The Man Who Was There*.

Henry (Hank) Rearden   Steel producer who invents a revolutionary new metal; joins with Dagny Taggart to build the John Galt Line in Ayn Rand's *Atlas Shrugged*.

Lillian Rearden   Wife of Henry Rearden, against whom she conspires to defeat, in Ayn Rand's *Atlas Shrugged*.

Nina (Madame Lecerf, Ninka) Toorovetz de Rechnoy   Russian woman whose letters V. finds in Sebastian Knight's apartment; V. tries to track her down after destroying the letters without reading them, according to Knight's instructions, in Vladimir Nabokov's *The Real Life of Sebastian Knight*.

Red   Bouncer murdered by Popeye; appears in William Faulkner's *Sanctuary* and *Requiem for a Nun*.

Red   Drug addict in Herbert Simmons's *Corner Boy*.

Mr. Redbrook   Reforming grassroots political organizer in Winston Churchill's *Mr. Crewe's Career*.

Eddie Win(g)field (Wing) Redburn   Major alto saxophonist in John Clellon Holmes's *The Horn*.

Wellingborough (Boots, Buttons, Jack, Jimmy Dux, Lord Stormont, Pillgarlic) Redburn   Narrator who sails to Liverpool and back to New York in Herman Melville's *Redburn*.

Red Clay (Lufki-Humma)   Natchez Indian who is an ancestor of Agricola Fusilier in George Washington Cable's *The Grandissimes*.

Fenwick (Fen, Uncle Wick) Redcliff   Father-in-law of Judith Redcliff; Charleston patriarch and entrepreneur in Josephine Pinckney's *Three O'Clock Dinner*.

Judith (Judy) Redcliff   Widow of a prominent Charlestonian; has a genteel job at the Fuel and Welfare Society in Josephine Pinckney's *Three O'Clock Dinner*.

Lucian Quintillian Redcliff   Half-brother of Fenwick Redcliff and real estate agent in Josephine Pinckney's *Three O'Clock Dinner*.

Tat Redcliff   Young brother-in-law of Judith Redcliff, part owner of several gas stations and a socialist; smitten by Lorena Hessenwinkle, whom he marries for a short time, not knowing she was his brother's lover, in Josephine Pinckney's *Three O'Clock Dinner*.

Joab Ellery Reddington   Well-educated but corrupt high school principal and clergyman who starts Gloria Wandrous sniffing ether and seduces her in John O'Hara's *Butterfield 8*.

Red-Eye   Huge, atavistic enemy of Big Tooth in Jack London's *Before Adam*.

Brian Redfield   Physician husband of Irene Redfield; charmed by Clare Kendry in Nella Larsen's *Passing*.

Irene ('Rene) Redfield   Chicago native, member of Harlem's social set, and wife of Brian Redfield; renews an acquaintance with Clare Kendry and keeps secret the knowledge that Clare is passing for white in Nella Larsen's *Passing*.

Redlaw   See Ben Redmond.

Red Man   Wrestling opponent of Laughing Boy; hopes to marry Slim Girl in Oliver La Farge's *Laughing Boy*.

Red Max   See Max.

Ben (Redlaw) Redmond   Lawyer who murders Colonel John Sartoris; appears in William Faulkner's *Sartoris (Flags in the Dust)*, *The Unvanquished*, and *Requiem for a Nun*.

Red Whiskers   Sailor aboard the *Indomitable* whom Billy Budd strikes in Herman Melville's *Billy Budd*.

Henry Reed   Neighbor and fiancé of Jane Bellmont, to whose money he is attracted; Jane rejects him in favor of George Means; later conspires with Mrs. Bellmont against Jenny Bellmont in Harriet E. Wilson's *Our Nig*.

Doctor Reefy   Winesburg physician who has a brief, platonic affair with Elizabeth Willard in Sherwood Anderson's *Winesburg, Ohio*.

Martha Goddard Reeves   School board member who speaks the Apache language and aids in spreading fear among whites concerning the ferocity of Agocho in Edwin Corle's *Fig Tree John*.

Vivian Sternwood Regan   Older daughter of General Sternwood; her husband Rusty Regan is murdered by her sister Carmen Sternwood, in Raymond Chandler's *The Big Sleep*.

Paul Reichelderfer   Yale classmate of Sidney Tate; introduces Tate to Grace Brock Caldwell in John O'Hara's *A Rage to Live*.

Rosa Reichl   Landlady of Charles Upton in Berlin in Katherine Anne Porter's *The Leaning Tower*.

Roberta Reid   See Roberta Reid Fairchild.

Frank (Weary) Reilley   Violent young man whom Studs Lonigan beats up in a fight in James T. Farrell's *Young Lonigan*; starts a fight at a football game in *The Young Manhood of Studs Lonigan*; reported to have raped a young woman in *Judgment Day*.

Reilly   Police lieutenant working with Jack Rose in Paul Cain's *Fast One*.

Harry Reilly   Socially ambitious and wealthy Irish-American in John O'Hara's *Appointment in Samarra*.

Dick Reinhart   Older university student who lives at the same boarding house as Lymie Peters and Spud Latham; confidant of Latham in William Maxwell's *The Folded Leaf*.

Mrs. Reinhart   White woman for whom Aunt Hager Williams washes clothes in Langston Hughes's *Not Without Laughter*.

Peter Reinick   Lover of Rita Salus and anti-Nazi who once ran an underground newspaper; caught and tortured by the Gestapo in Martha Gellhorn's *A Stricken Field*.

Mademoiselle Reisz   Ill-tempered pianist whose music inspires Edna Pontellier in Kate Chopin's *The Awakening*.

Renata (Contessa, Daughter)   Italian lover of Richard Cantwell in Ernest Hemingway's *Across the River and into the Trees*.

Renato   Young barber who serves as a kind of confessor for his patrons, and friend who listens to Paolo's stories of female conquest in Tennessee Williams's *The Roman Spring of Mrs. Stone*.

Corinna Rendlesham   Spinster choir leader at St. John's Episcopal Church in Constance Fenimore Woolson's *For the Major*.

Mr. Renling   Wealthy haberdasher for the carriage trade who, along with his wife, introduces Augie March to luxury and tries in vain to adopt him legally in Saul Bellow's *The Adventures of Augie March*.

Mrs. Renling   Wealthy haberdasher who, with her husband, wishes to adopt Augie Marsh legally and refine him in Saul Bellow's *The Adventures of Augie March*.

Amy (Baby) Rennsdale   Youngest member of the neighborhood dancing class; Penrod Schofield ruins her birthday party in Booth Tarkington's *Penrod and Sam*; her youth generally works to her disadvantage with other children in *Penrod* and *Penrod Jashber*.

Alfred Revere   Black sexton at Christ Church; patriarch of a family of respectable workers; failing in health and concerned about his approaching death in James Gould Cozzens's *By Love Possessed*.

Douglass Reynolds   Alcoholic suitor of Adah Logan; commits suicide in Susan Glaspell's *Judd Rankin's Daughter*.

Colonel Nathan Rhenn   Impoverished Southern gentleman and Unionist, supporter of the Reconstruction Acts, and chairman of the meeting to elect delegates to the Constitutional Convention in Albion W. Tourgee's *A Fool's Errand*.

George Rhewold   Physician who temporarily takes over the practice of the injured Doctor Caldwell; successfully courts William Caldwell in Mary Austin's *Santa Lucia*.

Leonard (Len) Rhodes   Rural politician severely beaten by Fee Guthrie in Mary Noailles Murfree's *In the "Stranger People's" Country*.

Leo (Lee) Rhynor   Dashing army corporal and romantic interest of Francie Nolan in Betty Smith's *A Tree Grows in Brooklyn*.

Giuseppe Ribaudo   Former illegal alien in the United States who becomes interpreter and assistant to Major Joppolo in John Hersey's *A Bell for Adano*.

Don Andrés de Ribera   Viceroy of Peru who fathers three children by Camila Perichole in Thornton Wilder's *The Bridge of San Luis Rey*.

Don Jaime de Ribera   Son of Camila Perichole and Don Andrés de Ribera; goes to Lima to be taught by his Uncle Pio; dies in the fall of the bridge in Thornton Wilder's *The Bridge of San Luis Rey*.

Francesca Ricci   Daughter of Michele Ricci; employed as a maid in the home of Mason Flagg, who rapes and kills her, in William Styron's *Set This House on Fire*.

Michele Ricci   Tubercular Italian peasant for whom Cass Kinsolving steals medicine; father of Francesca Ricci in William Styron's *Set This House on Fire*.

Bessie (Sister Bessie) Rice   Noseless, self-appointed evangelist who plans an automobile crusade with her teenaged husband, Dude Lester, in Erskine Caldwell's *Tobacco Road*.

Mrs. J. J. Rice   Perfectionistic white employer of Mrs. Annjee Rodgers in Langston Hughes's *Not Without Laughter*.

Richard   Common-law husband of Elizabeth Grimes and father of John Grimes; moves with Elizabeth to New York and commits suicide after he is falsely accused of armed robbery in James Baldwin's *Go Tell It on the Mountain*.

James (Black Jim) Richards   Grandfather of Hester Le Moyne and cousin of Red Jim Richards, whose land grant Black Jim fraudulently assumes, thus depriving Red Jim's descendants of a large tract of North Carolina land in Albion W. Tourgee's *Bricks Without Straw*.

James (Red Jim) Richards   New England shipowner/captain who holds the original land grant of which Mulberry Hill and Red Wing plantations are a part; dies in Philadelphia after executing a will leaving his property to his wife and daughter in Albion W. Tourgee's *Bricks Without Straw*.

Richardson   Doctor who tends to the dying Charlotte Rittenmeyer in William Faulkner's *The Wild Palms*.

Seth Richmond   Friend of George Willard; has a brief encounter with Helen White before his intended departure from Winesburg in Sherwood Anderson's *Winesburg, Ohio*.

Virginia Richmond   Mother of Seth Richmond; admires her son to the point that she is unable to be a proper parent to him in Sherwood Anderson's *Winesburg, Ohio*.

Carl Richter   German-born supporter of freedom who dies for the Union cause in Winston Churchill's *The Crisis*.

Rico   See Frederick.

Harry Riddle   Nice but feckless lover who absconds with Mrs. Sarah Temple in Winston Churchill's *The Crossing*.

Mrs. Evans Riddle   Proprietor of the Victory Thoughtpower Headquarters in New York City, for which Elmer Gantry teaches prosperity classes, in Sinclair Lewis's *Elmer Gantry*.

Mary Ridgeley   Friend of Sophia Westwyn; her discovery of a locket, featuring Sophia's likeness, that once belonged to Constantia Dudley, prompts Sophia to investigate Constantia's dire circumstances in Charles Brockden Brown's *Ormond*.

Evalina (Lina) Ridgely   See Evalina Ridgely Bowen.

Erwin Riemenschneider   Former convict who masterminds a million-dollar jewelry robbery and whose weakness for young women causes his capture in William Riley Burnett's *The Asphalt Jungle*.

Paul Riesling   Close friend and former college roommate of George Babbitt; accidentally shoots his wife in the shoulder during a domestic argument and is sentenced to prison in Sinclair Lewis's *Babbitt*.

Zilla Colbeck (Zil) Riesling   Wife of Paul Riesling; becomes religious after her husband shoots her in the shoulder during a domestic argument in Sinclair Lewis's *Babbitt*.

Riga   Russian-born captain of the *Highlander* in Herman Melville's *Redburn*.

Riggs   Servant of Frank Walker; kidnaps Halsey Innes in Mary Roberts Rinehart's *The Circular Staircase*.

Harvey Riggs   Go-between for Isaac Tracy and Frank Meriwether in the litigation over worthless land in John Pendleton Kennedy's *Swallow Barn*.

Gus J. (G. J., Gussie, Mouse, Mouso, Yanni, Yanny) Rigopoulos   Blustery Greek boyhood friend and hero of Jack Duluoz in Jack Kerouac's *Doctor Sax, Maggie Cassidy, Book of Dreams*, and *Desolation Angels*.

Rigs   Second mate aboard the *Highlander* in Herman Melville's *Redburn*.

Rinaldi   Lieutenant in the Italian army and a skilled surgeon; introduces Frederic Henry to Catherine Barkley in Ernest Hemingway's *A Farewell to Arms*.

B. P. (Rine, Rine the Runner) Rinehart   Well-dressed preacher and numbers man for whom the narrator is often mistaken in Ralph Ellison's *Invisible Man*.

John Ringman   Husband of Goneril; following his wife's death, he wears a widower's weed in his hat in Herman Melville's *The Confidence-Man*.

Ringo   See Marengo.

Jett Rink   Poor ruffian who becomes an oil baron; married and divorced several times in Edna Ferber's *Giant*.

Anne Riordan   Newspaper reporter and daughter of an honest police chief; she helps Philip Marlowe in Raymond Chandler's *Farewell, My Lovely*.

Maude Riordan   Talented young violinist loved by both Collin Fenwick and Riley Henderson; marries Riley after he becomes a successful businessman in Truman Capote's *The Grass Harp*.

Mike Riordan   One-legged, hard-drinking, Irish Catholic coal miner; friend of Tom Donovan and boyhood hero of Larry Donovan in Jack Conroy's *The Disinherited*.

Molly Riordan   Wife of Blue; raped by Clay Turner and burned in a fire Turner sets; molds Jimmy Fee into another Bad Man; accidentally killed when the mortally wounded Turner grabs her and Jimmy fires a shotgun in E. L. Doctorow's *Welcome to Hard Times*.

Polly Ann Ripley   Loving and capable pioneer wife of Tom McChesney; friend of David Ritchie in Winston Churchill's *The Crossing*.

Risley   Sheriff of the Nevada territory whose absence from Bridger's Wells when Greene brings word of the alleged murder of Larry Kinkaid convinces the townspeople to take the law into their own hands in Walter Van Tilburg Clark's *The Ox-Bow Incident*.

Rita   Good sport and traveling companion of Humbert Humbert, who picks her up after Dolores Haze abandons him, in Vladimir Nabokov's *Lolita*.

David (David Trimble, Davy) Ritchie   Orphan whose wanderings take him, during the Revolutionary War, to Kentucky, St. Louis, and New Orleans; husband of Hélène de St. Gré; narrator of Winston Churchill's *Coniston*.

Charlotte Rittenmeyer   Wife of Rat Rittenmeyer; dies as her lover Harry Wilbourne attempts to perform an abortion on her in William Faulkner's *The Wild Palms*.

Francis (Rat) Rittenmeyer   Husband of Charlotte Rittenmeyer in William Faulkner's *The Wild Palms*.

Dr. Morris Ritz   Charlatan brought from Chicago by Verena Talbo to market Dolly Talbo's dropsy medicine; flees after stealing Verena's money in Truman Capote's *The Grass Harp*.

Rivenoak   Wise Huron chief who captures and tortures Natty Bumppo for killing Le Loup Cervier in James Fenimore Cooper's *The Deerslayer*.

Condé (Condy, Conny) Rivers   Journalist/fictionist who successfully initiates his career as a writer with the aid of Travis Bessemer, falling in love with her during the process, in Frank Norris's *Blix*.

Connie Rivers   Husband of Rose of Sharon Joad Rivers and brother-in-law of Tom Joad II; abandons his wife after they move west in John Steinbeck's *The Grapes of Wrath*.

Don Rivers   Road superintendent and lover of Inez Charlesbois in Jessamyn West's *Cress Delahanty*.

Earl of Rivers   Grandfather of Mary Conant; leaves her a legacy in Lydia Maria Child's *Hobomok*.

Mrs. Lydia Ann Rivers   Nursery customer of Jess Birdwell; her fatal illness puts Birdwell's own worries into perspective in Jessamyn West's *The Friendly Persuasion*.

Reba (Miss Reba) Rivers   Proprietor of a Memphis brothel in William Faulkner's *Sanctuary, The Mansion*, and *The Reivers*.

Rose of Sharon Joad (Rosasharn) Rivers   Sister of Tom Joad II; strives, in the face of her family's difficult trek west, to keep intact her marriage to Connie Rivers in John Steinbeck's *The Grapes of Wrath*.

Ruthie (Ruthalle) Rivkin   Girlfriend of Harry Bogen, who leaves her because he thinks she looks too Jewish in Jerome Weidman's *I Can Get It for You Wholesale*; engaged to Murray Heimowitz in *What's in It for Me?*

Howard (Bricktop, Red) Roark   Creative architect and uncompromising hero in Ayn Rand's *The Fountainhead*.

Rob   Young black man who suffers at the hands of the Cresswells when he neglects his crop to care for his sick wife; lynched by Sheriff Colton's mob in W. E. B. Du Bois's *The Quest of the Silver Fleece*.

Robbins   Black resident of Catfish Row; killed by Crown after being accused of cheating in a crap game in DuBose Heyward's *Porgy.*

Arabella (Bella) Robbins   Romantic desperate for marriage; former girlfriend of Horace Larkin in Hjalmar Hjorth Boyesen's *The Mammon of Unrighteousness.*

Dwight Robbins   Boyish, self-consciously unacademic president of Benton College in Randall Jarrell's *Pictures from an Institution.*

Le Roy Robbins   See Henry Ritchie Clavering.

General Roberdeau   Leader of the Philadelphia militia who first denies and later supports Thomas Paine and the American Revolution in Howard Fast's *Citizen Tom Paine.*

Irene Roberdeau   Daughter of General Roberdeau; falls in love with Thomas Paine, only to marry another man when he rejects her, in Howard Fast's *Citizen Tom Paine.*

Roberto   Cuban revolutionary who kills Albert Tracy and shoots Harry Morgan in Ernest Hemingway's *To Have and Have Not.*

Dick Roberts   Real estate agent at Camp Morgan who is so despondent over the depression that his wife asks George Brush to watch him in order to keep him from committing suicide in Thornton Wilder's *Heaven's My Destination.*

Lieutenant (jg) Doug A. Roberts   Best-loved officer aboard the *Reluctant* and the only one with a desire to participate in World War II; battles the envious Captain Morton in Thomas Heggen's *Mister Roberts.*

Henry Roberts   Merchant from Wheeling, Virginia, in Herman Melville's *The Confidence-Man.*

Judson (Jud) Roberts   State secretary of the Y.M.C.A. who persuades Elmer Gantry to attend a prayer meeting, at which Gantry becomes religious, in Sinclair Lewis's *Elmer Gantry.*

Dutch Robertson   Ex-army private who turns unsuccessfully to crime when he is unable to make a living honestly in John Dos Passos's *Manhattan Tranfser.*

Robey   Eccentric millionaire and stutterer who employs Augie March briefly to assist him in writing a history of human happiness from the perspective of the wealthy, a book he intends to entitle "The Needle's Eye," in Saul Bellow's *The Adventures of Augie March.*

Freddi Robin   Son of Johannes Robin; freed from Dachau through the efforts of Lanny Budd in Upton Sinclair's *Dragon's Teeth.*

Johannes (Jascha Rabinowich) Robin   Jewish-German arms dealer naive to the Nazi threat to Jews; forced to give his fortune to the Nazis in Upton Sinclair's *Dragon's Teeth.*

Commodore Robinette   American naval officer imprisoned by Tripoli pirates; soldier of fortune, Indian trader, pioneer, and cofounder of a town in Oklahoma in H. L. Davis's *Harp of a Thousand Strings.*

Professor Robinolte   Owner of The Tattoo Palace; gives Malcolm a tattoo to prepare him for marriage in James Purdy's *Malcolm.*

Robinson (Robby)   Movie technician in F. Scott Fitzgerald's *The Last Tycoon.*

Doctor (Sawbones) Robinson   Accomplice of Injun Joe and Muff Potter; murdered by Injun Joe in Samuel Langhorne Clemens's *The Adventures of Tom Sawyer.*

Enoch Robinson   Artist who leaves Winesburg for New York; returns home when he is unable to find the solitude he craves in Sherwood Anderson's *Winesburg, Ohio.*

Galbraith (Horse-Shoe) Robinson   Patriot hero who is a guide for Arthur Butler; escapes captivity and guides the Lindsays to Cornwallis; rescues Butler in John Pendleton Kennedy's *Horse-Shoe Robinson.*

Helen Robinson   Wife of Tom Robinson; taunted by Bob Ewell in Harper Lee's *To Kill a Mockingbird.*

Horse-Shoe Robinson   See Galbraith Robinson.

Hyacinth (Hyacinthe Vivier) Robinson   Son of the impoverished French dressmaker Florentine Vivier and her lover Lord Frederick Purvis; becomes involved with a group of politically radical activists in Henry James's *The Princess Casamassima.*

Preston (Pres) Robinson   Controversial Sac Prairie history teacher who is suspected of being a communist and anti-Catholic; withstands church criticism for years before accepting a job in Madison in August Derleth's *The Shield of the Valiant.*

Thomas (Tom) Robinson   Black man falsely accused of raping and beating Mayella Ewell; killed by police while trying to escape in Harper Lee's *To Kill a Mockingbird.*

Patricia Robyn   Niece of Patricia Maurier and twin of Theodore Robyn; attends the yacht party in William Faulkner's *Mosquitoes.*

Theodore (Gus, Josh) Robyn   Nephew of Patricia Maurier and twin of Patricia Robyn; attends the yacht party in William Faulkner's *Mosquitoes.*

Maria Rocco   Italian who works at the American PX and falls in love with Moses Shulman in John Horne Burns's *The Gallery.*

Rochus   Son of the Saltmaster; appears to take advantage of the love of Benedicta in Ambrose Bierce's adaptation of *The Monk and the Hangman's Daughter.*

Marah Rocke   Deserted wife of Major Ira Warfield; raises their son, Traverse Rocke, in desperate poverty and serves as foster mother to Herberty Greyson in E.D.E.N. Southworth's *The Hidden Hand.*

Traverse Rocke   Disowned son of Major Ira Warfield; struggles through poverty to succeed brilliantly as a physician in E.D.E.N. Southworth's *The Hidden Hand.*

Gordon (Lord Stane) Roderick   Associate of Frank Cowperwood; in love with Berenice Fleming in Theodore Dreiser's *The Stoic.*

Mrs. Annjee (Annjelica Williams) Rodgers (Rogers)   Daughter of Aunt Hager Williams and mother of Sandy Rodgers; devotion to her adventurous, irresponsible husband leads her to leave home in Langston Hughes's *Not Without Laughter.*

James (Sandy) Rodgers (Rogers)   Son of Mrs. Annjee Rodgers; central character whose growth from childhood to adolescence is explored in Langston Hughes's *Not Without Laughter.*

Jimboy Rodgers (Rogers)   Freespirited husband of Mrs. Annjee Rodgers and father of Sandy Rodgers; leaves home frequently to find work in Langston Hughes's *Not Without Laughter.*

Seth Rodgers   Boyhood foe of Tom Bailey; becomes a grocer with Bill Conway in Thomas Bailey Aldrich's *The Story of a Bad Boy.*

Willy Roebuck   Deputy sheriff in Shelby Foote's *Follow Me Down.*

Elizabeth Browne Rogers   Early love of Langdon Towne; marries Major Robert Rogers and accompanies him to Michilimackinac in Kenneth Roberts's *Northwest Passage.*

Jimmie Rogers   Belligerent soldier who challenges Wilson and later is shot in battle in Stephen Crane's *The Red Badge of Courage.*

Milton K. Rogers   Former business partner of Silas Lapham; tries to involve Lapham in a shady investment deal in William Dean Howells's *The Rise of Silas Lapham.*

Patricia (Pat) Rogers   New Zealand Salvation Army worker and lover of Andy Hookans in Leon Uris's *Battle Cry.*

Major Robert Rogers   American commander of Rogers' Rangers during the French and Indian War; appointed royal governor of Michilimackinac; dreams of finding a route to the Pacific Ocean in Kenneth Roberts's *Northwest Passage.*

Tom Rogers   Colleague of Homer Zigler on the staff of the *San Francisco Tribune* in Clyde Brion Davis's *The Great American Novel.*

Dan Rolfe   Tubercular victim and companion to Dinah Brand in Dashiell Hammett's *Red Harvest.*

Loretta Lonigan Rolfe   See Loretta Lonigan.

Phillip (Phil) Rolfe   Jewish boyfriend of Loretta Lonigan; converts to Catholicism in James T. Farrell's *The Young Manhood of Studs Lonigan;* marries Loretta in *Judgment Day.*

Rolling Thunder   Indian chief and orator in James Kirke Paulding's *Koningsmarke.*

Indiana Frusk Rolliver   Rival of Undine Spragg when they are girls in Apex City and role model for Undine's habit of marrying to obtain social status in Edith Wharton's *The Custom of the Country.*

Bertrande (Madame Martin Guerre) de Rols   Wife of Martin Guerre; after being deserted by her husband, she lives with Arnaud du Tilh, who resembles Guerre and pretends to be him, in Janet Lewis's *The Wife of Martin Guerre.*

Pedro Romero   Young bullfighter from Pamplona; lover of Lady Brett Ashley in Ernest Hemingway's *The Sun Also Rises.*

Romilayu   Patient African guide who takes Eugene Henderson to his eventful encounters with the Arnewi and Wariri tribes in Saul Bellow's *Henderson the Rain King.*

Evy Rommely   See Evy Rommely Flittman.

Katie Rommely   See Katherine Rommely Nolan.

Mary (Granma) Rommely   Saintly wife of a brute and mother of four daughters; Austrian immigrant, storyteller, and believer in education; grandmother of Francie Nolan in Betty Smith's *A Tree Grows in Brooklyn.*

Sissy Rommely   Oldest child of Mary Rommely, energetic and zany wife of three husbands, and mother of eleven babies, ten of them born dead; Francie Nolan's favorite aunt and model of a stubborn spirit in Betty Smith's *A Tree Grows in Brooklyn.*

Dunstan Rondo   Methodist minister who officiates at the wedding of Dabney Fairchild and Troy Flavin in Eudora Welty's *Delta Wedding.*

Peter (Pete) Rood   Sullen, mysterious mountaineer who disgraces Mink Lorey in Mary Noailles Murfree's *In the Clouds.*

Miriam Rooth   Parisian actress loved by Peter Sherringham; marries Basil Dashwood in Henry James's *The Tragic Muse.*

Ropey   See Rope Yarn.

Rope Yarn (Ropey)   Landlubber aboard the *Julia* who dies at Papeetee in Herman Melville's *Omoo.*

Al Roquefort   Literary agent in Peter De Vries's *Comfort Me with Apples.*

Rosa (Roslin)   Concubine of Sir Philip Gardiner; disguises herself as a boy called Roslin in Catharine Maria Sedgwick's *Hope Leslie*.

Roscius (Roskus)   Husband of Phoebe and father of Thucydides in William Faulkner's *Go Down, Moses*.

Vernon (A. H. Dory, Verne) Roscoe   Oil investor who gets J. Arnold Ross to buy influence in the Harding administration; cheats Bunny and Bertie Ross out of most of their inheritance in Upton Sinclair's *Oil!*

Rose   Entertainer at the Congo cabaret; loves Jake Brown and wants to support him financially, if only he would be her man forever, in Claude McKay's *Home to Harlem*.

Jack (Jakie, Jake Rosencrancz) Rose   Gambler who plans to control Los Angeles in Paul Cain's *Fast One*.

Simon (Sim) Rosedale   Ambitious, social-climbing Jewish investor who falls in love with Lily Bart but refuses to marry her after her reputation becomes tarnished in Edith Wharton's *The House of Mirth*.

Rosemarie   See Rosemarie Buchanan.

Fernie Mae (Fern) Rosen   Southerner of black and Jewish heritage; the narrator is attracted to her but discovers she is emotionally beyond his understanding in Jean Toomer's *Cane*.

Gottfried Knosperl Rosenbaum   Jewish expatriate from Austria and husband of Irene Rosenbaum; teaches music at Benton College in Randall Jarrell's *Pictures from an Institution*.

Irene Rosenbaum   Retired singer of opera and lieder; wife and spiritual complement to Gottfried Rosenbaum in Randall Jarrell's *Pictures from an Institution*.

Harold Rosenblatt   Wise and scholarly colleague who tries to give Lee Youngdahl good advice in Mark Harris's *Wake Up, Stupid*.

Roseveldt   Shopkeeper who sells to Martinette de Beauvais the lute that formerly belonged to Constantia Dudley in Charles Brockden Brown's *Ormond*.

Edward (Ned) Rosier   Member of the American circle in Paris and suitor of Pansy Osmond in Henry James's *The Portrait of a Lady*.

Madame Rosita   Prostitute with whom Malcolm has his first sexual experience as preparation for his marriage to Melba in James Purdy's *Malcolm*.

Eino Roskinen   Dairy worker and rival of Cass Timberlane for the affections of Jinny Marshland; killed in World War II in Sinclair Lewis's *Cass Timberlane*.

Roskus   See Roskus Gibson and Roscius.

Roslin   See Rosa.

Alberta (Bertie, Birdie) Ross   Sister of Bunny Ross; disagrees with Bunny's political beliefs in Upton Sinclair's *Oil!*

Beulah (Sue) Ross   Prostitute murdered by her lover, Luther Eustis, in Shelby Foote's *Follow Me Down*.

Mrs. Cora Ross   Wife of Colonel Norman Ross; her intelligent observations and willingness to fulfill obligations bring her credit in James Gould Cozzens's *Guard of Honor*.

J. Arnold (Jim, Mr. Paradise) Ross   Millionaire father of J. Arnold Ross, Jr.; independent oil operator who becomes involved in a political scandal in Upton Sinclair's *Oil!*

J. Arnold (Bunny, Jim, Jr., Alex H. Jones) Ross, Jr.   Son of J. Arnold Ross; becomes involved in the labor movement and plans to start a labor college; marries Rachel Menzies in Upton Sinclair's *Oil!*

Larry Ross   Young and upcoming studio executive seen by Sammy Glick as a future threat in Budd Schulberg's *What Makes Sammy Run?*

Colonel Norman (Judge) Ross   Air Inspector of Ocanara Army Air Base whose reasoned understanding of human nature solves General Ira N. Beal's personnel crisis; moral center in James Gould Cozzens's *Guard of Honor*.

Rachel Menzies Ross   See Rachel Menzies.

Sybil Ross   Sister of Madeleine Lee; she and John Carrington inform Madeleine of Senator Ratcliffe's improper political dealings to keep her from marrying him in Henry Adams's *Democracy*.

Michael (Mike) Rossi   See Tomas Makris.

Earl of Rossmore   Father of Berkeley; annoyed by Mulberry Sellers's claim of the Rossmore title in Samuel Langhorne Clemens's *The American Claimant*.

Steffi Rostenkowski   Girlfriend of Bruno (Lefty) Bicek; remains faithful to Bicek after he betrays her into prostitution in Nelson Algren's *Never Come Morning*.

Sam Rothmore   Head of Paramount's New York office; hires Noel Airman as an assistant story editor in Herman Wouk's *Marjorie Morningstar*.

Chuck Rouncivale   Sportswriter for the Blue Mountain News in Katherine Anne Porter's *Pale Horse, Pale Rider*.

Janet Rowan   Rich, spoiled blonde who humiliates Ada Fincastle and who, through her father's social power, traps Ralph McBride into marrying her rather than Ada in Ellen Glasgow's *Vein of Iron*.

Roxana (Roxy) Slave of Percy Driscoll; fearing that her baby Valet de Chambre will be sold, she switches him with the baby Thomas à Becket Driscoll and rears Driscoll as her son in Samuel Langhorne Clemens's *Pudd'nhead Wilson*.

Roxie Black cook for the Battle Fairchild family in Eudora Welty's *Delta Wedding*.

Roy First morphine customer of William Lee and his partner in lush working in William S. Burroughs's *Junkie*.

Mrs. Roy American in Rome who is seeking a divorce under Pauline Privilege from the pope in Thornton Wilder's *The Cabala*.

Royal Bastard child of Gabriel Grimes and Esther, unacknowledged by his father; killed in a Chicago saloon in James Baldwin's *Go Tell It on the Mountain*.

Princess Royal Only daughter of Pharaoh, mother of Moses, and sister of Ta-Phar in Zora Neale Hurston's *Moses, Man of the Mountain*.

Charity Royall Daughter of Mary Hyatt and lover of Lucius Harney; eventually marries her guardian, Lawyer Royall; heroine of Edith Wharton's *Summer*.

Lawyer Royall Guardian and eventually husband of Charity Royall in Edith Wharton's *Summer*.

Enid Royce Devout prohibitionist; vegetarian Nebraskan who marries Claude Wheeler, only to depart for China to aid her ailing sister, in Willa Cather's *One of Ours*.

Rita Royce Blonde starlet who accompanies Sammy Glick to high-profile events in Budd Schulberg's *What Makes Sammy Run?*

Mama Rua Widowed mother of Terangi; visited by her husband's ghost; dies shortly before the hurricane in Charles Nordhoff and James Norman Hall's *The Hurricane*.

The Rube Junky friend deserted by William Lee in William S. Burroughs's *Naked Lunch;* undercover agent for the Nova Police and master of the reverse con in *Nova Express*.

Rubén Poor candymaker who falls in love with a gypsy; raids a neighboring village with Pepe Gonzales in order to steal the bones of a local hero in Josefina Niggli's *Mexican Village*.

Ruby Oldest of the orphaned girls under Rachel Cooper's care; reveals to Preacher that John and Pearl Harper are also in Cooper's care in Davis Grubb's *The Night of the Hunter*.

Sim Rudabaugh Carpetbagging Texas politician and rustler; tries to keep Del Sol cattle from getting to Kansas in Emerson Hough's *North of 36*.

Barry Rudd Ten-year-old genius and expert in biological classification and etymology; recruited as a brain specimen by Wissey Jones; subject of an investigation by the State Senate Standing Committee on Education, Welfare, and Public Morality in John Hersey's *The Child Buyer*.

Lambert Rudd Landscape painter from Boston; husband of Maizie Jekyll and lover of Leda March in Nancy Hale's *The Prodigal Women*.

Maud Purcells (Mrs. Paul Rudd) Rudd Mother of Barry Rudd; overcomes hardship to provide for Barry, but when she is threatened, intimidated, and bribed by Wissey Jones, she succumbs and permits the sale of her son in John Hersey's *The Child Buyer*.

May Rudge See May Rudge Harrington.

Jurgis (Michael O'Flaherty, Serge Reminitsky, Johann Schmidt) Rudkus Lithuanian immigrant to America and husband of Ona Rudkus; finds work in the Chicago stockyards in Upton Sinclair's *The Jungle*.

Ona Lukoszaite Rudkus Stepdaughter of Elzbieta and wife of Jurgis Rudkus; coerced into having sex with Phil Connor; dies during childbirth because of inadequate medical attention in Upton Sinclair's *The Jungle*.

Matthew Rudolph Servant to Prince Cabano; secret member of the Brotherhood of Destruction who arranges Estella Washington's escape from Cabano in Ignatius Donnelly's *Caesar's Column*.

Ruel See Jethro.

Hamm (Rufer Hammond) Rufe Son of Hallie Rufer Hammond and Michael Hammond; youthful runaway who assumes a new identity as an adult and returns to Franklin as a labor reporter; estranged husband of Stephani Kolhoff in Mari Sandoz's *Capital City*.

Marmaduke (Colonel Ruggles) Ruggles British valet who is won in a poker game by Egbert Floud, with whom Ruggles goes to the United States; narrator of Harry Leon Wilson's *Ruggles of Red Gap*.

Billy Rumbly Part-Indian brother of Henry Burlingame; civilized savage who marries Anna Cooke in John Barth's *The Sot-Weed Factor*.

Beatrice (Bea) Rumfoord Wife of Winston Niles Rumfoord and mate of Malachi Constant in Kurt Vonnegut's *The Sirens of Titan*.

Winston Niles Rumfoord Wealthy space and time traveler who enters a chronosynclastic infundibulum in Kurt Vonnegut's *The Sirens of Titan*.

Jacob Rumpel Stolid Pennsylvania farmer whose unaffected manner and good sense inspire Thomas Paine to revolutionary writing in Howard Fast's *Citizen Tom Paine*.

Sarah Rumpel Daughter of Jacob Rumpel; exemplifies a uniquely American civilization to Thomas Paine, who rejects her in favor of his revolutionary writing, in Howard Fast's *Citizen Tom Paine.*

Jack Rumsen Private detective hired by Ned Beaumont to help him find Bernie Despain in Dashiell Hammett's *The Glass Key.*

Frank Russel Cynical friend of Edward Clayton; rejects Edward's radicalism in favor of caution and acceptance of the local mores in Harriet Beecher Stowe's *Dred.*

Arthur Russell Summer-long boyfriend of Alice Adams; leaves her upon discovering her pretensions in Booth Tarkington's *Alice Adams.*

Puss and Emily Russell Society sisters in Winston Churchill's *The Crisis.*

Rusty Thug employed by Shad O'Rory in Dashiell Hammett's *The Glass Key.*

Helen Rutherford Alleged daughter of Leander Wapshot from a brief early marriage; believes that Wapshot abandoned her in infancy in John Cheever's *The Wapshot Chronicle.*

Miles Rutherford Churlish bully beaten by Ned Hazard in John Pendleton Kennedy's *Swallow Barn.*

Willie Rutledge Drownder preacher who bases his belief in brotherly love and a fervently spiritual life on a supernatural vision of heavenly glory in T. S. Stribling's *Unfinished Cathedral.*

Ada Rutter Trashy denizen of the Peaks of Laurel and scheming mother of Ada Belle Rutter in Andrew Lytle's *The Velvet Horn.*

Ada Belle Rutter Young mountain woman whom Lucius Cree marries when he learns she is pregnant with their child in Andrew Lytle's *The Velvet Horn.*

Pegeen Ryan Fiery redhead who teaches French and marries Patrick Dennis; appears in Patrick Dennis's *Auntie Mame* and *Around the World with Auntie Mame.*

Cynthia Ryder Mother of Sophia Grieve Ryder in Djuna Barnes's *Ryder.*

Japheth M. (Japh, Japhy) Ryder Oregon-born poet, Oriental scholar, and Zen Buddhist; idealized friend of Ray Smith in Jack Kerouac's *The Dharma Bums.*

Jonathan Buxton Ryder Father of Sophia Grieve Ryder in Djuna Barnes's *Ryder.*

Sophia Grieve Ryder Daughter of Jonathan Buxton Ryder and Cynthia Ryder, wife of John Peel and Alex Alexson, and mother of Wendell Ryder in Djuna Barnes's *Ryder.*

Wendell Ryder Son of John Peel and Sophia Grieve Ryder; husband of Amelia de Grier; lover of Kate Careless; father, by Amelia, of five children and father, by Kate, of three children; and lover of Molly Dance in Djuna Barnes's *Ryder.*

Nicholas (Nick) Sabb   London fence imprisoned in Australia; escapes from the penal colony and settles in Rotterdam in Charles Nordhoff and James Norman Hall's *Botany Bay*.

Timothy Sabb   Nephew of Nick Sabb; takes over Nick's illicit activities when Nick is taken to an Australian penal colony in Charles Nordhoff and James Norman Hall's *Botany Bay*.

Sabina   Woman who searches for herself in a series of affairs and has a failed lesbian relationship with Lillian in Anaïs Nin's *Ladders to Fire, Children of the Albatross, The Four-Chambered Heart,* and *A Spy in the House of Love*.

Sabino   Coroner who investigates Chalmers Egstrom's death and who enters into Marietta McGee-Chavéz's Spain in William Goyen's *In a Farther Country*.

Henri Guerlac de Sabrevois   British sympathizer and enemy of Steven Nason; abducts Mary Mallinson in Kenneth Roberts's *Arundel*.

Marie de Sabrevois   See Mary Mallinson.

Nicola (Nick) Sacco   Anarchistic Italian shoe-factory worker and night watchman who, unjustly charged with robbery and murder, is executed with Bartolomeo Vanzetti, to the horror of many, in Upton Sinclair's *Boston*.

Sackett   District attorney who fails to convict Frank Chambers for the murder of Nick Papadakis, but convicts him of murdering Cora Papadakis, who dies accidentally, in James M. Cain's *The Postman Always Rings Twice*.

Lorna Sackville   See Susan Lenox.

The Sailor   Heroin addict briefly mentioned in William S. Burroughs's *Junkie;* gatherer of reptile eggs and buyer of time in *Naked Lunch;* hangs himself in jail in *The Soft Machine;* mentioned in *Nova Express* and *Exterminator!*

Arthur St. Clair   Former British army officer; landowner in Hervey Allen's *The Forest and the Fort, Bedford Village,* and *Toward the Morning*.

Emilia St. Claire   Wealthy eccentric who buys a castle in Lowell, Massachusetts, and renames it Transcendenta in Jack Kerouac's *Doctor Sax*.

Amber St. Clare (Mrs. Luke Channell; Mrs. Samuel Dangerfield; Mrs. Edmund Mortimer, Countess of Radclyffe; Mrs. Gerald Stanhope, Countess of Danforth and Duchess of Ravenspur)   Fifteen-year-old country maid who becomes the mistress of King Charles II; unbeatable heroine who survives, among other trials, debtors' prison, a bout of plague, a murderous husband, the gossip of Court, and the London Fire, but cannot win the enduring affection and attention of her first love, Bruce Carlton, in Kathleen Winsor's *Forever Amber*.

Augustine St. Clare   Husband of Marie St. Clare and father of Eva St. Clare; second owner of Uncle Tom; influenced by Tom and Eva to replace his cynicism with faith before being stabbed to death in Harriet Beecher Stowe's *Uncle Tom's Cabin*.

Evangeline (Little Eva) St. Clare   Daughter of Marie and Augustine St. Clare; befriends Uncle Tom and inspires and reforms those around her, such as her father and Topsy, before dying of consumption in Harriet Beecher Stowe's *Uncle Tom's Cabin*.

Henrique St. Clare   Young cousin of Eva St. Clare; his aristocratic cruelty is tempered by Eva's admonitions in Harriet Beecher Stowe's *Uncle Tom's Cabin*.

Mammy St. Clare   See Mammy.

Marie St. Clare   Wife of Augustine St. Clare and mother of Eva St. Clare; suffers from debilitating headaches; disapproves of her husband's benevolent management of their slaves and sells Uncle Tom when she disposes of Augustine's estate in Harriet Beecher Stowe's *Uncle Tom's Cabin*.

Ophelia St. Clare   Vermonter who manages the New Orleans household of her cousin Augustine St. Clare in Harriet Beecher Stowe's *Uncle Tom's Cabin*.

Antoinette de St. Gré   Woman who marries Nick Temple in Winston Churchill's *The Crossing*.

Auguste de St. Gré   Degenerate son of Philippe de St. Gré and brother of Antoinette de St. Gré in Winston Churchill's *The Crossing*.

Hélène Victoire Marie de (Hélène d'Ivry-le-Tour) St. Gré   Widow; friend and later the wife of David Ritchie in Winston Churchill's *The Crossing*.

Philippe de St. Gré   Generous friend of David Ritchie and father of Antoinette and Auguste de St. Gré in Winston Churchill's *The Crossing*.

Captain St. Jermyn (Tyrrel)   British spy who induces Philip Lindsay to join the British and Tory forces at King's Mountain; hanged after the British defeat in John Pendleton Kennedy's *Horse-Shoe Robinson*.

Edgar St. Jermyn   Brother of Captain St. Jermyn; captured by Horse-Shoe Robinson and Christopher Shaw in John Pendleton Kennedy's *Horse-Shoe Robinson*.

Mary St. John   See Mary St. John Eaton.

Sakia (Love)   Wife of Paskingoe in James Kirke Paulding's *The Dutchman's Fireside*.

Salem   American sailor who confronts the English consul aboard the *Julia* and who fights Bembo in Herman Melville's *Omoo*.

Mac Sales   Airplane inspector in William Faulkner's *Pylon*.

Salo (Old Salo)   Tralfamadorian robot friend of Winston Niles Rumfoord and Malachi Constant in Kurt Vonnegut's *The Sirens of Titan*.

Saltmaster   Overseer of a salt mine; father of Rochus and, unknown to others, of Benedicta in Ambrose Bierce's adaptation of *The Monk and the Hangman's Daughter*.

Solly (Professor, Sparrow) Saltskin   Petty criminal forced to betray Frankie Machine, his best friend, in Nelson Algren's *The Man with the Golden Arm*.

Rita Salus   Lover of Peter Reinick and Communist refugee from the Nazis who is deported to Germany in Martha Gellhorn's *A Stricken Field*.

Doña Dolores (Grace Conroy) Salvatierra   Sister of Gabriel Conroy; poses as an Indian in Bret Harte's *Gabriel Conroy*.

Sam (Sammy-O)   Friend of Fish Tucker; enlists in the army and is sent to France in Richard Wright's *The Long Dream*.

Sam   Pedigreed foxhound named for a preacher and treated as a member of the family; Nunn Ballew buys him to chase King Devil in Harriette Arnow's *Hunter's Horn*.

Mr. Samm   Operator of the Go Hole in John Clellon Holmes's *The Horn*.

Cornelia (Corny) Samms   Schoolmate of Cress Delahanty and house party participant in Jessamyn West's *Cress Delahanty*.

Samoa   Upoluan aboard the Parki; married to Annatoo; killed by Aleema's sons in Herman Melville's *Mardi*.

Samuel   Abolitionist lecturer who falsely claims to be a fugitive slave; marries Frado, deserts her and their child, and dies of yellow fever in New Orleans in Harriet E. Wilson's *Our Nig*.

Reb Samuel   Chassidic immigrant owner of an umbrella store in Michael Gold's *Jews without Money*.

Samuele (Samuelino)   Narrator named by Alix d'Espoli after Alix's dog in Thornton Wilder's *The Cabala*.

Tony San Antonio   Saloonkeeper who makes a fortune during the Civil War by hoarding and selling cotton; becomes a wealthy financier in Grace King's *The Pleasant Ways of St. Médard*.

Dr. Sanborn   Physician, member of Chicago society, and proponent of the New Woman; marries Isabel Herrick in Hamlin Garland's *Rose of Dutcher's Coolly*.

Isabel Herrick Sanborn   See Isabel Herrick.

Sanchez   Faithful Mexican rider with the Del Sol herd in Emerson Hough's *North of 36*.

Pablo Sanchez   Poor, gluttonous friend of Pilon; released from jail and convinced by Pilon to live in Pilon's house, if Sanchez agrees to pay the rent, in John Steinbeck's *Tortilla Flat*.

James Sandage   County trustee and overseer of the Lane County, Tennessee, poor farm; guardian of Abner Teeftallow and murderer of Railroad Jones in T. S. Stribling's *Teeftallow*.

Sandbach   Intellectual and anarchist; rival of Jasper Ammen in Conrad Aiken's *King Coffin*.

Aleck Sander   Black friend of Chick Mallison in William Faulkner's *Intruder in the Dust* and *The Town*.

Billy Sanderlee   Pianist and friend who accompanies Harriett Williams in her singing act in Langston Hughes's *Not Without Laughter*.

Granny Sanders   Hag with a reputation for almost supernatural knowledge in Edward Eggleston's *The Hoosier School-Master*.

Luke Sanderson   Unambitious liar and thief; heir to Hill House in Shirley Jackson's *The Haunting of Hill House*.

Tommy Sanderson   Opportunist who is the supposed leader of the Union League but who is distrusted by the true Unionists in Albion W. Tourgee's *A Fool's Errand*.

Gus Sands   King of the bookies in Bernard Malamud's *The Natural*.

George Sandusky   Customer at the tailor shop who works at a hotel loading taxis in Henry Miller's *Black Spring*.

James (Jaky) Sandusky   Self-serving attorney who defends Toussaint Vaiden; appears in T. S. Stribling's *The Store* and *Unfinished Cathedral*.

Sandy (Alisande de la Carteloise)   Sixth-century wife of Hank Morgan; tells unending tales of knights' adventures in Samuel Langhorne Clemens's *A Connecticut Yankee in King Arthur's Court*.

Peter Sanford (Sandford)   Dashing army major who wishes to, avenge men's treatment by coquettes through his relationship with Eliza Wharton in Hannah Webster Foster's *The Coquette*.

Miss Amy Skully Sansom   Wife of Edward Sansom, whom she marries after her cousin, Randolph Skully, shot and paralyzed him, in Truman Capote's *Other Voices, Other Rooms*.

Edward R. (Ed) Sansom   Bedridden father of Joel Harrison Knox; unable to communicate except with red tennis balls after his accidental shooting in Truman Capote's *Other Voices, Other Rooms*.

Joel Harrison Knox Sansom   See Joel Harrison Knox.

Santiago   Old Cuban fisherman who catches a huge marlin, only to have it eaten by sharks before he can bring it to land, in Ernest Hemingway's *The Old Man and the Sea*.

El (Sordo) Santiago   Leader of a partisan group in Ernest Hemingway's *For Whom the Bell Tolls*.

Lee Sarason   Satanic secretary of state who deposes President Berzelius Windrip and succeeds him as president in Sinclair Lewis's *It Can't Happen Here*.

Kit Sargent   Mannish and assertive novelist and screenwriter who is instrumental in the formation of a Hollywood writers' guild; sometime girlfriend of Sammy Glick and later wife of Al Manheim in Budd Schulberg's *What Makes Sammy Run?*

Slim Sarrett   College boxer, poet, graduate student, and friend of Sue Murdock until she learns of his homosexuality; strangles her in Robert Penn Warren's *At Heaven's Gate*.

Father Sarria   Mission priest in the San Joaquin Valley who counsels Vanamee, whose fiancée has been raped and has died during childbirth, in Frank Norris's *The Octopus*.

Sarsefield   Lover of Euphemia Lorimer driven away by her brother, Arthur Wiatte, but eventually returns to marry her; friend and mentor of Edgar Huntly in Charles Brockden Brown's *Edgar Huntly*.

Bayard Sartoris (I)   Brother of Col. John Sartoris; killed in the Civil War; appears in William Faulkner's *Sartoris (Flags in the Dust)* and *The Unvanquished*.

Bayard Sartoris (II)   Son of Col. John Sartoris; mayor of Jefferson and president of a bank; kills Major Grumby, his grandmother's murderer; appears in William Faulkner's *Sartoris (Flags in the Dust)*; *The Unvanquished*; *The Hamlet*; *Go Down, Moses*; *Requiem for a Nun*; *The Town*; and *The Mansion*.

Bayard Sartoris (III)   Grandson of Bayard Sartoris II; killed while testing an airplane; appears in William Faulkner's *Sartoris (Flags in the Dust)*, *Requiem for a Nun*, *The Town*, and *The Mansion*.

Benbow (Bory) Sartoris   Son of Narcissa Benbow and Bayard Sartoris III in William Faulkner's *Sartoris (Flags in the Dust)*, *Sanctuary*, *The Town*, and *The Mansion*.

Drusilla Hawk Sartoris   Fearless young woman who fights with the regiment of Col. John Sartoris and becomes his second wife in William Faulkner's *The Unvanquished*.

Col. John Sartoris   First Sartoris in Yoknapatawpha County; Confederate officer and father of Bayard Sartoris II; murdered by his partner Ben Redmond; appears in William Faulkner's *Sartoris (Flags in the Dust)*; *The Sound and the Fury*; *Light in August*; *Absalom, Absalom!*; *The Unvanquished*; *The Hamlet*; *Go Down, Moses*; *Requiem for a Nun*; *The Town*; *The Mansion*; and *The Reivers*.

Narcissa Benbow Sartoris   Sister of Horace Benbow, second wife of Bayard Sartoris III, and mother of Benbow Sartoris; appears in William Faulkner's *Sartoris (Flags in the Dust)*, *Sanctuary*, *The Town*, and *The Mansion*.

Mr. de Sastago   Alleged marquis of Spain married to Honora Wapshot for eight months in her youth in John Cheever's *The Wapshot Chronicle*.

Cecily Saunders   See Cecily Saunders Farr.

Minnie Saunders   Wife of Robert Saunders I and mother of Cecily Saunders and Robert Saunders II in William Faulkner's *Soldiers' Pay*.

Robert Saunders (I)   Husband of Minnie Saunders and father of Cecily Saunders and Robert Saunders II in William Faulkner's *Soldiers' Pay.*

Robert Saunders (II)   Son of Robert and Minnie Saunders and brother of Cecily Saunders Farr in William Faulkner's *Soldiers' Pay.*

Savacol   Dissolute, egocentric gambler and first husband of Ruhama Warne in H. L. Davis's *Beulah Land.*

Eleanor Savage   Eccentric young woman with whom Amory Blaine is poetically involved in F. Scott Fitzgerald's *This Side of Paradise.*

Frank Savage   Demanding but successful commanding officer of the 918th Bomb Group in Beirne Lay, Jr., and Sy Bartlett's *Twelve O'Clock High!*

Richard Ellsworth Savage   Associate of J. Ward Morehouse's who has an affair with Anne Elizabeth Trent in Italy during World War I and refuses to marry her in John Dos Passos's *U.S.A.* trilogy.

Thomas (Tom) Savage   Lookout for men who try to ambush Comfort Servosse; after being injured and nursed back to health, he becomes a supporter of Servosse and warns the Regulators not to bother Servosse in Albion W. Tourgee's *A Fool's Errand.*

Miguel Saveda   Sailor whose corpse burns aboard the *Highlander* in Herman Melville's *Redburn.*

Maria Savor   Mother of a child that Annie Kilburn sends to the seaside for its health but which dies; with her husband, William, she forms the foundation of the Social Union in William Dean Howells's *Annie Kilburn.*

William Savor   Husband of Maria Savor and father of a deceased child in William Dean Howells's *Annie Kilburn.*

Pete Sawmill   Simple, free black man who has rapport with animals and nature; serves first as Rose Wentworth's servant and then as Barton Cathcart's bodyguard during the Civil War; helps Cathcart escape from Gettysburg in Henry Ward Beecher's *Norwood.*

Nancy Sawyer   Kindly old maid who aids the ill Shocky Thomson in Edward Eggleston's *The Hoosier School-Master.*

Sidney (Sid) Sawyer   Do-gooder half brother of Tom Sawyer in Samuel Langhorne Clemens's *The Adventures of Tom Sawyer.*

Taylor Sawyer   Wastrel brother of Sally Lacey in Mary Lee Settle's *O Beulah Land.*

Thomas (Sid, Tom) Sawyer   Mischievous boy who witnesses the murder of Dr. Robinson and finds $12,000 in gold in Samuel Langhorne Clemens's *The Adventures of Tom Sawyer;* helps Huck Finn free Jim and is shot in the process in *Adventures of Huckleberry Finn;* pilots a balloon across North Africa in *Tom Sawyer Abroad;* solves the murder Silas Phelps is accused of in *Tom Sawyer, Detective.*

Doctor (Adolphus Asher Ghoulens, King of Anti Evil, Raymond) Sax   Lurking, green-faced phantom who vows to destroy the Great World Snake; imaginary boyhood companion of Jack Duluoz in Jack Kerouac's *Doctor Sax;* also appears in *Book of Dreams.*

Gramma Julie Saxinar   Maternal grandmother of Neil and Robert Kingsblood in Sinclair Lewis's *Kingsblood Royal.*

Alethea Ann (Lethe) Sayles   Mountaineer loved by Mink Lorey and Ben Doaks in Mary Noailles Murfree's *In the Clouds.*

Herman Sayre   Wealthy alumnus of the College and father of Lily Sayre; overzealous supporter of Raymond Blent's eligibility to play football in Howard Nemerov's *The Homecoming Game.*

Lily Sayre   Daughter of Herman Sayre and girlfriend of Raymond Blent; loved by Dr. Charles Osman in Howard Nemerov's *The Homecoming Game.*

Giovanni Scabby   Underworld informer who seeks Rico Bandello in order to gain revenge on Bandello for having destroyed the Vettori mob in William Riley Burnett's *Little Caesar.*

Justina, (Cousin Justina) Wapshot Molesworth Scaddon   Ancient cousin of Leander and Honora Wapshot; former dancer and piano player who lives in the ramshackle castle Clear Haven and attempts to control Moses Wapshot's marriage to her ward, Melissa, in John Cheever's *The Wapshot Chronicle.*

Lucy Scanlan   Girlfriend of Studs Lonigan in James T. Farrell's *Young Lonigan;* although she has moved away, she remains the object of Lonigan's fantasies in *The Young Manhood of Studs Lonigan* and *Judgment Day.*

Timothy Scanlon   Father of Tom Scanlon and the real subject of Tom's autobiographical musings in Wright Morris's *The Field of Vision.*

Tom Scanlon   Father of Lois McKee; myopic, mythmaking frontiersman in Wright Morris's *The Field of Vision;* his ninetieth birthday is the central occasion in *Ceremony in Lone Tree;* appears also in *The World in the Attic.*

Scar   Best friend of Jake Adams; addicted to heroin; later tries the cure in Herbert Simmons's *Corner Boy.*

Miriam Schaefer   American artist in Italy who loves Donatello and signals him to kill Brother Antonio in Nathaniel Hawthorne's *The Marble Faun.*

Schatzi (Ernst)   German black marketeer in Thomas Berger's *Crazy in Berlin.*

Albert Schearl   Austrian immigrant ill-suited for life in New York; husband of Genya Schearl and father of David Schearl in Henry Roth's *Call It Sleep.*

David (Davy) Schearl   Son of Albert and Genya Schearl; absorbs the hectic conditions of Jewish immigrant life in New York in Henry Roth's *Call It Sleep.*

Genya Schearl   Wife of Albert Schearl; perceptive and protective mother of David Schearl in Henry Roth's *Call It Sleep.*

Nathan (Nate) Schild   Communist sympathizer and friend of Carlo Reinhart; murdered in Thomas Berger's *Crazy in Berlin.*

Richard (Dick) F. Schiller   Young man with job prospects in Alaska; husband of Dolores Haze and father of their stillborn child in Vladimir Nabokov's *Lolita.*

Ed Schindel   Friend of Hart Kennedy in John Clellon Holmes's *Go.*

Nicholas Schliemann   Socialist-anarchist theorist whose ideas inspire Jurgis Rudkus to work for socialism in Upton Sinclair's *The Jungle.*

Schlossberg   Journalist and Jewish patriarch whose wise humanism leads Asa Leventhal to aspire to the exactly human and to choose dignity in Saul Bellow's *The Victim.*

Achilles Schmidt   Legless giant whose obsession with the prostitute Hallie Breedlove causes him to cripple Dove Linkhorn in Nelson Algren's *A Walk on the Wild Side.*

Alma (Lorene) Schmidt   Prostitute at Gert Kipfer's brothel; has an affair with Robert E. Lee Prewitt and hides him after he kills Fatso Judson in James Jones's *From Here to Eternity.*

Herman H. (Dutch) Schnell   Manager of the New York Mammoths baseball team in Mark Harris's *The Southpaw, Bang the Drum Slowly, A Ticket for a Seamstitch,* and *It Looked Like For Ever.*

Connie Schoffstal   Best friend and confidante of Grace Brock Caldwell in John O'Hara's *A Rage to Live.*

Henry Passloe Schofield   Father of Penrod Schofield; administers corporal punishment to his son, when necessary, in Booth Tarkington's *Penrod, Penrod and Sam,* and *Penrod Jashber.*

Margaret Passloe Schofield   Sister of Penrod Schofield; her suitors, with the exception of Robert Williams, are driven away when they become the target of Penrod's antics in Booth Tarkington's *Penrod, Penrod and Sam,* and *Penrod Jashber.*

Mrs. Schofield   Mother of Penrod Schofield; she generally deals well with her son's creativity and energy in Booth Tarkington's *Penrod, Penrod and Sam,* and *Penrod Jashber.*

Penrod (George B. Jashber) Schofield   Boy whose imagination, creativity, and energy lead him into numerous adventures, experiments, and escapades in Booth Tarkington's *Penrod, Penrod and Sam,* and *Penrod Jashber.*

Marcus (Mark) Schouler   Friend of McTeague; upon believing that McTeague has cheated him, acts to have McTeague's license to practice dentistry revoked, thus triggering McTeague's economic and personal decline, in Frank Norris's *McTeague.*

Rudolph Schreiker   Kommisar of Warsaw after Nazi occupation in Leon Uris's *Mila 18.*

Peter (Dutchman) Schroeder   German immigrant whose house is robbed in Edward Eggleston's *The Hoosier School-Master.*

Schuldig   Messenger hired by Henry Miller; spends twenty years in prison for a crime he didn't commit; eventually goes insane in Henry Miller's *Tropic of Capricorn.*

Fran Natalie Schuschnigg   Governess-housekeeper employed by Arbogast von Hohengraetz; becomes Rudolf Stanka's *mamitsa* when he is restored to a noble position; marries Herr Ottokar Bukuwky in Louis Adamic's *Cradle of Life.*

Nancy Schuyler   Servant of the Demooths who is impregnated by a British soldier, runs away, and becomes an Indian squaw in Walter D. Edmonds's *Drums along the Mohawk.*

Manny Schwartz   Ruined movie producer who commits suicide in F. Scott Fitzgerald's *The Last Tycoon.*

Milton (Milt) Schwartz   Law partner of Lou Michaelson; marries Marjorie Morningstar in Herman Wouk's *Marjorie Morningstar.*

Roger Schwartz   Boyfriend of Rose MacMahon, about whose pregnancy he is concerned, in Robert Cantwell's *The Land of Plenty.*

Mattie Schwengauer   Innocent girlfriend of Dirk De Jong in Edna Ferber's *So Big.*

Zero Schwiefka   Owner of a Polish gambling house in Chicago and Frankie Machine's employer in Nelson Algren's *The Man with the Golden Arm.*

Scipio   Freed slave who accompanies Mark Littleton on the final part of Littleton's journey to the plantation in John Pendleton Kennedy's *Swallow Barn.*

General John Scott   Nearly toothless old slave on the Prosser plantation; serves as treasurer of the slave revolt in Arna Wendell Bontemps's *Black Thunder.*

Samuel (Honorable Sammy, Sam, Sammy) Scott   Leading black politician of Chicago; in reality, a shrewd businessman in W. E. B. Du Bois's *Dark Princess.*

Lieutenant Colonel Walter Scott   Good-humored battalion commander in Willa Cather's *One of Ours.*

Weeden Scott   Mining engineer who rescues White Fang from the dogfights and tames him into a loyal dog in Jack London's *White Fang.*

Louie Scurrah   Experienced woodsman who marries Genny Luckett; he deserts her and runs off with her sister Achsa Luckett to the western territories in Conrad Richter's *The Trees;* his death is mentioned in *The Fields.*

Sarah Seabrooke   Spinster great-aunt of Jim Calder and Clothilde Wright; considered by Calder to embody the New England tradition in Wickford Point in John P. Marquand's *Wichford Point.*

Lloyd Searight   Head of a nursing agency who falls in love with Ward Bennett but is alienated from him when he prevents her from doing her duty as a nurse in Frank Norris's *A Man's Woman.*

Harry Searle   Hack writer of soap operas who wants Lee Youngdahl to join his Dollar a Word Club in Mark Harris's *Wake Up, Stupid.*

Tobias Sears   Union officer who marries the mulatto Amantha Starr and makes her feel free in Robert Penn Warren's *Band of Angels.*

George Selby   Confederate colonel murdered by Laura Hawkins in Samuel Langhorne Clemens and Charles Dudley Warner's *The Gilded Age.*

T. Selby   Friend of J. Boyer; advises Boyer against further involvement with Eliza Wharton in Hannah Webster Foster's *The Coquette.*

Lawrence Selden   New York lawyer who loves and is loved by Lily Bart but whom she considers too poor to marry in Edith Wharton's *The House of Mirth.*

Father Seldon   Priest who introduces Cross Damon to Ely Houston in Richard Wright's *The Outsider.*

Colonel Beriah/Eschol/Mulberry (Berry, Earl of Rossmore) Sellers   Entrepreneur given to such wild schemes as the Salt Lick Pacific Extension and the Knobs Industrial University in Samuel Langhorne Clemens and Charles Dudley Warner's *The Gilded Age* (where he is known as Eschol, in the first edition, or as Beriah, in subsequent editions); plans to reincarnate spirits in Clemens's *The American Claimant* (where he is known as Mulberry and pretends to be the Earl of Rossmore).

Polly Sellers   Wife of Colonel Sellers in Samuel Langhorne Clemens's *The American Claimant* and Clemens and Charles Dudley Warner's *The Gilded Age.*

Sarah (Lady Gwendolen, Sally) Sellers   Daughter of Mulberry and Polly Sellers; falls in love with and marries Berkeley, whom she first knows as Howard Tracy, in Samuel Langhorne Clemens's *The American Claimant.*

Selvagee   Effeminate lieutenant aboard the *Neversink* in Herman Melville's *White-Jacket.*

Irving (Krankeit) Semite   Psychiatrist with bizarre theories and therapies in Terry Southern and Mason Hoffenberg's *Candy.*

Alfred Semple   Husband of Lillian Semple and shoestore owner; dies of pneumonia in Theodore Dreiser's *The Financier.*

Doña Maria Sepulvida   Fiery Latina and romantic interest of men, good and evil, in Bret Harte's *Gabriel Conroy.*

Mother Sereda   Mythical woman who bleaches the color from the cloth of life; flattered by Jurgen into granting him a year of youth, she sends her shadow along to observe his behavior; appears in various guises to Jurgen throughout his journeys in James Branch Cabell's *Jurgen.*

Serge   Russian truck driver who hires Henry Miller as an English teacher in exchange for a room and one meal a day in Henry Miller's *Tropic of Cancer.*

Mrs. May Server   Promiscuous woman who is supposedly using Guy Brissenden as a front for an affair, although she actually loves him, in Henry James's *The Sacred Fount.*

Servilia   Mother of Brutus; she urges her son to become part of the conspiracy against Caesar and hints that Brutus might even be Caesar's son in Thornton Wilder's *The Ides of March.*

Comfort (Fool) Servosse   Captain of the Peru Invincibles who buys Warrington Place after the Civil War; after moving South, he antagonizes his neighbors by associating with teachers from the freedmen's school; becomes disillusioned with the North's failure to protect freedmen and Unionists in the South; dies of yellow fever after a trip to Central America in Albion W. Tourgee's *A Fool's Errand.*

Lily (Lil) Servosse   Daughter of Comfort Servosse; she warns her father and Thomas Denton of the Ku Klux Klan's plans to ambush them; refuses to marry Melville Gurney without his father's approval in Albion W. Tourgee's *A Fool's Errand.*

Metta Ward Servosse   Wife of Comfort Servosse in Albion W. Tourgee's *A Fool's Errand.*

William Severance   Professor of English who teaches Lymie Peters, Hope Davison, and Sally Forbes at a midwestern university in William Maxwell's *The Folded Leaf.*

Birdie Sewall   Sister of Kivden Sewall and friend of Rena Janney in August Derleth's *The Shield of the Valiant.*

John Sewall   Banker who opposes the romance of his son Kivden Sewall and Rena Janney in August Derleth's *The Shield of the Valiant.*

Kivden (Kiv) Sewall   Boyfriend of Rena Janney; quits working in his father's bank and joins a Madison jazz band; enlists in the military at the beginning of World War II in August Derleth's *The Shield of the Valiant.*

William Seward   See William Lee.

Seymour   Murderous black cook and an instigator of the mutiny on the *Grampus;* killed when the ship is retaken by Arthur Gordon Pym, Augustus Barnard, and Dirk Peters in Edgar Allan Poe's *The Narrative of Arthur Gordon Pym.*

Frank Shabata   Jealous and spiteful husband of Marie Shabata; kills his wife and her lover Emil Bergson in Willa Cather's *O Pioneers!*

Marie Tovesky Shabata   Wife of Frank Shabata, who kills her and her lover Emil Bergson, in Willa Cather's *O Pioneers!*

Shah of Bratpuhr   Religious leader of the Kalhouri sect who visits the United States in Kurt Vonnegut's *Player Piano.*

Frank Shallard   Seminary student who, with his friend Elmer Gantry, works as an intern pastor at a country church; becomes a Baptist minister in Sinclair Lewis's *Elmer Gantry.*

Eileen Shallcross   Divorced stepdaughter of Sheridan Dale; falls in love and has an affair with Timothy Colt in Louis Auchincloss's *The Great World and Timothy Colt.*

Irene (Sister Monica) Shane   Daughter of Julia Shane; teaches English to millworkers and becomes a nun, Sister Monica, to the disappointment of her mother, in Louis Bromfield's *The Green Bay Tree.*

Julia Shane   Wealthy Protestant with two daughters in Louis Bromfield's *The Green Bay Tree.*

Lily Shane   Daughter of Julia Shane; after Lily becomes pregnant by the state governor, who will not marry her, her mother sends her to Europe, where she flourishes, in Louis Bromfield's *The Green Bay Tree.*

Father Shannon   Priest who preaches sermons against Sinclair Lewis and H. L. Mencken in James T. Farrell's *The Young Manhood of Studs Lonigan.*

Flo Shannon   Possessive, nagging, yet devoted mother of Margy Shannon in Betty Smith's *Tomorrow Will Be Better.*

Henny Shannon   Brooklyn shop worker; angry and argumentative husband of Flo Shannon and gentle, philosophical father of Margy Shannon in Betty Smith's *Tomorrow Will Be Better.*

Margaret (Margy) Shannon   Seventeen-year-old mail reader at the Thomson-Johnson Mail Order House; conscientious worker with unfulfilled dreams; child of Henry and Flo Shannon and wife of Frankie Malone in Betty Smith's *Tomorrow Will Be Better.*

Max Shapiro   Heroic marine commander killed at Saipan in Leon Uris's *Battle Cry.*

Norah Sharon   Lover of Jerry Fowler; rescued by Fowler and Issachar Bennet from a severe beating in Walter D. Edmonds's *Erie Water.*

Buckingham Sharp   Shrewd, manipulative lawyer and admirer of Adelaide Jones in T. S. Stribling's *Teeftallow;* confidant to Agatha Pomeroy and lawyer for Risdale Balus in *Bright Metal.*

Shattuck   Archaeologist friend of Leonard Rhodes; interested in the "stranger people's" graveyard in Mary Noailles Murfree's *In the "Stranger People's" Country.*

Christopher Shaw   Nephew of Allen Musgrove; helps Horse-Shoe Robinson capture Edgar St. Jermyn in John Pendleton Kennedy's *Horse-Shoe Robinson.*

Dorothy Shaw   Wisecracking brunette companion of Lorelei Lee in Anita Loos's *Gentlemen Prefer Blondes;* her impractical romances and marriages occupy most of the sequel, *But Gentlemen Marry Brunettes.*

Reggie Shaw   Doctor whose insensitivity and drinking are a mask for his despair over the inevitability of his patients' folly and death in James Gould Cozzens's *By Love Possessed.*

Margaret (Maggie) Rose Shawn   Sweetheart of Patrick Dennis Moore and namesake of his daughter, Maggie Moore; cause of the beating and public humiliation of Moore by her brother, Timothy Shawn, in Betty Smith's *Maggie-Now.*

Timothy (Big Red, Tim, Timmy) Shawn   Bowery police officer who avenges the honor of his sister, Maggie Rose Shawn; godfather to Maggie Moore in Betty Smith's *Maggie-Now.*

Esther Root Shawnessy   Second wife of John Wickliff Shawnessy, though half his age, in Ross Lockridge, Jr.'s *Raintree County.*

John Wickliff (Jack, Johnny) Shawnessy   Idealistic Indiana native whose dreams and disappointments mirror those of nineteenth-century America in Ross Lockridge, Jr.'s *Raintree County.*

Susanna Drake Shawnessy   See Susanna Drake.

Aunt Chloe Shelby   See Aunt Chloe.

George Shelby   Son of the owners of Uncle Tom, Aunt Chloe, and Eliza Harris; after having failed to save the venerated Uncle Tom from the hands of Simon Legree, George dedicates his life to the gradual emancipation of his remaining slaves in Harriet Beecher Stowe's *Uncle Tom's Cabin.*

Timothy (Tim) Shelby   Black politician who is lynched for having tried to kiss a white woman in Thomas Dixon's *The Leopard's Spots.*

Uncle Tom Shelby   See Uncle Tom.

P.G. Sheldon   Poet and good friend of Sebastian Knight and Clare Bishop; supplies V. with information about Knight in Vladimir Nabokov's *The Real Life of Sebastian Knight.*

Shenly   Foretopman aboard the *Neversink* who dies of pulmonary problems as White-Jacket tends to him in Herman Melville's *White-Jacket.*

Henry Shepard   Railroad stationmaster in Mudcat Landing, Missouri; hires Hugh McVey as an assistant and helps change Hugh's life for the better in Sherwood Anderson's *Poor White.*

Sarah Shepard   Wife of Henry Shepard; sets out to improve the life of Hugh McVey through his education and hard work in Sherwood Anderson's *Poor White.*

Shepherd   Father of Ophelia Shepherd and Mrs. Martin; enraged with Ophelia for her actions with Mr. Martin, but charges Martin with her seduction and death, in William Hill Brown's *The Power of Sympathy.*

Goode Shepherd   Dutiful but ineffective preacher; father of Mateel Shepherd in E. W. Howe's *The Story of a Country Town.*

Lawson Shepherd   Subordinate to Paul Proteus who eventually takes Proteus's job and wife in Kurt Vonnegut's *Player Piano.*

Mateel Shepherd   Daughter of Goode Shepherd; divorced by her first husband, Jo Erring, who kills her second husband, Clinton Bragg, in E. W. Howe's *The Story of a Country Town.*

Ophelia Shepherd   Sister of Mrs. Martin; commits suicide after having a child by Mr. Martin in William Hill Brown's *The Power of Sympathy.*

Harney Shepherdson   Member of the family that is feuding with the Grangerfords; elopes with Sophia Grangerford, thus precipitating a deadly battle between the two families, in Samuel Langhorne Clemens's *Adventures of Huckleberry Finn.*

Fred (Signor Rossello) Shepley   High rider, as Signor Rossello, for Huguenine's circus; enamored of Albany Yates in Walter D. Edmonds's *Chad Hanna.*

Moseley Sheppard   Virginia planter and gentleman in Arna Wendell Bontemps's *Black Thunder.*

Robin (Marse Robin) Sheppard   Young son of Moseley Sheppard; student at the College of William and Mary in Arna Wendell Bontemps's *Black Thunder.*

Randy Shepperton   Childhood friend of George Webber in Thomas Wolfe's *You Can't Go Home Again* and *The Web and the Rock.*

Colonel Sherburn   Upper-class Arkansan who talks a mob out of lynching him in Samuel Langhorne Clemens's *Adventures of Huckleberry Finn.*

Louisa Sheridan   Young schoolteacher from Lexington, Kentucky; accepts her first job in the remote Cal Valley; central character in Harriette Simpson Arnow's *Mountain Path.*

Nickie Sherman   Best friend, Wildean dramatic collaborator, and brother-in-law of Chick Swallow; sometime policeman, later private detective in Peter De Vries's *Comfort Me with Apples.*

Peter Sherringham   Brother of Julia Sherringham Dallow; diplomat who loves Miriam Rooth and is loved by Biddy Dormer in Henry James's *The Tragic Muse.*

Vida Sherwin   Gopher Prairie teacher and friend of Carol Kennicott in Sinclair Lewis's *Main Street.*

Shimerda   Bohemian weaver and musician; father of Ántonia Shimerda and an unsuccessful farmer who commits suicide in Willa Cather's *My Ántonia.*

Ambroz (Ambrosch) Shimerda   Sullen and surly brother of Ántonia Shimerda; a good farmer in Willa Cather's *My Ántonia.*

Ántonia Shimerda   Daughter of Shimerda and childhood friend of Jim Burden; plans to marry Larry Donovan, but he deserts her after impregnating her; happily married to Anton Cuzak in Willa Cather's *My Ántonia.*

Seth Shipley   Partner in Jim's business; marries Mag Smith after Jim's death and convinces her to abandon Frado to the Bellmont family in Harriet E. Wilson's *Our Nig.*

Helen Shires   Friend of Studs Lonigan in James T. Farrell's *Young Lonigan;* reported to be a lesbian in *The Young Manhood of Studs Lonigan.*

Shirley   Secretary to General Braddock and son of the Massachusetts governor; killed at Fort Duquesne in Mary Lee Settle's *O Beulah Land.*

Shirley   Prostitute in Key Bonita, Florida, who befriends Clinton Williams in James Leo Herlihy's *All Fall Down.*

Uncle Preston (Press) Shiveley   Proprietor of a toll station in Shoestring Valley, Oregon; father of Wade Shiveley and adoptive father of Clay Calvert in H. L. Davis's *Honey in the Horn.*

Wade Shiveley   Son of Uncle Preston Shiveley; ne'er-do-well accused of murdering four men; hanged by homesteaders in H. L. Davis's *Honey in the Horn.*

Hoover (Onnie Jay Holy) Shoats   Preacher in competition with Hazel Motes after Haze refuses to cooperate with him; hires false prophet Solace Layfield as a stand-in for Motes in Flannery O'Connor's *Wise Blood.*

Captain Godfrey Gerald Sholto   Revolutionary who is temporarily the favorite of Princess Casamassima in Henry James's *The Princess Casamassima.*

Earle Shoop   Arizona cowboy and model who is one of Faye Greener's lovers in Nathanael West's *The Day of the Locust.*

Shorty   Employee at the Sunk Creek ranch; killed by Trampas in Owen Wister's *The Virginian.*

Shorty (Cockney)   Cockney planter on Martair in Herman Melville's *Omoo.*

Mary Shrike   Wife of Willie Shrike; permits Miss Lonelyhearts to take physical liberties with her, but will not let him sleep with her, in Nathanael West's *Miss Lonelyhearts.*

Willie Shrike   Newspaper feature editor and Miss Lonelyhearts's humiliating boss in Nathanael West's *Miss Lonelyhearts.*

Moses (Moe) Shulman   Second lieutenant in love with Maria Rocco; shot and killed by a German officer in John Horne Burns's *The Gallery.*

Jack Shumann   Son of Laverne Shumann and either Roger Shumann or Jack Holmes in William Faulkner's *Pylon.*

Laverne Shumann   Wife of Roger Shumann and mother of Jack Shumann in William Faulkner's *Pylon.*

Roger Shumann   Husband of Laverne Shumann; stunt pilot killed in an airplane crash in William Faulkner's *Pylon.*

Reverend Dr. Alfred Shumway   Con man posing as a missionary; actually running contraband guns in Patrick Dennis's *Around the World with Auntie Mame.*

Rosemary Shumway   Con artist posing as Dr. Shumway's daughter in Patrick Dennis's *Around the World with Auntie Mame.*

Lady Caroline Sibly-Biers   Corrupt Englishwoman in F. Scott Fitzgerald's *Tender Is the Night.*

August Sieppe   Brother of Trina Sieppe; wets his pants while at the Orpheum theater, embarrassing his mother and sister before McTeague, in Frank Norris's *McTeague.*

Trina Sieppe   See Trina Sieppe McTeague.

Monica Ehrmann Sigelman   Sister of Noel Airman in Herman Wouk's *Marjorie Morningstar.*

Silas   Servant at Plumfield in Louisa May Alcott's *Little Men.*

Silas Rents His Ox   Pimp and drug dealer and mentor to Berry-berry Williams in James Leo Herlihy's *All Fall Down.*

Mr. Silbermann   Traveling businessman and former detective; meets V. in a train and helps him determine the identity of Sebastian Knight's former Russian mistress in Vladimir Nabokov's *The Real Life of Sebastian Knight.*

Solomon Moses David Menelik Silberstein   Card playing companion of William Demarest in Conrad Aiken's *Blue Voyage.*

Mrs. Tempe Williams Isles   Daughter of Aunt Hagar Williams and wife of a postal clerk; ashamed of her background, she joins the Episcopal Church in Langston Hughes's *Not Without Laughter.*

Dean Silva   Medical school dean in Sinclair Lewis's *Arrowsmith.*

Maria Silva   Poor woman from the South Pacific with whom Martin Eden boards in Jack London's *Martin Eden.*

Mattie (Matt) Silver   Cousin of Zenobia Frome and beloved of Ethan Frome, with whom she fails in a joint suicide attempt that leaves her an invalid, in Edith Wharton's *Ethan Frome.*

Sid Silver   University of Chicago student and part-time reporter for the *Daily Globe;* investigates the murder of Paulie Kessler and covers the trial of Artie Straus and Judd Steiner in Meyer Levin's *Compulsion.*

Mannie Silverhorn   Attorney for Elmer Gantry; ambulance chaser in Sinclair Lewis's *Elmer Gantry.*

Flem Simmons   Eccentric early settler in the mountains of Oregon who befriends Clay Calvert in H. L. Davis's *Honey in the Horn.*

Jake Simmons   Harlem cabaret owner who befriends Jule Jackson in George Wylie Henderson's *Jule.*

Maisie (Maise) Simmons   Wife of Jake Simmons and friend of Jule Jackson in George Wylie Henderson's *Jule.*

Mr. (Bee-lips) Simmons   Lawyer who sets up a deal between Harry Morgan and the Cubans in Ernest Hemingway's *To Have and Have Not.*

Payette Simmons   Sheepherder in H. L. Davis's *Honey in the Horn.*

Ralph (Enrico Del Credo, Sim) Simmons   American opera singer studying in Italy; gives civilian clothes to Frederic Henry after Henry deserts the Italian army in Ernest Hemingway's *A Farewell to Arms.*

Simms   Sidewalk preacher who pursues Jake Blount in Carson McCullers's *The Heart Is a Lonely Hunter.*

Rosalie Simms-Peabody   World traveler and adventurer; guest lecturer for the Ithaca Parlor Lecture Club in William Saroyan's *The Human Comedy.*

Simo   Father of Pamphilus and prominent trader and owner of warehouses and ships in Thornton Wilder's *The Woman of Andros.*

Simon   See Simon Strother.

Simonides   Elderly Jewish merchant and former slave who makes his fortune off the riches of the imprisoned/enslaved Hur family; raises his only daughter, Esther, without her knowing that they are legally slaves; is questioned by Judah Ben-Hur about the whereabouts of his mother and sister and confesses all, offering to return the fortune he has made to its rightful owner; is officially freed by Ben-Hur and becomes a trusted confidant and eventually Ben-Hur's father-in-law in Lew Wallace's *Ben-Hur: A Tale of the Christ*.

Elizabeth (Lizzie) Simpson   Daughter of Rev. Mr. Simpson; lover of Frederick Brent in Paul Laurence Dunbar's *The Uncalled*.

Homer Simpson   Iowa bookkeeper who shares a house with Faye Greener, who will not let him love her, in Nathanael West's *The Day of the Locust*.

Kermit Simpson   Rich, politically idealistic owner and editor of a liberal monthly newspaper and friend of John Laskell in Lionel Trilling's *The Middle of the Journey*.

Mark Simpson   Pennsylvania state senator and friend of Henry Mollenhauer in Theodore Dreiser's *The Financier*.

Rev. Mr. Simpson   Methodist preacher and father of Elizabeth Simpson in Paul Laurence Dunbar's *The Uncalled*.

Sam (Bub) Simpson   Discoverer of Roy Hobbs; takes Hobbs to Chicago to play baseball in Bernard Malamud's *The Natural*.

Chris Sims   Black youth murdered by an angry white mob for associating with white women in Richard Wright's *The Long Dream*.

Mr. Sing   Man who hires Harry Morgan to transport twelve Chinese men; killed by Morgan in Ernest Hemingway's *To Have and Have Not*.

John Singer   Lonely deaf-mute mistakenly idealized by Mick Kelly and other townspeople; commits suicide in despair over the death of his friend Spiros Antonapoulos in Carson Mc-Cullers's *The Heart Is a Lonely Hunter*.

Sergeant Singles   American prisoner of war in England who is married to Jenny, Israel Potter's boyhood sweetheart, in Herman Melville's *Israel Potter*.

Emily Singleton   Dying sister of Robert Singleton, takes refuge at the home of her uncle, Richard Walton, following the burning of her ancestral home in William Gilmore Simms's *The Partisan*.

Major Robert Singleton   Leader of a small band of partisans under Francis Marion in South Carolina in William Gilmore Simms's *The Partisan*.

Sam Singleton   American painter of small landscapes who travels in Europe looking for subject matter; finds Roderick Hudson dead at the bottom of a cliff in Henry James's *Roderick Hudson*.

Frank (J. Yák) Sinisterra   Counterfeiter who inadvertently kills Wyatt Gwyon's mother; his son is romantically involved with Gwyon's model Esme in William Gaddis's *The Recognitions*.

Valerie Sinnot   Screenwriter at Olympia Studios in Ludwig Bemelmans's *Dirty Eddie*.

Sinton   Black preacher and leader of the Princes and Potentates of Ethiopia, a benevolent association; works for equality, justice, and opportunity for blacks in T. S. Stribling's *Unfinished Cathedral*.

Henry De Soto (de Sota) Sippens   Real estate company owner and associate of Frank Cowperwood in Theodore Dreiser's *The Titan*; sent to London to investigate railway investments in *The Stoic*.

Dr. Archibald Sitgreaves   Comic military surgeon of the Virginia dragoons in James Fenimore Cooper's *The Spy*.

Suggie (Miss Suggie) Skeete   Flamboyant tenant of Silla Boyce and confidante of Selina Boyce; after a week of trying to

get ahead, rewards herself with rum and a new lover every weekend in Paule Marshall's *Brown Girl, Brownstones*.

Fradrik Skotoma   Iconoclastic philosopher whose benevolent conception of mankind, Ekwilism, first appeared as a pamphlet printed by Paduk's father and was later transformed by Paduk into a violent political doctrine in Vladimir Nabokov's *Bend Sinister*.

Percival Skrogg   Journalist who helps Wilkie Barron print the handbill that prompts Jeremiah Beaumont to kill Colonel Cassius Fort in Robert Penn Warren's *World Enough and Time*.

Randolph Lee Skully   Homosexual cousin of Amy Sansom; reclusive owner of Skully's Landing; person Joel Harrison Knox must finally turn to in Truman Capote's *Other Voices, Other Rooms*.

Ben Skutt   Lease-hound for J. Arnold Ross's oil company and spy for Petroleum Employers' Federation in Upton Sinclair's *Oil!*

Skyeman   See Jarl.

Senator Skypack   Philistine member of the committee investigating the attempted purchase of Barry Rudd by Wissey Jones; eager to allow the sale for alleged reasons of national defense in John Hersey's *The Child Buyer*.

Frank Slade   Son of Simon Slade; becomes a drunk and murders his father in T. S. Arthur's *Ten Nights in a Bar-Room*.

Simon Slade   Owner of the Sickle and Sheaf tavern, which is the source of Cedarville's corruption; murdered by his son Frank Slade in T. S. Arthur's *Ten Nights in a Bar-Room*.

The Great (Meester) Slashtubitch   Pornographic film star and director in William S. Burroughs's *Naked Lunch* and *The Wild Boys*.

Emmie Slattery   Mother, by Jonas Wilkerson, of illegitimate children in Margaret Mitchell's *Gone with the Wind*.

Mike Slattery   County political leader and mentor of Joe Chapin I in John O'Hara's *Ten North Frederick*.

Peg Slattery   Wife and confidante of Mike Slattery in John O'Hara's *Ten North Frederick*.

Slaughter   Farmhand and fellow employee of Ollie Miss on Uncle Alex's farm in George Wylie Henderson's *Ollie Miss*.

Nathan (Jibbenainosay, Nick of the Woods) Slaughter   Quaker pioneer who avenges his family's massacre by killing Indians and leaving the mark of the Jibbenainosay, or Nick of the Woods, who is believed to be an avenging spirit, in Robert Montgomery Bird's *Nick of the Woods*.

Jane Sligo   Wife of Salathiel Albine in Hervey Allen's *The Forest and the Fort*.

Slim   Jerkline skinner whose country wisdom helps George Milton care for Lennie Small in John Steinbeck's *Of Mice and Men*.

Slim Girl (Came With War, Lillian, Lily)   Beautiful Indian woman who struggles between leading Indian and white lifestyles; married to Laughing Boy; dies of an arrow wound in Oliver La Farge's *Laughing Boy*.

Mrs. Sliter   Cook for Clarissa and Edward Packard; fired for drunkenness in Caroline Gilman's *Recollections of a Housekeeper*.

Clere Sloane   Retired stage beauty married to Campbell Kitchen; Emma Lou Morgan is employed as her personal maid in Wallace Thurman's *The Blacker the Berry*.

Jaffrey (Sloco) Slocum   Cunning lawyer in Robert Herrick's *The Memoirs of an American Citizen*.

Annette and Cellie Slogum   Twin daughters of Gulla and Ruedy Slogum; prostituted by their mother in order to gain power over the Dumur County sheriff and county judge in Mari Sandoz's *Slogum House*.

Cash Slogum   Second son of Gulla and Ruedy Slogum; forced by his mother to commit crimes in order to help build the Slogum House property in Mari Sandoz's *Slogum House*.

Fannie Slogum   Fourth daughter of Gulla and Ruedy Slogum and twin of Ward Slogum; returns home from an eastern boarding school, suffering from frequent abortions, venereal disease, and consumption in Mari Sandoz's *Slogum House*.

Haber (Hab) Slogum   Oldest son of Gulla and, possibly, Ruedy Slogum; forced by his mother to commit crimes in order to help build the Slogum House property in Mari Sandoz's *Slogum, House*.

Libby Slogum   Oldest daughter of Gulla and Ruedy Slogum; responsible for the clean beds and good meals at Slogum House in Mari Sandoz's *Slogum Home*.

Regula Haber (Gulla) Slogum   Wife of Ruedy Slogum and mother of seven children; proprietor of the roadhouse, Slogum House, in Mari Sandoz's *Slogum House*.

Ruedy Slogum   Husband of Gulla Haber and father, by her, of seven children in Mari Sandoz's *Slogum Home*.

Ward Slogum   Third son of Gulla and Ruedy Slogum and twin of Fannie Slogum; beaten severely by the brothers of his Polish girlfriend after they are incited by his mother in Mari Sandoz's *Slogum House*.

Lazar Slonim   Jewish resistance fighter in Warsaw during the Nazi occupation; escapes through the ghetto wall, travels to the Treblinka death camp, and reveals the truth about the so-called Nazi resettlement of the Jews in John Hersey's *The Wall*.

Doctor Austin Sloper   Wealthy New York physician and widowed father of Catherine Sloper; determines to disinherit Catherine if she marries Morris Townsend, whom he despises, in Henry James's *Washington Square*.

Catherine Sloper   Daughter of Dr. Austin Sloper and niece of Lavinia Penniman; jilted by Morris Townsend in Henry James's *Washington Square*.

Harry Sloss   Associate of Paul Madvig's who, from a distance, witnesses the murder of Taylor Henry in Dashiell Hammett's *The Glass Key*.

Saul Slowns   Yankee soldier who stays on in Tennessee after the Civil War; bachelor friend of Peter Legrand in Andrew Lytle's *The Velvet Horn*.

Slug   See Dagny Taggart.

Dr. Henry Small   Young and apparently upright medical doctor who is actually the sinister leader of a band of robbers in Edward Eggleston's *The Hoosier School-Master*.

Lennie Small   Retarded companion of George Milton; helpless ranch worker whose misunderstood strength leads to his death in John Steinbeck's *Of Mice and Men*.

William Small   Small-minded principal of North Manual Trades High School in Evan Hunter's *The Blackboard Jungle*.

William Small   See Max Disher.

Smith   British lieutenant in William Faulkner's *A Fable*.

Smith Sheet music salesman from New Orleans and fictitious father of William Demarest in Conrad Aiken's *Blue Voyage*.

Alexander (John Adams, Alex, Reckless Jack) Smith Londoner, whose real name is John Adams, who signs aboard HMS *Bounty* as Alexander Smith; joins in the rebellion in Charles Nordhoff and James Norman Hall's *Mutiny on the Bounty*; treats the Tahitians humanely; as the sole survivor of Fletcher Christian's experiment with democracy, narrates the second half of *Pitcairn's Island*.

Beauty (Pinhead) Smith Yukon "Sour-dough" who buys White Fang to use in dogfights in Jack London's *White Fang*.

Boots Smith Cold, hard young black musician who works for Mr. Junto and is beaten to death by Lutie Johnson in Ann Petry's *The Street*.

Essie Meadowfill Smith Wife of McKinley Smith in William Faulkner's *The Mansion*.

Jack Tom Smith World War I navy buddy of Alfred Eaton; becomes a wealthy Texas oil man and befriends Eaton during World War II in John O'Hara's *From the Terrace*.

John Smith Soldier of fortune and founder of Virginia in John Pendleton Kennedy's *Swallow Barn*.

Capt. John Smith Colonial hero who saves himself from execution by Indians by successfully penetrating the impervious hymen of Pocahontas in John Barth's *The Sot-Weed Factor*.

Lafe Smith Junior senator from Iowa; playboy in his private life but an honorable politician and close friend of Sen. Brigham Anderson in Allen Drury's *Advise and Consent*.

Mag Smith White washerwoman who marries a black man, Jim, and gives birth to their daughter Frado; abandons Frado to the Bellmont family in Harriet E. Wilson's *Our Nig*.

McKinley Smith Texan who marries Essie Meadowfill in William Faulkner's *The Mansion*.

Miss Sarah Smith White schoolteacher from the North who comes to teach black children in Alabama and is instrumental in Zora's development; sister of Peter Charles Smith in W. E. B. Du Bois's *The Quest of the Silver Fleece*.

Mrs. Horace Smith Widow for whom Rabbit Angstrom works temporarily as a gardener in John Updike's *Rabbit, Run*.

Peter Smith Self-made man who rises from overseer to plantation owner and justice of the peace; father of Potestatem Dedimus Smith in Albion W. Tourgee's *Bricks Without Straw*.

Peter Charles Smith Senator who pays a high price for his seat when he represents interests not to his liking; brother of Sarah Smith in W. E. B. Du Bois's *The Quest of the Silver Fleece*.

Potestatent Dedimus Smith See Colonel Potern Desmit.

Raymond (Ray, Tiger) Smith Writer and cross-country traveler introduced to mountain climbing and asceticism by Japhy Ryder; narrator of Jack Kerouac's *The Dharma Bums*.

Roger Smith California newspaper editor; antiliberal sometime employer of Peter Gale in Louis Adamic's *Grandsons*.

Lieutenant Colonel John Dawson (Johnny) Smithers Anti-Semitic Georgian and U.S. infantry commander; becomes the lover of Dorothy Brock in Martha Gellhorn's *Wine of Astonishment*.

Smoke Black hotel porter lynched for allegedly assaulting a tough young man in Brand Whitlock's *J. Hardin & Son*.

Turk Smollet Isolated Winesburg wood chopper in Sherwood Anderson's *Winesburg, Ohio*.

Smothers Tiresias figure whose prophetic voice cannot prevent industrial disaster or save the souls of the steel mill workers in William Attaway's *Blood on the Forge*.

Maudel Smothers Best friend with whom Harriett Williams is arrested for prostitution in Langston Hughes's *Not Without Laughter*.

Wellington Smythe Supposed English aristocrat who is actually the son of a charwoman; advises southern women on fashion, manners, and entertainments in Mary Lee Settle's *Know Nothing*.

Aramintha Snead Churchwoman who seeks advice from N'Gana Frimbo in Rudolph Fisher's *The Conjure-Man Dies*.

Balso Snell Poet who crawls into a Trojan horse inhabited by unread writers in Nathanael West's *The Dream Life of Balso Snell*.

Clem (Private Ass Hole) Snide Protean character who ruins a sex/death cinema party in William S. Burroughs's *The Soft Machine*; appears briefly in *Naked Lunch*.

Abner (Ab) Snopes Father of Flem Snopes in William Faulkner's *The Unvanquished, The Hamlet, The Town*, and *The Mansion*.

Admiral Dewey Snopes Son of Eck Snopes in William Faulkner's *The Town* and *The Mansion*.

Bilbo Snopes Son of I. O. Snopes in William Faulkner's *The Town* and *The Mansion*.

Byron Snopes Brother of Virgil Snopes and father of the little Indian Snopeses; bank bookkeeper in William Faulkner's *Sartoris (Flags in the Dust), The Town*, and *The Mansion*.

Clarence Eggleston Snopes Son of I. O. Snopes; state senator in William Faulkner's *Sanctuary, The Town*, and *The Mansion*.

Doris Snopes   Son of I. O. Snopes in William Faulkner's *The Town* and *The Mansion*.

Eckrum (Eck) Snopes   Cousin of Flem Snopes and father of Wallstreet Panic and Admiral Dewey Snopes in William Faulkner's *The Hamlet, The Town,* and *The Mansion*.

Eula Varner Snopes   Daughter of Will Varner; has a child, Linda Snopes, by Hoake McCarron; marries Flem Snopes and has a long affair with Manfred de Spain; appears in William Faulkner's *The Hamlet, The Town,* and *The Mansion*.

Flem Snopes   Son of Ab Snopes and husband of Eula Varner; progresses from store clerk to bank president; appears in William Faulkner's *Sartoris (Flags in the Dust), As I Lay Dying, The Hamlet, The Town, The Mansion,* and *The Reivers*.

I. O. Snopes   Cousin of Flem Snopes and father of Bilbo, Clarence, Doris, Montgomery Ward, Saint Elmo, and Vardaman Snopes; appears in William Faulkner's *The Sound and the Fury, The Hamlet, The Town,* and *The Mansion*.

Isaac (Ike) Snopes   Cousin of Flem Snopes; loves Jack Houston's cow in William Faulkner's *The Hamlet*.

Launcelot (Lump) Snopes   Clerk, succeeding his cousin Flem Snopes, at Jody Varner's store in William Faulkner's *The Hamlet* and *The Mansion*.

Linda Snopes   See Linda Snopes Kohl.

Mink Snopes   Cousin of Flem Snopes; murders Jack Houston; appears in William Faulkner's *The Hamlet, The Town,* and *The Mansion*.

Montgomery Ward Snopes   Son of I. O. Snopes in William Faulkner's *Sartoris (Flags in the Dust), The Town,* and *The Mansion*.

Orestes (Res) Snopes   Farmer in William Faulkner's *The Mansion*.

Saint Elmo Snopes   Son of I. O. Snopes in William Faulkner's *The Hamlet*.

Vardaman Snopes   Son of I. O. Snopes in William Faulkner's *The Town* and *The Mansion*.

Virgil Snopes   Son of Wesley Snopes in William Faulkner's *Sanctuary, The Town,* and *The Mansion*.

Vynie Snopes   First wife of Ab Snopes in William Faulkner's *The Hamlet*.

Wallstreet Panic (Wall) Snopes   Son of Eck Snopes in William Faulkner's *The Hamlet, The Town,* and *The Mansion*.

Watkins Products Snopes   Carpenter in William Faulkner's *The Mansion*.

Wesley Snopes   Father of Virgil Snopes in William Faulkner's *The Mansion*.

Yettie Snopes   Wife of Mink Snopes in William Faulkner's *The Hamlet* and *The Mansion*.

Rev. Lazarus Snortgrace   Frontier preacher in James Kirke Paulding's *Westward Ho!*

Ernst (Ernie) Snow   Christ-driven husband of Stella Snow in John Hawkes's *The Cannibal*.

Stella Snow   Aristocratic personification of German nationalism; participates in the cannibalization of her nephew in John Hawkes's *The Cannibal*.

Uncle Snow   New Yorker who employs his nephew Tom Bailey in his counting house in Thomas Bailey Aldrich's *The Story of a Bad Boy*.

Mott (Pinky) Snyth   Husband of Vashti Hake Snyth; former cowhand who helps manage the Hake cattle operation in Edna Ferber's *Giant*.

Vashti Hake (Vash) Snyth   Daughter of a wealthy cattle rancher, wife of Pinky Snyth, and friend of Leslie Benedict in Edna Ferber's *Giant*.

Rita Greenough Sohlberg   Mistress of Frank Cowperwood; injured by the jealous Aileen Cowperwood in Theodore Dreiser's *The Titan*.

Ermentrude (Ermy) Solomon   Friend about whom Raymonde Ransome composes a poem in H. D.'s *Palimpsest*.

Leon Solomon   Philosophy professor and one of two teachers on whom Raymond Blent's eligibility to play football depends in Howard Nemerov's *The Homecoming Game*.

Dr. Isidore Solow   Selfless, socially conscious Lower East Side physician in Michael Gold's *Jews without Money*.

Henry Solum   Norwegian-American farmer who becomes a teacher in O. E. Rölvaag's *Giants in the Earth*; appears in *Peder Victorious*.

Sam Solum   Norwegian-American farmer who sells a farm to Store-Hans Holm (Hansa) and then goes west in O. E. Rölvaag's *Giants in the Earth* and *Peder Victorious*.

Lottie Somers   Widow Henry Miller attempts to seduce because she is now weak and vulnerable in Henry Miller's *Tropic of Capricorn*.

Julia Valette Somerville   Orphan adopted by Malcolm and Sarah Bedford; pretty coquette who marries Duncan Bedford in Stark Young's *So Red the Rose*.

Gustaf Sondelius   Famous soldier of science who travels the world promoting medical research and who later works with Martin Arrowsmith in Sinclair Lewis's *Arrowsmith*.

Sophie   German immigrant who is the cook for the Morison family in William Maxwell's *They Came Like Swallows*.

Sorenson   Longtime clipperman at the Past Bay Manufacturing Company factory; reluctant striker in Robert Cantwell's *The Land of Plenty*.

Bea Sorenson   Employee of Carol Kennicott; dies of typhoid fever in Sinclair Lewis's *Main Street*.

Sostrata   Wife of Simo and mother of Argo in Thornton Wilder's *The Woman of Andros*.

Brother Soulsby   Itinerant evangelist and husband of Candace Soulsby in Harold Frederic's *The Damnation of Theron Ware*.

Sister Candace Soulsby   Pragmatic evangelist and fundraiser; adviser and refuge of the disgraced Theron Ware in Harold Frederic's *The Damnation of Theron Ware*.

Allen Southby   Harvard professor and literary scholar who aspires to write the definitive novel about Wickford Point; second husband of Bella Brill in John P. Marquand's *Wickford Point*.

Space Wanderer   See Malachi Constant.

Sam Spade   Private detective hired by Brigid O'Shaughnessy first, ostensibly, to help find her missing sister and then to help her locate the jewel-encrusted statuette in Dashiell Hammett's *The Maltese Falcon*.

Major de Spain   Landowner and sheriff of Yoknapatawpha County; appears in William Faulkner's *Absalom, Absalom!; The Hamlet; Go Down, Moses; Intruder in the Dust; The Town; The Mansion;* and *The Reivers*.

Manfred de Spain   Son of Major de Spain; banker and mayor; appears in William Faulkner's *The Town, The Mansion,* and *The Reivers*.

Thomas (Tom) Spangler   Manager of the telegraph office where Homer Macauley works in William Saroyan's *The Human Comedy*.

Wolvert Spangler   Ballad-singing cobbler in James Kirke Paulding's *Koningsmarke*.

John Spaniard   Companion of Doctor Reefy in Sherwood Anderson's *Winesburg, Ohio*.

Patience (Patitia) Sparhawk   Orphaned daughter of an alcoholic mother; falsely accused of murdering her husband Beverly Peele, but is saved from execution by Garan Bourke in Gertrude Atherton's *Patience Sparhawk and Her Times*.

Sparicio   Louisiana fisherman who transports Julien La Brierre to Viosca's Point in Lafcadio Hearn's *Chita*.

Pammy Lee Sparkman   Black cook of Drusilla Lacefield Crowninshield; seduced by Jerry Catlin the Second and murdered by Ludus Meggs; appears in T. S. Stribling's *The Store* and *Unfinished Cathedral*.

Sparling   Surgeon-general of Java who offers relief for the men of the HMS *Bounty;* provides a place for Thomas Ledward to recall and record his ordeal in Charles Nordhoff and James Norman Hall's *Men against the Sea*.

Anne Sparrow   Teacher in Wayback, Illinois, whose fear of darkness leads to a brief relationship with Zury Prouder; marries John McVey, bears children by Prouder, and later marries Prouder in Joseph Kirkland's *Zury*.

Willard Sparser   Wild friend of Clyde Griffiths; involves Griffiths in a fatal hit-and-run accident in Theodore Dreiser's *An American Tragedy*.

Peter Spavic   Close friend of Agee Ward; responsible for maintaining and continuing Ward's album in Wright Morris's *The Man Who Was There*.

Mrs. Spearman   Elderly, virtuous housekeeper for Judge Honeywell in Ellen Glasgow's *The Romantic Comedians*.

Elsie Speers   Mother of Rosemary Hoyt in F. Scott Fitzgerald's *Tender Is the Night*.

Miss Mary (Cornelia) Spence   Teacher of Penrod Schofield; he sorely tries her patience in Booth Tarkington's *Penrod, Penrod and Sam,* and *Penrod Jashber*.

Maisie Spencer   Mac's wife whom he abandons along with their two young children to work for social revolution in John Dos Passos's *U.S.A.* trilogy.

Mr. Spencer   History teacher whom Holden Caulfield visits before leaving Pencey Prep in J. D. Salinger's *The Catcher in the Rye*.

Clement (Clem) Spender   Former suitor of Delia Ralston; jilted by Delia because he will not give up painting and become a lawyer; lover of Charlotte Lovell and father of their illegitimate child, Clementina Ralston, in Edith Wharton's *The Old Maid*.

Roderick (Rod) Spenser   Cincinnati reporter and aspiring playwright who takes Susan Lenox to New York, abandons her, and is later rescued from alcoholism by her in David Graham Phillips's *Susan Lenox*.

Spider   Dice player, gambler, and friend of Jake Adams and Scar; victim left crippled by a street gang in Herbert Simmons's *Corner Boy*.

Spirit of Alternatives (But on the Other Hand, Tu As Raison Aussi)   Intellectual discussant whom Joseph generates imaginatively for private colloquies on the nature of reality and morality in Saul Bellow's *Dangling Man.*

Spitz   Member of Buck's dog team; killed by Buck in a fight over control of the team in Jack London's *The Call of the Wild.*

Henry Spoffard   Wealthy and stingy censor of plays; Lorelei Lee marries him to finance a movie in which she will appear in Anita Loos's *Gentlemen Prefer Blondes;* he is further manipulated in *But Gentlemen Marry Brunettes.*

Icey Spoon   Wife of Walt Spoon; befriends Willa Harper after Ben Harper's execution in Davis Grubb's *The Night of the Hunter.*

Walt Spoon   Husband of Icey Spoon; store owner who employs Willa Harper out of charity in Davis Grubb's *The Night of the Hunter.*

Cherub Spooney   River barge deckhand in James Kirke Paulding's *Westward Ho!*

Sportin' Life   Carefree mulatto drug dealer who persuades Bess to take cocaine in DuBose Heyward's *Porgy.*

Abner E. Spragg   Father of Undine Spragg; his numerous business endeavors fund his daughter's zealous quest for social status in Edith Wharton's *The Custom of the Country.*

Leota B. Spragg   Ineffectual mother of Undine Spragg in Edith Wharton's *The Custom of the Country.*

Undine (Countess Raymond de Chelles, Undine Marvell, Undine Moffatt) Spragg   Relentlessly ambitious heroine who marries four times, twice to the same man, in her quest for wealth and acceptance in fashionable society in Edith Wharton's *The Custom of the Country.*

Clive Springer   Lover of Selina Boyce; aimless and nonproductive because of guilt heaped on him by his mother, Clytie Springer, in Paule Marshall's *Brown Girl, Brownstones.*

Clytie Springer   Mother of Clive Springer; uses her illnesses to keep him close to her in Paule Marshall's *Brown Girl, Brownstones.*

Frederick (Fred) Springer   Car dealer, husband of Rebecca Springer, and father of Janice Angstrom in John Updike's *Rabbit, Run* and *Rabbit Redux.*

Mr. Springer   Traveling drug salesman who frequently stays at the Beulah Hotel in Eudora Welty's *The Ponder Heart.*

Rebecca Springer   Wife of Fred Springer and mother of Janice Angstrom in John Updike's *Rabbit, Run* and *Rabbit Redux.*

Squeak   Sailor aboard the *Indomitable* who lies about Billy Budd in Herman Melville's *Billy Budd.*

Henrietta C. Stackpole   Brilliant and opinionated American journalist who is interested in Isabel Archer's life in Henry James's *The Portrait of a Lady.*

Ralph (Roaring Ralph) Stackpole   Loudmouth frontiersman and Indian fighter in Robert Montgomery Bird's *Nick of the Woods.*

Robert Stadler   Prominent scientist who surrenders his integrity to power-seeking government officials in Ayn Rand's *Atlas Shrugged.*

Lionel Stafford   Ill-fated intellectual-cum-coal miner in Jack Conroy's *The Disinherited.*

Maury Stafford   Rival of Richard Cleave for the affections of Judith Cary; sends a false order which disgraces Cleave and leads to the destruction of the Stonewall Brigade; confesses, and does penance in the trenches, in Mary Johnston's *The Long Roll* and *Cease Firing.*

Monroe Stahr   Brilliant movie producer who falls in love with Kathleen Moore in F. Scott Fitzgerald's *The Last Tycoon.*

Antrim Stairs   Biology professor who marries Julia Maybury in Mary Austin's *Santa Lucia.*

Julia Maybury Stairs   See Julia Maybury.

Jane (Janie) Staley   Cleaning woman and lover of Parkman's old men; grandmother of Edith Barclay in James Jones's *Some Came Running.*

Pat Stamper   Horse trader in William Faulkner's *The Hamlet* and *The Mansion.*

Constance Standish   See Constance MacKenzie.

Lord Stane   See Gordon Roderick.

Gerald Stanhope, Earl of Danforth and Duke of Ravenspur   Foppish fourth husband of Amber St. Clare; selected by King Charles II to offer respectability to Amber's pregnancy with the king's child in Kathleen Winsor's *Forever Amber.*

George Stanhope   Literary agent who helps Jim Calder revise Calder's writing in order to attain commercial success in John P. Marquand's *Wickford Point.*

James Staniford   Friend of Charley Dunham; marries Lydia Blood in William Dean Howells's *The Lady of the Aroostook.*

Lydia Blood Staniford   See Lydia Blood.

Rudolf Stanislaus (Rudek, Rudo) Stanka   Illegitimate son of Countess Zdenka von Studenitz and Crown Prince Rudolf von Hapsburg; reared by Dora Dugova, a Croatian peasant; uses his restored family position for the betterment of the peasants; narrator of Louis Adamic's *Cradle of Life.*

Zorka Dugova Stanka   See Zorka Dugova.

Stanley   Catholic organist who writes a concerto for his dying mother; buried in a church's collapse at the of William Gaddis's *The Recognitions*.

Joseph (Joe) Stanley   Caretaker at St. Jude's church in Sac Prairie in August Derleth's *The Shield of the Valiant*.

Glendinning (Glen) Stanly   Cousin of Pierre Glendinning III; tries to save Lucy Tartan from Pierre in Herman Melville's *Pierre*.

Dr. Stanpole   Physician at Devon School who performs the surgery during which Finny dies in John Knowles's *A Separate Peace*.

Charlotte Stant   School friend of Maggie Verver; marries Adam Verver in Henry James's *The Golden Bowl*.

Adam Stanton   Brother of Anne Stanton, friend of Jack Burden's youth, and physician whom Willie Stark selects to head his new hospital; assassinates Stark after learning of Stark's affair with Anne in Robert Penn Warren's *All the King's Men*.

Anne Stanton   Sister of Adam Stanton, mistress of Willie Stark, and later wife of Jack Burden in Robert Penn Warren's *All the King's Men*.

Governor Stanton   Father of Anne and Adam Stanton and friend of Judge Irwin in Robert Penn Warren's *All the King's Men*.

Gertrude Staple   Second wife of J. Ward Morehouse in John Dos Passos's *U.S.A.* trilogy.

Starbuck   Chief mate aboard the *Pequod* who is unable to challenge Ahab successfully in Herman Melville's *Moby-Dick*.

Lucy Stark   Wife of Willie Stark and mother of Tom Stark in Robert Penn Warren's *All the King's Men*.

Maylon Stark   Cook transferred to G Company; relates stories of Karen Holmes's sexual promiscuity at Fort Bliss to Milton Warden in James Jones's *From Here to Eternity*.

Tom Stark   Son of Willie and Lucy Stark; his sexual indiscretions cause political problems for Willie Stark; dies of a football injury in Robert Penn Warren's *All the King's Men*.

Willie (Cousin Willie, Boss, Governor) Stark   Lawyer, governor, father of Tom Stark, and employer of Jack Burden; rises from naive politico to ruthless demagogue in Robert Penn Warren's *All the King's Men*.

Oliver Reno Starkey   Mobster who is challenging Lew Yard for control of thievery in Personville in Dashiell Hammett's *Red Harvest*.

Joseph (Jody, Joe) Starks   Entrepreneur who becomes mayor of Eatonville, Florida, and Janie Crawford's second husband in Zora Neale Hurston's *Their Eyes Were Watching God*.

Berryben (Ben) Starnes (Ganchion)   Son of Malley and Walter Warren Starnes; wanderer who leaves his family in Charity in William Goyen's *The House of Breath*.

Jessy Starnes   Sickly daughter of Malley and Walter Warren Starnes; dies at the age of nineteen in William Goyen's *The House of Breath*.

Jimbob Starnes   Husband of Lauralee Starnes; father of Maidie and Swimma Starnes in William Goyen's *The House of Breath*.

Lauralee (Aunty) Starnes   Daughter of Granny Ganchion; wife of Jimbob Starnes and mother of Maidie and Swimma Starnes; dies in Dallas in William Goyen's *The House of Breath*.

Maidie Starnes   See Maidie Starnes Suggs.

Malley Ganchion Starnes   Daughter of Granny Ganchion; wife of Walter Warren Starnes and mother of Jessy and Berryben Starnes; becomes blind in William Goyen's *The House of Breath*.

Sue Emma (Swimma) Starnes   Daughter of Lauralee and Jimbob Starnes; becomes a model and actress, marries, and has several deformed children; finally operates a boardinghouse in Texas in William Goyen's *The House of Breath*.

Walter Warren Starnes   Husband of Malley Ganchion Starnes; father of Jessy and Berryben Starnes in William Goyen's *The House of Breath*.

Doctor Alexander Alexandrovich Starov   Physician of V.'s mother; meets Sebastian Knight by chance and treats him in his final illness in Vladimir Nabokov's *The Real Life of Sebastian Knight*.

Aaron Pendleton Starr   Father of Amantha Starr; refuses to accept his daughter's black blood and sends her to school in Ohio; dies unexpectedly without freeing her in Robert Penn Warren's *Band of Angels*.

Amantha (Manty, Mrs. Tobias Sears) Starr   Daughter and slave of Aaron Starr, slave and mistress of Hamish Bond, and wife of Tobias Sears; repeatedly asks, "Who am I?"; narrator of Robert Penn Warren's *Band of Angels*.

Walter Starr   Family friend who accompanies Andrew Lynch to the scene of the accident in which Jay Follet dies in James Agee's *A Death in the Family*.

Francis Starwick   Harvard schoolmate of Eugene Gant and secret homosexual in Thomas Wolfe's *Of Time and the River*.

Emil (Professor) Staubmeyer   Superintendent of schools in Fort Beulah and later a Minute Man officer in Sinclair Lewis's *It Can't Happen Here*.

Charlie Stavros   Lover of Janice Angstrom and salesman at her father's car dealership in John Updike's *Rabbit, Run* and *Rabbit Redux*.

Shep Stearns   Junior writer for a Hollywood film studio who, after submitting a screenplay for a college musical, is assigned to collaborate on the project with Manley Halliday, a writer whose work he greatly admires; not knowing that Halliday is an alcoholic, he presses him into sharing two bottles of champagne, inducing the drinking binge that will take Halliday's life in Budd Schulberg's *The Disenchanted*.

Margaret Gale (Maggie) Stedman   Granddaughter of Anton Galé in Louis Adamic's *Grandsons*.

Morgan Steele   Editor of the New York newspaper for which Patience Sparhawk works in Gertrude Atherton's *Patience Sparhawk and Her Times*.

Steelkilt   Lakeman aboard the *Town-Ho* who has an altercation with Radney in Herman Melville's *Moby-Dick*.

Steenie   See George Villiers.

Stefan (Corporal)   Soldier killed by a firing squad for leading a mutiny in William Faulkner's *A Fable*.

Harper Steger   Attorney for Frank Cowperwood in Theodore Dreiser's *The Financier and The Titan*.

Genevieve (Jenny) Steinbauer   Blonde who attends the yacht party with Pete Ginotta in William Faulkner's *Mosquitoes*.

Judah (Judd) Steiner, Jr.   Kidnapper and murderer (along with Artie Straus) of Paulie Kessler in Meyer Levin's *Compulsion*.

Judah Steiner, Sr.   Father of Judd Steiner and Chicago garment industry millionaire in Meyer Levin's *Compulsion*.

George W. Stener   Philadelphia city treasurer and agent for powerful politicians; refuses a loan to Frank Cowperwood in Theodore Dreiser's *The Financier*.

Uncle Birdie Steptoe   Drunken fisherman who befriends John Harper; discovers Willa Harper's body submerged in the river in Davis Grubb's *The Night of the Hunter*.

Felicia Sterling   Cousin of Rachel Winslow and resident of Chicago in Charles M. Sheldon's *In His Steps*.

Philip (Phil) Sterling   College friend of Henry Brierly and boyfriend of Ruth Bolton; unsuccessful at numerous jobs, but goes west with Brierly to make money from the railroads in Samuel Langhorne Clemens and Charles Dudley Warner's *The Gilded Age*.

Moran Sternersen   Largely uncivilized, amorally predatory woman with whom Ross Wilbur falls in love; killed on the *Bertha Millner* in Frank Norris's *Moran of the Lady Letty*.

Bertha Sternowitz   Enormous sister of Genya Schearl and possessor of a sharp Yiddish wit in Henry Roth's *Call It Sleep*.

Carmen Sternwood   Homicidal and nymphomaniacal younger daughter of General Sternwood in Raymond Chandler's *The Big Sleep*.

General Guy Sternwood   Dying father of Carmen and Vivian; Philip Marlowe's client in Raymond Chandler's *The Big Sleep*.

Dominie Stettinius   Clergyman and tutor of Sybrandt in James Kirke Paulding's *The Dutchman's Fireside*.

Steve   Friend of the Virginian in Owen Wister's *The Virginian*.

Don Stevens   Radical and abrasive newspaperman, an acquaintance of Eleanor Stoddard and Eveline Hutchins, he organizes a protest of the Sacco and Vanzetti execution with the help of Mary French in John Dos Passos's *U.S.A.* trilogy.

Dr. Stevens   Physician who nurses Arthur Mervyn to health following Mervyn's brush with yellow fever; becomes Mervyn's friend and adviser after listening to Mervyn tell about his adventures in Charles Brockden Brown's *Arthur Mervyn*.

Gavin Stevens   Attorney in William Faulkner's *Light in August*; *Go Down, Moses*; *Intruder in the Dust*; *Requiem for a Nun*; *The Town*; and *The Mansion*.

Gowan Stevens   Cousin of Gavin Stevens in William Faulkner's *The Town*; Temple Drake's husband in Faulkner's *Requiem for a Nun*; abandons his wife in Faulkner's *Sanctuary*.

Lemuel Stevens   Judge and father of Gavin and Margaret Stevens; appears in William Faulkner's *Intruder in the Dust, The Town, The Mansion,* and *The Reivers*.

Margaret Stevens   See Margaret Stevens Mallison.

Melisandre Backus Stevens   Wife of Gavin Stevens in William Faulkner's *The Mansion*.

Temple Drake Stevens   As Temple Drake, a flapper raped with a corncob by Popeye in William Faulkner's *Sanctuary*; wife of Gowan Stevens in *Requiem for a Nun*.

Stony Stevenson   Soldier friend of Malachi Constant in Kurt Vonnegut's *The Sirens of Titan*.

Agnes (Aggie, Jim) Stewart   Daughter of Jack Stewart and a woman of Ethiopian heritage; true love of Jean Baptiste in Oscar Micheaux's *The Homesteader*.

Col. Alexander Stewart   Copperhead, two-term Ohio legislator, and one of the oldest citizens of Dorbury, Ohio; father of Walter Stewart in Paul Laurence Dunbar's *The Fanatics*.

Cora Gordon Stewart   Sister of Harry Gordon and half sister of Nina and Tom Gordon; after having attempted to claim the Mississippi plantation left to her by her white husband, she is seized and thrown back into slavery; kills her children to prevent them from living enslaved, and is hanged as a murderess in Harriet Beecher Stowe's *Dred*.

Frances Stewart Beautiful courtesan who supplants Barbara Palmer as the chief interest of King Charles II; smallpox destroys her beauty and she finally becomes a close friend of Queen Catherine in Kathleen Winsor's *Forever Amber*.

Jack Stewart Scottish immigrant and farmer; father of Agnes Stewart in Oscar Micheaux's *The Homesteader*.

Walter Stewart Only son of Alexander Stewart; supports the Union during the Civil War and is denounced by his father in Paul Laurence Dunbar's *The Fanatics*.

Jerusalem Webster (Professor) Stiles Cynical, fraudulent professor and alter ego of John Wickliff Shawnessy in Ross Lockridge, Jr.'s *Raintree County*.

Sam Stillings Former butler at the Cresswell plantation who becomes Register of the Treasury in Washington, D.C., and marries Miss Caroline Wynn after he double-crosses Blessed Alwyn and Tom Teerswell in W. E. B. Du Bois's *The Quest of the Silver Fleece*.

Stilwell Gunner's mate second class who is at the helm of the USS *Caine* when the ship is seized by mutineers; obeys the mutineers in Herman Wouk's *The Caine Mutiny*.

Alec Stivvens Friend of Thomas Paine; thief in London's Gin Row who is hanged for stealing in Howard Fast's *Citizen Tom Paine*.

Stockton Failed merchant and friend of Clarissa and Edward Packard in Caroline Gilman's *Recollections of a Housekeeper*.

Bernice Stockton Domineering story writer who ignores her husband Bruce Dudley, whom she knows as John Stockton, because of his lack of ambition in Sherwood Anderson's *Dark Laughter*.

John Stockton See Bruce Dudley.

Stock Stockton Police officer who investigates Frederick Eichner's automobile accident in Terry Southern's *Flash and Filigree*.

Eleanor Stoddard Designer and eventual companion of J. Ward Morehouse who through hard work and skillful management of her image becomes a successful businesswoman and socialite in John Dos Passos's *U.S.A.* trilogy.

Hopton Stoddard Guilt-ridden philanthropist who commissions Howard Roark to build a temple in Ayn Rand's *The Fountainhead*.

David Stofsky Jobless homosexual poet and former Columbia University student who has visions in John Clellon Holmes's *Go*.

Bob Stone Scion of a former slaveholding family whose sexual attraction to Louisa leads to his death and the lynching of her black lover in Jean Toomer's *Cane*.

Hazel Stone Wife of Milton Stone II; administrative assistant to Senator Boyd Potter, whom she tries to stop from using the atomic bomb against the president of the United States, in Mari Sandoz's *The Tom-Walker*.

Hiram Stone Husband of Sarah Stone and father of Milton Stone; profit-raker during the Civil War in Mari Sandoz's *The Tom-Walker*.

Mrs. Karen (Miss Priss, The Pet) Stone Retired fifty-year-old actress who reflects on her marriage and stage career; sensing she is losing her beauty, she depends on gigolos for emotional and sexual gratification in Tennessee Williams's *The Roman Spring of Mrs. Stone*.

Lucinda Martin (Lucie) Stone Wife of Milton Stone I, whom she marries despite his loss of a leg; mother of Martin Stone in Mari Sandoz's *The Tom-Walker*.

Lyster Stone Bohemian artist and friend of Isabel Otis and John Gwynne; introduces Gwynne to the underside of San Francisco life in Gertrude Atherton's *Ancestors*.

Martin (Marty) Stone World War I veteran with gassed lungs; husband of Penny Turner Stone and father of three children; spends time in an insane asylum in Mari Sandoz's *The Tom-Walker*.

Milton (Milty) Stone (I) Civil War veteran with an iron peg leg who is the son of Sarah and Hiram Stone, the husband of Lucinda Martin Stone, and the father of Martin Stone in Mari Sandoz's *The Tom-Walker*.

Milton Stone (II) Son of Martin Stone and husband of Hazel Stone; World War II veteran with shrapnel located near his heart; knows the Portable Extradimensional Hole trick in Mari Sandoz's *The Tom-Walker*.

Penny Turner Stone Wife of Martin Stone and mother of three children; helps her husband homestead on a Wyoming ranch in Mari Sandoz's *The Tom-Walker*.

Sarah Stone Wife of Hiram Stone and mother of Milton Stone; plans her son's wedding to Lucinda Martin while unaware that he is returning from the Civil War as an amputee in Mari Sandoz's *The Tom-Walker*.

Thomas J. (Tom) Stone Childlike, impotent husband of Mrs. Karen Stone; his death from heart trouble leaves her alone in Tennessee Williams's *The Roman Spring of Mrs. Stone*.

Austin (Great Commoner) Stoneman United States congressman, legislative force behind Reconstruction, and father of Phil and Elsie Stoneman in Thomas Dixon's *The Clansman*.

Elsie Stoneman   Daughter of Austin Stoneman; influences Abraham Lincoln to pardon Ben Cameron, whom she loves, in Thomas Dixon's *The Clansman*.

Phil Stoneman   Union army captain who becomes sympathetic to the southern white cause; trades places with Ben Cameron, who is awaiting execution, and is rescued by the Ku Klux Klan in Thomas Dixon's *The Clansman*.

Paula Arnold Storm   Friend of Dirk De Jong; marries a man more than twice her age in Edna Ferber's *So Big*.

Raymond (Ray) Stothard   Drunkard who organizes an aggressive movement of poor white ruffians and corrupt politicians to assault the black contrabands in Paul Laurence Dunbar's *The Fanatics*.

Harvey Stovall   Attorney from Columbus, Ohio; adjutant for the 918th Bomb Group in Beirne Lay, Jr., and Sy Bartlett's *Twelve O'Clock High!*

Roma Stover   Yellow-haired girl from Roy Earle's boyhood in William Riley Burnett's *High Sierra*.

Joe Stowe   Friend and Harvard classmate of Jim Calder; first husband of Bella Brill; achieves critical and financial success as a writer of serious fiction in John P. Marquand's *Wickford Point*.

Ward Stradlater   Hotshot roommate of Holden Caulfield; Holden worries Stradlater might take advantage of Jane Gallagher in J. D. Salinger's *The Catcher in the Rye*.

Annabelle Marie Strang   Society girl who becomes pregnant by young J. Ward Morehouse, marries him, and aborts the pregnancy; he divorces her for being unfaithful in John Dos Passos's *U.S.A.* trilogy.

Arline Strange   Actress who employs Emma Lou Morgan as her maid in Wallace Thurman's *The Blacker the Berry*.

Laurentine Strange   Illegitimate mulatto daughter of Sarah Strange; courted successfully by Stephen Denleigh in Jessie Redmon Fauset's *The Chinaberry Tree*.

Sarah (Aunt Sal) Strange   Black servant and lover of the white Colonel Halloway; mother of Laurentine Strange in Jessie Redmon Fauset's *The Chinaberry Tree*.

Artie (James Singer) Straus   Kidnapper and murderer (along with Judd Steiner) of Paulie Kessler in Meyer Levin's *Compulsion*.

Randolph Straus   Father of Artie Straus and millionaire director of the Straus Corporation in Meyer Levin's *Compulsion*.

Lewis Lambert Strether   Middle-aged editor from Woollett, Massachusetts, engaged to Mrs. Newsome, who sends him to Paris to persuade her son Chad Newsome to stop his affair with Madame de Vionnet and return to a respectable life in America, in Henry James's *The Ambassadors*.

Luke Strett   London physician who encourages the dying Mildred Theale to enjoy life fully in Henry James's *The Wings of the Dove*.

Susan Shepherd Stringham   Elderly widow and writer who is Mildred Theale's traveling companion; schoolgirl friend of Maud Lowder in Henry James's *The Wings of the Dove*.

Simon Strother   Coachman for Bayard Sartoris II in William Faulkner's *Sartoris (Flags in the Dust)*; Marengo's father in *The Unvanquished*.

George Stroud   Executive editor of *Crimeways* magazine and husband of Georgette Stroud; unidentified witness who can link Earl Janoth to the murder of Pauline Delos, Stroud's sometime lover; a narrator of Kenneth Fearing's *The Big Clock*.

Georgette Stroud   Wife of George Stroud in and a narrator of Kenneth Fearing's *The Big Clock*.

Mrs. Lemuel Struthers   Wife of a millionaire shoe polish businessman whose soirees are initially deplored by old New York society but later accepted in Edith Wharton's *The Age of Innocence*.

Asa M. Stryker   Duck fancier turned commercial breeder of snapping turtles; murdered by Clarence Latouche in Edmund Wilson's *Memoirs of Hecate County*.

Charles Stuart (Charles II)   King of Restoration England and lover of Amber St. Clare in Kathleen Winsor's *Forever Amber*.

James (Jamie) Stuart, Duke of York   Controversy fomenting brother of King Charles II in Kathleen Winsor's *Forever Amber*.

Captain Stuart   English captain, late of the Gordon Highlanders, serving as commander of the bodyguard of President Alvarez of Olancho; killed during the overthrow of the government in Richard Harding Davis's *Soldiers of Fortune*.

Cornelius Stuart   Son-in-law of Montague Lacey; former Virginia congressman who opposes and fears secession in Mary Lee Settle's *Know Nothing*.

Henrietta Anne (Minette) Stuart   Physically delicate sister and closest friend of King Charles II in Kathleen Winsor's *Forever Amber*.

Jack Stuart   Leader of Jack Stuart and His Collegians; hires Rick Martin, but makes Martin play in a restrained style so the band will not sound like a black band in Dorothy Baker's *Young Man with a Horn*.

Jamie Stuart   Provincial officer, friend of Johnny Lacey, and beau of Sally Lacey's sister; killed in the battle at Fort Duquesne in Mary Lee Settle's *O Beulah Land*.

Lancelot Stuart Friend of Johnny Catlett; resigns a U.S. Army commission to join the Confederate army in Mary Lee Settle's *Know Nothing*.

Stubb Carefree second mate aboard the *Pequod* in Herman Melville's *Moby-Dick*.

Count Yaromir (Friend) von Studenitz Father of Countess Zdenka von Studenitz and maternal grandfather of Rudolf Stanka in Louis Adamic's *Cradle of Life*.

Countess Zdenka von Studenitz Daughter of Count Yaromir von Studenitz, lover of Rudolf von Hapsburg, and mother of Rudolf Stanka in Louis Adamic's *Cradle of Life*.

Ella Lowry Sturgis Promiscuous wife of Hector Sturgis and daughter of an Irish laborer in Shelby Foote's *Jordan County*.

Esther (Little Esther) Wingate Sturgis Wife of John Sturgis and domineering mother of Hector Sturgis in Shelby Foote's *Jordan County*.

Hector (Heck) Wingate Sturgis Ineffectual husband of Ella Lowry Sturgis; city planner, artist, failed farmer, and father in Shelby Foote's *Jordan County*.

John Sturgis Merchant, husband of Esther Wingate Sturgis, and father of Hector Sturgis in Shelby Foote's *Jordan County*.

Clyde Sturrock Childhood friend of Paul Hardin; unscrupulous lawyer and congressman; a drinker who seizes the cause of prohibition in Brand Whitlock's *J. Hardin & Son*.

Sue See Beulah Ross.

Sue Narrator of Helen Hooven Santmyer's *Herbs and Apples*.

Sugar-Boy (Roger/Robert O'Sheean) Irish driver and bodyguard for Willie Stark in Robert Penn Warren's *All the King's Men*.

Maidie Starnes Suggs Daughter of Lauralee and Jimbob Starnes; moves to Dallas, where she is unhappy, in William Goyen's *The House of Breath*.

Suleau (I) Father of Suleau II; police spy in H. L. Davis's *Harp of a Thousand Strings*.

Suleau (II) Son of Suleau I; journalist killed by a mob in Paris in H. L. Davis's *Harp of a Thousand Strings*.

Betty Sullivan Pianist married briefly to Stephen Lewis in Clyde Brion Davis's *The Great American Novel*.

Anna Summers See Anna Leath.

Dick Summers Veteran mountain man who teaches Boone Caudill the ways of the wilderness in A. B. Guthrie's *The Big Sky*; guide for a wagon train in *The Way West*.

Lucy Freeman Sumner Friend who counsels Eliza Wharton about the dangers of the adventurous life in Hannah Webster Foster's *The Coquette*.

Isaac (Ikey) Sumpter Son of the Reverend MacCarland Sumpter; exploits Jasper Harrick's being trapped in a cave and is partly responsible for Harrick's death in Robert Penn Warren's *The Cave*.

Reverend MacCarland (Brother Sumpter, Ole Mac) Sumpter Baptist preacher and father of Isaac Sumpter; goes into the cave and finds Jasper Harrick dead but lies to protect Isaac in Robert Penn Warren's *The Cave*.

Supercargo Enormous attendant of shell-shocked black veterans who rebel against him at the Golden Day bar in Ralph Ellison's *Invisible Man*.

Suratt Sewing machine salesman in William Faulkner's *Sartoris (Flags in the Dust)* and *As I Lay Dying*. See also V. K. Ratliff.

Susie Servant to Leonora and Captain Weldon Penderton in Carson McCullers's *Reflections in a Golden Eye*.

Susy See Gin-head Susy.

Bruce Sutherland British military commander of Cyprus who keeps secret his Jewish ancestry in Leon Uris's *Exodus*.

Clytemnestra (Clytie) Sutpen Daughter of Thomas Sutpen and a black slave; burns down the Sutpen mansion, killing Henry Sutpen and herself, in William Faulkner's *Absalom, Absalom!*

Ellen Coldfield Sutpen Second wife of Thomas Sutpen and mother of Henry and Judith Sutpen in William Faulkner's *Absalom, Absalom!*

Eulalia Bon Sutpen Probable first wife of Thomas Sutpen and probable mother, by Sutpen, of Charles Bon; Sutpen divorces her when he learns that she has black blood in William Faulkner's *Absalom, Absalom!*

Henry Sutpen Son of Thomas and Ellen Coldfield Sutpen and brother of Judith Sutpen; kills his half brother, Charles Bon, in William Faulkner's *Absalom, Absalom!*

Judith Sutpen Daughter of Thomas and Ellen Coldfield Sutpen and sister of Henry Sutpen; engaged to her half brother, Charles Bon, in William Faulkner's *Absalom, Absalom!*

Thomas Sutpen Probably the father, by Eulalia Bon Sutpen, of Charles Bon; father, by a black slave, of Clytemnestra Sutpen; by Ellen Coldfield Sutpen, of Henry and Judith Sutpen; by Milly Jones, of a daughter; killed by Milly's grandfather, Wash Jones; appears in William Faulkner's *Absalom, Absalom!*

Tobe Sutterfield Groom and minister in William Faulkner's *A Fable*.

Nessie Sutton   Milliner's assistant, mother of an illegitimate daughter by her lover Abner Teeftallow, and wife of A. M. Belshue in T. S. Stribling's *Teeftallow*.

Emiscah Svenson   Girlfriend of Charley Anderson who gets pregnant by his best friend and convinces Charley to marry her; he arranges an abortion and breaks off their engagement in John Dos Passos's *U.S.A.* trilogy.

Henry Swain   Father of Patty and Tom Swain; honest barrister and friend of Richard Carvel in Winston Churchill's *Richard Carvel*.

Patty Swain   Generous and hardworking woman who loves Richard Carvel in Winston Churchill's *Richard Carvel*.

Thomas (Tom) Swain   Wastrel son of Henry Swain and brother of Patty Swain in Winston Churchill's *Richard Carvel*.

Charles (Chick) Swallow   Writer who succeeds his father-in-law as *The Lamplighter* advice columnist in the Decency, Connecticut, *Picayune Blade;* narrator of Peter De Vries's *Comfort Me with Apples*.

Lila Swallow   Younger sister of Chick Swallow and wife of Nickie Sherman in Peter De Vries's *Comfort Me with Apples*.

Effingham Swan   Military judge of the Minute Men who sentences Fowler Greenhill to death; dies when Mary Jessup Greenhill crashes her airplane into his in Sinclair Lewis's *It Can't Happen Here*.

Ella Swan   Servant of the Loftig family and a follower of Daddy Faith in William Styron's *Lie Down in Darkness*.

Singleton Oglethorpe Swansdown   Plantation owner whose poetry Ned Hazard mocks; arbitrator in Isaac Tracy's litigation with Frank Meriwether over worthless land in John Pendleton Kennedy's *Swallow Barn*.

Aurelia Swartout   Wife of Jerry Catlin the Second; murdered by a group of blacks who are irate because of mortgage foreclosures in T. S. Stribling's *Unfinished Cathedral*.

Dame Swaschbuckler   Wife of Gottlieb Swaschbuckler in James Kirke Paulding's *Koningsmarke*.

Master Gottlieb Swaschbuckler   Village jailer in James Kirke Paulding's *Koningsmarke*.

Jason (Sweetie) Sweetwater   Son of an Episcopal bishop, union organizer opposing Bogan Murdock and father of Sue Murdock's aborted child in Robert Penn Warren's *At Heaven's Gate*.

Elizabeth Swift   Mother of Kate Swift in Sherwood Anderson's *Winesburg, Ohio*.

Kate Swift   Worldly Winesburg teacher; her attempt to counsel George Willard on his writing career becomes an aborted romantic encounter in Sherwood Anderson's *Winesburg, Ohio*.

Mark Swift   Model supported by his wife's dowry in Henry Miller's *Tropic of Cancer*.

Swift One   Mate of Big-Tooth; ancestor of the narrator in Jack London's *Before Adam*.

Pluto Swint   Obese and perspiring candidate for sheriff; suitor of Darling Jill Walden in Erskine Caldwell's *God's Little Acre*.

Sybil   Married white woman who simulates a rape with the narrator in Ralph Ellison's *Invisible Man*.

Colonel Sydenham   Coxcomb British officer in James Kirke Paulding's *The Dutchman's Fireside*.

Sydney Ben   Australian sailor who fights Bembo aboard the *Julia* in Herman Melville's *Omoo*.

Isaac Syfe   Jewish farmer and partner of Augustus M. Barr in Oscar Micheaux's *The Homesteader*.

Granville Sykes   Plantation owner who evicts Berry Lawson for having attended a Republican political meeting, and then, a few months later, sues Lawson for having left the plantation in Albion W. Tourgee's *Bricks Without Straw*.

Uncle Jim Sykes   Elderly black man who is accused of idleness by Harry Cresswell when he injures his leg and cannot work; eagerly attends Zora's meetings that promise freedom from such mistreatment in W. E. B. Du Bois's *The Quest of the Silver Fleece*.

Sylvain   Black leader of the attack on the home of de Kersaint I; killed by de Kersaint II in Lafcadio Hearn's *Youma*.

Pierre Sylvain   Owner of a printing establishment and friend of the young Diron Desautels in Arna Wendell Bontemps's *Drums at Dusk*.

Sylvester   Boyfriend of Tania in Henry Miller's *Tropic of Cancer*.

Robert Syverten   Aspiring director who narrates his experiences as Gloria Beatty's partner in a dance marathon; sentenced to be put to death for killing Beatty in accordance with her wishes in Horace McCoy's *They Shoot Horses, Don't They?*

Tachechana (the Skipping Fawn) Sioux Indian princess; daughter of Le Balafré and wife of Mahtoree; becomes the wife of the Pawnee chief Hard Heart, after he has defeated Mahtoree, in James Fenimore Cooper's *The Prairie*.

Tad Nephew of Gustus Griff; presumably killed when Griff's mill is destroyed in Mary Noailles Murfree's *In the Clouds*.

Tadlock Self-serving politician and captain of the wagon train in A. B. Guthrie's *The Way West*.

Tommy Taft One-legged retired sailor and town character who has a paternal interest in Barton Cathcart in Henry Ward Beecher's *Norwood*.

Dagny (Slug) Taggart Operations vice president of Taggart Transcontinental Railroad; heroine of Ayn Rand's *Atlas Shrugged*.

James (Jim) Taggart President of Taggart Transcontinental Railroad; compromises its control and ownership for political favors in Ayn Rand's *Atlas Shrugged*.

Dr. Tainkin Charlatan psychologist who loses the savings of Tommy Wilhelm in the stock market but who teaches him the difference between the true soul and the pretender soul and urges him to seize the day in Saul Bellow's *The Victim*.

Taji Narrator who pursues Yillah in Herman Melville's *Mardi*.

Dolly Augusta Talbo Unworldly maiden cousin who helps rear Collin Fenwick, becoming the boy's beloved friend and companion, in Truman Capote's *The Grass Harp*.

Verena Talbo Efficient, rich sister of Dolly Talbo; unmarried, she supports the household and controls the lives of the people in it in Truman Capote's *The Grass Harp*.

Mariana Talbot Wife of Mr. Talbot and mother of their four children in Grace King's *The Pleasant Ways of St. Médard*.

Mr. Talbot Wealthy lawyer with a thriving practice in New Orleans before the Civil War; forced to endure wartime poverty and hardship and to adjust to the loss of his position after the war in Grace King's *The Pleasant Ways of St. Médard*.

Charles (Charlie) Taliaferro Cousin of Lucinda McGehee, whom he loves; killed at Shiloh in Stark Young's *So Red the Rose*.

Bella Grantham Tallant Wife of Jimmy Tallant, who married her largely because of his friendship with her father, Bud Grantham, so that her expected child, not Tallant's, would not be branded illegitimate, in Elizabeth Spencer's *The Voice at the Back Door*.

Hugh Tallant American loyalist who seeks redress in England following the American Revolution; turns to crime and is imprisoned in Australia, but escapes from the penal colony and returns to England, where he is pardoned and marries Sally Munro, with whom he returns to Australia as a free settler; narrator of Charles Nordhoff and James Norman Hall's *Botany Bay*.

Jimmy Tallant Partner of Bud Grantham and one-time bootlegger; largely through the example of his friend and antagonist Duncan Harper, he undergoes a significant transformation of character in Elizabeth Spencer's *The Voice at the Back Door*.

Sally Munro Tallant Free Englishwoman who accompanies her father to Australia; falls in love with Hugh Tallant, whom she marries in England, whence they return to Australia as free settlers, in Charles Nordhoff and James Norman Hall's *Botany Bay*.

Ernest Talliaferro Widower who attends the yacht party in William Faulkner's *Mosquitoes*.

Jean-Lambert Tallien   French revolutionary politician/statesman and opponent of Robespierre in H. L. Davis's *Harp of a Thousand Strings.*

Taloufa   Nigerian former servant to an Englishman; supports the Back-to-Africa movement in Claude McKay's *Banjo.*

Tambur-Ola   Civil War veteran who marries Sörine Olsa in O. E. Rölvaag's *Peder Victorious;* also appears in *Their Father's God.*

Tanee (Pomaree-Tanee)   Henpecked husband of Queen Pomaree Vahinee in Herman Melville's *Omoo.*

Tanga   African servant of Louis Desrivières; tends to the slave children on Desrivières's plantation while their mothers work in the fields in Lafcadio Hearn's *Youma.*

Tania   Supposed girlfriend of Sylvester; tries to convince Henry Miller to live with her in Russia in Henry Miller's *Tropic of Cancer.*

Cornelia Tanner   Nurse who cares for Miranda in Katherine Anne Porter's *Pale Horse, Pale Rider.*

Psyche Tanzer   Young woman given a fatal dose of a drug by Victor Bruge in Theodore Dreiser's *The Bulwark.*

Ta-Phar   Son of Pharaoh, brother of Princess Royal, uncle of Moses, and second ruler of Egypt; frees the Hebrews and dies trying to reclaim them in Zora Neale Hurston's *Moses, Man of the Mountain.*

Oliver Tappan   Small-town boy who seeks his fortune in New York and Washington; becomes a congressman and marries a calculating society woman, Madeline Carter, in Hjalmar Hjorth Boyesen's *The Golden Calf.*

Tarleton   British colonel who prevents his foraging troops from burning the home of a deceased Patriot colonel's widow; courteously receives Mildred and Henry Lindsay at Cornwallis's camp in John Pendleton Kennedy's *Horse-Shoe Robinson.*

Mrs. Tarrant   Daughter of a Boston abolitionist; attempts to promote the speaking career of her daughter Verena Tarrant in Henry James's *The Bostonians.*

Doctor Selah Tarrant   Mesmeric healer who attempts to promote the speaking career of his daughter Verena Tarrant in Henry James's *The Bostonians.*

Verena Tarrant   Naive inspirational speaker who defies Olive Chancellor by going off to marry Basil Ransom in Henry James's *The Bostonians.*

Frederic Tartan   Older brother of Lucy Tartan, whom he tries to protect from Pierre Glendinning III, in Herman Melville's *Pierre.*

Lucy Tartan   Fiancée of Pierre Glendinning III; dies upon learning that Glendinning is married to his half sister Isabel Banford in Herman Melville's *Pierre.*

Francis Marion Tarwater   Fourteen-year-old country boy who goes to the city after the death of his great-uncle to learn whether what he has been taught is accurate; tries unsuccessfully to evade his calling as a prophet, but ends up baptizing his idiot cousin, Bishop Rayber, even as he drowns him in Flannery O'Connor's *The Violent Bear It Away.*

Mason Tarwater   Backwoods preacher and great-uncle of Francis Marion Tarwater, upon whom he lays the calling to be a prophet like himself and the instruction to baptize the idiot Bishop Rayber; his death motivates young Tarwater's visit to the city in Flannery O'Connor's *The Violent Bear It Away.*

Francis Tasbrough   Owner of a granite quarry; becomes the Minute Men District Commissioner in Sinclair Lewis's *It Can't Happen Here.*

Vasily Tashikov   Soviet ambassador to the United States; exhibits an open contempt for American leaders and the American political system in Allen Drury's *Advise and Consent.*

Tashtego (Tash)   American Indian who is Stubb's harpooner in Herman Melville's *Moby-Dick.*

Grace Brock Caldwell Tate   Beautiful, selfish daughter of the oldest, most respectable family in Fort Penn; lives on a Caldwell family farm with her husband Sidney Tate in John O'Hara's *A Rage to Live.*

Sheriff Heck Tate   Sheriff of Maycomb County, Alabama, who decides to proclaim that Bob Ewell fell on his knife rather than expose Boo Radley, Ewell's assailant, to the generosity of the townspeople in Harper Lee's *To Kill a Mockingbird.*

Norah (Nory) Tate   Poor Farm inmate who marries James Conboy, the superintendent's son, in Jessamyn West's *The Witch Diggers.*

Rosa (Aunt Piggie, Rosy) Tate (Tait)   Unmarried sister of Sarah Tate Bedford; lives at Portobello and helps instruct the Bedford children; dies of heart disease in Stark Young's *So Red the Rose.*

Sidney Tate   Yale-educated New Yorker who becomes a gentleman farmer after marrying the imperious Grace Brock Caldwell; establishes himself in the Fort Penn society in John O'Hara's *A Rage to Live.*

Tavi   Brother of Fakahau, husband of Marunga, and father of Mako and Hitia; storekeeper who survives the hurricane in Charles Nordhoff and James Norman Hall's *The Hurricane.*

Tawney   Old blackman aboard the *Neversink* who tells White-Jacket tales of the War of 1812 in Herman Melville's *White-Jacket.*

John Taylor Brother of Mary Taylor and confidential clerk for Grey and Easterly, Brokers; his interest in the cotton belt leads him to encourage his sister to teach in the South, where he meets and marries Helen Cresswell, in W. E. B. Du Bois's *The Quest of the Silver Fleece*.

Mary Taylor Sister of John Taylor and wife of Harry Cresswell; teacher at Miss Sarah Smith's school, where she never feels comfortable with the dark-skinned children and indistinct personalities of her colleagues; because she desires glory, she marries the cold and selfish Cresswell, who almost destroys her, in W. E. B. Du Bois's *The Quest of the Silver Fleece*.

Owen Taylor Mountaineer and mine owner who offers Rose Dutcher a life in the West, which she refuses, in Hamlin Garland's *Rose of Dutcher's Coolly*.

Weldon Taylor Student working to save money for dental school; first lover of Emma Lou Morgan in Wallace Thurman's *The Blacker the Berry*.

Tea Cake See Vergible Woods.

Teal Eye Daughter of a Piegan chief and lover of Boone Caudill in A. B. Guthrie's *The Big Sky*.

Zephi Teal First officer on river barges in James Kirke Paulding's *Westward Ho!*

The Technician Dyspeptic operator of sound and image control devices and consumer of bicarbonate of soda in William S. Burroughs's *Naked Lunch, Nova Express,* and *Exterminator!*

Ted Seventy-year-old Provincial soldier with Braddock's army; nurses his aching feet, warns Doggo Cutwright not to kill the visiting Catawbas, and is captured, tortured, and killed by the Shawnees in Mary Lee Settle's *O Beulah Land*.

Ted Blond teenaged driver of the soft-drink truck; backs into and breaks down part of the stone wall in John Updike's *The Poorhouse Fair*.

Abner (Ab) Teeftallow Ignorant and naive orphan; railroad construction worker, lover of Nessie Sutton and Adelaide Jones, and inheritor of large land claims from his grandfather in T. S. Stribling's *Teeftallow*.

Tom Teerswell Longtime escort of Caroline Wynn, until she meets Blessed Alwyn; plots with Sam Stillings to win her back but loses her forever when she marries Stillings in W. E. B. Du Bois's *The Quest of the Silver Fleece*.

Teganisoris Iroquois Indian chief whose tribe captures John Law and Sir Arthur Pembroke in Emerson Hough's *The Mississippi Bubble*.

Tehani Tahitian of royal birth who marries Roger Byam, by whom she has a daughter; dies shortly after Byam leaves Tahiti in chains in Charles Nordhoff and James Norman Hall's *Mutiny on the Bounty*.

Telemachus Son of Odysseus; visits Menelaos to learn what happened to Odysseus, only to be besotted by Helen, in John Erskine's *The Private Life of Helen of Troy*.

Telemachus Elderly slave who tells Peregrine Lacey Catlett when Johnny Catlett breaks the rules by going to the salt furnace; son of Jonathan Lacey and Lyddy in Mary Lee Settle's *Know Nothing*.

John Telfer Small-town idler who befriends young Sam McPherson in Sherwood Anderson's *Windy McPherson's Son*.

Juan (Spanish Johnny) Tellamantez Mexican laborer and musician; friend of Thea Kronborg in Willa Cather's *The Song of the Lark*.

Charlotte Temple Young British woman seduced by Jack Montraville; taken from her family to the United States, where Montraville abandons her and she dies shortly after giving birth to their child in Susanna Rowson's *Charlotte*.

Elizabeth (Bess) Temple Daughter of Judge Marmaduke Temple; twice rescued by Natty Bumppo; marries Oliver Effingham in James Fenimore Cooper's *The Pioneers*.

Henry Temple Husband of Lucy Eldridge Temple and father of Charlotte Temple; travels from England to the United States in hopes of rescuing Charlotte, but instead witnesses her death hours after his arrival in Susanna Rowson's *Charlotte*.

Lucy Eldridge Temple Doting mother of Charlotte Temple; despite the grief she suffers at Charlotte's death, she and her husband rear their motherless grandchild in Susanna Rowson's *Charlotte*.

Marmaduke Temple Leading citizen of Templeton and father of Elizabeth Temple; grants to Oliver Effingham the land Effingham claims in James Fenimore Cooper's *The Pioneers*.

Nicholas (Nick) Temple Adventurous and irresponsible friend of David Ritchie; marries Antoinette de St. Gré in Winston Churchill's *The Crossing*.

Sarah (Mrs. Clive, Sally) Temple Mother of Nicholas Temple; becomes repentant after taking a lover in Winston Churchill's *The Crossing*.

Colonel (Old Rocky) Templeton Marine officer who orders an unnecessary thirty-six-mile march for a group of out-of-shape reserve soldiers in William Styron's *The Long March*.

Jake Tench Heavy-drinking handyman who marries Mistress Bartram, although he knows that she is pregnant by another man, in Conrad Richter's *The Fields;* also appears in *The Trees* and *The Town*.

Rosa Tench   Illegitimate daughter of Mistress Bartram and Portius Wheeler in Conrad Richter's *The Fields;* loves her half brother Chancey Wheeler, but when the community censures this relationship, she commits suicide in *The Town.*

One-Eye Tenczara   Unforgiving police captain who arrests Bruno (Lefty) Bicek for murder in Nelson Algren's *Never Come Morning.*

Eve Tennant   Aristocratic daughter of the British port collector; liked by Johnny Fraser in James Boyd's *Drums.*

Joyce Tennant   Girlfriend of Felix Fay and secretary to her uncle in Floyd Dell's *Moon-Calf.*

Tennie   See Tennie Beauchamp.

Tennie's Jim   See James Thucydides Beauchamp.

Herman (Mr. T.) Teppis   Producer at Supreme Pictures in Norman Mailer's *The Deer Park.*

Terangi Matokia   Son of Mama Rua, husband of Marama, and father of Tita; leads people from Manukura to a nearby island to begin a new life; pardoned by the governor for an earlier altercation as a result of his valiant deeds during the hurricane in Charles Nordhoff and James Norman Hall's *The Hurricane.*

Ellen Terhune   Avant-garde composer and mistress of the Vallombrosa estate in Edmund Wilson's *Memoirs of Hecate County.*

Kermit Terkel   Agent who tries to find Martha Mills a job in Hollywood in Jerome Weidman's *What's in It for Me?*

Miss Terkle   Caseworker for Rock-a-Bye adoption agency in Peter De Vries's *The Tunnel of Love.*

Fats Terminal   Drug dealer who is a server of the Black Meat and knows the Algebra of Need in William S. Burroughs's *Naked Lunch;* mentioned in *Nova Express.*

Mamere Terrebonne   Oldest resident and spiritual mother of Isle aux Chiens, setting for Shirley Ann Grau's *The Hard Blue Sky.*

Terry   Grandson of Leah; idolizes Augie in Arna Wendell Bontemps's *God Sends Sunday.*

Terry   Young, married migrant woman with whom Sal Paradise becomes infatuated in Jack Kerouac's *On the Road.*

Gerald (Gerry) Tetley   Sickly, vacillating son of Major Willard Tedey; forced by his father to participate in the hanging of Donald Martin; commits suicide by hanging himself in his father's barn in Walter Van Tilburg Clark's *The Ox-Bow Incident.*

Major Willard Tetley   Former Confederate cavalry officer who leads the lynch mob; throws himself on his sword after learning of the suicide of his son Gerald Tetley in Walter Van Tilburg Clark's *The Ox-Bow Incident.*

Mrs. Thacher   Kindly widowed mother of Adeline Thacher Prince and grandmother of Nan Prince; cares for Nan in Sarah Orne Jewett's *A Country Doctor.*

Max Whisper Thaler   The criminal boss in charge of gambling in Personville in Dashiell Hammett's *Red Harvest.*

Flora Thangue   Gentle Englishwoman prevented from marriage by familial duty in Gertrude Atherton's *Ancestors.*

Ed Thatcher   Accountant, father of actress Ellen Thatcher in John Dos Passos's *Manhattan Transfer.*

Ellen Thatcher (Elaine, Elena)   Successful actress and journalist who is frustrated in her quest for true art in John Dos Passos's *Manhattan Transfer.*

Dr. Joe Thatcher   Physician and first mentor of Rose Dutcher in Hamlin Garland's *Rose of Dutcher's Coolly.*

Judge Thatcher   Father of Becky Thatcher in Samuel Langhorne Clemens's *The Adventures of Tom Sawyer* and *Adventures of Huckleberry Finn.*

Rebecca (Becky, Bessie) Thatcher   Daughter of Judge Thatcher and girlfriend of Tom Sawyer in Samuel Langhorne Clemens's *The Adventures of Tom Sawyer* and *Adventures of Huckleberry Finn.*

Susie Thatcher   Wife of Ed Thatcher and mother of Ellen Thatcher, whose birth is the opening scene of John Dos Passos's *Manhattan Transfer.*

Landry Thayer   Colorado ranch hand who falls in love with Mildred Osborne; saves her life during a cattle stampede and later proves himself a Victorian gentleman in Paul Laurence Dunbar's *The Love of Landry.*

Margaret Thayer   Helpful librarian at Waindell College and wife of Roy Thayer; suggests to Timofey Pnin that he board at the home of Laurence G. Clements in Vladimir Nabokov's *Pnin.*

Roy Thayer   Member of the English department at Waindell College, hypochondriac, expert in eighteenth-century poetry, and husband of Margaret Thayer, with whom he attends a party given by Timofey Pnin, in Vladimir Nabokov's *Pnin.*

Mildred (Milly) Theale   Wealthy American dying of an unnamed disease and in love with Merton Densher; discovering Densher's desire to marry her in order to inherit her wealth destroys her will to live in Henry James's *The Wings of the Dove.*

Theodora (Theo)   Spoiled, carefree telepath who forms a bond with Eleanor Vance at Hill House which the house determines to break in Shirley Jackson's *The Haunting of Hill House.*

Théodore   Orphan reared by Lafitte in Joseph Holt Ingraham's *Lafitte.*

Anne-Joseph Théroigne   Daughter of a small landholder in the village of Jean-Labert Tallien; political agitator in the French Revolution in H. L. Davis's *Harp of a Thousand Strings.*

Mrs. Therwald   Wife of a high Ku Klux Klansman; hints to her husband the importance of supporting Matthew Towns's release from prison in W. E. B. Du Bois's *Dark Princess.*

Clara Thicknesse   Quasi-mistress of Chick Swallow in Peter De Vries's *Comfort Me with Apples.*

Thomas   Cabin boy aboard the *Aroostook* and steward of Lydia Blood in William Dean Howells's *The Lady of the Aroostook.*

Thomas   Butler at Sunnyside; dies when he believes he sees Paul Armstrong's ghost in Mary Roberts Rinehart's *The Circular Staircase.*

Bigger Thomas   Twenty-year-old black man convicted and sentenced to death for the murder of Mary Dalton; murders his girlfriend, Bessie Mears, in Richard Wright's *Native Son.*

Buddy Thomas   Younger brother of Bigger Thomas in Richard Wright's *Native Son.*

Esther Thomas   Alienated, low-level employee of Glymmer, Read who is unaffected by the firm's bankruptcy in Nathan Asch's *The Office.*

Jack (Jackie) Thomas   Son of Robin Thomas and half brother of Morissa Kirk, who sends him to the safety of his father, in Mari Sandoz's *Miss Morissa.*

Joe Thomas   Thirty-nine-year-old postal worker pushed from a sixth-floor hotel window by Cross Damon in Richard Wright's *The Outsider.*

Marilla Thomas   Housekeeper to Dr. John Leslie; famous for her strange bonnets; crusty but kind to Nan Prince in Sarah Orne Jewett's *A Country Doctor.*

Mrs. Thomas   Mother of Bigger Thomas in Richard Wright's *Native Son.*

Robin Thomas   Father of Jack Thomas and stepfather of Morissa Kirk, whom he urges not to homestead, in Mari Sandoz's *Miss Morissa.*

Vera Thomas   Younger sister of Bigger Thomas in Richard Wright's *Native Son.*

Florabel Thompkins   Ultrafeminine twin of Idabel Thompkins, her opposite in all things, in Truman Capote's *Other Voices, Other Rooms.*

Idabel Thompkins   Tomboy who longs to be male; alternately Joel Knox's friend and nemesis; twin sister of Florabel Thompkins in Truman Capote's *Other Voices, Other Rooms.*

Thompson (Doctor)   Well-paid, religious, black cook aboard the *Highlander* in Herman Melville's *Redburn.*

Arthur and Herbert Thompson   Sons of Ellie and Royal Earle Thompson in Katherine Anne Porter's *Noon Wine.*

Caesar Thompson (Wharton)   Faithful black servant to the Whartons in James Fenimore Cooper's *The Spy.*

Ellen Bridges (Ellie) Thompson   Fragile, ailing wife of Royal Earle Thompson in Katherine Anne Porter's *Noon Wine.*

Ferris P. Thompson   Son of the richest farmer in Rock County, Indiana; marries Catherine Conboy in Jessamyn West's *The Witch Diggers.*

Henry T. Thompson   Father of Myra Thompson, father-in-law of George Babbitt, and partner in the Babbitt-Thompson Realty Company in Sinclair Lewis's *Babbitt.*

Colonel Marcus Thompson   Ku Klux Klansman who seeks the support of Negro voters in a race for sheriff of Rockford County; attacked in newspapers and handbills as the man responsible for murdering John Walters and for stealing two thousand dollars from Walters's body in Albion W. Tourgee's *A Fool's Errand.*

Miss Thompson   Neighborhood hairdresser and good friend of Selina Boyce in Paule Marshall's *Brown Girl, Brownstones.*

Rosamond Walden Thompson   Daughter of Ty Ty Walden and wife of Will Thompson in Erskine Caldwell's *God's Little Acre.*

Royal Earle Thompson   South Texas dairy farmer who kills Homer Hatch; although acquitted of the murder, he commits suicide in Katherine Anne Porter's *Noon Wine.*

Tommy Thompson   Chief of the American Embassy in Warsaw who helps direct American money and weapons to the Warsaw ghetto fighters; friend of Gabriela Rak in Leon Uris's *Mila 18.*

Will Thompson   Promiscuous weaver and strike leader who is killed by the company police in Erskine Caldwell's *God's Little Acre.*

Hannah Thomson   Eighteen-year-old bound into servitude upon her father's death; falls in love with Ralph Hartsook, whom she ultimately marries, in Edward Eggleston's *The Hoosier School-Master.*

Mrs. Thomson   Blind and widowed English-born mother of Hannah and Shocky Thomson; sent to the poorhouse upon the death of her husband in Edward Eggleston's *The Hoosier School-Master.*

W. J. (Shocky) Thomson   Orphan living with the family of John Pearson; most faithful and affectionate child in the school in Edward Eggleston's *The Hoosier School-Master.*

Margaretta Thorn White author of a testament to the veracity of Harriet E. Wilson's *Our Nig*.

Eleanor Thorne Head nurse at the Hauptman Clinic in Terry Southern's *Flash and Filigree*.

Derrick Thornton Midwesterner who goes to college in the East and works as a magazine editor in New York City in Helen Hooven Santmyer's *Herbs and Apples*.

Dr. Dick Thornton Physician in a small midwestern town who influences his daughter, Derrick Thornton, by permitting her to read any book in the house in Helen Hooven Santmyer's *Herbs and Apples*.

Frederick (Fritz) Thornton Wealthy New York uncle of Lex Porter and genial father-figure to Alfred Eaton in John O'Hara's *From the Terrace*.

John Thornton Gold prospector whose life Buck twice saves, but who is eventually killed by Indians in Jack London's *The Call of the Wild*.

Reneltje (Nell) Thornton Wife of Dick Thornton and mother of Derrick Thornton; rears a large family and then has no time for an artistic career in Helen Hooven Santmyer's *Herbs and Apples*.

Cornelia (Mrs. Nonna Cornell) Thornwell Spirited sixty-year-old widow of the former governor of Massachusetts who, after her husband's death, abandons her blue-blooded lifestyle and becomes a laborer; through her friendship with Bartolomeo Vanzetti she becomes a supporter, for a brief time, of oppressed workers; attempts to save Vanzetti from execution in Upton Sinclair's *Boston*.

Thorpe British pilot in William Faulkner's *A Fable*.

Mary Thorpe-Wharton Wealthy American traveling with her mother and boyfriend in Egypt; friend of Helen Fairwood in H. D.'s *Palimpsest*.

Sandor Thrilling Director at Olympia Studios in Ludwig Bemelmans's *Dirty Eddie*.

Sir Thicknesse Throgmorton Pompous British officer in James Kirke Paulding's *The Dutchman's Fireside*.

Thucydides Son of Roscius and Phoebe; marries Eunice before she gives birth to Tomasina in William Faulkner's *Go Down, Moses*.

Floyd Thursby Thug enticed by Brigid O'Shaughnessy to protect her during her search for the jewel-encrusted statuette; she initially hires Spade & Archer as part of a scheme to rid herself of him in Dashiell Hammett's *The Maltese Falcon*.

Mortimer Thynne London society thief who is imprisoned in Australia; becomes a bureaucrat in the new government, which leads to his refusal to join his friends in their escape from the penal colony, in Charles Nordhoff and James Norman Hall's *Botany Bay*.

George Tichnor Copyreader for the *Kansas City Times* and friend of Homer Zigler in Clyde Brion Davis's *The Great American Novel*.

Michael (Smiling Mike) Tiernan Saloon owner and first ward boss in Theodore Dreiser's *The Titan*.

Tig Personal slave of Johnny Catlett and husband of Toey; sold to Crawford Kregg, runs away, and is killed by a slave-hunter when Toey bears Johnny's child in Mary Lee Settle's *Know Nothing*.

Arnaud (Pansette) du Tilh Lover of Bertrande de Rols and father, by her, of two children, while pretending to be her husband, Martin Guerre, in Janet Lewis's *The Wife of Martin Guerre*.

Till Mother of Nancy and slave of Sapphira Dodderidge Colbert in Willa Cather's *Sapphira and the Slave Girl*.

Sue Annie Tiller Old midwife and most opinionated, free-thinking adult in Little Smokey Creek, Kentucky; neighbor of Nunn Ballew in Harriette Arnow's *Hunter's Horn*; mentioned in *The Dollmaker*.

Elijah Tilley Retired fisherman who takes the narrator to Elijah's house, which is a shrine to Tilley's dead wife, in Sarah Orne Jewett's *The Country of the Pointed Firs*.

Aunt Tillie Relative whom Henry Miller dislikes because she is ugly, smells of sweat, and has a dirty scalp in Henry Miller's *Tropic of Capricorn*.

Blanche Lebanon Timberlane See Blanche Lebanon Timberlane Boneyard.

Cass Timberlane Judge of Grand Republic in Sinclair Lewis's *Kingsblood Royal*; becomes disillusioned with his wife Jinny Marshland Timberlane and loses her to Bradd Criley in *Cass Timberlane*.

Virginia Marshland (Jinny) Timberlane Second wife of Cass Timberlane and lover of Bradd Criley in Sinclair Lewis's *Cass Timberlane*; also appears in *Kingsblood Royal*.

Jay Timlow Secessionist who taunts Hesden Le Moyne about being a Unioner, responds to Le Moyne's challenge by enlisting with him in the Confederate army, and becomes Le Moyne's friend and the cause of his losing his arm and horse in Albion W. Tourgee's *Bricks Without Straw*.

Solomon Tinkle Owner of the *Nancy Harkins* and friend of Daniel Harrow in Walter D. Edmonds's *Rome Haul*.

Robert Tinkler Midshipman aboard the HMS *Bounty* who saves Roger Byam from being hanged in Charles Nordhoff and

James Norman Hall's *Mutiny on the Bounty;* provides comic relief among those cast adrift in *Men Against the Sea*.

Tinor   Mother of Kory-Kory in Herman Melville's *Typee*.

Benjamin (Ben) Tipton   Husband of Minna Tipton and father of Tom Tipton; helps expose Minna as the false Lady Fauntleroy in Frances Hodgson Burnett's *Little Lord Fauntleroy*.

Dick Tipton   New York bootblack who is the brother of Ben Tipton and a friend of Cedric Errol in Frances Hodgson Burnett's *Little Lord Fauntleroy*.

Minna (Lady Faunderoy) Tipton   Wife of Ben Tipton; claims to be Lady Fauntleroy in Frances Hodgson Burnett's *Little Lord Fauntleroy*.

Tita   Daughter of Terangi and Marama; survives the hurricane in Charles Nordhoff and James Norman Hall's *The Hurricane*.

James (Buck) Titus   Horse breeder and cynical friend of Doremus Jessup; prints antigovernment leaflets for the New Underground and is sent to a concentration camp in Sinclair Lewis's *It Can't Happen Here*.

Tjerck   Old black servant of the Vancours in James Kirke Paulding's *The Dutchman's Fireside*.

Toad   See Paduk.

Joan Toast   London whore transformed by Ebenezer Cooke into a goddess of love in John Barth's *The Sot-Weed Factor*. See also Susan Warren.

Toby   Friend of Pacifica; wants to help restore the Hotel de las Palmas and become rich; his plans collapse when he discovers that Flora Quill, its proprietor, has very little money in Jane Bowles's *Two Serious Ladies*.

Toby   Companion of Tommo in Herman Melville's *Typee*.

Mike Todarescu   Director of the little theater at People's Liberal Church; marries Molly Calico in Peter De Vries's *The Mackerel Plaza*.

Almira Blackett (Almiry) Todd   Widowed landlady of the narrator; her engaging personality and skill with home remedies make her an ideal connection with people the narrator wishes to meet in Sarah Orne Jewett's *The Country of the Pointed Firs*.

Benton Todd   Son of Captain Todd; killed during the Bardsville raid on tobacco buyers' warehouses in Robert Penn Warren's *Night Rider*.

Captain Todd   Member of the board of directors of the Association of Growers of Dark Fired Tobacco, but a nonsupporter of its violent secret branch, the Free Farmers' Brotherhood of Protection and Control, in Robert Penn Warren's *Night Rider*.

Joanna Todd   Cousin of Almira Todd's late husband; lives and dies on the deserted Shell-Heap Island in Sarah Orne Jewett's *The Country of the Pointed Firs*.

Toey   Daughter of Peregrine Lacey Catlett and Minna, personal slave of Melinda Lacey Kregg, wife of Tig, and mother of Johnny Catlett's mulatto son in Mary Lee Settle's *Know Nothing*.

Bruce Tollifer   Hired diversion for the bored Aileen Cowperwood in Theodore Dreiser's *The Stoic*.

Senator Edmund Tolliver   Member of the board of directors of the Association of Growers of Dark Fired Tobacco; resigns when the organization becomes violent in Robert Penn Warren's *Night Rider*.

Ellen (Lilli Barr) Tolliver   Talented pianist whom Lily Shane helps leave a small town; becomes a star as Lilli Barr in Louis Bromfield's *The Green Bay Tree*.

Mr. Tolliver   Poor white farmer opposed to the aristocratic Cresswells; willing to sell his land to Sarah Smith in order to spite them in W. E. B. Du Bois's *The Quest of the Silver Fleece*.

Tom   Native African who is a slave at Glen-Eberley; Captain Porgy's loyal cook in William Gilmore Simms's *Woodcraft*.

Tomasina (Tomey)   Daughter of Carothers McCaslin and Eunice and mother of Tomey's Turl Beauchamp in William Faulkner's *Go Down, Moses*.

Tomasino   Fisherman who leads the villagers of Adano to resume fishing; his support heightens the respect earned by Major Joppolo in John Hersey's *A Bell for Adano*.

Salvatore (Sally) Tomato   Convict in Sing Sing prison whom Holly Golightly visits every Thursday for a fee in Truman Capote's *Breakfast at Tiffany's*.

Geneva Tomblin   Dance-marathon contestant who is introduced, with the fiancé she met during the contest, to the audience after her elimination in Horace McCoy's *They Shoot Horses, Don't They?*

Mama (Mama T.) Tomek   Aging, bitter prostitute and heroin addict who operates Bonifacy Konstantine's brothel in Nelson Algren's *Never Come Morning*.

Claas Tomeson   White captive tortured and killed by Indians in James Kirke Paulding's *Koningsmarke*.

Tomey   See Tomasina.

Tomey's Turl   See Tomey's Turl Beauchamp.

Tommo   Narrator who lives with the Typees and escapes from them in Herman Melville's *Typee*.

Tommy Bootlegger murdered by Popeye in William Faulkner's *Sanctuary.*

Tom the Tinker Chief of the Whiskey Rebels reduced to exhibiting his old kettles at the village fair, where Captain John Farrago encounters him, in Hugh Henry Brackenridge's *Modern Chivalry.*

Tomtit (Thomas) Comic grandson of Milly, whom he accompanies to freedom, in Harriet Beecher Stowe's *Dred.*

Tongue Overseer of Swallow Barn in John Pendleton Kennedy's *Swallow Barn.*

Tonoi Chief of the fishermen on Martair in Herman Melville's *Omoo.*

Kjersti Tönseten Wife of Syvert Tönseten in O. E. Rölvaag's *Giants in the Earth, Peder Victorious,* and *Their Father's God.*

Syvert Tönseten Leader of the local and then the state Norwegian community in O. E. Rölvaag's *Giants in the Earth, Peder Victorious,* and *Their Father's God.*

Ellsworth Monkton (Elsie, Monk) Toohey Pseudo-humanitarian journalist and villain in Ayn Rand's *The Fountainhead.*

Horne Tooke One of three Englishmen, sympathetic to the American cause, who sends Israel Potter as courier to Benjamin Franklin in Herman Melville's *Israel Potter.*

Rev. Wesley R. Toomis Methodist bishop who persuades Elmer Gantry to become the minister of a small church in Sinclair Lewis's *Elmer Gantry.*

Hamilton (Ham) Tooting Embittered party worker in Winston Churchill's *Mr. Crewe's Career.*

Too-wit Chief of the savage tribe on the island of Tsalal who leads the massacre of the crew of the *Jane Guy* in Edgar Allan Poe's *The Narrative of Arthur Gordon Pym.*

Julius Shaw Toppan Anarchist friend of Jasper Ammen; suggests to Ammen the idea of following strangers in Conrad Aiken's *King Coffin.*

Topsy (Tops) Young slave bought from the slave warehouse and given to Ophelia St. Clare to test her educational ideas in Harriet Beecher Stowe's *Uncle Tom's Cabin.*

Marty Tothero Former high school basketball coach of Rabbit Angstrom; introduces Rabbit to Ruth Leonard; suffers a stroke in John Updike's *Rabbit, Run.*

Daniel Tracy Touchett American banker and longtime resident of England; Isabel Archer's uncle in Henry James's *The Portrait of a Lady.*

Lydia Touchett Deliberate, eccentric wife of Daniel Tracy Touchett and mother of Ralph Touchett; invites her cousin, Isabel Archer, to Europe in Henry James's *The Portrait of a Lady.*

Ralph Touchett Clever, charming invalid who is emotionally supportive of his cousin Isabel Archer in Henry James's *The Portrait of a Lady.*

Toussaint Dreamy-eyed middle-aged coachman at Bréda and one of the few literate slaves; joins the revolt in Arna Wendell Bontemps's *Drums at Dusk.*

Marie Tovesky See Marie Tovesky Shabata.

Ann Potter Towne See Ann Potter.

Langdon Towne Member of Rogers' Rangers and admirer of Major Robert Rogers; successful painter of American Indians; narrator of Kenneth Roberts's *Northwest Passage.*

Matthew (George, Mat) Towns Black American who becomes disillusioned with democracy when he experiences the horrors of racism as a porter and a prisoner; allows himself to be used politically by Sammy Scott and Sara Andrews, his first wife, in W. E. B. Du Bois's *Dark Princess.*

Sara Andrews Towns Self-made and independent stenographer employed by Sammy Scott; first wife of Matthew Towns; organizes the Chicago Colored Woman's Council, a powerful political force, in W. E. B. Du Bois's *Dark Princess.*

Arthur Townsend Stockbroker married to Marian Almond; cousin of Morris Townsend in Henry James's *Washington Square.*

Edith (Edy) Townsend College roommate of and later resident of the same New York apartment with Derrick Thornton in Helen Hooven Santmyer's *Herbs and Apples.*

Marian Almond Townsend See Marian Almond.

Mary (Towney) Townsend Writer of Ye Towne Gossyp, a society column; friend of Miranda in Katherine Anne Porter's *Pale Horse, Pale Rider.*

Morris Townsend Handsome, mercenary suitor of Catherine Sloper, whom he jilts when her father resolves to disinherit her if she marries Morris, in Henry James's *Washington Square.*

Albert R. (Bert) Tozer Modern businessman and brother of Leora Tozer in Sinclair Lewis's *Arrowsmith.*

Mr. and Mrs. Andrew Jackson Tozer Parents of Bert and Leora Tozer; they persuade Martin Arrowsmith to live with them while he is establishing his medical practice in Sinclair Lewis's *Arrowsmith.*

Leora Tozer First wife of Martin Arrowsmith; supports her husband in his career and dies of the bubonic plague in Sinclair Lewis's *Arrowsmith.*

T. P   See T. P. Gibson.

Albert Tracy   Friend of Harry Morgan killed by Roberto; a narrator of Ernest Hemingway's *To Have and Have Not*.

Bel Tracy   Daughter of Isaac Tracy and fiancée of Ned Hazard; infatuated with medieval falconry in John Pendleton Kennedy's *Swallow Barn*.

Catharine Tracy   Educated daughter of Isaac Tracy in John Pendleton Kennedy's *Swallow Barn*.

Isaac Tracy   Revolutionary War veteran and widowered father of Bel, Catharine, and Ralph Tracy; obsessed with a lawsuit against Frank Meriwether for a worthless piece of swampland that separates their estates; distressed at the resolution of the litigation in his favor in John Pendleton Kennedy's *Swallow Barn*.

Ralph Tracy   Coarse son and heir of Isaac Tracy in John Pendleton Kennedy's *Swallow Barn*.

Viola (Vee) Tracy   Star of such movies as *The Virgin Vamp*; loves Bunny Ross, but does not accept his political activities, in Upton Sinclair's *Oil!*

Traddle   Illiterate weaver elected to the Pennsylvania assembly when Teague Oregan declines the honor in Hugh Henry Brackenridge's *Modern Chivalry*.

Trampas   Foe and shootout victim of the Virginian in Owen Wister's *The Virginian*.

Berwyn Phillips (Red) Traphagen   Crusty intellectual catcher for the New York Mammoths; later becomes a professor at San Francisco State College in Mark Harris's *The Southpaw*, *Bang the Drum Slowly*, *A Ticket for a Seamstitch*, and *It Looked Like For Ever*.

Adam Trask   California settler whose wife, Cathy Ames Trask, shoots and deserts him, leaving him to rear the twins, Caleb and Aron; later devastated financially when his lettuce shipment is ruined by a failure in his experimental refrigeration system; dies in John Steinbeck's *East of Eden*.

Aron (Aaron) Trask   Quiet and earnest twin brother of Caleb Trask; plans to become a minister, but when Caleb reveals to him that their mother, supposed to be dead, is living in Salinas, where she operates a successful brothel, he is devastated and runs off to join the army in John Steinbeck's *East of Eden*.

Caleb (Cal) Trask   Twin brother of Aron Trask; discovers the existence of his mother, the madam Kate Ames Trask, believed by the boys to be long dead, and uses this knowledge to destroy his brother, whom he believes their father Adam prefers to Caleb, in John Steinbeck's *East of Eden*.

Cathy Ames (Catherine Amesbury, Kate) Trask   Beautiful but cruel and deceitful woman who marries Adam Trask and who is the mother of Caleb and Aron Trask, whom she abandons soon after their birth; becomes madam of a successful Salinas brothel in John Steinbeck's *East of Eden*.

Charles Trask   Half brother of Adam Trask; seduced by Cathy Ames on the night of her marriage to Adam and is the true father of one or both of her twins, Caleb and Aron, in John Steinbeck's *East of Eden*.

Father Trask   Priest who leads a wake for Chalmers Egstrom in William Goyen's *In a Farther Country*.

Rutherford (Rusty) Trawler   Much-married millionaire; Holly Golightly considers marrying him, but her rival, Mag Wildwood, captures him in Truman Capote's *Breakfast at Tiffany's*.

Belinda Bolingbroke Treadwell   Wife of Cyrus Treadwell, whose stinginess forces her to sell her family silver, in Ellen Glasgow's *Virginia*.

Cyrus Treadwell   Wealthy tobacco manufacturer, leader of the New South, and father of Susan Treadwell in Ellen Glasgow's *Virginia*.

Henry (Harry) Treadwell   Spoiled, brilliant second child of Virginia Pendleton and Oliver Treadwell in Ellen Glasgow's *Virginia*.

Laura Treadwell   Aristocratic fiancée of Col. Henry French; rejects French because of his liberal racial attitudes in Charles W. Chesnutt's *The Colonel's Dream*.

Oliver Treadwell   Energetic, idealistic, and egocentric playwright; cousin of Susan Treadwell and unfaithful husband of Virginia Pendleton in Ellen Glasgow's *Virginia*.

Susan Treadwell   Independent, assertive, and sensible friend and foil of Virginia Pendleton in Ellen Glasgow's *Virginia*.

Virginia Pendleton Treadwell   See Virginia Pendleton.

Clay Tredgold   President of Steel Windmill Company and friend of Martin Arrowsmith in Sinclair Lewis's *Arrowsmith*.

Felix (Mrs. Hugo Gross) Treevly   Patient who is killed by his dermatologist, Frederick Eichner, in Terry Southern's *Flash and Filigree*.

John (Ezekiel Hook) Treeworgy   British sympathizer who sabotages Benedict Arnold's army in Kenneth Roberts's *Arundel*.

Silas Trefethen   Rivermouth grocer who buys old cannons in Thomas Bailey Aldrich's *The Story of a Bad Boy*.

Harriet Tremont   Aunt and surrogate mother of Patience Sparhawk in Gertrude Atherton's *Patience Sparhawk and Her Times*.

Charles Augustus (Gus) Trenor   Wealthy investor to whom Lily Bart becomes financially indebted in Edith Wharton's *The House of Mirth*.

Judy Trenor   Wealthy friend of Lily Bart; ends the friendship when she discovers that her husband, Gus Trenor, has given Bart a great deal of money in Edith Wharton's *The House of Mirth.*

Agnes Johnson Trent   College classmate of Jane Ward, successful writer and playwright, and wife of Jimmy Trent in Margaret Ayer Barnes's *Years of Grace.*

Anne Elizabeth Trent (Daughter)   Kind-hearted volunteer for the Near East Relief who has an affair with Richard Ellsworth Savage and becomes pregnant; in a final act of despair, she takes up with a French flier and is killed in a plane crash after she encourages him to daring maneuvers in Margaret Ayer Barnes's *Years of Grace.*

James (Jimmy) Trent   Composer and music critic; husband of Agnes Johnson Trent, but in love with Jane Ward, who rejects him; dies in World War I in Margaret Ayer Barnes's *Years of Grace.*

Joe Trent   College student who makes sexual advances toward Ellen Chesser in Elizabeth Madox Roberts's *The Time of Man.*

Harris (Bunk) Trevelyan   Tobacco farmer who joins the Free Farmers' Brotherhood of Protection and Control and is subsequently killed by members of the brotherhood in Robert Penn Warren's *Night Rider.*

Andrés Treviño   Owner of goats and friend of Pepe Gonzales, Bob Webster, and Porfirio; his wedding provides a funny scene in Josefina Niggli's *Mexican Village.*

Carlo Treviso   Famous music teacher who encourages and defends Veda Pierce's snobbery and alienation from her mother in James M. Cain's *Mildred Pierce.*

Agnes Trevor   Friend of Mary Ogden; engages in social work rather than express her passion in Gertrude Atherton's *Black Oxen.*

Marquise de Trézac (Nettie Wincher)   Young woman at a Virginia resort envied by Undine Spragg because of her higher social class; later provides Undine with advice about French society in Edith Wharton's *The Custom of the Country.*

Annabelle Puckett (Mrs. Duncan) Trice   Adulteress whose affair with Cass Mastern results in her husband's suicide in Robert Penn Warren's *All the King's Men.*

Caroline (Carolina) Trid   Wife of Chad Hanna and, as Carolina, lady high rider in Walter D. Edmonds's *Chad Hanna.*

Janet and Peter Trimble   Married friends of Arthur Ketcham in John Clellon Holmes's *Go.*

Tristessa   Mexican-Indian morphine addict idealized by the narrator of Jack Kerouac's *Tristessa;* mentioned in *Desolation Angels.*

Tom Tristram   American in Paris and friend of Christopher Newman in Henry James's *The American.*

Mrs. Tom Tristram   Wife of Tom Tristram; introduces Christopher Newman to Claire de Cintré in Henry James's *The American.*

Florrie Trotman   Friend who sympathizes with Silla Boyce's desire to own property in Paule Marshall's *Brown Girl, Brownstones.*

Captain Truck   Captain of the *Typhoon,* which takes Tom Bailey from New Orleans to Boston in Thomas Bailey Aldrich's *The Story of a Bad Boy.*

Trudchen   German teenager who sleeps with Carlo Reinhart in Thomas Berger's *Crazy in Berlin.*

Jim Trueblood   Black sharecropper who shocks Norton with the story of how Trueblood made his own daughter pregnant in Ralph Ellison's *Invisible Man.*

John Truman   President of and transfer agent for the Black Rapids Coal Company in Herman Melville's *The Confidence-Man.*

Louise Trunnion   Young woman with whom George Willard has his first sexual experience in Sherwood Anderson's *Winesburg, Ohio.*

George Tryon   Best friend of John Walden; falls in love with Rowena Walden but rejects her when he learns she is black in Charles W. Chesnutt's *The House Behind the Cedars.*

Dr. A. DeWitt Tubbs   Director of the McGurk Institute of Biology in Sinclair Lewis's *Arrowsmith.*

Euphus Tubbs   Jailer in William Faulkner's *Intruder in the Dust, Requiem for a Nun,* and *The Mansion.*

Emma (Mama) Tucker   Wife of Tyree Tucker and mother of Fish Tucker; tries to keep Fish in school and away from his father's illegal business establishments in Richard Wright's *The Long Dream.*

Rex (Fish, Fishbelly, Fishy-O) Tucker   Young man growing up in Clintonville, Mississippi; drops out of school to work for his father, is accused of raping a white woman, and spends three years in jail without being convicted; leaves Mississippi for France after his release in Richard Wright's *The Long Dream.*

Tyree (Papa) Tucker   Husband of Emma Tucker and father of Fish Tucker; owns a funeral home and illegal business establishments; murdered by Gerald Cantley, who believes Tucker to possess incriminating cancelled bribery checks, in Richard Wright's *The Long Dream.*

Edward (King Edward VI, Prince of Wales) Tudor   English prince who exchanges places with the impoverished Tom Canty and discovers the injustices of the English class system; vows to rule with compassion when he becomes king in Samuel Langhorne Clemens's *The Prince and the Pauper.*

Harry Tugman Supervisor of newspaper carriers and first boss of Eugene Gant in Thomas Wolfe's *Look Homeward, Angel.*

Cora and Vernon Tull Married couple in William Faulkner's *As I Lay Dying, The Hamlet, The Town,* and *The Mansion;* Vernon Tull is a farmer in Faulkner's *Sanctuary.*

Tunner Lover of Katherine Moresby and friend of Porter Moresby in Paul Bowles's *The Sheltering Sky.*

Second Lieutenant Amanda Turck WAC officer at Ocanara Army Air Base; intelligent and introspective divorcée who has a sexual encounter with Captain Nathaniel Hicks in James Gould Cozzens's *Guard of Honor.*

Turfmould Sexton and undertaker who buries Norwood's leading citizens in Henry Ward Beecher's *Norwood.*

Frank Turnbull Repentant womanizer, parishioner of Andrew Mackerel, and instigator of the Mackerel Plaza project in Peter De Vries's *The Mackerel Plaza.*

Steven (Steve, Stevie) Turnbull Seventeen-year-old son of Frank Turnbull; author of *Some Notes Toward an Examination of Possible Elements of Homosexuality in Mutt and Jeff* in Peter De Vries's *The Mackerel Plaza.*

Clay (Bad Man) Turner Sadistic killer who devastates the first Hard Times by killing people, raping prostitutes, and burning the town; wounded by Blue and killed by Jimmy Fee in E. L. Doctorow's *Welcome to Hard Times.*

Ellen Turner Younger sister of Marie Turner; worker at the Past Bay Manufacturing Company factory who falls in love with Johnny Hagen in Robert Cantwell's *The Land of Plenty.*

George Albert Turner High school teacher of Vridar Hunter; makes Hunter realize that masturbation does not lead to insanity and helps Hunter attain intellectual growth and honesty in Vardis Fisher's *In Tragic Life;* also appears in *Orphans in Gethsemane.*

Marie Turner Elder sister of Ellen Turner; worker at the Past Bay Manufacturing Company factory who becomes ill following an abortion; briefly kidnapped by Walt Connor in Robert Cantwell's *The Land of Plenty.*

Penny Turner See Penny Turner Stone.

Jacob Turnesa Peddler who gives Daniel Harrow a ride into Rome in Walter D. Edmonds's *Rome Haul;* also appears in *The Big Barn.*

Lucius Mamilius Turrinus Devoted friend and correspondent of Caesar; severely maimed in war; lives in self-imposed exile on Capri in Thornton Wilder's *The Ides of March.*

Arimithy (Grandma) Tussie Wife of Press Tussie and mother of Kim and Mott Tussie in Jesse Stuart's *Taps for Private Tussie.*

Ben Tussie Nephew of Press Tussie; moves in with the parvenu Tussies but reports them to the relief board in Jesse Stuart's *Taps for Private Tussie.*

George Tussie Brother of Press Tussie; fiddle-playing wanderer who marries Vittie Tussie in Jesse Stuart's *Taps for Private Tussie.*

Kim Tussie Son of Press and Arimithy Tussie; army private supposedly killed in the war who returns to reclaim his wife in Jesse Stuart's *Taps for Private Tussie.*

Mott Tussie Son of Press and Arimithy Tussie and brother of Kim Tussie; falsely identifies a corpse as Kim's in order to court Kim's wife, Vittie Tussie, in Jesse Stuart's *Taps for Private Tussie.*

Press (Grandpa) Tussie Father of Kim and Mott Tussie and patriarch of the shiftless Tussie clan; exploits the relief program through political power in Jesse Stuart's *Taps for Private Tussie.*

Sid Tussie Orphan and observer of the Tussie clan who learns that he is not a Tussie but is rather the illegitimate son of a wealthy mine owner and Vittie Tussie; narrator of Jesse Stuart's *Taps for Private Tussie.*

Vittie Tussie Wife of Kim Tussie and mother of Sid Tussie; inherits ten thousand dollars at Kim's supposed death and marries George Tussie before Kim returns in Jesse Stuart's *Taps for Private Tussie.*

Noah Tuttle Senior law partner who has long juggled trust funds to conceal a $200,000 embezzlement he committed to save investors in a bankrupt trolley line in James Gould Cozzens's *By Love Possessed.*

Twelvemough Writer of romantic fiction who defends America against Homos's criticisms in William Dean Howells's *A Traveler from Altruria.*

Kitty Twist Vagabond who briefly spends time with Dove Linkhorn in Nelson Algren's *A Walk on the Wild Side.*

Rick Tyler Fugitive whose escape, after he has been apprehended, is thought to have been arranged by Hiram Kelsey in Mary Noailles Murfree's *The Prophet of the Great Smoky Mountains.*

Mollie Tyndale Wife of Burt Parr, until the marriage is annulled, in Mari Sandoz's *Capital City.*

Typee (Paul) Narrator of Herman Melville's *Omoo.*

Tyrrel See Captain St. Jermyn.

Hattie Tyson Mistress of John Buddy Pearson before she uses voodoo to become his second wife in Zora Neale Hurston's *Jonah's Gourd Vine.*

U

Madame Fanny Uccelli   American expatriate and friend of Evalina Bowen in William Dean Howells's *Indian Summer*.

Florence Udney   See Florence Udney Parish.

Uhia   King of Ohonoo who desires to be king of Mardi in Herman Melville's *Mardi*.

Delly Ulver   Servant of the Glendinnings who is seduced by Ned and who accompanies Pierre Glendinning and Isabel Banford to the city in Herman Melville's *Pierre*.

Walter Ulver   Father of Delly Ulver; Isabel Banford stays with his family in Herman Melville's *Pierre*.

Uncas (le Cerf Agile)   Son of Chingachgook; killed trying to rescue his beloved Cora Munro, leaving his father as the last of their tribe, in James Fenimore Cooper's *The Last of the Mohicans*.

Uncle Buck   See Theophilus McCaslin.

Uncle Buddy   See Amodeus McCaslin.

Uncle Tom   Longtime faithful slave to the Shelby family; sold to the St. Clares and then to Simon Legree, who tortures him to death for maintaining his Christian principles, in Harriet Beecher Stowe's *Uncle Tom's Cabin*.

Uncle Willy   See Uncle Willy Christian.

Mary Underwood   Teacher who befriends young Sam McPherson, in Sherwood Anderson's *Windy McPherson's Son*.

Unk   See Malachi Constant.

Annabel Upchurch   Disillusioned daughter of Bella Upchurch; marries Gamaliel Bland Honeywell in order to get money for her mother in Ellen Glasgow's *The Romantic Comedians*.

Bella Upchurch   Widow whose pragmatism leads her to marry her daughter, Annabel, to Gamaliel Bland Honeywell in Ellen Glasgow's *The Romantic Comedians*.

Dr. Updike   Neighbor of the Fincastles who frequently intervenes to help them in Ellen Glasgow's *Vein of Iron*.

Charles Upton   Young American painter who visits Berlin during the depression in Katherine Anne Porter's *The Leaning Tower*.

John Ushant   Sexagenarian captain of the forecastle aboard the *Neversink* who refuses to have his beard shaved in Herman Melville's *White-Jacket*.

Pete Uspy   Agent for the Cracker Foundation who rescues Candy Christian from the police in Terry Southern and Mason Hoffenberg's *Candy*.

V Half brother of Sebastian Knight, whose biography V. is trying to write as the narrator of Vladimir Nabokov's *The Real Life of Sebastian Knight*.

Alberta Sydna Crowninshield Vaiden Daughter of Emory and Drusilla Lacefield Crowninshield, loved by Jerry Catlin the Second, second wife of Miltiades Vaiden, mother of Marsan Vaiden, and later the wife of Lucius Handback; appears T. S. Stribling's *The Store* and *Unfinished Cathedral*.

Augustus (Gus) Vaiden Son of Jimmie and Laura Vaiden; wounded in his first battle of the Civil War; appears in T. S. Stribling's *The Forge* and *The Store*.

Cassandra Vaiden Eldest daughter of Jimmie and Laura Vaiden; bluestocking spinster and a dominant influence in the Vaiden household; appears in T. S. Stribling's *The Forge* and *The Store*.

Gracie (Gracie Beekman, Gracie Dill, Gracie Light) Vaiden Unacknowledged quadroon daughter of Jimmie Vaiden and a black slave; mother of Toussaint Vaiden by Miltiades Vaiden; mistress to several white men; appears in T. S. Stribling's *The Forge*, *The Store*, and *Unfinished Cathedral*.

Jimmie Vaiden Patriarch of a large family of yeoman farmers in northern Alabama; father of the quadroon slave Gracie Vaiden in T. S. Stribling's *The Forge*.

Laura Vaiden Wife of Jimmie Vaiden and mother of Cassandra, Marcia, Miltiades, Augustus, and Polycarp Vaiden in T. S. Stribling's *The Forge*.

Lucy Lacefield Vaiden Educated black who marries Toussaint Vaiden and founds a school for black children at the former Lacefield Manor in T. S. Stribling's *The Store*.

Marcia (Marsh) Vaiden Sentimental and romantic daughter of Jimmie and Laura Vaiden and wife of Jerry Catlin; appears in T. S. Stribling's *The Forge* and *The Store*.

Marsan Vaiden Daughter of Miltiades and Sydna Crowninshield Vaiden and cousin of Jerry Catlin the Second; impregnated by Red McLaughlin; marries J. Adlee Petrie, her high school science teacher, in T. S. Stribling's *Unfinished Cathedral*.

Miltiades (Milt) Vaiden Son of Jimmie and Laura Vaiden, husband first of Ponny BeShears Vaiden and then of Sydna Crowninshield Vaiden, and father of Marsan Vaiden and the octoroon Toussaint Vaiden; store clerk, overseer of Lacefield Manor, colonel in the Fourth Alabama Regiment, leader of the Ku Klux Klan, and eventual bank president; appears in T.S. Stribling's *The Forge*, *The Store*, and *Unfinished Cathedral*.

Polycarp (Carp) Vaiden Son of Jimmie and Laura Vaiden and lover of Pormy BeShears; possibly killed by the Leatherwood gang in T. S. Stribling's *The Forge*.

Ponny BeShears Vaiden See Ponny BeShears.

Toussaint Vaiden Illegitimate son of Miltiades and Gracie Vaiden; victim of a lynch mob in T. S. Stribling's *The Store*.

Joseph (Blanchet) Vaillant French missionary and long-time friend of Bishop Latour; works with Latour in New Mexico and later works in Colorado in Willa Cather's *Death Comes for the Archbishop*.

Cardinal Vaini Eighty-year-old former missionary to China who has retired to Rome to read, meditate, and play with animals; his brilliant intellect holds him aloof from others; in an intellectual game, he undermines the faith of Marie-Astrée-Luce de Morfontaine, who later tries to shoot him, in Thornton Wilder's *The Cabala.*

Erik Valborg   Swedish tailor and lover of poetry who befriends Carol Kennicott in Sinclair Lewis's *Main Street.*

Magdalena Valdez   Mexican who is rescued from her murderous husband by Bishop Latour and who works for Latour until his death in Willa Cather's *Death Comes for the Archbishop.*

Basil Valentine   Art critic in league with Recktall Brown in art fraud; stabbed (but not killed) by Wyatt Gwyon in William Gaddis's *The Recognitions.*

Lee Valentine   Bandleader who hires Rick Martin away from Jack Stuart; takes Martin to New York in Dorothy Baker's *Young Man with a Horn.*

Dr. Valentini   Skilled Italian surgeon who removes shrapnel from Frederic Henry's knee in Ernest Hemingway's *A Farewell to Arms.*

Velma Valento (Mrs. Lewin Lockridge Grayle)   Former showgirl who marries a wealthy older man; object of Moose Malloy's quest in Raymond Chandler's *Farewell, My Lovely.*

Valeska   Secretary hired by Henry Miller; he falls in love with her and brings her home to meet his wife; gives Miller's wife a hundred dollars for an abortion and later commits suicide in Henry Miller's *Tropic of Capricorn.*

Valet de Chambre (Tom Driscoll)   Son of Roxy, who switches him at birth with Thomas à Becket Driscoll; reared as Tom Driscoll; murders York Leicester in Samuel Langhorne Clemens's *Pudd'nhead Wilson.*

Red Valsen   Soldier who unsuccessfully resists Sergeant Croft in Norman Mailer's *The Naked and the Dead.*

Marquesa Daisy de Valverde   Worldly Tangier socialite who tries to help Nelson Dyar in Paul Bowles's *Let It Come Down.*

Van   Finnish sailor aboard the *Julia* in Herman Melville's *Omoo.*

Harry Van   Composer and friend of Duff Conway in Shelby Foote's *Jordan County.*

Fred Van Ackerman   Junior senator from Wyoming and chief spokesman for a liberal group called COMFORT (Committee on Making Further Offers for a Russian Truce); eventually censured by the Senate for his unscrupulous and fanatical actions against Senator Brigham Anderson in Allen Drury's *Advise and Consent.*

Mr. Vanaker   Elderly garage employee, drunkard, and unhygienic inmate of the apartment house where Joseph lives; though he shares many of the same vices, Joseph vehemently denounces Vanaker's vulgarity, spying, and thievery in Saul Bellow's *Dangling Man.*

Vanamee   Wandering-shepherd figure who copes with the death of his fiancée by elaborating upon St. Paul's teachings concerning the resurrection in order to effect a denial of death itself in Frank Norris's *The Octopus.*

Abraham Van Brunt   Hired Dutchman who manages Fortune Emerson's farm; becomes Ellen Montgomery's loyal defender and later marries Fortune in Susan Warner's *The Wide, Wide World.*

Fortune Emerson Van Brunt   See Fortune Emerson.

Laura Van Brunt   See Laura Hawkins.

Mr. Van Brunt   Cantankerous old man who irritates Juan Chicoy by arguing with him about the danger of driving in a storm; has a stroke while waiting for the stranded bus to be rescued in John Steinbeck's *The Wayward Bus.*

Miss Van Campen   Supervising nurse at the American hospital in Milan; hastens Frederic Henry's return to the front by accusing him of self-inflicted alcoholic jaundice in Ernest Hemingway's *A Farewell to Arms.*

Eleanor (Nell) Vance   Thirty-two-year-old woman who, as a child, was the focus of poltergeist activity; invited to Hill House because of her susceptibility to spectral phenomena in Shirley Jackson's *The Haunting of Hill House.*

Margaret Vance   New Yorker who tries to introduce the Dryfoos sisters to high society; convinces Conrad Dryfoos to help the poor workers of New York in William Dean Howells's *A Hazard of New Fortunes.*

Mr. and Mrs. Vance   New York neighbors of Carrie Meeber and George Hurstwood, whom the Vances know as the Wheelers, in Theodore Dreiser's *Sister Carrie.*

Ariel (Auriel) Vancour   Youngest brother of the patroon family in James Kirke Paulding's *The Dutchman's Fireside.*

Catalina (Catty) Vancour   Daughter of Egbert and Madame Vancour; heroine of James Kirke Paulding's *The Dutchman's Fireside.*

Dennis Vancour   Middle brother of the patroon family in James Kirke Paulding's *The Dutchman's Fireside.*

Colonel Egbert Vancour   Oldest brother of the patroon family in James Kirke Paulding's *The Dutchman's Fireside.*

Madame Vancour   Wife of the patroon Egbert Vancour in James Kirke Paulding's *The Dutchman's Fireside.*

William Robespierre Vandamm   Bachelor uncle of Gloria Wandrous; provides for Gloria's education and supports her mother, his younger sister, in John O'Hara's *Butterfield 8.*

Clare Van Degen   Elegant, restless cousin of Ralph Marvel and wife of Peter Van Degen in Edith Wharton's *The Custom of the Country*.

Peter Van Degen   Wealthy socialite and womanizer who leaves his wife, Clare Van Degen, to become Undine Spragg's companion for several months in Edith Wharton's *The Custom of the Country*.

Gustavus (Van) Vanderbank   Handsome man who loves but does not marry Nanda Brookenham in Henry James's *The Awkward Age*.

Mrs. Vanderpool (née Wells)   Wealthy northern matron who refines Zora and ruins Mary Taylor Cresswell in society in W. E. B. Du Bois's *The Quest of the Silver Fleece*.

Caroline (Mrs. Erasmus Van de Weyer) Van de Weyer   Half sister of Peter Alden and socialite aunt of Oliver Alden in George Santayana's *The Last Puritan*.

Edith Van de Weyer   Cousin who rejects Oliver Alden's marriage proposal in George Santayana's *The Last Puritan*.

Mario (Marius, Vanny) Van de Weyer   Europeanized cousin of Oliver Alden in George Santayana's *The Last Puritan*.

Robert (Black Rider, Bob) Van Doren   Confederate soldier who falls in love with Mary Waters, a Union sympathizer; son of Stephen Van Doren in Paul Laurence Dunbar's *The Fanatics*.

Stephen Van Doren   Genteel white southerner and democrat who migrates to Dorbury, Ohio, and becomes a defender and protector of the northern black contrabands; father of Robert Van Doren in Paul Laurence Dunbar's *The Fanatics*.

Laura Nesbit Van Dorn   Daughter of James and Bedelia Nesbit; deserted by her husband Thomas Van Dorn; establishes a kindergarten for mine workers' families in William Allen White's *In the Heart of a Fool*.

Lila Van Dorn   Daughter of Thomas and Laura Van Dorn; marries Kenyon Adams in William Allen White's *In the Heart of a Fool*.

Thomas (Tom) Van Dorn   Materialistic judge who divorces Laura Nesbit Van Dorn to marry Margaret Müller Fenn; falls from power and social position in William Allen White's *In the Heart of a Fool*.

Vandover (Van)   Weak-willed, unanalytical artist who comes to ruin, suffering multiple physical and mental disorders as he degenerates, in Frank Norris's *Vandover and the Brute*.

Vane (Vanio)   Composer and lover of Julia Ashton in H. D.'s *Bid Me to Live*.

Austen (Aust) Vane   Reformist antirailroad lawyer and politician; marries Victoria Flint in Winston Churchill's *Mr. Crewe's Career*.

Hilary Vane   Father of Austen Vane; judge, railroad lawyer, and major political force in Winston Churchill's *Mr. Crewe's Career*.

Victoria Flint Vane   See Victoria Flint.

George Augustus Vane-Basingwell   Employer of the valet Marmaduke Ruggles; loses Ruggles to Egbert Floud in a poker game in Harry Leon Wilson's *Ruggles of Red Gap*.

Nevil (Earl of Brinstead) Vane-Basingwell   Brother of George Augustus Vane-Basingwell; tries to prevent his brother from marrying an unsuitable American woman, but marries her himself, in Harry Leon Wilson's *Ruggles of Red Gap*.

Edward Van Harrington   Unethical and rapacious youth who becomes a meatpacker and entrepreneur; husband of Sarah Gentles; narrator of Robert Herrick's *The Memoirs of an American Citizen*.

Van Horn (Skipper)   Captain of the *Arangi*, a ship taking indentured servants to the British Solomons; killed by Bashti in Jack London's *Jerry of the Islands*.

Madeleine Van Leyden   College roommate of and later resident of the same New York apartment with Derrick Thornton; serves in World War I in Helen Hooven Santmyer's *Herbs and Apples*.

Van Norden (Joe)   Jewish friend of Henry Miller; plans to write a book someday in Henry Miller's *Tropic of Cancer*.

Kate Van Schaak   Aristocratic New Yorker who directs the career of her husband, Horace Larkin, and attempts to buy a diplomatic post for him in Hjalmar Hjorth Boyesen's *The Mammon of Unrighteousness*.

Baltus (Captain, Skipper) Van Slingerland   Hudson River sloop captain in James Kirke Paulding's *The Dutchman's Fireside*.

Felice Van Verdighan   See Avis Cunningham Everhard.

Humphrey (Hump) Van Weyden   Narrator rescued at sea by the *Ghost*; saves the ship when the crewmen fight among themselves in Jack London's *The Sea-Wolf*.

Bartolomeo (Bart, Bartholomew) Vanzetti   Italian pastry cook and agnostic who immigrates to the United States to find a better life but sees such cruel exploitation of workers by the rich that he becomes an anarchist; unjustly charged with the murder of two men during a robbery; executed, despite the efforts of Cornelia Thornwell and others to save him, in Upton Sinclair's *Boston*.

Ludwig Varlett   Shoemaker and councilman killed by Indians in James Kirke Paulding's *Koningsmarke*.

Eula Varner   See Eula Varner Snopes.

Jody Varner　Son of Will Varner and store manager; appears in William Faulkner's *As I Lay Dying, Light in August, The Hamlet, The Town,* and *The Mansion.*

Will (Uncle Billy) Varner　Father of, among others, Jody Varner and Eula Varner Snopes; appears in William Faulkner's *As I Lay Dying, Light in August, The Hamlet, Intruder in the Dust, The Town,* and *The Mansion.*

Varvy　Deaf hermit who operates a still near Taloo in Herman Melville's *Omoo.*

Vanya (Danny Spellbinder) Vashvily　Hollywood producer who discovers Belinda in Ludwig Bemelmans's *Dirty Eddie.*

Whiskey Vassos　Thug employed by Shad O'Rory in Dashiell Hammett's *The Glass Key.*

Cecilia Vaughan　Friend of Alice Archer; in marrying Arthur Kavanagh, she causes Alice to die of a broken heart in Henry Wadsworth Longfellow's *Kavanagh.*

Colonel Ezekiel (Zeke) Vaughn　An original secessionist of Rockford County who never served in the Confederate army; surrenders to Comfort Servosse, takes financial advantage of him in the sale of Warrington plantation, but becomes his enemy when Servosse indignantly refuses to stop associating with the teachers at the freedmen's school; eventually accepts Servosse as harmless and tends to him during Servosse's final illness in Albion W. Tourgee's *A Fool's Errand.*

Zaza (Ali Zaza) Vauriselle　Mentally retarded adolescent given to masturbating in public; adopted by Jack Duluoz and his friends in Jack Kerouac's *Doctor Sax* and *Maggie Cassidy.*

Mrs. Vawse　Swiss native who lives on a remote mountain outside Thirlwall; befriends Ellen Montgomery and helps her learn French in Susan Warner's *The Wide, Wide World.*

Nancy Vawse　Mischievous young granddaughter of Mrs. Vawse; Ellen Montgomery overcomes her dislike of Nancy and befriends her in Susan Warner's *The Wide, Wide World.*

James Vayle　Fiancé of Helga Crane while both are teachers at a southern black school in Nella Larsen's *Quicksand.*

Agapito Vázquez de Anda　Wealthy banker and family tyrant who interferes with his son Domingo's desire to be a doctor and tries to force his son Cardito into being a banker in Josefina Niggli's *Step Down, Elder Brother.*

Brunhilda Vázquez de Anda　Extravagant daughter of the Vázquez de Anda family who is sent to New York to study piano; allies herself with her uncle Agapito and marries her brother Domingo's best friend in Josefina Niggli's *Step Down, Elder Brother.*

Domingo Vázquez de Anda　Oldest son torn between loyalty and duty to his family and his love for Márgara Bárcenas; fi-nally rebels against his tyrannical uncle; protagonist of Josefina Niggli's *Step Down, Elder Brother.*

Lucio (Uncle Lucio) Vázquez de Anda　Gentle failure in an illustrious family; takes correspondence courses in Josefina Niggli's *Step Down, Elder Brother.*

Ricardo (Cardito) Vázquez de Anda　Younger brother of Domingo Vázquez de Anda; impregnates the housemaid and flees all responsibility in Josefina Niggli's *Step Down, Elder Brother.*

Sofia Vázquez de Anda　Daughter thwarted in her business ambitions by stultifying traditions; marries out of her class, suggesting the social and economic changes beginning to bring Monterrey, Mexico, into a new era, in Josefina Niggli's *Step Down, Elder Brother.*

William Veal　Slave and butler on the McGehee estate; accompanies Agnes McGehee to Shiloh to find and bring home the dead Edward McGehee in Stark Young's *So Red the Rose.*

Vee-Vee　Dwarf and page to Media in Herman Melville's *Mardi.*

Veiled Lady　See Priscilla.

Constanza Velasquez　Betrothed of Count Alphonse D'Oyley; loved by Lafitte, who sacrifices much for her, in Joseph Holt Ingraham's *Lafitte.*

Felice Venable　Wife of Lewis Venable and mother of Sabra Venable Cravat; moves her family from Mississippi to the Midwest before the Civil War in Edna Ferber's *Cimarron.*

Lewis Venable　Husband of Felice Venable and father of Sabra Venable Cravat; supports Sabra's trek west in Edna Ferber's *Cimarron.*

Uncle Venner　Workman friend of Hepzibah and Clifford Pyncheon in Nathaniel Hawthorne's *The House of the Seven Gables.*

Edward Fairfax (Starry) Vere　Captain of the *Indomitable* who decides to have Billy Budd hanged in Herman Melville's *Billy Budd.*

Daniel (O. B. Haverton, Old Bitch Haverton, Virgin) Verger　Tubercular and masochistic former Harvard University student who lives in Spanish Harlem and has an affair with Georgia in John Clellon Holmes's *Go.*

Verman　Tongue-tied brother of Herman; his antics, both physical and verbal, provide comic relief for Penrod Schofield and his friends in Booth Tarkington's *Penrod, Penrod and Sam,* and *Penrod Jashber.*

T'ressa (Tessie) Vernacht　Daughter of German immigrants and wife of Denny Moore in Betty Smith's *Maggie-Now.*

Vernier   Colleague of Dr. Kersaint; patiently listens to Kersaint's story of the hurricane in Charles Nordhoff and James Norman Hall's *The Hurricane*.

Verrus   Roman esthete and lover of Hipparchia in H.D.'s *Palimpsest*.

Versh   See Versh Gibson.

Adam Verver   Wealthy American living in England; marries Charlotte Stant in Henry James's *The Golden Bowl*.

Charlotte Stant Verver   See Charlotte Stant.

Maggie (Mag, Princess) Verver   Wealthy woman whose attachment to her father, Adam Verver, threatens her marriage to Prince Amerigo in Henry James's *The Golden Bowl*.

Dred Vesey   Charismatic proselytizer of slave revolt based on Christian scriptures; inhabits the Dismal Swamp, where he hides and defends outlaw slaves until he is killed by Tom Gordon's gang, in Harriet Beecher Stowe's *Dred*.

Wilhelmina (Vesta Stover) Vesta   Illegitimate daughter of Jennie Gerhardt and George Brander; dies of typhoid fever in Theodore Dreiser's *Jennie Gerhardt*.

Anastasius Vetch   Violinist and friend of Amanda Pynsent and Hyacinth Robinson in Henry James's *The Princess Casamassima*.

Fleda Vetch   Heroine with great aesthetic appreciation; companion to Adela Gereth in Henry James's *The Spoils of Poynton*.

Maggie Vetch   Sister of Fleda Vetch in Henry James's *The Spoils of Poynton*.

Sam Vettori   Head of a Chicago gang and proprietor of the Club Palermo; pushed aside by Rico Bandello in William Riley Burnett's *Little Caesar*.

Paulette Viard   Beautiful but dangerous member of the aristocracy; suspected of masterminding the death of her late husband; rejected by Diron Desautels in Arna Wendell Bontemps's *Drums at Dusk*.

Terasina Vidavarri   First love of Dove Linkhorn in Nelson Algren's *A Walk on the Wild Side*.

Viking   See Jarl.

Chela Villareal   Homely daughter of the village mayor; Joaquin Castillo falls in love with her but she chooses the village professor in Josefina Niggli's *Mexican Village*.

Mimi Villars   Pretty waitress and free-love advocate whom Augie March nurses through a botched abortion in Saul Bellow's *The Adventures of Augie March*.

George Villiers, Duke of Buckingham   Cunning, powerful nobleman involved in many intrigues dangerous to himself and to King Charles II; cousin of Barbara Palmer in Kathleen Winsor's *Forever Amber*.

Marquis (Don Luis Guzman Sotomyer y O'Connell, conde de Azuaga) da Vincitata   Cuckolded husband of Maria Bonnyfeather; plots to kill Anthony Adverse, his wife's son, in Hervey Allen's *Anthony Adverse*.

Marquise da Vincitata   See Maria Bonnyfeather.

Viner   Trader on Tahiti who once sailed with John Jermin in Herman Melville's *Omoo*.

Sophy Viner   Vivacious, independent young woman who has a brief affair with George Darrow and later becomes governess for the daughter of Anna Leath, Darrow's fiancée, in Edith Wharton's *The Reef*.

Vineria (Vinie)   Much-admired pup treated like a family member; white female of the pair of pedigreed fox hounds that Nunn Ballew buys to chase King Devil in Harriette Arnow's *Hunter's Horn*.

Jeanne de Vionnet   Pretty daughter of Madame de Vionnet in Henry James's *The Ambassadors*.

Mme. Marie de Vionnet   Estranged wife of a French count; friend of Maria Gostrey, mother of Jeanne de Vionnet, and mistress of Chad Newsome in Henry James's *The Ambassadors*.

Carmen Viosca   Barcelonan wife of Feliu Viosca; rears their foster daughter, Conchita Viosca, to respect God and the sea in Lafcadio Hearn's *Chita*.

Conchita (Chita, Concha, Eulalie, Lil, Zouzoune) Viosca   Daughter of Julien La Brierre; found at sea following a storm and adopted by Feliu and Carmen Viosca in Lafcadio Hearn's *Chita*.

Feliu Viosca   Husband of Carmen Viosca; Spanish fisherman who rescues the baby Conchita after the storm that destroys Last Island in Lafcadio Hearn's *Chita*.

The Virginian   Gallant foreman at Sunk Creek ranch who upholds the laws of the West; has a shootout with Trampas in Owen Wister's *The Virginian*.

Popeye Vitelli   As Popeye Vitelli, a gangster in William Faulkner's *Requiem for a Nun*; as Popeye, a bootlegger and murderer who is hanged for a murder he did not commit in *Sanctuary*.

Florentine Vivier   Impoverished French dressmaker imprisoned for murdering her lover, Lord Frederick Purvis; mother, by Purvis, of Hyacinth Robinson in Henry James's *The Princess Casamassima*.

Hyacinthe Vivier   See Hyacinth Robinson.

Vladek   Illegitimate child reared by Dora Dugova and Yuro Dug; permitted to die in Louis Adamic's *Cradle of Life.*

Franz Vogelsang   Socialist political mentor of Felix Fay in Floyd Dell's *Moon-Calf.*

Baron Felix Volkbein   Orphan who marries Robin Vote, loses her, and rears their son Guido Volkbein in Djuna Barnes's *Nightwood.*

Guido Volkbein   Son of Felix Volkbein and Robin Vote in Djuna Barnes's *Nightwood.*

Robin Vote Volkbein   See Robin Vote.

Robin Vote   Wife of Felix Volkbein, mother of Guido Volkbein, and lover of Nora Flood and Jenny Petherbridge; teeters between her human and bestial natures in Djuna Barnes's *Nightwood.*

Captain de Vriess   Captain of the USS *Caine* prior to Captain Queeg in Herman Wouk's *The Caine Mutiny.*

Eileen Wade   Beautiful wife of Roger Wade, previously married to Terry Lennox; she murders Wade and Sylvia Lennox in Raymond Chandler's *The Long Goodbye*.

Ellen (Nelly) Wade   Eighteen-year-old dependent and relative by marriage of Esther and Ishmael Bush; helps free Inez de Certavallos; returns to the settlements with her beloved, Paul Hover, in James Fenimore Cooper's *The Prairie*.

Ida Wade   Woman who commits suicide after being seduced by Vandover and either being made pregnant or afflicted with a venereal disease by him in Frank Norris's *Vandover and the Brute*.

Roger Wade   Alcoholic writer murdered by his wife in Raymond Chandler's *The Long Goodbye*.

Elsa (Sarah) Wagner   Wife of Jacob Wagner; avoids arrest by the British by moving from North Carolina to Tennessee in Caroline Gordon's *Green Centuries*.

Jacob Wagner   North Carolina storekeeper and husband of Elsa Wagner; avoids arrest by the British by moving to Tennessee, where he establishes a grist mill, in Caroline Gordon's *Green Centuries*.

Wah-ta!-Wah (Hist-oh!-Hist)   Kidnapped lover of Chingachgook in James Fenimore Cooper's *The Deerslayer*.

Joseph Wainsworth   Harness maker in Bidwell, Ohio; because he is distressed at the coming industrialization, he goes crazy and kills Jim Gibson, his assistant, for having publicly humiliated him; shoots Steve Hunter for having opened the first factory in Bidwell; scratches and bites Hugh McVey for being the inventor who caused many of these changes in Sherwood Anderson's *Poor White*.

Edward Walcott   Harley College student who marries Ellen Langton in Nathaniel Hawthorne's *Fanshawe*.

Waldegrave   Brother of Mary Waldegrave; his murder initiates Edgar Huntly's derangement in Charles Brockden Brown's *Edgar Huntly*.

Mary Waldegrave   Sister of Waldegrave and sweetheart of Edgar Huntly in Charles Brockden Brown's *Edgar Huntly*.

Buck Walden   Son of Ty Ty Walden and husband of Griselda Walden; kills Jim Leslie Walden, who is courting Griselda, in Erskine Caldwell's *God's Little Acre*.

Darling Jill Walden   Voluptuous, sensual daughter of Ty Ty Walden in Erskine Caldwell's *God's Little Acre*.

Griselda Walden   Wife of Buck Walden; courted by Will Thompson and Jim Leslie Walden in Erskine Caldwell's *God's Little Acre*.

Jim Leslie Walden   Son of Ty Ty Walden; successful cotton broker who rejected his family; his passion for Griselda Walden causes Buck Walden to kill him in Erskine Caldwell's *God's Little Acre*.

John (John Warwick) Walden   Octoroon son of Molly Walden and elder brother of Rowena Walden; migrates to South Carolina, changes his name, and passes for white in Charles W. Chesnutt's *The House Behind the Cedars*.

Molly (Mis' Molly) Walden   Mulatto mother of John and Rowena Walden in Charles W. Chesnutt's *The House Behind the Cedars*.

Rosamond Walden   See Rosamond Walden Thompson.

Rowena (Rena) Walden   Octaroon daughter of Molly Walden and sister of John Walden; falls in love with George Tryon, who rejects her when he learns her true racial identity in Charles W. Chesnutt's *The House Behind the Cedars.*

Shaw Walden   Son of Ty Ty Walden in Erskine Caldwell's *God's Little Acre.*

Ty Ty Walden   Patriarch, prophet, and voyeur; Georgia farmer who digs for gold and does not plant the acre set aside for God in Erskine Caldwell's *God's Little Acre.*

Elaine (Estelle Walovsky) Wales   Young secretary of Phil Green; so ashamed of her heritage that she changed her name and cannot understand why anyone would admit to being Jewish in Laura Z. Hobson's *Gentleman's Agreement.*

Garvin Wales   Aging novelist who is the key to locating the missing money in Hamilton Basso's *The View from Pompey's Head.*

Lucy Devereaux Wales   Daughter of an old-line family who marries Garvin Wales for his fame and money in Hamilton Basso's *The View from Pompey's Head.*

Esther Walker   Society schemer who tries to swindle people into purchasing her husband's art; on a trip to Paris, tries to convince Aline Aldridge to have an affair with her in Sherwood Anderson's *Dark Laughter.*

Frank Walker   Physician who helps Paul Armstrong fake Armstrong's death; tries to force Louise Armstrong to marry him in Mary Roberts Rinehart's *The Circular Staircase.*

Joe Walker   Painter who lets his wife Esther Walker set up schemes to sell his inferior art in Sherwood Anderson's *Dark Laughter.*

Mrs. Jamison Walker   Married American aristocrat who gives Paolo ruby cuff links and pays the Contessa for his services before her husband beats Paolo up in Tennessee Williams's *The Roman Spring of Mrs. Stone.*

Susan Walker   Boston woman who enrolls freed slaves in northern colleges in Thomas Dixon's *The Leopard's Spots.*

Mrs. Waldo Wallace Walker   Mother of Caroline English in John O'Hara's *Appointment in Samarra.*

Mrs. Walker   American living in Rome; scandalized by Daisy Miller's disregard for her own reputation in Henry James's *Daisy Miller.*

Aubrey Wallace   See Arnold Armstrong.

Binny Wallace   Boyhood friend of Tom Bailey; lost at sea in Thomas Bailey Aldrich's *The Story of a Bad Boy.*

Freddy Wallace   Bar owner who lends Harry Morgan a boat in Ernest Hemingway's *To Have and Have Not.*

Lucien Wallace   Son of Lucy Haswell and Arnold Armstrong (Aubrey Wallace) in Mary Roberts Rinehart's *The Circular Staircase.*

Ina Inez Wallenius   Unpopular schoolmate befriended by Cress Delahanty in Jessamyn West's *Cress Delahanty.*

Mr. Wallenius   Father of Ina Wallenius; his disturbing behavior, including the torture of a gopher snake, forces Cress Delahanty to cut short her overnight stay with Ina in Jessamyn West's *Cress Delahanty.*

Evelyn Walling   Daughter of itinerant actors; adulterous lover of Paul Hardin in Brand Whitlock's *J. Hardin & Son.*

Estelle Walovsky   See Elaine Wales.

John Walters   Union League member who had refused to be conscripted into the Confederate army and who is murdered while attending the county nominating convention in Albion W. Tourgee's *A Fool's Errand.*

Mrs. Walters   Gossipy neighbor of Adam Moss in James Lane Allen's *A Kentucky Cardinal;* also appears in *Aftermath.*

Katharine (Kate) Walton   Daughter of Richard Walton and inamorata of both the British major Proctor and the partisan Robert Singleton in William Gilmore Simms's *The Partisan.*

Colonel Richard Walton   Important landholder who rejects offers of rank in the British service to join the American revolutionaries; captured at the Battle of Camden and sentenced to hang in William Gilmore Simms's *The Partisan.*

Gloria Wandrous   Beautiful brunette wanton leading a dissolute life in New York speakeasies in John O'Hara's *Butterfield 8.*

Mrs. (née Vandamm) Wandrous   Widowed mother of Gloria Wandrous; lives in Greenwich Village and is supported by her elder brother William Vandamm in John O'Hara's *Butterfield 8.*

Wang Lung   Peasant farmer who rises from poverty to wealth; ultimately leaves his mansion to retire to his land in Pearl Buck's *The Good Earth;* dies early in *Sons.*

Wang the Eldest, Wang the Landlord, Wang the Merchant, Wang the Second   See Nung En.

Wang the Third (Wang the Tiger)   Serious student who falls in love with Pear Blossom; when he discovers that she is his father's mistress, he joins the army in Pearl Buck's *The Good Earth;* warlord and husband of three women in *Sons;* weakened warlord disappointed with his son and finally defeated by bandits in Pearl Buck's *A House Divided.*

Betsey MacCaffery Wapshot   Discontented wife of Coverly Wapshot in John Cheever's *The Wapshot Chronicle;* identified as Betsey Marcus Wapshot in *The Wapshot Scandal.*

Coverly Wapshot   Second son of Leander Wapshot; good-hearted but ineffectual dreamer in John Cheever's *The Wapshot Chronicle* and *The Wapshot Scandal.*

Ezekiel Wapshot   Emigrant from England aboard the *Arbella* in 1630; founds the Wapshot line in New England in John Cheever's *The Wapshot Chronicle.*

Honora Wapshot   Eccentric matriarch of the current Wapshot family and patroness of her cousins Moses and Coverly Wapshot; sometime foil to Leander Wapshot's schemes in John Cheever's *The Wapshot Chronicle;* fugitive from income tax authorities in *The Wapshot Scandal.*

Leander Wapshot   Father of Moses and Coverly Wapshot and current male head of the Wapshot clan; captain of the excursion boat *Topaze* and compulsive chronicler of his own life in John Cheever's *The Wapshot Chronicle* and *The Wapshot Scandal.*

Melissa Scaddon Wapshot   Beautiful ward of Justina Wapshot and subsequently wife of Moses Wapshot in John Cheever's *The Wapshot Chronicle;* has an affair with a grocery boy and settles in Rome in *The Wapshot Scandal.*

Moses Wapshot   Elder son of Leander Wapshot and a youth of considerable promise which remains unfulfilled as he passes into alcoholic failure in John Cheever's *The Wapshot Chronicle* and *The Wapshot Scandal.*

Sarah Coverly Wapshot   Wife of Leander Wapshot, village club organizer, and keeper of a floating gift shop converted from her husband's excursion boat in John Cheever's *The Wapshot Chronicle* and *The Wapshot Scandal.*

Warbler   See Yoomy.

Lord Warburton   Upper-class English radical, friend of Ralph Touchett, and admirer of Isabel Archer in Henry James's *The Portrait of a Lady.*

Agee Ward   Orphan seeking knowledge of his past; title character reported missing in Wright Morris's *The Man Who Was There.*

Billy Ward   Thirteen-year-old boy who has suffered a nervous breakdown in Louisa May Alcott's *Little Men.*

Jane Ward   See Jane Ward Carver.

John Ward   Chicago businessman and father of Jane and Isabel Ward in Margaret Ayer Barnes's *Years of Grace* and *Wisdom's Gate.*

Lizzie Ward   Conventional wife of John Ward and mother of Jane and Isabel Ward in Margaret Ayer Barnes's *Years of Grace* and *Wisdom's Gate.*

Neal Dow Ward   Secretary to John Barclay and later editor of the Sycamore Ridge *Banner;* marries Jeanette Barclay when her father's wealth no longer threatens his moral integrity in William Allen White's *A Certain Rich Man.*

Ed Warden   Fellow railroad worker of Larry Donovan in Jack Conroy's *The Disinherited.*

Milton Anthony (Milt) Warden   First sergeant of G Company; has an affair with Karen Holmes, wife of his commanding officer, in James Jones's *From Here to Eternity.*

Alice Hastings Ware   Devoted wife of Theron Ware, who suspects her of infidelity with Levi Gorringe, in Harold Frederic's *The Damnation of Theron Ware.*

Cynthia Ware   See Cynthia Ware Wetherell.

Lugena Ware   See Lugena.

Nimbus Ware   See Nimbus.

Silas Ware   Overseer at Colonel Desmit's plantation and the person whose surname the freed slave Nimbus adopts in Albion W. Tourgee's *Bricks Without Straw.*

Reverend Theron Ware   Naive and intellectually pretentious Methodist minister whose exposure to free-thinkers leads to a breakdown, after which he gives up religion for the real estate business; husband of Alice Hastings Ware in Harold Frederic's *The Damnation of Theron Ware.*

Major Ira (Old Hurricane) Warfield   Guardian of Capitola Le Noir and proprietor of Hurricane Hall in E.D.E.N. Southworth's *The Hidden Hand.*

Ruth Warham   Cousin of Susan Lenox; wants to marry Lenox's boyfriend in David Graham Phillips's *Susan Lenox.*

Elison Warne   Half-white, half-Cherokee Indian younger daughter of Ewen Warne; wife of Savacol in H. L. Davis's *Beulah Land.*

Ewen Warne   Husband of Sedaya Gallet and father of Elison and Ruhama Warne in H. L. Davis's *Beulah Land.*

Ruhama Warne   Half-white, half-Cherokee Indian daughter of Ewen Warne; wife of Savacol and later of Askwani in H. L. Davis's *Beulah Land.*

Albert Warren   President of Longevity Life Insurance Company; forces Erskine Fowler into early retirement in Richard Wright's *Savage Holiday.*

Beth Evan (Baby) Warren   Unprincipled sister of Nicole Warren in F. Scott Fitzgerald's *Tender Is the Night.*

Charles (Devereux) Warren   Millionaire father and seducer of Nicole Warren in F. Scott Fitzgerald's *Tender Is the Night.*

Nicole Warren   See Nicole Warren Diver.

Robert Warren   Son of Albert Warren; given Erskine Fowler's position as district manager for Manhattan as a wedding present from his father in Richard Wright's *Savage Holiday*.

Susan (Susie) Warren   Swinemaid almost raped by Ebenezer Cooke; actually Joan Toast in disguise in John Barth's *The Sot-Weed Factor*.

Philpot (Philly) Wart   Revolutionary War veteran; attorney in whom Frank Meriwether confides in John Pendleton Kennedy's *Swallow Barn*.

John Warwick   See John Walden.

Great Grief Warwickson   Impoverished artist who shares an apartment with Billie Hawker in Stephen Crane's *The Third Violet*.

Estella Washington   Mistress, against her will, of Prince Cabano; rescued by Gabriel Weltstein, whom she marries, in Ignatius Donnelly's Caesar's *Column*.

General George Washington   American Revolutionary War commander-in-chief who relies on Thomas Paine to keep the soldiers loyal, only to forget about him when Washington is president of the United States and Paine is jailed in France, in Howard Fast's *Citizen Tom Paine*.

George (Harper) Washington   Commander-in-chief of the Continental army during the American Revolution in James Fenimore Cooper's *The Spy*.

Charles Waterlow   American painter in Paris who encourages Gaston Probert in Henry James's *The Reverberator*.

Bradford Waters   Prominent republican pioneer of Dorbury, Ohio, who sympathizes with the Union; father of Mary Waters in Paul Laurence Dunbar's *The Fanatics*.

John (Jack) Waters   Resident of the Puerto Rican section of Harlem who commits himself to a sanitarium in John Clellon Holmes's *Go*.

Mary Waters   Union sympathizer who falls in love with Robert Van Doren, a Confederate soldier; daughter of Bradford Waters in Paul Laurence Dunbar's *The Fanatics*.

Mrs. Waters   Prostitute and mother of Toby Waters; Ironside outsider and challenger of the village's values who saves Ada Fincastle from the village mob in Ellen Glasgow's *Vein of Iron*.

Rev. Mr. Waters   Aged minister whose religious doubts lead him to abandon his church and native land; confidant of Theodore Colville and friend of Evalina Bowen in William Dean Howells's *Indian Summer*.

Toby Waters   Young Ironside idiot, social outcast, and victim of basic appetites in Ellen Glasgow's *Vein of Iron*.

Eli (T. C. Brown) Watkins   Brother of Paul Watkins; radio preacher in Upton Sinclair's *Oil!*

Paul (Comrade Watkins) Watkins   Idealistic carpenter admired by Bunny Ross; member of the Communist Party who is beaten and killed to suppress his political beliefs in Upton Sinclair's *Oil!*

Belle Watling   Atlanta prostitute and mistress of Rhett Butler; lies to the Union soldiers in order to save the lives of Ashley Wilkes, Frank Kennedy, and other Confederate sympathizers in Margaret Mitchell's *Gone with the Wind*.

Bibleback Watrobinski   Witness to Bruno (Lefty) Bicek's murder of a nameless man; intimidated by Bonifacy Konstantine into turning Bicek in to the police in Nelson Algren's *Never Come Morning*.

Grover Watrous   Piano player with a clubfoot and a nose that runs like a sewer; believes it is a sin to bowl in Henry Miller's *Tropic of Capricorn*.

Anne Watson   Sister of Lucy Haswell and housekeeper at Sunnyside; confesses to murdering Arnold Armstrong in Mary Roberts Rinehart's *The Circular Staircase*.

Benjamin (Sailor Ben) Watson   Tattooed Nantucket sailor married to Kitty Collins; returns to her after a ten-year absence in Thomas Bailey Aldrich's *The Story of a Bad Boy*.

Johnnie Watson   Friend of William Baxter; one of Baxter's rivals for the affections of Miss Lola Pratt in Booth Tarkington's *Seventeen*.

Kenny Watson   Girlfriend of Scar; has difficulty finding employment after high school in Herbert Simmons's *Corner Boy*.

Kitty Watson   See Kitty Collins.

Miss Watson   Owner of the slave Jim, whom she frees in her will, in Samuel Langhorne Clemens's *Adventures of Huckleberry Finn*.

Phoeby Watson   Best friend of Janie Crawford in Eatonville, Florida, and person to whom Janie's life story is addressed in Zora Neale Hurston's *Their Eyes Were Watching God*.

Tom Watson   Lover of Nana; serenades her family in Aline Bernstein's *The Journey Down*.

Mr. Watterson   First officer aboard the *Aroostook* in William Dean Howells's *The Lady of the Aroostook*.

Mrs. Leora Watts   Prostitute who has the friendliest bed in town; Hazel Motes visits her on his arrival in Taulkinham to prove that sin is a meaningless concept in Flannery O'Connor's *Wise Blood*.

Ike Wayfish   Liquor-loving clown in Huguenine's circus in Walter D. Edmonds's *Chad Hanna*.

Mr. Waymarsh   American lawyer and friend of Lambert Strether, whom he accompanies to Paris; reports to Mrs. Newsome on Strether's failure to encourage Chad Newsome to return to America in Henry James's *The Ambassadors*.

Timothy (Varmounter) Weasel   Indian fighter in James Kirke Paulding's *The Dutchman's Fireside*.

Farmer Weatherbeat   Original owner of Dirty Eddie in Ludwig Bemelmans's *Dirty Eddie*.

Joseph Weatherby   Impoverished preacher who serves as minister to the wagon train in A. B. Guthrie's *The Way West*.

Twink Weatherby   Woman loved by Lem Forrester and Oliver Hutto; chooses Hutto over Forrester in Marjorie Kinnan Rawlings's *The Yearling*.

Harlan Weaver   Judge who presides over Frederic Manion's trial in Robert Traver's *Anatomy of a Murder*.

Robert Weaver   Childhood and college friend of Eugene Gant; his impulsiveness and love of alcohol lead Gant to suspect that rumors of insanity in the Weaver family might not be unfounded in Thomas Wolfe's *Of Time and the River*.

Samson Weaver   Owner of the Sarsey Sal, which Daniel Harrow owns upon Weaver's death, in Walter D. Edmonds's *Rome Haul*.

George Josiah (Monk, Monkus, Paul) Webber   Young writer who becomes a successful novelist in Thomas Wolfe's *You Can't Go Home Again* and *The Web and the Rock*; also appears in *The Hills Beyond*.

John Webber   Father of George Webber; causes a scandal in Libya Hills by abandoning his family to live openly with another man's wife in Thomas Wolfe's *The Hills Beyond* and *The Web and the Rock*.

Aaron Webster   Thoughtful and learned astronomer and pacifist; uncle and guardian of Holly Webster in Mark Harris's *The Southpaw*.

Holly Webster   See Holly Webster Wiggen.

Robert (Bob, Roberto Ortega Menéndez y Castillo) Webster   Mexican-American protagonist who comes to the town of Hidalgo to work as quarry manager; discovers his kinship with the ruling house of Castillo and fully accepts his Mexican heritage in Josefina Niggli's *Mexican Village*.

Thayer (Web) Webster   Aged Massachusetts Superior Court judge who, in his intense hatred of anarchists, conspires with the prosecuting attorney to make Sacco and Vanzetti look like antisocial, murderous villains, despite evidence of their innocence, in Upton Sinclair's *Boston*.

Rollie Weems   Idealistic worker and union man; led by faith in his union's strike to an early death in Jack Conroy's *The Disinherited*.

Isaac Weeps-by-Night   Indian who teaches the Sioux language to Aaron Gadd in Sinclair Lewis's *The God-Seeker*.

Nell Weil   Woman who identifies Joe Massara as a member of the gang that killed Jim Courtney in William Riley Burnett's *Little Caesar*.

Lieutenant Weincheck   Friend who shares Alison Langdon's appreciation of classical music; takes her and Anacleto to concerts in Carson McCullers's *Reflections in a Golden Eye*.

Thomas Welbeck   Forger and confidence man who attempts to use Arthur Mervyn in several schemes in Charles Brockden Brown's *Arthur Mervyn*.

John Welch   Orphaned cousin of Eva Birdsong; grows up to be a critical realist and to study medicine in Ellen Glasgow's *The Sheltered Life*.

Martin Welding   Mentally disturbed victim of social upheaval who seduces, impregnates, and abandons Milly Burden; marries Mary Victoria Littlepage in Ellen Glasgow's *They Stooped to Folly*.

Mary Victoria Littlepage Welding   Daughter of Victoria and Virginius Littlepage; nurse in the Balkans during World War I; virtuous idealist who, intrying to reunite Martin Welding and Milly Burden, eventually marries Welding in order to save him in Ellen Glasgow's *They Stooped to Folly*.

Arthur (Brother) Weldon   Meek, straw-hatted minister who travels the Nebraska countryside recruiting students for Temple College in Lincoln, where he teaches, in Willa Cather's *One of Ours*.

Augusta Welland   Daughter of Catherine Mingott, aunt of Ellen Olenska, and mother of May Welland in Edith Wharton's *The Age of Innocence*.

May Welland   Fiancée and then wife of Newland Archer; her conventionality contrasts with the independence of her cousin, Ellen Olenska, her rival for Archer's affections in Edith Wharton's *The Age of Innocence*.

Mr. Welland   Hypochondriacal father of May Welland and husband of Augusta Welland in Edith Wharton's *The Age of Innocence*.

Colmar (Cobby) Welles   Son of Susan Colmar Welles; president of the Franklin National Bank and Trust Company who commits suicide at the Kanewa Coronation in Mari Sandoz's *Capital City*.

Susan Colmar Welles   Widowed mother of Colmar Welles; owner of the Franklin National Bank and Trust Company in Mari Sandoz's *Capital City*.

Joe Welling   Standard Oil agent in Winesburg; courts Sarah King and befriends Tom and Edward King in Sherwood Anderson's *Winesburg, Ohio*.

Mercy Wellington   Beautiful socialite who marries Compton Keith in Janet Flanner's *The Cubical City*.

Colonel Wellmere   Cowardly British officer who courts Sarah Wharton and is about to marry her when Harvey Birch reveals that Wellmere is already married in James Fenimore Cooper's *The Spy*.

Plotinus Plinlimmon Welsh   See Plotinus Plinlimmon.

Gabriel Weltstein   Ugandan sheep rancher, friend of Maximilian Petion, and husband of Estella Washington; exposes the Oligarchy's plot to destroy the Brotherhood of Destruction; founds a utopian community in Uganda after civilization falls; as a letter writer, he is the narrator of Ignatius Donnelly's *Caesar's Column*.

Heinrich Weltstein   Recipient of the letters of his brother Gabriel in Ignatius Donnelly's *Caesar's Column*.

Victor Wenk   Hack writer who tries to simplify Lee Youngdahl's play sufficiently for it to appear on Broadway in Mark Harris's *Wake Up, Stupid*.

Wenonga   Shawnee chief responsible for the massacre of Nathan Slaughter's family; killed by Slaughter in Robert Montgomery Bird's *Nick of the Woods*.

Charlotte Wentworth   Steadfast daughter of William Wentworth; marries Mr. Brand in Henry James's *The Europeans*.

Clifford Wentworth   Son of William Wentworth; marries Lizzie Acton in Henry James's *The Europeans*.

Elizabeth Wentworth   See Elizabeth Wentworth Acton.

Gertrude Wentworth   High-spirited daughter of William Wentworth; marries Felix Young in Henry James's *The Europeans*.

Hugh Wentworth   White novelist who attends integrated social and charitable functions in Nella Larsen's *Quicksand* and *Passing*.

Katherine (Kate) Wentworth   Widow whose family, once plantation aristocrats, have lost their wealth and prominence; mother of Saint and Polly Wentworth, whom she desires to be recognized by elite Charleston society, in DuBose Heyward's *Mamba's Daughters*.

Polly Wentworth   Daughter of Kate Wentworth in DuBose Heyward's *Mamba's Daughters*.

Reuben Wentworth   Town physician and leading citizen of Norwood who espouses a natural philosophy, teaches his daughter Rose to love nature, and practices a holistic form of medicine in Henry Ward Beecher's *Norwood*.

Rose Wentworth   Intelligent, loving, and sensitive daughter of Reuben Wentworth, who teaches her to love nature; becomes a nurse during the Civil War, rejects the advances of Frank Esel and Thomas Heywood, and marries Barton Cathcart in Henry Ward Beecher's *Norwood*.

St. Julien de Chatigny (Saint) Wentworth   Artistic and materialistic son of Kate Wentworth; manager of the commissary at the Phosphate Mining Company in DuBose Heyward's *Mamba's Daughters*.

Valerie Land Wentworth   See Valerie Land.

William Wentworth   Reserved American uncle of Eugenia Münster and Felix Young; acts as their host in Henry James's *The Europeans*.

Wes   Doctor of Richard Cantwell in Ernest Hemingway's *Across the River and into the Trees*.

Wesley   Black man who helps Harry Morgan run a shipment of liquor to the Florida Keys in Ernest Hemingway's *To Have and Have Not*.

Emily (Aunt Wess) Wessels   Good-natured, simple aunt of Laura and Page Dearborn in Frank Norris's *The Pit*.

Arthur Francis (Artie) West   Student who threatens to knife Richard Dadier in Evan Hunter's *The Blackboard Jungle*.

Aurelia R. West   American from Rochester, New York, who travels through Europe with the Chatelaine in Henry Blake Fuller's *The Chatelaine of La Trinité*.

David West   Yacht steward in William Faulkner's *Mosquitoes*.

John Henry West   Bespectacled six-year-old cousin and playmate of Frankie Addams; dies of meningitis in Carson McCullers's *The Member of the Wedding*.

Josiah West   Internationally known painter in Brand Whitlock's *J. Hardin & Son*.

Julian West   Nineteenth-century Bostonian who, when he is hypnotized and awakens in the year 2000, learns how society has progressed; loves Edith Leete in Edward Bellamy's *Looking Backward*.

Tessie West   Friend of Ellen Chesser; Ellen runs away to find Tessie in Elizabeth Madox Roberts's *The Time of Man*.

Harold (Schultzy) Westbrook   Director of the *Cotton Blossom* company and husband of Elly Chipley in Edna Ferber's *Show Boat*.

Sybrandt Westbrook   Wilderness adventurer, fighter in the French and Indian War, and hero in James Kirke Paulding's *The Dutchman's Fireside*.

Mary Westerman   Gossip who describes Mabel Blake as an unfit mother in Richard Wright's *Savage Holiday*.

Jasper Western   American inland sailor who leads a relief expedition to the Thousand Islands; loves and marries Mabel Dunham in James Fenimore Cooper's *The Pathfinder*.

Professor Westervelt   Mesmerist who uses Priscilla as the Veiled Lady in Nathaniel Hawthorne's *The Blithedale Romance*.

John Westlock   Father of Ned Westlock; religious fanatic who deserts his wife and their son in E. W. Howe's *The Story of a Country Town*.

Ned Westlock   Son of John Westlock and husband of Agnes Deming; narrator of E. W. Howe's *The Story of a Country Town*.

Sophia Westwyn (Courdand)   Friend of Constantia Dudley; narrates the story of Constantia's battle with Ormond in Charles Brockden Brown's *Ormond*.

Caleb Wetherbee   Religious fanatic and cousin of Peter Alden; builds a Benedictine monastery in George Santayana's *The Last Puritan*.

Cynthia (Cynthy) Wetherell   Daughter of Cynthia Ware and William Wetherell; beloved ward of Jethro Bass following the death of her parents; marries Robert Worthington in Winston Churchill's *Coniston*.

Cynthia Ware (Cynthy) Wetherell   Beloved of Jethro Bass; marries William Wetherell; mother of Cynthia Wetherell in Winston Churchill's *Coniston*.

William (Will) Wetherell   Kind and loving, but ineffectual and sickly, husband of Cynthia Ware Wetherell; father of Cynthia Wetherell in Winston Churchill's *Coniston*.

Weucha   Treacherous Sioux warrior, a subordinate of Mahtoree; menaces Natty Bumppo and Bumppo's companions in James Fenimore Cooper's *The Prairie*.

Lottie Weyerhauser   Sister of Roberta Weyerhauser; convinces Roberta to marry George Brush and later convinces George to let Roberta divorce him in Thornton Wilder's *Heaven's My Destination*.

Roberta Weyerhauser   Young farm woman George Brush meets in Kansas; after they have sex, he searches for her, because, according to his beliefs, they are married; after finding her, he learns that she has been pregnant and apparently had an abortion; they marry and divorce in Thornton Wilder's *Heaven's My Destination*.

Weymouth   Friend of Waldegrave; his inquiry about money he gave to Waldegrave which Edgar Huntly planned to keep leads to Huntly's further derangement in Charles Brockden Brown's *Edgar Huntly*.

Rev. Quintus Whaley   Old-time black preacher who ministers to black workers at the Phosphate Mining Company in DuBose Heyward's *Mamba's Daughters*.

Walter (Whammer) Whambold   Famous home-run hitter who makes a bet with Sam Simpson over Roy Hobbs's pitching in Bernard Malamud's *The Natural*.

Eliza Wharton   Strong-willed society woman who dies because of her relationship with Peter Sanford in Hannah Webster Foster's *The Coquette*.

Frances Wharton   Younger daughter of Mr. Wharton; patriot sympathizer who marries Peyton Dunwoodie in James Fenimore Cooper's *The Spy*.

Henry Wharton   Son of Mr. Wharton; British army captain captured by the Virginia dragoons and condemned to death for espionage; escapes with the help of Harvey Birch in James Fenimore Cooper's *The Spy*.

M. Wharton   Affectionate and supportive mother of Eliza Wharton in Hannah Webster Foster's *The Coquette*.

Mr. Wharton   English father of Frances, Henry, and Sarah Wharton; secretly sympathizes with the royalists and lives on neutral ground hoping to escape the hostility of both sides in James Fenimore Cooper's *The Spy*.

Sarah Wharton   Elder daughter of Mr. Wharton flattered by the attention of British officers; suffers a breakdown when the existing marriage of her bridegroom, Colonel Wellmere, is revealed in James Fenimore Cooper's *The Spy*.

Gladys Wheatley   Detroit socialite, daughter of a wealthy banker, whom Charley Anderson marries and later abandons, prompting a financially crippling divorce in John Dos Passos's *U.S.A.* trilogy.

Bayliss Wheeler   Eldest son of the Wheeler family who runs a farm-implement business and is a prohibitionist and pacifist in Willa Cather's *One of Ours*.

Chancey Wheeler   Youngest child of Sayward and Portius Wheeler; after being favored by his mother, he becomes a rebel, rejecting the pioneering values of struggle and hard work; edits a newspaper in Cincinnati, which his mother ultimately underwrites so he can continue his writing, in Conrad Richter's *The Town*.

Claude Wheeler   Restless Nebraskan seeking the meaning of life as a private college student, farmer, and lieutenant in World War I in Willa Cather's *One of Ours*.

Evangeline Wheeler　Vermonter who goes to Nebraska to be a high school principal; she and her husband, Nat Wheeler, are the parents of Claude, Ralph, and Bayliss Wheeler in Willa Cather's *One of Ours.*

Guerdon Wheeler　Son of Sayward and Portius Wheeler; restless and hardworking man who marries a loose woman, kills one of her lovers, flees westward, and is never heard from again; appears in Conrad Richter's *The Fields* and *The Town.*

Colonel Isaiah Wheeler　Honest but combative Revolutionary War officer; Kike Lumsden turns to Wheeler for support against Enoch Lumsden in Edward Eggleston's *The Circuit Rider.*

Jason Wheeler　Former poet and former Communist, alcoholic pulp writer, friend of Leon Fisher, and resident of Twenty-Door City in Albert Halper's *Union Square.*

Nat Wheeler　Wealthy Nebraska farmland owner who is neighborly, charitable, and likeable; he and his wife, Evangeline Wheeler, are the parents of Claude, Ralph, and Bayliss Wheeler in Willa Cather's *One of Ours.*

Portius Wheeler　Lawyer who flees his family in Massachusetts and lives a reclusive life in the Ohio territory until he marries Sayward Luckett in Conrad Richter's *The Trees;* resumes the practice of law and fathers an illegitimate child in *The Fields;* prospers in the activities of the community, builds a huge town mansion, becomes a judge, and dies in *The Town.*

Ralph Wheeler　Younger brother of Claude Wheeler; chief mechanic of the Wheelers' Nebraska farm and a Colorado rancher in Willa Cather's *One of Ours.*

Resolve Wheeler　First child of Sayward and Portius Wheeler; studies at the local academy and reads law with his father in Conrad Richter's *The Fields;* becomes a lawyer and eventually is elected governor of Ohio in *The Town.*

Jenny Wheelwright　See Jenny Wheelwright Milbury.

Nathan (Shagpoke) Whipple　Former president of the United States and founder of the National Revolutionary party; convinces Lemuel Pitkin to seek his fortune in New York in Nathanael West's *A Cool Million.*

Silas Whipple　Pro-Union lawyer and judge; friend of Stephen Brice in Winston Churchill's *The Crisis.*

Laura Whitacre　Troubled wife of Michael Whitacre; moves with the fast set in Hollywood and New York and is finally divorced in Irwin Shaw's *The Young Lions.*

Michael Whitacre　Indecisive liberal and disillusioned stage director smothered by a sour marriage and stifled by the immoral life in Hollywood and New York; joins the army at the beginning of World War II and champions the ideals of patriotism and democracy in Irwin Shaw's *The Young Lions.*

Pepper Whitcomb　Boyhood friend of Tom Bailey, who accidentally shoots Pepper in the mouth with an arrow; captured in the snowball fight; becomes a judge in Thomas Bailey Aldrich's *The Story of a Bad Boy.*

Abiram White　Brother of Esther Bush, brother-in-law of Ishmael Bush, principal kidnapper of Inez de Certavallos, and murderer of Asa Bush, his nephew, in James Fenimore Cooper's *The Prairie.*

Florence J. (Florrie) White　Business associate and rival of Eugene Witla; strives to have Witla fired in Theodore Dreiser's *The "Genius."*

Helen White　Daughter of Winesburg's most prosperous citizen; has an occasional affair with George Willard in Sherwood Anderson's *Winesburg, Ohio.*

Wylie White　Screenwriter who hopes to marry Cecilia Brady in F. Scott Fitzgerald's *The Last Tycoon.*

White Fang　Part wolf, part dog; his vicious wolf nature is brought out by Lip-lip and Beauty Smith; his loyal dog nature, by Weeden Scott, in Jack London's *White Fang.*

White-Jacket　Narrator who, after many attempts, is finally able to rid himself of his jacket in Herman Melville's *White-Jacket.*

Sister Whiteside　Friend and neighbor of Aunt Hager Williams; gossips about sinners in the neighborhood and peddles vegetables in Langston Hughes's *Not Without Laughter.*

John Whitewood, Jr.　Wealthy son of a famous college professor; becomes Edward Colburne's rival for Lillie Ravenel Carter's affections after the death of John Carter in John William DeForest's *Miss Ravenel's Conversion from Secession to Loyalty.*

Ben Whitey　Friend who joins the Home Guard with Joshua Birdwell when the Rebels threaten Vernon, Indiana, in Jessamyn West's *The Friendly Persuasion.*

Whitfield　Minister in William Faulkner's *The Hamlet;* father of Addie Bundren's son Jewel Bundren in *As I Lay Dying.*

Psyche Whitmore　Lover of Japhy Ryder who has to be thrown off the boat on which Ryder sails for Japan in Jack Kerouac's *The Dharma Bums.*

Florence (Flo) Whittaker　Tactless and disorganized but ingenuous wife of Jerrold Whittaker in Randall Jarrell's *Pictures from an Institution.*

Jerrold Whittaker　Teacher of sociology, professed liberal, and pretender to a familiarity with French literature in Randall Jarrell's *Pictures from an Institution.*

Big Foot Whitten　Mountain man who is Don Joaquin MacGillivray's assistant in H. L. Davis's *Harp of a Thousand Strings.*

Arthur Wiatte Unsavory brother of Euphemia Lorimer; drives away Sarsefield; murdered by Clithero Edny; his death motivates the attempted murder of his sister in Charles Brockden Brown's *Edgar Huntly*.

Clarice Wiatte See Clarice.

Terry Wickett Chemist at the McGurk Institute of Biology and friend of Martin Arrowsmith in Sinclair Lewis's *Arrowsmith*.

Angela Wida Daughter of Angela Blue and Eugene Witla; her birth awakens her father's aesthetic sense in Theodore Dreiser's *The Genius*.

Eugene Tennyson (Genie, Henry Kingsland) Wida Failed artist and businessman who becomes successful following the birth of his daughter Angela; lover of many women in Theodore Dreiser's *The Genius*.

Harry Widener Playboy and junior partner with Glymmer, Read in Nathan Asch's *The Office*.

Catharine Pleyel Wieland Sister of Henry Pleyel and wife of Theodore Wieland; murdered by her husband in Charles Brockden Brown's *Wieland*.

Clara Wieland Sister of Theodore Wieland; forces Carwin to confess his culpability in the murders committed by her brother; narrator of Charles Brockden Brown's *Wieland*.

Theodore Wieland Brother of Clara Wieland and husband of Catharine Pleyel Wieland; led to kill his wife and their children by Carwin's biloquism in Charles Brockden Brown's *Wieland*.

Henry Whittier (Author, Hank) Wiggen Brash left-handed pitcher for the New York Mammoths; hero and not entirely literate narrator of Mark Harris's *The Southpaw, Bang the Drum Slowly, A Ticket for a Seamstitch*, and *It Looked Like For Ever*.

Holly Webster Wiggen Girlfriend, then wife of Henry Wiggen in Mark Harris's *The Southpaw, Bang the Drum Slowly, A Ticket for a Seamstitch*, and *It Looked Like For Ever*.

Harry Wilbourne Medical intern imprisoned for killing his lover, Charlotte Rittenmeyer, during an attempted abortion in William Faulkner's *The Wild Palms*.

Ross Wilbur Effeminate society man who is shanghaied in San Francisco and who "becomes a man" under the influence of his lover, Moran Sternersen, in Frank Norris's *Moran of the Lady Letty*.

Jack Wilcox American smuggler who lures Nelson Dyar to Tangier in Paul Bowles's *Let It Come Down*.

Jere Wilder-Halliday Unstable, aging flapper; Manley Halliday's ex-wife and the object of his obsessions in Budd Schulberg's *The Disenchanted*.

Arty Wildgans Head of the Wildgans Chase Agency in Ludwig Bemelmans's *Dirty Eddie*.

Margaret Thatcher Fitzhue (Mag) Wildwood Tall, elegant fashion model; competes with Holly Golightly for eligible rich men in Truman Capote's *Breakfast at Tiffany's*.

Tommy (Wilhelm Adler, Velvel, Wilky) Wilhelm Overweight, slovenly son of Dr. Adler, estranged husband, displaced father of two sons, unemployed former executive for the Rojax Corporation, and desperate struggler for a true identity and a better life; antihero badly advised and abandoned by quack psychologist Dr. Tamkin in Saul Bellow's *The Victim*.

Jonathan Wilk Defense attorney for Artie Straus and Judd Steiner; argues that his clients are products of their environment and are not deviant criminals in Meyer Levin's *Compulsion*.

Jonas Wilkerson Overseer at Tara; during Reconstruction, a carpetbagger who raises the taxes on Tara in order to claim it as his own plantation; father of Emmie Slattery's illegitimate children in Margaret Mitchell's *Gone with the Wind*.

Ashley Wilkes Husband of Melanie Hamilton; pursued relentlessly as a love interest by Scarlett O'Hara in Margaret Mitchell's *Gone with the Wind*.

India Wilkes Unmarried sister of Ashley Wilkes; accuses her brother and Scarlett O'Hara of being lovers, after witnessing them in a tender embrace, in Margaret Mitchell's *Gone with the Wind*.

Melanie Hamilton (Miss Melly) Wilkes Sister of Charles Hamilton, wife of Ashley Wilkes, and sister-in-law of Scarlett O'Hara; a devoted friend and defender of Scarlett in Margaret Mitchell's *Gone with the Wind*.

Joanna, Mary Jane, and Susan Wilks Sisters and heirs of their father's wealth; saved by Huckleberry Finn from the Duke of Bridgewater and the Dauphin's scheme to steal their inheritance in Samuel Langhorne Clemens's *Adventures of Huckleberry Finn*.

Elizabeth Willard Mother of George Willard and owner of the New Willard House hotel; has a brief platonic affair with Doctor Reefy shortly before her death in Sherwood Anderson's *Winesburg, Ohio*.

George Willard Aspiring writer and reporter for the *Winesburg Eagle*; his curiosity about human nature leads the townspeople to reveal their grotesqueries to him in Sherwood Anderson's *Winesburg, Ohio*.

Tom Willard Father of George Willard and marginally successful proprietor of the New Willard House hotel in Sherwood Anderson's *Winesburg, Ohio*.

Willatale Queen of the Arnewi tribe; bisexual and transcendental wise woman who sees in Eugene Henderson the spirit of vital life in Saul Bellow's *Henderson the Rain King*.

Eddie Willers   Personal secretary to Dagny Taggart in Ayn Rand's *Atlas Shrugged*.

Willett   Logging camp owner in William Dean Howells's *A Modern Instance*.

William   Watchman of the Bear Flag Restaurant; commits suicide with an ice pick following his rejection by the residents of the Palace Flophouse and Grill in John Steinbeck's *Cannery Row*.

Williams   Witty maintopman aboard the *Neversink* in Herman Melville's *White-Jacket*.

Williams   Patriot colonel who helps free Arthur Butler from captivity in John Pendleton Kennedy's *Horse-Shoe Robinson*.

Annabel Holznagel Williams   Wife of Ralph Williams and mother of Berry-berry and Clinton Williams in James Leo Herlihy's *All Fall Down*.

Annjelica Williams   See Mrs. Annjee Rodgers.

Berry-berry Williams   Wayward son of Ralph and Annabel Williams, older brother of Clinton Williams, and lover of Echo O'Brien; his treatment of Echo almost causes Clinton to murder him in James Leo Herlihy's *All Fall Down*.

Clinton (Clint, Willy) Williams   Teenaged son of Ralph and Annabel Williams and younger brother of Berry-berry Williams; travels to Florida in search of Berry-berry and falls in love with his brother's girlfriend, Echo O'Brien, in James Leo Herlihy's *All Fall Down*.

Del Williams   Cowboy who falls in love with Taisie Lockhart; murdered by Cal Dalhart, his rival, in Emerson Hough's *North of 36*.

Father Williams   Priest to Susie Dahoney Holm; tries to befriend her husband Peder Holm in O. E. Rölvaag's *Their Father's God*.

Aunt Hager Williams   Overbearing yet jovial Christian grandmother of Sandy Rodgers; washes clothes and tends to the sick for a living in Langston Hughes's *Not Without Laughter*.

Harriett (Harrietta) Williams   Prodigal daughter of Aunt Hager Williams; resents her mother's piety and becomes both a prostitute and a blues singer in Langston Hughes's *Not Without Laughter*.

Janey Williams   Ambitious stenographer and confidential secretary of J. Ward Morehouse in John Dos Passos's *U.S.A.* trilogy.

Jeffrey (Jeff) Williams   Black bandleader in Dorothy Baker's *Young Man with a Horn*.

Jennie Williams   Woman bludgeoned by the New York police when she accidentally appears in a crowd protesting the Sacco-Vanzetti executions in Nathan Asch's *Pay Day*.

Joe Williams   Sailor brother of Janey Williams who goes AWOL from the U.S. Navy, is arrested as a spy in England, and marries unhappily, in John Dos Passos's *U.S.A.* trilogy.

John Williams   Blacksmith aboard the HMS *Bounty* who joins the rebellion in Charles Nordhoff and James Norman Hall's *Mutiny on the Bounty*; helps precipitate the violence between Tahitians and whites by seducing a Tahitian wife in *Pitcairn's Island*.

Private L. G. (Ellgee) Williams   Young soldier and stablekeeper so infatuated with Leonora Penderton he spies on her while she sleeps; followed and eventually killed by Captain Weldon Penderton in Carson McCullers's *Reflections in a Golden Eye*.

Marion Averley Williams   Abandoned, vengeful wife of Stuart Williams; divorces him after an eleven-year separation in Susan Glaspell's *Fidelity*.

Mrs. Williams   Mother of Jennie Williams; lives in the same building as the Cowans in Nathan Asch's *Pay Day*.

Ralph Williams   Husband of Annabel Williams and father of Berry-berry and Clinton Williams; works jigsaw puzzles in the basement in James Leo Herlihy's *All Fall Down*.

Robert (Bob) Williams   Older brother of Sam Williams; he alone, of all of Margaret Schofield's suitors, wins Penrod Schofield's approval, thus avoiding Penrod's antics; appears in Booth Tarkington's *Penrod*, *Penrod and Sam*, and *Penrod Jashber*.

Samuel (Sam) Williams   Best friend of Penrod Schofield; blithely follows Penrod into numerous adventures and troubles in Booth Tarkington's *Penrod*, *Penrod and Sam*, and *Penrod Jashber*.

Stuart Williams   Midwestern businessman who leaves his wife, Marion Averley Williams, and runs away with Ruth Holland in Susan Glaspell's *Fidelity*.

T. T. Williams   Restaurant owner and suitor of Berenice Sadie Brown in Carson McCullers's *The Member of the Wedding*.

Wash Williams   Winesburg telegraph operator; his misogyny results from his wife's indiscretions and his mother-in-law's subsequent perverse attempt to reconcile the couple in Sherwood Anderson's *Winesburg, Ohio*.

Willie (Little Willie)   Twenty-year-old farmhand and, for a brief time, lover of Ollie in George Wylie Henderson's *Ollie Miss*.

Will Willing   Friend and biographer of George Apley; outdoes Apley in devotion to social convention in John P. Marquand's *The Late George Apley*.

Second Lieutenant Stanley M. Willis   Black officer struck by Benny Carricker for nearly causing the crash of General Ira N. Beal's plane; awarded a medal for an earlier exploit in James Gould Cozzens's *Guard of Honor*.

Stan Williston   Affluent gentile whose persistent apologies for Kirby Allbee are a constant source of chagrin to Asa Leventhal in Saul Bellow's *The Victim*.

John C. Willoughby   Millionaire playboy in William Riley Burnett's *Little Caesar*.

Tom Wills   Friend of Bruce Dudley; newspaperman who shares with Dudley Wills his love of art and his desire to do more with his writing ability in Sherwood Anderson's *Dark Laughter*.

Donald Willsson   Newspaper publisher, son of Elihu Willsson, who initially engages the Continental Detective Agency to investigate corruption in Personville in Dashiell Hammett's *Red Harvest*.

Elihu Willsson   Wealthy, corrupt patriarch of Personville in Dashiell Hammett's *Red Harvest*.

Billy Wilmerdings   Incorrigible son of a butcher; goes to sea in Henry Wadsworth Longfellow's *Kavanagh*.

George Wilmington   Husband of Lyra Wilmington and owner of the stocking mill in which his wife previously worked in William Dean Howells's *Annie Kilburn*.

Jack Wilmington   Nephew of Lyra Wilmington in William Dean Howells's *Annie Kilburn*.

Lyra Goodman Wilmington   Friend of Annie Kilburn; her marriage to an older, prosperous man causes scandal in William Dean Howells's *Annie Kilburn*.

Lee Wilshire   Girlfriend of Bernie Despain in Dashiell Hammett's *The Glass Key*.

Wilson   British consul on Tahiti in Herman Melville's *Omoo*.

Wilson   Loud soldier who comforts the wounded Henry Fleming and later fights alongside him in Stephen Crane's *The Red Badge of Courage*.

Baby Wilson   Niece of Biff Brannon and daughter of Lucile and Leroy Wilson; survives a gunshot wound in Carson McCullers's *The Heart Is a Lonely Hunter*.

David (Pudd'nhead) Wilson   Eccentric and intelligent lawyer and surveyor whom the residents of Dawson's Landing consider a fool; his long-term hobby of fingerprinting helps him solve the murder of York Driscoll in Samuel Langhorne Clemens's *Pudd'nhead Wilson*.

Edward (Beau) Wilson   Londoner killed in a duel by John Law in Emerson Hough's *The Mississippi Bubble*.

George B. Wilson   Husband of Myrtle Wilson; murders Jay Gatsby in F. Scott Fitzgerald's *The Great Gatsby*.

Leroy Wilson   Father of Baby Wilson; twice marries and twice deserts Lucile Wilson in Carson McCullers's *The Heart Is a Lonely Hunter*.

Lucile Wilson   Cosmetologist ambitious to develop the talents of her four-year-old daughter, Baby Wilson; wife of Leroy Wilson and sister-in-law of Biff Brannon in Carson McCullers's *The Heart Is a Lonely Hunter*.

Myrtle Wilson   Mistress of Tom Buchanan; killed in a hit-and-run accident by Daisy Buchanan in F. Scott Fitzgerald's *The Great Gatsby*.

Woodrow Wilson   Hard-drinking southern soldier in Norman Mailer's *The Naked and the Dead*.

Benjamin (Ben) Wilton   Inadequately Charleston-educated brother of Cornelia Wilton in Caroline Gilman's *Recollections of a Southern Matron*.

Cornelia Wilton   Submissive wife of Arthur Marion; nurse of both white and black plantation children; narrator of Caroline Gilman's *Recollections of a Southern Matron*.

Henry Wilton   Dashing, witty, and generous father of Cornelia Wilton Marion in Caroline Gilman's *Recollections of a Southern Matron*.

Richard (Dick) Wilton   Brother of Cornelia Wilton; injured in a college duel in Caroline Gilman's *Recollections of a Southern Matron*.

Luke Wimble   Orchardist whose praise of Ellen Chesser Kent restores her spirits in Elizabeth Madox Roberts's *The Time of Man*.

Erastus Winch   Farm equipment salesman and trader in cheese; conspires with fellow church trustee Loren Pierce to cheat Levi Gorringe in Harold Frederic's *The Damnation of Theron Ware*.

Nettie Wincher   See Marquise de Trézac.

Mrs. Winchester   Wealthy, cultured, kindly old aunt of Dick Dale in Sarah Orne Jewett's *A Marsh Island*.

Dr. Elizaveta (Lise, Liza) Innokentievna Bogolepov Pnin Wind   Former wife of Timofey Pnin; works as a psychologist with her second husband, Dr. Eric Wind, by whom she has the child Victor; goes on to marry twice again in Vladimir Nabokov's *Pnin*.

Dr. Eric Wind   Psychotherapist for whom Liza Pnin leaves her husband and with whom she collaborates on psychology projects in Vladimir Nabokov's *Pnin*.

Victor Wind   Enormously talented child artist and son of Drs. Eric and Liza Wind; fantasizes about an imaginary father and seems genuinely fond of Timofey Pnin, whom he visits one Easter vacation, in Vladimir Nabokov's *Pnin*.

Berzelius Noel Weinacht (Buzz) Windrip Democratic candidate for president who, when elected, turns the United States into a fascist state in Sinclair Lewis's *It Can't Happen Here.*

Cudge Windsor Owner of a pool hall in Stanton, Kansas, where many local black men and boys hang out; Sandy Rodgers goes to the pool hall to escape his snobbish aunt, Mrs. Tempy Siles, in Langston Hughes's *Not Without Laughter.*

Esther Pollard Wingate Mother of Esther Wingate Sturgis; successful farmer and land developer in Shelby Foote's *Jordan County.*

Ezra Wingate Barn owner whose stagecoach Tom Bailey and others steal in Thomas Bailey Aldrich's *The Story of a Bad Boy.*

Hector Wingate Husband of Esther Pollard Wingate and father of Esther Wingate Sturgis in Shelby Foote's *Jordan County.*

Jed Wingate Son of Jesse and Molly Wingate and brother of Little Molly Wingate in Emerson Hough's *The Covered Wagon.*

Jesse Wingate Leader of the Oregon-bound wagon train in Emerson Hough's *The Covered Wagon.*

Molly Wingate Wife of Jesse Wingate and mother of Jed and Little Molly Wingate in Emerson Hough's *The Covered Wagon.*

Molly (Little Molly) Wingate Daughter of Jesse and Molly Wingate; heroine of Emerson Hough's *The Covered Wagon.*

Stephen Wingate Financial agent for the imprisoned Frank Cowperwood in Theodore Dreiser's *The Financier.*

Barbara Winkle Governess and housekeeper at Swallow Barn in John Pendleton Kennedy's *Swallow Barn.*

Arthur Winner Junior Prosperous and respected lawyer who regards the passions as subverting order and who believes that youth's a kind of infirmity in James Gould Cozzens's *By Love Possessed.*

Arthur Winner Senior Dead father of Arthur Winner Junior; in his intellectual detachment and avoidance of emotional excess, epitomizes the Man of Reason in James Gould Cozzens's *By Love Possessed.*

Clarissa Henderson Winner Sensible and devoted younger wife of Arthur Winner Junior in James Gould Cozzens's *By Love Possessed.*

Winnie Tall Times Square night person; drug addict and thief in John Clellon Holmes's *Go.*

Rachel Winslow Prominent parishioner of Henry Maxwell; gifted singer and friend of Virginia Page in Charles M. Sheldon's *In His Steps.*

Mark Winsome Mystic who warns Frank Goodman to beware of Charlie Noble in Herman Melville's *The Confidence-Man.*

Winstock Army corporal who uses his authority to take the pistol from Richard Mast, who later steals it back, in James Jones's *The Pistol.*

Frederick Forsyth Winterbourne American in Europe fascinated with Daisy Miller and jealous of her relationship with Giovanelli; unable to decide if Daisy is respectable in Henry James's *Daisy Miller.*

Ed Winters Half-breed saw crewman at the Past Bay Manufacturing Company factory who proposes a walk-out to force Carl Belcher out as foreman; assaults Belcher during the power outage in Robert Cantwell's *The Land of Plenty.*

Hal Winters Winesburg farmhand who asks Ray Pearson for advice in Sherwood Anderson's *Winesburg, Ohio.*

Ralph Winwood Painter who secretly paints a portrait of his cousin Pierre Glendinning II in Herman Melville's *Pierre.*

Eva Wiseman Sister of Julius Kauffman and guest at the yacht party in William Faulkner's *Mosquitoes.*

Mrs. William Wallace Witcher Vice-president of the Mothers' League for Good Morals in Horace McCoy's *They Shoot Horses, Don't They?*

Witcikti (the Bald Eagle) Catawba warrior who accompanies the Shawnee raiding party that attacks Beulah; kills Jeremiah and Hannah Catlett and is killed by Ezekiel Catlett in Mary Lee Settle's *O Beulah Land.*

Witherby Dishonest Boston newspaper publisher in William Dean Howells's *A Modern Instance.*

Angela Blue Witla Wife of Eugene Witla; dies giving birth to Angela Witla in Theodore Dreiser's *The "Genius."*

Anthony (Antek the Owner) Witwicki Alcoholic owner of the Tug & Maul Bar in Nelson Algren's *The Man with the Golden Arm.*

Mrs. Wix Dowdy, much-loved governess of Maisie Farange; ignores textbooks to focus instead on her charge's sense of responsibility and moral development in Henry James's *What Maisie Knew.*

Dr. Woestijne Superintendent of Health for whom Martin Arrowsmith works in Sinclair Lewis's *Arrowsmith.*

Hat and Luke Wolf Sharecropper neighbors of Jerry and Judith Blackford in Edith Summers Kelley's *Weeds.*

Julia (Nancy Kane) Wolf Clyde Wynant's consort and confidential secretary with a criminal past who is murdered in Dashiell Hammett's *The Thin Man.*

Hugh Molly Wolfe   Oppressed laborer and artist who takes his life to avoid imprisonment in Rebecca Harding Davis's *Life in the Iron Mills*.

Old Wolfe   Welsh emigrant and laborer; father of Hugh Wolfe in Rebecca Harding Davis's *Life in the Iron Mills*.

John Wolff   Tory storekeeper who is imprisoned in a Connecticut mine, escapes, and searches vainly for his wife in Walter D. Edmonds's *Drums along the Mohawk*.

Meyer Wolfsheim   Racketeer who fixed the 1919 World Series; Jay Gatsby's partner in F. Scott Fitzgerald's *The Great Gatsby*.

Mary Stark (Molly) Wood   Vermont aristocrat who goes to the West to teach; marries the Virginian in Owen Wister's *The Virginian*.

Woodburn   Virginia colonel who is writing a book about the merits of slavery in William Dean Howells's *A Hazard of New Fortunes*.

Miss Woodburn   Daughter of Colonel Woodburn; marries Fulkerson in William Dean Howells's *A Hazard of New Fortunes*.

John Woodcock   One of three Englishmen sympathetic to the American cause who send Israel Potter as courier to Benjamin Franklin in Paris; dies of apoplexy while keeping Potter in a hidden chamber in Herman Melville's *Israel Potter*.

Samuel Payson (Sam) Woodhull   Wagon-train leader who contests with Will Banion for the love of Molly Wingate in Emerson Hough's *The Covered Wagon*.

Colonel (Woody) Woodman   Disgruntled alcoholic commander at Sellers Field who, passed over for advancement, commits suicide in James Gould Cozzens's *Guard of Honor*.

Bill Woodruff   Cuckold who gets revenge on his wife by beating her in Henry Miller's *Black Spring*.

Thurston Printise (Piney) Woods   Immature and unpredictable young catcher for the New York Mammoths in Mark Harris's *Bang the Drum Slowly* and *A Ticket for a Seamstitch*.

Vergible (Tea Cake) Woods   Hedonistic young man who becomes Janie Crawford's third husband; takes her from Eatonville, Florida, to the Everglades, where she shoots and kills him after he has been bitten by a rabid dog during a hurricane, in Zora Neale Hurston's *Their Eyes Were Watching God*.

Kerney Woolbright   Ambitious candidate for the state senate who for political gain betrays his friend Duncan Harper in Elizabeth Spencer's *The Voice at the Back Door*.

Dr. Emerson Woolcape   Black dentist in Sinclair Lewis's *Kingsblood Royal*.

Eliot Woolf   New York lawyer and Jewish convert to Episcopalianism who questions Noah Tuttle's irregular financial accounts in James Gould Cozzens's *By Love Possessed*.

Harrison Woolf   See Harrison Hawke.

Wooloo   Polynesian servant of Captain Claret aboard the *Neversink* in Herman Melville's *White-Jacket*.

Arnold (Little Arnie) Worch   Jewish gang chief run out of Chicago by Rico Bandello in William Riley Burnett's *Little Caesar*.

Belle Worsham   Spinster in William Faulkner's *Go Down, Moses*.

Doctor Worsham   Minister in William Faulkner's *The Unvanquished*.

Hamp Worsham   Brother of Molly Beauchamp and Belle Worsham's servant in William Faulkner's *Go Down, Moses*.

General Daniel Worth   Confederate general and plantation owner who disapproves of the romance of his daughter Sallie Worth with Charles Gaston in Thomas Dixon's *The Leopard's Spots*.

Sallie Worth   Daughter of General Daniel Worth; marries Charles Gaston against her father's wishes in Thomas Dixon's *The Leopard's Spots*.

Cynthia Wetherell Worthington   See Cynthia Wetherell.

Isaac Dudley Worthington   Father of Robert Worthington; rapacious businessman and opponent of Jethro Bass in Winston Churchill's *Coniston*.

Robert (Bob) Worthington   Principled son of Isaac Worthington; husband of the younger Cynthia Wetherell in Winston Churchill's *Coniston*.

Jack Worthy   Friend and correspondent of Tommy Harrington in William Hill Brown's *The Power of Sympathy*.

Wounded Face   Uncle of Laughing Boy; opposes his nephew's association with Slim Girl in Oliver La Farge's *Laughing Boy*.

Clothilde Brill Wright   Twice-widowed mother of Harry and Bella Brill; cousin of Jim Calder; lives on small income with her unemployed adult children in the decaying ancestral home Wickford Point in John P. Marquand's *Wickford Point*.

Tom Wright   Rival of Augie; a "bad nigger" who contends with Joe Baily for the affection of Florence Dessau in Arna Wendell Bontemps's *God Sends Sunday*.

Wrinkles (Wrink)   Starving artist; shares an apartment with Billie Hawker in Stephen Crane's *The Third Violet*.

Walter (Wally) Wronken   Assistant stage manager at South Wind camp for adults; pursues Marjorie Morningstar; becomes a successful playwright in Herman Wouk's *Marjorie Morningstar*.

Professor A. Wunsch   Drunken German musician who gives the young Thea Kronborg piano lessons in Willa Cather's *The Song of the Lark*.

Vida Sherwin Wutherspoon   See Vida Sherwin.

Ellis Wyatt   Ingenious oil producer who invents the means of extracting petroleum from shale; destroys his operation and disappears in protest against dictatorial government directives in Ayn Rand's *Atlas Shrugged*.

Tracy Wyatt   Multimillionaire who marries Donna Cravat in Edna Ferber's *Cimarron*.

Sidney (Books, Brown Skin) Wyeth   Author who sells his book throughout the South; eventually marries Mildred Latham in Oscar Micheaux's *The Forged Note*.

Wymontoo-Hee (Luff)   Native of Hannamanoo who joins the crew of the *Julia* in Herman Melville's *Omoo*.

Gail Wynand   Tabloid publisher who builds an empire by serving mediocrity in Ayn Rand's *The Fountainhead*.

Clyde Wynant   Eccentric inventor who is the missing person and title character of Dashiell Hammett's *The Thin Man*.

Dorothy Wynant   Daughter of the eccentric inventor Clyde Wynant; she enlists the help of Nick Charles in locating her missing father in Dashiell Hammett's *The Thin Man*.

Gilbert Wynant   Bookish son of Clyde Wynant and brother of Dorothy Wynant in Dashiell Hammett's *The Thin Man*.

Ashby Porsum Wyndham   Cousin of Private Porsum and poor white who quits his job with the Massey Mountain Lumber Company and becomes a religious witness; writes the Statement of Ashby Wyndham while in jail in Robert Penn Warren's *At Heaven's Gate*.

Miss Caroline (Carrie) Wynn   Schoolteacher who becomes involved in politics in an attempt to save her job; marries Sam Stillings because he has more money and position than her other suitors in W. E. B. Du Bois's *The Quest of the Silver Fleece*.

May (Marie Minotti) Wynn   Singer and girlfriend of Willie Keith in Herman Wouk's *The Caine Mutiny*.

Father Xavier   Childhood guardian of Anthony Adverse; tells Adverse that John Bonnyfeather is Adverse's grandfather in Hervey Allen's *Anthony Adverse*.

Yakima Shorty   Thug housebreaker shot by Elihu Willsson in Dashiell Hammett's *Red Harvest*.

Samuel (Sad Sam) Yale   Aging star pitcher for the New York Mammoths replaced by Henry Wiggen in Mark Harris's *The Southpaw*.

Lew Yard   The criminal boss in charge of thievery and fencing in Personville in Dashiell Hammett's *Red Harvest*.

Joab Yarkoni   Moroccan Jew and military trainer of refugee children in Leon Uris's *Exodus*.

Adelaide Yates   Wife of Stephen Yates; her comments about the stranger people's burial ground lead some to think her a murderess in Mary Noailles Murfree's *In the "Stranger People's" Country*.

Albany (Lady Lillian) Yates   Manipulator of men and school rider for Huguenine's circus; deserts the circus, but returns after being rescued from Burke and Walsh's circus by Chad Hanna, in Walter D. Edmonds's *Chad Hanna*.

Edward Hamilton Yates   Scottish lawyer who befriends Salathiel Albine and later becomes his partner; appears in Hervey Allen's *The Forest and the Fort, Bedford Village,* and *Toward the Morning*.

Stephen (Steve) Yates   Husband of Adelaide Yates; joins some outlaws while seeking a doctor for Leonard Rhodes, although people think he has disappeared mysteriously, in Mary Noailles Murfree's *In the "Stranger People's" Country*.

Hrant Yazdabian   Owner of a dress manufacturing firm; becomes a partner of Harry Bogen, but Bogen steals from their firm, in Jerome Weidman's *What's in It for Me?*

José Ybarra-Jaegar   Brazilian government official with whom Holly Golightly falls in love; deserts her when she is linked to a drug scandal in Truman Capote's *Breakfast at Tiffany's*.

Yellow Hand   Comanche Indian chief who punishes Sim Rudabaugh in Emerson Hough's *North of 36*.

Yellow Jim (Yaller Jim)   Slave sold by George Posey to buy an expensive mare; returns and assaults Jane Posey; killed by George Posey in Allen Tate's *The Fathers*.

Yillah   White woman saved from death by Taji, captured by Queen Hautia, and pursued by Taji in Herman Melville's *Mardi*.

August (Gus) Yoder   German immigrant who farms land adjacent to the Wheelers for thirty years and is charged with disloyalty at the outbreak of World War I in Willa Cather's *One of Ours*.

Yoky   Deformed king of Hooloomooloo, the island of cripples, in Herman Melville's *Mardi*.

Yoomy (Warbler)   Minstrel from Odo and Taji's companion in Herman Melville's *Mardi*.

York   See James Stuart, Duke of York.

Kakosan Yoshida   Exotic young Japanese woman taken up by Boston society; mistress of both Harry Morgan and Nathan Kadish in Jean Stafford's *Boston Adventure*.

Youma Loyal servant of Madame Léonie Peyronnette and lover of Gabriel; burned to death in a fire during a black riot in the West Indies in Lafcadio Hearn's *Youma.*

Edward (Ned) Young Midshipman aboard the HMS *Bounty* who sleeps through the rebellion but later joins the mutineers in Charles Nordhoff and James Norman Hall's *Mutiny on the Bounty;* survives the violence between Tahitians and whites, but dies of asthmatic complications shortly after teaching Alexander Smith to read and write in *Pitcairn's Island.*

Felix Young Bohemian artist and brother of Eugenia Münster; marries Gertrude Wentworth in Henry James's *The Europeans.*

Gertrude Wentworth Young See Gertrude Wentworth.

Linda (Lindy) Young Maid to Agatha Cramp and Fred Merrit; falls in love with Joshua (Shine) Jones in Rudolph Fisher's *The Walls of Jericho.*

Pansetta Young Classmate and first girlfriend of Sandy Rodgers; invites Sandy and other boys to her house while her mother works in Langston Hughes's *Not Without Laughter.*

Rosalie Young Accident victim who stays with the Wapshots while recovering; her intimacy with Moses Wapshot, inadvertently witnessed by Honora Wapshot, leads to his being sent out into the world to make his way in John Cheever's *The Wapshot Chronicle.*

Beth Youngdahl Pregnant wife of Lee Youngdahl in Mark Harris's *Wake Up, Stupid.*

Dee Youngdahl Brother of Lee Youngdahl in Mark Harris's *Wake Up, Stupid.*

Lee W. Youngdahl College teacher, playwright, former professional boxer, and dissatisfied protagonist of Mark Harris's *Wake Up, Stupid.*

I. Y. Yunioshi Neighbor of Holly Golightly in New York; photographer who discovers the carved wooden head of Holly in Africa years after she has fled New York in Truman Capote's *Breakfast at Tiffany's.*

Zar Russian immigrant who arrives with four prostitutes in Hard Times, where he builds a saloon; killed by one of Leo Jenks's wild shots in E. L. Doctorow's *Welcome to Hard Times.*

Countess Marie Ogden (Grifin, Countess Josef, Mary) Zattiany Fifty-eight-year-old woman faced with the choice between power and influence as the wife of an Austrian diplomat and rejuvenation as the wife of Lee Clavering in Gertrude Atherton's *Black Oxen.*

Pete Zavras Cameraman helped by Monroe Stahr in F. Scott Fitzgerald's *The Last Tycoon.*

Bolek Zbarski Son of Elzbieta Zbarski and brother of Magda Zbarski; loathes Yasha Mazur for bringing ignominy on Magda in Isaac Bashevis Singer's *The Magician of Lublin.*

Elzbieta Zbarski Widowed mother of Magda and Bolek Zbarski; obese, loquacious, and sorrowful, she depends on Yasha Mazur for income and sympathy in Isaac Bashevis Singer's *The Magician of Lublin.*

Magda Zbarski Mistress of Yasha Mazur, daughter of Elzbieta Zbarski, and sister of Bolek Zbarski; travels with Yasha and performs as an acrobat in his magic show; commits suicide when she believes Yasha will abandon her for another woman in Isaac Bashevis Singer's *The Magician of Lublin.*

Dr. Bruno Zechlin Professor at Mizpah Seminary whose career Elmer Gantry ruins in Sinclair Lewis's *Elmer Gantry.*

Zeftel Deserted wife of a prison escapee; peasant lover of Yasha, whom she follows to Warsaw; leaves Warsaw with Herman to become madam of their brothel in Isaac Bashevis Singer's *The Magician of Lublin.*

Baron Zeitgeist Amateur musician and scientist who admires the Chatelaine, whom he guides through the Tyrol, in Henry Blake Fuller's *The Chatelaine of La Trinité.*

Zeke (Keekee) American planter on Martair in Herman Melville's *Omoo.*

Marsha Zelenko Friend of Marjorie Morningstar at Hunter College; encourages Marjorie to act in Herman Wouk's *Marjorie Morningstar.*

Madam Zelma Clairvoyant who in attempting to help recover a lost fur cap predicts stormy times and then triumph ahead for the narrator of Aline Bernstein's *The Journey Down.*

Zenobia Daughter of Moodie and half sister of Priscilla; writer who lives at Blithedale and who apparently commits suicide by drowning in Nathaniel Hawthorne's *The Blithedale Romance.*

Zerkow Junk man whose mania for gold eventually leads to the murder of his wife, Maria Macapa, in Frank Norris's *McTeague.*

Zeusentell Participant in a drinking party; persuaded to recite "Patrick Clancy's Pig" in Stephen Crane's *George's Mother.*

Sabbatai Zevi Supposed Messiah who, with his followers, divides seventeenth-century Jewish communities in Europe; eventually forsakes his messianic claim and converts to Islam; appears in Isaac Bashevis Singer's *Satan in Goray, The Slave,* and *Shosha.*

Byron Zigler Son of Homer and Pearl Zigler in Clyde Brion Davis's *The Great American Novel.*

Homer Zigler   Journalist who, through successive newspaper jobs in Buffalo, Cleveland, Kansas City, San Francisco, and Denver, continues to cherish the ambition of writing a supreme work of fiction; diarist/narrator of Clyde Brion Davis's *The Great American Novel.*

Pearl Hawkins Zigler   Wife of Homer Zigler; oblivious to her husband's most fundamental feelings and ambitions in Clyde Brion Davis's *The Great American Novel.*

Heinz Zimmerman   Navigator in the 918th Bomb Group; commits suicide after having made an error in navigation in Beirne Lay, Jr., and Sy Bartlett's *Twelve O'Clock High!*

Zing   Foxhound owned by Nunn Ballew and considered the best hunting dog in the county; dies in pursuit of the elusive King Devil in Harriette Arnow's *Hunter's Horn.*

Zipporah   Midianite, eldest daughter of Jethro, and wife of Moses in Zora Neale Hurston's *Moses, Man of the Mountain.*

Zizendorf (Editor)   Insane neo-Nazi who plans to assassinate the American military overseer in Germany; narrator in John Hawkes's *The Cannibal.*

Zora   Invalid wife of Rango in Anaïs Nin's *The Four Chambered Heart.*

Zora   Wild, elflike girl who grows into a serious, productive young woman and challenges the entire sharecropping system when she fights to help her people in W. E. B. Du Bois's *The Quest of the Silver Fleece.*

Zsettlani   See Piotr.

Zuckor   Father-in-law of Goodman; daily opens the office of Glymmer, Read and greets the other employees in Nathan Asch's *The Office.*

Constantine (Connie, Ski) Zvonski   Marine radio operator killed at Guadalcanal in Leon Uris's *Battle Cry.*

Madame Zyszynski   Spiritual medium consulted by the Budds in Upton Sinclair's *Dragon's Teeth.*

VOLUME I
TITLE INDEX

VOLUME I
AUTHOR INDEX

LOUIS ADAMIC

Cradle of Life (1936)
Herr Ottokar Bukuwky
Yuro Dug
Dora (Doramamo) Dugova
Zorka Dugova
Don Franyo
Count Rudolf von Hapsburg
Prince Arbogast (Arbo) von Hohengraetz
Yozht Kozak
Matilda Nagy
Fran Natalie Schuschnigg
Rudolf Stanislaus (Rudek, Rudo) Stanka
Count Yaromir (Friend) von Studenitz
Countess Zdenka von Studenitz
Vladek

Grandsons (1935)
Beverly (Bev) Boyd
Andrew (Andy, George Andrews, Miles-Away Andrews) Gale, Jr.
Andrew (Andy) Gale, Sr.
Anthony Adams (Tony) Gale
Jack Gale
Mildred Adams Gale
Peter (Jack McLeish) Gale
Tony Gale
Anton Galé
Jesus Jiminez
L.
Roger Smith
Margaret Gale (Maggie) Stedman

HENRY ADAMS

Democracy (1892)
Mrs. Samuel Baker
John Carrington
Schuyler Clinton
Victoria Dare
Lord Dunbeg
Baron Jacobi
Madeleine Ross (Mrs. Lightfoot Lee) Lee
Senator Silas P. Ratcliffe
Sybil Ross

JAMES AGEE

A Death in the Family (1957)
Catherine Follet
Jay Follet
Mary Follet
Ralph Follet
Rufus Follet
Father Jackson
Andrew Lynch
Catherine Lynch
Hannah Lynch
Joel Lynch
Walter Starr

CONRAD AIKEN

Blue Voyage (1927)
Cynthia Battiloro
Seward Trewlove Clark
Daisy Dacey
Peggy Davis

William Demarest
Pauline Faubion
Clarence Hay-Lawrence
Major Kendall
Solomon Moses David Menelik Silber-
   stein
Smith

Great Circle (1933)
Andrew (Andy) Cather
Bertha (Berty) Cather
David Cather
Doris Cather
John Cather
Thomas (Tom) Lowell Crapo

King Coffin (1935)
Jasper Ammen
Gerta
Karl N. Jones
Sandbach
Julius Shaw Toppan

LOUISA MAY ALCOTT

Little Men (1871)
Thomas Buckminster (Tommy) Bangs
Ned Barker
Friedrich (Fritz) Bhaer
Robin (Rob, Robby) Bhaer
Nathaniel (Nat) Blake
Daisy (Posy, Mrs. Shakespeare Smith) Brooke
John Brooke
John (Demi, Demijohn) Brooke
Dick Brown

George (Stuffy) Cole
Dan
Emil
Jack Ford
Franz
Annie Harding
Bess Laurence
Theodore (Laurie, Teddy) Laurence
Amy Curtis (Mrs. Theodore Laurence)
  March
Jo (Mrs. Friedrich Bhaer) March
Margaret (Meg, Mrs. John Brooke)
  March
Adolphus (Dolly) Pettingill
Silas
Billy Ward

Little Women (1868)
Friedrich (Fritz) Bhaer
Daisy (Posy, Mrs. Shakespeare Smith)
  Brooke
John Brooke
John (Demi, Demijohn) Brooke
James Laurence
Theodore (Laurie, Teddy) Laurence
March
Amy Curtis (Mrs. Theodore Laurence)
  March
Aunt March
Elizabeth (Beth) March
Jo (Mrs. Friedrich Bhaer) March
Margaret (Meg, Mrs. John Brooke)
  March
Mrs. (Marmee) March
Hannah Mullett

THOMAS BAILEY ALDRICH

The Story of a Bad Boy (1923)
Phil Adams
Mat Ames
Thomas (Tom) Bailey
Harry Blake
Aunt Chloe
Kitty (Mrs. Benjamin Watson, Mrs.
  Catherine) Collins
Bill Conway
Widow Conway
Miss Dorothy Gibbs
Nelly Glentworth
Mr. Grimshaw
Gypsy (Zuleika)
Jack Harris
Wibird Hawkins

Dame Jocelyn
Fred Langdon
Charley Marden
Mr. Meeks
Grandfather (Captain) Nutter
Miss Abigail Nutter
Pettingil
Seth Rodgers
Uncle Snow
Silas Trefethen
Captain Truck
Binny Wallace
Benjamin (Sailor Ben) Watson
Pepper Whitcomb
Ezra Wingate

NELSON ALGREN

The Man with the Golden Arm (1949)
Record Head (Bednarski) (Bednar)
Louie (Nifty) Fomorowski
Violet Koskozka
Cousin Kvorka
Francis (Automatic, Frankie Machine)
  Majcinek
Sophie (Zoschka, Zosh) Majcinek
Molly (Molly N., Molly-O) Novotny
Blind Pig (Piggy-O)
Solly (Professor, Sparrow) Saltskin
Zero Schwiefka
Anthony (Antek the Owner) Witwicki

Never Come Morning (1942)
Casimir (Casey) Benkowski
Bruno (Lefty) Bicek
Finger Idzikowski
Fireball Kodadek
Bonifacy (The Barber) Konstantine
Catfoot Nowogrodski
Steffi Rostenkowski
One-Eye Tenczara
Mama (Mama T.) Tomek
Bibleback Watrobinski

Somebody in Boots (1935)
Dill Doak
Norah Egan
Luther Gulliday
Herman Hauser
Olin Jones
Matches
Bryan McKay
Cass McKay
Nancy McKay
Stuart (Stub, Stubby) McKay
Nubby O'Neill

A Walk on the Wild Side (1949)
Hallie Breedlove
Oliver Finnerty
Rhino (O-Daddy) Gross
Velma Gross
Hallie
Byron Linkhorn
Dove Linkhorn
Fitz Linkhorn
Luther (Fort)
Luther (Little Luke)
Achilles Schmidt
Kitty Twist
Terasina Vidavarri

HERVEY ALLEN

Action at Aquila (1938)
Judge Brisdine
Elizabeth Crittendon
Margaret Crittendon
Nathaniel T. (Nat) Franklin
Flossie Kiskadden

Anthony Adverse (1933)
Anthony (Toni) Adverse
Napoleon Bonaparte
John Bonnyfeather
Maria (Marquise da Vincitata) Bon-
  nyfeather
Dolores de la Fuente (y Someruelos)
Angela (Angela Maea) Guessippi
William (Sandy) McNab
Denis Moore
Vincent (Vinc) Nolte
Faith Paleologus
Florence Udney Parish
Marquis (Don Luis Guzman Sotomyer
  y O'Connell, conde de Azuaga) da
  Vincitata
Father Xavier

Bedford Village (1944)
Phoebe Davison
Simeon Ecuyer
Captain Jack Fenwick
James Callowhill Gladwin
Samuel Japson
James McArdle
Garrett Pendergass (Pendergrass)
Rose Pendergass

The Forest and the Fort (1943)
Salathiel (Little Turtle) Albine
Big Turtle

Simeon Ecuyer
Samuel Japson
Kaysinata
Mawakis
James McArdle
Nymwha
Garrett Pendergass (Pendergrass)
Rose Pendergass
Jane Sligo
Arthur St. Clair
Edward Hamilton Yates

Toward the Morning (1948)
Salathiel (Little Turtle) Albine
Bridget McCandliss
Frances Melissa O'Toole
Arthur St. Clair
Edward Hamilton Yates

JAMES LANE ALLEN

Aftermath (1895)
Georgiana Cobb
Joseph Cobb
Margaret Cobb
Sylvia Cobb
Adam Moss
Mrs. Walters

A Kentucky Cardinal (1898)
Georgiana Cobb
Joseph Cobb
Margaret Cobb
Sylvia Cobb
Adam Moss
Mrs. Walters

SHERWOOD ANDERSON

Dark Laughter (1925)
Ted (Teddy) Copeland
Bruce (John Stockton) Dudley
Rose Frank
Aline Aldridge Grey
Fred Grey
Sponge Martin
Bernice Stockton
Esther Walker
Joe Walker
Tom Wills

Poor White (1926)
Clara Butterworth
Tom Butterworth
Kate Chanceller

Ezra French
Jim Gibson
Judge Horace Hanby
Steve Hunter
Hugh McVey
Henry Shepard
Sarah Shepard
Joseph Wainsworth

Windy McPherson's Son (1916)
Janet Eberly
Mike McCarthy
Jane McPherson
John (Windy) McPherson
Kate McPherson
Sam McPherson
Colonel Tom Rainey
Sue Rainey
John Telfer
Mary Underwood

Winesburg, Ohio (1919)
Jesse Bentley
Katherine Bentley
Wing (Adolph Myers) Biddlebaum
Henry Bradford
Belle Carpenter
Ebenezer Cowley
Elmer Cowley
Ned Currie
Tom Foster
Ed Handby
Tandy Hard
Tom Hard
Albert Hardy
David Hardy
Harriet Hardy
John Hardy
Louise Bentley Hardy
Mary Hardy
Reverend Curtis Hartman
Will Henderson
Hop Higgins
Alice Hindman
Will Hurley
Edward King
Sarah King
Tom King
Mook
Adolph Myers
Doctor Parcival
Ray Pearson
Doctor Reefy
Seth Richmond
Virginia Richmond

Enoch Robinson
Turk Smollet
John Spaniard
Elizabeth Swift
Kate Swift
Louise Trunnion
Joe Welling
Helen White
Elizabeth Willard
George Willard
Tom Willard
Wash Williams
Hal Winters

HARRIETTE SIMPSON ARNOW
(See also Volume II)

The Dollmaker (1954)
Homer Anderson
Mrs. Anderson
John (Old John, Uncle John) Ballew
Battle John Brand
Andy Hull
Henley Kendrick
Mrs. Kendrick
Mrs. McKeckeran (Mrs. McBales)
Sophronie Meanwell
Whit Meanwell
Amos Nevels
Cassie Marie Nevels
Clovis Nevels
Clytie Nevels
Enoch Nevels
Gertie Kendrick Nevels
Reuben Nevels
Sue Annie Tiller

Hunter's Horn (1949)
Jaw Buster Anderson
John (Old John, Uncle John) Ballew
Lee Roy Ballew
Lucy Ballew
Milly Ballew
Nunnely Danforth (Nunn) Ballew
Suse Ballew
William Danforth (Bill Dan) Ballew
Battle John Brand
Keg Head Cramer
Lureenie Cramer
Mark Cramer
Rans Cramer
King Devil
J. D. Duffey

Andrew Haynes
Andy Hull
Sam
Sue Annie Tiller
Vineria (Vinie)
Zing

Mountain Path (1936)
Chris Bledsoe
Corie (Corie Cal) Calhoun
Haze (Haze Cal) Calhoun
Lee Buck Calhoun
Mabel Calhoun
Rie (Rie Cal) Calhoun
Lee Buck Cal
Samanthetie Pedigo
Louisa Sheridan

T. S. ARTHUR

Ten Nights in a Bar-Room (1854)
Harvey Green
Willy Hammond
Lyman
Joe Morgan
Mary Morgan
Frank Slade
Simon Slade

NATHAN ASCH

The Office (1925)
Henry Clarke
Jim Denby
Gertrude (Gert, Gerty) Donovan
Edward (Eddie) Foley
John T. Glymmer
Goodman
Samuel (Sammy) Jacobs
Miss James
Marc Krantz
Read
Esther Thomas
Harry Widener
Zuckor

Pay Day (1930)
Daisy Patricia Cowan
Eugene Cowan
James (Jim) Cowan
Martha Cowan
Helen
Phillip Laurie
Eddie Mitchell
Paddy

Jennie Williams
Mrs. Williams

GERTRUDE ATHERTON

Ancestors (1907)
Dolly Boutts
Anabel Colton
Thomas (Tom) Colton
John Elton Cecil (Jack) Gwynne
Lady Victoria Gwynne
Julia Kaye
Leslie
Anne Montgomery
Isabel Otis
Lyster Stone
Flora Thangue

Black Oxen (1923)
Lee (Clavey) Clavering
Gora Dwight
Prince Moritz Franz Ernst Felix von
   Hohenauer
James (Jim) Oglethorpe
Jane Oglethorpe
Janet Oglethorpe
Agnes Trevor
Countess Marie Ogden (Grifin, Count-
   ess Josef, Mary) Zattiany

Patience Sparhawk and Her Times
(1908)
Miss Beale
Garan Bourke
Honora Tremont Mairs
Beverly Peele
Harriet (Hal) Peele
Patience (Patitia) Sparhawk
Morgan Steele
Harriet Tremont

WILLIAM ATTAWAY

Blood on the Forge (1941)
Chinatown (China) Moss
Mat (Big Mat) Moss
Melody Moss
Smothers

LOUIS AUCHINCLOSS
(See also Volume II)

The Great World and Timothy Colt
(1956)
Ann Colt

Timothy (Timmy) Colt
Sheridan Dale
Larry Duane
George Emlen
David Fairchild
Henry Knox
Eileen Shallcross

MARY AUSTIN

Santa Lucia (1908)
Luella Bixby
Dr. Edward (Ned) Caldwell
William (Billy) Caldwell
James J. (Jim) Halford
Edward K. (Jap) Jasper
Evan Lindley
Serena Haven Lindley
Julia Maybury
George Rhewold
Antrim Stairs

A Woman of Genius (1912)
Thomas (Tommy) Bettersworth
Sarah Croyden
Mark Eversley
Helmeth Garrett
Leon Griffin
Ephemia (Effie) Lattimore
Forester (Forrie) Lattimore
Olivia May Lattimore
Sally Lattimore
Leon (Griffin) Lawrence
Gerald (Jerry) McDermott
Henry Mills
Pauline Allingham Mills
Morris Polatkin
Henrietta Rathbone

DOROTHY BAKER

Young Man with a Horn (1944)
Arthur (Art) Hazard
Daniel (Dan, Smoke) Jordan
Edward Richard (Rick) Martin
Amy (Doctor) North
Jack Stuart
Lee Valentine
Jeffrey (Jeff) Williams

JAMES BALDWIN
(See also Volume II)

Giovanni's Room (1956)
David

Giovanni
Guillaume
Hella

Go Tell It on the Mountain (1953)
Esther
Deborah Grimes
Elizabeth Grimes
Florence Grimes
Gabriel Grimes
John Grimes
Roy Grimes
Richard
Royal

DJUNA BARNES

Nightwood (1937)
Nora Flood
Dr. Matthew O'Connor
Jenny Petherbridge
Baron Felix Volkbein
Guido Volkbein
Robin Vote

Ryder (1928)
Alex Alexson
Molly Dance
Amelia de Grier
Kate-Careless
Dr. Matthew O'Connor
John Peel
Cynthia Ryder
Jonathan Buxton Ryder
Sophia Grieve Ryder
Wendell Ryder

MARGARET AYER BARNES

Wisdom's Gate (1938)
Alden Carver, Junior
Jane Ward (Mumsy) Carver
Stephen Carver
Flora Furness
Lily Furness
Cicily Carver Bridges Lancaster
Muriel Lester Lancaster
Jane Ward
John Ward
Lizzie Ward

Years of Grace (1930)
Alden Carver, Junior
Cicily (Silly) Carver
Jane Ward (Mumsy) Carver

Stephen Carver
André Duroy
Flora Furness
Lily Furness
Agnes Johnson
Albert Lancaster
Cicily Carver Bridges Lancaster
Muriel Lester Lancaster
Agnes Johnson Trent
James (Jimmy) Trent
Jane Ward
John Ward
Lizzie Ward

JOHN BARTH
(See also Volume II)

The Sot-Weed Factor (1960)
Henry Burlingame III
Bertrand Burton
Charles Calvert, Lord Baltimore
John Cooke
Anna Cooke
Ebenezer (Eben) Cooke
Pocahontas
Billy Rumbly
Capt. John Smith
Joan Toast
Susan (Susie) Warren

HAMILTON BASSO

The View from Pompey's Head (1954)
Dinah Blackford Higgins
Wyeth Blackford
Phillip (Phil) Greene
Mico (Mickey) Higgins
Anna Jones
Anson Page
Meg Page
Garvin Wales
Lucy Devereaux Wales

HENRY WARD BEECHER

Norwood (1868)
Hiram Beers
Agate Bissell
Buell
Abiah Cathcart
Alice Cathcart
Barton Cathcart
Rachel Liscomb Cathcart

Frank Esel
Thomas J. Heywood
Jerry Marble
Pete Sawmill
Tommy Taft
Turfmould
Reuben Wentworth
Rose Wentworth

EDWARD BELLAMY

Looking Backward (1917)
Edith Bartlett
Barton
Leete
Edith Leete
Julian West

SAUL BELLOW
(See also Volume II)

The Adventures of Augie March (1954)
Hymie Bateshaw
Stella Chesney
William Einhorn
Thea Fenchel
Sophie Geratis
Grandma Lausch
Augie (Bolingbroke) March
Georgie March
Mama March
Harold Mintouchian
Kayo Obermark
Manny Padilla
Mr. Renling
Mrs. Renling
Robey
Mimi Villars

Dangling Man (1944)
Myron (Mike) Adler
Amos
Kitty Daumler
Etta
Iva (née Almstadt)
Joseph
Spirit of Alternatives (But on the Other Hand, Tu As Raison Aussi)
Mr. Vanaker

Henderson the Rain King (1959)
Atti

Dahfu
Eugene H. (Captain Henderson, Gene,
 Henderson-Sungo, Leo E., Rain King,
 Sungo) Henderson
Itelo
Mtalba
Romilayu
Willatale

The Victim (1947)
Dr. Adler
Kirby Allbee
Daniel Harkavy
Asa Leventhal
Schlossberg
Dr. Tainkin
Tommy (Wilhelm Adler, Velvel, Wilky)
 Wilhelm
Stan Williston

LUDWIG BEMELMANS

Dirty Eddie (1947)
Betsy Allbright
Belinda (Marie O'Neill)
Belladonna
Maurice (Joe) Cassard
Beverly Copfee
Raoul de Bourggraff
Dirty Eddie
Envelove
Moses Fable
Grippenwald
Ma Gundel
Jerome (Jerry) Hack
Buddy van der Lynn
Casey McMahon
Ludlow Mumm
Arthur Nightwine
Miss Princip
Valerie Sinnot
Sandor Thrilling
Vanya (Danny Spellbinder) Vashvily
Farmer Weatherbeat
Arty Wildgans

THOMAS BERGER
(See also Volume II)

Crazy in Berlin (1958)
Bach
Veronica Leary
James T. (Jimmy) Marsala
Schatzi (Ernst)

Nathan (Nate) Schild
Trudchen

ALINE BERNSTEIN

The Journey Down (1938)
Amelia
Carl
Daddy
Mr. Flick
Francie
Cousin Julia
Mrs. Lindow
Aunt Mamie
Nana (Mrs. Greenfield, Ray)
Tom Watson
Madam Zelma

WENDELL BERRY
(See also Volume II)

Nathan Coulter (1960)
Big Ellis
Kate Helen Branch
Burley (Uncle Burley) Coulter
David (Dave) Coulter
Jarrat Coulter
Nathan Coulter
Tom Coulter
Jig Pendleton

AMBROSE BIERCE

*The Monk and the Hangman's
Daughter* (1892)
Ambrosius
Amula
Andreas
Benedicta
Rochus
Saltmaster

ROBERT MONTGOMERY
BIRD

Nick of the Woods (1939)
Richard Braxley
Colonel Bruce
Pardon Dodge
Abel Doe
Telie Doe
Captain Roland Forrester
Edith Forrester

Major Roland (Roly) Forrester
Nathan (Jibbenainosay, Nick of the
 Woods) Slaughter
Ralph (Roaring Ralph) Stackpole
Wenonga

ARNA WENDELL BONTEMPS

Black Thunder (1936)
Ben (Old Ben)
Alexander Biddenhurst
Bundy (Old Bundy)
Creuzot
Ditcher
Drucilla
Juba
Laurent
Melody
Mingo
Pharoah
Gabriel (Gen'l Gabriel) Prosser
Thomas (Marse Prosser) Prosser
General John Scott
Moseley Sheppard
Robin (Marse Robin) Sheppard

Drums at Dusk (1939)
Angélique
Annette
Boukman
Choucoune
Claire
Diron Desautels
Philippe Desautels
Captain Frounier
Céleste Juvet
Hugo Juvet
Mme. Jacques Juvet
Bayou de Libertas
Mars Plasair
Count Armand De Sacy
Pierre Sylvain
Toussaint
Paulette Viard

God Sends Sunday (1931)
Augie (Little Augie, Little Poison)
Joe Baily
Biglow (Papa Biglow) Brown
Horace (Woody) Church-Woodbine
Mississippi Davis
Florence Dessau
Bad-foot (Mistah Bad-foot Man) Dixon
Della Green
Barney Jones

Leah
Lissus
Parthenia
Count (Rags) Ragsdale
Terry
Tom Wright

JANE BOWLES

Two Serious Ladies (1943)
Arnold
Ben
Frieda Copperfield
J. C. Copperfield
Lucie Gamelon
Christina Goering
Andrew (Andy) McLane
Pacifica
Flora Quill
Toby

PAUL BOWLES

Let It Come Down (1952)
Thami Beidaoui
Nelson Dyar
Eunice Goode
Hadi Ja
Marquesa Daisy de Valverde
Jack Wilcox

The Sheltering Sky (1949)
Eric Lyle
Mrs. Lyle
Katherine (Kit) Moresby
Porter (Port) Moresby
Tunner

JAMES BOYD

Drums (1925)
Hugh Clapton
Nathaniel (Nat, Sir Nat) Dukinfield
Captain Flood
John (Johnny) Fraser, Jr.
John (Dadder) Fraser
John Paul Jones
Sally Merrillee
Eve Tennant

Through the Wheat (1923)
John R. Adams
Lieutenant Bedford

King Cole
Kerfoot (Carl) Harriman
William Hicks
Kitty Kahl
Captain Powers
Jack Pugh

HJALMAR HJORTH BOYESEN

The Golden Calf (1892)
Cyrus Carter
Madeline Carter
Dr. Habicht
Ferdinand Habicht
Minna Habicht
Oliver Tappan

The Mammon of Unrighteousness (1891)
Dr. Archibald Hawk
Alexander (Aleck) Larkin
Gertrude (Gertie) Larkin
Horace Larkin
Obed Larkin
Arabella (Bella) Robbins
Kate Van Schaak

HUGH HENRY BRACKENRIDGE

Modern Chivalry (1937)
Monsieur Douperie
Captain John Farrago
Duncan Ferguson
Marquis de Marnessie
Kate Maybone
M'Donald
Mutchkin
M'Whorter
Teague Oregan (O'Regan)
Peter Porcupine
Tom the Tinker
Traddle

RAY BRADBURY

Fahrenheit 451 (1953)
Beatty
Faber
Granger
Clarisse McClellan
Guy Montag
Mildred Montag

LOUIS BROMFIELD

The Green Bay Tree (1924)
René de Cyon
Governor
William (Willie) Harrison
Stepan Krylenko
Irene (Sister Monica) Shane
Julia Shane
Lily Shane
Ellen (Lilli Barr) Tolliver

CHARLES BROCKDEN BROWN

Arthur Mervyn (1799)
Achsa Fielding
Mr. Hadwin
Arthur Mervyn
Dr. Stevens
Thomas Welbeck

Edgar Huntly (1799)
Clarice
Clithero Edny
Edgar Huntley
Euphemia Wiatte Lorimer
Queen Mab (Old Deb)
Sarsefield
Waldegrave
Mary Waldegrave
Weymouth
Arthur Wiatte

Ormond (1799)
Balfour
Sarah Baxter
Helena (Hellen) Cleves
Thomas Craig
Martinette de Beauvais (Ursula Monrose)
Constantia (Constance) Dudley
Stephen Dudley
Malcolm M'Crea
Mr. Melbourne
Ormond
Mary Ridgeley
Roseveldt
Sophia Westwyn (Courdand)

Waveland (1798)
Thomas Cambridge
Francis Carwin
Judith
Henry Pleyel
Catharine Pleyel Wieland

Clara Wielend
Theodore Wieland

WILLIAM HILL BROWN

The Power of Sympathy (1789)
Harriot (Rosebud) Fawcet
Maria Fawcet
Fidelia
Mrs. Francis
Amelia Harrington
J. Harrington
Myra Harrington
Tommy Harrington
Henry
Mrs. Eliza Holmes
Mr. Martin
Mrs. Martin
Shepherd
Ophelia Shepherd
Jack Worthy

PEARL BUCK

The Good Earth (1931)
O-lan
Pear Blossom
Ching
Cuckoo
Lord (Old Lord) Hwang
Lotus (Lotus Flower)
Wang Lung
Nung En (Elder, Wang the Eldest, Wang the Landlord)
Nung Wen (Wang the Second, Wang the Merchant)
Old Lord
Wang the Third (Wang the Tiger)

A House Divided (1935)
Nung En (Elder, Wang the Eldest, Wang the Landlord)
Nung Wen (Wang the Second, Wang the Merchant)
Pig Butcher
Wang the Third (Wang the Tiger)

Sons (1932)
Pear Blossom
Elder
Hawk
Leopard
Wang Lung
Nung En (Elder, Wang the Eldest, Wang the Landlord)

Pig Butcher
Nung En (Wang the Second, Wang the Merchant)
Wang the Third (Wang the Tiger)

FRANCES HODGSON BURNETT

Little Lord Fauntleroy (1886)
Earl of Dorincourt
Captain Cedric Errol
Cedric (Ceddie, Lord Fauntleroy) Errol
John Arthur Molyneux (Earl of Dorincourt) Errol
Mrs. Cedric (Dearest) Errol
T. Havisham
Silas Hobbs
Minna (Lady Fauntleroy) Tipton
Benjamin (Ben) Tipton
Dick Tipton

WILLIAM RILEY BURNETT

The Asphalt Jungle (1949)
Louis (Schemer) Bellini
Bob Brannom
Charles (Cobby) Cobb
Joe Cool
Eddie Donato
Alonzo D. (Lon) Emmerich
Lou Farbstein
Angela Finlay
Dolph Franc
Dix (Dixie, William Tuttle Jamieson) Handley
Theo J. Hardy
Dorothy (Doll) Pelky
Erwin Riemenschneider

High Sierra (1940)
John (Johnny) Dillinger
Roy (Mad Dog) Earle
Marie Garson
Jim Goodhue
Velma Goodhue
Vince Healy
Barmy Johnson
Kramner
Louis Mendoza
Big Mac M'Gann
Arnold Francis (Babe) Milnik
Doc Parker
Joseph (Red) Potter

Lon Preiser
Roma Stover

Little Caesar (1929)
Cesare (Rico) Bandello
Blondy Belle
Jim Courtney
DeVoss
Jim Flaherty
Magdalena (Ma)
Joe (Gentleman Joe) Massara
Father McConagha
Pete Montana
James Michael (Big Boy) O'Doul
Ramón (The Greek) Otero
Tony (Antonio Passalacqua) Passa
Giovanni Scabby
Sam Vettori
Nell Weil
John C. Willoughby
Arnold (Little Arnie) Worch

JOHN HORNE BURNS

The Gallery (1947)
Chaplain Bascom
Father Donovan
Ginny
Giulia
Hal
Sergeant Joe (Jo-Jo)
Louella
Monuna
Major Motes
Michael Patrick
Maria Rocco
Moses (Moe) Shulman

WILLIAM S. BURROUGHS
(See also Volume II)

Junkie (1953)
Gene Doolie
Bill Gains
Herman
Ike (Old Ike)
William (Bill, Billy, Lee the Agent, El Hombre Invisible, Inspector J. Lee, Klinker, William Seward)
Pat
Roy
The Sailor

Naked Lunch (1959)
A. J. (Merchant of Sex)

Dr. (Doc) Benway
The County Clerk (Arch Anker)
Clem Ergot
Jody Ergot
Bill Gains
Mr. Hyslop
Ike (Old Ike)
Johnny
William (Bill, Billy, Lee the Agent, El
  Hombre Invisible, Inspector J. Lee,
  Klinker, William Seward)
Salvador Hassan (After Birth Tycoon,
  K. Y. Ahmed, Pepe El Culito, Hassan,
  Placenta Juan)
Carl Peterson
The Rube
The Sailor
The Great (Meester) Slashtubitch
Clem (Private Ass Hole) Snide
The Technician
Fats Terminal

JAMES BRANCH CABELL

Jurgen (1928)
Dame Anaitis (Lady of the Lake)
Chloris
Koshchei the Deathless
Dorothy la Désirée (Heart's Desire,
  Madame Dorothy)
Florimel
Princess Guenevere (Phyllida)
Jurgen
Dame Lisa (Adelais)
Nessus
Mother Sereda

GEORGE WASHINGTON CABLE

The Grandissimes (1908)
Bras Coupé
Clemence
Joseph Frowenfeld
Agricola (Agricole) Fusilier
Achille Grandissime
Honoré Grandissime
Honoré Grandissime f.m.c.
Sylvestre Grandissime
Raoul Innerarity
Doctor Charlie Keene
Charlie Mandarin
Aurore De Grapion Nancanou
Clotilde De Grapion Nancanou

Palmyre (Madame Inconnue) la
  Philosophe
Red Clay (Lufki-Humma)

JAMES M. CAIN

Mildred Pierce (1941)
Montgomery (Monty) Beragon
  (Bergoni)
Wally Burgan
Lucy Gessler
Herbert (Bert) Pierce
Mildred Pierce
Moire (Ray) Pierce
Veda Pierce
Carlo Treviso

The Postman Always Rings Twice
(1934)
Madge Allen (Kramer)
Frank Chambers
Katz
Cora Smith Papadakis
Nick (the Greek) Papadakis
Sackett

PAUL CAIN

Fast One (1932)
Shep Beery
John R. (Boss) Bellmann
Crotti
Lee Fenner
S. Granquist
Gerry Kells
Reilly
Jack (Jakie, Jake Rosencrancz) Rose

ERSKINE CALDWELL

God's Little Acre (1960)
Dave Dawson
Pluto Swint
Rosamond Walden Thompson
Will Thompson
Buck Walden
Darling Jill Walden
Griselda Walden
Jim Leslie Walden
Shaw Walden
Ty Ty Walden

Tobacco Road (1960)
Lov Bensey
Pearl Lester Bensey

Ada Lester
Dude Lester
Ellie May Lester
Jeeter Lester
Mother Lester
Bessie (Sister Bessie) Rice

ROBERT CANTWELL

The Land of Plenty (1934)
Gil Ahab
Carl Belcher
Walt Connor
Digby
Vin Garl
Hagen
John (Johnny) Hagen
Little Rock
Charles (Mac) MacMahon
Rose (Kitten, Kitty) MacMahon
Morley (Molly)
Roger Schwartz
Sorenson
Ellen Turner
Marie Turner
Ed Winters

TRUMAN CAPOTE
(See also Volume II)

Breakfast at Tiffany's (1958)
Joe Bell
O. J. Berman
Fred
Doc Golightly
Holiday (Holly, Lulamae Barnes) Go-
  lightly
Salvatore (Sally) Tomato
Rutherford (Rusty) Trawler
Margaret Thatcher Fitzhue (Mag)
  Wildwood
José Ybarra-Jaegar
I. Y. Yunioshi

The Grass Harp (1951)
Judge Charlie Cool
Catherine Creek
Collin Talbo Fenwick
Riley Henderson
Little Homer Honey
Sister Ida Honey
Maude Riordan
Dr. Morris Ritz
Dolly Augusta Talbo
Verena Talbo

Other Voices, Other Rooms (1948)
Pepe Alvarez
Jesus Fever
Missouri (Zoo) Fever
Ellen Kendall
Joel Harrison Knox
Edward R. (Ed) Sansom
Joel Harrison Knox Sansom
Miss Amy Skully Sansom
Randolph Lee Skully
Little Sunshine
Florabel Thompkins
Idabel Thompkins
Miss Wisteria

WILLA CATHER

Death Comes for the Archbishop
(1929)
Kit (Christóbal) Carson
Jesus de Baca
Bernard Ducrot
Eusabio
Gallegos
Jacinto
Jean Marie Latour
Marino Lucero
Antonio José Martinez
Baltazar Montoya
Antonio Olivares
Isabella Olivares
Joseph (Blanchet) Vaillant
Magdalena Valdez

A Lost Lady (1923)
Henry Collins
Francis Bosworth (Frank) Ellinger
Ed Elliott
Captain Daniel Forrester
Marian Ormsby (Maidy) Forrester
Niel Herbert
Constance Ogden
Ivy (Poison Ivy) Peters
Judge Pommeroy

My Ántonia (1926)
Jim Burden
Gaston Cleric
Wycliffe (Wick) Cutter
Anton Cuzak
Larry Donovan
Otto Fuchs
Peter Krajiek
Lena Lingard
Pavel and Peter

Shimerda
Ambroz (Ambrosch) Shimerda
Ántonia Shimerda

One of Ours (1922)
Olive de Courcy
Augusta Erlich
Lieutenant Tod Fanning
Gladys Farmer
Lieutenant David Gerhardt
Ernest Havel
Mme. Joubert
Mahailey
Captain Harris Maxey
Victor Morse
Barclay (Julius Caesar) Owens
Emd Royce
Lieutenant Colonel Walter Scott
Arthur (Brother) Weldon
Bayliss Wheeler
Claude Wheeler
Evangeline Wheeler
Nat Wheeler
Ralph Wheeler
August (Gus) Yoder

O Pioneers! (1941)
Alexandra Bergson
Emil Bergson
John Bergson
Lou Bergson
Mrs. Bergson
Oscar Bergson
Crazy Ivar
Carl Linstrum
Frank Shabata
Marie Tovesky Shabata

Sapphira and the Slave Girl (1940)
Betty Blake
Mary (Molly) Blake
Michael Blake
Rachel Colbert Blake
Mrs. Bywaters
Henry Colbert
Martin Colbert
Rachel Colbert
Sapphira Dodderidge (Sapphy Mistress) Colbert
Jefferson (Jeff)
Jezebel
Nancy
Till

The Song of the Lark (1943)
Doctor Howard Archie

Madison Bowers
Andor Harsanyi
Ray H. Kennedy
Mr. and Mrs. Peter Kronborg
Thea Kronborg
Philip Frederick Ottenburg
Juan (Spanish Johnny) Tellamantez
Professor A. Wunsch

RAYMOND CHANDLER

The Big Sleep (1939)
Lash Canino
Arthur Gwynn Geiger
Philip Marlowe
Eddie Mars
Mona Mars
Vivian Sternwood Regan
Carmen Sternwood
General Guy Sternwood

Farewell, My Lovely (1940)
Jules Amthor
Lewin Lockridge Grayle
Moose Malloy
Philip Marlowe
Lindsay Marriott
Anne Riordan
Velma Valento (Mrs. Lewin Lockridge Grayle)

The Long Goodbye (1953)
Sylvia Lennox
Terry Lennox
Linda Loring
Philip Marlowe
Mendy Menendez
Bernie Ohls
Harlan Potter
Eileen Wade
Roger Wade

JOHN CHEEVER
(See also Volume II)

The Wapshot Chronicle (1957)
Ray Badger
Uncle Peepee (George Humbolt) Marshmallow
Pancras
Helen Rutherford
Mr. de Sastago
Justina (Cousin Justina) Wapshot Molesworth Scaddon
Betsey MacCaffery Wapshot

Coverly Wapshot
Ezekiel Wapshot
Honora Wapshot
Leander Wapshot
Melissa Scaddon Wapshot
Moses Wapshot
Sarah Coverly Wapshot
Rosalie Young

CHARLES W. CHESNUTT

The Colonel's Dream (1905)
William Fetters
Col. Henry French
Laura Treadwell

The House Behind the Cedars (1900)
George Tryon
John (John Warwick) Walden
Molly (Mis' Molly) Walden
Rowena (Rena) Walden

The Marrow of Tradition (1901)
Major Philip Carteret
Dr. William Miller

LYDIA MARIA CHILD

Holbrook (1824)
Charles Brown
John Collier
Sally Oldham Collier
Charles Hobomok Conant
Mary Conant
Mrs. Mary Conant
Roger Conant
Corbitant
Governor Endicott
Hobomok
James Hopkins
Earl of Rivers

KATE CHOPIN

The Awakening (1899)
Alcée Arobin
Madame Lebrun
Robert Lebrun
Dr. Mandelet
Edna Pontellier
Etienne Pontellier
Léonce Pontellier
Raoul Pontellier
Adèle Ratignolle
Mademoiselle Reisz

WINSTON CHURCHILL

Coniston (1906)
Jethro Bass
Sally Broke
Jane Merrill
Stephen (Steve) Merrill
Susan Merrill
Lucretia Penniman
Ephraim (Eph) Prescott
David (David Trimble, Davy) Ritchie
Cynthia (Cynthy) Wetherell
Cynthia Ware (Cynthy) Wetherell
William (Will) Wetherell
Isaac Dudley Worthington
Robert (Bob) Worthington

The Crisis (1901)
Captain Elijah (Lige) Brent
Margaret Brice
Stephen Atterbury (Steve) Brice
Colonel Comyn Carvel
Virginia (Jinny) Carvel
George Catherwood
Tom Catherwood
Clarence Colfax
Ephum
Eliphalet Hopper
Carl Richter
Puss and Emily Russell
Silas Whipple

The Crossing (1904)
Gignoux
Thomas (Tom) McChesney
Harry Riddle
Polly Ann Ripley
Antoinette de St. Gré
Auguste de St. Gré
Hélène Victoire Marie de (Hélène
    d'Ivry-le-Tour) St. Gré
Philippe de St. Gré
Nicholas (Nick) Temple
Sarah (Mrs. Clive, Sally) Temple

The Inside of the Cup (1913)
Gordon Atterbury
Horace Bentley
Richard Garvin
Sally Grover
Alison Parr Hodder
John Hodder
Kate Marcy
Reverend Mister McCrae
Alison Parr

Eldon Parr
Preston Parr

Mr. Crewe's Career (1908)
Brush Bascom
Jacob (Jake) Botcher
Euphrasia (Phrasie) Cotton
Alice Pomfret Crewe
Humphrey Crewe
Augustus P. (Gus) Flint
Victoria Flint
Thomas (Tom) Gaylord
Adam B. Hunt
Jabe Jenney
Zebulun (Zeb) Meader
Alice Pomfret
Fanny Pomfret
Mr. Redbrook
Hamilton (Ham) Tooting
Austen (Aust) Vane
Hilary Vane
Victoria Flint Vane

Richard Carvel (1914)
Reverend Allen
Grafton Carvel
Lionel Carvel
Philip Carvel
Richard (Dick) Carvel
Duke of Chartersea
Captain Daniel Clapsaddle
Lord (Jack) Comyn
Dorothy (Dolly) Manners
Margaret Manners
Marmaduke Manners
Henry Swain
Patty Swain
Thomas (Tom) Swain

WALTER VAN TILBURG CLARK

The Ox-Bow Incident (1940)
Amigo
Bartlett
Canby
Gil Carter
Art Croft
Arthur Davies
Harley Drew
Jeff Farnley
Greene
Jenny (Ma) Grier
Alva Hardwick
Laurence Liam (Larry) Kinkaid

Donald Martin
Juan (Francisco Morez) Martinez
Risley
Major Willard Tetley
Gerald (Gerry) Tetley

SAMUEL LANGHORNE CLEMENS (MARK TWAIN)

Adventures of Huckleberry Finn (1884)
Dauphin (Edmund Kean, Alexander Blodgett, Looy the Seventeen, Harvey Wilks)
Widow Douglas
Duke of Bridgewater (Bilgewater, David Garrick, William Wilks)
Huckleberry (George Jackson, George Peters, Huck, Sarah Mary Williams, Tom Sawyer) Finn
Pap Finn
Colonel Saul Grangerford
Emmeline Grangerford
Sophia Grangerford
Jim
Aunt Polly
Thomas (Sid, Tom) Sawyer
Harney Shepherdson
Colonel Sherburn
Judge Thatcher
Rebecca (Becky, Bessie) Thatcher
Miss Watson
Joanna, Mary Jane and Susan Wilks

Adventures of Tom Sawyer (1876)
Widow Douglas
Huckleberry (George Jackson, George Peters, Huck, Sarah Mary Williams, Tom Sawyer) Finn
Pap Finn
Joseph (Joe) Harper
Injun Joe
Amy Lawrence
Aunt Polly
Muff Potter
Doctor (Sawbones) Robinson
Sidney (Sid) Sawyer
Thomas (Sid, Tom) Sawyer
Judge Thatcher
Rebecca (Becky, Bessie) Thatcher

A Connecticut Yankee in King Arthur's Court (1889)
Arthur (Jones)
Clarence (Amyas le Poulet)

Dinadan
Guenever
M. T.
Merlin
Morgan le Fay
Hank (The Boss) Morgan
Sandy (Alisande de la Carteloise)

The Prince and the Pauper (1881)
John Canty
Tom Canty
Earl of Hertford
Miles Hendon
Edward (King Edward VI, Prince of Wales) Tudor

Pudd'nhead Wilson (1894)
Luigi and Angelo Capello
Percy Northumberland Driscoll
Thomas à Becket (Chambers, Valet de Chambre) Driscoll
York Leicester Driscoll
Pembroke Howard
Roxana (Roxy)
Valet de Chambre (Tom Driscoll)
David (Pudd'nhead) Wilson

Tom Sawyer Abroad (1894)
Huckleberry (George Jackson, George Peters, Huck, Sarah Mary Williams, Tom Sawyer) Finn
Jim
Aunt Polly
Thomas (Sid, Tom) Sawyer

Tom Sawyer, Detective (1896)
Brace Dunlap
Jake Dunlap
Jubiter Dunlap
Huckleberry (George Jackson, George Peters, Huck, Sarah Mary Williams, Tom Sawyer) Finn
Benny Phelps
Aunt Polly
Thomas (Sid, Tom) Sawyer

SAMUEL LANGHORNE CLEMENS AND CHARLES DUDLEY WARNER

The American Claimant (1892)
Barrow
Kirkcudbright Llanover Marjoribanks Sellers (Howard Tracy), Berkeley
Dan'l
Earl of Rossmore

George Washington Hawkins
Hattie (Puss) Marsh
Rachael Marsh
One-armed Pete
Colonel Beriah/Eschol/Mulberry (Berry, Earl of Rossmore) Sellers
Poly Sellers
Sarah (Lady Gwendolen, Sally) Sellers

The Gilded Age (1873)
Ruth Bolton
Henry (Harry) Brierly
Abner Dilworthy
George Washington Hawkins
Henry Clay Hawkins
Laura Van Brunt Hawkins
George Selby
Colonel Beriah/Eschol/Mulberry (Berry, Earl of Rossmore) Sellers
Polly Sellers
Philip (Phil) Sterling

EVAN CONNELL (See also Volume II)

Mrs. Bridge (1959)
Madge Arlen
Grace Barron
Virgil Barron
Carolyn (Corky) Bridge
Douglas Bridge
India Bridge
Ruth Bridge
Walter Bridge
Dr. Foster
Harriett
Alice Jones
Julia

JACK CONROY

The Disinherited (1933)
Helen Baker
Jasper Collins
Larry Donovan
Tom Donovan
Hans
Bonny Fern Haskin
Nat Moore
Mike Riordan
Lionel Stafford
Ed Warden
Rollie Weems

JAMES FENIMORE COOPER

The Deerslayer (1841)

Nathaniel (Deerslayer, Hawkeye, Leather-stocking, la Longue Carabine, Natty, Pathfinder) Bumppo
Chingachgook (Great Serpent, Indian John, John Mohegan)
Hist-oh!-Hist
Hetty Hutter
Judith Hutter
Thomas (Thomas Hovey) Hutter
Le Loup Cervier
Henry (Hurry Harry) March
Rivenoak
Wah-ta!-Wah (Hist-oh!-Hist)

The Last of the Mohicans (1826)

Nathaniel (Deerslayer, Hawkeye, Leather-stocking, la Longue Carabine, Natty, Pathfinder) Bumppo
Chingachgook (Great Serpent, Indian John, John Mohegan)
David Gamut
Duncan Heyward
Magua (le Renard Subtil)
Montcalm (Louis de Saint Véran, Marquis of Montcalm)
Alice Munro
Colonel Munro
Cora Munro
Uncas (le Cerf Agile)

The Pathfinder (1840)

Arrowhead
Nathaniel (Deerslayer, Hawkeye, Leather-stocking, la Longue Carabine, Natty, Pathfinder) Bumppo
Charles Cap
Chingachgook (Great Serpent, Indian John, John Mohegan)
Duncan of Lundie
Mabel (Magnet) Dunham
Serjeant Dunham
David (Davy) Muir
Jasper Western

The Pioneers (1823)

Nathaniel (Deerslayer, Hawkeye, Leather-stocking, la Longue Carabine, Natty, Pathfinder) Bumppo
Chingachgook (Great Serpent, Indian John, John Mohegan)
Hiram Doolittle
Oliver (Oliver Edwards) Effingham
Louisa Grant
Hector
Richard (Dickon) Jones
Elizabeth (Bess) Temple
Marmaduke Temple

The Prairie (1827)

Obed (Dr. Battius) Bat
Nathaniel (Deerslayer, Hawkeye, Leather-stocking, la Longue Carabine, Natty, Pathfinder) Bumppo
Asa Bush
Esther (Eester) Bush
Ishmael (the Great Buffalo) Bush
Inez de Certavallos
Hard Heart
Hector
Paul (Mr. Bug Gatherer) Hover
Le Balafré
Mahtoree
Duncan Uncas Middleton
Tachechana (the Skipping Fawn)
Ellen (Nelly) Wade
Weucha
Abiram White

The Spy (1821)

Harvey Birch
Peyton Dunwoodie
Elizabeth (Betty) Flanagan
Captain John (Jack) Lawton
Jeanette Peyton
Dr. Archibald Sitgreaves
Caesar Thompson (Wharton)
George (Harper) Washington
Colonel Wellmere
Frances Wharton
Henry Wharton
Mr. Wharton
Sarah Wharton

EDWIN CORLE

Fig Tree John (1935)

Agocho (Agocho Koh Tli-chu, Fig Tree John, John, Red Fire Bird)
Joe
Jose
Kai-a (Bi-Tli-Kai, Nalin, White Deer's Daughter)
George Mack
Johnny (Fig Tree Junior, Great Spirits, Juanito Fig Tree, N'Chai Chidn) Mack
Maria
Paul
Petterman
Martha Goddard Reeves

JAMES GOULD COZZENS

By Love Possessed (1957)

J. Jerome (Jerry) Brophy
Fred Dealey
Helen Detweiler
Ralph Detweiler
Julius Penrose
Marjorie Penrose
Polly Pratt
Alfred Revere
Reggie Shaw
Noah Tuttle
Arthur Winner Junior
Arthur Winner Senior
Clarissa Henderson Winner
Eliot Woolf

Guard of Honor (1948)

Captain Donald Andrews
Major General Ira N. (Bus) Beal
Lieutenant Colonel Benny Carricker
Captain Clarence Duchemin
First Lieutenant James A. Edsell
Captain Nathaniel Hicks
Colonel Mowbray
Brigadier General (J. J., Jo-Jo) Nichols
Master Sergeant Dominic (Danny) Pellerino
Colonel Norman (Judge) Ross
Mrs. Cora Ross
Second Lieutenant Amanda Turck
Second Lieutenant Stanley M. Willis
Colonel (Woody) Woodman

STEPHEN CRANE

George's Mother (1896)

Blue Billie
Bleecker
Fidsey Corcoran
Maggie (Mag) Johnson
Charley (Charlie) Jones
George (Georgie, Kel') Kelcey
Zeusentell

Maggie: A Girl of the Streets (1893)

Blue Billie
Johnson
Jimmie Johnson
Maggie (Mag) Johnson
Mary Johnson

Nellie
Pete

The Red Badge of Courage (1895)
Jim Conklin
Henry (Flem) Fleming
Tom Jamison
Jimmie Rogers
Wilson

The Third Violet (1897)
Grace Fanhall
William (Billie, Will) Hawker
Florinda (Splutter) O'Connor
Jem Oglethorpe
Pennoyer (Penny)
Great Grief Warwickson
Wrinkles (Wrink)

COUNTEE CULLEN

One Way to Heaven (1932)
Constancia Brown (Constance, Lady
  Macbeth, Mrs. Shakespeare) Brandon
Dr. George Brandon
Professor Seth Calhoun
Mary (Duchess of Uganda) Johnson
Mattie Johnson
Sam Lucas
Aunt Mandy

H . D .
(See also Volume II)

Bid Me to Live (1960)
Julia Ashton
Rafe Ashton
Lett Barnes
Bella Carter
Frederick (Frederico, Rico)
Elsa Frederick
Vane (Vanio)

Hedylus (1928)
Demetrius
Demion
Douris
Hedyle
Hedylus
Irene

Palimpsest (1926)
Julia Cornelia Augusta
Helen Fairwood
Hipparchia

Mavis Landour
Marius
Olivia
Philip
Captain Rafton
Fred (Freddie) Ransome
Raymonde Ransome
Ermentrude (Ermy) Solomon
Mary Thorpe-Wharton
Verrus

CLYDE BRION DAVIS

The Great American Novel (1938)
Paul Clark
Frances Harbach
Syra Morris
Harvey O'Brien
John Penny
Tom Rogers
Betty Sullivan
George Tichnor
Byron Zigler
Homer Zigler
Pearl Hawkins Zigler

H. L. DAVIS

Beulah Land (1949)
Askwani
Hube Dakens
Sedaya (Sede) Gallet
Grandma Luttrell
Maruca
Perrault
Savacol
Elison Warne
Ewen Warne
Ruhama Warne

Harp of a Thousand Strings (1947)
Apeyahola (Indian Jory)
Melancthon Crawford
Marquis René-Victor de Bercy
Jeanne-Marie Ignace Thérèse Cabarrus
  de Fontenay
Fouché
Father Jarnatt
Don Joaquin MacGillivray
Ouvrard
Commodore Robinette
Suleau (I)
Suleau (II)
Jean-Lambert Tallien

Anne-Joseph Théroigne
Big Foot Whitten

Honey in the Horn (1935)
Clark Burdon
Clay Calvert
Orlando Geary
Pappy Howell
Foscoe Leonard
Isaac Luz (Luce)
Serphin Moss
Uncle Preston (Press) Shiveley
Wade Shiveley
Flem Simmons
Payette Simmons

REBECCA HARDING DAVIS

Life in the Iron Mills (1861)
Clarke
Deborah (Deb)
Janey
Kirby
John May
Mitchell
Hugh Molly Wolfe
Old Wolfe

RICHARD HARDING DAVIS

Soldiers of Fortune (1897)
Madame (Manueleta [Manuelata] Her-
  nandez) Alvarez
President Alvarez
Robert Clay
Reginald (Reggie) King
Alice Langham
Andrew Langham
Hope Langham
Theodore Langham
MacWilliams
General Mendoza
Captain Stuart

JOHN WILLIAM DEFOREST

*Miss Ravenel's Conversion from Se-
cession to Loyalty* (1867)
John T. Carter
Lillie Ravenel Carter
Ravenel (Ravvie) Carter
Edward (Cap) Colburne
Major Gazaway
Mrs. Larue

Doctor Ravenel
John Whitewood, Jr.

FLOYD DELL

Moon-Calf (1920)
Thomas (Tom, Tommy) Alden
Miss Croly
Felix Fay
Stephen Frazer
Rose Henderson
Lulu (L. L.) Miller
Nathan
Helen Raymond
Joyce Tennant
Franz Vogelsang

PATRICK DENNIS

Around the World with Auntie Mame (1958)
Dwight Babcock
Elmore Jefferson Davis Burnside
Vera Charles
Mame (Auntie Mame) Dennis
Michael Dennis
Patrick Dennis
Captain Basil Fitz-Hugh
Hermione Gravell-Pitt
Baron (Putzi) von Hodenlohern
Ito
Pegeen Ryan
Reverend Dr. Alfred Shumway
Rosemary Shumway

Auntie Mame (1955)
Dwight Babcock
Beauregard Jackson Pickett (Beau)
  Burnside
Vera Charles
Mame (Auntie Mame) Dennis
Michael Dennis
Patrick Dennis
Pegeen Dennis
Agnes Gooch
Ito
Norah Muldoon

AUGUST DERLETH
(See also Volume II)

Evening in Spring (1941)
Grandfather Adams
Constance (Connie) Estabrook

Margery Estabrook
Stephen (Steve) Grendon
Will and Rose Grendon
Simolean (Sim) Jones
May (Aunt May)

The Shield of the Valiant (1945)
Grandfather Adams
Stephen (Steve) Grendon
Mrs. Janney
Rena (Miss Lolly C., Mouse, Renchen)
  Janney
Simolean (Sim) Jones
Miss Mergan
Father Peitsch
Preston (Pres) Robinson
Birdie Sewall
John Sewall
Kivden (Kiv) Sewall
Joseph (Joe) Stanley

PETER DE VRIES
(See also Volume II)

Comfort Me with Apples (1956)
Frank Carmichael
Pete (The Smoothie) Cheshire
Crystal Chickering
Harry Clammidge
Al Roquefort
Nickie Sherman
Charles (Chick) Swallow
Lila Swallow
Clara Thicknesse

The Mackerel Plaza (1958)
Jack Analysis
Molly Calico
Pippa Calico
George (Fat) Chance
Charlie Comstock
Ida May Mackerel
Reverend Andrew Mackerel
Arthur (Henry, Junior) Meesum
Joseph Meesum
Hester Pedlock
Mike Todarescu
Frank Turnbull
Steven (Steve, Stevie) Turnbull

The Tunnel of Love (1957)
Audrey
Aurora
Hugh Blair
Cornelia Bly

Dick
Mrs. Mash
Terry McBain
Ernest (Putsi) Mills
Augie Poole
Isolde Poole
Miss Terkle

THOMAS DIXON

The Clansman (1905)
Augustus (Gus) Caesar
Ben Cameron
Margaret Cameron
Richard Cameron
Jake
Alexander (Uncle Aleck) Lenoir
Jeannie Campbell Lenoir
Marion Lenoir
Abraham Lincoln
Silas Lynch
Austin (Great Commoner) Stoneman
Elsie Stoneman
Phil Stoneman

The Leopard's Spots (1902)
Flora Camp
Tom Camp
Stuart Dameron
Dick
Mrs. John Durham
Rev. John Durham
Charles (Charlie) Gaston
Nelson (Nelse) Gaston
George Harris
Simon Legree
Everett Lowell
Allan McLeod
Hose Norman
Timothy (Tim) Shelby
Susan Walker
General Daniel Worth
Sallie Worth

E. L. DOCTOROW
(See also Volume II)

Welcome to Hard Times (1960)
Bert Albany
Avery
John Bear
Helga Bergenstrohm
Swede Bergenstrohm
Blue

Mrs. Clement
Fee
Jimmy Fee
Hayden Gillis
Hausenfield
Leo (Dead-Eye) Jenks
Ezra Maple
Isaac Maple
Angus Mcellhenny
Jack Millay
Alf Moffet
Munn
Molly Riordan
Clay (Bad Man) Turner
Zar

IGNATIUS DONNELLY

Caesar's Column (1890)
Frederika Bowers
Nathan Brederhagan
Prince Cabano (Jacob Isaacs)
Christina Jansen (Christina Carlson)
Caesar Lomellini
Maximilian (Arthur Phillips) Petion
Jacob Quincy
Matthew Rudolph
Estella Washington
Gabriel Weltstein
Heinrich Weltstein

JOHN DOS PASSOS

Manhattan Transfer (1953)
George Baldwin
Anna Cohen
Congo
Stan Emery
Joe Harland
Jimmy Herf
Jo-Jo
Nevada Jones
Bud Korpenning
Gus McNiel
Nellie McNiel
James Merivale
Jefferson Merivale
Dutch Robertson
Ellen Thatcher (Elaine, Elena)
Ed Thatcher
Susie Thatcher

   U.S.A. (1946)
   Charley Anderson

Joe Askew
G. H. Barrow
Nat Benton
Doc Bingham
Ben Compton
Gladys Compton
Margo Dowling
Mary French
Tony Garido
George (Ike) Hall
Bill Haywood
Fred Hoff
Eveline Hutchins
Mac
Agnes Mandeville
Frank Mandeville
Dirk McArthur
Fenian Fainy McCreary (Mac)
J. Ward Morehouse
Tim O'Hara
Jose O'Riely
Richard Ellsworth Savage
Maisie Spencer
Gertrude Staple
Don Stevens
Eleanor Stoddard
Annabelle Marie Strang
Emiscah Svenson
Anne Elizabeth Trent (Daughter)
Gladys Wheatley
Janey Williams
Joe Williams

THEODORE DREISER

An American Tragedy (1925)
Hortense Briggs
Sondra Finchley
Asa Griffiths
Clyde (Baker, Clifford Golden, Carl
   Graham, Harry Tenet) Griffiths
Elvira Griffiths
Samuel Griffiths
Roberta (Mrs. Clifford Golden, Mrs.
   Carl Graham, Ruth Howard) Alden
Willard Sparser

The Bulwark (1946)
Benecia Wallin Barnes
Etta Barnes
Hannah and Rufus Barnes
Solon Barnes
Stewart (Stew) Barnes
Victor Bruge

Willard Kane
Volida La Porte
Psyche Tanzer

The Financier (1912)
Edward Malia (Eddie) Butler
Aileen Butler (Ai, Mrs. Montague)
   Cowperwood
Frank Algernon (Dickson, Montague)
   Cowperwood
Henry Worthington Cowperwood
Lillian Semple (Anna Wheeler) Cow-
   perwood
Seneca Davis
Henry A. Mollenhauer
Alfred Semple
Mark Simpson
Harper Steger
George W. Stener
Stephen Wingate

The "Genius" (1915)
Stella Appleton
Christina Channing
Anatole Charles
Suzanne Dale
Margaret (Margy) Duff
Miriam Finch
Ruby (Rube) Kenny
Florence J. (Florrie) White
Angela Wida
Eugene Tennyson (Genie, Henry Kings-
   land) Wida
Angela Blue Witla

Jennie Gerhardt (1911)
George Sylvester Brander
Letty Pace Gerald
Genevieve (Jennie, Mrs. J. G. Stover)
   Gerhardt
William Gerhardt
Archibald Kane
Lester Kane
Letty Pace Gerald Kane
Robert Kane
Wilhelmina (Vesta Stover) Vesta

Sister Carrie (1900)
Bob Ames
Sister Carrie
Charles H. (Charlie) Drouet
Minnie Meeber Hanson
George W. (George Wheeler) Hurstwood
Julia Hurstwood
Caroline (Carrie Madenda, Sister Car-
   rie, Mrs. Wheeler) Meeber
Mr. and Mrs. Vance

The Stoic (1947)
Marigold Shoemaker Brainerd
Hattie (Hattie Starr) Carter
Aileen Butler (Ai, Mrs. Montague)
    Cowperwood
Frank Algernon (Dickson, Montague)
    Cowperwood
Lillian Semple (Anna Wheeler) Cow-
    perwood
Berenice (Bevy, Kathryn Trent) Fleming
Montague Greaves
Philip Henshaw
Jefferson James
Willard Jarkins
Lorna Maris
Gordon (Lord Stane) Roderick
Henry De Soto (de Sota) Sippens
Lord Stane
Bruce Tollifer

The Titan (1914)
Judah Addison
Claudia Carlstadt
Hattie (Hattie Starr) Carter
Aileen Butler (Ai, Mrs. Montague)
    Cowperwood
Frank Algernon (Dickson, Montague)
    Cowperwood
Lillian Semple (Anna Wheeler) Cow-
    perwood
Berenice (Bevy, Kathryn Trent) Fleming
Forbes Gurney
Augustus M. Haguenin
Cecily Haguenin
Caroline Hand
Hosmer Hand
Edwin L. Kaffrath
Patrick (Emerald Pat) Kerrigan
Peter Laughlin
Polk Lynde
General MacDonald
Truman Leslie MacDonald
Antoinette Nowak
Stephanie Platow
Henry De Soto (de Sota) Sippens
Rita Greenough Sohlberg
Harper Steger
Michael (Smiling Mike) Tiernan

ALLEN DRURY

Advise and Consent (1959)
Brigham M. (Brig) Anderson
Celestine Barre

Raoul Barre
Seabright B. (Seab) Cooley
Mrs. Phelps (Dolly) Harrison
Harley M. Hudson
Krishna (K. K.) Khaleel
Orrin Knox
Robert A. (Bob) Leffingwell
Lady Kitty Maudulayne
Lord Claude Maudulayne
Robert Durham (Bob) Munson
The President
Lafe Smith
Vasily Tashikov
Fred Van Ackerman

W. E. B. DU BOIS

Dark Princess (1928)
Mr. Amos
Mrs. Beech
Mr. Cadwalader
Corruthers
Congressman Doolittle
Jimmie Giles
Miss Gillespie
Mr. Graham
Mr. Green
Brother John Jones
Princess Kautilya (Dark Princess, Ma-
    haranee of Bwodpur)
Miguel Perigua
Samuel (Honorable Sammy, Sam,
    Sammy) Scott
Mrs. Therwald
Matthew (George, Mat) Towns
Sara Andrews Towns

The Quest of the Silver Fleece (1911)
Blessed (Bles) Alwyn
Bertie
Colton
Colonel St. John Cresswell
Harry Cresswell
Helen Cresswell
Mary Taylor Cresswell
Edward Easterly
Elspeth
Emma
Mr. Job Grey
Mrs. Grey
Johnson
Jones
Aunt Rachel
Rob

Miss Sarah Smith
Peter Charles Smith
Sam Stillings
Uncle Jim Sykes
John Taylor
Mary Taylor
Tom Teerswell
Mr. Tolliver
Mrs. Vanderpool (née Wells)
Miss Caroline (Carrie) Wynn
Zora

PAUL LAURENCE DUNBAR

The Fanatics (1901)
Nigger Ed (Negro Ed)
Col. Alexander Stewart
Walter Stewart
Raymond (Ray) Stothard
Robert (Black Rider, Bob) Van Doren
Stephen Van Doren
Bradford Waters
Mary Waters

The Love of Landry (1900)
Anna Annesley
Arthur Heathcote
Helen Osborne
John Osborne
Mildred Osborne
Landry Thayer

The Sport of the Gods (1902)
Berry (Be'y) Hamilton
Fannie (Fannie Gibson) Hamilton
Joe Hamilton
Kitty (Kit) Hamilton
Col. Maurice Oakley
Francis (Frank) Oakley

The Uncalled (1898)
Frederick (Fred, Freddie) Brent
Margaret (Mag, Margar't) Brent
Tom Brent
Eliphalet (Brother Hodges, 'Liph,
    'Liphalet) Hodges
Hester Prime
Elizabeth (Lizzie) Simpson
Rev. Mr. Simpson

WALTER D. EDMONDS

The Big Barn (1929)
Daniel (Dan, Dan'l) Harrow
Jacob Turnesa

Chad Hanna (1940)
Bastock
B. D. Bisbee
Caroline Trid Hanna
Chad Hanna
Alonzo Dent (A. D.) Huguenine
Bettina (Bettina Billings) Huguenine
Oscar
Elias Proops
Fred (Signor Rossello) Shepley
Caroline (Carolina) Trid
Ike Wayfish
Albany (Lady Lillian) Yates

Drums along the Mohawk (1936)
Blue Back
Joe Boleo
Adam Helmer
Nicholas Herkimer
Gilbert (Gil) Martin
Magdelana Borst (Lana) Martin
Sarah McKlennar
Nancy Schuyler
John Wolff

Erie Water (1933)
Issachar Bennet
Lester Charley
Harley Falk
Jeremiah (Jerry) Fowler
Mary Goodhill Fowler
Betsey (Ma) Halleck
Caleb Hammil
Dorothy and Robert Melville
Norah Sharon

Rome Haul (1929)
Joseph P. (Gentleman Joe) Calash
Fortune Friendly
Lucy Gurget
Daniel (Dan, Dan'l) Harrow
Sam Henderson
Jotham Klore
Molly Larkins
Solomon Tinkle
Jacob Turnesa
Samson Weaver

EDWARD EGGLESTON

The Circuit Rider (1874)
Brady
Lewis (Marcus Burchard, Lew, Pinkey)
  Goodwin
Morton (Mort) Goodwin

Captain Enoch (Nuck) Lumsden
Hezekiah (Kike) Lumsden
Patty Lumsden
Mr. Magruder
Ann Eliza Meacham
Dr. Morgan
Henrietta (Nattie) Morgan
Colonel Isaiah Wheeler

The Hoosier School-Master (1871)
Henry (Hank) Banta
George H. Bronson
Ralph Hartsook
Martha Hawkins
Squire Hawkins
Walter Johnson
Peter (Pete) Jones
Israel W. (Bud) Means
Jack Means
John Pearson
Granny Sanders
Nancy Sawyer
Peter (Dutchman) Schroeder
Dr. Henry Small
Hannah Thomson
Mrs. Thomson
W. J. (Shocky) Thomson

RALPH ELLISON
(See also Volume II)

Invisible Man (1952)
A. Hebert Bledsoe
Lucius Brockway
Brother Tod Clifton
Brother Hambro
Brother Jack
Norton
Mary Rambo
Ras the Exhorter (Ras the Destroyer)
B. P. (Rine, Rine the Runner) Rinehart
Supercargo
Sybil
Jim Trueblood

JOHN ERSKINE

The Private Life of Helen of Troy (1954)
Adraste
Aegisthus
Agamemnon
Charitas
Clytemnestra
Damastor

Eteoneous
Helen
Hermione
Idomeneus
Menelaos
Orestes
Paris
Pyrrhus
Telemachus

JAMES T. FARRELL

Judgment Day (1935)
Catherine Banahan
Father (Gilly) Gilhooley
Dennis P. (Dinny) Gorman
Frances (Fran, Frances Dowson) Lonigan
Loretta (Fritzie) Lonigan
Mary Lonigan
Patrick J. (Paddy, Pat) Lonigan
William (Bill, Studs) Lonigan
Frank (Weary) Reilley
Phillip (Phil) Rolfe
Lucy Scanlan

Young Lonigan (1932)
Father (Gilly) Gilhooley
Dennis P. (Dinny) Gorman
Paul (Paulie) Haggerty
Frances (Fran, Frances Dowson) Lonigan
Loretta (Fritzie) Lonigan
Mary Lonigan
Patrick J. (Paddy, Pat) Lonigan
William (Bill, Studs) Lonigan
Danny O'Neill
Frank (Weary) Reilley
Lucy Scanlan
Helen Shires

The Young Manhood of Studs Lonigan (1934)
Father (Gilly) Gilhooley
Dennis P. (Dinny) Gorman
Paul (Paulie) Haggerty
Frances (Fran, Frances Dowson) Lonigan
Loretta (Fritzie) Lonigan
Mary Lonigan
Patrick J. (Paddy, Pat) Lonigan
William (Bill, Studs) Lonigan
Danny O'Neill
Frank (Weary) Reilley
Phillip (Phil) Rolfe
Lucy Scanlan
Father Shannon
Helen Shires

HOWARD FAST
(See also Volume II)

Citizen Tom Paine (1943)
Robert Aitken
Richard Bache
Joel Barlow
William Blake
Napoleon Bonaparte
Danton
Nicholas de Bonneville
Benjamin Franklin
General Nathanael Greene
Thomas (Tom) Jefferson
Jordan
Doctor Kearsley
Lafayette
Mary Lambert
Thomas Paine
General Roberdeau
Irene Roberdeau
Jacob Rumpel
Sarah Rumpel
Alec Stivvens
General George Washington

WILLIAM FAULKNER
(See also Volume II)

Absalom, Absalom! (1936)
Charles Bon
Charles Etienne Saint-Valery Bon
Eulalia Bon
Jim Bond
Ellen Coldfield
Goodhue Coldfield
Rosa Coldfield
Quentin Compson (I)
Jason Lycurgus Compson (II)
Jason Lycurgus Compson (III)
Alexander Holston
Ikkemotubbe (Doom)
Milly Jones
Wash Jones
Luster
Shrevlin (Shreve) McCannon
Theophilus (Uncle Buck) McCaslin
Pettibone
Col. John Sartoris
Major de Spain
Clytemnestra (Clytie) Sutpen
Ellen Coldfield Sutpen
Eulalia Bon Sutpen
Henry Sutpen

Judith Sutpen
Thomas Sutpen

As I Lay Dying (1930)
Henry Armstid
Martha (Lula) Armstid
Addie Bundren
Anse Bundren
Cash Bundren
Darl Bundren
Dewey Dell Bundren
Jewel Bundren
Vardaman Bundren
Lafe
Flem Snopes
Suratt
Cora and Vernon Tull
Jody Varner
Will (Uncle Billy) Varner
Whitfield

A Fable (1954)
Philip Manigault Beauchamp
Bidet
Bridesman
Buchwald
Casse-tête
Collyer
Marthe (Magda) Demont
Charles Gragnon
Harry
Jean
Lallemont
Lapin
Gerald David Levine
Luluque
Mannock
Marya
McCudden
Middleton
Morache
Picklock
Piotr (Pierre Bouc, Zsettlani)
Polchek
Smith
Stefan (Corporal)
Tobe Sutterfield
Thorpe

Go Down, Moses (1942)
Henry Beauchamp
Hubert Beauchamp
James Thucydides (Tennie's Jim,
   Thucydus) Beauchamp
Lucas Quintus Carothers McCaslin
   Beauchamp

Molly (Mollie) Beauchamp
Samuel Worsham Beauchamp
Sophonsiba Beauchamp
Tennie Beauchamp
Tomey's Turl Beauchamp
Jason Lycurgus Compson (II)
Carothers (Roth) Edmonds
Carothers McCaslin (Old Cass) Ed-
   monds
Zachary Taylor (Zack) Edmonds
Eunice
Walter Ewell
Sam Fathers
Boon Hogganbeck
Ikkemotubbe (Doom)
Issetibbeha
Will Legate
Lion
Amodeus (Uncle Buddy) McCaslin
Isaac (Ike) McCaslin
Lucius Quintus Carothers (Old
   Carothers) McCaslin
Sophonsiba Beauchamp McCaslin
Theophilus (Uncle Buck) McCaslin
Old Ben
Phoebe (Fibby)
Roscius (Roskus)
Bayard Sartoris (II)
Col. John Sartoris
Major de Spain
Gavin Stevens
Thomas Sutpen
Thucydides
Tomasina (Tomey)
Tomey's Turl
Belle Worsham
Hamp Worsham

The Hamlet (1940)
Henry Armstid
Martha (Lula) Armstid
Odum Bookwright
Major Grumby
Hope (Hub) Hampton (I)
Buck Hipps
Jack (Zack) Houston
Labove
Mrs. Little John
Hoake McCarron
Isaac (Ike) McCaslin
Theophilus (Uncle Buck) McCaslin
Rosa (Granny) Millard
Lucius Quintus Peabody
V. K. Radiff

Giant (1952)
Baldwin (Bawley) Benedict
Jordan (Jordy) Benedict the Fourth
Jordan (Bick) Benedict the Third
Juana Benedict
Leslie Lynnton (Les) Benedict
Luz Benedict (I)
Luz Benedict (II)
Bob (Bobby) Dietz
Jett Rink
Mott (Pinky) Snyth
Vashti Hake (Vash) Snyth

Show Boat (1926)
Steve Baker
Kenneth Cameron
Kim Ravenal Cameron
Elly Chipley (Lenore La Verne)
Julie Dozier
Captain Andy Hawks
Parthenia Ann (Parthy) Hawks
Gaylord Ravenal
Magnolia Hawks Ravenal
Harold (Schultzy) Westbrook

So Big (1924)
Julie Hempel Arnold
Dirk (So Big, Sobig) Dejong
Pervus Dejong
Selina Peake Dejong
August (Aug) Hempel
Dallas O'Mara
Widow Paarlenberg
Simeon Peake
Klaas Pool
Maartje Pool
Roelf Pool
Mattie Schwengauer
Paula Arnold Storm

LAWRENCE FERLINGHETTI

Her (1960)
Andalous (Andy) Raffine

RUDOLPH FISHER

The Conjure-Man Dies (1932)
John Archer
Bubber Brown
Martha Crouch
Samuel (Easley Jones) Crouch
Perry Dart
N'Gana Frimbo
Jinx Jenkins

Easley Jones
N'Ogo
Henry (Pat) Patmore
Aramintha Snead

The Walls of Jericho (1928)
Bubber Brown
Agatha Cramp
Jinx Jenkins
Joshua (Shine) Jones
Fred Merrit
Henry (Pat) Patmore
J. Pennington Potter
Linda (Lindy) Young

VARDIS FISHER

In Tragic Life (1932)
Charley Bridwell
Jed Bridwell
Lela Bridwell
Neloa (Nell) Doole
Diana Hunter
Dock Hunter
Joseph Charles (Joe) Hunter
Mertyl (Mert) Hunter
Neloa Doole Hunter
Prudence Branton Hunter
Vridar Baroledt (Vreed) Hunter
George Albert Turner

No Villain Need Be (1936)
Robert (Bob, David Hawke) Clark
Neloa (Nell) Doole
David Hawke
Harrison (Woolf) Hawke
Diana Hunter
Joseph Charles (Joe) Hunter
Mertyl (Mert) Hunter
Prudence Branton Hunter
Vridar Baroledt (Vreed) Hunter
Athene Marvell
Harrison Woolf

Orphans in Gethsemane (1960)
Jed Bridwell
Robert (Bob, David Hawke) Clark
Neloa (Nell) Doole
David Hawke
Harrison (Woolf) Hawke
Angele Lorelei Lee Hunter
Diana Hunter
Dock Hunter
Joseph Charles (Joe) Hunter
Mertyl (Mert) Hunter

Prudence Branton Hunter
Vridar Baroledt (Vreed) Hunter
George Albert Turner
Harrison Woolf

Passions Spin the Plot (1935)
Neloa (Nell) Doole
Diana Hunter
Joseph Charles (Joe) Hunter
Mertyl (Mert) Hunter
Prudence Branton Hunter
Vridar Baroledt (Vreed) Hunter
A. M. (Forenoon) McClintock

We Are Betrayed (1936)
Neloa (Nell) Doole
Diana Hunter
Joseph Charles (Joe) Hunter
Mertyl (Mert) Hunter
Prudence Branton Hunter
Vridar Baroledt (Vreed) Hunter
Athene Marvell

F. SCOTT FITZGERALD

The Beautiful and Damned (1922)
Joseph Bloeckman (Black)
Richard (Dick) Caramel
Gloria Gilbert
Maury Noble
Adam J. Patch
Anthony Patch
Gloria Gilbert Patch
Dorothy Raycroft

The Great Gatsby (1925)
Jordan Baker
Daisy Fay Buchanan
Tom Buchanan
Nick Carraway
Dan Cody
Jay (James Gatz) Gatsby
Henry C. Gatz
Ewing Klipspringer
Owl Eyes
George B. Wilson
Myrtle Wilson
Meyer Wolfsheim

The Last Tycoon (1941)
Cecilia Brady
Pat Brady
Brimmer
Kathleen Moore
Robinson (Robby)
Manny Schwartz

WILLIAM GADDIS
(See also Volume II)

The Recognition (1955)
Anselm (Arthur, Saint Anselm)
Recktall Brown
Esme
Camilla Gwyon
Esther Gwyon
Reverend Gwyon
Wyatt (Stephan Asche, Stephen)
  Gwyon
Otto (Gordon) Pivner
Frank (J. Yák) Sinisterra
Stanley
Basil Valentine

ZONA GALE

Miss Lulu Bett (1920)
Lulu Bett
Mrs. Bett
Neil Cornish
Diana (Di) Deacon
Dwight Herbert (Bertie) Deacon
Ina Bett (Inie) Deacon
Ninian Deacon
Bobby Larkin

HAMLIN GARLAND

Rose of Dutcher's Coolly (1895)
Carl
John Dutcher
Rose (Rosie) Dutcher
Caroline Harvey
Elbert Harvey
Willis Harvey
Isabel Herrick
Warren Mason
Dr. Sanborn
Owen Taylor
Dr. Joe Thatcher

MARTHA GELLHORN

A Stricken Field (1940)
Lord Balham
Louis Berthold
Mary Douglas
General Labonne
Tom Lambert
Frau Markheim
Peter Reinick
Rita Salus

Wine of Astonishment (1948)
Dorothy (Dotty) Brock
William (Bill) Gaylord
Bert Hammer
Heinrich
Major Gordon Jarvis
Jacob (Jake, Jawn) Levy
Kathe Limpert
Royal (Roy) Lommax
Sergeant-Major Postalozzi
Lieutenant Colonel John Dawson
  (Johnny) Smithers

CAROLINE GILMAN

Recollections of a Housekeeper (1834)
Ma'am Bridge
Nancy
Clarissa Gray (Clara) Packard
Edward Packard
Mrs. Philipson
Polly
Mrs. Sliter
Stockton

Recollections of a Southern Matron (1838)
Anna Allston
Bill Barnwell
Lewis Barnwell
Josep Bates
Charles Duncan
Arthur Marion
Benjamin (Ben) Wilton
Cornelia Wilton
Henry Wilton
Richard (Dick) Wilton

ELLEN GLASGOW

Barren Ground (1925)
Doctor Burch
Bob Ellgood
Geneva Ellgood
James (Jim) Ellgood
Doctor Faraday
Aunt Mehitable Green
Doctor Greylock
Jason Greylock
Mr. Kettledrum
Fluvanna Moody
Dorinda (Dorindy, Dorrie) Oakley
Eudora Abernethy Oakley
Joshua Oakley

Josiah Oakley
Rufus Oakley
John Abner Pedlar
Lena Pedlar
Nathan Pedlar
Rose Emily Milford Pedlar

The Romantic Comedians (1926)
Alberta
Dabney Birdsong
Colonel Bletheram
Angus Blount
Edmonia Honeywell Bredalbane
Ralph Bredalbane
Doctor Buchanan
Annabel Upchurch Honeywell
Judge Gamaliel Bland Honeywell
Amanda Lightfoot
Mrs. Spearman
Annabel Upchurch
Bella Upchurch

The Sheltered Life (1932)
Uncle Abednego
Cora (Mamma) Archbald
Etta (Aunt Etta) Archbald
General David (Grandfather) Archbald
Isabella (Aunt Isabella) Archbald
Jenny Blair Archbald
Delia Barron
Eva Howard Birdsong
George Birdsong
Joseph Crocker
Memoria
Bena Peyton
John Welch

They Stooped to Folly (1929)
Colonel Bletheram
Milly Burden
Amy Paget Dalrymple
Louisa Goddard
Agatha (Aunt Agatha) Littlepage
Curle Littlepage
Duncan Littlepage
Marmaduke Littlepage
Victoria Brooke Littlepage
Virginius Curle Littlepage
Martin Welding
Mary Victoria Littlepage Welding

Vein of Iron (1935)
Minna Bergen
Mr. Black
Ada Fincastle
Grandmother Fincastle
John (Father) Fincastle

Maggie (Aunt Maggie) Fincastle
Mary Evelyn (Mrs. John, Mother) Fin-
    castle
Abigail (Aunt Abigail) Geddy
Ada Fincastle McBride
Mrs. McBride
Ralph McBride
Ranny McBride
Janet Rowan
Dr. Updike
Mrs. Waters
Toby Waters

Virginia (1913)
Miss Priscilla Batte
Mandy
Gabriel Pendleton
Lucy Pendleton
Virginia (Jinny) Pendleton
Belinda Bolingbroke Treadwell
Cyrus Treadwell
Henry (Harry) Treadwell
Oliver Treadwell
Susan Treadwell

SUSAN GLASPELL

Fidelity (1915)
Edith Lawrence Blair
Amy Forrester Franklin
Dr. Deane Franklin
Annie Morris Herman
Cyrus (Cy) Holland
Ruth Holland
Ted Holland
Marion Averley Williams
Stuart Williams

Judd Rankin's Daughter (1945)
Gerald Andrews
Stuart Jackson
Adah Elwood (Cousin Adah) Logan
Joe Logan
Frances Rankin Mitchell
Judson Mitchell
Leonard (Len) Mitchell
Madeleine (Maddie) Mitchell
Judd (Juddie) Rankin
Douglass Reynolds

MICHAEL GOLD

Jews without Money (1930)
Dr. Marcus J. Axelrod
Joey Cohen
Esther Gold

Herman Gold
Katie Gold
Michael (Mikey) Gold
Nigger
Louis One Eye
Reb Samuel
Dr. Isidore Solow

CAROLINE GORDON

Green Centuries (1941)
Francis (Frank) Dawson
Archy Outlaw
Jocasta Dawson (Cassy) Outlaw
Orion (Rion) Outlaw
Elsa (Sarah) Wagner
Jacob Wagner

WILLIAM GOYEN
(See also Volume II)

The House of Breath (1950)
Hattie Clegg
Boy Ganchion
Christy Ganchion
Folner (Follie) Ganchion
Hannah (Granny) Ganchion
Berryben (Ben) Starnes (Ganchion)
Jessy Starnes
Jimbob Starnes
Lauralee (Aunty) Starnes
Malley Ganchion Starnes
Sue Emma (Swimma) Starnes
Walter Warren Starnes
Maidie Starnes Suggs

In a Farther Country (1955)
Sister Angelica
Thwaite Cumberly
Eddie
Chalmers Egstrom
Jack Flanders
Lois Fuchs
Louisa
Thomas Harold MacDougal
Marietta McGee-Chavéz
Oris
Sabino
Father Trask

SHIRLEY ANN GRAU
(See also Volume II)

The Hard Blue Sky (1958)
Julius Arcenaux

Ignatius (Inky) D'Alfonso
Adele Landry
Alistair (Al) Landry
Annie Landry
Henry Livaudais
Pete Livaudais
Mamere Terrebonne

ANNA KATHARINE GREEN

The Leavenworth Case (1878)
Amy Belden
Hannah Chester
Henry Ritchie (Le Roy Robbins)
    Clavering
Thomas Dougherty
Ebenezer Gryce
James Trueman Harwell
Eleanore Leavenworth
Horatio Leavenworth
Mary Leavenworth
Morris (Q)
Everett Raymond

DAVIS GRUBB

The Night of the Hunter (1953)
Bart
Macijah Blake
Clara
Rachel Cooper
Miz Cunningham
Ben Harper
John Harper
Pearl Harper
Willa Harper
Mary
Harry (Preacher) Powell
Ruby
Icey Spoon
Walt Spoon
Uncle Birdie Steptoe

A. B. GUTHRIE

The Big Sky (1947)
Boone (Zeb Calloway) Caudill
Jim Deakins
Jourdonnais
Dick Summers
Teal Eye

The Way West (1949)
Brownie Evans
Lije Evans

Rebecca (Becky) Evans
Henry (Hank) McBee
Mercy McBee
Dick Summers
Tadlock
Joseph Weatherby

NANCY HALE

The Prodigal Women (1942)
Hector Connolly
Betsy Jekyll
Minnie May Jekyll
Minnie May (Maizie) Jekyll
Thomas (Tom) Jekyll
Adèle Macomb
James March
Leda March
Treat March
Lambert Rudd

ALBERT HALPER

Union Square (1933)
Miss Allen
Henry (Hank) Austin
Milly Boardman
Quincy (Boardie) Boardman
Celia Chapman
Natasha and Otto (Vanya) Drollinger
Leon Fisher
Andre Franconi
Pete Garolian
Helen Jackson
Margie
Terence McGuffy
José Morales
James Nicholson
Old Running Water
Jason Wheeler

DASHIELL HAMMETT

The Glass Key (1931)
Ned Beaumont
Bernie Despain
M. J. Farr
Jeff Gardner
Janet Henry
Senator Ralph Bancroft Henry
Taylor Henry
Walter Ivans
Opal Madvig
Paul Madvig

Eloise Matthews
H. K. Matthews
Shad O'Rory
Jack Rumsen
Rusty
Harry Sloss
Whiskey Vassos
Lee Wilshire

The Maltese Falcon (1930)
Iva Archer
Miles Archer
Joel Cairo
Wilmer Cook
Lieutenant Dundy
Mr. Freed
Casper Gutman
Rhea Gutman
Capt. Jacobi
Brigid O'Shaughnessy (Miss Wonderly)
Effie Perine
Tom Polhaus
Sam Spade
Floyd Thursby

Red Harvest (1929)
Helen Albury
Robert Albury
Dinah Brand
Ike (Al Kennedy) Bush
The Continental Op
Charles Proctor Dawn
Dick Foley
Myrtle Jennison
Stanley Lewis
Mickey Linehan
Bob MacSwain
Noonan
Tim Noonan
Pete the Finn
Bill Quint
Dan Rolfe
Yakima Shorty
Oliver Reno Starkey
Max Whisper Thaler
Donald Willsson
Elihu Willsson
Lew Yard

The Thin Man (1934)
Asta
Studsy Burke
Nick Charles
Nora Charles
John Guild
Christian Jorgensen (Sidney Kelterman)

Mimi Jorgensen
Georgia Kelterman
Herbert Macaulay
Shep Morelli
Arthur Nunheim (Albert Norman)
Miriam Nunheim
Harrison Quinn
Julia (Nancy Kane) Wolf
Clyde Wynant
Dorothy Wynant
Gilbert Wynant

MARK HARRIS
(See also Volume II)

Bang the Drum Slowly (1956)
Sidney Jerome (Sid) Goldman
Katie
Patricia Moors
Bruce William Pearson, Jr.
Pop
Herman H. (Dutch) Schnell
Berwyn Phillips (Red) Traphagen
Henry Whittier (Author, Hank) Wiggen
Holly Webster Wiggen
Thurston Printise (Piney) Woods

The Southpaw (1953)
Sidney Jerome (Sid) Goldman
Bradley Lord
Patricia Moors
Michael J. (Mike) Mulrooney
Pop
Herman H. (Dutch) Schnell
Berwyn Phillips (Red) Traphagen
Aaron Webster
Henry Whittier (Author, Hank) Wiggen
Holly Webster (Wiggen)
Samuel (Sad Sam) Yale

A Ticket for a Seamstitch (1957)
Sidney Jerome (Sid) Goldman
Patricia Moors
Herman H. (Dutch) Schnell
Berwyn Phillips (Red) Traphagen
Henry Whittier (Author, Hank) Wiggen
Holly Webster Wiggen
Thurston Printise (Piney) Woods

Wake Up, Stupid (1959)
Clinton W. Blalock
Gabriella Bodeen
Bartholomew Enright
Louis Garafolo
Whizzer Harlow

Richard (Dick, Ricardo) Cantwell
Gran Maestro (Grand Master)
T5 Ronald Jackson
Renata (Contessa, Daughter)
Wes

A Farewell to Arms (1929)
Bartolomeo Aymo
Catherine Barkley
Aldo Bonello
Helen (Fergy) Ferguson
Count Greffi
Frederic Henry
Meyers
Mrs. Meyers
Ettore Moretti
Luigi Piani
Rinaldi
Ralph (Enrico Del Credo, Sim) Simmons
Dr. Valentini
Miss Van Campen

For Whom the Bell Tolls (1940)
Andés
Anselmo
Augustin
Lieutenant Paco Berrendo
Eladio
Fernando (Fernandito)
Comrade General Golz (Hotze)
Captain Rogelio Gomez
Joaquin
Robert (Inglés, Roberto) Jordan
Karkov
Maria
André Marty
Captain Mora
Pablo
Pilar
Primitivo
Rafael
El (Sordo) Santiago

The Old Man and the Sea (1952)
Manolin
Santiago

The Sun Also Rises (1926)
Lady Brett Ashley
Jacob (Jake) Barnes
Michael (Mike) Campbell
Frances Clyne
Robert Cohn
Bill Gorton
Count Mippipopolous
Pedro Romero

To Have and Have Not (1937)
Captain Willie Adams
Frankie
Helen Gordon
Richard (Dick) Gordon
Frederick Harrison
Mr. Johnson
John MacWalsey (McWalsey)
Eddie (Eddy) Marshall
Harry Morgan
Marie Morgan
Roberto
Mr. (Bee-lips) Simmons
Mr. Sing
Albert Tracy
Freddy Wallace
Wesley

GEORGE WYLIE HENDERSON

Jule (1946)
Alex (Uncle Alex)
Bob Benson
Bertha Mae
Rollo Cage
Caroline
Louise (Lou) Davis
Old Douglas
Jeff Gordon
Zell Ingram
Jule (Mr. Man, Schoolboy) Jackson
Jule (Big Jule)
Boykin Keye
Lucius (Dr. Mootry) Kimbell
Ollie (Ollie Miss)
Jake Simmons
Maisie (Maise) Simmons

Ollie Miss (1935)
Alex (Uncle Alex)
Caroline
Della Dole
Jule (Big Jule)
Knute Kelly
Mack MacLeod
Ollie (Ollie Miss)
Slaughter
Willie (Little Willie)

JAMES LEO HERLIHY
(See also Volume II)

All Fall Down (1960)
Bernice (Mrs. W. B.) O'Brien

Echo Malvina O'Brien
Arthur Ramirez
Shirley
Silas Rents His Ox
Annabel Holznagel Williams
Berry-berry Williams
Clinton (Clint, Willy) Williams
Ralph Williams

ROBERT HERRICK

The Memoirs of an American Citizen
(1905)
John Carmichael
Hillary Cox
Henry Iverson Dround
Jane Dround
Sarah Gentles
Reverend Hardman
Edward Harrington
May Rudge Harrington
Will Harrington
Jaffrey (Sloco) Slocum
Edward Van Harrington

JOHN HERSEY

A Bell for Adano (1944)
Sergeant Leonard Borth
Matteo Cacopardo
Errante Gaetano
Zito Giovanni
Major Victor Joppolo
Lieutenant Crofts Livingston
General Marvin
Mayor Nasta
Captain N. Purvis
Giuseppe Ribaudo
Tomasino

The Child Buyer (1960)
Donald R. Broadbent
Sean Cleary
Dr. Frederika Gozar
Wissey Jones
Senator Aaron Mansfield
Charity M. Perrin
Barry Rudd
Maud Purcells (Mrs. Paul Rudd) Rudd
Senator Skypack

The Wall (1950)
Rachel (Little Mother) Apt.
Dolek Berson
Noach Levinson

Rutka Mazur
Henryk Rapaport
Lazar Slonim

DUBOSE HEYWARD

Mamba's Daughters (1929)
George P. Addnson
Lissa Atkinson
Proctor (Proc) Baggart
Gilly (Prince) Bluton
Thomas Broaden
Rev. Thomas Grayson
Hagar (Baxter)
Valerie (Val) Land
Mamba
Maum Netta (Mauma)
Frank North
Charles Raymond
Katherine (Kate) Wentworth
Polly Wentworth
St. Julien de Chatigny (Saint) Wentworth
Rev. Quintus Whaley

Porgy (1925)
Alan Archdale
Bess
Crown
Simon Frasier
Jake
Maria
Peter
Porgy
Robbins
Sportin' Life

LAURA Z. HOBSON

Gentleman's Agreement (1947)
Anne Dettrey
Dave Goldman
Philip (Phil, Schuyler) Green
Tom (Tommy) Green
Belle King
Katherine (Kathy) Lacey
John Minify
Elaine (Estelle Walovsky) Wales

JOHN CLELLON HOLMES

Go (1952)
Albert Ancke
Liza Adler
Bill Agatson

Ben
Bianca
Christine
Will Dennison
Dinah
Estelle
Georgia
Rocco (Little Rock, Little Rock Harmony, Rock) Harmonia
Kathryn (Cousin Angie) Hobbes
Paul (H.) Hobbes
Hart Kennedy
Arthur Ketcham
Margo
Max
May
Gene Pasternak
Ed Schindel
David Stofsky
Janet and Peter Trimble
Daniel (O. B. Haverton, Old Bitch Haverton, Virgin) Verger
John (Jack) Waters
Winnie

The Horn (1958)
Walden Blue
Cleo
Kelcey Crane
Geordie Dickson
Thomas (Colonel, Curn, Curny) Finnley
Billy James Henry
Metro (Met)
Willy (Owlie) Owls
Edgar (Eddie, Horn) Pool
Junius (June, Juny) Priest
Eddie Win(g)field (Wing) Redburn
Mr. Samm

EMERSON HOUGH

The Covered Wagon (1922)
William Hays (Will) Banion
Jim Bridger
Christopher (Kit) Carson
Bill Jackson
Rob't Kelsey
Jed Wingate
Jesse Wingate
Molly Wingate
Molly (Little Molly) Wingate
Samuel Payson (Sam) Woodhull

The Mississippi Bubble (1902)
Mary Connynge

Du Mesne
Lady Catherine (Lady Kitty) Knollys
Catherine Law
John (Beau, Jack, Jean L'as, Jessamy) Law
Will (Guillaume Las) Law
Sir Arthur (Pem) Pembroke
Philippe of Orléans (Duke of Orléans, Grace Philippe)
Teganisoris
Edward (Beau) Wilson

North of 36 (1923)
Alamo
Cinquo, (Sinker) Centavos
Cal Dalhart
Colonel Sandy Griswold
Wild Bill Hickok
Anastasie (Taisie) Lockhart
Joe McCoyne
Daniel (Dan) McMasters
Jim Nabours
Sim Rudabaugh
Sanchez
Del Williams
Yellow Hand

E. W. HOWE

The Story of a Country Town (1883)
Damon Barker
Lyde (Little) Biggs
Clinton Bragg
Agnes Deming
Jo Erring
Goode Shepherd
Mateel Shepherd
John Westlock
Ned Westlock

WILLIAM DEAN HOWELLS

Annie Kilburn (1888)
Oliver Bolton
Pauliny Bolton
Percy Brandreth
Emmeline Gerrish
William B. (Bill) Gerrish
Annie Kilburn
Judge Rufus Kilburn
James Morrell
Mrs. Munger
Idella Peck

Rev. Julius W. Peck
Ellen Putney
Ralph Putney
Winthrop (Win) Putney
Maria Savor
William Savor
George Wilmington
Jack Wilmington
Lyra Goodman Wilmington

A Hazard of New Fortunes (1889)
Angus Beaton
Christine (Chris) and Mela (Mely)
  Dryfoos
Conrad Dryfoos
Jacob Dryfoos
Fulkerson
Alma Leighton
Berthold Lindau
Basil March
Isabel March
Margaret Vance
Woodburn
Miss Woodburn

Indian Summer (1886)
Mrs. Amsden
Effie Bowen
Evalina Ridgely (Lina) Bowen
Theodore Colville
Imogene Graham
Mrs. Graham
Maddalena
Jenny Wheelwright Milbury
Mr. Morton
Paolo
Evalina (Lina) Ridgely
Madame Fanny Uccelli
Rev. Mr. Waters

The Lady of the Aroostook (1879)
Lydia (Lily, Lurella, Lyddy) Blood
Charley Dunham
Mrs. Dunham
Henshaw Erwin
Josephine Erwin
Miss Hibbard
Mr. Hicks
Captain Jenness
Deacon Latham
Maria Latham
Mr. Mason
James Staniford
Thomas
Mr. Watterson

A Modern Instance (1882)
Atherton
Henry Bird
Squire Gaylord
Ezra Ben Halleck
Bartley Hubbard
Marcia Gaylord (Marsh) Hubbard
Kinney
Mrs. Macallister
Hannah Morrison
Willett
Witherby

The Rise of Silas Lapham (1885)
Anna Bellingham Corey
Bromfield Corey
Tom Corey
Bartley Hubbard
Marcia Gaylord (Marsh) Hubbard
Irene Lapham
Penelope (Pen) Lapham
Persis (Pert) Lapham
Silas Lapham
Milton K. Rogers

Their Wedding Journey (1872)
Kitty Ellison
Richard and Fanny Ellison
Basil March
Isabel March

A Traveler from Altruria (1894)
Reuben (Reub) Camp
Homos (Altrurian)
Lumen
Mrs. Makely
Twelvemough

LANGSTON HUGHES

Not Without Laughter (1930)
Buster (Bus)
Madam Fannie Rosalie de Carter
Uncle Dan Givens
Earl James
Sister Sarah Johnson
Willie-Mae Johnson
Jimmy (Jimmie) Lane
Mingo
Mr. Prentiss
Mrs. Reinhart
Mrs. J. J. Rice
James (Sandy) Rodgers (Rogers)
Jimboy Rodgers (Rogers)

Mrs. Annjee (Annjelica Williams)
  Rodgers (Rogers)
Billy Sanderlee
Mrs. Tempy Williams Siles
Maudel Smothers
Sister Whiteside
Aunt Hager Williams
Harriett (Harrietta) Williams
Cudge Windsor
Pansetta Young

EVAN HUNTER

The Blackboard Jungle (1954)
Anne Dadier
Richard (Richie, Rick) Dadier
Josh Edwards
Lois Hammond
Solly Klein
Gregory (Greg) Miller
William Small
Arthur Francis (Artie) West

ZORA NEALE HURSTON

Jonah's Gourd Vine (1934)
Amy Crittenden
Ned Crittenden
Sally Lovelace
Alf Pearson
Hattie Pearson
John Buddy Pearson
Lucy Ann Potts
Hattie Tyson

Moses, Man of the Mountain (1939)
Aaron
Amram
God
Jethro (Ruel)
Jochebed
Joshua
Mentu
Miriam
Moses
Pharaoh
Princess Royal
Ta-Phar
Zipporah

Seraph on the Suwanee (1948)
Alfredo Corregio
Arvay (Arvie) Henson
Hatton Howland
Dessie Kelsey

Joe Kelsey
Angeline Meserve
Earl David Meserve
James Kenneth (Kenny) Meserve
Jim Meserve
Carl Middleton
Larraine (Raine) Henson Middleton

Their Eyes Were Watching God (1937)
Janie Mae Crawford
Logan Killicks
Nanny
Joseph (Jody, Joe) Starks
Phoeby Watson
Vergible (Tea Cake) Woods

JOSEPH HOLT INGRAHAM

Lafitte (1836)
Cudjoe
Count Alphonse (Henri) D'Oyley
Juana
Lafon
Lalittle (Achille)
Gertrude Langueville
Théodore
Constanza Velasquez

SHIRLEY JACKSON
(See also Volume II)

The Haunting of Hill House (1959)
Arthur
Dudley
Mrs. Dudley
Dr. John Montague
Mrs. Montague
Luke Sanderson
Theodora (Theo)
Eleanor (Nell) Vance

HENRY JAMES

The Ambassadors (1903)
John Little Bilham
Maria Gostrey
Chadwick (Chad) Newsome
Mrs. Newsome
Jim Pocock
Mamie Pocock
Sarah (Sally) Newsome Pocock
Lewis Lambert Strether
Jeanne de Vionnet

Mme. Marie de Vionnet
Mr. Waymarsh

The American (1877)
Catherine Bread
Claire de Bellegarde de Cintré
Emmeline de Bellegarde
Henri-Urbain de Bellegarde
Madame Urbain de Bellegarde
Urbain de Bellegarde
Valentin de Bellegarde
Lord Deepmore
Stanislas Kapp
Christopher Newman
Nioche
Noémie Nioche
Mrs. Tom Tristram
Tom Tristram

The Awkward Age (1899)
Fernanda (Nanda) Brookenham
Mrs. Edward (Mrs. Brook) Brookenham
Mrs. Harry (Tishy) Grendon
Duchess Jane
Lady Julia
Mr. Longdon
Mitchy Mitchett
Gustavus (Van) Vanderbank

The Bostonians (1886)
Miss Birdseye
Henry Burrage
Mrs. Burrage
Olive Chancellor
Mrs. Farrinder
Mr. Filer
Mr. Gracie
Adeline Luna
Matthias Pardon
Doctor Mary J. Prance
Basil Ransom
Doctor Selah Tarrant
Mrs. Tarrant
Verena Tarrant

Daisy Miller (1879)
Mrs. Costello
Eugenio
Giovanelli
Annie P. (Daisy) Miller
Mrs. Miller
Randolph Miller
Mrs. Walker
Frederick Forsyth Winterbourne

The Europeans (1878)
Elizabeth (Lizzie) Acton
Mrs. Acton
Robert Acton
Augustine
Azarina
Mr. Brand
Baroness Eugenia-Camilla-Dolores
   Münster
Charlotte Wentworth
Clifford Wentworth
Elizabeth Wentworth
Gertrude Wentworth
William Wentworth
Felix Young

The Golden Bowl (1904)
Prince Amerigo
Col. Robert (Bob) Assingham
Fanny Assingham
Mr. Blint
Lady Castledean
Dotty and Kitty Lutch
Mrs. Noble
Principino
Mrs. Rance
Charlotte Stant
Adam Verver
Maggie (Mag, Princess) Verver

The Portrait of a Lady (1881)
Isabel Archer
Caspar Goodwood
Madame Serena Merle
Gilbert Osmond
Pansy Osmond
Edward (Ned) Rosier
Henrietta C. Stackpole
Daniel Tracy Touchett
Lydia Touchett
Ralph Touchett
Lord Warburton

The Princess Casamassima (1886)
Prince Casamassima
Millicent (Milly) Henning
Lady Aurora Langrish
Christina (Princess Casamassima) Light
Paul Muniment
Eustache Poupin
Lord Frederick Purvis
Amanda (Pinnie) Pynsent
Hyacinth (Hyacinthe Vivier) Robinson
Captain Godfrey Gerald Sholto
Anastasius Vetch
Florentine Vivier

RANDALL JARRELL

SARAH ORNE JEWETT

JOSEPHINE JOHNSON

MARY JOHNSTON

Hagar (1913)
Colonel Argall Ashendyne
Hagar Ashendyne
Medway Ashendyne
Rachel Bolt
Ralph Coltsworth
John Fay
Denny Gayde
Edgar Laydon
Roger Michael

Lewis Rand (1908)
Aaron Burr
Fairfax Cary
Ludwell Cary
Edward Churchill
Jacqueline Churchill
Unity Dandridge
Adam Gaudylock
Thomas Jefferson
Lewis Rand

The Long Roll (1911)
Edward Cary
Fauquier Cary
Judith Jacqueline Cary
Lucy Cary
Richard (Dick, Philip Deaderick) Cleave
Steven (Steve) Dagg
Allan Gold
General Thomas Jonathan (Stonewall) Jackson
Joseph Eggleston Johnston
Maury Stafford

JAMES JONES
(See also Volume II)

From Here to Eternity (1951)
Andy Anderson
Blues Berry
Isaac Nathan Bloom
Chief Choate
Salvatore (Friday, Sal) Clark
Lieutenant Culpepper
Ike Galovitch
Captain Dana E. (Dynamite) Holmes
Karen Holmes
James (Fatso) Judson
Mrs. Gert Kipfer
Angelo Maggio
John J. (Jack) Malloy
Violet Ogure
Robert E. Lee (Prew) Prewitt
Alma (Lorene) Schmidt

Maylon Stark
Milton Anthony (Milt) Warden

The Pistol (1959)
Thomas Burton
Fondriere
Grace
Richard Mast
Musso
O'Brien
Paoli
Pender
Winstock

Some Came Running (1957)
Edith Barclay
Raymond Cole
Wallace French (Wally) Dennis
William Howard Taft ('Bama) Dillert
Doris Frederic
Guinevere (Gwen) French
Robert Ball French
Vic (Old Man) Herschmidt
Clark Hubbard
Agnes Marie Towns Hirsh
David L. (Dave, David Herschmidt) Hirsh
Dawn (Dawnie) Hirsh
Mrs. Elvira Hirsh
Frank Hirsh
Walter Hirsh
Geneve Lowe
Ginnie Moorehead
Jane (Janie) Staley

EDITH SUMMERS KELLEY

Weeds (1923)
Jerry Blackford
Judith Pippinger (Judy) Blackford
Jabez Moorhouse
Annie and Bill Pippinger
Lizzie May and Luella Pippinger
Hat and Luke Wolf

JOHN PENDLETON KENNEDY

Horse-Shoe Robinson (1835)
Walter (Wat, Watty) Adair
Arthur Butler
Cornwallis
James (Peppercorn) Curry
Nancy Dimock
Endymion

Ferguson
Stephen (Steve) Foster
Hugh Habershaw
Innis
Isaac
Henry Lindsay
Mildred Lindsay
Philip Lindsay
Mistress Morrison
Allen Musgrove
Mary Musgrove
David Ramsay
John Ramsay (Ramsey).
Galbraith (Horse-Shoe) Robinson
Christopher Shaw
Captain St. Jermyn (Tyrrel)
Edgar St. Jermyn
Tarleton
Williams

Swallow Barn (1832)
Abe
Ben
Hafen Blok
Mike Brown
Absalom Bulrush
Carey
Chub
Crab
Mammy Diana
Edward Hazard
Ned Hazard
Walter Hazard
Zachary (Zack) Huddlestone
Mark Littleton
Lucy
Francis (Frank) Meriwether
Lucretia Hazard Meriwether
Lucy Meriwether
Philip (Rip) Meriwether
Prudence (Pru) Meriwether
Victorine Meriwether
Harvey Riggs
Miles Rutherford
Scipio
John Smith
Singleton Oglethorpe Swansdown
Tongue
Bel Tracy
Catharine Tracy
Isaac Tracy
Ralph Tracy
Philpot (Philly) Wart
Barbara Winkle

Margery Bellew
Dave Freeland
Felise Freeland
Bob Kendry
Clare Kendry
Gertrude Martin
Brian Redfield
Irene ('Rene) Redfield
Hugh Wentworth

Quicksand (1928)
Dr. Robert Anderson
Helga Crane
Katrina Nilssen Dahl
Poul Dahl
Reverend Mr. Pleasant Green
Anne Grey
Miss Hartley
Jeanette Hayes-Rore
Peter Nilssen
Axel Olsen
James Vayle
Hugh Wentworth

BEIRNE LAY, JR., AND SY BARTLETT

Twelve O'Clock High! (1948)
Jesse Bishop
Joe R. Cobb
Keith Davenport
Ben Gately
Ed Henderson
Don (Doc) Kaiser
Pamela (Pam) Mallory
Sergeant McIllhenny
Patrick (Pat) Pritchard
Frank Savage
Harvey Stovall
Heinz Zimmerman

HARPER LEE

To Kill a Mockingbird (1960)
Aunt Alexandra
Miss Maudie Atkinson
Calpurnia
Miss Stephanie Crawford
Mayella Violet Ewell
Robert E. Lee (Bob) Ewell
Atticus Finch
Jean Louise (Scout) Finch
Jeremy Atticus (Jem) Finch
Charles Baker (Dill) Harris

Miss Rachel Haverford
Arthur (Boo) Radley
Helen Robinson
Thomas (Tom) Robinson
Sheriff Heck Tate

MEYER LEVIN

Compulsion (1956)
Charles Kessler
Jonas Kessler
Martha Kessler
Paulie Kessler
Sid Silver
Judah (Judd) Steiner, Jr.
Judah Steiner, Sr.
Artie (James Singer) Straus
Randolph Straus
Jonathan Wilk

JANET LEWIS

The Wife of Martin Guerre (1941)
Carbon Bareau
Jean Espagnol
Martin Guerre
Monsieur Guerre
Pierre Guerre
Sanxi Guerre
Bertrande (Madame Martin Guerre) de
  Rols
Arnaud (Pansette) du Tilh

SINCLAIR LEWIS

Arrowsmith (1925)
Martin Arrowsmith
Clif Clawson
Angus Duer
Madeline Fox
Professor Max Gottlieb
Dr. Rippleton Holabird
Latham Ireland
Joyce Lanyon
Dr. Oliver Marchand
Ross McGurk
Henry Novak
Fatty Pfaff
Dr. Almus Pickerbaugh
Dean Silva
Gustaf Sondelius
Albert R. (Bert) Tozer
Leora Tozer

Mr. and Mrs. Andrew Jackson Tozer
Clay Tredgold
Dr. A. DeWitt Tubbs
Terry Wickett
Dr. Woestijne

Babbitt (1922)
George F. (Georgie) Babbitt
Katherine (Tinka) Babbitt
Myra Thompson Babbitt
Theodore Roosevelt (Ted) Babbitt
Verona (Rone) Babbitt
Rev. John Jennison Drew
William Washington Eathorne
Kenneth Escott
Stanley Graff
Vergil Gunch
Tanis Judique
Eunice Littlefield
Howard Littlefield
Theresa McGoun
Paul Riesling
Zilla Colbeck (Zil) Riesling
Henry T. Thompson

Cass Timberlane (1945)
Blanche Lebanon Timberlane Boneyard
Rev. Evan Brewster
Avis Criley
Bradd Criley
Dr. Roy Drover
Avis Criley Elderman
Sweeney Fishberg
Lucius Fliegend
Christabel Grau
Tilda Hatter
Mrs. Higbee
Jay Laverick
Rose Timberlane Pennloss
John William Prutt
Eino Roskinen
Cass Timberlane
Virginia Marshland (Jinny) Timberlane

Dodsworth (1929)
Fernande (Nande) Azeredo
Edith Cortright
Brent Dodsworth
Frances Voelker (Fran) Dodsworth
Samuel (Sam, Sammy) Dodsworth
Major Clyde Lockert
Emily Dodsworth McKee
Harry McKee
Count Kurt von Obersdorf
Thomas J. (Tub) Pearson

One Eye
Weeden Scott
Beauty (Pinhead) Smith
White Fang

HENRY WADSWORTH LONGFELLOW

Kavanagh (1849)
Alice Archer
Alfred Churchill
Mary Churchill
Mr. Churchill
Hiram Adolphus Hawkins
Martha Amelia Hawkins
Arthur Kavanagh
Lucy
Sally Manchester
Mr. Pendexter
Cecilia Vaughan
Billy Wilmerdings

ANITA LOOS

But Gentlemen Marry Brunettes (1928)
Charlie Breene
Lorelei Lee
Lester
Frederick Morgan
Dorothy Shaw
Henry Spoffard

Gentlemen Prefer Blondes (1925)
Sir Francis (Piggie) Beekman
Gus Eisman
Gerald Lamson
Lorelei Lee
Gilbertson Montrose
Dorothy Shaw
Henry Spoffard

ANDREW LYTLE

A Name for Evil (1947)
Ellen Brent
Henry Brent
Major Brent

The Velvet Horn (1957)
Captain Joe Cree
Lucius Cree
Beverly Cropleigh
Dickie Cropleigh

Duncan Cropleigh
Jack (Uncle Jack) Cropleigh
Julia Cropleigh
Peter Legrand
Ada Rutter
Ada Belle Rutter
Saul Slowns

ROSS MACDONALD

The Moving Target (1950)
Lew Archer

ELIZABETH MADOX ROBERTS

The Great Meadow (1930)
Diony Hall (Diny) Jarvis
Elvira Jarvis

NORMAN MAILER
(See also Volume II)

Barbary Shore (1951)
Willie Dinsmore
Ed Leroy Hollingsworth
Michael (Mike) Lovett
Lannie Madison
Beverly Guinevere McLeod
William (Bill) McLeod
Monina

The Deer Park (1955)
Charles Francis (Charley) Eitel
Elena Esposito
Marion (Marion O'Faye) Faye
Lulu Meyers
Carlyle (Collie) Munshin
Dorothea O'Faye
Sergius (Gus, Mac, Slim, Spike)
  O'Shaugnessy
Teddy (Mr. T) Pope
Herman (Mr. T) Teppis

The Naked and the Dead (1948)
Sergeant William (Willie) Brown
Staff Sergeant Samuel (Sam) Croft
Major General Edward Cummings
Casimir (Polack) Czienwicz
Major Dalleson
Roy Gallagher
Joey Goldstein
Lieutenant Robert (Bobby) Hearn
Sergeant Julio Martinez
Steve Minetta

Red Valsen
Woodrow Wilson

BERNARD MALAMUD
(See also Volume II)

The Assistant (1957)
Frank Alpine
Helen Bober
Ida Bober
Morris Bober
Nick Fuso
Julius Karp
Louis Karp
Ward Minogue

The Natural (1952)
Bump Baily
Judge Goodwill Banner
Harriet Bird
Pop Fisher
Roy Hobbs
Iris Lemon
Memo Paris
Gus Sands
Sam (Bub) Simpson
Walter (Whammer) Whambold

WILLIAM MARCH

The Bad Seed (1954)
Monica Breedlove
Claude Daigle
Burgess, Claudia, and Octavia Fern
Leroy, Jessup
Christine Penmark
Kenneth Penmark
Rhoda Penmark

JOHN P. MARQUAND

H. M. Pulham, Esquire (1941)
Bo-Jo Brown
Bill King
Marvin Myles
Henry Moulton (Harry, H. M.) Pulham
Cornelia Motford (Kay) Pulham

The Late George Apley (1937)
Catharine Bosworth Apley
Eleanor (El) Apley
George William Apley
John Apley
Thomas Apley
William Apley

Mary Monahan
O'Reilly
Will Willing

Point of No Return (1949)

Roger Blakesley
Malcolm (Malc) Bryant
Anthony (Tony) Burton
Charles (Charley) Gray
John Gray
Nancy (Nance) Gray
Jessica (Jessie) Lovell
Laurence Lovell
Jack (Jackie) Mason

Wickford Point (1939)

Bella (Belle) Brill
Clothilde Brill
Harry Brill
Jim Calder
Patricia (Pat) Leighton
Sarah Seabrooke
Allen Southby
George Stanhope
Joe Stowe
Clothilde Brill Wright

PAULE MARSHALL
(See also Volume II)

Brown Girl, Brownstones (1959)

Deighton Boyce
Ina Boyce
Selina (Deighton Selina) Boyce
Silla (Silla-gal) Boyce
Beryl Challenor
Percy Challenor
Virgie Farnum
Iris Hurley
Maritze
Miss Mary
Suggie (Miss Suggie) Skeete
Clive Springer
Clytie Springer
Miss Thompson
Florrie Trotman

WILLIAM MAXWELL
(See also Volume II)

The Folded Leaf (1945)

Hope Davison
Alfred Delmer
Sally Forbes

Charles (Spud) Latham
Evans Latham
Helen Latham
Mrs. Latham
Lymie Peters
Lymon Peters
Dick Reinhart
William Severance

They Came Like Swallows (1937)

Ethel Blaney
Boyd (B. H.) Hiller
Irene Blaney Hiller
Elizabeth Blaney (Bess) Morison
James B. Morison
Peter (Bunny) Morison
Robert Morison
Clara Morison Paisley
Sophie

Time Will Darken It (1948)

Alice (Alie) Beach
Lucy Beach
Miss Ewing
Martha Hastings
Abbey (Ab) King
Austin King
Martha Hastings King
Nora Potter
Randolph Potter
Reuben S. Potter
Rachel

JULIAN MAYFIELD
(See also Volume II)

The Hit (1957)

Sister Clarisse
Gertrude Cooley
Hubert Cooley
James Lee Cooley
John Lewis

The Long Night (1958)

Frederick (Steely) Brown
Mae Brown
Paul Brown

HORACE McCOY

They Shoot Horses, Don't They? (1935)

Mack Aston
Lillian Bacon
Mattie Barnes

James Bates
Ruby Bates
Gloria Beatty
Vincent (Socks) Donald
Jere Flint
Freddy
Rocky Gravo
Mary Hawley
Mrs. J. Franklin Higby
Kid Kamm
Mrs. Layden
Rosemary Loftus
Vee Lovell
John Maxwell
Jackie Miller
Monk
Pedro Ortega
Rollo Peters
Mario (Giuseppe Lodi) Petrone
Robert Syverten
Geneva Tomblin
Mrs. William Wallace Witcher

CARSON McCULLERS
(See also Volume II)

The Heart Is a Lonely Hunter (1940)

Spiros Antonapoulos
Jake Blount
Alice Brannon
Bartholomew (Biff) Brannon
Benedict Mady Copeland
Grandpapa Copeland
William (Willie) Copeland
Lancy Davis
Highboy
Love Jones
Junebug
Bill Kelly
Etta Kelly
George (Baby-Killer, Bubber) Kelly
Hazel Kelly
Mick Kelly
Ralph Kelly
Wilbur Kelly
Harry Minowitz
Charles Parker
Portia
Simms
John Singer
Baby Wilson
Leroy Wilson
Lucile Wilson

The Member of the Wedding (1946)
Frances (F. Jasmine, Frankie) Addams
Jarvis Addams
Royal Quincy Addams
Berenice Sadie Brown
Honey Camden Brown
Janice Evans
Ludie Freeman
Mary Little John
Barney MacKean
John Henry West
T. T. Williams

Reflections in a Golden Eye (1941)
Anacleto
Firebird
Alison Langdon
Major Morris (The Buffalo) Langdon
Capt. Weldon (Captain Flap-Fanny) Penderton
Leonora (The Lady) Penderton
Susie
Lieutenant Weincheck
Private L. G. (Ellgee) Williams

CLAUDE McKAY

Banjo (1929)
Buchanan Malt (Malty) Avis
Jake Brown
Lincoln Agrippa (Banjo) Daily
Sister Geter
Goosey
Latnah
Lonesome Blue
Raymond (Ray)
Taloufa

Home to Harlem (1928)
Agatha
Billy Biasse
Jake Brown
Miss Lavinia Curdy
Uncle Doc
Felice
Gin-head Susy (Susy)
Zeddy Plummer
Raymond (Ray)
Rose

HERMAN MELVILLE

Billy Budd (1924)
William (Baby, Beauty, Billy) Budd
John (Jemmy Legs) Claggart

The Dankster (Board-Her-in-the-Smoke)
Red Whiskers
Squeak
Edward Fairfax (Starry) Vere

The Confidence-Man (1857)
Black Guinea (Ebony, Guinea)
China Aster
Charlemont
Coonskins
William Cream
Egbert
Thomas (Happy Tom) Fry
Goneril
Francis (Frank) Goodman
James Hall
John Moredock
Charles Arnold (Charlie) Noble
Orchis (Doleful Dumps)
Pitch (Coonskins)
John Ringman
Henry Roberts
John Truman
Mark Winsome

Israel Potter (1855)
Ethan (Ticonderoga) Allen
James (John) Bridges
Benjamin Franklin
George III
Jenny
John Paul Jones
John Millet
Captain Pearson
Benjamin Potter
Israel (Peter Perkins, Yellow-hair) Potter
Sergeant Singles
Horne Tooke
John Woodcock

Mardi (1849)
A
Abrazza
Alanno
Aleema
Almanni
Annatoo
Babbalanja
Bardianni
Bello
Borabolla
Donjalolo (Fonoo)
Hautia
Hello

Hevaneva
Hivohitee
I
Jarl (Skyeman, Viking)
Lombardo
Media
Mohi (Braid-Beard)
Nimni
O
Ohiro-Moldona-Fivona
Oh-Oh
Pani
Peepi
Piko
Samoa
Taji
Uhia
Vee-Vee
Yillah
Yoky
Yoomy (Warbler)

Moby-Dick (1851)
Ahab
Bildad
Bulkington
Daggoo
Elijah
Fedallah
Flask (King-Post)
Ishmael
Father Mapple
Moby-Dick
Peleg
Perth
Pip (Pippin)
Queequeg (Quohog)
Radney
Starbuck
Steelkilt
Stubb
Tashtego (Tash)

Omoo (1847)
Arfretee
Arheetoo
Baltimore
Beauty (Chips)
Bell
Bembo (Mowree)
Bungs
Crash
Guy (Cabin Boy, Paper Jack)
Lem (Hardee-Hardee) Hardy
John Jermin

GRACE METALIOUS

OSCAR MICHEAUX

Jack Stewart
Isaac Syfe

HENRY MILLER

Black Spring (1936)
Albert F. Bendix
H. W. Bendix
R. N. Bendix
Jabberwhorl (Jab) Cronstadt
Katya Cronstadt
George (Crazy George) Denton
Paul Dexter
Brother Eaton
Baron Carola von Eschenbach
Katya
Julian Legree
Paul Melia
Tante Melia
Henry V. (Joe) Miller
Tom Moffatt
Patsy O'Dowd
Ferd Pattee
Rob Ramsay
George Sandusky
Bill Woodruff

Tropic of Cancer (1934)
Bessie
Boris
Borowski
Carl (Joe)
Mlle. Claude
Collins
Jabberwhorl (Jab) Cronstadt
Elsa
Fillmore
Germaine
Ginette
Kepi
Kruger
Macha
Marlowe
Henry V. (Joe) Miller
Moldorf
Mona
Nanantatee
Olga
Walter Pach
Peckover
Serge
Mark Swift
Sylvester
Tania
Van Norden (Joe)

Tropic of Capricorn (1939)
Mr. Burns
Carnashan
Aunt Caroline
Mr. Clancy
Clausen
Curley
Father
Francie
Georgiana
Joe (Joey) Gerhardt
Griswold
Roy Hamilton
Pauline Janowski
Hymie Laubscher
Jack Lawson
MacGregor
McGovern
Henry V. (Joe) Miller
Monica
Gottlieb Leberecht Müller
Uncle Ned
Lola Niessen
O'Mara
O'Rourke
Dr. Rausch
Schuldig
Lottie Somers
Aunt Tillie
Valeska
Grover Watrous

MARGARET MITCHELL

Gone with the Wind (1936)
Eugenie Victoria Butler
Rhett K. Butler
Charles (Charlie) Hamilton
Sarah Jane Hamilton
Frank Kennedy
Mammy
Gerald O'Hara
Scarlett O'Hara
Emmie Slattery
Belle Watling
Jonas Wilkerson
Ashley Wilkes
India Wilkes
Melanie Hamilton (Miss Melly) Wilkes

WRIGHT MORRIS
(See also Volume II)

Ceremony in Lone Tree (1960)
Gordon Boyd

Daughter (Mrs. Boyd)
W. B. Jennings
Calvin McKee
Eileen McKee
Gordon Scanlon McKee
Lois Scanlon McKee
Walter McKee
Bud Momeyer
Etoile Momeyer
Lee Roy Momeyer
Maxine Momeyer
Charlie Munger
Tom Scanlon

The Field of Vision (1956)
Gordon Boyd
Paul (Paula) Kahler
Dr. Leopold Lehmann
Gordon Scanlon McKee
Lois Scanlon McKee
Walter McKee
Timothy Scanlon
Tom Scanlon

The Home Place (1948)
Eddie Cahow
Bobby (Will) Muncy
Clara Cropper Muncy
Clyde Muncy
Harry (Uncle Harry) Muncy
Peg Muncy
Peggy Muncy
Grace Osborn

The Huge Season (1954)
Lou Garbo (Left Bank, Montana Lou)
   Baker
Peter Nielson Foley
Charles Gans Lawrence
Richard Olney (Dickie) Livingston III
Jesse Lasky Proctor

Love among the Cannibals (1957)
Eva (Greek) Baum
Billie Harcum
Earl Horter
Dr. Leggett
Irwin K. (Mac) Macgregor

Man and Boy (1951)
Myrtle Dinardo
Private Lipido
Violet Ames (Mother) Ormsby
Virgil Ormsby
Warren K. Ormsby

The Man Who Was There (1945)
Eddie Cahow
Grandmother Herkimer
Roger Burns Lakeside
Augusta (Gussie) Newcomb
Grace Osborn
Christian Reagan
Peter Spavic
Agee Ward

My Uncle Dudley (1942)
Cupid
Furman
Kid
The Kid
Dudley (Uncle Dudley) Osborn

The Works of Love (1952)
Mickey Ahearn
Ethel Bassett
Willy Brady, Jr.
Will Jennings Brady
Gertrude Long
T. P. Luckett
Opal Mason
Manny Plinski

The World in the Attic (1949)
Angeline (Angie) Hibbard
Bud Hibbard
Caddy Hibbard
Clinton Hibbard
Nellie Hibbard
Ralph Moody
Bobby (Will) Muncy
Clyde Muncy
Peg Muncy
Peggy Muncy
Grace Osborn
Lemuel T. Purdy
Tom Scanlon

MARY NOAILLES MURFREE

In the Clouds (1886)
Ben Doaks
Gustus Thomas (Gus, Tom) Griff
James (Jeemes, Jim) Gwinnan
Bob Harshaw
Reuben (Mink) Lorey
Peter (Pete) Rood
Alethea Ann (Lethe) Sayles
Tad

In the "Stranger People's" Country (1891)
Ephraim (Eph) Guthrie
Felix (Fee) Guthrie
Letitia (Litt) Pettingill
Leonard (Len) Rhodes
Shattuck
Adelaide Yates
Stephen (Steve) Yates

The Prophet of the Great Smoky Mountains (1885)
Dorinda (Wrindy) Cayce
John Cayce
Gid Fletcher
Micajah ('Cajah) Green
Hiram (Hi) Kelsey
Rick Tyler

VLADIMIR NABOKOV (See also Volume II)

Bend Sinister (1947)
Dr. Alexander
President Azureus
Linda (Lin) Bachofen
Mariette (Mariechen) Bachofen
Mr. Ember
Professor Hedron
David Krug
Olga Krug
Professor Adam (Adamka, Adam the Ninth, Mugakrad, Gumakrad) Krug
Maximov
Anna Petrovna Maximov
Paduk (Toad, Leader)
Fradrik Skotoma
Toad

Lolita (1955)
Mona Dahl
Jean Farlow
John Farlow
Gaston Godin
Dolores (Dolly, Lo, Lolita) Haze
Charlotte Becker Haze Humbert
Humbert (Edgar H. Humbert, Hummy) Humbert
Annabel Leigh
Clare (Cue) Quilty
John Ray, Jr.
Rita
Richard (Dick) F. Schiller

Pnin (1957)
Betty Bliss
Laurence G. Clements
Jack Cockerell
Herman Hagen
Alexandr Petrovich (Al Cook) Kukolnikov
Susan Marshall (Susanna Karlovna) Kukolnikov
Timofey (Timosha) Pavlovich Pnin
Margaret Thayer
Roy Thayer
Dr. Elizaveta (Lise, Liza) Innokentievna Bogolepov Pnin Wind
Dr. Eric Wind
Victor Wind

The Real Life of Sebastian Knight (1941)
Clare Bishop
Mr. Goodman
Sebastian Knight
Virginia Knight
Alexis Pan
Helen Pratt
Nina (Madame Lecerf, Ninka) Toorovetz de Rechnoy
P. G. Sheldon
Mr. Silbermann
Doctor Alexander Alexandrovich Starov
V

HOWARD NEMEROV

The Homecoming Game (1957)
Arthur Barber
Raymond (Ray) Blent
Lou Da Silva
Mr. Giardineri
Coach Hardy
President Harmon Nagel
Dr. Charles Osman
Herman Sayre
Lily Sayre
Leon Solomon

JOSEFINA NIGGLI

Mexican Village (1945)
Alejandro Castillo
Joaquin Castillo
Maria de las Garzas
Pepe Gonzales
Tia Magdalena

Anita O'Malley
Porfirio
Rubén
Andrés Treviño
Chela Villareal
Robert (Bob, Roberto Ortega Menéndez y Castillo) Webster

Step Down, Elder Brother (1947)
Márgara Bárcenas
Mateo Chapa
Agapito Vásquez de Anda
Brunhilda Vásquez de Anda
Domingo Vázquez de Anda
Lucio (Uncle Lucio) Vázquez de Anda
Ricardo (Cardito) Vázquez de Anda
Sofia Vázquez de Anda

ANAÏS NIN
(See also Volume II)

Children of the Albatross (1947)
Lillian Beye
Djuna
Donald
Faustin the Zombie
Jay
Lawrence
Matilda
Michael
Paul
Uncle Philip
Sabina

The Four-Chambered Heart (1950)
Djuna
Jay
Paul
Rango
Sabina
Zora

Ladders to Fire (1946)
Adele
Lillian Beye
Djuna
Gerard
Jay
Larry
Lillian
Nanny
Paul
Sabina

A Spy in the House of Love (1954)
Alan

Cold Cuts
Djuna
Donald
Jay
John
The Lie Detector
Mambo
Philip
Sabina

CHARLES NORDHOFF AND
JAMES NORMAN HALL

Botany Bay (1941)
Moll Cudlip
Robert Fleming
Nat Garth
Bella Goodwin
Dan Goodwin
Nellie Garth Goodwin
Ned Inching
Phoebe Thynne Oakley
Tom Oakley
Arthur Phillip
Nicholas (Nick) Sabb
Timothy Sabb
Hugh Tallant
Sally Munro Tallant
Mortimer Thynne

The Hurricane (1936)
Ah Fong
Arai
Fakahau
Farani
Hitia
Kauka
Kersaint
Eugene de Laage
Germaine Anne Marie de Laage
Mako
Marama
Marunga
Mata
Terangi Matokia
George Nagle
Father Paul
Mama Rua
Tavi
Tita
Vernier

Men against the Sea (1934)
William Bligh
William Cole

William Elphinstone
John Fryer
Thomas Hayward
Thomas Ledward
David Nelson
John Norton
William Purcell
Sparling
Robert Tinkler

Mutiny on the Bounty (1934)
John Adams
Joseph Banks
William Bligh
Roger Byam
Fletcher Christian
William Cole
Edward Edwards
William Elphinstone
John Fryer
Hamilton
Thomas Hayward
Hitihiti
Thomas Ledward
Maimiti
William McCoy
David Nelson
John Norton
William Purcell
Matthew Quintal
Alexander (John Adams, Alex, Reckless Jack) Smith
Tehani
Robert Tinkler
John Williams
Edward (Ned) Young

Pitcairn's Island (1934)
John Adams
Fletcher Christian
Maimiti
William McCoy
Minarii
Alexander (John Adams, Alex, Reckless Jack) Smith
John Williams
Edward (Ned) Young

FRANK NORRIS

Blix (1899)
Travis (Blix) Bessemer
Blix
Captain Jack
Condé (Condy, Conny) Rivers

A Man's Woman (1900)
Adler
Ward Bennett
Richard (Dick) Ferriss
Lloyd Searight

McTeague (1899)
Miss Baker
Cribbens (Crib)
Old Grannis
Maria Miranda Macapa
McTeague (Mac)
Trina Sieppe McTeague
Marcus (Mark) Schouler
August Sieppe
Trina Sieppe
Zerkow

Moran of the Lady Letty (1898)
Josie (Jo) Herrick
Captain Hodgson
Captain Alvinza Kitchell
Moran Sternersen
Ross Wilbur

The Octopus (1901)
Annixter
S. Behrman
Caraher
Mr. Cedarquist
Mrs. Cedarquist
Delaney
Annie Derrick
Harran Derrick
Lyman Derrick
Magnus Derrick
Dyke
Genslinger
Minna Hooven
Mrs. Hooven
Osterman
Presley (Pres)
Father Sarria
Vanamee

The Pit (1903)
Sheldon Corthell
Landry Court
Carrie Cressler
Charles (Charlie) Cressler
Laura Dearborn
Page Dearborn
Samuel (Sam) Gretry
Curtis (J.) Jadwin
Laura Dearborn Jadwin
Emily (Aunt Wess) Wessels

Vandover and the Brute (1914)
Flossie
Charlie Geary
Dolliver (Dolly) Haight
Turner Ravis
Vandover (Van)
Ida Wade

FLANNERY O'CONNOR

The Violent Bear It Away (1960)
Bernice Bishop
Lucette Carmody
Mr. Meeks
Buford Munson
Bishop Rayber
Mr. Rayber
Francis Marion Tarwater
Mason Tarwater

Wise Blood (1952)
Enoch Emery
Mrs. Flood
Asa Hawks
Sabbath Lily Hawks
Mrs. Wally Bee Hitchcock
Onnie Jay Holy
Solace Layfield
Hazel (Haze) Motes
Hoover (Onnie Jay Holy) Shoats
Mrs. Leora Watts

JOHN O'HARA
(See also Volume II)

Appointment in Samarra (1934)
Caroline Walker English
Julian McHenry English
William Dilworth English
Luther Leroy (Lute) Fliegler
Al (Ed Charney, Anthony Joseph
  Murascho) Grecco
Helene Holman
Anthony Joseph (Tony) Murascho
Harry Reilly
Mrs. Waldo Wallace Walker

Butterfield 8 (1935)
Major Boam
Eddie Brunner
Norma Day
Emily Liggett
Weston Liggett
Jimmy Malloy
Joab Ellery Reddington

William Robespierre Vandamm
Gloria Wandrous
Mrs. (née Vandamm) Wandrous

From the Terrace (1958)
Martha Johnson Eaton
Mary St. John Eaton
Natalie Benziger Eaton
Raymond Alfred Eaton
Rowland Eaton
Samuel Eaton
James Duncan MacHardie
Alexander Thornton (Lex) Porter
Jack Tom Smith
Mary St. John
Frederick (Fritz) Thornton

A Rage to Live (1949)
Roger Bannon
Brock Caldwell
Julian McHenry English
Catherine (Katty) Grenville
John (Jack) Hollister
Charlie Jay
Betty Martindale
Paul Reichelderfer
Connie Schoffstal
Grace Brock Caldwell Tate
Sidney Tate

Ten North Frederick (1955)
Charley Bongiorno
Joseph Benjamin (Joby, Joe) Chapin, Jr.
Ann Chapin
Benjamin Chapin
Charlotte Hofman Chapin
Edith Stokes Chapin
Joseph (Joe) Benjamin Chapin
Kate Drummond
William Dilworth English
Harry Jackson
Arthur McHenry
Mike Slattery
Peg Slattery

JAMES KIRKE PAULDING

The Dutchman's Fireside (1831)
Mr. Aubineau
Mrs. Aubineau
Colonel Barry Fitzgerald Macartney
  Gilfillan
Sir William Johnson
Dame (Aunt) Naunqe
Paskingoe (One-eye)

Miss Morissa (1955)
Calamity Jane (Martha Jane Canary)
Martha Jane Canary
Edward Elton (Ed, Eddie) Ellis
Morissa Kirk Ellis
Morissa (Issy) Kirk
Tris Polk
Jack (Jackie) Thomas
Robin Thomas

Slogum House (1937)
René Dumur
Butch (Butch Braley) Haber
Leo Platt
Annette and Cellie Slogum
Cash Slogum
Fannie Slogum
Haber (Hab) Slogum
Libby Slogum
Regula Haber (Gulla) Slogum
Ruedy Slogum
Ward Slogum

The Tom-Walker (1947)
Senator Boyd Potter
Milton (Milty) Stone (I)
Milton Stone (II)
Hazel Stone
Hiram Stone
Lucinda Martin (Lucie) Stone
Martin (Marty) Stone
Penny Turner Stone
Sarah Stone

GEORGE SANTAYANA

The Last Puritan (1935)
Harriet Bumstead Alden
Nathaniel Alden
Oliver Alden
Peter Alden
Dr. Bumstead
Austin Darnley
James (Jim, Lord Jim) Darnley
Rose Darnley
Letitia (Letty) Lamb
Caroline (Mrs. Erasmus Van de Weyer)
  Van de Weyer
Edith Van de Weyer
Mario (Marius, Vanny) Van de Weyer
Caleb Wetherbee

HELEN HOOVEN SANTMYER
(See also Volume II)

Herbs and Apples (1925)
Jack Devlin
Frances Higginson
Alice McIntyre
Sue
Derrick Thornton
Dr. Dick Thornton
Reneltje (Nell) Thornton
Edith (Edy) Townsend
Madeleine Van Leyden

WILLIAM SAROYAN

The Human Comedy (1943)
Mr. Byfield
Lionel Cabot
Tobey George
August (Auggie) Gottlieb
William (Willie) Grogan
Miss Hicks
Homer Macauley
Marcus Macauley
Ulysses Macauley
Rosalie Simms-Peabody
Thomas (Tom) Spangler

BUDD SCHULBERG

The Disenchanted (1950)
Professor Connolly
Professor Crofts
Douglas Halliday
Jere Halliday
Manley Halliday
Al Harper
Ann (Annie) Loeb
Victor Milgrim
Hank Osborne
Shep Stearns
Jere Wilder-Halliday

What Makes Sammy Run (1941)
Julian Blumberg
Sheik Dugan
Sidney Fineman
Sammy (Sammele Glickstein) Glick
Israel Glickstein
Rosalie Goldbaum
Harrington
Laurette Harrington
Al Manheim
Billie Rand

Larry Ross
Rita Royce
Kit Sargent

GEORGE S. SCHUYLER

Black No More (1931)
Dr. Shakespeare Agamemnon Beard
Madame Sisseretta (Mrs. Sari Blandine)
  Blandish
Bunny Brown
Dr. Samuel Buggerie
Dr. Junius (Doc) Crookman
Max (Matthew [Matt] Fisher, William
  Small) Disher
Helen Givens
Reverend Henry Givens
Rev. Alex McPhule
William Small

CATHARINE MARIA
SEDGWICK

Hope Leslie (1827)
Everell Fletcher
William Fletcher
Sir Philip Gardiner
Faith Leslie
Hope Leslie
Magawisca
Mononotto
Nelema
Oneco
Rosa (Roslin)

MARY LEE SETTLE
(See also Volume II)

Know Nothing (1960)
Stuart Brandon
Lawyer Carver
Maury Carver
Preston Carver
Johnny Catlett
Leah Cutwright Catlett
Lewis Catlett
Mamie Brandon Catlett
Peregrine Lacey Catlett
Sara Lacey (Mrs. Lewis Catlett) Catlett
Cuffee
Jim
Brandon Kregg
Crawford (Fish) Kregg
Dr. Noah Kregg

Lacey Kregg
Melinda Lacey Kregg
Brandon Lacey
Peregrine Lacey
Sally Crawford (Sal) Lacey
Sally Sawyer (Sal) Lacey
Loady
Maria (Rachel)
Reverend Charles McAndrews
Gideon McKarkle
Jeb McKarkle
Mr. McKarkle
Minna
Napoleon
Dan Neill
James Peregrine Neill
Lydia Catlett (Liddy, Liddy Boo) Neill
Annie Brandon O'Neill (Neill)
Big Dan O'Neill (Neill)
Little Dan O'Neill.
Molly O'Neill
Teeny O'Neill
Rachel
Squire (Josiah Devotion, Charles Ed-
  ward Montmorency) Raglan
Wellington Smythe
Cornelius Stuart
Lancelot Stuart
Telemachus
Tig
Toey

O Beulah Land (1956)
Baucis
Backwater Brandon
Ralph Burton
Mother Carver
Ezekiel (Zeke) Catlett
Hannah Bridewell Catlett
Jeremiah Catlett
Rebecca (Becky) Catlett
Sara Lacey (Mrs. Ezekiel Catlett) Catlett
Ensign Peregrine Cockburn
Mister Corey
Brandon Crawford
Doggo Cutwright
Jacob Cutwright
Maggie Cutwright
Christopher Gist
Colonel (Sir Peter) Halkett
Azariah Keel
Moses Kregg
Sanhedron Kregg
Jonathan (Johnny) Lacey

Montague Crawford Bacchus Lacey
Peregrine Lacey
Spotteswood Lewis
Joe Little Fox
Lydia (Lyddy)
Mrs. Stacy McAndrews Mason
Ben McKarkle
Solomon McKarkle
Tad McKarkle
Herr Mittelburger
Mary Martha O'Keefe
Captain Robert Orme
Jarcey Pentacost
Philemon
Tom Preston
Squire (Josiah Devotion, Charles Ed-
  ward Montmorency) Raglan
Taylor Sawyer
Shirley
Jamie Stuart
Ted
Witcikti (the Bald Eagle)

IRWIN SHAW

The Young Lions (1948)
Noah Ackerman
Johnny Burnecker
Christian Diestl
Gretchen Hardenburg
Lieutenant Hardenburg
Hope Plowman
Laura Whitacre
Michael Whitacre

CHARLES M. SHELDON

In His Steps (1899)
Rev. Calvin Bruce
Jasper Chase
President Donald Marsh
Henry Maxwell
Edward Norman
Virginia Page
Rollin Page
Alexander Powers
Felicia Sterling
Rachel Winslow

HERBERT SIMMONS
(See also Volume II)

Corner Boy (1957)
Jake Adams

Old Man Adams
Armenta Arnez
Edna Arnez
Henry Arnez
Booker
Georgia Garveli
Pop Garveli
Maxine Goldstein
Evelyn Keyes
Monk
Red
Scar
Spider
Kenny Watson

WILLIAM GILMORE SIMMS

The Partisan (1835)
Moll (Mother Blonay) Blonay
Ned (Goggle) Blonay
John (Jack) Davis
General Johann De Kalb
Frampton
Lancelot (Lance) Frampton
Captain Amos Gaskens
General Horatio Gates
Walter (Wat) Griffin
Sergeant Hastings
Bella (Bell) Humphries
Richard (Old Dick) Humphries
William (Bill) Humphries
Francis (The Swamp Fox) Marion
Dr. Oakenburg (Oakenburger)
Lieutenant Porgy
Major Proctor
Emily Singleton
Major Robert Singleton
Katharine (Kate) Walton
Colonel Richard Walton

Woodcraft (1854)
Mrs. Eveleigh
Lancelot (Lance) Frampton
Mrs. Griffin
Sergeant Millhouse
M'Kewn
Lieutenant Porgy
Tom

UPTON SINCLAIR

Boston (1928)
Elizabeth Thornwell (Betty) Alvin
Governor Alvin Tufts (Allie) Fuller

TERRY SOUTHERN AND MASON HOFFENBERG (AS MAXWELL KENTON)

Candy (1958)
Candy Christian
Jack Christian
Livia Christian
Sidney Christian
Doctor J. Dunlap
Emmanuel
Grindle
Howard Johns
Doctor Irving Krankeit
Professor Mephesto
Irving (Krankeit) Semite
Pete Uspy

E.D.E.N. SOUTHWORTH

The Hidden Hand (1888)
Clara Day
Black Donald
Nancy Grewell
Herbert Greyson
Capitola (Cap Black) Le Noir
Craven Le Noir
Gabriel Le Noir
Old Hurricane
Marah Rocke
Traverse Rocke
Major Ira (Old Hurricane) Warfield

ELIZABETH SPENCER

The Light in the Piazza (1960)
Clara Johnson
Margaret Johnson
Noel Johnson
Fabrizio Naccarelli
Signor Naccarelli

The Voice at the Back Door (1956)
Beckwith Dozer
Willard Follansbee
Bud Grantham
Duncan (Happy) Harper
Louise Taylor (Tinker) Harper
Jason Hunt
Marjorie Angeline (Cissy) Hunt
Nan Hunt
Marcia Mae Hunt O'Donell
Bella Grantham Tallant
Jimmy Tallant
Kerney Woolbright

JEAN STAFFORD

Boston Adventure (1944)
Countess Berthe von Happel
Nathan Kadish
Hermann Marburg
Ivan Marburg
Shura Korf Marburg
Sonia (Sonie) Marburg
Hopestill (Hope) Mather
Dr. Philip (Perly) McAllister
Harry Morgan
Miss Lucy Pride
Kakosan Yoshida

WALLACE STEGNER
(See also Volume II)

The Big Rock Candy Mountain (1943)
Jud Chain
Miss Hammond
Heimie Hellman
Bruce Mason
Chester (Chet) Mason
Elsa Norgaard Mason
Harry G. (Bo) Mason
Laura Mason
George Nelson
Kristin Norgaard Nelson
Elaine Nesbitt
Karl Norgaard
Nels Norgaard
Sarah Norgaard

JOHN STEINBECK
(See also Volume II)

Cannery Row (1945)
Horace Abbeville
Alfred (Alfy)
Lee Chong
Doc
Eddie
Dora Flood
Frankie
Mack
William

East of Eden (1952)
Abra Bacon
Samuel (Sam) Hamilton
Will Hamilton
Lee (Ching Chong)
Adam Trask
Aron (Aaron) Trask

Caleb (Cal) Trask
Cathy Ames (Catherine Amesbury, Kate) Trask
Charles Trask

The Grapes of Wrath (1939)
Jim Casy
Muley Graves
Al Joad
John (Uncle John) Joad
Ma Joad
Noah Joad
Tom (Pa) Joad (I)
Tom (Tommy) Joad (II)
Connie Rivers
Rose of Sharon (Rosasharn) Joad Rivers

In Dubious Battle (1936)
Alfred (Al) Anderson
Doc Burton
Dick
Joy
London
McLeod (Mac)
Jim Nolan

Of Mice and Men (1937)
Candy
Crooks
Curley
George Milton
Slim
Lennie Small

The Pearl (1947)
Coyotito
Juan Tomás
Juana
Kino

Tortilla Flat (1935)
Jesus Maria Corcoran
Danny
Pilon
Pirate
Big Joe Portagee
Pablo Sanchez

The Wayward Bus (1947)
Edward (Ed, Kit, Pimples) Carson
Alice Chicoy
Juan Chicoy
Ernest Horton
Louie
Norma
Camille Oaks
Bernice Pritchard

Elliott Pritchard
Mildred Pritchard
Mr. Van Brunt

DONALD OGDEN STEWART

Mr. and Mrs. Haddock Abroad (1924)
Harriet N. Q. (Hattie) Haddock
Mildred Haddock
William P. (Will) Haddock

HARRIET BEECHER STOWE

Dred (1856)
Frederic Augustus Carson
Anne Clayton
Edward Clayton
Judge Clayton
John Cripps
Sue Seymour (Suse) Cripps
Dred
Harry Gordon
John Gordon
Lisette Gordon
Nina Gordon
Thomas (Tom) Gordon
Aunt Katy
Milly
Louisa (Aunt Loo) Nesbit
Old Hundred (John)
Tiff (Old Tiff) Peyton
Frank Russel
Cora Gordon Stewart
Tomtit (Thomas)
Dred Vesey

Uncle Tom's Cabin (1852)
Senator and Mrs. Bird
Cassy (Miss Cassy)
Aunt Chloe
Emmeline
Dan Haley
Rachel Halliday
Eliza Harris
George Harris
Harry Harris
Simon Legree
Tom Loker
Mammy
Augustine St. Clare
Evangeline (Little Eva) St. Clare
Henrique St. Clare
Mammy St. Clare
Marie St. Clare

Ophelia St. Clare
George Shelby
Topsy (Tops)
Uncle Tom

T. S. STRIBLING

The Forge (1926)
Cyrus U. (Beeky) Beekman
Alexander (Alex) BeShears
Ponny BeShears
Marcia (Marsh) Vaiden
Drusilla Lacefield (Dru) Crowninshield
Emory Crowninshield
John Handback
A. Gray Lacefield
Caruthers Lacefield
Bill Leatherwood
Lump Mowbray
Bennie Mulry
Augustus (Gus) Vaiden
Cassandra Vaiden
Gracie (Gracie Beekman, Gracie Dill,
   Gracie Light) Vaiden
Jimmie Vaiden
Laura Vaiden
Marcia (Marsh) Vaiden
Miltiades (Milt) Vaiden
Polycarp (Carp) Vaiden

The Store (1932)
Cyrus U. (Beeky) Beekman
Alexander (Alex) BeShears
Ponny BeShears
Alex Cady
Jeremiah Catlin
Jerry Catlin the Second
Drusilla Lacefield (Dru) Crowninshield
John Handback
Lucius Handback
A. Gray Lacefield
Landers
Mayhew
Lump Mowbray
Terry O'Shawn
James (Jaky) Sandusky
Pammy Lee Sparkman
Alberta Sydna Crowninshield Vaiden
Augustus (Gus) Vaiden
Cassandra Vaiden
Gracie (Gracie Beekman, Gracie Dill,
   Gracie Light) Vaiden
Lucy Lacefield Vaiden
Marcia (Marsh) Vaiden

Miltiades (Milt) Vaiden
Toussaint Vaiden

Teeftallow (1926)
Tug Beavers
A. M. Belshue
Roxie Biggers
Blackman (Big Bertha of Heaven)
Peck Bradley
Ditmas
Adelaide (Addy) Jones
David (Railroad) Jones
Perry Northcutt
Zed Parrum
James Sandage
Buckingham Sharp
Nessie Sutton
Abner (Ab) Teeftallow

Unfinished Cathedral (1934)
Jefferson Ashton
Jim Blankenship
William Yancey Bodine
Eph Cady
Jerry Catlin the Second
Drusilla Lacefield (Dru) Crowninshield
Lucius Handback
James Vaiden Hodige
Red McLaughlin
Ludus Meggs
Junior Petman
Marvin Petman
J. Adlee Petrie
Phineas Delfase Ponniman
Willie Rutledge
James (Jaky) Sandusky
Sinton
Pammy Lee Sparkman
Aurelia Swartout
Alberta Sydna Crowninshield Vaiden
Gracie (Gracie Beekman, Gracie Dill,
   Gracie Light) Vaiden
Marsan Vaiden
Miltiades (Milt) Vaiden

JESSE STUART

Taps for Private Tussie (1943)
George Rayburn
Arimithy (Grandma) Tussie
Ben Tussie
George Tussie
Kim Tussie
Mott Tussie
Press (Grandpa) Tussie

Sid Tussie
Vittie Tussie

WILLIAM STYRON
(See also Volume II)

Lie Down in Darkness (1951)
Dolly Bonner
Carey Carr
Daddy Faith
Helen Peyton Loftis
Maudie (Maudie-poo) Loftis
Milton (Bunny, Cap'n Milton, Milt)
  Loftis
Peyton Loftis
Ella Swan

The Long March (1956)
Lieutenant Jack Culver
Corporal Hobbs
Major Billy Lawrence
Captain Al Mannix
Sergeant O'Leary
Colonel (Old Rocky) Templeton

Set This House on Fire (1960)
Celia Flagg
Mason Flagg
Cass Kinsolving
Poppy Kinsolving
Rosemarie de Laframboise
Peter Charles Leverett
Luigi Migliore
Francesca Ricci
Michele Ricci

BOOTH TARKINGTON

Alice Adams (1921)
Alice (Lady Alicia, Alys Tuttle) Adams
Mrs. Adams
Virgil (Virg) Adams
Walter (Wallie) Adams
J. A. Lamb
Mildred Palmer
Arthur Rusell

The Magnificent Ambersons (1918)
George Amberson
Isabel Amberson
Major Amberson
Fanny Minafer
George Amberson (Georgie) Minafer
Isabel Amberson Minafer
Wilbur Minafer

Eugene Morgan
Lucy Morgan

Penrod (1914)
Georgie (The Little Gentleman) Bassett
Roderick Magsworth (Roddy) Bitts,
  Junior
Rupe (Rupie) Collins
Della
Duke
Herman
Marjorie Jones
Mitchell (Mitchy-Mitch) Jones
Kinosling
Maurice Levy
Queenie
Amy (Baby) Rennsdale
Henry Passloe Schofield
Margaret Passloe Schofield
Mrs. Schofield
Penrod (George B. Jashber) Schofield
Miss Mary (Cornelia) Spence
Verman
Robert (Bob) Williams
Samuel (Sam) Williams

Penrod and Sam (1916)
Georgie (The Little Gentleman) Bassett
Roderick Magsworth (Roddy) Bitts,
  Junior
Della
Duke
Herman
Marjorie Jones
Maurice Levy
Amy (Baby) Rennsdale
Henry Passloe Schofield
Margaret Passloe Schofield
Mrs. Schofield
Penrod (George B. Jashber) Schofield
Miss Mary (Cornelia) Spence
Verman
Robert (Bob) Williams
Samuel (Sam) Williams

Penrod Jashber (1929)
Georgie (The Little Gentleman) Bassett
Roderick Magsworth (Roddy) Bitts,
  Junior
Herbert Hamilton Dade
Della
Duke
Herman
Marjorie Jones
Maurice Levy

Amy (Baby) Rennsdale
Henry Passloe Schofield
Margaret Passloe Schofield
Mrs. Schofield
Penrod (George B. Jashber) Schofield
Miss Mary (Cornelia) Spence
Verman
Robert (Bob) Williams
Samuel (Sam) Williams

Seventeen (1916)
Freddie Banks
Wallace Banks
Jane (Little Jane) Baxter
Mrs. Baxter
William Sylvanus (Silly Bill) Baxter
Miss Boke
Joe Bullitt
Clematis (Clem)
George Crooper
Flopit
Genesis
Mr. Genesis
Mary Randolph (Rannie) Kirsted
May Parcher
Mr. Parcher
Miss Lola Pratt
Johnnie Watson

ALLEN TATE

The Fathers (1938)
Lacy Gore Buchan
Major Lewis Buchan
Semmens (Brother Semmens) Buchan
John Langton
George (Brother George) Posey
Jane Posey
Aunt Jane Anne Posey
Susan Buchan (Susie) Posey
Yellow Jim (Yaller Jim)

WALLACE THURMAN

The Blacker the Berry (1929)
Alva
Mrs. Blake
Bobbie
Billy Bocksfuss
Braxton
Benson Brown
Jasper Crane
Tony Crews
Geraldine

Grace Giles
Goat-Boy
Anise Hamilton
Uncle Joe
John
Gwendolyn Johnson
Campbell Kitchen
Maria Lightfoot
Samuel Lightfoot
Alma Martin
Hazel Mason
Jane Lightfoot Morgan
Jim Morgan
Uncle Joe Morgan
Clere Sloane
Arline Strange
Weldon Taylor

JEAN TOOMER

Cane (1923)
Avey
King Barlo
Becky
Tom (Big Boy) Burwell
Carma
Esther Crane
Dorris
Bona Hale
Fred Halsey
Samuel Hanby
Paul Johnson
Karintha
Louisa
Fernie Mae (Fern) Rosen
Bob Stone
Ralph Kabnis

ALBION W. TOURGEE

Bricks without Straw (1880)
Mollie Ainslie
Oscar Ainslie
Colonel Potem (Potestatem Dedimus
   Smith) Desmit
Lorency Desmit
Lucy Ellison
Washington Goodspeed
Colonel Walter Greer
Eliab Hill
Jordan Jackson
Berry Lawson
Sally Ann Lawson
Casaubon Le Moyne

Hesden Le Moyne
Hester Richards Le Moyne
Hildreth Le Moyne
Julia Lomax Le Moyne
Hetty Lomax
Lorency
Lugena
Nimbus (George Nimbus, Nimbus
   Desmit, Nimbus Ware)
Theron Pardee
James (Black Jim) Richards
James (Red Jim) Richards
Peter Smith
Granville Sykes
Jay Timlow
Silas Ware

A Fool's Errand (1879)
Andy
Jayhu (Jehu) Brown
John Burleson
Alice E. Coleman
Claris Coleman
Exum Davis
Thomas Denton
Mr. Eyebright
George D. Garnett (Garnet)
Louisa Garnett (Garnet)
Dr. Gates
General Marion Gurney
Melville Gurney
Nat Haskell
Jerry (Uncle Jerry) Hunt
Jesse Hyman
Squire Nathaniel Hyman
Theophilus Jones
Ralph Kirkwood
Bob Martin
David Nelson
Colonel Nathan Rhenn
Tommy Sanderson
Thomas (Tom) Savage
Comfort (Fool) Servosse
Lily (Lil) Servosse
Metta Ward Servosse
Colonel Marcus Thompson
Colonel Ezekiel (Zeke) Vaughn
John Walters

B. TRAVEN

The Treasure of the Sierra Madre (1935)
Curtin (Curtis, Curty)
Dobbs (Dobby)

Joaquin Escalona
Howard (Howy)
Robert W. Lacaud
Pat McCormick
Miguel

ROBERT TRAVER

Anatomy of a Murder (1958)
Max Battisfore
Paul (Polly) Biegler
Claude Dancer
Julian Durgo
Gregory W. Harcourt
Sulo Kangas
Mr. Lemon
Mitch Lodwick
Sonny Loftus
Maida
Frederic (Manny) Manion
Laura Manion
Parnell Emmett Joseph (Parn) McCarthy
Duane (Duke) Miller
Alphonse (Al) Paquette
Mary Pilant
Barney Quill
Harlan Weaver

LIONEL TRILLING

The Middle of the Journey (1947)
Duck Caldwell
Emily Caldwell
Susan Caldwell
Arthur Croom
Nancy (Nan) Croom
Miss Debry
Alwin Folger
Eunice (Eunie) Folger
Mrs. Folger
Elizabeth (E. F.) Fuess
Dr. Graf
Mr. Gurney
John Laskell
Gifford (Giff) Maxim
Nerissa Paine
Kermit Simpson

DALTON TRUMBO

Johnny Got His Gun (1939)
Kareen Birkman
Mike Birkman
Joe Bonham

MARK TWAIN. See SAMUEL LANGHORNE CLEMENS

JOHN UPDIKE
(See also Volume II)

The Poorhouse Fair (1959)
Walter Andrews
Dr. Angelo
Stephen Conner
Tommy Franklin
Grace
Billy Gregg
August Hay
Elizabeth Heinemann
John F. (Hookie) Hook
Mary (Bessie) Jamiesson
Mrs. Johnson
Fred Kegerise
Buddy Lee
George R. Lucas
Martha (Marty) Lucas
Mendelssohn
Amelia (Amy) Mortis
Ted

Rabbit, Run (1960)
Earl Angstrom
Harry (Rabbit) Angstrom (*See also* Volume II)
Janice (Jan) Springer Angstrom (See also Volume II)
Mary Angstrom
Miriam (Mim) Angstrom
Nelson Frederick Angstrom (See also Volume II)
Rebecca June Angstrom
Jack Eccles
Lucy Eccles
Fritz Kruppenbach
Ruth Leonard
Mrs. Horace Smith
Frederick (Fred) Springer
Rebecca Springer
Charlie Stavros
Marty Tothero

LEON URIS
(See also Volume II)

Battle Cry (1953)
Cyril Brown
Daniel (Danny) Forrester
Joseph (Joe, Spanish) Gomez

Mortimer (Mort, Speedy, Tex) Gray
Andrew (Andy) Hookans
Samuel (Sam) Huxley
Lamont Quincy (L. Q.) Jones
Jake Levin
Shining Lighttower
Mac
Patricia (Pat) Rogers
Max Shapiro
Constantine (Connie, Ski) Zvonski

Exodus (1957)
David Ben Ami
Akiva Ben Canaan
Ari Ben Canaan
Barak Ben Canaan
Jordana Ben Canaan
Karen Hansen Clement
Katherine (Kitty) Fremont
Dov Landau
Ernest Lieberman
Mark Parker
Bruce Sutherland
Joab Yarkoni

Mila 18 (1960)
Andrei Androfski
Alexander (Alex) Brandel
Wolf Brandel
Deborah Androfski Bronski
Paul Bronski
Rachael Bronski
Horst von Epp
Franz Koenig
Christopher (Chris) de Monti (De Monti)
Gabriela (Gaby) Rak
Rudolph Schreiker
Tommy Thompson

KURT VONNEGUT
(See also Volume II)

Player Piano (1952)
Bud Calhoun
Katharine Finch
Edward Francis (Ed) Finnerty
Elmo C. Hacketts, Jr.
Edgar Rice Burroughs Hagstrohm
Doctor Ewing J. Halyard
Reverend James J. Lasher
Anita Proteus
Paul Proteus
Shah of Bratpuhr
Lawson Shepherd

The Sirens of Titan (1959)
Boaz
Chrono
Malachi (Space Wanderer, Unk) Constant
Bobby Denton
Kazak
Beatrice (Bea) Rumfoord
Winston Niles Rumfoord
Salo (Old Salo)
Stony Stevenson

LEW WALLACE

Ben-Hur: A Tale of the Christ (1880)
Quintus Arrius
Balthasar
Judah Ben-Hur
Tirzah Ben-Hur
Esther
(the Generous) Sheik Ilderim
Iras
Messala
Simonides

SUSAN WARNER

The Wide, Wide World (1852)
Ellen Chauncey
Fortune Emerson
Alice Humphreys
John Humphreys
Mr. Humphreys
Mr. Lindsay
Mrs. Lindsay
George Marshman
Mr. Marshman
Captain Morgan Montgomery
Ellen (Ellie) Montgomery
Mrs. Montgomery
Abraham Van Brunt
Fortune Emerson Van Brunt
Mrs. Vawse
Nancy Vawse

ROBERT PENN WARREN

All the King's Men (1946)
Ellis (Scholarly Attorney) Burden
Jack (Jackie, Jackie-Bird, Jackie-Boy) Burden
Sadie Burke
Tiny Duffy
Judge Montague M. (Monty) Irwin

Gummy Larson
Mortimer Lonzo Littlepaugh
Cass Mastern.
Hugh Miller
Adam Stanton
Anne Stanton
Governor Stanton
Lucy Stark
Tom Stark
Willie (Cousin Willie, Boss, Governor)
  Stark
Sugar-Boy (Roger/Robert O'Sheean)
Annabelle Puckett (Mrs. Duncan) Trice

At Heaven's Gate (1943)
Gerald (Bull's-eye, Jerry) Calhoun
Bogan Murdock
Sue Murdock
Private Milt Porsum
Slim Sarrett
Jason (Sweetie) Sweetwater
Ashby Porsum Wyndham

Band of Angels (1955)
Hamish (Old Man Bond, 'Sieur 'Amsh,
  Alec Hinks, Captain Strike-down-
  then-make-the-Palaver) Bond
Lieutenant Oliver Cromwell Jones
Mrs. Herman (Miss Idell, Mrs. Morgan
  Morton, Mrs. Seth Parton) Muller
Seth Parton
Charles de Marigny Prieur-Denis
Rau-Ru (the k'la, Lieutenant Oliver
  Cromwell Jones)
Tobias Sears
Aaron Pendleton Starr
Amantha (Manty, Mrs. Tobias Sears)
  Starr

The Cave (1959)
Jo-Lea Bingham
Timothy Bingham
Celia Hornby (Baby, Ceeley, Doll-Baby,
  Honey-Baby) Harrick
Jasper (Big Bubba) Harrick
John T. (Jack, Jumping Jack, Ole Jack)
  Harrick
Jebb Holloway
Nicholas (Nick, Pappy the Greek) Pa-
  padoupalous
Isaac (Ikey) Sumpter
Reverend MacCarland (Brother
  Sumpter, Ole Mac) Sumpter

Night Rider (1939)
Professor Ball

Bill Christian
Lucille (Sukie) Christian
Doctor (Mac) MacDonald
May Cox Munn
Percy (Barclay, Perse) Munn
Willie (Man-with-hair-white-like-
  wind-on-water) Proudfit
Benton Todd
Captain Todd
Senator Edmund Tolliver
Harris (Bunk) Trevelyan

World Enough and Time (1950)
Wilkie Barron
Jeremiah (Jerry, William K. Grierson)
  Beaumont
Rachel Jordan Beaumont
Colonel Cassius (Old Cass) Fort
Gran Boz (La Grand' Bosse, Louis
  Caddo, Louis Cadeau, Ole Big Hump)
Morton Marcher
Percival Skrogg

JEROME WEIDMAN

I Can Get It for You Wholesale (1937)
Theodore (Teddy) Ast
Meyer Babushkin
Harry (Heshalle, Heshie) Bogen
Mrs. Bogen
Mrs. Heimowitz
Tootsie Maltz
Martha Mills
Maurice (Mr. P.) Pulvermacher
Ruthie (Ruthalle) Rivkin

What's in It for Me? (1938)
Theodore (Teddy) Ast
Harry (Heshalle, Heshie) Bogen
Mrs. Bogen
Mrs. Heimowitz
Murray Heimowitz
Martha Mills
Leonard (Lenny) Nissem
Ruthie (Ruthalle) Rivkin
Kermit Terkel
Hrant Yazdabian

EUDORA WELTY
(See also Volume II)

Delta Wedding (1946)
Battle (Fire-eater) Fairchild
Dabney (Miss Dab) Fairchild
Ellen Dabney Fairchild

George Fairchild
India Primrose Fairchild
Jim Allen Fairchild
Maureen Fairchild
Primrose Fairchild
Roberta Reid (Robbie) Fairchild
Roy Fairchild
Shelley Fairchild
Troy Flavin
Maureen Fairchild (Great-Aunt Mac)
  Laws
Mary Lamar Mackey
Laura McRaven
Shannon Fairchild (Great-Aunt Shan-
  non) Miles
Parthenia (Partheny)
Dunstan Rondo
Roxie

The Ponder Heart (1954)
DeYancey Clanahan
Tip Clanahan
Narciss
Bonnie Dee Peacock Ponder
Daniel Ponder
Edna Earle Ponder
Sam Ponder
Teacake (Miss Teacake) Sistrunk Magee
  Ponder
Mr. Springer

The Robber Bridegroom (1942)
Mike Fink
Goat
Little Harp
Jamie Lockhart
Rosamond Musgrove Lockhart
Amalie Musgrove
Clement Musgrove
Salome Thomas Musgrove

JESSAMYN WEST
(See also Volume II)

Cress Delahanty (1953)
Miss Iris (Aunt Iris) Bird
Inez Dresden Charlesbois
Luther Charlesbois
Frank (Frankie, Mark) Cornelius
Joyce Cornelius
Avis Davis
Mavis Davis
Bernadine (Nedra) Deevers
Crescent (Cress, Cressy) Delahanty
Gertrude Delahanty

The Old Maid (1924)
Lanning Halsey
Sillerton Jackson
Charlotte (Chatty) Lovell
Clementina Lovell
Henry van der Luyden
Louisa Dagonet van der Luyden
Catherine Spicer (Mrs. Manson Mingott) Mingott
Clementina (Teeny, Tina) Lovell Ralston
Delia Lovell Ralston
James (Jim) Ralston
Joseph (Joe) Ralston
Clement (Clem) Spender

The Reef (1912)
Madame de Chantelle
George Darrow
Anna Leath
Effie Leath
Fraser Leath
Owen Leath
Mrs. Murrett
Adelaide Painter
Sophy Viner

Summer (1917)
Annabel Balch
Lucius Harney
Miss Hatchard
Ally Hawes
Julia Hawes
Liff Hyatt
Mary Hyatt
Verena Marsh
Dr. Merkle
Mr. Miles
Charity Royall
Lawyer Royall

WILLIAM ALLEN WHITE

A Certain Rich Man (1909)
Jane Mason Barclay
Jeanette Barclay
John (Johnnie) Barclay
Elijah Westlake (Lige) Bemis
Adrian Pericles Brownwell
Molly Culpepper Brownwell
Martin (Mart) Culpepper
Robert (Bob) Hendricks
Watts McHurdie
Neal Dow Ward

In the Heart of a Fool (1918)
Amos Adams
Grant Adams
Kenyon Adams
Mary Sands Adams
Henry Fenn
Violet Mauling Hogan
Margaret (Duchess of Müller, Mag, Maggie) Müller
Bedelia Satterthwaite Nesbit
James Nesbit
Nathan Perry
Laura Nesbit Van Dorn
Lila Van Dorn
Thomas (Tom) Van Dorn

BRAND WHITLOCK

J. Hardin & Son (1923)
Billie Dyer
Malcolm Dyer
Winona (Winifred, Winnie) Dyer
J. (Joshua) Hardin
Paul Hardin
Winona Dyer Hardin
Matilda (Mat)
Hosea Ortman
Smoke
Clyde Sturrock
Evelyn Walling
Josiah West

THORNTON WILDER
(See also Volume II)

The Bridge of San Luis Rey (1927)
Captain Alvarado
Doña Clara
Esteban
Don Jaime
Bother Juniper
Mañuel
Doña Clara de Montemayor
Doña Maria (Marquesa de Montemayor) de Montemayor
Pepita
Camila (Micaela Villegas) Perichole
Madre Maria del Pilar
Uncle Pio
Don Andrés de Ribera
Don Jaime de Ribera

The Cabala (1926)
Mme. Agoropoulos

Madame Anna Bernstein
James Blair
Léry Bogard
Julia (Donna Julia) d'Aquilanera
Leda Matilda Colonna, La Duchessa d'Aquilanera
Marcantonio d'Aquilanera
Princess Alix d'Espoli
Elizabeth Grier
Mademoiselle Marie-Astrése-Luce de Morfontaine
Ottima
Frederick Perkins
Mrs. Roy
Samuele (Samuelino)
Cardinal Vaini

Heaven's My Destination (1934)
Bat
Reverend Doctor James Bigelow
Doremus (Reme) Blodgett
George Marvin (George Busch, James Bush, Jim) Brush
George Burkin
Judge Darwin Carberry
Judge Leonidas Corey
Mississipi Corey
Marcella L. (Queenie) Craven
Mrs. Crofut
Mrs. Efrim
Louie
Elizabeth Martin
Herbert (Herb) Martin
Jessie Mayhew
Mrs. Margie (Marge) McCoy
Mrs. Ella McManus
Father Pasziewski
Dick Roberts
Lottie Weyerhauser
Roberta Weyerhauser

The Ides of March (1948)
Marc Antony
Marcus Junius Brutus
Gaius Julius Caesar
Calpurnia
Gaius Valerius Catullus
Cicero
Cleopatra
Cytheris
Julia Marcia
Cornelius Nepos
Octavius
Asinius Pollio
Pompeia

Porcia
Clodia (Claudilla, Mousie) Pulcher
Publius Clodius Pulcher
Servila
Lucius Mamilius Turrinus

The Woman of Andros (1930)
Apraxine
Argo
Chremes
Chrysis
Glycerium
Mysis
Niceratus
Pamphilus
Philocles
Philumena
Simo
Sostrata

TENNESSEE WILLIAMS (See also Volume II)

The Roman Spring of Mrs. Stone (1950)
Meg Bishop
Contessa
Signora Coogan
Al Cook
Fabio
Paolo
Renato
Mrs. Karen (Miss Priss Pet) Stone
Thomas J. (Tom) Stone
Mrs.Jamison Walker

EDMUND WILSON

I Thought of Daisy (1929)
Hugo Bamman
Pete Bird
Rita Cavanagh
Daisy Meissner Coleman
Ray Coleman
H. M. Grosbeake
Bobby McIlvaine
Lawrence (Larry) Mickler

Memoirs of Hecate County (1946)
Si Banks
Wilbur Flick
Jo Gates
Flagler Haynes
Clarence Latouche
Anna Lenihan (Lenihanova)
Imogen Loomis

Warren Milholland
Asa M. Stryker
Ellen Terhune

HARRIET WILSON

Our Nig (1859)
Aunt Abby (Nab)
Alfrado (Frado, Nig)
James Bellmont
Jane Bellmont
Jenny Bellmont
John Bellmont
John (Jack) Bellmont
Lewis Bellmont
Mary Bellmont
Mrs. Bellmont
Susan Bellmont
Mrs. Capon
Pete Greene
Mrs. Hale
Mrs. Hoggs
Jim
Miss March
George Means
Mrs. Moore
Henry Reed
Samuel
Seth Shipley
Mag Smith
Margaretta Thorn

HARRY LEON WILSON

Merton of the Movies (1922)
Jeff Baird
Amos G. Gashwiler
Merton (Clifford Armytage) Gill
Sarah Nevada (Flips) Montague

Ruggles of Red Gap (1915)
Effie (Mrs. Effie, Mrs. Senator James
    Knox Floud) Floud
Egbert G. Floud
Mrs. Judson
Kate Kenner
Marmaduke (Colonel Ruggles) Ruggles
George Augustus Vane-Basingwell
Nevil (Earl of Brinstead) Vane-Basingwell

KATHLEEN WINSOR

Forever Amber (1944)
Almsbury
Lady Emily Almsbury

Amber
Nan Britton
Buckingham
Lady (Corinna) Carlton
Lord (Bruce) Carlton
Castlemaine
Queen Catherine (Infanta Catherine of
    Portugal)
Luke Channell
Charles II
Clarendon
Edward Hyde, Earl of Clarendon
Bess Columbine
Danforth
Samuel Dangerfield
Michael Godfrey
Nell (Nelly) Gwynne
Anne Hyde
Black Jack Mallard
Minette
Capt. Rex Morgan
Edmund Mortimer (Radclyffe)
Mother Red-Cap
Barbara Palmer, Lady Castlemaine
John Randolph, Earl of Almsbury
Ravenspur
Amber St. Clare (Mrs. Luke Channell;
    Mrs. Samuel Dangerfield, Mrs. Ed-
    mund Mortimer, Countess of Rad-
    clyffe, Mrs. Gerald Stanhope,
    Countess of Danforth, and Duchess of
    Ravenspur)
Gerald Stanhope, Earl of Danforth and
    Duke of Ravenspur
Steenie
Frances Stewart
Charles Stuart (Charles II)
James (Jamie) Stuart, Duke of York
Henrietta Anne (Minette) Stuart
George Villiers, Duke of Buckingham

OWEN WISTER

The Virginian (1902)
Judge Henry
Shorty
Steve
Trampas
Virginian
Mary Stark (Molly) Wood

THOMAS WOLFE

The Hills Beyond (1941)
Hugh Fortescue

Edward Joyner
Emily Drumgoole Joyner
Gustavus Adolphus (Dolph, Silk) Joyner
Robert Joyner
Theodore Joyner
William (Bear) Joyner
Zachariah (Zack) Joyner
George Josiah (Monk, Monkus, Paul)
    Webber
John Webber

Look Homeward, Angel (1929)
Benjamin (Ben) Harrison Gant
Eliza E. Pentland Gant
Eugene Gant
Oliver Gant
George Graves
Laura James
Margaret Leonard
Hugh McGuire
Harry Tugman

Of Time and the River (1935)
Ann
Elinor
Benjamin (Ben) Harrison Gant
Eliza E. Pentland Gant
Eugene Gant
James Graves Hatcher
Hugh McGuire
Bascom Pentland
Francis Starwick
Robert Weaver

The Web and the Rock (1939)
Gerald (Jerry) Alsop
Nebraska (Bras) Crane
Esther Jack
Frederick (Fritz) Jack
Mag Joyner
Mark Joyner
Maw Joyner
James Heyward (Jim) Randolph
Randy Shepperton
George Josiah (Monk, Monkus, Paul)
    Webber
John Webber

You Can't Go Home Again (1940)
Nebraska (Bras) Crane
Foxhall (Fox) Edwards
Esther Jack
Frederick (Fritz) Jack
Mag Joyner
Mark Joyner
Maw Joyner

Else von Kohler
Lloyd McHarg
Randy Shepperton
George Josiah (Monk, Monkus, Paul)
    Webber

CONSTANCE FENIMORE WOOLSON

For the Major (1883)
Senator Godfrey Ashley
Madam Marion More Morris Carroll
Sara Carroll
Scar Carroll
Major Scarborough Carroll
Louis Eugene (Julian Morris) Dupont
Mrs. Greer
Frederick Owen
Corinna Rendlesham

HERMAN WOUK
(See also Volume II)

The Caine Mutiny (1951)
Captain Blakely
Lieutenant Commander Jack Challee
Ensign Farrington
Walter Feather
Lieutenant Barney Greenwald
Roland Keefer
Thomas (Tom) Keefer
Edwin (Ed, Eddy, Keggsy) Keggs
Mrs. Keith
Willis Seward (Keither, Willie) Keith
Lieutenant Stephen (Steve) Maryk
Ensign Paynter
Lieutenant Commander Philip Francis
    Queeg
Stilwell
Captain de Vriess
May (Marie Minotti) Wynn

Marjorie Morningstar (1955)
Noel (Saul Ehrmann) Airman
George Drobes
Michael (Mike) Eden
Billy Ehrmann
Saul Ehrmann
Samson-Aaron (The Uncle) Feder
Guy Flamm
Sandy Goldstone
Maxwell Greech
Lou Michaelson
Arnold Morgenstern

Marjorie (Marjorie Morningstar) Mor-
    genstern
Rose Kupperberg Morgenstern
Seth Morgenstern
Geoffrey Quill
Sam Rothmore
Milton (Milt) Schwartz
Monica Ehrmann Sigelman
Walter (Wally) Wronken
Marsha Zelenko

RICHARD WRIGHT
(See also Volume II)

The Long Dream (1958)
James (Jim) Bowers
Fats Brown
Dr. Bruce (Doc)
Gerald (Chief) Cantley
Gladys
Zeke (Zeki-O) Jordan
Gloria Mason
Harvey McWilliams
Sam (Sammy-O)
Chris Sims
Emma (Mama) Tucker
Rex (Fish, Fishbelly, Fishy-O) Tucker
Tyree (Papa) Tucker

Native Son (1940)
Mr. Britten
David A. Buckley
Henry G. Dalton
Mary Dalton
Mrs. Dalton
Jan Erlone
Gus
Reverend Hammond
Max
Bessie Mears
Peggy O'Flagherty
Bigger Thomas
Buddy Thomas
Mrs. Thomas
Vera Thomas

The Outsider (1953)
Mr. Blimin
Eva Blount
Gilbert (Gil) Blount
Cross (Lionel Lane) Damon
Gladys
Langley Herndon
John (Jack) Hilton
Ely Houston

Robert (Bob) Hunter
Sarah Hunter
Jenny
Rose Lampkin
Herbert Menti
Dorothy (Dot) Powers
Father Seldon
Joe Thomas

Savage Holiday (1954)
Mabel Blake

Tony Blake
Erskine Fowler
Minnie
Albert Warren
Robert Warren
Mary Westerman

STARK YOUNG

So Red the Rose (1934)
Duncan Bedford

Malcolm (Mac) Bedford
Sarah Tate (Sallie, Tait) Bedford
Mary Cherry
Agnes Bedford McGehee
Edward McGehee
Hugh McGehee
Lucinda (Lucy) McGehee
Julia Valette Somerville
Charles (Charlie) Taliaferro
Rosa (Aunt Piggie, Rosy) Tate (Tait)
William Veal

CONTRIBUTORS

Katherine Anne Ackley
Scott W. Allen
Suzanne A. Allen
Lisa L. Antley
Leonard R. N. Ashley
Robert D. Attenweiler
Ken Autrey
Max L. Autrey
James R. Bailey
Elizabeth B. Baker
Jan Bakker
Rae Galbraith Ballard
Sandra Ballard
Sarah Barnhill
Vanu "Bill" W. Barrett
Anne I. Barton
Gay Barton
Judith S. Baughman
Ronald Baughman
Harry McBrayer Bayne
Gloria J. Bell
Elaine Bender
Kristin Berkey-Abbott
Edith Blicksilver
Edward B. Borden
William K. Bottorff
Maureen Boyd
Muriel Wright Brailey
Marlena E. Bremseth
Stephen C. Brennan
Jean M. Bright
J. M. Brook
Mary Hughes Brookhart
Charles D. Brower
Donald M. Brown

Wylie Brown
Matthew Joseph Bruccoli
Beth L. Brunk
J. A. Bryant, Jr.
Paul T. Bryant
Martin Bucco
Ron Buchanan
Linda K. Bundtzen
David G. Byrd
John Calabro
Joseph Caldwell
Roseanne V. Camacho
John Canfield
Delores Carlito
Thomas Carmichael
Diane Carr
David J. Carroll
Jean W. Cash
Leonard Casper
William H. Castles, Jr.
Ronald Cella
Jim C. Chin
Mona Choucair
Henry A. Christian
Gary M. Ciuba
Samuel Coale
Carol Bebee Collins
R. G. Collins
Daniel T. Cornell
Karen F. Costello-McFeat
Carol Cumming
Tom Dabbs
Christopher C. Dahl
Thomas E. Dasher
Joan F. Dean

S. Renee Dechert
Laurie Bernhardt Demarest
Marc Demarest
Carolyn C. Denard
James E. Devlin
R. H. W. Dillard
Joanne Dobson
Sharon D. Downey
Paul A. Doyle
Margaret Dunn
Joyce Dyer
Wilton Eckley
Catherine A. Eckman
Peter G. Epps
Barbara J. Everson
Ann Dahlstrom Farmer
Carol Farrington
Kathy A. Fedorko
Rebecca E. Feind
Dianne S. Fergusson
Benjamin Franklin Fisher
Mathew D. Fisher
Joseph M. Flora
Erwin H. Ford II
Edward Halsey Foster
Elaine Dunphy Foster
Abigail Franklin
Rebecca Jane Franklin
Benjamin Franklin V
June M. Frazer
Timothy C. Frazer
Joan Frederick
Robert S. Frederickson
Michael J. Freeman
Linda Garner

Helen S. Garson
Lisa L. Gay
Robert F. Geary Jr.
Boyd W. Geer
Gary Geer
Marcia Kinder Geer
Kelly S. Gerald
Sinda Gregory
Donald J. Greiner
Johnanna L. Grimes
James A. Grimshaw, Jr.
Virginia B. Guilford
Susan Elizabeth Gunter
Judith Giblin Haig
Robert L. Haig
Lee Emling Harding
Herbert Hartsook
Melissa Walker Heidari
Australia Henderson
Suzann Hick
Sharon K. Higby
William Higgins
Dorothy Combs Hill
James W. Hipp
E. Jens Holley
Susan Luck Hooks
Steven P. Horowitz
Brooke Horvath
Helen R. Houston
Lillie P. Howard
Glenda A. Hudson
Theodore R. Hudson
Heather L. Hughes
Rebecca E. Hurst
Vernon Hyles
Laura Ingram
Betty J. Irwin
Dennis Isbell
Michael Jasper
David K. Jeffrey
Greg Johnson
Thomas L. Johnson
Allan Johnston
Kirkland C. Jones
Norma R. Jones
James L. de Jongh
Richard A. Kallan
Steven G. Kellman
Alison M. Kelly
Mary Lou Kete
Sue Lashe Kimball
Jackie Kinder
Harriet L. King
Seema Kurrup

Janet Sanders Land
Ellen B. Lane
Jim E. Lapeyre
Doris Lucas Laryea
Helen T. Lasseter
Norman Lavers
Leota S. Lawrence
Richard Layman
Suzanne Leahy
Frank H. Leavell
Dan Lee
Dawn Lee Terry Leonard
Peggy J. Lindsey
May Harn Liu
Leslie P. Lochamy
Charlene Loope
Barbara Lootens
Susan T. Lord
Robert E. Lougy
Charles F. Loveless
Dennis Loyd
Mark T. Lucas
Gary D. MacDonald
Jane Compton Mallison
Daniel Marder
Seth D. Martin
Amanda Gwyn Mason
Wanda L. Mattress
John R. May
Jo Mayer
Len McCall
Charlotte S. McClure
Joseph R. McElrath, Jr.
Warren McInnis
Nellie Y. McKay
Mary H. McNulty
Mary Cease Megra
Gary B. Meyer
Joseph Milicia
Paul W. Miller
Joseph R. Millichap
Eva Mills
Carey S. Minderhout
Judith B. Mobley
Rayburn S. Moore
Steven Moore
Gregory L. Morris
Stephanie Morris
Patrick D. Morrow
Lynn M. Morton
Charmaine A. Mosby
Michael Mullen
Robert M. Myers
Charles C. Nash

Peter Nazareth
Christine Nelson
Emmanuel S. Nelson
Jennifer Castillo Norman
Jennifer Norton
Douglas A. Noverr
Lance Olsen
Steven E. Olsen
Kevin Hunter Orr
Jacqueline E. Orsagh
Julie M. Overton
Clark W. Owens
Donna Padgett
Jeffrey D. Parker
Robert L. Phillips, Jr.
Edward J. Piacentino
Roxane V. Pickens
M. Gilbert Porter
Robert E. Preissle
Barbara J. Price
Diane Dufva Quantic
Elizabeth Lee Rametta
Jennifer L. Randisi
J. R. Raper
Michael W. Raymond
Peter J. Reed
Edward C. Reilly
Josephine Rentz
Katheryn L. Rios
Barbara Rippey
Carmen S. Rivera
William Roba
William M. Robins
Donna Brumback Romein
Kimberly Roppolo
Walter W. Ross
Stephen J. Rubin
Judith Ruderman
Edward J. Ruggero
Christine A. Rydel
Robert M. Ryley
Elaine B. Safer
Arthur M. Saltzman
Leslie Sanders
Michael J. Sasso
Linda Schlafer
Richard J. Schrader
Mitzi Schrag
Richard R. Schramm
Elizabeth Schultz
Lucille M. Schultz
Katherine C. Schwartz
Marilyn J. Seguin
Dean Shackelford

David Shelter
Allan Shepherd
Thelma J. Shinn
Carl R. Shirley
Paula W. Shirley
Alan Shucard
Michael K. Simmons
Jean Sims
Thomas R. Smith
Virginia Whatley Smith
Kathryn Snell
Andew B. Spencer
Teresa Steppe
Cynthia L. Storm
Robert D. Sturr
Suzanne T. Stutman
Jack R. Sublette
Jon Christian Suggs
Guy Szuberla

Stephen L. Tanner
David M. Taylor
Estelle W. Taylor
Richard C. Taylor
Heidi Thompson
Eleanor Q. Tignor
Lindsey S. Tucker
Richard Tuerk
Susan Hayes Tully
Nancy Lewis Tuten
Gordon Van Ness III
Ronald Walcott
Joseph S. Walker
Richard Walser
Mary Ellen Williams Walsh
Virginia Weathers
Robert W. Weathersby II
Carolyn E. Wedin
William Wehmeyer

Sylvia H. Weinberg
Jennifer Welsh
Holly Westcott
Warren Westcott
Mary Ellen R. Westmoreland
John Whalen-Bridge
Heather L. Williams
Kathleen Murat Williams
Crystal Williamson
J. Randall Woodland
Hammett Worthington-Smith
Mary E. Wright
Joseph J. Wydeven
Delbert E. Wylder
Deborah L. Yerkes
Pamela A. Zager
Anne R. Zahlan